The Transcendentalists

AN ANTHOLOGY

The Transcendentalists

AN ANTHOLOGY

PERRY MILLER

HARVARD UNIVERSITY PRESS

Cambridge, Massachusetts

1950

LONDON · GEOFFREY CUMBERLEGE · OXFORD UNIVERSITY PRESS

FOR

GERTRUDE EDDY MILLER

ACKNOWLEDGMENT

This book has been constructed mainly out of texts furnished by the Harvard College Library and Houghton Library; to them my thanks are due for making the materials available and for their coöperation. To the Massachusetts Historical Society, I am indebted for permission to use the hitherto unpublished sermon of George Ripley, and to Mr. George Bluestone for the transcription. Mr. Frederic W. Pratt generously gave permission to use unpublished portions of the journals of Bronson Alcott; I have profited from Mr. Murray Murphey's transcription of these journals and from his Alcott researches. Mr. Warner Berthoff gave me the benefit of his study of Jones Very. Mr. J. C. Levenson guided my treatment of Cranch. I am indebted throughout to Miss Vivian C. Hopkins for her exhaustive knowledge of the period, and especially for help on the Emerson-Norton controversy. Mr. Sherman Paul and Mr. Leo Marx have supplied innumerable suggestions; Mr. Paul read the proof and prepared the index. Like every student in the field I have profited by the works of Professor Ralph L. Rusk and of Professor Odell Shepard. Miss Edith Warren assisted substantially in the preparation. I had the constant assistance of Elizabeth Williams Miller.

.P. M.

CONTENTS

3 Emergence

4 *Annus Mirabilis*

5 *Miracles*

xii CONTENTS

6 *Manifestoes*

7 The Movement: *Philosophical and Religious*

8 The Movement: *Literary and Critical*

9 The Movement: *Political and Social*

10 *Recollections*

The Transcendentalists

AN ANTHOLOGY

There is a small class of scholars whose aims and pursuits are of a different character. They value literature not as an end, but as an instrument to help the solution of problems, that haunt and agitate the soul. They wish to look into the truth of things. The Universe, in its mysterious and terrible grandeur, has acted on them. Life is not regarded by them as a pageant or a dream; it passes before their eye in dread and solemn beauty; thought is stirred up from its lowest depths; they become students of God unconsciously; and secret communion with the divine presence is their preparation for a knowledge of books, and the expression of their own convictions. Their writings, accordingly, whenever they appear, will be alive. They will probably offend or grieve many, who make the state of their own minds the criterion of truth; but, at the same time, they will be welcomed by others, who find in them the word which they were waiting to hear spoken.

—GEORGE RIPLEY

INTRODUCTION

This volume exists primarily on the level of what the Transcendentalists called the Understanding, or what Emerson called "Commodity." It aims to make available articles and books that by now can be found only in a few special libraries. I have endeavored to arrange the selections so that they tell the story of themselves, and to include at least one example of all the major phases or concerns. I have deliberately withheld comment of my own, confining myself to essential biographical and historical annotations. My conviction, which I trust the book will confirm, is that the group who composed the "Transcendental movement" of the 1830's were writers of extraordinary abilities and of still more extraordinary intensities. They have suffered in reputation largely because, their works being locked up in rare publications, they are no longer seen in their true perspective. If they be permitted to speak for themselves, they are, I am persuaded, quite capable of holding their own.

Through the florescence of historical scholarship over the last generation, at least the names of the figures ranged around Emerson and Thoreau have gradually gained currency, but the student still has difficulty in finding out what they did, and even more what they said. Some of these—Brownson, Margaret Fuller, Parker, Alcott, Very—have recently received critical re-evaluations, and biographies have been written, but the best of their creations have not been sifted out and recognized. In the schools of graduate study an increasing amount of research is being devoted to the period and the people; out of this is shaping a clearer and more accurate picture of the movement than we have hitherto possessed, but even so, the truism would still hold that the sources themselves are the fact upon which all interpretation must be founded.

As a record of the facts, this volume must confess at once to a serious incompletion: it omits, except for a few unavoidable citations, Emerson and Thoreau. The reason is frankly utilitarian; there is not enough space. Moreover, the works of these two men are easily accessible, at least in anthologies. Were Emerson's part in the pageant to be here represented in accordance with its central importance, all his publications between 1836 and 1850 would need to be reprinted, and the volume would become unmanageable. At the risk of trying to construct a *Hamlet* with Hamlet left out—not only once but twice over—I have sacrificed Emerson and Thoreau to make room for Brownson and Ripley.

This rigor has been regretfully maintained even when we come to 1836 and to *Nature*. This essay is so clearly the pivotal utterance that without it the book may have no center and little coherence; however, it is so widely reprinted that any student can consult it in connection with Chapter IV. I have, however, felt obliged to find room for at least the first half of Emerson's *Historic Notes;* although it is contained in the standard edition, it is all too little known there, and to reread it against the array of its contemporaries will be, I wager, to find in it meanings that at first sight are hidden. The other extracts from Emerson, his preface for *The Dial* and his presentations of the younger Channing, are not usually included in his *Works;* their omission has been a loss.

The problem of Thoreau is somewhat different, since he published his two books after the years on which this collection is focused. To include all his earlier writings would again be to consume space needed for lesser known productions. On the other hand, in order to correct certain excesses of recent interpretation, I would like to convey some sense of how Thoreau made his bow among the Transcendental brotherhood—when it was far from evident that he was a major artist. I have tried to strike a balance by reprinting five of his verses from *The Dial* along with the other *Dial* poets. Also, I have placed the gist of his "Natural History of Massachusetts" among the philosophical selections in order deliberately to emphasize what modern criticism too often forgets, that his formative years were molded by the concepts and theories of Transcendentalism. Though from the beginning he strove for a greater concreteness than the others, his approach to the particular presumed an abstract rationale. He did not underrate the value of any fact, because any given fact *could* flower into a truth. I believe that if this, his first sustained essay, be read in the company of its fellows, it becomes the clue to a more perceptive reading of *Walden* than is normally attained even by the most ardent Thoreauvians. The omission of his "Civil Disobedience" from Chapter IX leaves that section fatally impaired, but since the essay is by now widely disseminated, I leave the reader to consult it elsewhere.

In still another respect the book belies the promise of its title and its table of contents: the articles are edited, and most of them are severely cut down. That generation was, by our standards, terribly verbose. Furthermore, writers on all sides of the Transcendental question were members of the same communion, at least at the beginning; they realized that for two hundred years

New England had been riven by sterile controversies, and all the camps had recently learned from the new literature of Europe an ideal of spaciousness which they were eager to imitate. Hence they strove to be polite, and to this effort devoted pages of bowing, scraping, preliminary conciliation, and a display of erudition. Considering both the spatial limits and modern impatience, I have assumed the right to throw out irrelevancies and arid passages; I have tried to preserve only the hard core and the basic themes. The onus of the choice rests, of course, entirely upon me; students of the sources may well quarrel with my decisions, but on the whole I believe that the excised portions can, for the purposes of this narrative, be dispensed with. Even so vigorous a writer as Brownson was highly repetitious—especially when he had a whole issue of his *Quarterly* to fill up by himself—and although *The Laboring Classes* keeps up the fervid pace for over a hundred pages, the heart of the matter is, I am certain, within the parts I have selected. Because of the obvious importance of Parker's *Transient and Permanent,* I have reproduced it without abridgment. For those who wish to consult the other texts in their entirety, I have indicated the proveniences.

Finally, in order that this anthology may represent the group as they actually figured in history, I have limited the selection to what appeared at the time as public record, to what was published or was spoken in public. In the annotations I have sometimes used passages from journals and letters that were then private, but only to facilitate our understanding of what, so far as the world could know, was the Transcendentalism of New England. And for clarity I have corrected their frequent typographical errors.

To leave the plane of these dreary mechanical or editorial considerations for something closer to what the Transcendentalists might call that of the Reason, the problem then becomes: why make an anthology of the Transcendentalists at all? Emerson, and Thoreau even more, have won secure positions in the world's literature, but why exhume Christopher Cranch?

An answer may be constructed, well within the limits of critical proportion, by contending that even though the specific achievements of these writers were seldom of the very first order, yet the achievement of the group as a whole—even with Emerson and Thoreau hugely omitted—remains a significant episode in the American experience. Even in Dublin, the restless Finnegan dreams about "Concord on the Merrymaking." In their recollections of the movement, both Parker and Emerson insist that it was constituted by pitifully few persons, and that even these were far from attaining organized unanimity or anything resembling a coherent program. There was, as Emerson says, "no concert"; there were only a number of disparate individuals who fell of themselves "upon Coleridge and Wordsworth and Goethe, and then on Carlyle, with pleasure and sympathy." The biographies of these discoverers are so dissociated that there seems really very little warrant for dignifying them into a "movement." Nevertheless, Emerson proclaimed in ringing tones —at least when the business was at its height—a "party of the Future," which he rallied against "the party of the Past." In the *Discourse of Matters Pertaining to Religion,* Parker so analyzed the history of New England—he was a sufficiently cosmopolitan scholar to appreciate the configurations of intellectual development in universal terms—as to assign to the Transcendental band a vital role in the march of American thought. At the end of his life, tired and battered, Parker blessed the fate that had cast his youth amid these creative years.

All this is a plea, offered by the Transcendentalists themselves, that their efforts may still be worth preserving. But better inducements are afforded by their enemies. The greatest and most formidable of these was Professor Andrews Norton of the Harvard Divinity School. He did not mince matters: he called them, privately and publicly, infidels. In New England, this was not a charge to be made lightly. Furthermore, it was not a charge to be made without due forethought by a Unitarian. Unitarians had smarted under the accusation for decades; they had been described as being themselves such abandoned heretics that they were bereft of even the conception of heresy. And then, being a Unitarian and a Harvard man, Norton was schooled in the discipline of dignity and in the avoidance of name-calling. He was surely goaded beyond endurance by the time he cast good manners to the wind and assaulted these renegades before the world. There was every reason that he be considerate and tactful: they were his own students, products of his institution. Ripley, Emerson, Clarke, Cranch, the younger Channings, were not upstart vulgarians; they were Harvard Brahmins. Norton had known their fathers. If despite these considerations he assailed them, he must have felt that they had become so vicious as to call for desperate remedies. And if, in the heat of his exasperation, he fell back, liberal though he was, upon the ancient battle cry of Puritan New England—if he shouted "infidelity" at them, and so invoked a slogan that carried the connotations of suppression, the hangman, and mob violence—it was because in his eyes (and in the eyes of the pundits, many of the priests, and most of the pew-holders for whom he spoke) the Transcendentalists were guilty of exactly that enormity. In the context of New England, infidelity meant more than a relish for Wordsworth and Coleridge, and even more than a fascination with Goethe: it meant a falling out of line both in theology and in sociology. It meant that the culprit was a threat both to the church and to the state. If Transcendentalism was anywhere near so serious a matter as Norton's polemic declared, then it is a matter worth investigating.

In other words, however few or confused or faltering were the so-called Transcendentalists, they were, often despite themselves, caught up in a crisis of the spirit and of the nation, a crisis that carries immense implications for the American predicament not only in their time but also in ours. It may be a backhanded way of introducing a bevy of writers to plead that they builded better than they knew, or that they reveal more than they intended to say— especially when they happened to pride themselves on the exquisiteness of their perceptions. But the fact is that because of their highly sensitized awareness of the plight of American culture in the 1830's, although they were often thereby betrayed into sentimentality or into affectation, they managed to get into print enough pertinent and penetrating things about the nature of this society, or to give expression in poetry and criticism to aspirations at work deep within it, to achieve in the sum total of their work a significance that really does transcend the boundaries of their time and their place, and even the limitations of their peculiar idiom.

The most telling objection against any claim for a larger implication in this material arises from the indisputable fact that all of it was composed in the neighborhood of Boston or else, as with the writers for *The Western Messenger,* by Bostonians in exile. It seems therefore to add up, at best, to a parochial disturbance. Although the members fancied that there were great differences among themselves, which they took with an ostentatious and often exaggerated seriousness, still from our point of view they can be seen as pretty much of a single stripe: they were all young Unitarians who between 1830 and 1840 revolted against Unitarianism (even those who came from non-Unitarian backgrounds, like Alcott and Brownson, had to move through a Unitarian stage in order thereafter to become Transcendentalists by rejecting it!). And Unitarianism was notoriously indigenous to eastern Massachusetts; a heresy within so localized a sect may well be thought of little interest or significance for the rest of an immense country.

In certain basic respects, this observation is altogether true; the sections omitted from these texts are largely devoted to topics that are now of interest only to the New England antiquarian. But the fascination of this particular tempest, even though it took place in the Boston teacup, is precisely that it churned up prophetic issues. Unitarianism, viewed in the larger perspective of modern intellectual history, was a form, the most institutionalized form, in which rationalism, "liberalism," and the cult of social conformity rather than of emotional intensity, were established in America. The protest of these few troubled spirits against what their society had confidently assumed was the crowning triumph of progress and enlightenment is therefore a portent for America, all the more because their protest was the result of no organized indoctrination, but was entirely spontaneous and instinctive. It was as native to the soil as the birch tree. It was an assertion that men in New England, and so in the New World, will refuse to live by sobriety and decorum alone, that there are requirements of the soul which demand satisfaction even though respectability must be defied and shocked. The Transcendentalists did not need to be unified upon any one creed or platform because they were already united in the community of the heart; they had all grown miserable and disgusted within what Emerson called "the corpse-cold Unitarianism of Brattle Street and Harvard College." This was the ethos of their youth; their ultimate condemnation of this ethos, after an agony of soul-searching and fumbling, is nothing less than the first of a succession of revolts by the youth of America against American Philistinism.

Which is to imply something that I hope these massed quotations will make clear, namely, that the Transcendental movement is most accurately to be defined as a religious demonstration. The real drive in the souls of the participants was a hunger of the spirit for values which Unitarianism had concluded were no longer estimable. It had, to all appearances irrevocably, codified into manageable and safe formularies appetites that hitherto in America had been glutted with the terrors of hell and the ecstasies of grace. Unless this literature be read as fundamentally an expression of a religious radicalism in revolt against a rational conservatism, it will not be understood; if it is so interpreted, then the deeper undertone can be heard. Once it is heard, the literature becomes, even in its more fatuous reaches, a protest of the human spirit against emotional starvation. The time had come, Margaret Fuller wrote after listening to a pulpit exposition on the "rational" exercise of the will, for reinterpreting old dogmas. "For one I would now preach the Holy Ghost as zealously as they have been preaching Man, and faith instead of the understanding, and mysticism instead, etc." She broke off because she could not bear to continue; but she packed into one exclamation about the Unitarian congregation more concerning the origins of Transcendentalism than can be found in a hundred learned monographs: "That crowd of upturned faces, with their look of unintelligent complacency!"

This inherently religious character of New England Transcendentalism has not been widely appreciated, mainly because most students are not acquainted with all the writings, and so fall into the habit of judging the whole by the more familiar, but not always typical, works of Emerson and Thoreau. But also, the misapprehension gains credence because all the insurgents strove, like Emerson and Thoreau, to put their cause into the language of philosophy and literature rather than of theology. In this respect, once more, the fact that they were children of New England enabled them to speak, as no other group in the America of their time could speak, for a tendency that pertains as much to all America as to little New England, although elsewhere the tendency was to become explicit only with the passing of more time. That is, they derived from a society in which theological disputation and fine logical distinguishing had long been a major industry; New England, sooner than other regions, had grown sick and tired of it. Unitarianism taught the youth that it was no longer fruitful or necessary to argue the problems of life and the intellect in the crabbed language of systematic divinity. "Unitarianism," said Brownson, "has demolished Calvinism, made an end in all thinking minds of everything like dogmatic Protestantism." Therefore this revival of religion had to find new forms of expression instead of new formulations of doctrine, and it found them in literature. It found them in patterns supplied by Cousin, Wordsworth, Coleridge, and Carlyle. But the self-consciously literary character of the movement should not deceive us into regarding it as no more than a school of aestheticians, as only a New England version of the Pre-Raphaelites or the Imagists (although sometimes it does indeed resemble the Dadaists). Remembrance of the affair has been chiefly kept alive by students of literature, or by readers won through the literary skill of Emerson and Thoreau, but Transcendentalism was not primarily a literary phenomenon. Neither Emerson nor Thoreau conceived of himself as an artist, but each of them came close—perilously close perhaps—to imagining himself a prophet. Or else, as Emerson put it, "a chartered libertine, free to worship and free to rail." If the railing was exhilarating, and if in Thoreau it could become authentic invective, still for both of them, as for all their confreres, worship remained the controlling motive. Transcendentalism was fed by deeper springs than mere aesthetics, although the situation was such that there was almost no other direction in which the waters could flow than into a doctrine and an attempted practice of the beautiful. Though the movement was asserted through poems in *The Dial,* Orphic apothegms, and lyric passages upon the woodchuck, it was, as the tendency of these selections will make clear, an effort to create a living religion without recourse to what it supposed the obsolete jargon of theology. For this reason, Parker's *Discourse,* which most trenchantly separated the "permanent" from the "transient," is one of the two supreme articulations of the endeavor.

Because they desperately needed forms and concepts in which to embody a passion that arose out of domestic pressures, the Transcendentalists appropriated with avidity the new literature of "romanticism" that came to them through Wordsworth and Coleridge and the new philosophy of German idealism that came to them at secondhand through Cousin and Carlyle. Here again, in a second respect, Transcendentalists exhibit a pattern of behavior which has wide implications for all America, rather than for the local scene alone: here is a neat exemplification of the perennial problem of Europe and America. Here is a test-tube model of the process of assimilation that had been at work even before the declaration of political independence, and is still at work. How the American artist or thinker, laboring under compulsions set up in America, with his character and the bent of his interests already determined by the environment, yet reaches out for the results of an older and more complex culture, how he reworks them and refashions them to suit his own needs, and so perturbs and enriches the life of America—all this is illustrated in the emergence and formulation of Transcendentalism. Little wonder, therefore, that the movement has been of the greatest interest to students of literature, or that they have understandably erred by presenting it as exclusively a literary and critical enterprise. How the members took over their German, French, and English (and later their Oriental) literature, and how they used it or imitated it, and yet contrived, while masquerading as poets and critics, to rephrase the ancient religious preoccupations of New England, seems to me the most striking theme to emerge from the simple grouping together of these selections. It is all the more arresting there because it emerges, as the reader must acknowledge, unmistakably and of itself.

In the peculiar context of New England there is a third moral that impresses itself upon the reader of these fragments, and this likewise may be taken as a recurrent lesson of cultural history. Unitarianism was the culmination of a century-long campaign for freedom, elegance, and liberality. Men like Andrews Norton and Francis Bowen quite properly regarded themselves as the guardians of a great tradition, as being progressive and forward-looking men. Furthermore, it was Unitarianism that overcame the provincial hostility of Puritan New England to belles-lettres and to the fine arts, that pried open the doors of those enchanting vistas that were spread before the generation of the 1830's. Buckminster, Everett, and Channing set the model for a minister who could be literate rather than pedantic, who could quote poetry rather than eschatology, who could be a stylist and could scorn controversy. Buckminster and Emerson's own father founded the Boston Athenaeum—and without its library, its subscriptions to periodicals, and its casts of the Greek sculptures, the young Transcendentalists could hardly have found their way to romanticism and idealism. Unitarians like the two Everetts conducted *The North American Review* and *The Christian Register*. Edward Everett's lectures on German literature were, as Emerson tells us, a new morning for even the rudest undergraduate in Harvard Hall.

Hence it is not difficult to sympathize with the distress, the bewilderment, and then with the rage, of the older generation when they heard themselves consigned by ungrateful and unnatural children to the party of the Past. To them, the Transcendentalists seemed all too clearly a generation of vipers; they bit the hands that had nourished them. Norton and Bowen believed ardently that the line of thought they were furthering was the highway to civilization. Emerson and Parker were throwbacks to the messy emotionalism and the dangerous mysticism that "liberal Christianity" had striven for a century to exorcise. To sober, judicious, rational Brattle Street and Harvard College, Transcendentalism was really "infidelity"; it was a betrayal of the citadel from within, it was a rebellion against the fathers. Their temper was not improved when they heard the traitors calling the Harvard Divinity School, where most of the rebels had been handsomely educated, an "icehouse." It is therefore revealing of the state that affairs had reached by 1840 that Andrews Norton, the uncrowned "Pope" of the Unitarians, who for decades had been the most aggressive fighter among them against "orthodoxy," should not only be reduced to accusing his former pupils of infidelity, but to seeking for allies against them among his former foes. It is both ironic and pathetic that he, being hard pressed by Ripley, Hildreth, Brownson, and Parker, should republish in Cambridge, with his open endorsement, articles from *The Princeton Review,* from the very stronghold of orthodoxy, in which three Calvinist theologians castigated Emerson and the Transcendentalists. He was so desperately harried that he printed these texts without alteration, even though one of the points scored most heavily by the Princetonians was that the Unitarians had only themselves to blame for what had befallen them, because, by becoming Unitarians in the first place, they had opened Pandora's box. Norton feared the jibes of his erstwhile enemies less than he did the mutiny among his disciples. Nothing is more illustrative of a recurrent unfolding in American society than the complaint of these good Unitarians that the younger generation of Transcendentalists were arrogant, self-opinionated, precious, and censorious. What they failed to appreciate was that the youngsters had reached back into an older Puritan manner, which Emerson's Aunt Mary Moody once made vivid for him by declaring, "I was never patient with the faults of the good."

In other words, then, we have in the emergence of the group one of those mysterious conflicts that have been staged a thousand times in modern culture, particularly in what has been called "bourgeois" society, and for that reason perhaps nowhere more violently than in America. It is one more instance of the rift between the generations. Here, even within the confines of the Unitarian fold, where it might be supposed that continuity would have best been preserved, no sooner was the victory won, no sooner had the elders begun to relax in the confidence that their sons would carry on, than a coterie of the most gifted among them turned on their fathers and reviled them. The selections thus make clear that about 1825–1835 students at Harvard College and in the Divinity School were in actuality receiving two distinct and disparate educations: one in the classroom, administered by Professors Norton and Bowen, and one in the dormitory, where they were poring over European importations. The rapid emergence of the Transcendental point of view— which can be traced in Chapter III through the procession of articles in *The Christian Examiner,* the organ of literate Unitarianism—into the barrage of books and articles that exploded in 1836, is a story of the triumph of the self-instilled education of the dormitory over the official tuition of the lecture room. The most moving observation to be made upon the debate (in Chapter V) of Norton and Bowen versus Emerson, Ripley, Brownson, and Parker is that, although the two contending parties belonged to a common culture and shared an articulated heritage, by the late 1830's they had so deeply diverged that they could no longer understand each other. What each assumed as the obvious premise was to the other no longer even comprehensible. The whole narrative is thus a cogent and instructive demonstration of how in America, even under the freest and most enlightened aegis, successive generations have repeatedly risen against their predecessors and so set in motion a series of revolutions, each one of which has struck the elder victims as the surrender of the national birthright and as a reprehensibly un-American activity.

In this case, as in the others, the controversy between the generations threatened, by the time division had become irreparable, to involve more than tastes in poetry and philosophy. Here we encounter the fourth, and perhaps the most relevant respect, in which the Transcendental movement has meaning for the whole sweep of American history. These insurgents had ideas about politics and economics, and about relations between the sexes, as well as about woodchucks and sunsets. If the latter sort of their notions seemed to proper Boston to be absurd, the former sort were downright subversive. I believe that this element in the story has been most lost sight of today, and for that reason I suspect that Chapter IX—where the chief exhibits are, of course, Brownson and Parker—is the most important in the book. That the revolutionary threat to the established order contained in the Transcendental premises has been forgotten is to be accounted for mainly on the ground that little or nothing ever came of it. Reasons for this evaporation of the social thrust are numerous and do not concern this study; it is enough to say, or to let the selections say, that by the early 1840's the critique of Unitarian Boston had become also a critique of State Street and investment banking. As studies of our society, as formulations of the meaning of democracy and of freedom in what had suddenly become (and remains) a "business" culture, these documents are as alive as the day they were written, even though in historical fact they produced no more earth-shaking actions than Brook Farm or Brownson's opposition to President Harrison. They raised, at any rate, the issue, and nowhere more ominously than in Dr. Loring's interpretation of *The Scarlet Letter* as an indictment of the social morality of the dominant classes—although Dr. Loring himself was so fearful of what he had to say, and so timid about his aspersions upon the absolute validity of chastity, that he took pains to keep his article anonymous.

The fact that these writings did produce few tangible effects, and that after a slight turmoil about them, American society went on its way undisturbed, is no doubt a comment upon the movement, and a warning against magnifying its importance. Surely, if it once did contain revolutionary implications for society, by 1850 or thereabouts these were no longer visible. In fact, as a movement in any sense of the word, by then it had virtually ceased to be, and for that reason I have not attempted the amorphous task of tracing ultimate ramifications. One reason—possibly a sufficient reason—for the disappearance of the movement was simply that it won its point, or at any rate most of its points. As the generation of Norton died off, younger ministers, tinged with Emersonianism, took over the pulpits, and strife between the church and the "new school" ceased. The steadily mounting success of Emerson, his life-long demonstration that Transcendentalism did not mean immorality but rather virtue, and the veneration in which he was finally held (Thoreau being dead, and all but forgotten), ended by covering his colleagues with the mantle of his respectability. The channelizing of reforming energies into the antislavery crusade also helped to make Transcendentalism respectable. And finally, in America of the late nineteenth century, when religion became less of a battleground and anxieties were centered upon the economic problem, Transcendentalism—or what little was left of it—seemed no more than a harmless exhortation to self-reliance and optimism. Vice-presidents of banks have been known to hang framed mottoes from Emerson on the walls of their offices.

Thus the picture of the movement as a charming idyll in a pastoral America became, by the end of the century, the stereotype. It has been perpetuated to our own day by writers whose dread of an industrialized and mechanized civilization bred a nostalgia for simplicity and rural quietude; they have fled to a New England that never existed and have presented the whole affair in elegiac prose as a gentle "flowering" that was accompanied by some quaint eccentricities of behavior.

It must therefore be insisted upon that if Transcendentalism did not remain a disturbing force, the reason is not alone that America adopted it and made it orthodox, but also that it consumed, shattered, and destroyed its adherents. Margaret Fuller fled to Europe, to violence and to death; Cranch took refuge in Florence and in cultivated dilettantism. Parker killed himself with overwork, and Thoreau expended himself; Emerson dissolved into aphasia, Ripley subsided into disillusion, Hedge became a Harvard professor, and Jones Very kept himself out of the lunatic asylum only by writing versified platitudes on the Atlantic cable. Brownson became a Catholic, as did Sophia Ripley, and Elizabeth Peabody became a "character"; Bancroft became a politician, and the Sturgis girls got married; J. S. Dwight became the dean of Boston music critics, and Ellery Channing spent a life of futility. Bronson Alcott alone endured to the end as the irreducible and indestructible Transcendentalist, but he lived a life of meditative leisure shamelessly parasitic on the labors of his wife and daughters.

The point, I believe, is that the Transcendental episode was not all dreamy and not all benignity. It was a struggle with ideas, a struggle in earnest, under devastating handicaps. In the final reckoning, what counts is not what the people did, but what the ideas meant. They broached these ideas, and so gave them to the American tradition. Had Transcendentalism been in fact—or did it amount upon analysis to no more than—a somewhat ludicrous cerebral frenzy, these fugitive pieces would hardly be worth rescuing. But the excitement—though assuredly it had its comic aspects—was a profound stirring of certain souls under conditions imposed by the cultural situation; their response to these conditions is an indispensable chapter in the making of the American mind. Granted that their service to the ideas was hindered by their shortcomings, by their lack of scholarship and sophistication, by their ignorance of history and logic, and most of all by their precommitment to making literature a substitute for religion, and religion a substitute for philosophy—still, the Transcendental movement was the most energetic and extensive upsurge of the mind and spirit enacted in America until the intellectual crisis of the 1920's. For those who would understand the character of this country, a firsthand knowledge of the ideas that generated and sustained the movement is important—as long as that knowledge includes also an awareness of the historical and social conditions. Whatever the historian or the critic may try to make out of the Transcendentalists, they themselves must be acknowledged the ultimate authorities for what they felt and attempted. In the hope of recovering for our literature this substantial body of material, I have undertaken to put together this anthology.

1

Forerunners

The finite is something real as well as the infinite. We must reconcile the two in our theology. It is as dangerous to exclude the former as the latter. God surpasses all human thought; yet human thought, mysterious, unbounded, "wandering through eternity," is not to be contemned. God's sovereignty is limitless; still man has rights. God's power is irresistible; still man is free. On God we entirely depend; yet we can and do act from ourselves, and determine our own characters. These antagonistic ideas, if so they may be called, are equally true, and neither can be spared.

—WILLIAM ELLERY CHANNING

1. Joseph Stevens Buckminster (1784–1812)
The Peculiar Blessings of Our Social Condition as Americans

[Ralph Waldo Emerson barely remembered his father, who died in 1811 when Waldo was eight. In 1850 Emerson looked over his father's papers and advised his brother that there was no justification for publishing them. At best, he reported, they showed no more than that "candour and taste, or I should almost say, docility, the principal merit possible to that early, ignorant and transitional Month-of-March, in our New England culture."

Emerson wrote thus out of an assured eminence, confirmed not only by his own achievement but by what everybody acknowledged, the immense coming-of-age that had been enacted in New England between his father's generation and his own. He could afford to speak condescendingly of the tentative efforts of the first decade of the nineteenth century because to him it was evident that the intellectual level had been radically elevated. In all filial piety, and yet with critical objectivity, Emerson would claim no more for his father than that "he fostered the Anthology and the Athenaeum." But, he added—hitting upon the precise names that in his view and in ours constitute the precursors of the epoch—"These things ripened in Buckminster, Channing and Everett."

Joseph Stevens Buckminster, born in Portsmouth, New Hampshire, and graduated from Harvard in 1800, was called in 1805 to the Brattle Street Church, the largest and most fashionable in Boston. He was, by universal consent, the outstandingly brilliant young man among that segment of the clergy who were already distinguishing themselves under the label of "liberal Christianity," and who were soon to become avowedly Unitarian. The Reverend William Emerson, pastor of the more ancient but less influential First Church, gravitated into Buckminster's sphere, and became his lieutenant in organizing the Anthology Club, which produced *The Monthly Anthology,* a pioneer attempt at an American literary magazine in imitation of the great English journals. In 1806 Buckminster traveled for a year in Europe, returning with a collection of 3,000 volumes, most of them texts hitherto unavailable in provincial New England. These became the nucleus of the Boston Athenaeum, in the founding of which William Emerson, along with the other leaders of liberal Boston, followed Buckminster's leadership. The death of Buckminster, just as he was appointed to the Dexter Lectureship at Harvard, was felt by all this circle to be a cutting off before his prime of the most accomplished and cosmopolitan figure of the age.

Buckminster's eloquence became a legend, and to the youth of the 1830's the legend meant form and elegance, culture and fluency, the domestication of European graces in ungainly New England. Most of his sermons were published posthumously, so that for a period of twenty years, until Webster and Everett surpassed him, Buckminster remained the highest reach of "eloquence," as that word was to be employed by Emerson and his friends, which America had yet produced. The following selection is taken from the edition of his *Sermons* published in Boston in 1829 (pp. 247–263); it is a fair sample of his tone and that of early Unitarianism. It is all the more relevant to the later story because it announces— even though in a diction redolent of the eighteenth century—an identification of American uniqueness with the economic opportunities of America, a theme that was never to be lost sight of in the literature of Transcendentalism. At the same time, the sermon sounds the note of spiritual distrust of a sheerly material prosperity that was to receive, in the 1830's, a more incisive emphasis.]

Our social and domestic condition is . . . distinguished by a diffusion of competence and of the means of prosperity, in which every man has a share. When do we find families, or individuals, who do not, in some comfortable degree partake of all the essential comforts, which wealth can procure? Who is driven out of society because he is too poor to partake, in some form, of its pleasures? Every morning's sun, as it rises, brings to every man a provision for the day, or lights him to the means of procuring it. How much may be retrenched from every station in society, before poverty can be even perceptible? and how much more, before we should hear the cry of want? Who among us returns in the evening to his family, to have his heart broken by the cries of his children clinging to his knees for bread? Whose sleep is disturbed by the thin phantoms of tomorrow's difficulties? So general is our prosperity, that if we would find distress we must look for it; it does not obtrude itself upon our notice. The miseries which really exist, do not throng upon us so fast that the hand of charity is exhausted before it can effectually relieve them. We see frequent changes from luxury to mediocrity, but how faint and rare is the cry of real and incurable wretchedness. Contrivances for comfort meet us at every door we enter. Everywhere the table is spread, and the cup is filled; everywhere, we find men ascending from convenience to comfort, to neatness, to elegance, to luxury, to profusion . . . In the prodigious extent of an unoccupied country behind us, there seems to be left a common fund for every man's exigencies. The reduced and the unfortunate change their residence, and if we hear of them again, it is only to hear of their prosperity. We look around for the poor, and we meet with here and there the infirm, the diseased, the aged, the imprudent, and the profligate foreigner, but for native, irremediable want, we search in vain . . . Truly the lines have fallen to us in pleasant places, and we have a goodly heritage . . .

Our common prosperity is indeed unexampled, but it is not out of the reach of injury. While it lasts, it is the duty of every man to contribute what he can to preserve it. If you would advance the glory of your age, and make it worthy of being remembered by those who shall come after you, beware of the encroachments of luxury. Nothing will so much tend to make you insensible to the best gifts of Providence, and callous to the purest pleasures of life, as the love of noisy and frivolous distinctions, the pursuit of vicious pleasures, and the tyranny of fashion. Consider whether you do not contribute to the corruptions of the age, by an immoderate pursuit of amusement. Consider how easily the minds of those who are coming into life, are enfeebled and deluded by the doubtful examples of those whom they are taught to consider as giving the tone to the manners of the age.

To preserve our social pleasures in any good degree of purity, nothing will so much contribute as the cultivating a taste for domestic life and the quiet and affectionate pleasures which it affords. In such a state of society as ours, also, there is danger lest the love of money, or of merely sensual idleness, should overwhelm the rising generation. To obviate these evils it is much to be desired, that the love of literature and of intellectual pursuits should be greatly encouraged; for though the passion for knowledge is no proof of a principle of virtue, it is often a security against the vices and temptations of the world. Everything which you contribute to the institutions of sound learning and to promote a correct and pious education, you contribute to the peace, the purity, and the glory of the age.

2. Edward Everett (1794–1865)

Oration Pronounced at Cambridge, Before the Society of Phi Beta Kappa, August 26, 1824

[Everett performed his greatest service for the Transcendental generation as Eliot Professor of Greek Literature at Harvard between 1819 and 1824; the nature of his effect was to be most precisely stated by Emerson (see pp. 496–498). No account of Transcendentalism is even comprehensible unless it includes a consideration of what seemed, during the 1820's, the unearthly magic of his eloquence. If the whole group, and especially Emerson, were committed to the belief that oratory is among the supreme manifestations of art, they were persuaded not only by such forensic giants as Webster and Clay, but more particularly by Everett, who was one of their own kind. Here at last was a New England scholar who appeared the master of all that European culture could offer, who in native terms made articulate, in a style that could compete with Burke and Pitt and Sheridan, everything that America held precious. The spectacular success that followed upon this very oration became a measuring rod for literature. Later on, the Transcendentalists were to be disillusioned by Everett, and recognized in him the hollow voice of the Cotton Whigs and the compromisers, but they all bore the imprint of his earliest example, when he seemed the spontaneous triumph of American genius, when he defined the function of the intellectual in such vital and grandiloquent terms as would sustain a hundred youths even beyond what appeared to be Everett's own abject surrender.

Born in Dorchester, Everett graduated from Harvard with highest honors in 1811, and immediately upon receiving his M.A. in 1814 was called to Buckminster's pulpit at the Brattle Street Church. Named to the Harvard professorship in 1815, he departed for four years in Europe to prepare himself, receiving at Göttingen in 1817 the first Ph.D. bestowed upon an American. Assuming his professorship in 1819, he also became an editor of *The North American Review,* and in 1822 married Charlotte Brooks, daughter of one of the most powerful capitalists in New England.

He delivered this oration to the Phi Beta Kappa Society with Lafayette present; he so overwhelmed the audience with the torrent of his speech, and particularly with his peroration to the Revolutionary hero, that a group of citizens immediately nominated him for Congress and secured his election in November.

Thereafter he was Congressman, Governor of Massachusetts, Minister to England (where he scored a social success), President of Harvard (1846–1849— an unhappy interval), Secretary of State, and Senator. As a politician he was willing to preserve the Union at the cost of accommodating the slaveholders, and so came to grief over the Kansas-Nebraska bill, but between 1861 and his death in 1865 he performed prodigious services as an inspiriter of morale by delivering, at a fatal physical expense, rousing orations throughout the North.

Evidence for the impact of Everett upon the youth of the 1820's is voluminous; by 1832 Emerson could observe that on the same platform with a Cherokee Indian, Everett sounded stuffy and that he sat down "as if one would say the mind of man can scarce steadily contemplate the grandeur of my effort." But Margaret Fuller, even while recognizing that Everett's material was becoming hackneyed, confessed that there was still "the manner, the *manner,* the delicate inflections of voice, the elegant and appropriate gesture, the sense of beauty produced by the whole, which thrilled us all to tears."

Because in such irresistible tones Everett in 1824 called upon the intellectuals of America—who in New England parlance were called the "scholars"—to assume a vital function in the society, he remained for them, despite his subsequent derelictions, a trumpeter of the New England awakening.

This selection is from Everett's *Orations and Speeches* (Boston, 1836, pp. 9–40).]

The most powerful motives call on us, as scholars, for those efforts, which our common country demands of all her children. Most of us are of that class, who owe whatever of knowledge has shone into our minds, to the free and popular institutions of our native land. There are few of us, who may not be permitted to boast, that we have been reared in an honest poverty or a frugal competence, and owe every thing to those means of education which are equally open to all. We are summoned to new energy and zeal by the high nature of the experiment we are appointed in Providence to make, and the grandeur of the theatre on which it is to be performed. When the old world afforded no longer any hope, it pleased Heaven to open this last refuge of humanity. The attempt has begun, and is going on, far from foreign corruption, on the broadest scale, and under the most benignant prospects; and it certainly rests with us to solve the great problem in human society, to settle, and that forever, the momentous question—whether mankind can be trusted with a purely popular system? One might almost think, without extravagance, that the departed wise and good of all places and times, are looking down from their happy seats to witness what shall now be done by us; that they who lavished their treasures and their blood of old, who labored and suffered, who spake and wrote, who fought and perished, in the one great cause of Freedom and Truth, are now hanging from their orbs on high, over the last solemn experiment of humanity. As I have wandered over the spots, once the scene of their labors, and mused among the prostrate columns of their Senate Houses and Forums, I have seemed almost to hear a voice from the tombs of departed ages; from the sepulchres of the nations, which died before the sight. They exhort us, they adjure us to be faithful to our trust. They implore us, by the long trials of struggling humanity, by the blessed memory of the departed; by the dear faith, which has been plighted by pure hands, to the holy cause of truth and man; by the awful secrets of the prison houses, where the sons of freedom have been immured; by the noble heads which have been brought to the block; by the wrecks of time, by the eloquent ruins of nations, they conjure us not to quench the light which is rising on the world . . .

Here then a mighty work is to be fulfilled, or never, by the race of mortals. The *man*, who looks with tenderness on the sufferings of good men in other times; the *descendant of the pilgrims*, who cherishes the memory of his fathers; the *patriot*, who feels an honest glow at the majesty of the system of which he is a member; the *scholar*, who beholds with rapture the long sealed book of unprejudiced truth opened for all to read; these are they, by whom these auspices are to be accomplished. Yes, brethren, it is by the intellect of the country, that the mighty mass is to be inspired; that its parts are to communicate and sympathize with each other, its bright progress to be adorned with becoming refinements, its strong sense uttered, its character reflected, its feelings interpreted to its own children, to other regions, and to after ages.

3. William Ellery Channing (1780–1842)
Likeness to God

[William Ellery Channing, minister of the Federal Street Church from 1803 until 1842, was the chief spokesman for New England Unitarianism. His sermon, "Unitarian Christianity," delivered at Baltimore in 1819 for the ordination of Jared Sparks, was the classic formulation of the liberal creed, and it remains one of the focal documents in American intellectual history. Emerson called him "our bishop" and never lost a chance to stress his importance for the later group (see pp. 500–501). Neither did any of the others; despite his shortcomings, said Hedge, Channing "could from the spiritual height on which he stood, by mere dint of gravity, send his word into the soul with more searching force than all the orators of his time."

Although, because he was an early student of Richard Price, Channing was not, like the rest of his fellow Unitarians, an unquestioning follower of John

Locke, still, as the event proved, he was no Transcendentalist. He was what the textbooks glibly call a "transitional" figure. A small man, a valetudinarian, shy, socially remote, cautious and hesitant, he was also a man of consuming devotion to principle, an eloquent though measured speaker, and a discoverer of passages which he refused himself to explore beyond the threshold. The Transcendental generation grew up in adoration of him, improved his every hint to an imperative, and continued to worship him even after he shuddered at their excesses. In the second number of *The Dial* either Emerson or Ripley declared that Channing embodied "the creed of the youth of this country, who are beginning not so much to protest against the past, as to live in the present and construct for the future."

Properly to represent the effect of the great Dr. Channing upon these youths would be to fill pages with his utterances. To epitomize his message, especially that which the insurgent group took more literally than he quite intended, a portion of the sermon he preached for the ordination of F. A. Farley at Providence in 1828 will serve. Here we have the commencement of themes that were to become standards among the more passionate of his adherents: namely, that nature is the revelation of the divine rather than formal dogma, and that the approach to nature is properly to be made through insight and not through a systematized and sterilized theology. In this sermon Channing attained his most "Transcendental" limit and practically asserted the supremacy of the intuitive assurance over all inductive reasoning; but even in his most reckless moment, he was far from casting off his eighteenth-century inheritance, and even while glorifying the innate propensities of the mind, he enjoined a "caution" which some of his listeners were soon cheerfully to transcend.

The text is from Channing's *Works* (Boston, 1880, pp. 291–302).]

I begin with observing, what all indeed will understand, that the likeness to God, of which I propose to speak, belongs to man's higher or spiritual nature. It has its foundation in the original and essential capacities of the mind. In proportion as these are unfolded by right and vigorous exertion, it is extended and brightened. In proportion as these lie dormant, it is obscured. In proportion as they are perverted and overpowered by the appetites and passions, it is blotted out. In truth, moral evil, if unresisted and habitual, may so blight and lay waste these capacities, that the image of God in man may seem to be wholly destroyed . . .

It is plain, too, that likeness to God is the true and only preparation for the enjoyment of the universe. In proportion as we approach and resemble the mind of God, we are brought into harmony with the creation; for in that proportion we possess the principles from which the universe sprung; we carry within ourselves the perfections of which its beauty, magnificence, order, benevolent adaptations, and boundless purposes are the results and manifestations. God unfolds himself in his works to a kindred mind. It is possible that the brevity of these hints may expose to the charge of mysticism what seems to me the calmest and clearest truth. I think, however, that every reflecting man will feel that likeness to God must be a principle of sympathy or accordance with his creation; for the creation is a birth and shining forth of the Divine Mind, a work through which his spirit breathes. In proportion as we receive this spirit we possess within ourselves the explanation of what we see. We discern more and more of God in every thing, from the frail flower to the everlasting stars. Even in evil, that dark cloud which hangs over the creation, we discern rays of light and hope, and gradually come to see, in suffering and temptation, proofs and instruments of the sublimest purposes of wisdom and love . . .

That man has a kindred nature with God, and may bear most important and ennobling relations to him, seems to me to be established by a striking proof. This proof you will understand by considering, for a moment, how we obtain our ideas of God. Whence come the conceptions which we include under that august name? Whence do we derive our knowledge of the attributes and perfections which constitute the Supreme Being? I answer, we derive them from our own souls. The divine attributes are first developed in ourselves, and thence transferred to our Creator. The idea of God, sublime and awful as it is, is the idea of our own spiritual nature, purified and enlarged to infinity. In ourselves are the elements of the Divinity. God, then, does not sustain a figurative resemblance to man. It is the resemblance of a parent to a child, the likeness of a kindred nature . . .

I am aware that it may be objected to these views, that we receive our idea of God from the universe, from his works, and not so exclusively from our own souls. The universe, I know, is full of God. The heavens and earth declare his glory. In other words, the effects and signs of power, wisdom, and goodness, are apparent through the whole creation. But apparent to what? Not to the outward eye; not to the acutest organs of sense; but to a kindred mind, which interprets the universe by itself. It is only through that energy of thought by which we adapt various and complicated means to distant ends, and give harmony and a common bearing to multiplied exertions, that we understand the creative intelligence which has established the order, dependencies, and harmony of nature. We see God around us because He dwells within us. It is by a kindred wisdom that we discern his wisdom in his works. The brute, with an eye as piercing as ours, looks on the universe; and the page, which to us is radiant with characters of greatness and goodness, is to him a blank. In truth, the beauty and glory of God's works are revealed to the mind by a light beaming from itself. We discern the impress of God's attributes in the universe by accordance of nature, and enjoy them through sympathy . . .

I would offer another answer to this objection, that God's infinity places him beyond the resemblance and approach of man. I affirm, and trust that I do not speak too strongly, that there are traces of infinity in the human mind; and that, in this respect, it bears a likeness to God. The very conception of infinity is the mark of a nature to which no limit can be prescribed. This thought, indeed, comes to us not so much from abroad as from our own souls. We ascribe this attribute to God, because we possess capacities and wants which only an unbounded being can fill, and because we are conscious of a tendency in spiritual faculties to unlimited expansion. We believe in the divine infinity through something congenial with it in our own breasts. I hope I speak clearly, and if not, I would ask those to whom I am obscure to pause before they condemn. To me it seems that the soul, in all its higher actions, in original thought, in the creations of genius, in the soarings of imagination, in its love of beauty and grandeur, in its aspirations after a pure and unknown joy, and especially in disinterestedness, in the spirit of self-sacrifice, and in enlightened devotion, has a character of infinity. There is often a depth in human love which may be strictly called unfathomable. There is sometimes a lofty strength in moral principle which all the power of the outward universe cannot overcome. There seems a might within which can more than balance all might without. There is, too, a piety which swells into a transport too vast for utterance, and into an immeasurable joy. I am speaking, indeed, of what is uncommon, but still of realities. We see, however, the tendency of the soul to the infinite in more familiar and ordinary forms. Take, for example, the delight which we find in the vast scenes of nature, in prospects which spread around us without limits, in the immensity of the heavens and the ocean, and especially in the rush and roar of mighty winds, waves, and torrents, when, amidst our deep awe, a power within seems to respond to the omnipotence around us. The same principle is seen in the delight ministered to us by works of fiction or of imaginative art, in which our own nature is set before us in more than human beauty and power. In truth, the soul is always bursting its limits. It thirsts continually for wider knowledge. It rushes forward to untried happiness. It has deep wants, which nothing limited can appease. Its true element and end is an unbounded good. Thus, God's infinity has its image in the soul; and through the soul, much more than through the universe, we arrive at this conception of the Deity . . .

To complete my views of this topic, I beg to add an important caution.

I have said that the great work of religion is to conform ourselves to God, or to unfold the divine likeness within us. Let none infer from this language that I place religion in unnatural effort, in straining after excitements which do not belong to the present state, or in any thing separate from the clear and simple duties of life. I exhort you to no extravagance. I reverence human nature too much to do it violence. I see too much divinity in its ordinary operations to urge on it a forced and vehement virtue. To grow in the likeness of God we need not cease to be men. This likeness does not consist in extraordinary or miraculous gifts, in supernatural additions to the soul, or in any thing foreign to our original constitution; but in our essential faculties, unfolded by vigorous and conscientious exertion in the ordinary circumstances assigned by God. To resemble our Creator we need not fly from society, and entrance ourselves in lonely contemplation and prayer. Such processes might give a feverish strength to one class of emotions, but would result in disproportion, distortion, and sickliness of mind. Our proper work is to approach God by the free and natural unfolding of our highest powers—of understanding, conscience, love, and the moral will.

2

Impact

In a state of society like our own, with institutions so free from abuse and so full of mercifulness, it is hard to comprehend why there should be such a feverish sensibility in favor of the abandoned, and so intense a wish for something better than the laws.

—NATHANIEL L. FROTHINGHAM

1. Alexander H. Everett (1790–1847)
History of Intellectual Philosophy

[The first generation of Unitarian intellectuals—editors of *The Monthly Anthology* and importers of European culture, men like Buckminster and Edward Everett—conscientiously endeavored to prove that New Englanders, or at least their sort of New Englanders, could cast off the hereditary vice of New England: its concentration upon theology. Therefore, as publicly as possible, they advertised their receptivity to "literature." By that term they understood what had been written in Europe and England throughout the last century. They meant Pope, Addison, and Dr. Johnson. They had not the slightest suspicion, as Channing was soon ruefully to confess, that by confidently opening the port of Boston to European literature, any other frigates than the Augustan would enter.

They went to Europe in search of "the regular, elaborate, harmonious strains" that would reinforce and confirm their regular and harmonious theology. The Athenaeum serenely subscribed to the English periodicals. By the middle of the 1820's the Unitarian leaders got their first glimmering realization that they were bringing in items which meant (if they meant anything) that Unitarianism was obsolete. By resolutely establishing channels of communication, these noble figures worked their own undoing. Despite what they had heard about the French Revolution and Napoleon, they were utterly unaware that the Europe with which they made contact was undergoing an intellectual revolution more profound than the political. In the expectation of furnishing New England libraries with the elegancies of Pope and Addison, they managed to give their pupils the barbarities of Wordsworth, Coleridge, and Cousin.

The Augustan literature, Channing had to acknowledge, is now being accused —he would not say how justly—of playing only on the surface of nature and of the heart. "Men want and demand a more thrilling note, a poetry which pierces beneath the exterior of life to the depths of the soul, and which lays open its mysterious workings, borrowing from the whole outward creation fresh images and correspondences, with which to illuminate the secrets of the world within us." The first reaction of the rational Unitarians was sheer consternation. They could not grasp these ideas; they knew only that this was not the Europe they had gone in search of. The new literature held up for American admiration (and imitation) not a Europe of decorum, but of "gross violations both of taste and moral sentiment." It was much too late to retreat into isolation; Buckminster, Everett, and the Athenaeum did their work all too well. There was nothing for editors of *The North American Review* to do but to try to meet the uninvited guest at the water's edge, and by explaining that this was not what they had meant at all, to turn him back before he could work havoc in the Harvard Yard.

To the credit of these men, let it be said, they did not shirk the challenge; they advanced to meet it. In July of 1829, only three years after Victor Cousin had published his first important book—while he was still the sensation of Paris and before any of his works were translated into English—the *Review* (XXIX, 67–123) attempted to dispose of him before hardly anybody in America had heard even so much as his name.

In this case the *Review* had the benefit of intelligences closer to the scene of action than Boston. Alexander Hill Everett, elder by four years to his more stately brother, a Harvard graduate of 1806 and a youthful member of the Anthology Club, first went abroad as private secretary to John Quincy Adams in the mission to Moscow. From 1815 to 1824 he was a diplomat at The Hague. In 1825 Adams made him minister to Spain. Hence he knew Europe and could detect the danger in Victor Cousin when on Beacon Hill it was known only that a French professor was making some sort of stir at the Ecole Normale.

Everett came home the next year, 1830, and succeeded Jared Sparks as editor of *The North American Review*. American influences worked upon him in unpredictable ways; he deserted the Whig party and became a Democrat, to the great embarrassment of Edward Everett and his friends. He finally died in Canton, as United States Commissioner to China. But at the moment he sent this article to the *Review,* he was an emissary in Europe not only of the United States government but of Unitarian Boston, and he recognized at once that Cousin was a foe. So, he undertook to demolish him.

He succeeded—as did the editors and professors of his generation—only in making the object of his attack sound alluring. His younger readers, recognizing in Everett's standards of condemnation exactly what they were becoming bored with, were forced to the conclusion that Cousin must be what they were groping for. Instead of quarantining his charges, Everett exposed them to the infection, and for the next decade the contagion raged.

Emerson later spoke scornfully of Cousin and his eclecticism, but he betrayed how large a part in the formation of Transcendentalism Cousin had actually played by remembering how astonished he had been in 1833 to find that Wordsworth knew only the name of Cousin, "whose lectures we had all been reading in Boston." Parker's acknowledgment of Cousin's influence is more explicit (see pp. 487–488). Others in the 1830's, notably Brownson and Ripley, rated him the greatest name in modern philosophy. With the translation of his *History of Philosophy* by H. G. Linberg in 1832 and *Elements of Psychology* by C. S. Henry in 1834, Cousin became a decisive factor in the intellectual life of hundreds of young New Englanders.

In modern intellectual history, as we now view it, Victor Cousin (1792–1867) is memorable chiefly because he popularized German idealism in a simple—indeed, a much too simple—style. He smoothed over the break between the nineteenth and eighteenth centuries by offering, under the banner of eclecticism, a method of accepting the Kantian metaphysics without altogether rejecting the sensationalism of Locke and the Enlightenment. Still, the weight of his influence was all against Locke, and upon Locke and his psychology the Unitarian edifice was constructed. He studied in Germany in 1817 and published his *Fragmens philosophiques* in 1826. His return in 1828 to the chair at the Ecole Normale—of which he had been deprived in 1821–22 for political reasons—was the signal for a liberal demonstration, and for three years his lectures were the most thronged performances in the capital. Ultimately Cousin became Director of the Ecole under Louis Philippe, and his reputation is so identified with the bourgeois monarchy that he is known only among historians of the period. But for the times Cousin's simplification, or even vulgarization, of German idealism exerted an influence over all Europe as well as in Boston. He was especially useful in supplying formulations to those incapable of reading German, such as the concept of a universal and impersonal "Reason" in which individuals merely participate, and the concept of the history of philosophy as being the central thread of social and cultural history.

Everett's article is all the more remarkable because it exhibits the immediate alarm of the Unitarians upon hearing that Locke was under fire. Everett shows only a cursory understanding of Cousin, but he clearly demonstrates what Locke meant to the Unitarian way of thinking. Thus he succeeds, as early as 1829, in drawing the line that was to divide the Unitarian mentality from the Transcendental. He reveals the handicap under which the Unitarians, to their vast surprise, were obliged to fight: no sooner had they freed liberalism from Calvinism on the basis of their version of the Lockean doctrine than they found the most advanced philosophers in Europe accusing Locke of being the author of the Deism and atheism of the French Philosophes. Also, from these sources, and equally to their surprise, the Unitarians learned that it was universally assumed in Europe that Hume had destroyed Locke.

Everett's line of attack is also revealing: he accounts for Cousin's nonsense on political grounds. He sees it as a result of the frenzies of the French Revolution. The inference is thus obvious: America is a sane and sober country where such horrors are unthinkable. Hence, these ideas are utterly foreign to the American scene, and no true American will ever regard them as anything but fantastic.]

I⊤ is the glory of Newton and Locke, to have directed their labors at once, and with all the necessary zeal and perseverance, to the most important subjects in physical and intellectual science; and the splendor of the results corresponded with, or even surpassed, all that might have been expected from the excellence of the new method, and the extraordinary talent of those who made the application of it . . . The great principles of the Newtonian system had been suspected even by the ancients, and were probably taught in the schools of Pythagoras; but . . . they never took deep hold on the public opinion, and were afterwards lost. In modern times they . . . would, perhaps, have been lost again, had not the genius and patience of Newton fixed them for ever upon the basis of rigorous demonstration. In the same way, the leading principles of intellectual science had floated loosely for centuries upon the chaos of public opinion, sometimes adopted, sometimes rejected, but in either case on insufficient grounds, and always mixed up with a large alloy of fiction and absurdity. The sagacious and powerful mind of Locke seized upon them as they lay in this unsettled and corrupted state, divested them of the extraneous matter with which they were connected, placed them on a solid foundation of clear and satisfactory argument, and arranged them into a regular and symmetrical system. In the "Essay on the Human Understanding," intellectual science appeared for the first time in a clear and intelligible shape, unmingled with the vain and visionary fancies which had previously disfigured it, and accessible to the plain good sense of every cultivated mind. This great work is, and will probably always remain, the textbook of the noblest branch of human learning . . .

The political revolutions of the last thirty years have created a large and active party on the Continent, the adherents of which habitually denounce the "Essay on the Human Understanding," as the real fountain of all the mischief which more superficial professors of the same doctrine have attributed to Voltaire and Rousseau, and which sounder thinkers than those of either class, would perhaps account for by causes much more deeply seated

than the publications of any contemporary or recent writers. Accustomed as
we are to look up to Locke with reverence, as one of the great teachers of
intellectual, moral, and religious truth; aware that he has not only established
in his great work the doctrines of natural religion, but was also a firm believer in revelation, in defence of which he published a separate treatise; rec-
ollecting that he adorned the splendid elevation of his genius by a private
life of remarkable disinterestedness and exemplary moral beauty; looking
at his character, we say, under this point of view, which is common to the
whole English public on both sides of the water, it is not without some
astonishment as well as pain, that we find him branded at the present day
by a party on the Continent, as the great apostle of irreligion, immorality,
impurity, and sedition . . .

[Cousin] belongs to a school of philosophy which may be looked upon
as a reaction or indirect result of the French Revolution. The long rain of
disasters which accompanied that great political crisis, naturally excited strong
prejudice against the moral and political theories which prevailed about the
time of its opening, and were supposed to be, to a certain extent, the causes
of its occurrence and of the unfortunate direction which it pursued for so
many years. These moral and political theories were also believed, whether
correctly or not, to be essentially connected with the metaphysical systems of
the day; and the latter again, having been published and generally received
as deductions from the philosophy of Locke, were somewhat too hastily
identified with his opinions. Under these circumstances it appeared necessary
in order to furnish a complete refutation of the political doctrines of the
French revolutionists, to go back to the source of evil, in the "Essay on the
Human Understanding." The leading principle of this work, that all our
ideas are either received through the senses or obtained by reflection upon
such as are so received, was looked upon as the root of all the modern heresies;
and was therefore to be set aside at all hazards. In order to contest this principle with success, it was necessary to show, that such of our notions as are
not the immediate results of sensation are original possessions of the mind.
This is the old theory of *innate ideas,* which has accordingly been revived
with a sort of passion by most of the anti-revolutionary philosophers of the
present day, and has even been adopted . . . by many of the adherents of the
liberal political school; who while they approve the results of the Revolution,
are anxious to shake off all responsibility for most of the acts and even opinions of its authors . . .

At about the same time when this doctrine was growing up in Scotland,
another came into notice in the North of Germany, which engaged for many

years a large share of the public attention, and indeed excited a stronger immediate sensation than any philosophical system which has ever been promulgated. We allude of course to the *Transcendental Philosophy,* founded by the celebrated Kant, a professor at the University of Konigsberg in Prussia. This writer states in the introduction to his *Criticism on Pure Reason,* that having been convinced by the arguments of Hume that the idea of *power* is not obtained by sensation or reflection . . . he drew the conclusion that it must be an original or innate possession of the mind. Having come to this opinion respecting our notion of *power,* or the relation between causes and effects, he was naturally led to inquire whether there were not other ideas which were also independent of sensation and reflection, and which formed, as it were, a part of our intellectual substance. The result of his researches was, that there are a considerable number of ideas of this kind, which he arranges under the two heads of *sensible* and *intellectual* ideas. The first division includes only the two notions of *space* and *time;* the second, that of *power,* and some ten or twelve more, which we need not recapitulate. The rule adopted by Kant for discovering which of our ideas are innate, was the following.—On reviewing your ideas, whenever you come to one which strikes you as necessary, so that having once obtained it, you cannot possibly suppose it not to exist, you may be sure that it is not the product of sensation or reflection, but an original possession of the mind. Thus we can easily conceive the non-existence of all extended objects, but having once obtained the idea of *extension* or *space,* we cannot conceive its non-existence. The notion of *extension* or *space* is therefore transcendental and original, while those of the qualities of particular extended objects are the results of sensation. These two classes of ideas we naturally connect together in the habitual exercise of our intellectual powers, so that all our notions of individual objects are combinations of one or more ideas belonging to each class; just as the idea which a man, looking through a piece of colored glass, forms of the object before him is a combined result of the sensible qualities of the object and of the color of the glass . . . Hence we know nothing of the real character of the external world, because we never see it except in combination with some ingredient furnished by our own minds; but we are certain of the reality of our transcendental notions, because they are immediate objects of consciousness, as they exist in their own nature, and unmingled with any other element. Kant therefore abandons the external world to the skeptics, and founds the certainty of our knowledge upon the supposed reality of the notions originally inherent in our own understanding . . .

By those who are acquainted with the theory of innate or original ideas, only through the detailed, and in general to us very satisfactory refutation of it given by Locke, it may perhaps be deemed a mere chimera, long since exploded, and unworthy of the least notice at the present day. It is nevertheless a doctrine that has in all ages, including the present, been held by many philosophers of the highest rank; and is indeed represented, not without some appearance of correctness, by the writer now before us, as one of the two leading answers that have been given, alike in ancient and in modern times, to the problem of the origin of our knowledge . . .

There seems to be a restlessness in our nature, which leads us, when in the progress of improvement we have attained the truth, not to be satisfied with it, but still to wander in search of new discoveries, although every step we take necessarily carries us farther from the point at which we profess to aim. We see this disposition plainly exemplified in the department of the fine arts, where a period of good taste is uniformly followed by one, of which the predominant characteristic is extravagance, and a hankering after the exploded errors of a barbarous age. The principle no doubt exercises its influence with equal certainty in philosophy . . .

Idealism, therefore, historically viewed, presents itself as an unsubstantial dream, which charms the infantile period of intellectual philosophy, rather than as one of two opinions which have nearly divided the thinking men of all ages and nations. Critically viewed, the system has, we think, the same general characteristics. There is a wild and ethereal air about it, that catches the attention and delights the fancy. It fills the mind with lofty and glorious imaginations, transports us from the cold and formal realities of the world around us, into empyreal regions, the perpetual abodes of light, truth, purity, and happiness. It gratifies our longing after a nobler and a loftier destiny than that which we can here aspire to, by bringing our minds into nearer contact,—identifying them, indeed, by some mysterious and inexplicable bond of union,—with the sublime spirit whose energy pervades and governs the Universe. It lends itself easily to all the beauties of rhetorical embellishment, and when it appears in its natural dress, always wears the seductive graces of an elegant style . . . Kant and his followers, the only idealists who pretend to strict and logical forms of expression, have given their language the same indistinctness and obscurity which belongs to that of all the rest, by employing a new and almost unintelligible nomenclature. Their terms not being settled by familiar usage or precise explanation, really convey, notwithstanding their exact and scientific air, no definite meaning to the mind of the reader and serve, on the contrary, to shroud the author's opinions under a misty veil, equivalent in effect, though by no means in attraction, to the wild and vague poetical imagery of the preceding writers of the same class . . .

Notwithstanding the imposing appearance which idealism makes, under the formidable terminology of Kant, and the seductive graces which it wears in the charming style of Plato, we cannot upon the whole regard it, when reduced to its simple expression, and rigorously examined, as anything but a mass of palpable absurdities . . . Intellectual science is now fixed; but the mind, ever restless, and ever dissatisfied with its own possessions, under-values the truths it has acquired, and still pushing forward on its perpetual voyage of discovery, arrives at length at the region of materialism and sensuality,—of sophists and skeptics,—of Epicurus, Pyrrho, Condillac, Helvetius, and Hume. It is now affirmed, that because the mind can only communicate with external objects, through the senses, it is in fact nothing more than a faculty attached to the body; and the system is pushed into its consequences until it ends in the denial of the immortality of the soul, and the existence of God. Alarmed for these sacred and cherished principles, which, as we have already remarked, man will make any sacrifice rather than relinquish, and casting about with anxious impatience for the means of securing them, the mind, in the first moments of uncertainty, rejects *en masse* the whole improved doctrine which has apparently involved such fatal results, and oscillates back to the visions of its childhood, content to embrace the ideal theory, with all its absurdity, rather than abandon the glorious truths with which it is for the time supposed to be connected. Such appears to have been the origin of the second Platonism of antiquity, and of the revival of idealism in modern Europe . . . by Kant and his followers, and by the French writers of the present day. But this period of reaction is obviously in its nature a transitory one, and when the false alarm created by the sophists has subsided, the enlightened opinion of the public will quietly settle down again in the conclusions of Locke and Aristotle, which, in our view of them at least, as they exhaust the science and leave no room, on essential points, for the farther progress of real discovery, must form in all ages the creed of judicious men, and the standard to which those who may be led astray by the false lights of other theories, will be gradually rallied back from their different vagaries.

2. James Marsh (1794–1842)
Preliminary Essay

[James Marsh, born on a farm at Hartford, Vermont, and educated at Dartmouth, was converted there, during a revival in 1815, to orthodox Calvinism. He studied at Andover Theological Seminary, was ordained in 1824, and in 1826 became president of the University of Vermont. He resigned that office in 1833, but continued as professor of philosophy. He read German fluently and translated Herder; he left an impression upon the university that still is felt.

It is indicative of the total situation in New England that the introduction of Coleridge should be made by an orthodox Calvinist to whom both Unitarianism and Transcendentalism were reprehensible. In editing Coleridge's *Aids to Reflection* at Burlington, Vermont, in 1829, and publishing it with this "Preliminary Essay," Marsh was striking not at Boston or Harvard—which he ignored—but was contending against what he considered the real centers of New England thought, Andover and Yale. In the middle of the eighteenth century, Jonathan Edwards rephrased Calvinism in the language of Locke; by the end of the century, his version generally triumphed. The debate between the orthodox and the Unitarians was conducted upon a common acceptance of Lockean premises. But meanwhile dissensions sprang up among the Calvinists, and to Marsh it seemed that the time had come to rally them upon new, more creative, and less argumentative grounds. Coleridge designed his "philosophy" to support orthodox Christian conclusions, and so Marsh invoked it in the hope of making a new departure in American Christianity.

Thus he put into the hands of Emerson, Parker, Alcott, and their group the book that was of the greatest single importance in the formation of their minds. This was entirely beside Marsh's intention, but it happened. He made clear, as no one had yet done in this country, the utter opposition of the new philosophy to that upon which the Unitarians had builded. The rebels disregarded Coleridge's and Marsh's doctrinal conclusions, but were excited by the method, particularly with the central distinction between "Reason" and the "Understanding." In the early stages, this was the principal instrument of Transcendental analysis. Writing to his brother in 1834, Emerson reveals how decidedly second nature it had by then become for him to use these terms:

Philosophy affirms that the outward world is only phenomenal & the whole concern of dinners of tailors of gigs of balls whereof men make such account is a quite relative & temporary one—an intricate dream—the exhalation of the present state of the Soul—wherein the Understanding works incessantly as if it were real but the eternal Reason when now & then he is allowed to speak declares it is an accident a smoke nowise related to his permanent attributes.

Whereupon, realizing that he was speaking in a yet novel vein, Emerson continued, "Now that I have used the words, let me ask you do you draw the distinction of Milton Coleridge & the Germans between Reason & Understanding. I think it a philosophy itself & like all truth very practical." (The exposition he then offers his brother is one of the best of the early statements; see *Letters*, I, 412–413.)

Marsh was thus of tremendous assistance to the burgeoning movement, and not only in presenting Coleridge but, by following the clue of Coleridge, in proclaiming that in Germany and France the Coleridgian type of thought was on the march. When he proclaimed the empire of Locke at an end, he assured the youth of Boston and Cambridge that in revolting against the Understanding in the name of the Reason they were launching upon the wave of the future. Within a matter of months, Margaret Fuller was putting into her journals her great veneration of Coleridge, "a conviction that the benefits conferred by him on this and future ages are as yet incalculable." Though it is significant of the entire tone of the Coleridgian cult that she had to add, "To the unprepared he is nothing, to the prepared, everything."]

In regard to the distinguishing character and tendency of the Work itself, it [is] didactic, and designed to aid reflection on the principles and grounds of truth in our own being; but in another point of view, and with reference to my present object, it might rather be denominated A PHILOSOPHICAL STATEMENT AND VINDICATION OF THE DISTINCTIVELY SPIRITUAL AND PECULIAR DOCTRINES OF THE CHRISTIAN SYSTEM . . . The methods by which he accomplishes this, either in regard to the terms in which he enunciates the great doctrines of the Gospel, or the peculiar views of philosophy by which he reconciles them with the subjective grounds of faith in the universal reason of man, need not be stated here. I will merely observe, that the key to his system will be found in the distinctions, which he makes and illustrates between *nature* and *free-will,* and between the *understanding* and *reason.* It may meet the prejudices of some to remark farther, that in philosophizing on the grounds of our faith he does not profess or aim to solve all mysteries, and to bring all truth within the comprehension of the understanding. A truth may be mysterious, and the primary ground of all truth and reality must be so. But though we may believe what *passeth all understanding,* we *can not* believe what is *absurd,* or contradictory to *reason* . . .

Enlightened Christians, and especially Christian instructors, know it to be their duty, as far as possible, to prepare the way for the full and unobstructed influence of the Gospel, to do all in their power to remove those natural prejudices, and those errors of the understanding, which are obstacles to the truth, that the word of God may find access to the heart, and conscience, and reason of every man, that it may have *free course, and run, and be glorified*. My own belief, that such obstacles to the influence of truth exist in the speculative and metaphysical opinions generally adopted in this country, and that the present Work is in some measure at least calculated to remove them, is pretty clearly indicated . . . But, to be perfectly explicit on the subject I do not hesitate to express my conviction, that the natural tendency of some of the leading principles of our prevailing system of metaphysics, and those which must unavoidably have more or less influence on our theoretical views of religion, are of an injurious and dangerous tendency, and that so long as we retain them, however we may profess to exclude their influence from our theological inquiries, and from the interpretation of Scripture, we can maintain no consistent system of Scriptural theology, nor clearly and distinctly apprehend the spiritual import of the Scripture language . . .

Let it be understood, then, without further preface, that by the prevailing system of metaphysics, I mean the system, of which in modern times Locke is the reputed author, and the leading principles of which, with various modifications, more or less important, but not altering its essential character, have been almost universally received in this country . . . Yet I have reasons for believing there are some among us, and that their number is fast increasing, who are willing to revise their opinions on these subjects, and who will contemplate the views presented in this work with a liberal, and something of a prepared feeling of curiosity. The difficulties in which men find themselves involved by the received doctrines on these subjects, in their most anxious efforts to explain and defend the peculiar doctrines of spiritual religion, have led many to suspect that there must be some lurking error in the premises. It is not that these principles lead us to mysteries which we can not comprehend; they are found, or believed at least by many, to involve us in absurdities which we can comprehend . . .

I know that some whose moral and religious feelings had led them to a full belief in the doctrines of spiritual religion, but who at the same time had been taught to receive the prevailing opinions in metaphysics, have found these opinions carrying them unavoidably, if they would be consequent in their reasonings, and not do violence to their reason, to adopt a system of religion which does not profess to be spiritual, and thus have been compelled to choose between their philosophy and their religion. In most cases indeed, where men reflect at all, I am satisfied that it requires all the force of authority, and all the influence of education, to carry the mind over these difficulties;

and that then it is only by a vague belief that, though we can not see how, there must be some method of reconciling what seems to be so contradictory . . .

It must have been observed by the reader . . . that I have used several words, especially *understanding* and *reason,* in a sense somewhat diverse from their present acceptation; and the occasion of this I suppose would be partly understood from my having already directed the attention of the reader to the distinction exhibited between these words in the Work, and from the remarks made on the ambiguity of the word "reason" in its common use. I now proceed to remark, that the ambiguity spoken of, and the consequent perplexity in regard to the use and authority of reason, have arisen from the habit of using, since the time of Locke, the terms understanding and reason indiscriminately, and thus confounding a distinction clearly marked in the philosophy and in the language of the older writers . . . The misfortune is, that the powers of understanding and reason have not merely been blended and confounded in the view of our philosophy;—the higher and far more characteristic, as an essential constituent of our proper humanity, has been as it were obscured and hidden from our observation in the inferior power, which belongs to us in common with the brutes which perish . . .

We do indeed find in ourselves then, as no one will deny, certain powers of intelligence, which we have abundant reason to believe the brutes possess in common with us in a greater or less degree. The functions of the understanding, as treated in the popular systems of metaphysics, its faculties of attention, of abstraction, of generalization, the power of forethought and contrivance, of adapting means to ends, and the law of association, may be, so far as we can judge, severally represented more or less adequately in the instinctive intelligence of the higher order of brutes. But . . . do these, or any and all the faculties which we discover in irrational animals, satisfactorily account to a reflecting mind for all the *phenomena* which are presented to our observation in our own consciousness? Would any supposable addition to the *degree* merely of those powers which we ascribe to brutes, render them *rational* beings, and remove the sacred distinction, which law and reason have sanctioned, between things and persons? Will any such addition account for our having—what the brute is not supposed to have— the pure *ideas* of the geometrician, the power of ideal construction, the intuition of geometrical or other necessary and universal truths? Would it give rise, in irrational animals, to a *law of moral rectitude* and *to conscience*— to the feelings of moral *responsibility* and *remorse?* Would it awaken them to a reflective self-consciousness, and lead them to form and contemplate the *ideas* of the *soul,* of *free-will,* of *immortality,* and of God? It seems to me, that we have only to reflect for a serious hour upon what we mean by these, and then to compare them with our notion of what belongs to a brute, its inherent powers and their correlative objects, to feel that they are utterly incompatible—that in the blessing of these we enjoy a prerogative, which we can not disclaim without a violation of reason, and a voluntary abasement of ourselves—and that we must therefore be possessed of some *peculiar* powers— of some source of ideas *distinct* from the understanding, differing *in kind* from any and all of those which belong to us in common with inferior and irrational animals . . .

It is our peculiar misfortune in this country, that while the philosophy of Locke and the Scottish writers has been received in full faith, as the only rational system, and its leading principles especially passed off as unquestionable, the strong attachment to religion, and the fondness for speculation, by both of which we are strongly characterized, have led us to combine and associate these principles, such as they are, with our religious interests and opinions, so variously and so intimately, that by most persons they are considered as necessary parts of the same system; and from being so long contemplated together, the rejection of one seems impossible without doing violence to the other. Yet how much evidence might not an impartial observer find in examining the theological discussions which have prevailed, the speculative systems which have been formed and arrayed against each other, for the last seventy years, to convince him that there must be some discordance in the elements, some principle of secret but irreconcilable hostility between a philosophy and a religion, which, under every ingenious variety of form and shaping, still stand aloof from each other and refuse to cohere. For is it not a fact, that in regard to every speculative system which has been formed on these philosophical principles—to every new shaping of theory which has been devised and has gained adherents among us,—is it not a fact, I ask, that to all, except those adherents, the *system*—the philosophical theory—has seemed dangerous in its tendency, and at war with orthodox views of religion—perhaps even with the attributes of God? Nay, to bring the matter still nearer and more plainly to view, I ask, whether at this moment the organs and particular friends of our leading theological seminaries in New England, both devotedly attached to an orthodox and spiritual system of religion, and expressing mutual confidence as to the *essentials* of their mutual faith, do not each consider the other as holding a philosophical *theory* subversive of orthodoxy? . . .

I can not but add, as a matter of simple justice to the question, that however our prevailing system of philosophizing may have appealed to the authority of Lord Bacon, it needs but a candid examination of his writings, especially the first part of his *Novum Organum,* to be convinced that such an appeal is without grounds; and that in fact the fundamental principles of his philosophy are the same with those taught in this work. The great distinction especially, between the understanding and the reason, is fully and clearly recognized; and as a philosopher he would be far more properly associated with Plato, or even Aristotle, than with the modern philosophers, who have miscalled their systems by his name . . . In our own times, moreover, there is abundant evidence, whatever may be thought of the principles of this Work here, that the same general views of philosophy are regaining their ascendency elsewhere. In Great Britain there are not few, who begin to believe that the deep-toned and sublime eloquence of Coleridge on these great subjects may have something to claim their attention besides a few peculiarities of language. In Paris, the doctrines of a rational and spiritual system of philosophy are taught to listening and admiring thousands by one of the most learned and eloquent philosophers of the age; and in Germany, if I mistake not, the same general views are adopted by the serious friends of religious truth among her great and learned men.

Such—as I have no doubt—must be the case, wherever thinking men can be brought distinctly and impartially to examine their claims; and indeed to those who shall truly study and comprehend the general history of philosophy, it must always be matter of special wonder, that in the Christian community, anxiously striving to explain and defend the doctrines of Christianity in their spiritual sense, there should have been a long-continued and tenacious adherence to philosophical principles, so subversive of their faith in every thing distinctively spiritual; while those of an opposite tendency, and claiming a near relationship and correspondence with the truly spiritual in the Christian system, and the mysteries of its sublime faith, were looked upon with suspicion and jealousy, as unintelligible or dangerous metaphysics.

3. Timothy Walker (1802–1856)
Signs of the Times

["Before we knew his name, we knew *him*." In the late 1820's readers in New England, assiduously trying to keep up with the latest issues of the British periodicals, *The Foreign Review* and *The Edinburgh Review,* easily detected, in the style of certain articles, "a new power coming up in the literary republic." This anonymous power did not charm all his readers. Possibly because Timothy

Walker sensed that some of the younger people were responding altogether too extravagantly to this "wild bugle-call," he took occasion in *The North American Review* for July 1831 (XXXIII, 122–126), to rebuke the as yet unidentified author.

Timothy Walker had graduated as first scholar from Harvard in 1826 and then studied law; in 1830 he began to practice in Cincinnati. Later he was to become distinguished in the field of legal theory and to organize a law school that ultimately grew into the Law School of Cincinnati College. By pitching in 1831 upon "The Signs of the Times" (which had appeared in *The Edinburgh Review* in June 1829) he attacked the one of Carlyle's early broadsides that most effectively riddled the Unitarian position. As with Everett's attack on Cousin, Walker may have gratified readers of the *Review,* but to those whom he was trying to shield against this deleterious influence, he only made the object of his scorn seem the more enthralling. So, he deepened the already widening cleavage.]

We cannot help thinking, that this brilliant writer has conjured up phantoms for the sake of laying them again. At all events, we can see nothing but phantoms in what he opposes. In plain words, we deny the evil tendencies of Mechanism, and we doubt the good influences of his Mysticism. We cannot perceive that Mechanism, as such, has yet been the occasion of any injury to man. Some liberties, it is true, have been taken with Nature by this same presumptuous intermeddler. Where she denied us rivers, Mechanism has supplied them. Where she left our planet uncomfortably rough, Mechanism has applied the roller. Where her mountains have been found in the way, Mechanism has boldly levelled or cut through them. Even the ocean, by which she thought to have parted her quarrelsome children, Mechanism has encouraged them to step across. As if her earth were not good enough for wheels, Mechanism travels it upon iron pathways. Her ores, which she locked up in her secret vaults, Mechanism has dared to rifle and distribute. Still further encroachments are threatened. The terms uphill and downhill are to become obsolete. The horse is to be unharnessed, because he is too slow; and the ox is to be unyoked, because he is too weak. Machines are to perform all the drudgery of man, while he is to look on in self-complacent ease.

But where is the harm and danger of this? Why is every lover of the human race called on to plant himself in the path, and oppose these giant strides of Mechanism? Does this writer fear, that Nature will be dethroned, and Art set up in her place? Not exactly this. But he fears, if we rightly apprehend his meaning, that mind will become subjected to the laws of matter; that physical science will be built up on the ruins of our spiritual nature; that in our rage for machinery, we shall ourselves become machines . . .

On the face of the matter, is it likely that mechanical ingenuity is suicidal in its efforts? Is it probable that the achievements of mind are fettering and enthralling mind? Must the proud creator of Mechanism stoop to its laws? By covering our earth with unnumbered comforts, accommodations, and delights, are we, in the words of this writer, descending from our "true dignity of soul and character"? Setting existing facts aside, and reasoning in the abstract, what is the fair conclusion? To our view directly the contrary. We maintain, that the more work we can compel inert matter to do for us, the better will it be for our minds, because the more time shall we have to attend to them . . . If machines could be so improved and multiplied, that all our corporeal necessities could be entirely gratified, without the intervention of human labor, there would be nothing to hinder all mankind from becoming philosophers, poets, and votaries of art. The whole time and thought of the whole human race could be given to inward culture, to spiritual advancement. But let us not be understood as intimating a belief, that such a state of things will ever exist. This we do not believe, nor is it necessary to our argument. It is enough, if there be an approach thereto. And this we do believe is constantly making. Every sober view of the past confirms us in this belief . . .

When we attempt to convey an idea of the infinite attributes of the Supreme Being, we point to the stupendous machinery of the universe. From the ineffable harmony and regularity, which pervade the whole vast system, we deduce the infinite power and intelligence of the Creating Mind. Now we can perceive no reason, why a similar course should not be pursued, if we would form correct conceptions of the dignity and glory of man . . . Before we conclude that man's dignity is depreciated in the contrivance and use of this machinery, let us remember, that a precisely analogous course of reasoning must conduct us to the conclusion, that the act of Creation subtracted from the glory of the Creator; that the Infinite Mind, as it brooded from eternity over chaos, was more transcendently glorious, than when it returned from its six days' work, to contemplate a majestic world. We accordingly believe there is nothing irreverent in the assertion, that the finite mind in no respect approximates so nearly to a resemblance of the Infinite Mind, as in the subjugation of matter, through the aid of Mechanism, to fixed and beneficial laws,—to laws ordained by God, but discovered and applied by man . . .

But this writer has not confined his warfare to the world as a whole. He has divided mankind into classes, and attacked them in detail. We shall try to follow him through his campaign . . . "With its whole, undivided might, it [this age] forwards, teaches, and practices, *the great art of adapting means to ends.* Nothing is now done directly, or by hand; all is by rule, and calculated contrivance. For the simplest operation, some helps and accompaniments, some cunning, abbreviating process is in readiness." Now take away the lurking sneer with which this is said, and we see not how it would be possible to crowd more praise into a smaller compass. It is no small part of wisdom, to possess "the capacity of adapting means to ends." What would the writer have us do? Pursue ends without regard to means? . . .

The next thrust is made at Metaphysics. And here we are informed that nobody has gone to work right. The whole world are now, and always have been, totally in the wrong. Even Locke, the great master, was at fault in the outset. But to avoid mis-statement, let the reviewer speak for himself. "The whole doctrine of Locke is mechanical, in its aim and origin, in its method and results. It is a *mere* discussion concerning the origin of our consciousness, or ideas, or whatever else they may be called; a genetic history of what we see *in* the mind. But the *grand secrets* of Necessity and Free-will, of the mind's vital or non-vital dependence on matter, of our *mysterious relations* to Time and Space, to God, to the Universe, are not in the faintest degree touched on." So because Locke confined his inquiries to what can be known, instead of meddling with "grand secrets," and "mysterious relations," he is a mere mechanic. Commend us to such mechanics. Give us Locke's Mechanism, and we will envy no man's Mysticism. Give us to know the "origin of our ideas," to comprehend the phenomena "which we see in the mind," and we will leave the question of the mind's essence to transcendental speculators. So of Necessity and Free-will; mechanical as the age is, we have heard of no machinery which can be brought to bear upon their explanation. And as to "the mind's vital or non-vital dependence upon matter," we are compelled to plead ignorance of what it means. We are bound, however, to suppose it has a deep meaning, since Locke did not get at the bottom of it. And should the writer give some of his leisure moments to the investigation, we hope the world may have the benefit of his researches. He may next find it profitable to undertake with Entities, Quiddities, Essences, and Sensible Forms, those stubborn secrets which did so puzzle some of the schoolmen. After brushing away these mists, there will still remain a rich field for discovery, in "our mysterious relations to Time and Space." And these relations being fully ascertained, the way will be cleared for a discussion of the celebrated question,—Whether spirits can pass from one point of space to another, without passing through the intervening space . . .

We have no wish to disguise the feeling of strong dissatisfaction, excited in us, by the article under consideration. We consider its tendency injurious, and its reasoning unsound. That it has some eloquent passages must be admitted, but when we hear distinguished philosophers spoken of as "logic-mills,"—the religion of the age as "a working for wages,"—our Bible societies as "supported by fomenting of vanities, by puffing, intrigue, and chicane,"—and all descriptions of men "from cartwright up to the code-maker," as mere "mechanists"; when we further hear "the grand secrets of necessity and free-will,"—"our mysterious relations to time and space,"—and "the deep, infinite harmonies of nature and man's soul,"—brought repeatedly forward under the most varied forms of statement, as the legitimate objects of philosophical inquiry, and the most illustrious of the living and the dead, men whom we never think of but as benefactors of our race, made the objects of satire and ridicule, because they have preferred the *terra firma* of mechanical philosophy to the unstable quagmire of mystic conjecture;—we find it difficult not to regard the Essay rather as an effort of paradoxical ingenuity,—the sporting of an adventurous imagination with settled opinions,—than as a serious inquiry after truth.

4. James Freeman Clarke (1810–1888)

The Influence of Carlyle

[James Freeman Clarke was the step-grandson of James Freeman, who led King's Chapel into Unitarianism and who was a prophet of the movement second in influence only to Dr. Channing. Brought up in Dr. Freeman's household, Clarke was thoroughly educated in liberal Christianity before he went to college. He graduated from Harvard in 1829 and from the Divinity School in 1833. He then joined a band of gallant young Harvard men who went West to bring culture and Unitarianism to Louisville and Cincinnati. Their principal implement was *The Western Messenger,* a monthly magazine, of which Clarke was an editor from 1836 to 1839.

Practically all of this group found their way back, more or less defeated, to New England. Clarke established the Church of the Disciples in Boston in 1841 and eventually became a leading and influential citizen. One of the chief spokesmen for Transcendentalism, he insisted throughout that he was nevertheless a Christian. He was a fine scholar, of great dignity and charm.

Clarke repeatedly, in his old age, paid tribute to the arousing effect of Carlyle on the generation of 1830. He made for us, said Clarke, "a new heaven and a new earth, a new religion and a new life." In 1831, when Timothy Walker tried to dismiss Carlyle, the younger generation had no magazine in which they could reply. The young group in Cincinnati forged the *Messenger* and in it made clear their break with their teachers. So, within seven years of Walker's tirade, Clarke could comment on the effect of Carlyle as being long since achieved. He made this point in *The Western Messenger* for March 1838 (V, 417–423).]

For ourselves, we hardly know how to describe the feelings with which we first perused his articles in some old numbers of the Foreign Review which we happened upon, one day, in the Boston Athenaeum. There was a freshness and unworn life in all he said, new and profound views of familiar truths, which seemed to open a vista for endless reflection. It was as if we saw the angels ascending and descending in a Jacob's dream. It was, as it sometimes happens when we are introduced to a person with whom we have strong affinities—in ten minutes we are wholly intimate—we seem to have known him all our life. It makes us smile now, to remember how we used to walk into the reading room every day, to spend our leisure hour in reading the same articles again and again, at the foot of the group of Laocoön . . .

When he began to write, eight or ten years ago, what did we know of German writers? Wieland's Oberon, Klopstock's Messiah, Kotzebue's plays, Schiller's Robbers, Goethe's Werther, a dim notion of his Faust, and what we could learn from Madame de Staël's L'Allemagne,—this was about the substance of what well educated Englishmen understood as constituting the modern masterpieces of German genius. Of the massive and splendid structure of philosophy, which Kant had founded, and men of like talent built up, we had only to say, "mystical," "transcendental"—and having pronounced these two pregnant words, we judged ourselves excused from all further examination. And yet, this very time, there existed a literature unsurpassed in the history of the world for genius, variety, and extent. Goethe's Werther had been forgotten in his splendid series of dramatic, aesthetic, and philosophical writings. His Egmont, Tasso, and Iphigenia; his Hermann and Dorothea; his exquisite lyrics; his philosophical romances; and his profound treatises on art and science, had quite eclipsed the dazzling products of his youthful pen. Schiller's Robbers was looked upon as a youthful indiscretion, and pardoned for the sake of the Joan of Arc, the Maria Stuart, the William Tell, the Wallenstein,—ripe fruits of his maturer taste and more developed genius. Richter, Novalis, Tieck, and a whole crowd of master-spirits, had carved out for themselves a home in the intellectual community. But of all this we knew little. Much praise then, to Mr. Carlyle, for having introduced us to this fair circle of gifted minds.

5. Orestes A. Brownson (1803–1876)

The Everlasting Yes

[Orestes Augustus Brownson was born in the old faith of New England, came from hard-scrabble rural backgrounds, and was not a Harvard man. In many respects the most powerful of the Transcendentalists—at any rate, the hardest hitting—there was always a kind of peasantlike crudity in him, and an instability that was manifested in his histrionic conversions and retractions.

Born in Stockbridge, Vermont, and brought up in poverty on a farm, he was entirely self-taught. In 1822 he underwent a religious experience and joined the Presbyterian Church. In 1824 he became a Universalist and was ordained in 1826, afterwards preaching in various pulpits in Vermont and upstate New York. Rejecting Universalism, he was associated with Robert Dale Owen and Fanny Wright in New York City, where he organized the Workingmen's Party. Then, announcing himself a Unitarian, he preached at Walpole, New Hampshire, 1832–1834, and in 1834 came to Canton, Massachusetts. He thus became a part of the Unitarian community around Boston, contributed to the journals, and immediately made his vitality felt.

He responded as fervently as the others to the new influences, to Coleridge and Carlyle, and to the German literature, but Cousin became his divinity, and he appointed himself a kind of American agent for eclecticism. In 1838 he founded *The Boston Quarterly Review,* which he conducted with great dash, often having to write most of it himself. He took the presidential campaign of 1840 very seriously and propagandized against the Whigs.

Between 1834 and 1844 he was certainly one of the major spokesmen for the new school—in terms of popular reaction possibly the most conspicuous spokesman. Hence his conversion to Catholicism in 1844 was a shock to the entire community, and Brownson's reputation among the Transcendentalists suffered; their opinion has been preserved in most histories, so that the immense contribution of Brownson during his Transcendental phase has been shamefully neglected.

In 1857 he wrote an autobiography, *The Convert; or, Leaves from My Experience;* it is mainly a history of his shifts in religious belief and his struggle for faith, but in this passage (from the second edition, New York, 1877, pp. 122–124) he looks back upon the situation in the vicinity of Boston in the 1830's and says perhaps the most penetrating thing upon it that survives from the literature of that decade. Of course, Brownson is here looking down upon the past from the heights of his conversion, but even so, he could remember with tenderness and pity the spiritual drives that produced the Transcendental outbreak.]

Irreligious ideas and sentiments are disorganizing and destructive in their nature, and cannot be safely cherished for a single moment after the work of destruction is completed. When the work to be done is that of construction, of building up, of organizing, of founding something, we must resort to religious ideas and sentiments, for they, having love for their principle, are plastic, organic, constructive, and the only ideas and sentiments that are so. They are necessary to the new organization or institution of the race demanded; and the organization or institution, which I called the church, is necessary to the progress of man and society, or the creation of an earthly paradise. The first thing to be done is to cease our hostility to the past, discontinue the work of destruction; abandon the old war against the Papacy, which has no longer any significance, and in a spirit of universal love and conciliation, turn our attention to the work of founding a religious institution, or effecting a new church organization, adapted to our present and future wants.

This we are now, I thought, in a condition to attempt. Men are beginning to understand that Protestantism is no-churchism, is no positive religion; and while it serves the purpose of criticism and destruction, it cannot meet the wants of the soul, or erect the temple in which the human race may assemble to worship in concord and peace. Unitarianism has demolished Calvinism, made an end in all thinking minds of everything like dogmatic Protestantism, and Unitarianism itself satisfies nobody. It is negative, cold, lifeless, and all advanced minds among Unitarians are dissatisfied with it, and are craving something higher, better, more living, and lifegiving. They are weary of doubt, uncertainty, disunion, individualism, and crying out from the bottom of their hearts for faith, for love, for union. They feel that life has wellnigh departed from the world; that religion is but an empty name, and morality is mere decorum or worldly prudence; that men neither worship God, nor love one another. Society as it is, is a lie, a sham, a charnel-house, a valley of dry bones. O that the Spirit of God would once more pass by, and say unto these dry bones, "Live!" So I felt, and so felt others; and whoever enjoyed the confidence of the leading Unitarian ministers in Boston and its vicinity from 1830 to 1840, well knows that they were sick at heart with what they had, and were demanding in their interior souls a religious institution of some sort, in which they could find shelter from the storms of this wintry world, and some crumbs of the bread of life to keep them from starving. Not only in Boston was this cry heard. It came to us on every wind from all quarters,—from France, from Germany, from England even; and Carlyle, in his *Sartor Resartus,* seemed to lay his finger on the plague-spot of the age. Men had reached the centre of indifference; under a broiling sun in the Rue d'Enfer, had pronounced the everlasting "No." Were they never to be able to pronounce the everlasting "Yes"?

6. James Freeman Clarke (1810–1888)
Autobiography

[Clarke remained a Transcendentalist to the end of his days, a militant one. In his last years he wrote an *Autobiography* (published in Boston, 1891) in which he described the situation at Harvard College and the Harvard Divinity School in the 1830's. The passage (pp. 38–40) is an excellent statement of the two educations, the official and the private, which these students were receiving, and of the immediacy of their response to ideas that were circulating outside the lecturerooms.]

When I recall what my classmates were interested in doing, I find it was not college work, which might have given them rank, but pursuits outside of the curriculum. They did not put their strength into college themes, but into articles for the "Collegian." They did not read Thucydides and Xenophon, but Macaulay and Carlyle. We unearthed old tomes in the college library, and while our English professors were teaching us out of Blair's "Rhetoric," we were forming our taste by making copious extracts from Sir Thomas Browne, or Ben Jonson. Our real professors of rhetoric were Charles Lamb and Coleridge, Walter Scott and Wordsworth. I recall the delight which George Davis and I took in an old copy of Sir Thomas Browne which we stumbled upon in the college library. We had scarcely heard the name; but by a sure instinct we discovered the wit, originality, and sagacity of this old writer. It was about the time of our senior year that Professor Marsh, of Vermont University, was reprinting Coleridge's "Friend," his "Aids to Reflection," and his "Biographia Literaria." These books I read from time to time during several years, and they gave, in a high degree, incitement and nourishment to my intellect. Coleridge the poet I had known and loved. Coleridge the philosopher confirmed my longing for a higher philosophy than that of John Locke and David Hartley, the metaphysicians most in vogue with the earlier Unitarians down to the time of Channing.

The books of Locke, Priestly, Hartley, and Belsham were in my grandfather Freeman's library, and the polemic of Locke against innate ideas was one of my earliest philosophical lessons. But something within me revolted at all such attempts to explain soul out of sense, deducing mind from matter, or tracing the origin of ideas to nerves, vibrations, and vibratiuncles. So I concluded I had no taste for metaphysics and gave it up, until Coleridge showed me from Kant that though knowledge begins *with* experience it does not come *from* experience. Then I discovered that I was born a transcendentalist; and smiled when I afterwards read, in one of Jacobi's works, that he had gone through exactly the same experience.

Thus I became a great reader of Coleridge, and was quite ready to accept his distinction between the reason and the understanding judging by sense. This distinction helped me much in my subsequent studies in theology. It enabled me to distinguish between truth as seen by the reason, and its statement as formulated by the understanding. It enabled me to put logic in its proper place, and see that its function was not the discovery of truth, but that of arranging, methodizing, and harmonizing verbal propositions in regard to it. I could see that those who had the same spiritual experience, and who beheld the same truth, might differ in their statements concerning it, and that while truth was unchanging and eternal, theology might alter and improve from age to age.

3

Emergence

I am now employed something in the way in which I trust I am destined to pass my life; and if the profession I have chosen is in any degree as rich in sources of delight as the study of it, my lot is indeed a happy one. I expect to pass a life of poverty, and I care not if of obscurity; but give me my Bible and the studies which relate to its interpretation, give me that philosophy which explains our moral faculty and intellect, and I ask not for wealth or fame. I can be useful to my fellow man . . . Let the world say what it pleases; truth, and truth unpopular and odious,—aye, and that which is stigmatized as heresy and sin,—must be sought and professed by the consistent Christian.

—GEORGE RIPLEY

1. Sampson Reed (1800–1880)
Oration on Genius

[Sampson Reed is a fascinating but obscure figure. Born in Weymouth, the son of a liberal minister, he graduated from Harvard in 1818 and, entering the Divinity School, appeared launched upon the typical career. In the privacy of his study—again illustrating the divergence of the educations, he being in fact the pioneer example—he read Swedenborg and underwent so profound an alteration as disqualified him, he knew, for the Unitarian pulpit. He took his M.A. in 1821, then found employment as a clerk in an apothecary shop; he soon opened a store of his own and finally became the leading wholesale druggist of New England. He devoted his wealth to his chief interest, the Swedenborgian church and *The New Jerusalem Magazine*.

Emanuel Swedenborg (1688–1772) is a pervasive influence upon New England Transcendentalism, as fundamental as Coleridge and Carlyle. Emerson, Parker, W. H. Channing, Thoreau, and all the Brook Farmers read him; yet it may be suggested that they came to him more through Reed than by themselves and that Reed represented Swedenborg to them, much as Coleridge and Cousin represented Kant or as Carlyle the German literature. The classic statement of the

Transcendental conception of him is in Emerson's *Representative Men*. What the Transcendentalists got from him can be pretty well covered by the word "correspondence." Emerson expounded this idea by a quotation from Swedenborg: "If we choose to express any natural truth in physical and definite vocal terms, and to convert these terms only into the corresponding and spiritual terms, we shall by this means elicit a spiritual truth, or theological dogma, in place of the physical truth or precept." The power of this theory in the early nineteenth century is attested by the devotion of Blake, Balzac, and Baudelaire. The response to it of the young New Englanders constitutes one respect in which they can clearly be regarded as manifestations of "Romanticism."

Reed delivered the "Oration on Genius" as he received his M.A. in 1821. He was, indirectly, saying farewell to academic security and respectability. Emerson heard the speech, and it lived in his mind for years as an epochal experience; he borrowed it and made a copy, which he "kept as a treasure." The manuscript circulated among the initiated. In 1842 Emerson could find no higher praise for an effort of Charles Newcomb's than: "more native gold than anything we have seen since Sampson Reed's Oration on Genius." Eventually, in 1849, when Elizabeth Peabody attempted to start a Transcendental periodical and got as far as one issue of *Aesthetic Papers,* the oration was belatedly printed (pp. 59–65). By then, it had long since wrought its effect, but its importance for the early years was universally conceded.

It is not difficult to see why the speech so stirred Emerson and his contemporaries. It was the first admonitory indictment of formalism in the liberal church and pointed the way for an appeal from institutional legalities to a fresh and creative approach to nature; it insinuated that the first requirement would be a rejection of Locke. And then, it took as its subject "genius"—with the implication that all who turned to nature could become geniuses. It excited the expectation of a new day, and it did so in an oracular, cryptic style, such as had not been heard in New England before, no accent of which was lost on the delighted eighteen-year-old Waldo Emerson.]

THE world was always busy; the human heart has always had love of some kind; there has always been fire on the earth. There is something in the inmost principles of an individual, when he begins to exist, which urges him onward; there is something in the centre of the character of a nation, to which the people aspire; there is something which gives activity to the mind in all ages, countries, and worlds. This principle of activity is love: it may be the love of good or of evil; it may manifest itself in saving life or in killing; but it is love.

The difference in the strength and direction of the affections creates the distinctions in society. Every man has a form of mind peculiar to himself.

The mind of the infant contains within itself the first rudiments of all that will be hereafter, and needs nothing but expansion; as the leaves and branches and fruit of a tree are said to exist in the seed from which it springs . . .

Man has often ascribed to his own power the effects of the secret operations of divine truth. When the world is immersed in darkness, this is a judgment of the Most High; but the light is the effect of the innate strength of the human intellect . . .

The intellectual eye of man is formed to see the light, not to make it, and it is time that, when the causes that cloud the spiritual world are removed, man should rejoice in the truth itself, and not that *he* has found it. More than once, when nothing was required but for a person to stand on this world with his eyes open, has the truth been seized upon as a thing of his own making. When the power of divine truth begins to dispel the darkness, the objects that are first disclosed to our view—whether men of strong understanding, or of exquisite taste, or of deep learning—are called geniuses. Luther, Shakespeare, Milton, Newton, stand with the bright side toward us . . .

The arts have been taken from nature by human invention; and, as the mind returns to its God, they are in a measure swallowed up in the source from which they came. We see, as they vanish, the standard to which we should refer them. They are not arbitrary, having no foundation except in taste: they are only modified by taste, which varies according to the state of the human mind. Had we a history of music, from the war-song of the savage to the song of angels, it would be a history of the affections that have held dominion over the human heart. Had we a history of architecture, from the first building erected by man to the house not made with hands, we might trace the variations of the beautiful and the grand, alloyed by human contrivance, to where they are lost in beauty and grandeur. Had we a history of poetry, from the first rude effusions to where words make one with things, and language is lost in nature, we should see the state of man in the language of licentious passion, in the songs of chivalry, in the descriptions of heroic valor, in the mysterious wildness of Ossian; till the beauties of nature fall on the heart, as softly as the clouds on the summer's water. The mind, as it wanders from heaven, moulds the arts into its own form, and covers its nakedness. Feelings of all kinds will discover themselves in music, in painting, in poetry; but it is only when the heart is purified from every selfish and worldly passion, that they are created in real beauty; for in their origin they are divine.

Science is more fixed. It consists of the laws according to which natural things exist; and these must be either true or false. It is the natural world in the abstract, not in the concrete. But the laws according to which things exist, are from the things themselves, not the opposite. Matter has solidity: solidity makes no part of matter. If, then, the natural world is from God, the abstract properties, as dissected and combined, are from him also. If, then, science be from Him who gave the ten commandments, must not a life according to the latter facilitate the acquirement of the former? Can *he* love the works of God who does not love his commandments? It is only necessary that the heart be purified, to have science like poetry its spontaneous growth. Self-love has given rise to many false theories, because a selfish man is disposed to make things differently from what God has made them. Because God is love, nature exists; because God is love, the Bible is poetry. If, then, the love of God creates the scenery of nature, must not he whose mind is most open to this love be most sensible of natural beauties? But in nature both the sciences and the arts exist embodied . . . But this inspiration has been esteemed so unlike religion, that the existence of the one almost supposes the absence of the other. The spirit of God is thought to be a very different thing when poetry is written, from what it is when the heart is sanctified . . .

It needs no uncommon eye to see, that the finger of death has rested on the church. Religion and death have in the human mind been connected with the same train of associations . . . It is not strange, then, that genius, such as could exist on the earth, should take its flight to the mountains. It may be said, that great men are good men. But what I mean is, that, in the human mind, greatness is one thing, and goodness another; that philosophy is divorced from religion; that truth is separated from its source; that that which is called goodness is sad, and that which is called genius is proud.

Since things are so, let me take care that the life which is received be genuine. Let the glow on the cheek spring from the warmth of the heart, and the brightness of the eyes beam from the light of heaven . . . When the heart is purified from all selfish and worldly affections, then may genius find its seat in the church . . .

Here is no sickly aspiring after fame,—no filthy lust after philosophy, whose very origin is an eternal barrier to the truth. But sentiments will flow from the heart warm as its blood, and speak eloquently; for eloquence is the language of love. There is a unison of spirit and nature. The genius of the mind will descend, and unite with the genius of the rivers, the lakes, and the woods. Thoughts fall to the earth with power, and make a language out of nature . . .

Science will be full of life, as nature is full of God. She will wring from her locks the dew which was gathered in the wilderness. By science, I mean natural science. The science of the human mind must change with its subject. Locke's mind will not always be the standard of metaphysics. Had we a description of it in its present state, it would make a very different book from "Locke on the Human Understanding."

The time is not far distant. The cock has crowed. I hear the distant lowing of the cattle which are grazing on the mountains. "Watchman, what of the night? Watchman, what of the night? The watchman saith, The morning cometh."

2. Sampson Reed (1800–1880)
Observations on the Growth of the Mind

[In 1826 Reed published in Boston a forty-four-page pamphlet, *Observations on the Growth of the Mind,* which Emerson told his brother was "in my poor judgment the best thing since Plato of Plato's kind, for novelty & wealth of truth." He noted that "it was all writ in the shop." For the next twenty years the brotherhood held it in high esteem. It had a steady circulation for decades, the eighth edition being published in 1886.

Herein Reed was clearly expounding Swedenborg, though he was clever enough to conceal the name. For the Transcendentalists the booklet was chiefly important as supplying them with the basic content of their revolutionary—or so they supposed it—aesthetic theory. It gave to the function of the artist a dignity that hitherto had not been even suspected in America, and so prepared the way for the Transcendental vocation. It formulated the essentials of the organic style in asserting that the artist achieves form by giving direct expression to the arrangements of nature, not by imposing artificial proportions and groupings upon nature. It announced that the organic principle, if piously observed, cannot fail to achieve coherence by the method of surrender and receptivity, because the correspondence of idea and object, of word and thing, is inherent in the universe. Nature is therefore not the inert subject matter of physics, but a language; and in order to interpret this language, which is a poetry rather than a prose, the artist must cultivate an absolute reliance upon his own intimations and intuitions.]

Nothing is a more common subject of remark than the changed condition of the world. There is a more extensive intercourse of thought, and a more powerful action of mind upon mind, than formerly. The good and wise of all nations are brought nearer together, and begin to exert a power, which, though yet feeble as infancy, is felt throughout the globe. Public opinion, that helm which directs the progress of events by which the world is guided to its ultimate destination, has received a new direction. The mind has attained an upward and onward look, and is shaking off the errors and prejudices of the past. The structure of the feudal ages, the ornament of the desert, has been exposed to the light of heaven; and continues to be gazed at for its ugliness, as it ceases to be admired for its antiquity. The world is deriving vigor, not from that which is gone by, but from that which is coming; not from the unhealthy moisture of the evening, but from the nameless influence of the morning. The loud call on the past to instruct us, as it falls on the rock of ages, comes back in echo from the future. Both mankind, and the laws and principles by which they are governed, seem about to be redeemed from slavery. The moral and intellectual character of man has undergone, and is undergoing, a change; and as this is effected, it must change the aspect of all things, as when the position-point is altered from which a landscape is viewed. We appear to be approaching an age which will be the silent pause of merely physical force before the powers of the mind; the timid, subdued, awed condition of the brute, gazing on the erect and godlike form of man . . .

There prevails a most erroneous sentiment, that the mind is originally vacant, and requires only to be filled up; and there is reason to believe, that this opinion is most intimately connected with false conceptions of time. The mind is originally a most delicate germ, whose husk is the body; planted in this world, that the light and heat of heaven may fall upon it with a gentle radiance, and call forth its energies. The process of learning is not by synthesis, or analysis. It is the most perfect illustration of both. As subjects are presented to the operation of the mind, they are decomposed and reorganized in a manner peculiar to itself, and not easily explained . . .

The mind must grow, not from external accretion, but from an internal principle. Much may be done by others in aid of its development; but in all that is done, it should not be forgotten, that even from its earliest infancy, it possesses a character and a principle of freedom, which *should* be respected, and *cannot* be destroyed. Its peculiar propensities may be discerned, and proper nutriment and culture supplied; but the infant plant, not less than the aged tree, must be permitted, with its own organs of absorption, to separate that which is peculiarly adapted to itself; otherwise it will be cast off as a foreign substance, or produce nothing but rottenness and deformity . . .

The best affections we possess will find their home in the objects around us, and, as it were, enter into and animate the whole rational, animal, and vegetable world. If the eye were turned inward to a direct contemplation of these affections, it would find them bereft of all their loveliness; for when they are active, it is not of them we are thinking, but of the objects on which they rest. The science of the mind, then, will be the effect of all the other sciences. Can the child grow up in active usefulness, and not be conscious of the possession and use of his own limbs? The body and mind should grow together, and form the sound and perfect man, whose understanding may be almost measured by his stature. The mind will see itself in what it loves and is able to accomplish. Its own works will be its mirror; and when it is present in the natural world, feeling the same spirit which gives life to every object by which it is surrounded, in its very union with nature it will catch a glimpse of itself, like that of pristine beauty united with innocence, at her own native fountain . . .

The natural world was precisely and perfectly adapted to invigorate and strengthen the intellectual and moral man. Its first and highest use was not to support the vegetables which adorn, or the animals which cover, its surface; nor yet to give sustenance to the human body;—it has a higher and holier object, in the attainment of which these are only means. It was intended to draw forth and mature the latent energies of the soul; to impart to them its own verdure and freshness; to initiate them into its own mysteries; and by its silent and humble dependence on its Creator, to leave on them, when it is withdrawn by death, the full impression of his likeness.

It was the design of Providence, that the infant mind should possess the germ of every science. If it were not so, they could hardly be learned . . . As well might the eye see without light, or the ear hear without sound, as the human mind be healthy and athletic without descending into the natural world and breathing the mountain air. Is there aught in eloquence, which warms the heart? She draws her fire from natural imagery. Is there aught in poetry to enliven the imagination? There is the secret of all her power. Is there aught in science to add strength and dignity to the human mind? The natural world is only the body, of which she is the soul. In books science is presented to the eye of the pupil, as it were in a dried and preserved state; the time may come when the instructor will take him by the hand, and lead him by the running streams, and teach him all the principles of science as she comes from her Maker, as he would smell the fragrance of the rose without gathering it . . .

It is in this way the continual endeavor of Providence, that the natural sciences should be the spontaneous production of the human mind. To these should certainly be added, poetry and music; for when we study the works of God as we should, we cannot disregard that inherent beauty and harmony in which these arts originate. These occasion in the mind its first glow of delight, like the taste of food, as it is offered to the mouth; and the pleasure they afford, is a pledge of the strength and manhood afterwards imparted by the sciences.

By poetry is meant all those illustrations of truth by natural imagery, which spring from the fact, that this World is the mirror of Him who made it. Strictly speaking, nothing has less to do with fiction than poetry. The day will come, and it may not be far distant, when this art will have another test of merit than mere versification, or the invention of strange stories; when the laws by which poetry is tested will be as fixed and immutable as the laws of science; when a change will be introduced into taste corresponding to that which Bacon introduced into philosophy, by which both will be confined within the limits of things as they actually exist. It would seem that genius would be cramped; that the powers of invention would be destroyed; by confining the human mind, as it were, at home, within the bounds which nature has assigned. But what wider scope need it have? It reaches the throne of God; it rests on his footstool. All things spiritual and natural are before it. There is as much that is true as false; and truth presented in natural imagery, is only dressed in the garments which God has given it . . .

Fiction in poetry must fall with theory in science, for they depend equally on the works of creation. The word fiction, however, is not intended to be used in its most literal sense; but to embrace whatever is not in exact agreement with the creative spirit of God. It belongs to the true poet to feel this spirit, and to be governed by it; to be raised above the senses; to live and breathe in the inward efforts of things; to feel the power of creation, even before he sees the effect; to witness the innocence and smiles of nature's infancy, not by extending the imagination back to chaos, but by raising the soul to nature's origin. The true poetic spirit, so far from misleading any, is the strongest bulwark against deception. It is the soul of science. Without it, the latter is a cheerless, heartless study, distrusting even the presence and power of Him to whom it owes its existence. Of all the poetry which exists, that only possesses the seal of immortality, which presents the image of God which is stamped on nature. Could the poetry which now prevails be viewed from the future, when all partialities and antipathies shall have passed away, and things are left to rest on their own foundations; when good works shall have dwindled into insignificance, from the mass of useless matter that may have fallen from them, and bad ones shall have ceased to allure with false beauty; we might catch a glimpse of the rudiments of this divine art, amid the weight of extraneous matter by which it is now protected, and which it is

destined to throw off. The imagination will be refined into a chaste and sober
view of unveiled nature. It will be confined within the bounds of reality. It
will no longer lead the way to insanity and madness, by transcending the
works of creation, and, as it were, wandering where God has no power to
protect it; but finding a resting-place in every created object, it will enter
into it and explore its hidden treasures, the relation in which it stands to
mind, and reveal the love it bears to its Creator . . .

There is a language, not of words, but of things. When this language shall
have been made apparent, that which is human will have answered its end;
and being as it were resolved into its original elements, will lose itself in
nature. The use of language is the expression of our feelings and desires—
the manifestation of the mind. But every thing which is, whether animal or
vegetable, is full of the expression of that use for which it is designed, as of
its own existence. If we did but understand its language, what could our
words add to its meaning? It is because we are unwilling to hear, that we
find it necessary to say so much; and we drown the voice of nature with the
discordant jargon of ten thousand dialects. Let a man's language be confined
to the expression of that which actually belongs to his own mind; and let
him respect the smallest blade which grows, and permit it to speak for itself.
Then may there be poetry, which may not be written perhaps, but which
may be felt as a part of our being. Everything which surrounds us is full of
the utterance of one word, completely expressive of its nature. This word is its
name; for God, even now, could we but see it, is creating all things, and
giving a name to every work of his love, in its perfect adaptation to that for
which it is designed. But man has abused his power, and has become insensible to the real character of the brute creation; still more so to that of inanimate nature, because, in his selfishness, he is disposed to reduce them to slavery. Therefore he is deaf. We find the animal world either in a state of savage
wildness, or enslaved submission. It is possible, that, as the character of man
is changed, they may attain a midway condition equally removed from both.
As the mind of man acknowledges its dependence on the Divine Mind,
brutes may add to their instinct submission to human reason; preserving an
unbroken chain from our Father in Heaven, to the most inanimate parts of
creation. Such may be supposed to have been the condition of the animal on
which the King of Zion rode into Jerusalem; at once free and subject to the
will of the rider. Everything will seem to be conscious of its use; and man
will become conscious of the use of everything . . .

Syllogistic reasoning is passing away. It has left no permanent demonstration but that of its own worthlessness. It amounts to nothing but the discern-

ment and expression of the particulars which go to comprise something more general; and, as the human mind permits things to assume a proper arrangement from their own inherent power of attraction, it is no longer necessary to bind them together with syllogisms. Few minds can now endure the tediousness of being led blindfold to a conclusion, and of being satisfied with the result merely from the recollection of having been satisfied on the way to it. The mind requires to view the parts of a subject, not only separately, but together; and the understanding, in the exercise of those powers of arrangement, by which a subject is presented in its just relations to other things, takes the name of reason. We appear to be approaching that condition which requires the union of reason and eloquence, and will be satisfied with neither without the other. We neither wish to see an anatomical plate of bare muscles, nor the gaudy daubings of finery; but a happy mixture of strength and beauty. We desire language neither extravagant nor cold, but blood-warm. Reason is beginning to learn the necessity of simply tracing the relations which exist between created things, and of not even touching what it examines, lest it disturb the arrangement in the cabinet of creation—and as, in the progress of moral improvement, the imagination (which is called the creative power of man) shall coincide with the actively creative will of God, reason will be clothed with eloquence, as nature is with verdure . . .

It becomes us, then, to seek and to cherish this *peculium* of our own minds, as the patrimony which is left us by our Father in Heaven—as that by which the branch is united to the vine—as the forming power within us, which gives to our persons that by which they are distinguished from others; and, by a life entirely governed by the commandments of God, to leave on the duties we are called to perform the full impress of our real characters. Let a man's ambition to be great disappear in a willingness to be what he is; then may he fill a high place without pride, or a low one without dejection. As our desires become more and more concentrated to those objects which correspond to the peculiar organization of our minds, we shall have a foretaste of that which is coming, in those internal tendencies of which we are conscious. As we perform with alacrity whatever duty presents itself before us, we shall perceive in our own hearts a kind of preparation for every external event or occurrence of our lives, even the most trivial, springing from the all-pervading tendency of the Providence of God, to present the opportunity of being useful wherever there is the disposition.

Living in a country whose peculiar characteristic is said to be a love of equal liberty, let it be written on our hearts, that the end of all education is a life of active usefulness. We want no education which shall raise a man out of the reach of the understanding, or the sympathies of any of his species. We are disgusted with that kind of dignity which the possessor is himself obliged to guard; but venerate that, which having its origin in the actual character of the man, can receive no increase from the countenance of power, and suffer no diminution from the approach of weakness—that dignity in which the individual appears to live rather in the consciousness of the light which shines from above, than in that of his own shadow beneath . . . Truth is the way in which we should act; and then only is a man truly wise when the body performs what the mind perceives. In this way, flesh and blood are made to partake of the wisdom of the spiritual man; and the palms of our hands will become the book of our life, on which is inscribed all the love and all the wisdom we possess. It is the light which directs a man to his duty; it is by doing his duty that he is enlightened—thus does he become identified with his own acts of usefulness, and his own vocation is the silken cord which directs to his heart the knowledge and the blessings of all mankind.

3. George Ripley (1802–1880)
Charles Follen's Inaugural Discourse

[George Ripley, one of the noblest and most appealing Americans of his time, was born in Greenfield, Massachusetts. A precocious scholar, he graduated from Harvard in 1823, easily at the head of his class. In 1826, upon completing his studies at the Divinity School—where he was regarded as the white hope of Unitarianism—he was immediately called to a newly organized church in Purchase Street, Boston. In 1827 he married Sophia Willard Dana, whose intelligence and sensitivity were as fine as his own. He read widely, and began in 1832 to publish in *The Christian Examiner,* the organ of Unitarian scholarship, a series of essays that are among the most distinguished of the period.

By 1836 he had become a recognized leader of the new school and was a charter member of the Transcendental Club. He supervised the publication of *Specimens of Foreign Standard Literature* (see p. 294) and assisted Margaret Fuller in the conduct of *The Dial.*

In 1841 he resigned his pulpit and in April became president of the Brook Farm Association. He and his wife poured their life's blood into the enterprise, and its collapse in 1847 left them in despair. They moved to New York; Mrs. Ripley became a Catholic and died in 1861. For years they were in desperate poverty, struggling to pay the debts of the Farm and of its periodical, *The Harbinger,* which Ripley had edited. He succeeded Margaret Fuller as literary critic for Horace Greeley's *Tribune* (for which he did many extraordinary articles), and made a living from journalism and editorial hack-work. In 1865 he married a young German widow and enjoyed a rich though belated tour of Europe. In his last years he let lapse almost all his ties with New England or with the surviving Transcendentalists.

The impulse, generated by the Unitarian emancipation of the New England mind, toward a widening of cultural horizons resulted at Harvard in 1816 in the appointment of George Ticknor to the newly endowed Smith Professorship of Modern Languages. Ticknor, who perfectly embodied all the virtues of Unitarian culture, taught French and Spanish; by 1825 the growing prestige of German induced the Corporation to venture into that language. Charles Follen (1796–1840) was a German liberal who had fought in the wars of liberation and taught at Jena. He fled from the Prussian regime in 1820 and arrived in Boston in 1824. The next year he was made tutor at Harvard and in 1831 was elevated to a professor. He taught German language and law, and introduced organized gymnastics. He was not a romantic, but he was a faithful reporter and helped make the romantic literature available. Intellectually he was at home in Cambridge, and frequently preached in Unitarian pulpits; but he was also a true liberal, and became an abolitionist. In 1835 Harvard chose not to renew his appointment, an action that has been widely judged a blot on its record.

Sampson Reed inaugurated no school of literature, because those to whom his words were winged were still too young to commence creating one, nor could they follow him into the Swedenborgian church. The years 1826 to 1832 were for men like Emerson, Clarke, and Ripley years of intense soul-searching, of a slow finding out what they stood for, and a great reluctance to break with their masters and elders. By 1832 the influences of Swedenborg, Cousin, Coleridge, Carlyle, and German literature were beginning to be absorbed, and their meanings mastered. In September 1831 Follen delivered his "Inaugural Discourse"; Ripley reviewed it in *The Christian Examiner* for January 1832 (XI, 373–380).

The review is still a hesitant effort, an apology that strives to exonerate the Germans from slurs cast by editors of *The North American Review* or by respected professors at the Divinity School. But even as apology, it is symptomatic of a growing appreciation of those very qualities which were supposed to be the defects of German literature. Ripley is almost ready to contend—though he does not quite dare say it—that even if the Germans are guilty, their crimes are in reality Transcendental virtues. Thus, the article is the first overt sign of the still hidden rift in the Unitarian ranks.]

The literature of Germany has, hitherto, received comparatively little attention from the best educated scholars in this country. In this respect, they have followed too closely the bad example of our English brethren. Until within a recent period, the treasures of philosophy, poetry, history, and critical speculation, with which that remarkable literature is filled, have, for the most part, been sealed up from foreign eyes. A few bold adventurers only have preferred to see for themselves, rather than to trust the casual reports of others.

Our University, for some time past, has made liberal provision for the instruction of its pupils in the more popular modern languages, but has afforded scanty facilities for acquiring a thorough knowledge of the German. We suppose that few more able lectures are anywhere delivered, than the annual courses from the Professor of the French and Spanish languages and literature; but an equally able course, we think, should long since have been given, to satisfy the just claims of the most profound, the most original, and most various literature of modern Europe. We are much gratified by the establishment of the Professorship which has given occasion to the present interesting Discourse . . .

It is not difficult to assign the reasons which have caused this branch of study to be so much neglected among us. They are the same, to a great degree, with those which have excited strong prejudices against the writings of German scholars in England and France,—principally, a confused idea, taken up with very little or no examination, that they are all given to mysticism, rhapsody, wild and tasteless inventions in poetry, and dark and impenetrable reasonings in metaphysics . . .

The charge of mysticism and obscurity . . . has been vehemently exaggerated. We have made up our opinions from wretched translations of extravagant authors, or from incoherent patches and portions of great systems, which give no better an idea of the magnificent whole, than the fool's brick did of his palace,—and then pronounced a dogmatical sentence of condemnation on the mysticism of German literature, and the obscurity of German philosophy. Thus we often hear a summary and contemptuous decision on the merits of Kant,—a writer and reasoner from whom the great questions, which man as an intellectual, accountable, and immortal being will never cease to ask of his own consciousness, have received more light than from any uninspired person, since the brightest days of Grecian philosophy,—which seems to us as fair and well-founded, as the decisions of a ship-master, who knew only enough to work his reckoning, on the astronomy of Sir Isaac Newton. For instance, it is a common thing to compare Kant with Coleridge, and then doom them both to the same dark abyss. Nothing shows more forcibly the blinding influence of a popular prejudice, than to hear this stale conceit from the mouths of men at whose feet we would gladly sit and learn wisdom, and who would be the first to discard it, should they study each of those great writers as they deserve. In truth, without expressing an opinion as to their respective merits, we believe that scarcely two minds could be found, agreeing in important matters of opinion, which are more unlike in character than those of Coleridge and Kant. The general spirit of their philosophy, to be sure, is the same; for they are both the zealous advocates of the great spiritual truths, which are at the foundation of all real morality and religion, and which have been called in question by skeptical and sensual reasoners, from the time of the Greek sophists to that of the French atheists. But in every thing else, as it respects mental peculiarities, they are in almost direct opposition to each other. We see nothing in common between the cool, far-reaching, and austere habits of thought which characterize the German philosopher, and the impassioned, bold, and excursive conceptions of the English poet. The severe logic, the imperturbable patience, the mathematical precision, and the passionless exhibition of the results of pure reason, which distinguish Kant from all other writers on philosophy, are in striking contrast with the moody restlessness, the feverish irritability, the incoherent ramblings, and the bright flashes of imagination playing over the dark obscurity of his page, which, in the writings of Coleridge, mark the philosopher struggling with the poet, and finally yielding the victory.

Still it is said that the German philosophy is obscure. And what great science, we would ask, is not obscure, before its nomenclature is understood, and its definitions studied? . . . We ask, again, if the German writers are more obscure than other writers who have treated the same subjects? Is Kant difficult to be understood? Neither is Aristotle perfectly easy reading. Are Fichte and Schelling mysterious? Plato has been thought to utter nonsense, by the uninitiated. The truth, we imagine, is, that no philosophy which explains, or attempts to explain, the grand mysteries of the universe, to the solution of which man is called by the strong impulses of his nature, can be made intelligible to those who have not a congenial spirit with the writers whom they study. There is a great variety in the intellectual appetites and powers of assimilation. Some minds thrive only on plain matters of fact. Some breathe most freely in the high regions of poetry. Others regard all works of fiction as the devil's inventions. Many eschew mathematics. Few can digest solid metaphysics. Every one has his own gift. And in this infinite diversity of endowments, many will be found destitute of all taste for the philosophy, which unfolds the secrets of their own nature, the deep things of God and of his universe. To such minds we do not recommend German philosophy. They have no use for it. It can do them no good. It is no fault of theirs, it is no disgrace to them, that it cannot. They are made for something else,—it may be, for something better. We hope that they are; but let them not deride every thing out of their own vocation. Others there always have been, there are now, there always will be, to whom the desire of knowing themselves, of fathoming the mysterious life which we are passing, and that still more mysterious life for which we hope, is a perfect passion, an inwrought element of their being. To such minds we do not recommend German philosophy. We need not do it. They will find it out by the strong instinct which leads every creature of God to its appropriate aliment.

4. Convers Francis (1795-1863)
Natural Theology

[Whether by accident or design, Ripley's article was followed in the same issue of the *Examiner* by a review from one of the editors, the Reverend W. B. O. Peabody, of Lord King's life of John Locke. It celebrates Locke's "calm judgment," praises him for treating religion "as a reasonable thing," and concludes that he was "a manly, sagacious, and independent, as well as a pious, humble and fervent Christian." No question of mysticism and obscurity here! In the Unitarian cosmos, for which Locke and not Kant or Coleridge was the ideal Christian, there existed no such thing as a "mysterious life" to be fathomed.

In the next issue of the *Examiner,* May 1832 (XII, 193–220), appeared an article by Convers Francis, whom the younger men then regarded as one of them and whose essay—a review of Alexander Crombie, *Natural Theology*—much enheartened them. Francis, born in West Cambridge, was a brother of Lydia Maria Child; graduated from Harvard College in 1815, he attended the Divinity School and in 1819 became pastor of the First Church of Watertown. A meticulous and erudite scholar, an early student of German, he proved also fearful and timid. Intellectually capable of understanding the new ideas, and apparently of embracing them, he fell away when the social hazards became too great. Although he attended early meetings of the Transcendental Club, and a pamphlet of his in 1836—*Christianity as a Purely Internal System*—was hailed as a proclamation along with Ripley's and Brownson's, he soon retreated into conformity, and in 1842 succeeded Henry Ware, Jr., as professor of pulpit eloquence at the Divinity School.

In the light of his character, this hymn to the inward powers of the soul, with its generosity toward the doctrine of a universal Divine Mind, is not to be taken too seriously, but it is an evidence of how the new philosophy was straining toward formulation in New England, and so marks a further stage in the emergence of a recognizable "movement."]

There is a part of our nature, which perceives and judges of truth, comprehends the relations and proportions of things, explores the labyrinths of nature, follows the winding and intricate chain of causes and effects, investigates the several departments of the animal, mineral, and vegetable kingdoms, measures the distances and traces the laws of systems, reduces to an exact science the movements of revolving worlds, constructs elaborate and profound systems of policy, refines and elevates society with countless inventions and improvements, kindles and transmits along the generations of men that light of thought, which time cannot quench . . . There are sympathies, springing up spontaneously with the growth of our moral powers, strengthening and brightening the bond that unites us in the social state at first, and then keeps us together amidst the darkness, the storms, and the disasters of life, multiplying and sweetening the relations among mankind, and causing them so to act and react on one another, that no one liveth for himself alone and no one dieth for himself. All these are parts of our constitution, the existence of which is a simple matter of fact. Now with regard to their origin and purpose, what is the conclusion to which unvitiated reason would lead us? What but that our moral and intellectual nature is the work of One, who "hath made man in the image of His own eternity"? What but that the principle of thought and of moral feeling is an emanation from the fountain itself of heavenly light? The religious philosophy of old, which taught that the human soul is a particle of the Divine Mind, was the ready and natural expression of such a conclusion: and however mysterious or romantic might be some of the conceptions associated with this doctrine, the foundation of it was laid in a great and beautiful truth. The spiritual nature had a consciousness of its high origin, which it could not shake off; it heard from the depths of its own existence intimations of its birth-place, from which it seemed to itself to have wandered far away; it deemed its residence in the body an exile, a banishment from its native home, to which in its contemplative hours of reflection and of pure feeling it sought with ardent longing to return. We may well pardon such a philosophy many of its erratic fancies, when we remember that the nucleus, around which it is gathered, unquestionably lies in the very nature of our intellectual and moral frame, and that it gave a noble and elevated turn to the speculations of its votaries . . .

We have no apprehension, indeed, that religion can ever be driven from society. The hand of the Omnipotent has placed a strong guard around this consecrated interest, which the poor delusions of man will in vain essay to break down. All history shows, that, though atheism and reckless skepticism may from certain causes spread to some extent, yet men are at length carried back to the fundamental principles of religion by an irresistible tendency of their moral constitution. But even the temporary and partial mischief, which this folly may occasion, is sufficiently fearful to excite the deepest interest in every friend of mankind. Nothing can be more important, than that the religious sentiment of the community should be enlightened, guarded, and strengthened. All the sources, from which it may receive purity and warmth, whether in nature or in revelation, should be opened upon the mind; and man should be accustomed to feel that he stands, as a priest, in the midst of the magnificent temple of God's creation, to offer the praise of a devout heart, and to render the service of reverence, of love, and of duty.

5. George Ripley (1802–1880)
James Mackintosh

[In January 1833 (*The Christian Examiner*, XIII, 311–332), Ripley reviewed James Mackintosh, *A General View of the Progress of Ethical Philosophy*. Here he was obliged to deal with a delicate problem: American Unitarianism claimed Locke as its philosopher, yet found intensely distasteful the Utilitarianism of Bentham and James Mill. But rumors from Europe indicated that in many quarters Utilitarianism was regarded as an offshoot of Locke. Ripley was speaking for Unitarianism in general as he rejected the calculations of Bentham, but he could not quite bring himself to condemn them without appealing to the higher moral sanction of the "intuitive perception"—which was a little more than most of his colleagues (except Dr. Channing) were willing to admit even existed.

At the same time, he could not check himself from revealing a still more uncomfortable implication in his line of defense: if there is an intuitive rule of right, then by that rule society is to be judged. If Unitarianism was reluctant to be tarred with the brush of Utilitarianism, then had it any other grounds for moral certainty except the inward perception? But if this has a royal prerogative, above and beyond the useful, what is to prevent society as a whole, as well as particular individuals, from being called to account by it? Here, the possibilities of a social as well as a theological radicalism, implicit in the Transcendental philosophy, are for the first time suggested.]

It is evident, that there are many instances, in which the utility of an action convinces us that the action is right, and that we are under a moral obligation to perform it. Now is utility the sole and ultimate ground upon which the obligation rests, or can we discover, after further analysis, a more general element, which constitutes the ground of obligation? We think there is an element more general than utility, and which, in fact, gives to utility its binding power. It is conformity to our moral relations, as intuitively perceived, in the final analysis, by the moral faculty. From all the relations, which man is called to sustain, proceed a corresponding order of duties, the perception of which is as intuitive to the mature mind, as the perception of the first principles of philosophy, or the axioms of mathematics. These intuitive perceptions are the foundation of moral science, and the ultimate standard by which we settle all questions of practical duty . . .

There is a far more intimate connexion between sound theoretical principles, and the advancement and prosperity of society, than is generally imagined. It has been abundantly verified by experience, that when the primitive and sublime sentiment of Duty, engraved by the finger of God on the heart of man, has been lost sight of, or merged in an inferior order of principles, a slow but fatal poison has preyed upon the vital interests of the community. We cannot but regret, that there is so strong a tendency at the present day, among a great number of benevolent and philanthropic men, who, we are sure, have deeply at heart the welfare of their race, to forget the eternal distinctions of right and wrong, and to substitute in their place, as the criterion of actions, and the motives of conduct, merely empirical considerations, derived from an exaggerated sense of public utility, and connected, as they generally are, with exclusive appeals to private interest. We yield to none, in our earnest desire to see the measures of governments, and the institutions of public policy, brought to the test of utility, so far as that is conformable to the dictates of unchangeable justice; we cherish the deepest conviction, that the performance of duty is the best security for private happiness; but we can never believe, that the interests of states or of individuals are best provided for, when the primitive nature of man is obscured, and the immutable perceptions of his reason, and the noble sentiments of his heart, are commuted for uncertain and selfish calculations, which exercise only a small portion of his faculties, and those of the least exalted and venerable character.

6. Frederic Henry Hedge (1805–1890)

Coleridge

[The son of Levi Hedge, professor of logic at Harvard, Frederic Hedge was born to the Brahmin purple, and proved it by memorizing Virgil at the age of seven. His father sent him, aged thirteen, in the care of George Bancroft, to Germany. There he acquired the language and—as he later put it—"an early initiation into the realm of German idealism, then to our people an unknown world." Returning in 1822, he took his Harvard degree in 1825, and spent four years in the Divinity School. From 1829 to 1835 he was minister in West Cambridge, whence he began to exert the prestige that was his to command as the one American who really had read Kant in the original. His essays in *The Christian Examiner*, along with those of Ripley and Brownson, brought the Transcendental movement into being.

In 1835 Hedge accepted the call from Bangor, Maine, where he remained officially until 1850, although he visited Boston frequently; after 1836, his trips became the occasions for gatherings of the Transcendental Club—which Emerson always called the "Hedge Club." In 1848 he brought out *Prose Writers of Germany,* a carefully constructed anthology. While pastor at Brookline from 1857 to 1872 he also served as professor of ecclesiastical history in the Harvard Divinity School, and after 1872 was professor of German literature in the College. He was a distinguished teacher, and in his last years was also a power in the Unitarian Association. His *Reason in Religion* (1865) is perhaps the classic statement of Transcendentalized Christianity.

Hedge was something of a puzzle to his contemporaries, as he remains to us —for with his advantages, intelligence, and talents, he ought to have made more of a mark than he did. "One of the sturdiest little fellows I have come across for many a day," wrote Carlyle of him. "A face like a rock, a voice like a howitzer; only his honest kind grey eyes reassure you a little." He evidently needed constantly to give his friends such reassurances. In 1840, in a moment of uncharacteristic annoyance, Emerson exploded to Margaret Fuller that he and Hedge could never quite meet—"there is always a fence betwixt us." But two years later, after a day of Hedge's company, Emerson confessed that he had underestimated the man: "How rare to find a man so well mixed & so intellectual: In this country a nonpareil."

Asked in 1877 what his part in the movement had been, Hedge replied that it was of no importance except that in *The Christian Examiner* for March 1833 (XIV, 109–129), he wrote an article on Coleridge, which, he modestly but accurately declared, was "the *first word,* so far as I know, which any American had uttered in respectful recognition of the claims of Transcendentalism." Coleridge and Carlyle had predisposed many "to the rejection of the old sensualistic ideas," but no American except himself had really mastered the German metaphysics in German. Emerson's reaction was somewhat more indicative of the impression the essay made in 1833: "a living leaping Logos," Emerson called it.

The article marks the point at which Transcendentalism went over to the offensive. Hedge here first spoke with that assumption of profundity which infuriated the opponents. He blandly told them that those who had not experienced the Transcendental vision could hardly be expected to understand the literature. Refusing any longer to apologize for the Germanic or Coleridgean "obscurity," he in effect told the elder generation that if they were incapable of following this metaphysic, they were simply stupid. The Hedge of this article is the Hedge who could reply, upon being told that the facts were against him, "So much the worse for the facts."]

There is no writer of our times whose literary rank appears so ill-defined as that of Mr. Coleridge. Perhaps there is no one whose true standing in the literary world it is so difficult to determine. For ourselves we know not a more doubtful problem in criticism than this author and his works present . . .

As to the charge of obscurity, so often and obstinately urged against Mr. Coleridge's prose writings, we cannot admit it in any thing like the extent in which it has been applied. So far as there is *any* ground for this complaint, it is owing to the author's excessive anxiety to make himself intelligible, an anxiety which leads him to present a subject in so many points of view, that we are sometimes in danger of losing the main topic amid the variety of collateral and illustrative matter which he gathers round it . . . He is certainly not a shallow writer, but, as we think, a very profound one, and his style is for the most part as clear as the nature of his thoughts will admit. To those only is he obscure who have no depths within themselves corresponding to his depths . . .

In a review of Mr. Coleridge's literary life, we must not omit to notice that marked fondness for metaphysics, and particularly for German metaphysics, which has exercised so decisive an influence over all his writings. Had it been given to him to interpret German metaphysics to his countrymen, as Mr. Cousin has interpreted them to the French nation, or had it been possible for him to have constructed a system of his own, we should not have regretted his indulgence of a passion which we must now condemn as a source of morbid dissatisfaction with received opinions, unjustified by any serious attempt to introduce others and better . . . But though so ill-qualified for the work of production, one would think the translator of Wallenstein might have interpreted for us all that is most valuable in the speculations of Kant and his followers. It has been said that these works are untranslatable, but without sufficient grounds. That they are not translatable by one who has not an intimate acquaintance with the transcendental philosophy, is abundantly evident . . . But in this respect, and indeed in every respect, Mr. Coleridge is eminently fitted for such a task; and it is the more to be regretted that he has not undertaken it, as the number of those who are thus fitted is exceedingly small, while the demand for information on this subject is constantly increasing. We are well aware that a mere translation, however perfect, would be inadequate to convey a definite notion of transcendentalism to one who has not the metaphysical talent necessary to conceive and reproduce in himself a system whose only value to us must depend upon our power to construct it for ourselves from the materials of our own consciousness, and which in fact exists to us only on this condition.

While we are on this ground, we beg leave to offer a few explanatory remarks respecting German metaphysics, which seem to us to be called for by the present state of feeling among literary men in relation to this subject. We believe it impossible to understand fully the design of Kant and his followers, without being endowed to a certain extent with the same powers of abstraction and synthetic generalization which they possess in so eminent a degree. In order to become fully master of their meaning, one must be able to find it in himself. Not all are born to be philosophers, or are capable of becoming philosophers, any more than all are capable of becoming poets or musicians. The works of the transcendental philosophers may be translated word for word, but still it will be impossible to get a clear idea of their philosophy, unless we raise ourselves at once to a transcendental point of view. Unless we take our station with the philosopher and proceed from his ground as our starting-point, the whole system will appear to us an inextricable puzzle. As in astronomy the motions of the heavenly bodies seem confused to the geocentric observer, and are intelligible only when referred to their heliocentric place, so there is only one point from which we can clearly understand and decide upon the speculations of Kant and his followers; that point is the interior consciousness, distinguished from the common consciousness, by its being an active and not a passive state. In the language of the school, it is a free intuition, and can only be attained by a vigorous effort of the will. It is from an ignorance of this primary condition, that the writings of these men have been denounced as vague and mystical. Viewing them from the distance [as] we do, their discussions seem to us like objects half enveloped in mist; the little we can distinguish seems most portentously magnified and distorted by the unnatural refraction through which we behold it, and the point where they touch the earth is altogether lost. The effect of such writing upon the uninitiated, is like being in the company of one who has inhaled an exhilarating gas. We witness the inspiration, and are astounded at the effects, but we can form no conception of the feeling until we ourselves have experienced it. To those who are without the veil, then, any *exposé* of transcendental views must needs be unsatisfactory. Now if any one chooses to deny the point which these writers assume, if any one chooses to call in question the metaphysical existence of this interior consciousness, and to pronounce the whole system a mere fabrication, or a gross self-delusion,—to such a one the disciples of this school have nothing further to say; for him their system was not conceived. Let him content himself, if he can, with "that compendious philosophy which talking of mind, but thinking of brick and mortar, or other images equally abstracted from body, contrives a theory of spirit, by nicknaming matter, and in a few hours can qualify the dullest of its disciples to explain the *omne scibile* by reducing all things to impressions, ideas, and sensations." The disciples of Kant wrote for minds of quite another stamp, they wrote for minds that seek with faith and hope a solution of questions which that philosophy meddles not with,—questions which relate to spirit and form, substance and life, free will and fate, God and eternity. Let those who feel no interest in these questions, or who believe not in the possibility of our approaching any nearer to a solution of them, abstain for ever from a department of inquiry for which they have neither talent nor call. There are certain periods in the history of society, when, passing from a state of spontaneous production to a state of reflection, mankind are particularly disposed to inquire concerning themselves and their destination, the nature of their being, the evidence of their knowledge, and the grounds of their faith. Such a tendency is one of the characteristics of the present age, and the German philosophy is the strongest expression of that tendency; it is a striving after information on subjects which have been usually considered as beyond the reach of human intelligence, an attempt to penetrate into the most hidden mysteries of our being. In every philosophy, there are three things to be considered, the object, the method, and the result. In the transcendental system, the *object* is to discover in every form of finite existence, an infinite and unconditioned as the ground of its existence, or rather as the ground of our knowledge of its existence, to refer all phenomena to certain *noumena,* or laws of cognition. It is not a *ratio essendi,* but a *ratio cognoscendi;* it seeks not to explain the existence of God and creation, objectively considered, but to explain our knowledge of their existence. It is not a skeptical philosophy; it seeks not to overthrow, but to build up; it wars not with the common opinions and general experience of mankind, but aims to place these on a scientific basis, and to verify them by scientific demonstrations.

The method is synthetical, proceeding from a given point, the lowest that can be found in our consciousness, and deducing from that point "the whole world of intelligences, with the whole system of their representations." The correctness or philosophical propriety of the construction which is to be based upon this given point, this absolute thesis, must be assumed for a while, until proved by the successful completion of the system which it is designed to establish. The test by which we are to know that the system is complete, and the method correct, is the same as that by which we judge of the correct construction of the material arch,—continuity and self-dependence. The last step in the process, the keystone of the fabric, is the deduction of time, space, and variety, or, in other words (as time, space, and variety include the elements of all empiric knowledge), the establishing of a coincidence between the facts of ordinary experience and those which we have discovered within ourselves, and scientifically derived from our first fundamental position. When this step is accomplished, the system is complete, the hypothetical frame-work may then fall, and the structure will support itself . . .

If now it be asked, as probably it will be asked, whether any definite and substantial good has resulted from the labors of Kant and his followers, we answer, Much. More than metaphysics ever before accomplished, these men have done for the advancement of the human intellect. It is true the immediate, and if we may so speak, the calculable results of their speculations are not so numerous nor so evident as might have been expected: these are chiefly comprised under the head of method. Yet even here we have enough to make us rejoice that such men have been, and that they have lived and spoken in our day. We need mention only the sharp and rightly dividing lines that have been drawn within and around the kingdom of human knowledge; the strongly marked distinctions of subject and object, reason and understanding, phenomena and noumena;— the categories established by Kant; the moral liberty proclaimed by him as it had never been proclaimed by any before; the authority and evidence of law and duty set forth by Fichte; the universal harmony illustrated by Schelling. But in mentioning these things, which are the direct results of the critical philosophy, we have by no means exhausted all that that philosophy has done for liberty and truth. The pre-eminence of Germany among the nations of our day in respect of intellectual culture, is universally acknowledged; and we do fully believe that whatever excellence that nation has attained in science, in history, or poetry is mainly owing to the influence of her philosophy, to the faculty which that philosophy has imparted of seizing on the spirit of every question, and determining at once the point of view from which each subject should be regarded,—in one word, to the transcendental method. In theology this influence has been most conspicuous. We are indebted to it for that dauntless spirit of inquiry which has investigated, and for that amazing erudition which has illustrated, every corner of biblical lore. Twice it has saved the religion of Germany,—once from the extreme of fanatic extravagance, and again, from the verge of speculative infidelity. But, though most conspicuous in theology, this influence has been visible in every department of intellectual exertion to which the Germans have applied themselves for the last thirty years. It has characterized each science and each art, and all bear witness to its quickening power. A philosophy which has given such an impulse to mental culture and scientific research, which has done so much to establish and to extend the spiritual in man, and the ideal in nature, needs no apology; it commends itself by its fruits, it lives in its fruits, and must ever live, though the name of its founder be forgotten, and not one of its doctrines survive.

7. Frederic Henry Hedge (1805-1890)
Progress of Society

[Having found his voice, a year after his piece on Coleridge, Hedge wrote in *The Christian Examiner* of March 1834 (XVI, 1–21), a review of an oration by Edward Everett on the hackneyed theme of the progress of society. Quickly leaving Everett aside, Hedge worked out a ringing statement of social optimism, identifying the hope of mankind with America; but his version differed from the conventional Phi Beta Kappa address, such as Everett's, because it phrased the social expectation in Transcendental terms. The crux of the problem, as he saw it, is nature: the interaction of man and nature is the key to social prosperity, and therefore in America—where nature is most abundant—resides the prospect. Hedge went beyond mere patriotism by disdaining the crude spread-eagle Americanism of Everett; he appealed to the "universal Man," who happens to find his best chance for universality in America, not because he is an American, but because here he can most directly confront nature. Again, Hedge was demonstrating that Transcendental metaphysics led inescapably to a social philosophy, and to a critique of existing institutions. Hedge was breaking ground for Emerson's *American Scholar*.]

It has been maintained by some, that the progress of society is necessarily limited; that the bounds of civilization are distinctly marked; that they have already, in several instances, been attained, or very nearly approached. This is inferred from the fact, that many individuals and states, and many departments of the human intellect, among the nations of antiquity, have attained a degree of refinement and perfection which has never been surpassed, or even equalled, in modern times; and furthermore, from the fact that all nations, after a certain degree of culture, have uniformly declined, and a savage people and a barbarous age succeeded. The supporters of this doctrine point us to the turning crises in the history of nations; they bid us mark the ebbing tide of wealth, refinement, and social improvement, and tell us that such is the destination of society to the end of time. The error which lies at the foundation of this doctrine, consists in not accurately distinguishing between the progress of society, and the advancement of a single people, or the perfection of the individual mind. There can be no doubt that individual minds and particular provinces of genius have, in repeated instances, reached the highest degree of earthly perfection, and attained to a power and glory which will never be surpassed. It is probable that single nations have advanced to the uttermost limits of national power and glory; and it is certain, that the outward aspect of society, so far from displaying a constant and uniform increase of culture and refinement, has exhibited thus far only a constant succession of light and darkness. Alternate civilization and barbarism make up the apparent history of man. Nevertheless, society, we believe, has always been moving onward. Notwithstanding the perpetual flux and reflux which appears on the surface of things, there has been an under-current of improvement, coëxtensive with the whole course of time. There never was an age in which some element of humanity was not making progress. Even in those periods of the world, which seem darkest to the superficial historian, there has ever been some process at work, in which the best interests of mankind were involved. In the dark ages, emphatically so called, more was done for society, than during the whole period of ancient history. For, what is society? It is not a single people or generation, it is not a collection of individuals as such; but it is an intimate union of individuals, voluntarily coöperating for the common good, actuated by social feelings, governed by social principles, and urged onward by social improvements. Society, in this sense, has always been advancing, not uniformly, indeed, far from it,—sometimes the motion has not been perceptible, sometimes, it may be, there has been no motion at all,—but it has never lost ground;—whenever it has moved at all, it has moved forward. The human mind, the source of this progress, has acted like the animal heart, not by a constant effort, but by successive pulsations, which pulsations, however, unlike those of the animal heart, must be reckoned, not by seconds, but by ages. Each pulsation has sent forth into the world some new sentiment or principle, some discovery or invention, which, like small portions of leaven, have successively communicated their quickening energy to the whole mass of society. It is the first duty of the philosophic historian to trace and exhibit these successive impulses. He who can do this, and he only, will be able to furnish a systematic history of Man; something very different from, and infinitely more important than the histories we now have of dynasties and tribes . . .

It is common in this country to connect the hope of man's advancement with the destinies of our own land. Nor is this connexion wholly without foundation. So far as outward circumstances are concerned, the prospect of social improvement is certainly brighter with us than in any other portion of the globe. Where *can* man advance if not in a country where all the elements of civilization abound? But is there no danger of carrying this notion too far? Our political destinies are written in the very features of the soil we inhabit. Its lakes, its rivers, its rich mines, its fertile valleys, utter but one prophecy. It is impossible to misinterpret such signs as these. They promise,— so long as peace shall unite these realms,—a perpetual increase of prosperity and glory. But what augury shall insure an equal increase of intellectual prosperity and moral glory? Shall we infer it from the institutions of this age? Alas! they are not, like the physical features of our country, fixed and permanent tokens. They are the creations of the day, they can vouch only for the passing generation. Not to these, but to the principles which they represent, let us look for salvation. Let these be our pledge for the fulfilment of all that the imagination has ever pictured of the destination of man. The institutions of this country have sometimes been represented as an experiment, on the issue of which the cause of universal improvement, and all the best interests of humanity, in some measure depend. If these fail, it is said, then farewell all farther hope of liberty and social progress. We love not to believe that a stake so precious is pending on a cast so doubtful. These institutions may fail, they certainly will fail, whenever, in the course of our advancement, they shall cease to be faithful expressions of the wisdom and the power of the age. Like seared foliage, at the touch of Autumn, they will wither and drop whenever their brief destination is fulfilled. It may be they are destined to a less timely end. The tempest may pluck them now in all their prime,

> "And, with forced fingers, rude,
> Shatter their leaves before the mellowing year."

But let us not, therefore, for a moment, cease to believe in the practicability of that which these institutions were designed to realize. Let us rest our hope of liberty and social improvement on something more decisive than the issue of a single experiment, or the fate of a single people. Let our trust have a surer foundation than the land of Washington, though there be a spell in that name above all earthly names; let it have a pledge more infallible than the seed of the pilgrims, though there be a virtue in that race which the world cannot match. Let us ground it on universal Man, on the might of the human will, and on the boundless resources of the human mind.

8. Isaac Ray (1807–1881)
Moral Aspects of Phrenology

[In the early 1830's the intellectual serenity of rational Unitarians—who like James Walker were proclaiming in *The Christian Examiner* that this was a period of rapid and perceptible progress because it was marked by "the disappearance of a thousand weak and debasing superstitions"—was upset not only by the influx of a strange and mystical philosophy, but by the intrusion into respectable quarters of a weird craze that made pretensions to being a science. In substance, phrenology purported to be a way of deciphering character from the configurations of the skull; its vogue in America dates from the publication in Boston in 1829 of George Combe's *Constitution of Man*—which did for Kaspar Spurzheim what Reed's *Observations* did for Swedenborg.

The young Transcendentalists were immediately fascinated. Emerson gave way in 1830 to the extent of calling Combe's book "the best Sermon I have read for some time." He later checked his enthusiasm, particularly as the practice of phrenology became associated with mesmerism, which he distrusted as being an invasion of personality; he cautioned his eager young friends, Caroline Sturgis and Margaret Fuller, against "your flights in the sky." But both he and Parker, in their summaries of the period, testify to the provocative effect of the craze, at least to the extent that it was a criticism of the sterile science of the academicians (see pp. 487, 499).

Unitarians were aghast at the spread of this cult, not only because it seemed, on rational grounds, fantastic, but because it raised in a totally new form the spectre of determinism, which they thought they had got rid of when they renounced Calvinism. In the guise of a physical analysis, it seemed to say that an immortal spirit is conditioned by his anatomical form. If phrenology were true, could a man be anything but what the shape of his cranium dictated?

Somewhat belatedly, after it could no longer afford to disregard the fad, *The Christian Examiner* decided to take notice of Combe's book and entrusted the review to Isaac Ray. The editors probably expected a destructive critique. (At any rate, their notices hereafter were to be uniformly unfavorable, one of them, two issues later, being by Hedge, who termed phrenology "materialistic and fatalistic.") They had every reason to suppose that Ray would excoriate the pseudo science, because he was a levelheaded scientist. A graduate of Bowdoin, he studied medicine in Boston under Dr. George Shattuck, and at the time the review appeared, was practicing in Eastport, Maine. Later on Isaac Ray was to gain fame as superintendent of the Maine Insane Hospital and from 1846 to 1866 as superintendent of the Butler Hospital in Providence. He is a pioneer of psychiatry in America and his *A Treatise on the Medical Jurisprudence of Insanity* (1838) is

still authoritative. But to the distress of the Unitarian community, Ray offered a
defense of phrenology, or at least, if not a justification for it on scientific grounds,
a plea for tolerance in terms of its philosophical intentions (*The Christian Examiner*, May 1834, XVI, 221–248). Clearly Dr. Ray had been more than infected with
the new metaphysics, and instead of seeing in phrenology a crude fatalism, he beheld in it an effort toward reading the "correspondence" of spirit and matter, a
welcome deliverance from the sensational psychology of John Locke.

In the history of Transcendentalism, the article is of importance since it
pointed the way in which Transcendentalists might continue to hail phrenology
as a sign of the times and employ it against the "sensualists," without having
necessarily to take it literally—just as they also employed Swedenborg's theology.
In his public utterances Emerson took a mischievous pleasure in praising those
who introduce questionable facts into their cosmogenies, such as palmistry, mesmerism, and phrenology, because these are "the certificate we have of departure
from routine, and that here is a new witness." More than that, phrenology was
an exploration of the parallelism between idea and nature, and therefore, instead of preaching fatalism it taught the Transcendental kind of freedom. For
Margaret Fuller phrenology was to be an even more rewarding study: "The mind
presses nearer home to the seat of consciousness the more intimate law and rule
of life, and old limits become fluid beneath the fire of thought."

If the Transcendentalists were always a bit ambiguous in their attitude toward
phrenology—and though the more Christian of them, like Hedge, would have
none of it—still their interest in it, and their partial endorsement, became another point on which they parted company with the rational Unitarianism of their
fathers, and the effect upon them of this enthusiasm was materially to widen the
breach.]

Phrenology recommends itself to us, at the first glance, by avoiding
the fruitful sources of error to which the metaphysicians have laid themselves open, in their neglect of the connexion between mind and matter, of
the mental manifestations of the inferior animals, and of the special purpose
of every particular power of which the general economy is composed. The
present state of our knowledge warrants us in rejecting any ethical or metaphysical system, that does not recognise and explain the adaptation of the
human constitution to the circumstances in which it is placed, its reference,
in every particular, to its sphere of action and the purpose of its being, and
furnish a clear and satisfactory theory of the varieties of individual and national character. Phrenology, therefore, establishes the fundamental principle,
that for every special end and object of our existence, nature has provided us
with an original and distinct power, by the exercise of which this end or object is accomplished, and demonstrates the power and its results to be neces-

sary in maintaining the relations of the constitution, as an harmonious and consistent whole, to the world around it. Seeing that the bodily organs are constituted in reference to external circumstances, it assumes also the same adaptation of the higher powers to the objects of their activity; and, from the same necessity that certain forms of organization are required by peculiarities of food, climate, &c., it is inferred that the moral and intellectual conditions are determined by the sphere and destinies of the individual. If for every and the smallest bodily function, an organ is provided that performs its office with perfect regularity and exactness, who, not utterly blinded by prejudice, will deny the existence, or at least the reasonableness, of a similar provision for the due preparation for and attainment of the highest and noblest purposes of our being? Phrenology looks for the material instruments whereby the subtler powers of our nature are exercised, defines their respective extent of action, examines the result of their combined operation and reciprocal influence, and furnishes a complete and consistent analysis of the moral and intellectual manifestations. If in a carnivorous animal we expect to find limbs adapted for overtaking its prey, claws and teeth for seizing and tearing it in pieces, senses for discerning it at a distance, and a stomach for digesting it, ought we not, in consistence with the same principle, to search for that stranger power that gave the spontaneous impulse to attack and destroy? While the Phrenologist sees the smallest process in the bodily economy accomplished by powers acting independent of volition, he believes that philosophy to be dishonorable to the Builder of his frame, that would deny an equal care for the nobler processes of the mental economy. While he is as willing as his opponents to admit the effects of education and other external circumstances, he contends for some definite and original faculty *to be* affected in this manner, and that the influence of these agents is confined by determinate limits. The truth is, though little suspected we fear, that since Locke's attack on the doctrine of innate ideas, people have become so accustomed to attribute the phenomena of mind to the influence of habit, association, &c., that the *mind itself* seems to be entirely lost sight of, and practically, if not theoretically, believed to be what Hume would make it, a mere bundle of perceptions. From such a philosophy, which makes the most wonderful phenomena of our nature the mere creature of the material world, Phrenology delivers us, and presents in its place a rational and intelligible exposition of the mental powers, and shows their relations to the moral, organic, and physical laws. That it has done all it professes to have done, we are not very anxious to contend; but that it has been successful to a certain extent, is now, we believe, denied by few who have taken the trouble to acquaint themselves with the subject, by a tolerably unprejudiced and thorough investigation. It must also be remembered, that these results are not necessarily dependent on any theory of the structure of the brain, but may stand, though every anatomical doctrine of Gall and Spurzheim should be swept away before the progress of discovery. Striving, as Phrenology now is, for the spread of a pure, practical morality, battling manfully with the forces that ignorance and selfishness have always arrayed against the rights of humanity, and laboring with the philanthropists of every sect and nation, wherever an opening is offered, in the great cause of human improvement, neither Phrenology, nor any other science acting in such a spirit, can be pronounced a visionary speculation, worthy of utter contempt and rejection. The spirit that glowed in the heart of that founder of the science whose voice is yet ringing in our ears, and preëminently entitled him to be called the "friend of man," is the spirit of Phrenology, and this should be sufficient to protect it from the scoffs of sciolists, and the sneers of the conceited adherents of an old philosophy.

9. Frederic Henry Hedge (1805–1890)
Schiller

[The reception in the office of *The Christian Examiner* of a life of Schiller in English meant, by now, that Hedge was the obvious man to review it. He took the occasion, in the issue of July 1834 (XVI, 365–392), to read his countrymen a further lecture on German literature, to teach them how to discriminate among German writers instead of lumping them all together under one rubric of scorn, and to make a further proclamation of the modern spirit. The dominant notes, he said, are a "fierce disquietude" and a "dissatisfaction with the whole mechanism of society." This was not what Boston and Harvard had understood by modernism.]

He who is called to be a prophet in his generation,—whose office it is to unfold new forms of truth and beauty,—enjoys, among other prerogatives peculiar to his calling, the privilege of a two-fold life. He is at once a dweller in the dust, and a denizen of that land where all truth and beauty spring. The genius that is linked with him, has its own world, and his earthly fortunes are chiefly memorable as the conditions of its development, or as the fruits of its action. While his mortal part, according to necessary and everlasting laws, fulfills its destiny in the great circle of Nature, the free spirit labors joyfully in that invisible kingdom to whose service it has been called. Ofttimes, however, the mortal and the spiritual, the earthly calling and the high calling, the prophet and the man, are so interwoven, that it becomes almost impossible to distinguish the one from the other. Hence the biography of such an one, when conceived in the spirit of this double nature, is a task of peculiar difficulty. The biographer must not only exhibit each part of his subject in its individual distinctness and fulness, but he must also explain the relation between them; he must show how the intellectual life has sprung from the earthly condition, and how the earthly condition has in turn been modified by the intellectual life. Now it is evident, that none but an *auto*-biography can fully satisfy the conditions of such a problem, inasmuch as the whole mystery of the connexion between the mortal and the spiritual, can be known only to individual consciousness. But so far as it *is* possible for one mind to interpret another,—so far as it is possible for the disciple of one nation or literature to comprehend and exhibit the intellectual offspring of a different nation and literature, so far this object has been accomplished in the work before us. The "Biography of Schiller" is a production of no ordinary merit, from whatever point of view we regard it; to us, it is chiefly remarkable as one of the very few instances in which full justice has been rendered by an English mind, to the character and claims of a foreign writer. Exclusiveness has been ever the besetting sin of that nation. Possessing a literature of their own, unequalled since the Greek, they seem never to have dreamed that any thing could be gained by a free intercourse with the genius of other climes. And yet there is no literature so rich, but it may be improved by grafts of foreign growth. The Germans have acted in this respect more liberally and more wisely. By means of translations, which seem rather to reproduce, than to interpret their respective originals, these indefatigable cultivators have succeeded in naturalizing the choice products of every zone. Their late luxuriant harvest of native produce has been rendered more luxuriant still, by a matchless collection of exotics; and an acquaintance with the German has now become an introduction to all that is beautiful and good of every age and clime.

The "Life of Schiller" is distinguished by its clear and happy method, its luminous critiques, and its just appreciation of the characteristic excellences and deficiencies of the poet whom it portrays. From scanty materials the author has constructed a work full of instruction, and pregnant with more than romantic interest. A life unusually barren of vicissitude, is made to appear eventful in the strong light which is thrown upon the revolutions of a master mind. In short, this biography is what the biography of a poet should always be,—the history of a mind rather than the history of a person, a record of thoughts and feelings rather than of events, a faithful exposition of the struggles and vicissitudes, the trials and the triumphs, which have befallen a human intellect in the service of truth . . .

The class of writings, to which this work belongs, is peculiar, we believe, to modern times. It is characterized by a spirit of fierce disquietude, a dissatisfaction with the whole mechanism of society, and a presumptuous questioning of all that God or man has ordained. It represents a state of being which no word or combination of words can exactly express; a disease peculiar to ardent natures, in early life:

"The flash and outbreak of a fiery mind;
A savageness of unreclaimed blood;"

a keen sensibility to all that is absurd and oppressive in social life, a scorning of authority and custom, a feeling that all the uses of this world are weary and unprofitable, together with the consciousness of high powers, bright visions of ideal excellence, and a restless yearning after things not granted to man. To those who are not acquainted with German works of this description, Shelley's and Byron's poetry may serve as English samples. "The Robbers" is, on the whole, the most innocent work of the kind to which it belongs. Heinse's "Ardinghello," a contemporary production of the same class, is a very impure book, the tendency of "Werter" is questionable, and that of "Faust" still more so; but Schiller's drama, we will venture to affirm, never did injury to the morals of any one. The allegation that young men have been made highwaymen by it, is unsupported by any evidence that we have been able to discover. It seems to us just about as probable that "The Robbers" should produce this effect, as that any one should be induced by one of Cooper's novels to join a tribe of Indians. Our author has said with truth, that the publication of "The Robbers" forms an era in the literature of the world. With the exception of "Faust," we know of no work since Shakespeare, that possesses half its power; we mean that kind of power which is evinced by fertility of imagination, and by vivid expression of passionate emotions. In this latter respect, "The Robbers" exceeds every thing of the kind. "The Corsair" and "The Giaour" are pastoral eclogues compared with it . . .

The most prominent quality in Schiller's intellectual character,—that which formed the foundation of his success as a poet,—was, unquestionably, his creative power, his ability to produce finished works of art, characterized by unity of purpose, continuity of interest, and entireness of effect. Works of this kind are more rare in German, than in any other literature. Possessed with the love of philosophizing peculiar to their countrymen, the writers of fiction in that language have ever some other object in view than the regular and harmonious development of the subject before them. The progress of a story, the interest of a plot, are with them matters of secondary importance; it is the exhibition of some variety of human nature, or some form of human life; the exercise of the imagination, the indulgence of personal or general satire, or the illustration of some philosophical truth, which chiefly occupies them. The story is nothing more than a pretence for bringing these things before the public. This is particularly true of their better novels, which differ, in this respect, from those of every other nation. They have nothing epic, they pursue no straight-forward course; the reader is not, as in one of Scott's or Miss Edgeworth's compositions, hurried irresistibly along by a single thread of narrative, which holds him captive until the work is finished, but is placed in a labyrinth of striking thoughts and beautiful illustrations, having no necessary connexion or dependence, through which he is left to find his way as he can. This it is, that so perplexes English readers on their first introduction to German literature. Unacquainted with this species of composition, they sit down to a German novel as they would to an English work of the same title, never doubting but that they are to be entertained with a pleasant story; instead of which, they are treated to a series of philosophical disquisitions.

This species of composition, as it has been managed by Goethe and Jean Paul, seems to us to hold a much higher rank than the historical novel. That it should be less attractive to the mass of readers, we can easily conceive; but we are persuaded that no person of cultivated mind who takes up one of Goethe's novels, knowing what he is to expect, and not judging according to rules drawn from the works of other countries, will find them deficient in interest. This feature in German works of fiction proceeds rather from a peculiarity of taste, than from want of epic power, the existence of which, in that nation, has been sufficiently proved by many of their lighter works, particularly by those of Tieck, Hoffman, and Baron Motte Fouqué. In general, however, it must be allowed that the German genius is too expansive for epic composition, it loves to lose itself in airy speculations, and wants that contractile power which is necessary to concentrate the interest of a work around a single point. To this general rule, Schiller forms a remarkable exception. There never was a poet in whose works unity and wholeness, harmony of form and concentration of interest, were more conspicuous than in his. In this respect he seems less intimately related to his own country than most of his contemporaries. We cannot subscribe to the sentence which has pronounced him a peculiarly *national* poet. We know of no German writer, unless it be Tieck, who is less German.

10. James Walker (1794–1874)
Foundations of Faith

[James Walker was, along with Convers Francis, one of the few among the slightly older generation to whom the Transcendentalists looked with respect and with the hope of communion. Born in Woburn, Massachusetts, graduated from Harvard in 1814, he studied under Henry Ware, Jr., and was settled at Charlestown in 1818. He immediately became a leader of the liberal forces and was second only to Dr. Channing himself in organizing the American Unitarian Association. An impressive and handsome man, he was learned in philosophy and was genuinely tolerant. As editor of *The Christian Examiner* from 1831 to 1839, he tried as long as possible to let both sides have their say, and it is to his liberality that Ripley, Hedge, and Brownson were indebted for the chance to publish their radical ideas in the official Unitarian journal. In 1839 he was to become Alford Professor of Natural Religion at Harvard, and in 1840 to deliver an address in vindication of philosophy, which *The Dial* could still find admirable. But Walker was, however broad-minded, a disciple of the Scottish realists, an editor of textbook versions of Dugald Stewart and Thomas Reid, and no encourager of Transcendental nonsense. However, in 1834 he published an address in the *Examiner* (September, XVII, 1–15), in which he tried to dissociate Unitarianism from a strict sensationalism, and so gave a halfhearted blessing to the new tendencies. From 1853 to 1860, Walker was President of Harvard; he left the library a valuable collection of philosophical works.]

Modern philosophy has revived an important distinction, much insisted on by the old writers, between what is *subjectively* true and real, that is to say, true and real so far as the mind itself is concerned, and what is *objectively* true and real, that is to say, true and real independently of the mind. Thus we affirm of things, the existence of which is reported by the senses, that they really exist both subjectively and objectively; that is to say, that the mind is really affected as if they existed, and that, independently of this affection of the mind, the things themselves exist. In other words, we have an idea of the thing really existing *in* the mind, and this is subjective truth and reality; and there is also an object answering to that idea really existing *out of* the mind, and this is objective truth and reality. One sense, therefore, there certainly is, in which the most inveterate skeptic must allow that religion has a real and true existence to the really and truly devout. Subjectively it is real and true, whether objectively it is real and true, or not. All must admit that it is true and real so far as the mind itself is concerned, even though it cannot be shown to have existence independently of the mind. It is a habit or disposition of soul, and, in any view of the matter, the habit or disposition truly and really exists. It is a developement of our nature, a developement of character, and, as such, is as true and real as any other developement of nature and character. Even if it feeds on illusions, it is not itself an illusion. Even if, in its springing up, it depends on nothing better than a fancy, a dream,—its growth in the soul, and the fruits of that growth, are realities,—all-important, all-sustaining realities . . .

Most of you, I presume, are apprized of the extravagances of skepticism into which men have been betrayed by insisting on a *kind* of evidence of which the nature of the case does not admit. Some have denied the existence of the spiritual world; others have denied the existence of the sensible world; and others again have denied the existence of both worlds, contending for that of impressions or perceptions alone. These last, if we are to believe in nothing but the facts of sensation, and what can be *logically* deduced from these facts, are unquestionably the only consistent reasoners. For what logical connexion is there between a fact of sensation, between an impression or perception, and the real existence of its object, or of the mind that is conscious of it? None whatever. I do not mean that a consistent reasoner will hesitate to admit the real existence of the objects of sensation. Practically speaking he cannot help admitting their real existence, if he would. Every man, woman, and child believes in his or her own existence, and in that of the outward universe or sensible world; but not because the existence of either is susceptible of proof by a process of reasoning. Not the semblance, not the shadow of a sound logical argument can be adduced in proof of our own existence, or that of the outward universe. We believe in the existence of both, it is true; but it is only because we are so constituted as to make it a matter of intuition. Let it be distinctly understood, therefore, that our conviction of the existence of the sensible world does not rest on a logical deduction from the facts of sensation, or of sensation and consciousness. It rests on the constitution of our nature. It is resolvable into a fundamental law of belief. It is held, not as a logical inference, but as a first principle. With the faculties we possess, and in the circumstances in which we are placed, the idea grows up in the mind, and we cannot expel it if we would.

Now the question arises, On what evidence does a devout man's conviction of the existence and reality of the *spiritual world* depend? I answer;—On the very same. He is conscious of spiritual impressions or perceptions, as he also is of sensible impressions or perceptions; but he does not think to demonstrate the existence and reality of the objects of either by a process of reasoning. He does not take the facts of his inward experience, and hold to the existence and reality of the spiritual world as a logical deduction from these facts, but as an intuitive suggestion grounded on these facts. He believes in the existence and reality of the spiritual world, just as he believes in his own existence and reality, and just as he believes in the existence and reality of the outward universe,—simply and solely because he is so constituted that with his impressions or perceptions he cannot help it. If he could, it would be to begin by assuming it to be possible that his faculties, though in a sound state and rightly circumstanced, may play him false; and if he could begin by assuming this as barely possible, there would be an end to all certainty. Demonstration itself, ocular or mathematical, would no longer be ground of certainty. It is said that sophistical reasoning has sometimes been resorted to in proof of the existence and reality of the spiritual world; and this perhaps is true; but the error has consisted in supposing that any reasoning is necessary. It is not necessary that a devout man's conviction of the existence and reality of the spiritual world should rest on more or on better evidence, than his conviction of the existence and reality of the sensible world;—it is enough that it rests on as much, and on the very same. It is enough that both are resolvable, as I have shown, into the same fundamental law of belief; and that, in philosophy as well as in fact, this law ought to exclude all doubt in the former case, as well as in the latter.

11. Orestes A. Brownson (1803–1876)
Benjamin Constant

[In 1834 Brownson came to Canton, and the new school at last had its bulldog. George Ripley quickly became his friend, and later was to insist that Brownson's career—considered, of course, before Brownson's conversion to Catholicism—"presents a cheering example of the influence of our institutions to bring forward the man rather than the scholar, to do justice to the sincere expression of a human voice, while the foppery of learning meets with nothing but contempt." His early life had indeed been passed, as Ripley understated it, "in scenes foreign to the pursuits of literature," and he wrote, not out of a desire for reputation, but because he had an earnest conviction "that must needs be spoken out."

He announced his presence, in no uncertain tones, by publishing in *The Christian Examiner* for September 1834 (XVII, 63–77) a review of Benjamin

Constant, *De la religion, considérée dans sa source, ses formes et ses développements,* which Brownson was capable of reading and understanding without the help of a translation. He used the opportunity to deliver the most explicit blast yet uttered in Boston against religious institutionalism (no one could mistake that he meant his fellow Unitarians) and against the intellectualism of Unitarian psychology, in the name of the superior and anterior "sentiments."]

In these works, Benjamin Constant attempts to reduce our religious history to a science, and to verify its laws . . .

He begins his work with the position, that all beings, created or uncreated, animate or inanimate, rational or irrational, have their laws. These laws constitute the nature of each species, and are the general and permanent cause of each one's mode of existence. We do not know, we cannot know, the origin of these laws. All we know, or need know, is, that they exist, and in all our attempts to explain any partial phenomena, we must assume their existence, as our point of departure . . .

But if man is determined to religion by a fundamental law of his being, how comes it that men, even wise and virtuous men, at various epochs, are either indifferent or opposed to it? To solve this problem, we must distinguish between the religious sentiment, and religious institutions. The sentiment results from that craving, which we have, to place ourselves in communication with invisible powers; the institutions, the form, from that craving which we also have, to render the means of that communication, we think to have discovered, regular and permanent . . . Hence the necessity of religious institutions, the reason why the sentiment is always clothed with some form.

But every positive form, however satisfactory it may be for the present, contains a germ of opposition to future progress. It contracts, by the very effect of its duration, a stationary character, that refuses to follow the intellect in its discoveries, and the soul in its emotions, which each day renders more pure and delicate. Forced to borrow images more and more material, in order to make the greater impression upon its adherents, the religious form soon comes to present man, wearied with this world, only another very little different. The ideas it suggests are daily narrowed down to the terrestrial ideas, of which they are only a copy, and the epoch arrives when it presents to the mind only assertions which it cannot admit, and to the soul only practices which can no longer satisfy it. The sentiment now breaks away from that form, which, if one may so speak, has become petrified; it asks another form, one which will not wound it, and it ceases not its exertions till it obtains it. Here is the history of religion; but without the distinction between the sentiment and the form, it would be for ever unintelligible. The sentiment is lodged in the bottom of the soul, always the same, unalterable, and eternal; the form is variable and transitory . . .

We think the time has come for us to clothe the religious sentiment with a new form, and to fix upon some religious institution, which will at once supply our craving for something positive in religion, and not offend the spirituality which Christianity loves, and towards which the human race hastens with an increasing celerity. We think, we see indications, that this presents itself to many hearts as desirable. And we think we see this especially among our own friends. Every religious denomination must run through two phases, the one destructive, the other organic. Unitarianism could commence only by being destructive. It must demolish the old temple, clear away the rubbish, to have a place whereon to erect a new one. But that work is done; that negative character which it was obliged to assume then, may now be abandoned. The time has now come to rear the new temple,—for a positive work, and, if we are not mistaken, we already see the workmen coming forth with joy to their task. We already see the germ of re-organization, the nucleus, round which already gravitate the atoms of a new moral and religious world. The work of elaboration is well nigh ended, the positive institutions, so long sought, will soon be obtained, and the soul, which has so long been tossed upon a sea of dispute, or of skepticism, will soon find that repose, after which it so deeply sighs and yearns.

Here, perhaps, we ought to close; but we cannot let the occasion pass without offering some remarks upon a point very distinctly recognised in the interesting Preface to the first volume of the first of the works we have named. The point to which we allude is, that religion and morality rest not on the understanding, not on logical deductions, but on an interior sentiment. Here is an important recognition,—a recognition of two distinct orders of human faculties. This recognition is not always made by metaphysicians, but it never escapes popular language. It is found in the distinction between the head and the heart, the mind and the soul, the understanding and the affections, which obtains in all languages. And this is not strange. One cannot have made the least progress in psychological observation, without being struck with internal phenomena, which can by no means be classed with the operations of the understanding. There belong to human nature, passions, emotions, sentiments, affections, of which, the understanding, properly so called, can take no account, which pay no deference to its ratiocinations, and even bid defiance to its laws. The feeling which we have, when contemplating a vast and tranquil sea, distant mountains with harmonious outlines, or, when marking an act of heroism, of disinterestedness, or of generous self-sacrifice for others' welfare, rises without any dependence on the understanding. We feel what we then feel, not because we have convinced ourselves by logical deductions that we ought so to feel. Reasoning may come afterwards and justify the feeling; but it did not precede it, and, if it had, it could not have produced it. The understanding cannot feel; it cannot love, hate, be pleased, be angry, nor be exalted or depressed. It is void of emotion. It is calm, cold, calculating. Had we no faculty but those it includes, we should be strangers to pity, to sympathy, to benevolence, to love, and,—what is worse,—to enthusiasm. Bring the whole of man's nature within the laws of the understanding, and you reduce religion, morality, philosophy, to a mere system of logic; you would, in the end, pronounce every thing which does not square with dry and barren dialectics, chimerical, and every thing which interest cannot appropriate, mischievous.

But we not only contend for the distinction of the mental phenomena into two different orders, but we contend, that the sentiments are as worthy of reliance, as the understanding; that, to speak in popular language, the testimony of the heart is as legitimate, as that of the head. We are aware, that the philosophy of sensation will condemn this position. Be it so. The philosophy of sensation reigned during the last half of the last century, and it is, as far as we have any philosophy, still the philosophy of our own country; but it is no great favorite of ours. It undoubtedly has its truth; but, taken exclusively, freed from its inconsequences, and pushed to its last results, it would deprive man of all but a merely mechanical life, divest the heart of all emotion, wither the affections, dry up the sentiments, and sink the human race into a frigid skepticism. The testimony of the senses requires an internal sanction, and, in the last analysis, that of the understanding is not credited till it is corroborated by that of consciousness. Neither our senses, nor our understanding, can prove to us, that we exist, and yet it is impossible for us, in a healthy state of mind to doubt our existence; neither our senses nor our understanding can prove to us the existence of an external world, nor the objective reality of any thing, yet we should justly regard him as insane, who should not believe in the existence of an external world, and there is no one, who, listening to the sweet strains of music, will not believe they come to his heart from some objective reality. It is a law of our nature, of which reasoning cannot divest us, that in these, and in a vast variety of cases, we must believe on the simple testimony of consciousness, or, in other words, we believe so, because our nature,—the very laws of our being,—compel us to believe so. But the moment we recur to the testimony of consciousness, to the laws of our nature, we desert the understanding, we leave the power of ratiocination, and have recourse to an entirely different order of testimony . . .

But we would not merely rely on this order of our faculties, which we call the sentiments. We would have them appealed to, as the most essential part of our nature. We do not mean to depreciate the understanding; we would not underrate the power of ratiocination, nor, in any case, dispense with sound logic. We value man's whole nature; man's whole nature is essential. We should think clearly, reason closely, powerfully; but we should also feel justly and energetically. We should retain and develope all our faculties, each in its place, so as to preserve unbroken harmony through the whole man. But if we do this, we shall find, that the sentiments, the feelings, are entitled to a much higher rank than it has been customary to assign them for the last century. To us the sentiments seem to be peculiarly the human faculties. They give to man his distinctive character. They supply him with energy to act, and prompt him to the performance of grand and noble deeds. We fear that their power is seldom suspected, that little attention is paid to the mission which is given them to accomplish. We have schools for the intellect. We take great pains to educate the reasoning faculty, but we almost, at least so far as our schools are concerned, entirely neglect the sentiments. We cannot but regret this; for knowledge when not coupled with just feelings, strong reasoning powers when not under the guidance of pure and holy sentiments, only so much the better fit one for a career destructive to the best interests of humanity. And, let it be understood, men are not reasoned into good feelings, for the feelings do not depend on the intellect. Just sentiments are not the result of just knowledge. A man may know the truth, be able to defend it in language and with arguments that fix attention, and flash instantaneous conviction, and yet have no just, honorable, or benevolent feelings. It is an old saying, that men know better than they do;

> "Video meliora, proboque;
> Deteriora sequor."

It will be so, as long as we trust to merely intellectual education to give right feelings. We would, therefore, without in the least neglecting the intellect, turn attention to the sentiments, appeal to them on all occasions, and make it the leading object of all education to develope them, to fit them for strong and beneficent action.

12. George Ripley (1802–1880)
Herder

[Emboldened by the assistance which Hedge and Brownson had now rendered the cause, Ripley could take up an English translation of Herder's *The Spirit of Hebrew Poetry* in *The Christian Examiner* for May 1835 (XVIII, 167–221) with a confidence he had been far from commanding when he reviewed Follen three years before. In describing Herder, Ripley presented, although under a Germanic alias, a sketch of the ideal theologian as he might be conceived in Transcendental terms. The point would seem to be—although Ripley is still not too definite—that the truly religious man derives more from the "organic forces of nature" than from any formulae and that German "mysticism" may be the expression of a truly exalted spirituality. The article is guarded, but conveys an unmistakable hint of more to come.]

The poetry of Germany, with the other branches of its elegant literature, has begun to receive in our mother country some degree of the attention, which is due to the products of the genius and culture of a kindred nation . . . Under the auspices of sound and liberal scholars, like Carlyle, Hayward, and Mrs. Austin, the English public are in a fair way of obtaining access to the literary treasures of their Teutonic neighbours; and even we, who are not within the borders of European cultivation, may hope to receive some share of the spoils.

We cannot make so favorable a report of the prospects of German Theology. Neither that, nor any of the various schools of philosophy, which have sprung up in Germany, within the last fifty years, has received tolerable justice at the hands of English scholars. We are by no means in possession of the results produced by the intense and powerful action of the masterly intellects, which have been directed to those interesting subjects, since the skepticism of Hume spread a general alarm, and awakened the adherents of a traditional faith to inquiry and examination. It is rather singular, that, in our own country, where a zeal for religion and a love of speculation, form a part of our birthright, we should have given so little attention to the labors of others, who have explored every part of the field on which we are employed ourselves. It is said that the great points, which have been made the subject of theological discussion among us, the nature and evidences of revelation, the foundation of religion in the human soul, and character of Christianity, the connexion between Jesus Christ and God, the hope of immortality, have been so thoroughly discussed by the divines and philosophers of Germany, that there is hardly a theory or a doctrine that has not been examined; and it would not be extravagant to believe, that, amid the comparison of so many opinions, by men of learning and sense, some light would be struck out, that would well repay the trouble of giving it an attentive considera- tion. We are by no means so enthusiastic as to suppose, that a knowledge of German theology would settle any controversies now pending; but we think it very possible, that a sober examination of its achievements might present some facts or points of view, which would be of service to us in our inquiries, although they had escaped our notice in the course of our own personal studies. At any rate, the massive learning, which we believe it is universally admitted the German theologians possess, might be of great use to many of us, who are so involved in the practical business of life, as to have little opportunity for original investigation, but who still like to be informed as to what wise men have thought before us . . .

Herder is one of the great historical names in German literature. His theological works are a treasure of learning, refined from the dross and base admixtures of the mine, and wrought up into the most beautiful and winning forms. It is seldom that we meet with a writer, whose soul is so penetrated with the true spirit of antiquity, and who is so capable of bringing up the faded past in vivid reality before the eye. "It seems, in reading him," says Madame de Staël, "as if we were walking in the midst of the old world with an historical poet, who touches the ruins with his wand and erects anew all the fallen edifices." He brings to his subject a freshness, a gushing enthusiasm, which spreads a charm over the driest details, and reminds us more of the eloquent conversation of a friend than of the learned discussions of a critic. Every thing is in motion, every thing has life, he is never languid himself, and he never permits languor in others; and we are led on from page to page of profound learning, of curious research, of wide and scholar-like in- vestigation, with as little feeling of satiety or fatigue, as if we were reading a fascinating novel. He is unrivalled in the power of giving a picturesque beauty to the most barren subjects, so that the wilderness springs up into bloom and luxuriance under his magic touch. His own pure and noble spirit breathes through his productions. They seem to bring us into the presence of the author, where we hear his deep and thrilling voice, gaze upon his serene brow, and receive a revelation of his inmost heart. We cannot read them without knowing and loving the mind, from whose inspiration they pro- ceeded. The great object of his life was the spiritual elevation of humanity; and, in his view, the means of its accomplishment was to infuse the spirit of Christ and his religion into the hearts of men. Such fervent love of man, such deep sympathy with Christ, such filial and noble conceptions of the great Father of all, are rarely united in any character; and these are so distinctly impressed on the whole face of his writings, that, in reading them, we feel that we are enjoying the intimate communion of an exalted and holy mind . . .

In his views with regard to the physical world, he has been accused of a tendency to mysticism, and, in the present state of science, it cannot be denied that there is some foundation for this reproach. He believed that there were certain powers of nature and of the soul, not yet explained by philosophy, in accordance with each other and with the known laws of the universe, upon which the human mind is yet to receive further light. He was acquainted with the writings of the most celebrated mystics, but they did not satisfy him. He believed with them, however, that there are moments of inward abstraction, when the purified mind enjoys glimpses of the future and foresees the shadowy approach of coming events. With the genius of Shakespeare, which cast such deep glances into the hidden world of spirits, he cherished a lively sympathy, and on this account, besides his admiration of his great powers, preferred him to all other poets. His mind was in a constant state of communion with the invisible world. He was wont to indulge in presentiments concerning the future, and often expressed his firm conviction that he should not live to be old.

The organic forces of nature were always a favorite subject of investigation. He wished to penetrate into her secret laboratory, in order, if possible, to discover the laws of her spiritual activity. On this account, he took a deep interest in the progress of the physical sciences. The recent discovery of Galvanism, the improvements that were to be expected in Electricity and Magnetism, the geological system of Werner, the investigations of Camper and Sömmering in Physiology, and even the theories of Dr. Gall on the brain, strongly attracted his attention; and he often lamented that he was born too soon to be a witness of their results to science and humanity. The discovery of the laws of nature, and of their union and harmony with each other and with the universe, even in a moral point of view, was his favorite wish. He was accustomed to say, that "the progress of the human mind in scientific discoveries had introduced a clearer and more certain light into the world; in this path we must carry on the grand structure, and seek for greater certainty and truth, in our knowledge of nature's laws. We must no longer dwell in the twilight of former ages; but the germ of all human knowledge and action, which we have received from them, must become to us the germ of new life and new virtue. We must cultivate this germ, according to our present modes of conception, and the knowledge and power which we have acquired from the past; so that every truth, of which we become certain, may lead us more freely to the great spiritual objects of our being. As physical science receives new light, the operation of spiritual powers is confirmed, and the soul of man is elevated in reverence and love towards the Supreme Creator."

13. Orestes A. Brownson (1803–1876)
Progress of Society

[For the next issue of *The Christian Examiner,* July 1835 (XVIII, 345–368), the irrepressible Brownson seized the chance of reviewing an anonymous essay on the moral constitution of man to return to the theme that Hedge had uncovered in March of the previous year, and to proclaim aloud that the Transcendental metaphysic had no intention whatsoever of sparing the existing social arrangements. The prevailing assumption in Unitarian circles was that the present had no reason to accuse itself of any serious shortcomings, particularly in America, where all the evidences of progress were so conspicuous. As against this confidence, Brownson bluntly declared that inequalities of wealth are basically incompatible with genuine Christianity. From the vantage point of a conception of Christianity that had been somehow identified with "nature," Brownson served emphatic notice that the dreams of mankind cannot safely be contradicted by the so-called realities of economics.]

In a former article we spoke of the progress which Christianity has effected. We advanced the doctrine of the Essay before us, that mankind collectively has a growth precisely analogous to that of the individual. This is a doctrine which enables us to recall the past without wrath or bitterness. All past social institutions have had and fulfilled their mission. They are not to be tried by the present, but by that epoch in the progress of society to which they belonged. Tried by this standard, most of the institutions which we now condemn, will be found to have been good in their day, and the evil which is charged against them belonged, not to their origin, but resulted from their lingering too long, from their outliving their time . . .

But, if we acquit the past, we must not forget the duty of the present. We must neither feel nor act as if all progress was ended, and man had attained all the perfection of which he is capable. There is to be a progress through all the future, as there has been one through all the past; but the future progress must always be elaborated in the present. The child prepares the youth, the youth prepares the man; and in like manner this generation must prepare its successor, and that must prepare the one to come after it. The duty of the present, then, is great; its position is one of great consequence; it can act on all future time, and hasten or retard, in some degree, the progress of society through all coming generations. It will discharge its duty very much in proportion to its estimate of itself and its hopes for the future. If it be satisfied with itself, or if it believe that nothing better is possible, its exertions will be feeble, and its contributions to future progress will be hardly worth naming. For ourselves, we believe the present greatly superior to whatever has gone before it; but it does not satisfy us. We do not declaim against it, we attempt to comprehend it; we contemplate it with gratitude to God, but it does not come up to our idea of good. There flit across our mental vision the shadows, at least, of something immeasurably better.

That all will agree with us in our estimate of the present, or in our hopes for the future, is more than we expect. Men's notions of society are much influenced by the position from which they view it. He who is at ease himself, rich, enjoying ample leisure, and associating only with the most favored individuals in the community, will call society as it is, very nearly, if not quite, perfect; he will be prone to forget, or not to suspect, the vast amount of suffering that lies beyond him; and, unless perchance he has learned something more of Christianity than its dogmas, he will be very liable to look upon the manual laborer, not as a fellow immortal, with rights, duties, interests, and feelings, sacred as his own, but as a mere instrument of his wealth or pleasure, made to be used for his service, and sufficiently provided for if fed and clothed and comfortably lodged. It will be difficult for him to comprehend any measures taken to benefit the working men as a class, and any interest shown in their behalf will seem to him to flow from a Jacobinical spirit, or from an over-refined sentimentalism. But the poor man who trudges daily to his toil, feeling himself hardly more respected than an implement of husbandry, and able, with all his exertions, barely to keep his wife and children from starving, will believe society as it is, very imperfect; he will call this a bad world, and hard and bitter thoughts will pass through his mind, as he gazes on the palace of the rich, or sees its lordly owner roll by him in his carriage.

We do not censure or approve either. The views of both are natural, if not inevitable, if we take into the account their respective positions. The guinea often slips between men's eyes and the truth; and, from not seeing the truth, it is very natural that they should come to deny it. For ourselves, we share fully the views of neither of the two individuals we have introduced as the representatives of the two extremes of society. It has been our lot to see society on more than one side. Indeed we have seen it on all sides. We know what it can give, and what it requires to be endured, and we say again, it does not satisfy us. We cannot avoid dreaming,—if dreaming it prove to be,—of something greatly its superior. We see endured by all classes a vast amount of evil, to which we cannot reconcile our love of humanity. We see noble energies misdirected, false modes of judging adopted, factitious distinctions to obtain and be defended. All over the world, even in its most favored portions, there is an inequality in wealth, in moral, intellectual, and social advantages, which we believe wholly inconsistent with full exercise of Christian love. Everywhere one part of our fellow beings are wasting away in luxury, indolence, listlessness, and dissipation; and another part pining in want and neglect, devoured by discontent and envy; and when we see this, we can call it neither good nor necessary. We ask that it may be cured, and we turn to the future with full faith that it will be.

14. George Ripley (1802–1880)
Herder's Theological Opinions and Services

[Returning to the discussion of Herder, Ripley took an English edition of his works, along with the German original, in the November 1835 issue of *The Christian Examiner* (XIX, 172–204), in order to complete his portrait of the Transcendental theologian to whom nature as well as revelation is the gift of God. Toward the close of his sketch he was obliged to confront—though still under the guise of reporting Herder's opinions—the issue upon which there could be no possible accommodation between the new school and the old: the question of the historicity of the miracles recorded in the Bible, especially those in the New Testament performed by Christ himself. In the next twelve months dispute over this doctrine was hopelessly to split the Unitarian community.

As Ripley here presents it, the issue seems no more than a cloud on the horizon the size of a man's hand, but the storm that the cloud contained had long been brewing. The most poignant element in the story is that Ripley, who first broached the problem—although in this indirect fashion—was one who genuinely did believe that the miracles had taken place exactly as Scripture tells them. Yet in all honesty and courage, he could not restrain himself from reporting Herder's belief that doctrines depend not upon miracles but upon their own intrinsic worth, or from indicating, by the tone of his treatment, his sympathy with that belief.

For the moment, professors at the Harvard Divinity School and leaders of Unitarian opinion could disregard Ripley's paragraph. He was, after all, merely retailing Herder, and he did not yet say, in his own person, that miracles were irrelevant. But his implication seemed clear enough, and it was a fair warning to the majority of his colleagues. From their point of view, it was all very well to learn German and to inform New England about the notions of obscure Germans like Herder, but if Ripley and the Germanophiles were to identify themselves with these un-Christian theories, then the Unitarian leaders would need to take steps—especially as their Calvinist opponents were watching the sequence of *Examiner* articles with interest, prepared, as soon as the end was reached, to accuse all Unitarianism of having forfeited its last pretension to the name of Christianity.]

[Herder's] views of the general subject of revelation, though admitting a direct communication from God, were somewhat at variance with the ideas that have usually prevailed with regard to it. He believed in a constant and intimate connexion between the human soul and the Spirit of God. He regarded every mental endowment, as the gift of divine Providence. In accordance with their natural powers, he supposed, that a higher degree of light had been granted to favored individuals, by which they were made the special messengers of God to their fellow men. The collection of truths, which they taught, under the influence of this light, he regarded as the substance of divine revelation. The effect of the Holy Spirit upon the mind, he maintains, is not to impair its healthy action, but on the contrary, to call forth its noblest powers in order and harmony. This view, according to his opinion, coincides with the sentiments of the ancient world, which always understood by divine inspiration, a state of the highest energy and of entire freedom. The favorite conception of modern times, however, has been of a lower character. The subject of inspiration has been regarded as no more than the pipe of an organ, through which the wind is blown,—a mere hollow medium, deprived of his own thought and activity. A more desolate condition of human nature can hardly be imagined . . .

This narrow procedure of theologians was entirely opposed to Herder's favorite mode of thinking. Nature and revelation, in his view, were both the gift of God. There was no hostility between them, until it was called forth by the disputes of men. They both have the same object, they aim at the same result, and they should, accordingly, exist together in mutual peace . . .

Among other topics which early attracted his attention in the study of the Bible, the account of the creation and primitive state of man appears to have presented peculiar charms . . .

It is the love of scholastic forms, Herder repeats, which has caused so many of the most acute scholars of modern times to lose their talents, their time, and their labor, in the interpretation of this passage. They wished to take the whole of it in a doctrinal sense. But they saw that it was ridiculous to understand all according to the letter. This tempted so many good heads to escape the difficulty by subtile and ingenious inventions. They wished by all means to preserve its doctrinal significance. And to do this, they have spun out, sometimes philosophical defences, sometimes physical hypotheses, sometimes mystical dreams, sometimes chronological tables of days, sometimes philological theories, to the perversion of the true sense of the words. In this way, the understanding has been shackled and cast into the dust. Until within a recent period, there has scarcely been a respectable critic, who ventured to call the first chapters of the Bible poetry; and although, at the present day, the name is often repeated, yet their true point of view, as remains of national songs, is too much kept out of sight. Yet, this would naturally be the most simple and easy explanation, which would need only to be stated, in order to commend itself to the unprejudiced inquirer. It remains true to its principal aim from beginning to end, without entering into vexatious details; it is free from all physical and dogmatic systems, and follows only the genius of the passage, of the language, of the nation, and of the clime in which it was produced; it seeks out the meaning of all that is in the passage, but has no desire, no reason, to find a single iota in it, more than it actually contains. "If nine and ninety paths," asks Herder, "lead astray; may not the hundredth still be the way to the simple truth? And what if that way should be the easiest of all?" . . .

A course of reasoning similar to this was pursued by Herder, with regard to the nature and purposes of the miracles recorded in the New Testament. He did not call in question their historical truth. In his opinion they could not be separated from the narratives of the Evangelists, without doing violence to the plainest laws of literary criticism. He admitted, moreover, that there was no antecedent improbability, which should lead us to reject them, without examining their historical evidence. They are so interwoven with the whole history of our Saviour, so appropriate to his person and character as the Messiah, that Christ would be no longer Christ, if we denied these facts concerning him. We are not, however, to rest the divine authority of Christianity upon the evidence of miracles. Our Saviour himself never regarded them as the criterion of truth, nor as a gift, the value of which could be compared with that of moral endowments. It is in fact impossible, argues Herder, to establish the truth of any religion, merely on the ground of miracles. Suppose that we call religion, a system of doctrinal instruction. How can a miracle prove the truth of a doctrine, unless this has first proved itself through the conviction of the understanding? A miracle may direct attention to the doctrine, it may clothe the person of the teacher with outward consideration, it may even give him external credibility, according to the notions of the age; but the truth of the doctrine, it can never prove; and this was acknowledged by Christ himself. His words were spirit and life; he presented living waters for the refreshment and sustenance of the soul. He announced truth, which should make the heart of man alive and free. And the proof of this, he placed in the experience of every individual. To this, outward miracles could contribute nothing. If a teacher were to come before us at the present day, with the demand that we should believe his doctrine merely on account of his miracles, would not every one, who had common sense reply, "Let us discriminate here, my friend; I will first examine your doctrine and then your miracles, for they are two very different things" . . .

It was in this mode, that Herder was accustomed to argue in defence of revealed religion. He wished to bring the conviction of its truth to the individual consciousness of man, instead of resting it merely on the ground of tradition and authority; and this he believed could be done only by appealing to its inward character, and demonstrating its accordance with our better nature . . . While he cherished the doctrine of the Divinity of Christ, as it was set forth by the sacred writers, free from the confused explanations of modern theologians, he loved to regard him chiefly in his human relations, as a being possessing all human sympathies, subject to all human feelings, clothed with all human virtues, in truth, as the type and complete expression of perfect humanity.

15. Cornelius C. Felton (1807–1862)
Wordsworth's Yarrow Revisited

[In the second issue of *The Dial,* for October 1840, Emerson was to say that which most precisely chronicles Wordsworth's part in the formation of American Transcendentalism:

The fame of Wordsworth is a leading fact in modern literature, when it is considered how hostile his genius at first seemed to the reigning taste, and with what limited poetic talents his great and steadily growing dominion has been established. More than any poet his success has been not his own but that of the idea which he shared with his coevals, and which he has rarely succeeded in adequately expressing.

The interesting point is that the children of Harvard, as contrasted with William Cullen Bryant in the Berkshires, had difficulty appreciating Wordsworth the poet until they had become indoctrinated through the prose of Coleridge and Cousin with the "idea." Emerson's struggle is typical. In 1826—the first Boston edition of Wordsworth having appeared only two years before—he found the poet deficient in elegance and too prone to "pantheism." Not until 1831—his study of Reed and Coleridge behind him—could Emerson perceive Wordsworth in the perspective he expounded in *The Dial,* and resolve therefore to seek him out on his trip to Europe as one of the master spirits of the age.

By 1835, however, it was evident that Wordsworth was well established in the affections of the younger generation. When his *Yarrow Revisited* was published in Boston by James Munroe, the editors of *The Christian Examiner,* hoping to offend neither party, entrusted the review to Professor Cornelius C. Felton. He, presumably, was safe.

Felton, born in Newbury and self-supported, earned his Harvard degree in 1827, became a tutor in 1829, and in 1832 was made professor of Greek. He was an austere scholar, but no mere philologist. In the last two years of his life he served as president of Harvard.

Being an honest classicist, Felton could not really approve of Wordsworth, but being an honest man, he had to confess that by now there existed a circle of devotees who most emphatically did. His notice is testimony to the gulf that, by the date of his review (*The Christian Examiner,* January 1836, XIX, 375–383) could no longer be ignored.]

Mr. Wordsworth has striven to undo all the ties that artificial life has bound around him. He has attempted to go back to the simplicity of primitive man. He tries to look on nature as if she had never been looked on before, and to express the elemental feelings of the heart, as if they had never been expressed before. All his errors and weaknesses grow out of the excess to which he carries this principle; and the volume before us is not free from these unfortunate peculiarities. But if it shows too much egotism in the allusions to his character as a poet, and to his "Rydalian laurels," it must be confessed the vanity is almost justified by the worship of an increasing school of devoted disciples, and the growing disposition of the world at large to do him homage. We cannot, however, entirely rid ourselves of an unpleasant impression, that he is often poetical because he feels it his duty to be poetical,— that he sets out, *with malice prepense,* to be poetically affected by the contemplation of a scene in nature, and that he is deliberately inspired with it, because he has a sort of professional character to support. Now this perpetual consciousness of being a poet, and having certain poetical duties to perform at all times, cannot be very graciously regarded by readers beyond the circle of the initiated. But, with all these deductions, the poems of Mr. Words-

worth will always be ranked among the most remarkable monuments of reflective genius, that our age has produced.

16. George Ripley (1802–1880)
Schleiermacher as a Theologian

[Ripley was now on the verge of the irrevocable step. In March of 1836
he published in *The Christian Examiner* (XX, 1–46) a study of Schleiermacher
which is a transparent allegory for New England. If instead of Supernaturalism
one reads the Calvinists and instead of Rationalism the Unitarians, then the inference is obvious that the younger generation—repelled by Rationalism but incapable of fleeing back to Supernaturalism—have only the one choice of going
forward, like Schleiermacher, toward the "primitive consciousness." Ripley was
here desperately striving to convince the two great religious bodies of New England that Transcendentalism was not a cult, but a synthesis and reconciliation of
their tragic controversy.]

The problem of Schleiermacher's life was determined by the historical relations which preceded and accompanied the period of his literary activity. This problem . . . was to reconcile the conflicting claims of religion
and science, as they were exhibited in the state of intellectual cultivation in his
own country. In the solution of this problem, Schleiermacher developed certain theological principles, which may be said to form a new era in the history of the science, and which have certainly created a large and increasing
school among the modern theologians of Germany. A few brief statements
will be sufficient to illustrate the position which he occupied.

The writings of the English Deists were for the most part translated into
the German language, and produced a deep impression on the minds of
thinking men, both within and without the official precincts of theology.
This impression was increased by the spirit of the French Revolution and
the tendency of the King of Prussia towards a superficial literature and a
material philosophy. The prevailing opinions in the Lutheran Church were
not competent to present a barrier against the approaching torrent of skepticism and infidelity. The consequence was, that, after the Scriptures had been
submitted to a critical examination of great extent and thoroughness, the doctrines of theology discussed on all sides with the utmost freedom, and the
philosophy of religion made the subject of new and profound investigations,
a new form of Christianity was presented, which admitted the essential truth
of the ideas revealed by Jesus Christ, and their divine authority as coming

from God, but denied their claims to a miraculous or supernatural character. This is the leading principle of the system of Rationalism. This system, the result of a scientific examination of the records of religion, but unaccompanied with a profound estimate of its inward spirit, has prevailed until within the last fifteen or twenty years, among the most celebrated theologians of Germany without any effectual opposition. About that time a reaction began to take place. Many, who had formerly been ardently attached to it, relaxed in their zeal, or took a new tendency in the opposite direction. The want of a more spiritual religion was distinctly and loudly expressed. Rationalism was charged with coldness and inefficiency, with being destitute of a deep philosophical foundation, and with inadequacy to meet the necessities of the religious nature of man. Still it was seen, that no help could be obtained from the literal and precise orthodoxy of the ancient standards of the Lutheran church. The common ideas on inspiration, on the nature of revelation, on the character of the sacred books, on the evidences of Christianity, and on the doctrines of the Christian faith, which were maintained in those formularies, could not be brought into harmony with the improved science of modern times, or the results of sound and thorough critical investigations. It appeared, that the prevailing Rationalism would not do, and that the ancient Supernaturalism would do still less. The problem then was to discover some scientific principles, by which the merits of both systems could be secured and their defects avoided.

The solution of this problem was the mission of Schleiermacher's life . . . He admitted the validity of critical investigations to their fullest extent. These, he could not but perceive, had abolished the foundation on which the prevailing views of the Bible had reposed. Hence, it was necessary to draw the sharpest line of distinction between religion in its essential elements, and religion in its outward manifestations. Instead then of taking his stand in the written letter, he commenced with the religious consciousness of human nature. He aimed not so much to carry over the spirit of Christianity into the soul, as to awaken the soul itself to a sense of its affinity with the essential revelations of the Gospel, and to lead it to embrace them with a consciousness of sympathy and relationship. But here two grand points were clearly to be settled as the condition of all further progress; first, what is the essential character of religion in the soul; and second, what is the peculiar spirit of Christianity, to which this character corresponds. These points are discussed by Schleiermacher with all the logical acuteness which was eminently characteristic of his mind. The results at which he arrives may be stated in a few words. Religion, he supposes, in its primitive elements, is neither knowledge

nor action, but a sense of our dependence on God, and of our need of redemption from sin. The seat of this feeling is the primitive consciousness of
human nature. As to the second point, the essential spirit of Christianity is
to be found in those principles, which have universally prevailed in the Christian church, from the time of the Apostles to the present day. These, of
course, are not always to be taken in their literal sense, and never in that of
the symbols and illustrations, with which it has been attempted to make
clear to the understanding. There have ever been great differences in the
modes of conceiving essential ideas. And the difficulty has been, that these
various modes have been confounded with the primitive and unchanging
truth. In all general conceptions of religion, then, as well as in the records of
revelation, we must not fail to look beyond the letter to the spirit, to separate
the central and absolute idea from the temporary forms with which it is surrounded. In this mode, Schleiermacher attempts to demonstrate the validity of
the primary truths of the Gospel, in their relation to the religious consciousness of man, as they have been held in some form or other, by the great body
of believers in the church from the time of its foundation.

If we are now asked, whether Schleiermacher is to be classed among the
Rationalists or the Supernaturalists, as they are arranged in German theology,
we answer that he belongs to both, inasmuch as he admits the most valuable
distinctions and principles of each of those schools. He holds, with perfect
faith, to the supernatural character, the miracles, and the divine mission of
Jesus Christ; and at the same time he would reinstate the authority of reason,
and establish the claims of religion in harmony with those of a sound philosophy. He perceives, in the revelation of the Gospel, a fountain, which corresponds with the wants of our religious nature, and which flows directly
from the throne of God; and at the same time he does not forget, that the
streams which issue from this fountain must partake of the character of the
soil and other accidental influences, to which they are exposed. He regards
the spirit of Christ as having been filled with all the fulness of God, and, at
the same time, he remembers the human relations in which this spirit was
manifested. Schleiermacher thus reconciles some of the most perplexing
antitheses between the two opposing systems, and lays a broad foundation
for a faith which is equally in accordance with the results of science and the
wants of the heart.

A question, perhaps, of still greater interest may now be asked by our
readers; With which of the two great religious divisions in this country, is
Schleiermacher to be ranked? We answer, With neither. He occupied a station which has found no representative in our own theological progress. We

add, that his views are capable of doing service to both of the leading schools in this country. If in no other respect, he may inspire us all with a feeling of the importance of connecting philosophy and theology in the most intimate harmony, by pointing out to each its peculiar province,—of exercising a spirit of tolerance and charity towards the faithful strivings of every seeker of truth,—and of recognising, in the nature of man, the same signatures of Divinity which authenticate the Gospel of Christ.

17. Orestes A. Brownson (1803–1876)
Education of the People

[In the next issue of the *Examiner* (May 1836, XX, 153–169), Brownson continued hammering on the social theme, pressing the responsibility so relentlessly upon the clergy that his colleagues had little alternative to going along with him except to disown him.]

We say the dominant sentiment of our epoch is that of social progress. We think we cannot be mistaken in this. If the development and growth of the social element be not the dominant sentiment of the age, we would ask, what mean these demands for social reform which come to our ears on every breeze, from every land? What mean these movements among the people, these combinations of even workingmen to meliorate society? What mean these shakings of thrones, these fears, which penetrate the hearts of kings, fill courts with consternation, and make those who live by existing abuses turn pale? There is no mistaking the spirit of the times. We see it everywhere, we see it in new sects, in the abortive attempts of the Saint-Simonians, in the new French Catholic Church, insignificant as it may be. We saw it in the deep sensation produced by the whimsical Owen, when he first announced his new social system; we felt it in the thrill which ran through our hearts, and heard it in the loud burst of sympathy which broke from the whole civilized world, at the news of the French Revolution of July, 1830. We see it in the influence of such writers as Jeremy Bentham, Byron, and Bulwer. We see it, and not the least plainly, in the humble but powerful ministry to the poor in *this* city as well as in some others. All these and a thousand other circumstances, we could mention, had we room, are proofs to us, that men's minds and hearts are busy with the social state, and that the real sentiment of our epoch is the sentiment of social progress. To this sentiment the clergy must attach themselves. The time for star-gazing has gone by. They must look on the earth, and exert themselves to make it the abode of peace and love. This is the only way in which they can recover a permanent influence, and be widely and lastingly useful. They neglected to accept the social element, when they might have done it to better advantage. That element is now mainly in the hands of laymen, and to a great extent in the hands of men who either disavow or do not love religion. In their hands it is abused, it takes a tinge of infidelity, receives a character and a direction foreign to its nature. The clergy should now be instant to redeem their past neglect, to recover and accept the rejected element, to cultivate it and give it a religious direction. By so doing they will recover their influence, so far as they ought to recover it, and be again in men's minds and hearts, with power to lead them up to God.

18. Nathaniel L. Frothingham (1793–1870)

Sartor Resartus

[No one would be more astonished or distressed to find himself included in a collection of the Transcendentalists than Nathaniel Langdon Frothingham. The most stalwart of the Unitarian rationalists, he had so little sympathy with the movement that he virtually disowned his son, Octavius Brooks, upon discovering that the boy had yielded to the seductions of Theodore Parker.

Graduated from Harvard in 1811, Frothingham studied under the elder Henry Ware and was summoned to the First Church of Boston. He married a daughter of Peter Chardon Brooks, thus becoming brother-in-law to Edward Everett and Charles Francis Adams. A man of massive dignity, his very handwriting, said Emerson, was "Parnassian." Nothing vulgar could be associated with him, Emerson continued—long after the parting of the ways was evident—although Frothingham's fame "was bought by many years' steady rejection of all that is popular with our saints, and [a] persevering study of books which none else reads, and which he can convert to no temporary purpose." Frothingham, whose scholarship had, as Emerson readily testified (see p. 498), assisted the saints on their way, would magisterially have turned off this comment as flippant. In 1835, upon the twentieth anniversary of his installation, he mentioned the word "Unitarian" in his pulpit for the first time, explaining that hitherto, in the ethos he had created at the First Church, explicit avowal had been unnecessary. "We silently assumed the ground, or rather found ourselves standing upon it." He compressed what from his point of view was the essence of liberal Christianity into a sentence: "We have made more account of the religious sentiment than of theological opinions."

The editors of *The Christian Examiner* again were acting judiciously when they asked Frothingham to review *Sartor Resartus* for the September number in

1836 (XXI, 74–79). The old Roman was justice itself, and gave what praise he could to sheer eccentricity. But what he had most simply to say was that the divergence of reactions to this book would make for a divergence of parties; he was prepared, by being critically generous, to prove that his wing of the Unitarian community was not lacking in some degree of comprehension.]

      In giving our readers some account of this singular production, we will begin by reversing the usual method of our vocation, and instead of a review utter a prophecy. Indeed the book is so very odd, that some departure from the common course seems the most appropriate to any notice of it. We predict, then, that it will not be read through by a great many persons, nor be liked by all its readers. Some will pronounce it unintelligible, or boldly deny that it has any good sound meaning. Some will be deterred by its Latin porch and German decorations from having any thing to do with what seems not intended for their accommodation; while perhaps their neighbour, attracted by the quaintness of the title, "Sartor Resartus,"—*The Tailor Sewed Over,*—and thinking only of being amused in a passive way, will soon find his mistake, and declare himself imposed upon. The taste of some will be offended by what they will call its affectation and mannerism, and you shall not easily dispossess them of the notion, that the style is a jargon and the philosophy stark nought.

      These are they that will rise up to defame and vilipend the elaborate and mystic book of The Philosophy of Clothes, by Dr. Diogenes Teufelsdröckh (Asafœtida), Professor of Things in General at the University of Weiss-nichtwo (Know-not-where), and living in the attic floor of the highest house in its Wahngasse (Whimsey Street). Even his choice phrases and profoundest speculations shall be as unsavoury to them as the drug, from which he has rather unaccountably,—to say the least of it,—taken his name. But then we plainly foresee that there will be others, who will make very different account of our Professor's lucubrations. They will admire his wildest extravagances, and discover in his most playful disportings a hidden wisdom; even as the worshippers of Goethe found, and find still, a perfect system of philosophy and a whole canon of Scripture in the wondrous *diablerie* of the *Faust*. They will admit nothing in him to be obscure, nothing tedious. They will talk rather mystically about him at times, and as if they would form round him a special school of the initiated. Every novelty of the least pretension being now-a-days "a new revelation of man to himself," they will adjudge this "philosophy of clothes" to be among the leading phenomena of modern thought. Its style will be copied by young aspirants for literary fame. It will be quoted from the pulpit. It will be read aloud to enthusiastic circles of most intelligent persons . . .

It loves to bring together the low and the lofty, the learned and vulgar, the strange and familiar, the tragic and comic, into rather violent contrasts. We cannot say that it is always clear and sprightly. The words are often unusual, the digressions bewildering, the objects in view not very manifest. But it will seldom fail to repay a careful attention. The device of making a book by pretending to edit the papers of another person may appear to be rather a stale one, and has certainly been of late pressed quite unconscionably into the service. But in the present instance it was absolutely essential to the management of the author's plan, and has been so ingeniously availed of as quite to reconcile us to it . , .

Whether congenial or not with our tastes and intellectual habits, it is certainly one of the most extraordinary works of our day. It is wrought with great learning and ingenuity, though without the appearance of effort. It throws out the noblest conceptions as if at play, and its sparkling expressions seem kindled by the irrepressible fervor of a brilliant mind. It has imagination enough to give a poet renown; more sound religion and ethics than slumber in the folios of many a body of divinity; more periods that one would copy down in his note-book, to read and read again, than are to be found in all the writings together of many a one who has made himself famous everywhere for having written well. It is not equally sustained in every part; how should it be?—but we can scarcely look where we shall not find something of tenderness or sublimity or wit or wisdom;—something that makes us feel, and makes us reflect too, as deeply as some more pretending "Aids to Reflection."

4

Annus Mirabilis

I find that George Ripley is publishing *Discourses on the Philosophy of Religion;* besides, Brownson is out with his *New Views,* and Alcott with *Questions on the Gospels,* for Children. Then there is Furness' book, *Remarks on the Gospels,* so that it seems the spiritualists are taking the field in force. I have long seen that the Unitarians must break into two schools—the old one, or English School, belonging to the sensual and empiric philosophy, and the new one, or the German School (perhaps it may be called), belonging to the spiritual philosophy.

—CONVERS FRANCIS

1. Orestes A. Brownson (1803–1876)

Victor Cousin

[In September 1836 Harvard celebrated its second centennial. Ripley, Hedge, and Emerson—finding the society flat and foolish—agreed that the present state of opinion was "very unsatisfactory." They decided to summon a further assembly, with the hope of finding out "what precisely we wanted." On September 16, at Ripley's house, they met with Francis, Clarke, Brownson—and with Alcott (Emerson having insisted upon his inclusion). This became the so-called Transcendental Club, which thereafter met at intervals, depending upon Hedge's incursions from Bangor. Dr. Channing and George Bancroft came once; the other more or less regular members were Parker, Cranch, Dwight, W. H. Channing, Cyrus Bartol, Caleb Stetson. Adventurously deciding to be truly modern, they admitted women, so that Margaret Fuller, Sophia Ripley, and Elizabeth Peabody came. The second meeting, held at Alcott's house in October, was devoted to a topic propounded by Emerson: "'T was pity that in this Titantic continent, where nature is so grand, genius should be so tame."

The Club, as a club, achieved nothing more than such top-lofty symposia; its importance, however, resides not in anything it wrought, but in the mere fact that it existed. That these people, each having come his separate route, could converge so infallibly upon a common ground, and that they then discovered in each other a shared experience, is a disclosure of the intellectual forces, greater than any individual among them, that had been at work in the community for a decade. And that they did thus fall together, even into so haphazard an assemblage, in the very month of September 1836 is even more significant; for at that precise moment the ideas that had been maturing through the decade of exploration had come—it is hardly too much to say that they had come of themselves—to the point where they could no longer be denied their final and declarative form.

On September 9, Emerson's *Nature* was published. In the perspective of today, this work gathered up and organized the disparate theses which Reed, Ripley, Hedge, and Brownson had been patiently extracting out of Swedenborg, Coleridge, and Cousin. As I have explained, *Nature* is not printed in this collection solely for reasons of space; in all justice, it ought, at this point, to be inserted. However, in terms of the immediate public reaction, Emerson's pamphlet did indeed, first off, attract a minimum of attention. Only within the next months, as the lengthening and searching controversy made plain how it anticipated every point at issue, did its preëminence dawn. Only after all were obliged to confess that Emerson had hit upon the neatest way of stating the propositions did they have to acknowledge his control over their thinking.

For the moment, in September of 1836, a more immediate impact was being registered by an article on Victor Cousin, written by Orestes Brownson, in the current issue of *The Christian Examiner* (XXI, 33–64). It was—at a very long last—a Transcendental rebuttal of Alexander Everett's tirade of seven years before. By this time Brownson had become the self-appointed apostle of Cousin in America (and had carried Ripley with him); although Emerson was weary of Cousin—whose eclecticism now seemed to him "pompous"—still the motifs of Brownson's essay turn out to be so close to those of *Nature* that many pages of the latter, particularly some of its obscure pages, are wonderfully illuminated by comparison with this contemporaneous effort. Brownson was here being allowed to review Linberg's translation of *The History of Philosophy,* which had appeared in 1832, and Henry's translation of the *Elements of Psychology,* which was published in 1834; the delay of the *Examiner* was probably inspired, but Brownson was not a man to be muzzled for long.]

WHOEVER would see the American people as remarkable for their philosophy as they are for their industry, enterprise, and political freedom, must be gratified that these works have already attracted considerable attention among us, and are beginning to exert no little influence on our philosophical speculations. It is a proof that our philosophical speculations are taking a wholesome direction, and especially that the great problems of mental and moral science are assuming in our eyes a new importance, and calling to their solution a greater and an increasing amount of mind. We are, in fact, turning our attention to matters of deeper interest, than those which relate merely to the physical well-being of humanity. We are beginning to perceive that Providence, in the peculiar circumstances in which it has placed us, in the free institutions it has given us, has made it our duty to bring out the ideal man, to prove, by a practical demonstration, what the human race may be, when and where it has free scope for the full and harmonious development of all its faculties. In proportion as we perceive and comprehend this duty, we cannot fail to inquire for a sound philosophy, one which will enumerate and characterize all the faculties of the human soul, and determine the proper order and most efficient means of their development . . .

But the philosophy, which has hitherto prevailed, and whose results now control our reasonings, cannot sustain religion. Everybody knows, that our religion and our philosophy are at war. We are religious only at the expense of our logic. This accounts for the fact, that, on the one hand, we disclaim logic, unchurch philosophy, and pronounce it a dangerous thing to reason; while, on the other, we reject religion, declaim against the clergy, and represent it exceedingly foolish to believe. This opposition cannot be concealed. It is found not only in the same community, but to a great extent in the same individual. The result cannot be doubtful. Philosophy will gain the victory. The friends of religion may seek to prevent it, labor to divert men's minds from inquiry by engaging them in vast associations for practical benevolence, or to frighten them from philosophizing by powerful appeals to hopes and fears; but the desire to philosophize, to account to ourselves for what we believe, cannot be suppressed. Instead, then, of quarrelling with this state of things, instead of denouncing the religious as do professed free inquirers, or the philosophizers, as is the case with too many of the friends of religion, we should reëxamine our philosophy, and inquire if there be not a philosophy true to human nature, and able to explain and verify, instead of destroying, the religious belief of mankind? We evidently need such a philosophy; such a philosophy we believe there is, and we know of no works so well fitted to assist us in finding it, as those of M. Cousin . . .

The principal peculiarity of M. Cousin's system results from the fact, that he makes psychology the foundation, but not the superstructure, the beginning, but not the end of philosophy. By making psychology the basis of philosophy, he connects his philosophical enterprise with modern philosophy itself, which from Descartes, Bacon, and Locke, tolerates only the experimental method. In this he does not dissent from the philosophy which reigned in France during the last century. That philosophy was indeed sensualism, but it was also experimental; as experimental M. Cousin accepts, though he modifies, continues it. This deserves the especial notice of those, who have supposed that he rejects experience and ought to be confounded with the hypothesis-constructing Germans. In method, he is as free from hypothesis as he is from skepticism. By beginning with psychology, making it the only door of entrance into the temple of philosophy, he not only connects himself with the old French, but separates himself from the new German school. The new German school, represented by Schelling and Hegel, begins where he ends, and ends where he begins. It begins by an hypothesis, rises at once with means, or by means of which it takes no account, to the Absolute, to the Being of beings, and attempts to reach nature and humanity through ontology. When we have once placed ourselves in ontology, in absolute being, the passage to the phenomenal, to nature and humanity, is without difficulty; psychology may most assuredly be found in ontology; but how can we attain to ontology? How shall we place ourselves in the Absolute as our point of observation? We must attain the summit by a slow and toilsome ascent from the valley, where is our starting-point, not by dropping from the heavens. Our only true method is to begin by ascertaining what is; from what is, the actual, we may pass to its origin, from that to its legitimacy, and thus attain the Absolute. Should we adopt the method of the new German school, and by some lucky devination obtain the truth, which M. Cousin considers to be the case with the school in question, the truth thus obtained, not having been scientifically obtained, would be without any scientific validity . . .

M. Cousin recognizes in the consciousness three classes of phenomena, which result from the great elementary faculties which comprehend and explain all the rest. These faculties are Sensibility, Activity, and Reason. They are never found isolated one from another. Yet they are essentially distinct, and a scrupulous analysis distinguishes them in the complex phenomena of intellectual life without dividing them. To sensibility belong all the internal phenomena, which are derived from sensation, through our senses, from the external world; to the activity belong those, which we are conscious that we ourselves produce; and under the head of reason must be arranged all our ideas of the Absolute, the Supersensible, and all the internal facts which are purely intellectual, which we know we do not produce, and which cannot be derived through sensation from external nature. The activity is developed only by sensation. Activity and sensibility can generate no idea without the reason; and without sensibility and activity the reason would have no office . . .

The Sensualist school admits and studies with great success the facts of the sensibility; but overlooking those of the activity and the reason, or not making a sufficient account of them it mutilates the soul, and becomes false in its inductions. The Scotch school avoids this error; it distinguishes between the reason and sensibility, but without much scientific precision. The Kantian school has done it with more care and accuracy; it has also described with great clearness and precision the laws of the reason, but it has not discerned with sufficient exactness the distinction between the reason and the activity. This deficiency has ruined the school . . . To deprive the reason of all but a subjective authority, to allow it no validity out of the sphere of our own personality, is to deprive it of all legitimate authority, and to place philosophy on the route to a new and original skepticism. If the reason have no authority out of the sphere of the personality, out of the individual consciousness in which its phenomena appear, it can reveal to us no existences which lie beyond ourselves. Such may be the laws of our nature, that we cannot help believing that we are, that there is an external world, and God; but our belief can repose on no scientific basis. There is nothing to assure us, that it is not a mere illusion; nothing can demonstrate to us, that any thing really exists to respond to it. All certainty resolves itself into a mere personal affection. To this conclusion all are driven who assert the subjectivity of the reason . . .

To avoid this extravagance, we must distinguish between the reason and the activity, and show that, though intimately connected, they are nevertheless fundamentally distinct. The reason, though appearing in us, is not our *self*. It is independent of us, and in no sense subject to our personality. If it depended on our personality, or if it constituted our personality, we could control its conceptions, prescribe its laws, and compel it to speak according to our pleasure . . . We may say, "my actions, my crimes, my virtues," for we consider ourselves very justly as their cause; we may even say, "my error," for our errors are in some degree attributable to ourselves; but who dares say *"my* truth"? Who does not feel, who does not know, that the truth is not his,—is nobody's, but independent of everybody? If, then, we are conscious that the conceptions of the reason are not ours, that the truths it reveals are not our truths, are not truths which are in any sense dependent on us, we must admit that the reason is independent of us, and, though appearing in us, is not ours, is not our *self* . . .

The reason, once established in its true nature and independence, becomes a legitimate authority for whatever it reveals. A true analysis of it shows, that, instead of being imprisoned in the consciousness and compelled to turn for ever within the sphere of the subjective, it extends far beyond, and attains to beings as well as to phenomena. It reveals to us God and the world on precisely the same authority as our own existence, or the slightest modification of it. Ontology thus becomes as legitimate as psychology; since it is psychology, which, by disclosing to us the true nature of the reason, conducts of itself to ontology . . .

If this analysis of a fact of consciousness be accurate, we are authorized to say that no fact of consciousness is possible without the conception of our own existence, the existence of the world, and that of God. The ideas, of ourselves as a free personality, of nature, and of God as the substance, the cause, of both us and nature, constitute a single fact of the consciousness, are its inseparable elements, and without them consciousness is impossible. Ourselves, nature, and God are, then, necessarily asserted in every word, in every affirmation, in every thought. The skeptic who professes to doubt their existence, in that he can assert that he doubts, asserts that they exist. Atheism is, then, impossible; some men may want the term, the word, but all men believe in God . . .

It should be remarked, that we do not *infer* the Absolute from the relative, the Infinite from the finite, God from nature and humanity. The Absolute is no logical creation, no production of reasoning. It could not be deduced from the realtive. No dialectical skill has ever yet been able to draw the infinite from the finite, the unconditioned from the conditioned. Both terms are given together, both are primitive *data,* without which no reasoning could possibly take place. Remove from man the idea of the infinite, or of the finite, and he would be incapable of a single intellectual act. A man, to reason, must assert something, and must assert something to be either infinite or finite. But no man can say that a thing is finite without having at the same time the conception of the infinite; or that a thing is infinite without at the same time conceiving the finite. Neither, then, can be deduced from the other; both coexist in the intelligence as its fundamental elements, and not only coexist, but coexist as cause and effect. Hence the ideas of the infinite, the finite and their relation, not of mere coexistence but as cause and effect, are inseparable and essential elements of all intellection. This being true, all three, embracing all existence, ourselves, God, and the world, must have existed in the understanding, before ever an intelligent act was possible. They are, then, so far from being inferred, some from the others, that all [of them] must exist before an inference is possible. They are the primitive *data* of the intellect, the starting-points of all reasoning . . .

But if the absolute logically precedes the relative, and if the conceptions of the infinite, the finite, and their relation be indispensable conditions of all reasoning, it follows of course that our belief in God, in nature, in our own existence, is the result of no reasoning. When we first turned our minds inward in the act of reflection, we found that belief. We had it, and every man has it, from the first dawn of the intellect. It does not proceed then from reflection; and as reflection is the only intellectual act in which we have any agency, it follows that it does not exist in consequence of any thing we have willed or done. It is prior to *our* action, and independent of it. Whence then its origin? It must be a primitive, spontaneous belief, the result of the spontaneity of the reason. The reason sees by its own light, is itself active; and, being in relation with the objective and the absolute, it can and does of itself reveal to the consciousness God and the world, giving by its own vigor the belief in question. The reason, being in its nature independent, and in its spontaneity acting independently of us, and though developing itself in us, is a good and legitimate witness for what lies beyond us, and exists independent of us . . .

The reason can reveal nothing which it has not in itself. If it reveal the absolute, it must itself be absolute. If absolute, it must be the Being of beings, God himself. The elements of the reason are then the elements of God. An analysis of the reason gives, as its elements, the ideas of the infinite, the finite, and their relation as cause and effect. Then those ideas are the elements of all thought, of thought in itself, of God. God then, is thought, reason, intelligence in itself. An intelligence which does not manifest itself, is a dead intelligence, a dead thought; but a dead thought, a dead intelligence, is inconceivable. To live, to exist, intelligence must manifest itself. God, being thought, intelligence in itself, must necessarily manifest himself. To manifest himself is to create, and his manifestation is creation . . .

But God can manifest only what is in himself. He is thought, intelligence itself. Consequently there is in creation nothing but thought, intelligence. In nature, as in humanity, the supreme Reason is manifested, and there, where we had fancied all was dead and without thought, we are now enabled to see all living and essentially intellectual. There is no dead matter, there are no fatal causes; nature is thought, and God is its personality. This enables us to see God in nature, in a new and striking sense . . . Well may we study nature, for, as a whole and in the minutest of its parts, it is a manifestation of the Infinite, the Absolute, the Everlasting, the Perfect, the universal Reason,— God. It should be loved, should be reverenced, not merely as a piece of mechanism, but as a glorious shining out of the Infinite and the Perfect . . .

This is not Pantheism. Pantheism considers the universe as God; but this presents God as the cause, and the universe as the effect. God is as inseparable from the universe as the cause is inseparable from the effect; but no one who can discern any distinction between an appearance and that which appears, between the phenomenon and being, the manifestation, can ever confound him with the universe . . . The universe is his intention. It is what he will, and he is in it, the substance of his volition; it is what he speaks, and he is in it, as a man is in his words; but he is distinct from it, by all the distinction there is between the energy that wills, and that which is willed, between him who speaks, and the words he utters . . .

The reason is God; it appears in us, therefore God appears in us. The light of reason, the light by which we see and know all that we do see and know, is truly the light of God. The voice of the spontaneous reason is the voice of God; those who speak by its authority, speak by the authority of God, and what they utter is a real revelation. This explains inspiration, accounts for the origin of prophecies, pontificates, and religious rites, and justifies the human race for having believed that some men had been the confidants and interpreters of God. He in whom the spontaneous reason was more active than in his fellow beings, had a closer communion with God, could better interpret him than they, and was rightly termed the inspired, for he was inspired;— not indeed in a sense different from the rest of mankind, but in a different, a special degree . . .

Man's intellectual life begins with the spontaneous reason. We believe, we confide before we reflect. In the infancy of the individual and of the race, God himself, as a tender father, is the guide and teacher. The child a little advanced, wishes to go alone, to be guided by his own light, to follow his own will, and rely on his own strength. A dangerous wish; but one which must be gratified, if the child is ever to become a man. After a while man finds he has believed, and he desires to know why he has believed, to account to himself for the phenomena he discovers. There is now a new element developed within him, the reflective reason; and henceforth, instead of confiding, he must reflect, and instead of faith he must have philosophy. No more repose, no more careless glee of the child; active life begins: its cares, its burdens, its duties must be met and borne and performed. The father gives the child his blessing, his counsel, and sends him, at his request, forth into the world to seek his fortunes as best he may.

Philosophy begins, the day that man begins to reflect; it is the creation of reflection, and, since reflection is our act, it is our creation. It is to humanity, what nature and humanity are to God. As there can be nothing in nature and humanity which is not in God, so there can be nothing in philosophy which is not in humanity. He who comprehends humanity, comprehends not only true philosophy, but all systems of philosophy which have heretofore obtained, or which can obtain hereafter. He who comprehends all the systems of philosophy which have been, comprehends humanity as far as it is now developed. The study of human nature then, throws light on the history of philosophy, and the study of the history of philosophy in return, throws light on human nature. Since all the systems of philosophy which have been, embrace the entire development of humanity in the past, it follows that he who should comprehend those systems, would comprehend thus far the whole history of our race. History in general, as throwing light on humanity, the history of philosophy in particular, as enlightening all other branches of history, and as the practical, the experimental test of a philosophy, should be ranked among the very highest objects of human study . . .

We must be eclectics, excluding no element of humanity, but accepting and melting all into one vast system, which will be a true representative of humanity so far as it is as yet developed. We must take broad and liberal views, expect truth and find it in all schools, in all creeds, in all ages, and in all countries. The great mission of our age is to unite the infinite and the finite. Union, harmony, whence proceed peace and love, are the points to be aimed at. We of the nineteenth century appear in the world as mediators. In philosophy, theology, government, art, industry, we are to conciliate hostile feelings, and harmonize conflicting principles and interests. We must bind together the past and the future, reconcile progress and immobility, by preserving what is good and studying to advance, that is, by meliorating instead of destroying; enable philosophy and theology to walk together in peace and love, by yielding to theology the authority of the spontaneous reason,—inspiration,—and vindicating for philosophy the absolute freedom of reflection.

2. Orestes A. Brownson (1803–1876)
New Views of Christianity, Society, and the Church

[Within two months (the Preface is dated November 8) Brownson followed his article on Cousin with a booklet, his New Views. In small compass it proposed a novel conception of modern history, whereby America was placed against a background of western European development. Brownson's reading of the Middle Ages was no doubt sketchy; but his interpretation of the eighteenth century and of the French Revolution—and more strikingly, his linking of the American Revolution with that epoch—sprang from a historical sense that could not, in 1836, find many appreciators in this country. (To twentieth-century students it may even sound commonplace.) From his studies in Cousin and the French socialists, particularly Saint-Simon, Brownson was able to comprehend that American society, including the society of liberal Boston, was a product of the Enlightenment and therefore was caught in the toils of the failure of the Enlightenment—a realization to which few or no Americans had yet been brought.

To Brownson it seemed rather too clear that the liberal surge of the two revolutions could, in this later phase, be consolidated only by a program of social cohesion. He set himself to oppose the atomistic and individualistic legends which inheritors of the two revolutions persuaded themselves had been the meaning of those events. Indeed, looked at from today, Brownson's pamphlet is nothing less than prophetic—if it were not that in 1840 he was to become even more prophetic —but there is little difficulty in comprehending why, in 1836, his message fell upon ears totally unprepared to understand a syllable he was saying. Their owners, already nonplused by the new metaphysics, could not begin to follow the logic— to us become familiar—through which the romantic philosophy of history became a basis for "UNION."

For the year 1836, the one clear meaning of Brownson's treatise was its condemnation of rational Unitarianism as pertaining to a dead past. Furthermore he rode roughshod over the whole matter of historical miracles—which the pundits of liberal Massachusetts had decided was the line beyond which they could concede nothing more to the radicals. In fact, Brownson's whole historical vision—his identification, for example, of "Protestantism" with "Materialism"—was so be-wildering to well-mannered New Englanders it is little wonder they decided thereupon that the new school must be insane. Still, try as they would, they could not laugh off a historical analysis that found inherent connections between Protestantism, industrialism, and the literary style of the eighteenth century; and so they could not help sensing a possible method in the madness that arrayed against these powers—with the indisputable help of modern literature—a spirit which purported to be that of the nineteenth century and which demanded outright a more stringent egalitarianism than liberalism had been able to imagine.]

Two systems then disputed the Empire of the World; Spiritualism * represented by the Eastern world, the old world of Asia, and Materialism represented by Greece and Rome. Spiritualism regards purity or holiness as predicable of Spirit alone, and Matter as essentially impure, possessing and capable of receiving nothing of the Holy,—the prison house of the soul, its only hindrance to a union with God, or absorption into his essence, the cause of all uncleanness, sin, and evil, consequently to be contemned, degraded, and as far as possible annihilated. Materialism takes the other extreme, does not recognize the claims of Spirit, disregards the soul, counts the body everything,

* I use these terms, Spiritualism and Materialism, to designate two social, rather than two philosophical systems. They designate two orders, which, from time out of mind, have been called *spiritual* and *temporal* or carnal, *holy* and *profane, heavenly* and *worldly,* &c.

earth all, heaven nothing, and condenses itself into the advice, "Eat and drink, for to-morrow we die" . . .

This antithesis generates perpetual and universal war. It is necessary then to remove it and harmonize the two terms. Now, if we conceive Jesus as standing between Spirit and Matter, the representative of both—God-Man— the point where both meet and lose their antithesis, laying a hand on each and saying, "Be one, as I and my Father are one," thus sanctifying both and marrying them in a mystic and holy union, we shall have his secret thought and the true Idea of Christianity . . .

Everything must have its time. The Church abused, degraded, vilified Matter, but could not annihilate it. It existed in spite of the Church. It increased in power, and at length rose against Spiritualism and demanded the restoration of its rights. This rebellion of Materialism, of the material order against the Spiritual, is Protestantism . . .

What we call the Reformation is really a Revolution in favor of the material order. Spiritualism had exhausted its energies; it had done all it could for Humanity; the time had come for the material element of our nature, which Spiritualism had neglected and grossly abused, to rise from its depressed condition and contribute its share to the general progress of mankind. It rose, and in rising it brought up the whole series of terms the Church had disregarded. It brought up the state, civil liberty, human reason, philosophy, industry, all temporal interests.

In Protestantism, Greece and Rome revived and again carried their victorious arms into the East. The Reformation connects us with classical antiquity, with the beautiful and graceful forms of Grecian art and literature, and with Roman eloquence and jurisprudence, as the Church had connected us with Judea, Egypt, and India . . .

Philosophy is a human creation; it is the product of man, as the universe is of God. Under Spiritualism, then, which—in theory—demolishes man, there can be no philosophy; yet as man, though denied, exists, there is a philosophical tendency. But this philosophical tendency is always either to Skepticism, Mysticism, or Idealism. Skepticism, that philosophy which denies all certainty, made its first appearance in modern times in the Church. The Church declared the reason unworthy of confidence, and in doing that gave birth to the whole skeptical philosophy . . . On the other hand, the Church having its point of view in Spirit, consulted the soul before the body, became introspective, fixed on the Inward to the exclusion of the Outward. It overlooked the Outward; and when that is overlooked it is hardly possible that it should not be denied. Hence Idealism or Mysticism.

Under the reign of Materialism all this is changed. There is full confidence in the reason. The method of philosophizing is the experimental. But as the point of view is the Outward—Matter—Spirit is overlooked; Matter alone admitted. Hence philosophical Materialism. And philosophical Materialism, in germ or developed, has been commensurate with Protestantism. When the mind becomes fixed on the external world, inasmuch as we become acquainted with that world only by means of our senses, we naturally conclude that our senses are our only source of knowledge. Hence Sensualism, the philosophy supported by Locke, Condillac, and even by Bacon, so far as it concerns his own application of his method. And from the hypothesis that our senses are our only inlets of knowledge, we are compelled to admit that nothing can be known which is not cognizable by some one or all of them. Our senses take cognizance only of Matter; then we can know nothing but Matter. We can know nothing of the spirit or soul. The body is all that we know of man. That dies, and there ends man—at least all we know of him. Hence no immortality, no future state. If nothing can be known but by means of our senses, God, then, inasmuch as we do not see him, hear him, taste him, smell him, touch him, cannot be known; then he does not exist for us. Hence Atheism. Hence Modern Infidelity, in all its forms, so prevalent in the last century, and so far from being extinct even in this . . .

Properly speaking, Protestantism has no religious character. With Protestants, religion has existed; but as a reminiscence, a tradition . . . If the religion of the Protestant world be a reminiscence, it must be the religion of the Church. It is, in fact, only Catholicism continued. The same principle lies at the bottom of all Protestant churches, in so far as they are churches, which was at the bottom of the Church of the middle ages. But Materialism modifies their rites and dogmas. In the practice of all, there is an effort to make them appear reasonable. Hence Commentaries, Expositions, and Defences without number. Even where the authority of the reason is denied, there is an instinctive sense of its authority and a desire to enlist it. In mere forms, pomp and splendor have gradually disappeared, and dry utility and even baldness have been consulted. In doctrines, those which exalt man and give him some share in the work of salvation have gained in credit and influence. Pelagianism, under some thin disguises or undisguised, has become almost universal. The doctrine of man's Total Depravity, in the few cases in which it is asserted, is asserted, more as a matter of duty than of conviction. Nobody, who can help it, preaches the old-fashioned doctrine of God's Sovereignty, expressed in the dogma of unconditional Election and Reprobation. The vicarious Atonement has hardly a friend left. The Deity of Jesus is questioned, his simple Humanity is asserted and is gaining credence. Orthodox is a term which implies as much reproach as commendation; people are beginning to laugh at the claims of councils and synods, and to be quite merry at the idea of excommunication.

In Literature and Art there is the same tendency. Poetry in the last century hardly existed, and was, so far as it did exist, mainly ethical or descriptive. It had no revelations of the Infinite. Prose writers under Protestantism have been historians, critics, essayists, or controversialists; they have aimed almost exclusively at the elevation or adornment of the material order, and in scarcely an instance has a widely popular writer exalted God at the expense of Man, the Church at the expense of the State, Faith at the expense of Reason, or Eternity at the expense of Time. Art is finite, and gives us busts and portraits, or copies of Greek and Roman models. The Physical sciences take precedence of the Metaphysical, and faith in Rail-roads and Steam-boats is much stronger than in Ideas.

In governments, the tendency is the same. Nothing is more characteristic of Protestantism, than its influence in promoting civil and political liberty. Under its reign all forms of governments verge towards the Democratic. "The King and the Church" are exchanged for the "Constitution and the People." Liberty, not Order, is the word that wakes the dead, and electrifies the masses. A social science is created, and the physical well-being of the humblest laborer is cared for, and made a subject of deliberation in the councils of nations.

Industry has received in Protestant countries its grandest developments. Since the time of Luther, it has been performing one continued series of miracles. Every corner of the globe is explored; the most distant and perilous seas are navigated; the most miserly soil is laid under contribution; manufactures, villages and cities spring up and increase as by enchantment; canals and rail-roads are crossing the country in every direction; the means of production, the comforts, conveniences and luxuries of life are multiplied to an extent hardly safe to relate.

Such, in its most general aspect, in its dominant tendency, is Protestantism. It is a new and much improved edition of the Classics. Its civilization belongs to the same order as that of Greece and Rome. It is in advance, greatly in advance, of Greece and Rome, but it is the same in its ground-work. The Material predominates over the Spiritual. Men labor six days for this world and at most but one for the world to come. The great strife is for temporal goods, fame or pleasure. God, the Soul, Heaven, and Eternity, are thrown into the back ground, and almost entirely disappear in the distance. Right yields to Expediency, and Duty is measured by Utility. The real character of Protestantism, the result to which it must come, wherever it can have its full development, may be best seen in France, at the close of the last century. The Church was converted into the Pantheon, and made a resting place for the bodies of the great and renowned of earth; God was converted into a symbol of the human reason, and man into the Man-Machine; Spiritualism fell, and the Revolution marked the complete triumph of Materialism . . .

The Eighteenth Century will be marked in the annals of the world for its strong faith in the material order. Meliorations on the broadest scale were contemplated and viewed as already realized. Our Republic sprang into being, and the world leaped with joy that "a man child was born." Social progress and the perfection of governments became the religious creed of the day; the weal of man on earth, the spring and aim of all hopes and labors. A new paradise was imaged forth for man, inaccessible to the serpent, more delightful than that which Adam lost, and more attractive than that which the pious Christian hopes to gain. We of this generation can form only a faint conception of the strong faith our fathers had in the progress of society, the high hopes of human improvement they indulged, and the joy too big for utterance, with which they heard France in loud and kindling tones proclaim LIBERTY and EQUALITY. France for a moment became the centre of the world. All eyes were fixed on her movements. The pulse stood still when she and her enemies met, and loud cheers burst from the universal heart of Humanity when her tri-colored flag was seen to wave in triumph over the battle field. There was then no stray thought for God and eternity. Man and the world filled the soul. They were too big for it. But while the voice of Hope was yet ringing, and *Te Deum* shaking the arches of the old Cathedrals,—the Convention, the reign of Terror, the exile of patriots, the massacre of the gifted, the beautiful and the good, Napoleon and the Military Despotism came, and Humanity uttered a piercing shriek, and fell prostrate on the grave of her hopes!

The reaction produced by the catastrophe of this memorable drama was tremendous . . . Men never feel what they felt but once. The pang which darts through their souls changes them into stone.—From that moment enthusiasm died, hope in social melioration ceased to be indulged, and those who had been the most sanguine in their anticipations, hung down their heads and said nothing; the warmest friends of Humanity apologized for their dreams of Liberty and Equality; Democracy became an accusation, and faith in the perfectibility of mankind a proof of disordered intellect.

In consequence of this reaction, men again despaired of the earth; and when they despair of the earth, they always take refuge in heaven; when man fails them, they always fly to God . . . They turned back and sighed for the serene past, the quiet and order of old times, for the mystic land of India, where the soul may dissolve in ecstasy and dream of no change.

At the very moment when the sigh had just escaped, that mystic land reappeared. The English, through the East India Company, had brought to light its old Literature and Philosophy, so diverse from the Literature and Philosophy of modern Europe or of classical antiquity, and men were captivated by their novelty and bewildered by their strangeness. Sir William Jones gave currency to them by his poetical paraphrases and imitations; and the Asiatic Society by its researches placed them within reach of the learned of Europe. The Church rejoiced, for it was like bringing back her long lost mother, whose features she had remembered and was able at once to recognise.—Germany, England, and even France became Oriental. Cicero, and Horace, and Virgil, Æschylus, Euripides, and even Homer, with Jupiter, Apollo and Minerva were forced to bow before Hindoo Bards and Gods of uncouth forms and unutterable names.

The influence of the old Braminical or spiritual world, thus dug up from the grave of centuries, may be traced in all our Philosophy, Art, and Literature. It is remarkable in our poets. It moulds the form in Byron, penetrates to the ground in Wordsworth, and entirely predominates in the Schlegels. It causes us to feel a new interest in those writers and those epochs which partake the most of Spiritualism. Those old English writers who were somewhat inclined to mysticism are revived; Plato, who travelled in the East and brought back its lore which he modified by Western genius and moulded into Grecian forms, is reëdited, commented on, translated and raised to the highest rank among philosophers. The middle ages are reëxamined and found to contain a treasure of romance, acuteness, depth and wisdom, and are deemed by some to be "dark ages" only because we have not light enough to read them . . .

We cannot then go back either to exclusive Spiritualism, or to exclusive Materialism. Both these systems have received so full a development, have acquired so much strength, that neither can be subdued. Both have their foundation in our nature, and both will exist and exert their influence. Shall they exist as antagonist principles? Shall the spirit forever lust against the flesh, and the flesh against the spirit? Is the bosom of Humanity to be eternally torn by these two contending factions? No. It cannot be. The war must end. Peace must be made.

This discloses our Mission. We are to reconcile spirit and matter; that is, we must realize the atonement. Nothing else remains for us to do.—Stand still we cannot. To go back is equally impossible. We must go forward, but we can take not a step forward, but on the condition of uniting these two hitherto hostile principles. PROGRESS is our law and our first step is UNION . . .

But we can do this only by a general doctrine which enables us to recognise and accept all the elements of Humanity. If we leave out any one element in our nature, we shall have antagonism. Our system will be incomplete and the element excluded will be forever rising up in rebellion against it and collecting forces to destroy its authority . . .

To reject human nature and declare it unworthy of confidence as the Church did, and as all sects now do, is— whether we know it or not—to reject all grounds of certainty, and to declare that we have no means of distinguishing truth from falsehood. Truth itself is nothing else to us than that which our nature by some one or all of its faculties compels us to believe. The fact that God has made us a revelation does not in the least impair this assertion. God has revealed to us truths which we could not of ourselves have discovered. But how do we know this? What is it but the human mind that can determine whether God has or has not spoken to us? What but the human mind can ascertain and fix the meaning of what he may have communicated? If we may not trust the human mind, human nature, how can we ever be sure that a revelation has been made? or how distinguish a real revelation from a pretended one? By miracles? But how determine that what are alleged to be miracles, really are miracles? or the more difficult question still, that the miracles, admitting them to be genuine, do necessarily involve the truth of the doctrines they are wrought to prove? Shall we be told that we must believe the revelation is a true one, because made by an authorized teacher? Where is the warrant of his authority? What shall assure us that the warrant is not a forgery? Have we any thing but our own nature with which to answer these and a hundred more questions like them and equally important? . . .

Unitarianism belongs to the material order. It is the last word of Protestantism, before Protestantism breaks entirely with the Past. It is the point towards which all Protestant sects converge in proportion as they gain upon their reminiscences. Every consistent Protestant Christian must be a Unitarian. Unitarianism elevates man; it preaches morality; it vindicates the rights of the mind, accepts and uses the reason, contends for civil freedom, and is social, charitable, and humane. It saves the Son of man, but sometimes loses the Son of God.

But it is from the Unitarians that must come out the doctrine of universal reconciliation; for they are the only denomination in Christendom that labors to rest religious faith on rational conviction; that seeks to substitute reason for authority, to harmonize religion and science, or that has the requisite union of piety and mental freedom, to elaborate the doctrine which is to realize the Atonement. The orthodox, as they are called, are disturbed by their memory. Their faces are on the back side of their heads. They have zeal, energy, perseverance, but their ideas belong to the past. The Universalists can do nothing till some one arises to give them a philosophy. They must comprehend their instincts, before they can give to their doctrine of reconciliation that character which will adapt it to the wants of entire Humanity.

But Unitarians are every day breaking away more and more from tradition, and every day making new progress in the creation of a philosophy which explains Humanity, determines its wants and the means of supplying them. Mind at this moment is extremely active among them, and as it can act freely it will most certainly elaborate the great doctrine required. They began in Rationalism. Their earlier doctrines were dry and cold. And this was necessary. They were called at first to a work of destruction. They were under the necessity of clearing away the rubbish of the old Church, before they could obtain a site whereon to erect the new one. The Unitarian preacher was under the necessity of raising a stern and commanding voice in the wilderness, "Prepare ye the way of the Lord, make his paths straight." He raised that voice, and the chief Priests and Pharisees in modern Judea heard and trembled, and some have gone forth to be baptised. The Unitarian has baptised them with water unto repentance, but he has borne witness that a mightier than he shall come after him, who shall baptise them with the Holy Ghost and with fire . . .

In this country more than in any other is the man of thought united in the same person with the man of action. The people here have a strong tendency to profound and philosophic thought, as well as to skillful, energetic, and persevering action. The time is not far distant when our whole population will be philosophers, and all our philosophers will be practical men. This is written on almost every man's brow in characters so plain that he who runs may read. This characteristic of our population fits us above all other nations to bring out and realize great and important ideas. Here too is the freedom which other nations want, and the faith in ideas which can be found nowhere else. Philosophers in other countries may think and construct important theories, but they can realize them only to a very limited extent. But here every idea may be at once put to a practical test, and if true will be realized. We have the field, the liberty, the disposition and the faith to work with ideas. It is here then that must first be brought out and realized the true idea of the Atonement. We already seem to have a consciousness of this, and it is therefore that we are not and cannot be surprised to find the union of popular inspiration with profound philosophical thought manifesting itself more clearly here than any where else . . .

I do not misread the age. I have not looked upon the world only out from the window of my closet; I have mingled in its busy scenes; I have rejoiced and wept with it; I have hoped and feared, and believed and doubted with it, and I am but what it has made me. I cannot misread it. It craves union. The heart of man is crying out for the heart of man. One and the same spirit is abroad, uttering the same voice in all languages. From all parts of the world voice answers to voice, and man responds to man. There is a universal language already in use. Men are beginning to understand one another, and their mutual understanding will beget mutual sympathy, and mutual sympathy will bind them together and to God.

And for the progress too the whole world is struggling. Old Institutions are examined, old opinions criticised, even the old Church is laid bare to its very foundations, and its holy vestments and sacred symbols are exposed to the gaze of the multitude; new systems are proclaimed, new institutions elaborated, new ideas are sent abroad, new experiments are made, and the whole world seems intent on the means by which it may accomplish its destiny. The individual is struggling to become a greater and a better being. Every where there are men laboring to perfect governments and laws. The poor man is admitted to be human, and millions of voices are demanding that he be treated as a brother. All eyes and hearts are turned to education. The cultivation of the child's moral and spiritual nature becomes the worship of God. The priest rises to the educator, and the school-room is the temple in which he is to minister. There is progress; there will be progress. Humanity must go forward. Encouraging is the future. He, who takes his position on the "high table land" of Humanity, and beholds with a prophet's gaze his brothers, so long separated, coming together, and arm in arm marching onward and upward towards the Perfect, towards God, may hear celestial voices chanting a sweeter strain than that which announced to Judea's shepherds the birth of the Redeemer, and his heart full and overflowing, he may exclaim with old Simeon, "Lord, now lettest thou thy servant depart in peace, for mine eyes have seen thy salvation."

3. William Henry Furness (1802–1896)
Remarks on the Four Gospels

[A native Bostonian and a schoolmate of Emerson at the Latin School, Furness was his life-long (and possibly his only really intimate) friend. He was to preach Emerson's funeral sermon. Graduated from Harvard College in 1820 and from the Divinity School in 1823, he was called to the Unitarian Church in Philadelphia, where he had a long and distinguished career. He became a leader of antislavery sentiment.

His major passion was the quest of the historical Jesus. His *Remarks,* published in Philadelphia in 1836, was the first in a series of researches; his ties with Boston were close, so that the book was received there as soon as it was published.

In the guise of Biblical criticism, it is a prosaic *Nature.* Though it claims also to be specifically Christian, to the regular Unitarians it appeared a surrender of any such title. It celebrates the religion of nature as the substratum of all religion, and endorses Christianity only because Christ adhered to the universal teaching. In this light, Furness makes short work of the miracles. He accuses those who insisted that certain historical events were supernatural of degrading everything else. If nature is seen as itself divine—and the Christian will see it no otherwise—then no particular set of phenomena can be distinguished from any other on the score of being miraculous. Thus the sensational philosophy, which requires such props, shows itself at heart a mere skepticism, kept from acknowledging its real character only by a specious pretense. In other words, by Furness' logic, rational Unitarians are forever debarred, by their idolatry of John Locke, from attaining a semblance of Christian faith. Clearly, there is no hope in them.]

Taking up the first four books of the New Testament as human compositions, forgetting as far as possible all that has been said of their authority and inspiration, . . . I propose to point out those characteristics of these writings which have produced in my mind a new and lively conviction of their truth . . . I wish only to state what I have seen with my own eyes, and felt with my own heart . . . My fondest hope, so far as others are concerned, will be fulfilled, if these pages serve to create in minds better qualified to pursue the work, a belief in the exceeding riches of a region, as yet so imperfectly explored . . .

There is one characteristic of [Jesus'] religion, as it was taught by himself, to which I would ask a moment's attention. It is the entire absence of all that is vulgarly termed speculation—theory. Every sentiment uttered by Jesus, admits of being understood as the expression of a fact—an eternal and essential truth. His religion, as a revelation, is a revelation of things true from all eternity. The great topics of his teaching were not the fancies, the creations of his own mind. They existed in the nature of things . . . Even in that startling declaration, "Whoso liveth and believeth in me, shall never die," we have an indisputable fact. Is it not inevitably and unchangeably true, that death ceases to be death to him whose feelings and views accord with the spirit of this great Teacher? . . . Examine his language on all occasions with this view, and you will be struck with its truth. We call the principles which he inculcated by his name, but not because he originated them, for they are older than the creation. But he did originate a new manifestation of them. He not only asserted them with an unprecedented clearness, he gave them a new and living force in his own being . . . In his doings and sufferings, the true sacred writing—the characters and symbols by which the Divine mind expresses itself, the great facts and principles of the moral world were revealed anew. If we cannot always discern the whole of the truths he uttered in nature and life, we can at least discover some intimations, some germs of them there. Affecting no peculiarity of language, he freely expressed himself in the popular religious phraseology of the day, but interpreted, as the language of every man should be, by the general tone of his life, we see that it was used by him metaphorically . . . Even the sublime doctrine of a future life, which is so frequently represented as a peculiar doctrine of Christianity, is nowhere formally asserted by Jesus. It is rather taken for granted—treated as if it were a plain and indisputable fact. And if theologians were not so anxious to exalt the Gospel at the expense of reason and nature, it might be perceived that the immortality of man, like all the other truths of the New Testament, is written in our very nature, and that in all his allusions to it, Jesus regarded it as a natural truth . . .

But why, it may be asked, why call the truths of Religion by his name, if they were taught so long ago and by so many mighty teachers, if they were, long before he appeared, engraven upon the ancient tables of the human heart? For a plain and emphatic reason. The life of Jesus of Nazareth, his words, acts and sufferings, being real, being facts, are a part of the grand and all-instructive system of Creation,—they constitute a page, nay, a chapter, and at once, the profoundest and clearest chapter in the vast volume of God. Nowhere do I see spiritual and eternal things so clearly revealed, so touchingly expressed, as in his life. The truth which all else teaches is presented by him and in him with a new significance, an original beauty. Let it be that he taught nothing more than the religion of Nature, still by concentrating all its force and loveliness in his individual being, by incorporating it with his life, and so teaching it as it had never been taught by any other, he made natural religion, HIS religion, HIS truth. He has given a new illustration of it. Regard his life as only a part and portion of the great system of Nature, the grand chain of Providence,—still I say that from no quarter of the grand whole come there such all-enlightening beams as from him. His history amidst all objects and events is by far the most luminous point. It is the grand Interpretation of Nature—the Revelation of her mysteries. There the truth shines forth with satisfying clearness. Therefore do I hold it to be true and right to call the truth he preached through his own being, *his* truth— *Christian* truth. When it is so denominated, it is not meant that he appropriated it to himself. On the contrary, in the sense in which it is *his*, it is more effectually put within the reach of all men, and imparted to all, and we are made to feel that it is natural and eternal truth . . .

The next aspect under which we may contemplate the character of Christ is in relation to those extraordinary works of power and benevolence ascribed to him. It is interesting to see how they illustrate his moral elevation . . .

Miracles are usually conceived of and represented as departures from the natural order of things,—interruptions, violations of the laws of Nature. They are so understood and designated by Dr. Channing in his Dudleian Lecture . . .

The chief objection to [this] reasoning . . . is, that it is based upon the merest assumption. It takes for granted, that the whole order of Nature is known to us, that the limits of our knowledge are commensurate with all the laws and modes of existence. Because, if it is not so, if our knowledge is not thus complete, how can we presume so much as to speak even of a *violation* of, or a *departure* from the order of Nature? The truth is, and it would seem only necessary to hint at it, to bring it to mind with overpowering force, our knowledge, so far from possessing anything like completeness, is most imperfect. We stand but on the borders of the tremendous abyss of being. We have caught but a distant glimpse of its great author. "How faint the whisper we have heard of him!" We see but a portion of Nature, and that portion, how superficially! . . .

With our very limited knowledge of Nature, how, I ask again, shall we pronounce an alleged fact a violation of its order? Is it because it is referrible to no cause but a moral and intelligent Being, a super-physical Agency, a Supreme Will? But to what else, pray, is any event, however common, to be ascribed, but an invisible, supernatural Power? We are accustomed, it is true, to ascribe power to physical causes; and because one phenomenon is always preceded by another of a certain description, to refer the former to the latter, as to its efficient cause. The sun shines, the rain descends, and the grass grows; and we conclude that the sun and the rain possess in themselves the power to cause the grass to grow. But there is no reason for this conclusion, except the familiarity of this sequence, which is no reason at all. For aught we perceive, the shining of the sun and the falling of the rain might have been followed by directly opposite consequences. All that we perceive, and all that we can affirm, so far as our perceptions go, is, that one event is invariably followed by another of a certain description. It is now conceded by eminent philosophical writers, that in what are commonly termed physical causes we perceive no inherent power to produce the effects by which they are followed . . .

"The falseness of the analogy," says Dugald Stewart, alluding to the opinion of those who conceive that the universe is a machine formed and put in motion by the Deity, "appears from this, that the moving force in every machine is some *natural* power, such as gravity and elasticity; and, therefore, the very idea of mechanism presupposes the existence of those active powers of which it is the professed object of a mechanical theory of the universe to give an explanation" . . . How long oftentimes is the interval between the rejection of an error and the full admission of the opposite truth! We reject the mechanical theory of the universe: but how does it continue to vitiate our reasonings and deaden our sensibilities! The universe is not a machine, many are ready to admit, but then they turn away as if this were the end, when it is but the beginning of the whole matter. If the creation is not a machine, what then is it? What do we see, when we look upon the objects and changes around us? Nothing, so the reply is commonly expressed, nothing but Mind—nothing but the agency of God. Nothing but the agency of God! In the name of Heaven, what would we have more to stir up the deepest springs of curiosity, wonder and awe, and make us feel that a new world of thought is opened before us! It must put all things in new lights. The familiar must become novel, the novel, familiar. Natural facts become supernatural, and miracles become natural, when all are regarded as manifestations of an Invisible Mind, an Infinite Will . . .

Let us look now at the extraordinary facts related in the New Testament . . . When these facts are considered, under all the circumstances under which they are represented to have taken place, no man can affirm that they lie beyond the boundaries of possibility. They fall not, it is true, within the limits of our experience; but it cannot be maintained that they are impossible in the nature of things, because the nature of the things concerned is but very partially known. For the same reason, they cannot be pronounced interruptions of the laws of nature . . . I say again, then, that we are not at liberty to pronounce the restoration of a dead man to life, a natural impossibility, or a violation of nature, until we know what death is, and life; what the influence of the mind upon the body, and when that influence ceases, and, more than all, what are the limits of the power with which God may possess a mind of unequalled purity, wisdom and exaltation, like the mind of Jesus Christ, without any violation of the laws of its being. A phenomenon, the elements whereof are but so imperfectly known, purporting to take place through the agency of such a being as the man of Nazareth, is not to be regarded as essentially incredible on the one hand, nor as an interruption of the laws of Nature on the other, without—so I venture to conclude—a manifest disregard of the soundest principles of thought . . .

In denying that the order of Nature has been violated, I may be charged with helping to perpetuate that narrowing influence which the observation of this order has sometimes exerted, and which Dr. Channing has so well described . . . On the contrary, I maintain, it is the common idea of the Christian miracles, as interruptions or violations of the natural order of things, that contributes to this unhappy effect. It virtually concedes that a divine spiritual agency is in nature indirect. It allows nature to be conceived of as a sort of labour-saving contrivance, a machine without any intrinsic worth or beauty, going by itself, with only an indirect dependence upon a higher Power. It promotes in men's minds the idea of a separation between the common works and ways of the creation and the Creator himself, and so induces them to contemplate the former, without any necessary reference to the latter. Whereas, establish the miracles as demonstrations of a supreme spiritual force, existing in the nature of things, and acting in a manner kindred to, and in harmony with, all the other agencies that we witness; and then the power of physical causes over the mind is broken. God, who was afar off, is brought near and enthroned in Nature . . .

We cannot see the miracles of Jesus as natural facts, except as we are ascending that eminence of Faith, from which we look abroad and recognise the supernatural everywhere in the natural. The common idea of the miracles is based upon a mechanical philosophy—a philosophy of the senses. We conceive of the universe as a piece of mechanism, going in some sort of itself; so our ideas of the Divine nature and agency are fashioned upon a false, human analogy, which blinds that spiritual sense within us, the principle of faith, and impedes our approach unto God. We say indeed that all power was originally from God, but we conceive of him as having delegated certain measures of power to what we call the general laws, the order of Nature, so that now, as things are, He stands in the same relation to his creation that a man does to the machine he has invented, and if any departure from our experience occurs, we set it down as a peculiar interposition—a stretching forth of the arm which otherwise hangs comparatively idle and at rest! Our ideas of the Divinity are thus narrowed, and we flatter ourselves that we know him when we know him not.

4. George Ripley (1802–1880)

Martineau's Rationale

[In the November number of *The Christian Examiner* (XXI, 225–254), Ripley at last spoke openly on the question of miracles. Reviewing James Martineau, *The Rationale of Religious Enquiry,* he went out of his way to use this stalwart English liberal as a bludgeon with which to beat the American Unitarians. He read them such a lecture as they could not disregard, and for which they were never to forgive him.

What most offended and scandalized the Unitarians was his open assertion— for all the world to hear—that inside the liberal church, even after the great emancipation had been wrought, the human heart was more "pulverized" than it had been under Calvinism. Dr. Channing had put the essential Unitarian thesis, once and for all: "To rob man of his dignity is as truly to subvert religion as to strip God of his perfection." Well, here the most brilliant student in the post-Channing generation arraigned his elders—by implication even Dr. Channing— of robbing man of his dignity more shamefully—because more slyly—than did the preachers of total depravity. They insulted mankind by their dogmatic insistence upon the literal veracity of recorded miracles. For three decades these liberals had been daily accusing their Calvinist opponents of annihilating the image of God in the human spirit; for them it was a disaster to be accused, by a rationale they could hardly comprehend, of doing exactly the same thing. At this point Ripley began to experience how astonishingly illiberal outraged liberals can become.

There was no longer any way of evading the question of miracles, for upon it depended all the other issues between the new school and the old. Liberal Christianity had stood, with what it had thought was courage, for the dignity of man; then it required that this dignity be insured by miracles. Ripley was willing to concede that the miracles had happened; his point was that they were not necessarily miraculous and that in any event, they were irrelevant to the main contention, the high estimate of human nature. In other words, the real point of the discussion was "Nature"—the nature of Nature. Here was a crisis in modern liberalism, reaching deeper into the foundations of the creed than an academic debate over the historicity of certain events might at first sight suggest.

This was the form in which America was first confronted with that problem of which Albert Schweitzer has been only one, although the most distinguished, historian. The real question in 1836 was one of sincerity: the elder liberals were embarrassed in the extreme, for if Ripley (along with Furness, Emerson, and Brownson) was correct, they stood convicted of duplicity. They had publicly renounced the doctrine of original sin, but they had secretly hung onto it by requiring the dignity of man to be sustained through supernatural intervention. They did not, after all, trust humanity. Despite their professions, they were reactionaries. Ripley called upon them to go the whole way with their own proclamations, even to the point of accepting, as the only revelation known to man, the naked and unsupported "human consciousness."]

It was supposed that the science of theology sprang at once into perfection from the heads of the Reformers; and every attempt to modify its character, was regarded as an offence, and almost as a blasphemy. In this way, it has been left encrusted with ancient errors, while the work of purification has been going on in every other department of inquiry and thought. Astronomy has been separated from astrology, chemistry from the search after the philosopher's stone, medicine from the incantations of magic; but between theology and mythology, a sharp line of distinction yet remains to be drawn. It is a problem, which we who speak the English tongue have hardly looked in the face; but one which we must be prepared to meet, before the claims of science and religion can be reconciled,—before "an open and solemn marriage between faith and reason can be celebrated." The time has come when a revision of theology is demanded, as the commencement of a reform; when no solemn mutterings can present a charm to keep away the hand of bold research; when the veil must be wholly lifted up from the face of the statue, before which men have so long bowed in darkness and dread, and a clear, piercing light be admitted into the temple of our faith and the mysteries of our worship. Systems of divinity we have, indeed, had in abundance; but how unworthy of the name! Where can we find one which has not failed in the very thing that science demands as essential to a system,—a rigid method and a comprehensive unity? The science of Divinity, regarded in its true light, is the noblest that the mind can be conversant with, for it is the science of the Divine, of the Infinite, of God in Nature, in History, in Humanity, in the Heart of Man. It should be filled with the dewy freshness of the morning, it should breathe an atmosphere of unclouded light, it should move with the freedom and grace of conscious inspiration, and gather around itself all that is attractive, beautiful, and glorious, in the whole compass of creation.

But what are our prevailing systems of theology? What claim do they present, as now organized, upon the attention of the philosopher or the lover of nature? It is hard to imagine a study more dry, more repulsive, more perplexing, and more totally unsatisfactory to a scientific mind, than theology, as it is presented in the works of by far the greater part of English writers on the subject.

It is no wonder that the heart is pulverized, that the freshness of life is exhausted, under their influence. It is no wonder, that the most vigorous efforts of sacred eloquence have been made by those, who have avoided, as much as possible, the hard abstractions of our technical systems; who have studied divinity in communion with their own nature and with the universe or who have not studied it at all. We respond, with living sympathy, to the earnest voice that comes to us from beyond the sea, calling for a new organ of theology, and presenting us a specimen of its scientific culture. We long to see the educated mind of England awakening to the importance of this subject, seeking for an instrument wherewith this vast and holy science may be raised to its becoming rank among other intellectual pursuits, redeemed from the petty subtleties which have planted thorns around it, and brought out of bondage and darkness into the stately light of day . . .

In like manner, we know of no unerring test, by which to distinguish a miracle of religion from a new manifestation of natural powers, without a previous faith in the divinity of the performer. The phenomena of electricity and magnetism exhibit wonders surpassing the ordinary agencies of nature. Upon their first discovery, they presented all the characteristics by which we designate miracles, except their application to religious purposes. If a miracle is said to have been wrought by one whom we already know to be in possession of supernatural gifts, there is a strong presumption that it may be true; but if the evidence of supernatural endowments is made to depend on the miracle, we ask how we are to know that what appears to be a miracle is, in fact, supernatural, and not a new development of nature.

If, then, a firm faith in Christianity may be cherished independently of miracles; if the purpose of miracles be to operate within the sphere of action rather than of thought; and if there be great difficulties in the proof of miracles, without a previous conviction of the divine authority of him who is said to exhibit them, we hold it to be an unsound method to make a belief in them the essential foundation of Christian faith, or the ultimate test of Christian character.

It will be perceived, that in the foregoing remarks, we have not been inclined to controvert the truth of the Christian miracles. They are subjects of historical inquiry, and are to be settled by historical considerations, including that of the character and position of their author. We wish only to maintain what we deem a better mode of examining the evidence of Christianity than that which is usually pursued in the study of theology. The adoption of this mode, we are persuaded, would remove some of the strongest objections of infidels, and convert the timid and wavering faith of multitudes into strong and masculine conviction. Let the study of theology commence with the study of human consciousness. Let us ascertain what is meant by the expression, often used, but little pondered,—the Image of God in the Soul of Man. Let us determine whether our nature has any revelation of the Deity within itself; and, if so, analyze and describe it. If we there discover, as we firmly believe we shall, a criterion of truth, by which we can pass judgment on the Spiritual and Infinite, we shall then be prepared to examine the claims of a Divine Revelation in history.

5. George Ripley (1802–1880)
Discourses on the Philosophy of Religion

[Ripley's review of Martineau's *Rationale* in the *Examiner* so aroused Professor Andrews Norton that he took what was, considering the standards of decorum then reigning in Boston, the extreme step of writing a letter to the newspapers (see p. 158). Ripley thereupon published, at the end of 1836, a forty-page pamphlet, a digest of sermons he had been delivering over the last two years: *Discourses on the Philosophy of Religion Addressed to Doubters Who Wish to Believe*.

The article had perforce been "negative"—an attack on the doctrine of miracles. Here he put his "positive" case—and the case for Transcendentalism. His great point is that the miraculous—which is to say the distinction between the divine and the natural—ceases to mean anything at all when nature is seen as a divine language.

But then, there follows, or here for the first time seems to be following, an odd consequence: there are evidently differences among men in their abilities to read the language. Does the difference between those who perceive Nature through the Reason and those who view it only with the Understanding suggest a more ancient distinction? Can it be that the former are saints and the latter the sort of unfortunates who in the seventeenth century were more bluntly called reprobates?]

I have been thought by some esteemed friends to have exhibited views in a recent number of one of our theological journals that are liable to many serious objections. I fear also that I may have unconsciously given pain to some devout and timid minds, who think that discussions of this nature serve only to unsettle the foundations of Christian faith. I have the most heartfelt sympathy with such minds. I would sooner never speak again than do aught which tends to cloud the blessed light of a serene and confiding piety. It was my purpose, in the discussion alluded to, to suggest a mode of considering the evidences of Christianity which should free it from certain difficulties under which it has been thought to labor. No one who has read my article understandingly can suppose that I intended to cast any doubt on the reality of the Christian miracles—or that I doubted them myself. I do not. Their certainty being once established, by what I deem the only valid proof, they are no less holy and precious to me than to others.

The fears which are entertained by many, who are not theologians by profession, with regard to the effect of free discussion, often arises from the want of an intelligent and vigorous faith. They dread lest the progress of inquiry should bring to light some hidden defect in the grounds of our religion. They are, in fact, doubters, though they know it not. They wish to believe. They cannot bear to hear a word said which implies that any cherished view is wrong. But this arises from a lurking suspicion that there is something unsound in the fabric of their faith. To such minds these discourses are addressed. I would frankly point out to them the principles on which my own faith is built; and I cannot but hope that theirs will gain strength by the exposition. The interests of speculative science and of practical piety appear to me so intimately blended, that it would cause me deep sorrow to think that I had laid a rude hand on either. What I have recently published explains the negative side of my faith. I here give the positive; and one should read both the statements in connexion, in order to perceive the complete whole in which I venture to think my views exist in my own mind . . .

The religious man is, indeed, conversant with invisible objects. His thoughts expatiate in regions, which eye hath not seen, but which God has revealed to him, by his spirit. He reposes as firm faith in those ideas, which are made known to him by his Reason, as in those facts, which are presented to his notice by the senses. He has no belief that human nature is so shackled and hemmed in, even in its present imperfect state, as to be confined to the objects made known by the eye of sense, which is given us merely for the purposes of our temporal existence, and incapable of ascending to those higher spheres of thought and reality, to which the eternal elements of our being belong.

But, allowing this, it by no means follows, that the religious man is a visionary, in any just sense of that word, because, in the first place, he need not neglect the objects, with which he is at all times surrounded, and which are appropriate to the province of sense, and in the second place, the invisible objects, with which he is conversant, have no less truth and reality, than those which are seen.

The religious man need not see less, in the sphere of the senses, than any other man. There is nothing in his faith in the Invisible, which should blind him to any perceptions, within the sphere of the visible. Indeed, he ought to give his understanding a generous culture, that it may be acute and ready to decide on all objects, that come within its province. One part of his nature is not to be educated at the expense of another. One portion of his existence is not to be sacrificed to the claims of another. The present, with its duties, its enjoyments, and its dangers, is not to be forgotten, amid the hopes and prospects of the future. It is a most pernicious mistake, which leads men to suppose, that they must give up the interests of this world in order to prepare for another, instead of making their preparation for another, to consist in a faithful discharge of all the claims and trusts of this. The visible is of great importance to every man on earth. Our Maker has made us conscious of life, in the most intimate connexion with it. He has surrounded us with objects, addressed to the senses, on a proper use of which, the religious improvement of life essentially depends. It is our duty, as immortal beings, not to neglect the present. It is our duty to provide for its wants. It is our duty to obtain a wise acquaintance with its necessities. The truly religious man feels this as much as another. The enlightened Christian, who understands the spirit of his Master, and who is resolved to cultivate it, should not be confounded with the dreaming visionary, who in the fancied care for his soul, cares for nothing else; who is so absorbed in the contemplation of the Invisible as to lose sight of the important realities before his eyes; whose mystic speculations on heaven spoil him for the duties of earth, like the ancient philosopher, who, in gazing at the stars, fell into a pit. This is not the course pursued by the truly-instructed Christian. He knows that every thing has its place and its importance, that all duties and all thoughts should preserve a just proportion among themselves, and if he sees those things which are invisible, he should give none the less heed to those which are visible.

But, again, the invisible objects, with which the religious man is conversant, possess as much reality, as those within the sphere of the outward senses. Do not call him a visionary, until you have proved that he is dealing with visions. What if the objects of his attention should be found to have a more substantial existence than any thing which we now see? Do not deem him a man of fantastic mind, until you have proved that he is following phantoms. What if the things that are not seen, should turn out to be enduring realities, while the things that appear, are only transitory appearances? It may be that this is the case. We have great reason to hold that it is probable. Nay, we have the words of inspiration, declaring that it is a fact. "For the things which are seen are temporal, but those which are unseen are eternal". . .

In pursuing this subject, I would first remark, that the things which are unseen possess the only independent reality. This assertion, I know, is contrary to our usual modes of conception. The objects of sense make so early and so strong an impression upon our minds, that we soon learn to regard them as more real than any others. Our first connexion is with the material universe. We are awakened, in the first instance, to a consciousness of our own being, through the influence which it exerts upon our frames. We learn to know ourselves, by having previously learned the changes which we experience from the agency of outward objects. The universe, with its varied beauty and splendor, is spread forth in our presence, it addresses every faculty and excites every feeling, we behold its vast and complicated changes with reverence and awe, and it is not surprising that we should regard it as clothed with original and independent reality. But, in truth, the things which are seen were not made of things which do appear. The material universe is the expression of an Invisible Wisdom and Power. It has its origin in the will of the Infinite, who has made it what it is, endowed it with all its properties, impressed it with all its tendencies, assigned it all its laws, and by whose energy it is ever constantly sustained. The creation in itself, without reference to the Almighty Spirit from which it sprung, is formless and without order—a mass of chaotic objects, of whose uses we are ignorant, and whose destiny we cannot imagine. It is only when its visible glory leads our minds to its unseen Author, and we regard it as a manifestation of Divine Wisdom, that we can truly comprehend its character and designs. To the eye of sense, what does the external creation present? Much less than we are generally apt to suppose. Consider every thing which we learn from it, merely through our bodily organization, you will be surprised to find how small an amount can be summed up. Deduct all the pleasure it gives us, through the medium of our higher nature, all the associations which it suggests to thought and feeling, all the indications of a spiritual presence and glory, which its significant symbols reveal to our souls, and you will find that what remains, is of far less interest and importance than you would at first have imagined. The outward creation, indeed, exhibits an ever-changing variety of forms, of colors, and of motions, which excite the perception of beauty and produce intense delight in the mind of the beholder. But what is it that the external eye per-

ceives, when it contemplates this? Merely the different arrangements of matter, the various degrees and directions in which the light falls on the object
admired, and the change of position with regard to space. This is all that is
seen. The rest is felt. The forms are addressed to the eye, but the perception
of beauty is in the soul. And the highest degree of this is perceived, when the
outward creation suggests the wisdom of the Creator. Without that, it is
comparatively blank and cold and lifeless. It is his existence which furnishes
the ground for the existence of that, and connected with Him, as the Primal
Fountain of Being, it derives all the reality which it possesses, from his
Sovereign Will. How unwise, then, to confine our attention merely to the
outward form, and to forget the inward spirit, which it represents! How unworthy of the character of a man, to be so occupied with the mere outside,
the dry husk and shell of matter, as to lose sight of the Infinite and Divine
Energy, from which it draws the reality of its being.

The things that are seen, moreover, are dependent, in a great measure,
upon our own souls. We have another instance, here, of the relation between
the visible and the invisible, and the subjection of the former to the latter.
It is often said, I am aware, that the soul is dependent for its character and
growth, on the external forms of matter, with which it is connected, and that
it is greatly influenced by them is a fact, which no observer of human nature
can deny; but it is no less true, that the outward universe is to a great degree,
dependent upon our souls for its character and influence, and that by changes
in our inward condition, a corresponding change is produced in the objects
with which we are surrounded. It is from the cast and disposition of our
souls, that external nature derives its hues and conformation. Place two men
of different character, in the same outward scenes, how different is the effect
which takes place. To one, perhaps, whose heart is tuned to the praises of his
Maker, every thing suggests the presence of Divine Wisdom and Love. The
voice of God is heard in the rushings of the wind and the whisperings of
the breeze, in the roar of the thunder and the fall of the rain; his hand is
visible in the glories of the midnight sky and the splendor of the opening
morn, in the fierce majesty and might of winter, and in the greenness and
beauty of the returning spring; every object is an image of the goodness of
God; every sound, a call for his adoration; every spot a hallowed temple for
his praise. But to the heart of the other, no such feelings are suggested. He
looks coldly on, amid the fair scene of things, in which he is placed. No emotions of admiration or of gratitude penetrate his soul. No sound comes to
him from the depths of nature, answering to an accordant sound within
the depths of his own heart. He views all that is before him, with a spirit

of calculation or a spirit of indifference. Yet he sees precisely the same objects with his companion. The same outward universe is unfolded to his view. The same material sights meet his eye; the same material sounds touch his ear; the same forms and colors and motions, are addressed to his senses. But is it in fact, the same world that is beheld in the two cases? In one, it is a living image, speaking forth the glory of God; in the other, a mute and dead mass of material forms. Whence is this difference? Whence, but from the souls of the two spectators? It is upon the inward condition that the outward reality depends. The visible universe is to us what our invisible souls choose to make it. Here, then, we have a reason for looking at the things which are unseen—for making them the chief object of our attention. In so doing, we become conversant with the primal source of reality. We ascend to the original fountain of Being, from which the streams that flow forth receive their properties and their direction . . .

Let us see if there is any thing in the nature of man, which may enable him to become a partaker of the divine nature—any capacities, which may be the germ of qualities in his character, similar to those which we reverence in the character of God.

I. When we examine the nature which we possess, we perceive at once, that it has a power of a remarkable character, which seems to bear some resemblance to one of the divine attributes—the power of perceiving truth. Man has a faculty, which enables him not merely to count, to weigh, and to measure, to estimate probabilities and to draw inferences from visible facts, but to ascertain and determine certain principles of original truth. He sees not merely that one thing is, and another thing is not, that one object of sense is present and another is absent, but that one proposition, relating to abstract and invisible subjects of thought, is true, and another is false. An assertion may be made, concerning an object which he has never seen and never can see,—which cannot be submitted to the cognizance of the senses, and yet he has the power, which enables him to say, with absolute certainty, whether it is true or false. It is this power, by which all science is created. It was the possession of this power in a remarkable degree, which enabled the solitary thinkers, in the retirement of their closets, whose labors have shed the greatest light on science, to make those discoveries, by which the arts of life have been promoted, and aid given in the pursuit of the great interests of society. This power is Reason. It gives us the immediate perception of Truth. It is the ultimate standard, in judging on all subjects of human inquiry. Whatever appears to be true to our Reason, we believe to be true; whatever appears false to that, we believe to be false. Existing in different degrees, in different men, it is found in some degree in all. There are certain points on which the judgment of all men is alike—certain propositions, which every one would pronounce true, certain others which all would declare false. We are compelled to this by the nature of our Reason. It is not subject to the control of our will. We cannot say, that we choose to have two and two appear equal to five, and therefore they are so in the sight of Reason; but this faculty exercises its own judgment, announces its own decisions, enforces its own authority, from which there is no appeal. Does not this show, that Reason though within us is not created by us; though belonging to human nature, originates in a higher nature; though shining in the mind of man, is an emanation from the mind of God? Is not the faculty of reason similar to the wisdom of God? As he has the power of perceiving the pure and absolute truth on all subjects, has he not endowed man with the similar power of perceiving truth on a limited number of subjects? In this respect, then, I believe that the nature of man has powers by which he may become a partaker of the divine nature—may exhibit qualities of a similar character to those which we reverence in God.

II. Again, man has the faculty of recognising moral distinctions. Of two courses of conduct that are presented to his choice, he is able to say that one is Right and that the other is Wrong. He perceives not merely what would be for his advantage, his interest, what will gratify his passions, or promote the happiness of society, but he sees that certain actions, though they might gratify his selfish inclinations, are forbidden by the law of Duty, and he feels an inward obligation to obey that law. Man does not obtain this knowledge through the medium of any of his senses. It is not the result of that part of his nature which calculates and compares. It is not subject to his own will. A man may be tempted to do a wrong action, and may yield to the temptation;—he may turn away his mind from the contemplation of its character, and thus be blind to its real nature;—but, as long as he gives his attention to an action, not blinded by passion, nor warped by prejudice, but in the pure light of conscience, he cannot make the unjust appear to be just, the wrong appear to be right. A voice within speaks, which he cannot but hear, and tells him the character of the action which he is about to perform. It is common to call this voice within us, this conscience which speaks out its clear behests, whether we will hear or whether we will forbear, the voice of God—and is there not a truth of deep significance in the expression? Is not conscience in the human soul, a quality similar to that attribute of God, which makes him the righteous judge of all the earth? Is not conscience, the voice of God, the word of Him who is of purer eyes than to behold iniquity, and who separates between the evil and the good? As God discerns with his all-seeing eye, the real character of every action, so has he imparted to the human soul, a portion of his spirit, which gives it a similar power, and arms the decisions of conscience with a divine authority. Here then, is an element, by the cultivation of which man may become a partaker of the divine nature. Let him reverence his conscience, and it will acquire a power similar to that justice, which we adore in God. Let him listen to the faintest whispers of that voice, which speaks in his moral nature, and he will preserve, in its original brightness, the image of his Maker, which has been impressed upon his soul.

III. Again, man has the power of disinterested Love. I do not say, how frequently it is exercised. That is not requisite for the argument I have in view. It is of no consequence, how many instances to the contrary may be adduced from the experience of life, to show that its actual existence is rare. They only prove that the original element, upon which it is founded, has failed of its proper culture; not, that it is wanting in human nature. It is enough to know that the ground of disinterested, self-sacrificing love is placed within the heart of man, and we have at once an element, by which he may be made a partaker of the divine nature. And that this germ does exist in the human soul, who can deny? Has it not been displayed in examples of benevolence, which had no selfish object in view, but which went steadily forward to the accomplishment of their purpose, in the midst of peril and sacrifice? It was displayed in the example of Jesus Christ, who so loved the world,—who was so interested in the spiritual welfare of mankind,—so intent on promoting the highest happiness of the human race, that he forgot himself, forsook every earthly interest, suffered every outward deprivation, and at last sacrificed his life, in the cause which was dearer to him than any personal advantage which could be desired. It was displayed in the example of his apostles, whose hearts burned within them for the promotion of truth, and who laid down every earthly blessing at the foot of the cross. It is felt by the philanthropist, who is ready, at the expense of his tears and his blood, to alleviate the miseries of the human race. It is felt by the friend, who would willingly renounce his own life in behalf of his friend. It is felt by the parent, who knows that the happiness of his children is dearer to him than his own, and who would give up every thing himself to confer it upon them. It is felt by every good man, who has so devoted himself to a righteous cause, that he regards his own interests as but chaff and dust, compared with the promotion of the cause which he has at heart. And this love is the very essence of the Divine character. God is Love, and whoso dwelleth in Love, dwelleth in God and God in him. It is not of Earth, but of Heaven. It is the great attribute which binds the Almighty to the heart of Man. The more we possess of this quality, the more we resemble God. The germ of it, which exists in our hearts, is the foundation for our growing likeness to the Creator, and when it is fully developed within us, we have become partakers of the Divine Nature.

IV. Once more, man has the power of conceiving of a perfection higher than he has ever reached. Not only so. He can make this perfection a distinct object of pursuit. He has faculties which the present can never satisfy. After he has done his best, he feels how much better it might have been done. He can always form a conception of a higher model, than any which he can actually realize. And his nature impells him to follow this ideal standard—not to rest content in imperfection—to forget the things that are behind—and to press forward to higher attainments, to diviner excellence. The artist sees this vision of perfection in his mind, and attempts to embody it in the materials that are subject to his skill; but the result is never equal to his conception, he still imagines more glorious forms of beauty, than any which he has produced, his soul communes with an ideal perfectness, that no human hand can ever call into being. The good man sees this vision of perfection, when he compares himself with what he ought to be, with the unspotted virtue, which he can conceive, but which was never realized, except in him, "who possessed the Spirit of the Father without measure." And this power, belonging to the human soul, is another element, by which man may become partaker of the divine nature. It is the germ of resemblance to God. It is intended to lead us on from strength to strength, from glory to glory, in an ever-growing likeness to the Infinite Source of Beauty, and Goodness and Love.

Consider then, my friends, these four principles of human nature, the power of perceiving Truth—of recognising moral distinctions—of exercising disinterested love—and of aspiring after illimitable perfection, and tell me, if we were not made to become partakers of the Divine Nature? Does not the soul of Man bear the impress of God? Are we not created to exhibit the Image of our Maker in its divine purity and splendor? And if such be our destiny, how solemn is our responsibility!

6. Elizabeth Palmer Peabody (1804–1894)

Record of a School

[Born in Billerica, but brought up mainly in Salem, Elizabeth Peabody was the daughter of a brilliant and eccentric physician. Her sister Sophia married Hawthorne in 1842 and in 1843 her sister Mary married Horace Mann. She herself was an intellectual spinster who lived to become a Boston institution, a never-ending advocate of reform and of all new ideas. She taught in private schools in Lancaster and Boston, became the friend and secretary of Dr. Channing. She assisted Alcott at his school with great enthusiasm in 1834, but in 1836 retreated to Salem and is generally thought to have failed him in his hour of need. Yet they remained fast friends for fifty years.

In 1839 she opened a bookshop in West Street, which became a meeting place for Boston intelligentsia. She published *The Dial,* wrote textbooks on grammar and history, and in 1860 founded the first American kindergarten.

She met Alcott on his first visit to Boston in 1828, and later said that as soon as she saw him with a child she realized his surpassing genius for education. "I am vain enough to say that you are the only one I ever saw who, I soberly thought, surpassed myself in the general conception of this divinest of arts." She brought Alcott and Dr. Channing together, and secured the great Doctor's blessing upon their enterprise, the school which she and Alcott opened in the Masonic Temple in Tremont Street, September 1834.

The premise of Transcendentalism was bound to lead to an examination of education, and to a revolt against the prevailing, external and "sensational" methods. Alcott was the man, appointed by the Over-Soul and by himself, to represent the Transcendental surge on the educational front. In his journals for 1834 he summed up the doctrine in a passage as fundamental for the movement as any in Emerson or Ripley:

> Education is that process by which *thought* is opened out of the soul, and, associated with outward . . . things, is reflected back upon itself, and thus made conscious of its reality and shape. It is *Self-Realization.* As a means, therefore, of educating the soul out of itself, and mirroring forth its ideas, the external world offers the materials. This is the dim glass in which the senses are first called to display the soul, until, aided by the keener state of imagination, . . . it separates those outward types of itself from their sensual connection, in its own bright mirror recognizes again itself, as a *distinctive* object *in* space and time, but *out of it* in *existence,* and painting itself upon these, as emblems of its inner and super-sensual life which no outward thing can fully portray . . . A language is to be instituted between [the child's] spirit and the surrounding scene of things in which he dwells . . . He who is seeking to know himself, should be ever seeking himself in external things, and by so doing will he be best able to find, and explore his inmost light.

Alcott's and Elizabeth's school was thus a stroke for the new philosophy. That its import should not be lost, Elizabeth wrote this account, illustrated with stenographic reports on the conduct, and published it in July 1835.

To the first edition she appended a theoretical exposition, "General Principles of Education," which proved so difficult of comprehension, even to the initiated, that in the second edition (1836) she substituted a possibly more intelligible "Explanatory Preface." The 1835 discourse was a mélange of her own ideas and Alcott's; it is one of the more engaging documents in American Transcendentalism, with its contention that human nature is compacted of three principles—Happiness, Love, Faith—and that education is a method of realizing them in consciousness. Still, since even the "class of minds" that Elizabeth attempted to address found "no meaning in my words," the modern reader may be spared the ordeal. In the second edition, *Record of a School: Exemplifying the General Principles of Spiritual Culture* (Boston, 1836), she hoped she was more cogent; she sought to separate herself somewhat from Alcott and to criticize his theories (he reading and correcting the proof!). A few passages from her preface and her summation give an adequate notion of Miss Peabody's contribution.

The record itself is substantially the same in both editions; the story can be illustrated as easily by any one section as by any other, but a good impression of the year's activities is contained in the first and last days of Alcott's academic year, with two characteristic sessions in between.]

EXPLANATORY PREFACE

To contemplate Spirit in the Infinite Being, has ever been acknowledged to be the only ground of true Religion. To contemplate Spirit in External nature, is universally allowed to be the only true Science. To contemplate Spirit in ourselves and in our fellow men, is obviously the only means of understanding social duty, and quickening within ourselves a wise Humanity.—In general terms, Contemplation of Spirit is the first principle of Human Culture; the foundation of Self-education.

This principle, Mr. Alcott begins with applying to the education of the youngest children. Considering early education as a leading of the young mind to self-education, he would have it proceed on the same principles . . .

Instead, therefore, of making it his aim to make children investigate External nature, after Spirit, Mr. Alcott leads them in the first place, to the contemplation of Spirit as it unveils itself within themselves. He thinks there is no intrinsic difficulty in doing this, inasmuch as a child can as easily perceive and name pleasure, pain, love, anger, hate and any other exercises of soul, to which himself is subjected, as he can see the objects before his eyes, and thus a living knowledge of that part of language, which expresses intellectual and moral ideas, and involves the study of his own consciousness of feelings and moral law, may be gained, External nature being only made use of, as imagery, to express the inward life which he experiences. Connected with this self contemplation, and constantly checking any narrowing effect of egotism, or self complacency, which it may be supposed to engender, is the contemplation of God, that can so easily be associated with it. For as the word finite gives meaning to the word infinite, so the finite virtue always calls up in the mind, an Idea which is henceforth named, and becomes an attribute of the Eternal Spirit. Thus a child, having felt what a just action is, either in himself or another, henceforth has an Idea of Justice, which is pure and perfect, in the same ratio, as he is unsophisticated; and is more and more comprehensive of particular applications, as his Reason unfolds. How severe and pure it often is, in a child, thousands have felt! . . .

The first object of investigation is also in the highest degree fruitful for the intellect. Spirit, as it appears within themselves, whether in the form of feeling, law, or thought, is universally interesting. No subject interests children so much as self-analysis. To give name to inward movements of heart and mind, whether in themselves or others, is an employment of their faculties which will enchain the attention of the most volatile. There is no one class of objects in external nature, which interests all children; for children are very differently gifted with respect to their sympathies with nature. But all are conscious of something within themselves which moves, thinks, and feels; and as a mere subject of curiosity and investigation, for the sake of knowledge, it may take place of all others. In order to investigate it, a great many things must be done, which are in themselves very agreeable. Mr. Alcott reads, and tells stories, calculated to excite various moral emotions. On these stories, he asks questions, in order to bring out from each, in words, the feelings which have been called forth. These feelings receive their name, and history, and place in the moral scale. Then books, and passages from books are read, calculated to exercise various intellectual faculties, such as Perception, Imagination, Judgment, Reason (both in apprehension and comprehension); and these various exercises of mind are discriminated and named. There can be no intellectual action more excellent than this, whether we consider the real exercise given to the mind, or its intrinsic interest to the children, and consequently the naturalness of the exercise. And its good influence with respect to preparing for the study of Science is literally incalculable. There is not a single thing that cannot be studied with comparative ease, by a child, who can be taught what faculties he must use, and how they are to be brought to bear on the subject, and what influence on those faculties the subject will have, after it is mastered . . .

PLANS

Mr. Alcott re-commenced his school in Boston, after four years' interval, September, 1834, at the Masonic Temple, No. 7.

Believing that the objects which meet the senses every day for years, must necessarily mould the mind, he felt it necessary to choose a spacious room, and ornament it, not with such furniture as only an upholsterer can appreciate, but with such forms as would address and cultivate the imagination and heart.

In the four corners of the room, therefore, he placed upon pedestals, fine busts of Socrates, Shakespeare, Milton, and Sir Walter Scott. And on a table, before the large gothic window by which the room is lighted, the Image of Silence, "with his finger up, as though he said, beware." Opposite this gothic window, was his own table, about ten feet long, whose front is the arc of a circle, prepared with little desks for the convenience of the scholars. On this, he placed a small figure of a child aspiring. Behind was a very large bookcase, with closets below, a black tablet above, and two shelves filled with books. A fine cast of Christ, in basso-relievo, fixed into this bookcase, is made to appear to the scholars just over the teacher's head. The bookcase itself, is surmounted with a bust of Plato . . .

The desks for the scholars, with conveniences for placing their books in sight, and with black tablets hung over them, which swing forward, when they wish to use them, are placed against the wall round the room, that when in their seats for study, no scholar need look at another. On the right hand of Mr. Alcott, is a sofa for the accommodation of visitors, and a small table, with a pitcher and bowl. Great advantages arise from this room, every part of which speaks the thoughts of Genius. It is a silent reproach upon rudeness.

About twenty children came the first day. They were all under ten years of age, excepting two or three girls. I became his assistant, to teach Latin to such as might desire to learn.

Mr. Alcott sat behind his table, and the children were placed in chairs, in a large arc around him; the chairs so far apart, that they could not easily touch each other. He then asked each one separately, what idea he or she had of the purpose of coming to school? To learn; was the first answer. To learn what? By pursuing this question, all the common exercises of school were brought up by the children themselves; and various subjects of art, science, and philosophy. Still Mr. Alcott intimated that this was not all; and at last some one said "to behave well," and in pursuing this expression into its meanings, they at last decided that they came to learn to feel rightly, to think rightly, and to act rightly. A boy of seven years old suggested, and all agreed, that the most important of these three, was right action.

Simple as all this seems, it would hardly be believed what an evident exercise it was to the children, to be led of themselves to form and express these conceptions and few steps of reasoning. Every face was eager and interested. From right actions, the conversation naturally led into the means of bringing them out. And the necessity of feeling in earnest, of thinking clearly, and of school discipline, was talked over. School discipline was very carefully considered; both Mr. Alcott's duty, and the children's duties, also various means of producing attention, self-control, perseverance, faithfulness. Among these means, punishment was mentioned; and after a consideration of its nature and issues, they all very cheerfully agreed, that it was necessary; and that they preferred Mr. Alcott should punish them, rather than leave them in their faults, and that it was his duty to do so. Various punishments were mentioned, and hurting the body was decided upon, as necessary and desirable in some instances. It was universally admitted that it was desirable, whenever words were found insufficient to command the memory of conscience.

After this conversation, which involved many anecdotes, many supposed cases, and many judgments, Mr. Alcott read "The Peaches," from Krummacher's fables, a story which involves the free action of three boys of different characters; and questioned them respecting their opinion of these boys, and the principles on which it was seen by analysis that they acted. Nearly three hours passed away in this conversation and reading; and then they were asked, how long they had been sitting; none of them thought more than an hour. After recess Mr. Alcott heard them read; and after that, spell. All could read in such a book as Miss Edgeworth's Frank. Each was then asked what he had learned, and having told, they were dismissed one by one. The whole effect of the day seemed to be a combination of quieting influences, with an awakening effect upon the heart and mind . . .

It was soon found that Mr. Alcott, with all his mildness, was very strict. When sitting at their writing, he would not allow the least intercommunication, and every whisper was taken notice of. When they sat in the semicircle around him, they were not only requested to be silent, but to appear attentive to him; and any infringement of the spirit of this rule, would arrest his reading, and he would wait, however long, it might be, until attention was restored. For some time, the acquirement of this habit of stillness and attention was the prominent object; for it was found that many of the children had very little self-control, very weak attention, very self-indulgent habits. Some had no humility, and defended themselves in the wrong; there was some punishment, consisting of impression upon the body, (on the hand;) but still, in every individual instance, it was granted as necessary, not only by the whole school, but, I believe no bodily punishment was given, without the assent of the individual himself, and it was never given in the room. In many of the punishments,—in the pauses of the reading, for instance,—the innocent were obliged to suffer with the guilty. Mr. Alcott wished both parties to feel that this was the inevitable consequence of moral evil in this world; and that the good, in proportion to the depth of their principle, always feel it to be worth while to share the suffering, in order to bring the guilty to rectitude and moral sensibility.

On these occasions, he conversed with them; and, by a series of questions, led them to come to conclusions for themselves upon moral conduct in various particulars; teaching them how to examine themselves, and to discriminate their animal and spiritual natures, or their outward and inward life; and showing them how the inward moulds the outward. They were deeply interested in these conversations, as they would constantly declare; although, at first, those, who were very often revealing to themselves and others their hitherto unrecognized weaknesses and faults, were so deeply mortified, that it was often painful. The youngest scholars were as much interested as the oldest, and although it was necessary to explain language to them rather more, it was found less necessary to reason on moral subjects. They did not so often inquire the history of an idea, or feeling; but they analysed the feelings which prompt action better. It was very striking to see how much nearer the kingdom of heaven (if by this expression is meant the felt authority of moral principles,) were the little children, than were those who had begun to pride themselves on knowing something. We could not but often remark to each other, how unworthy the name of knowledge was that superficial acquirement, which has nothing to do with self-knowledge; and how much more susceptible to the impressions of genius, as well as how much more apprehensive of general truths, were those who had not been hackneyed by a false education . . .

JOURNAL

January 14 . . . He proceeded to the word *type*. What is a type? said he. One boy said, a type is a metal letter which is used to stamp a sign upon paper. What is a word the sign or type of? said Mr. Alcott. They severally said, of a thought; of an idea; of a feeling; of an object; of an action; of a quality. Language, said Mr. Alcott, is typical of whatever goes on within us, or is shaped out of us. What is the body a type of? Of the mind. What is the earth a type of? Of God; mind; heaven; were the several answers. I would go on much farther, said Mr. Alcott, if there was time. There are people who think and say, that the world and outward things are all; because they do not know what they are typical of. I could show you that all outward things are produced out of those spiritual realities, of which they are types. But the clock now typifies the hour of recess: and you may go out . . .

February 2 . . . *Birth* was the first word. Mr. Alcott remarked that we had once before talked of birth, and their ideas had been brought out. Now I am going to speak of it again, and we shall read Mr. Wordsworth's Ode. He then asked the youngest child present, how old he was, and found he was four. The oldest was twelve. He said, that little boy, in four years, has not had time to make that comparison of thoughts and feelings which makes up conscious life. He asked those who understood him, to hold up their hands. Several held up their hands. Those who do not understand these words, may hold up their hands. A great many of the younger ones held up their hands . . .

Mr. Wordsworth had lived, when he wrote this ode, many years, and consequently had felt changes, and he expresses this in the lines I am about to read . . .

> It is not now as it has been of yore,
>   Turn whereso'er I may,
>   By night or day
> The things which I have seen I now can see no more.

He here stopped, and asked why Mr. Wordsworth could not see the things which he had seen before; had they changed, or had he changed? He had changed, said a boy of ten. Have you had any degree of this change? Yes, and more in this last year, than in all my life before. Mr. Alcott said he thought that there were periods in life, when great changes took place: he had experienced it himself.

He then said: but let us all look back six months; how many of you look at things, and feel about them differently from what you did six months ago? How many of you feel that this school-room is a different place from what it was the first week you were here? Almost every one, immediately, with great animation, held up his hand. He then asked those who knew why this was, to hold up their hands. Many did. And when called on to answer, they severally said, because we know more, because we think more, because we understand you, because you know us, because you have looked inside of us. Mr. Alcott said, the place is very different to me; and why? They give similar answers; but he said they had not hit it. At last one said: because we behave better. Yes, said he, you have it now; knowledge is chaff of itself; but you have taken the knowledge and used it to govern yourselves, and to make yourselves better. If I thought I gave you knowledge only, and could not lead you to use it, to make yourselves better, I would never enter this school-room again! . . .

ANALYSIS OF A HUMAN BEING. GENERAL SURVEY OF THE ANALYSIS

Mr. Alcott called the class to analysis, for the last time. He said we had now gone through the scale; but it had often been changed since we began, for almost every week had improved it . . .

We began with Love; and then went to Faith; and then to Conscience, speaking of Obedience, Temptation, and Will; and then to the Appetites, Affections, and Aspirations of the Soul; and then we went to Mind, and spoke of Imagination, Judgment, and Insight . . .

He here stopped and said that one of the boys in this school had said that he did not know before he came to this school, that he had inward eyes; but now he felt that they were open. They began to guess who it was, but they did not guess the right one. Mr. Alcott said that many of them, when they came, were blind, were in midnight. And then he went on reading different passages of the Gospels. He ended with, the light of the body is the eye; what eye? This eye, said a little boy of five. That is the body's eye; what is the spirit's eye? That eye which can see every thing that it wants to see, and which can see God; the body's eye cannot see what it wants to, but the spirit's eye can; and Mr. Alcott, I think that when we are asleep, the spirit goes out of the body, and leaves the body dead; and bye and bye it goes back again, and makes the body alive again. But is the body entirely dead, in sleep? said Mr. Alcott. Why, perhaps a little spirit stays in the body to keep it alive. But almost all the spirit goes out, and sees and hears with its inward eyes and ears, and that is dreaming . . .

Who think that we must know ourselves, in order to know God? All. Who thinks he cannot know God, till he knows himself a great deal? All. Who think that they can know God by studying outward things? None. What are outward things? Shadows of inward things, said the little girl, who was generally the subject of analysis. The Representation of Mind, said a boy of nine. Who was called the Image of God? Jesus Christ, said the whole school. Yes, the outward world is the image of the perfect Mind; and Jesus Christ was the Image of God; or his nature was all Spirit, as he said. Who think that until we study ourselves, we cannot study outward things to much advantage? Many.

Mr. Alcott then remarked that many naturalists who never studied themselves, but studied outward things, did not believe in any spirit; and some who believed in spirit, yet did not think it was the most important, and did not therefore believe in Christianity, or what Jesus Christ taught about spirit. Others have gone out into the outward world, thinking it a shadow of the inward, and followed on until they found the Spirit that was in themselves, and God. One boy said, if I study botany, can I go from it and find God? Mr. Alcott explained, but I could not hear him, as he walked to a place, where he stood with his back to me . . .

I intend you shall learn outward things too: I shall get people to come and tell you about many outward things, which I do not know much about myself. I can teach better about the inward things. Next quarter I am going to teach you about inward things, not in yourselves, but in another—a Perfect Being. In Jesus Christ? asked some. Yes; we will study Jesus Christ; how many will be glad to do this? They all held up their hands. How many have learned something from the analysis—they are very sure; they know it? Almost all held up their hands. How many are sorry these lessons are over? Several. Some said they were glad the next subject was coming. Who would like to hear the Record of the Analysis read? All.

Mr. Alcott then recurred to the blackboard, and said he would read the scale. This diagram had been altered, many times, during the quarter. It was intended merely to systematize the conversations in a degree; and never was presented to the children as a complete map of the mind. Some have objected to these diagrams, as if they would be fetters on the minds of the children. But their constant renewal and changes preclude the possibility of their being regarded as any thing but what they are. After having read the scale through, he began at the end asking the meaning of each word, and as they were defined, he obliterated them, until all were gone.

CONCLUSION

It may seem to some persons rather out of place, to bring philosophy to bear upon taking care of babies. But here is the starting point of education . . . The principles growing out of the few primal facts of human nature which are stated above, carried out into the whole education—this is Mr. Alcott's system. He would teach children to discriminate spiritual happiness from that bodily ease and enjoyment, which too often takes its place; to cherish the principle of love, by feeding it on beauty and good, and not on illusion; and to clarify and strengthen faith, by getting knowledge in the right way; not by accumulation, but by growth; for there is something at the foundation of the human soul, analogous to the organization of a plant, which does indeed feed on the earth from which it springs, the air in which it flourishes, the light of heaven which comes upon it from afar; but which admits nothing that it cannot assimilate to itself. We may assist a plant, if we will study its nature, but there are things which might be put round one plant, which would destroy another. And so we may assist a soul; but there is only one way. We must study its nature; we must offer the individual those elements alone, which it needs, and at the time it needs them, and never too much, and always enough. Then we shall find that each soul has a form, a beauty, a purpose of its own. And we shall also find, that there are a few general conditions never to be shut out: that, as the light of heaven, the warmth of earth, and space to expand, are necessary to the plants; so knowledge of God, the sympathy of human love, and liberty to act from within outward, are indispensable to the soul.

7. Amos Bronson Alcott (1799–1888)
Conversations with Children on the Gospels

[At the age of seventy-eight Bronson Alcott meditated on himself:

My long apprenticeship in the school of leisure appears to be drawing to a close, and it is coming none too soon for one who has come to something like late ripeness of gifts for usefulness in his time. It was taken at first with not a little of restlessness, and a sense of injustice withal; but the passage of years brought reconcilement, and, I may add, acceptance, as it were the drill of discipline for such as myself, without which I might have proved a waste power in my time.

That he should complacently regard seventy-eight years of his life as a preparation, and congratulate himself upon schooling himself to so extended a leisure—combined with the fact that his success had been paid for by the killing exertions of his wife and daughters and by the charity of his friends—summarizes the career of this Transcendental egoist who was also the movement's preëminent saint, and furthermore one of the shrewdest judges of men and events in recorded American history.

He was born in rural poverty, at Spindel Hill near Wolcott, Connecticut, and had little or no formal schooling. From 1818 to 1822 he was a Yankee peddler, mainly in Virginia, where he learned grand manners from the planters. He taught schools in small Connecticut towns where, with some help from stray books but mainly out of his own invention, he made such innovations as organized play, the honor system, pleasant rooms, and the abolition of physical chastisement. In 1828 he opened a school in Boston, heard the Boston ministers, and—although he was older than the rest of the younger group, his lack of formal education enabled him to respond to the new stimulations—began to read the new authors.

In 1830 he married Abigail May, who always adored him. He and she conducted a school in Germantown, Pennsylvania, 1831–1834 (where he read Coleridge with avidity), returned to Boston in 1834, and in September he opened the Temple School.

The failure and collapse of this enterprise, with all its scandal, left him with no occupation, crying in his solitude:

> Save me, O ye destinies, from idleness, from tame and servile engagements, from compliance with the vulgar aims and pursuits of my age! Lift me above its low maxims, and make me a light shining amidst darkness!

He conducted "conversations"—on the principle of "Only God defines, man can but confine"—lived mainly in Concord (largely on Emerson's bounty), had a triumphal visit to London in 1842 (financed by Emerson and other friends), and in 1844 tried the disastrous experiment of a communal society at Fruitlands, near Harvard, Massachusetts. The success of Louisa's *Little Women* in 1868 supplied him with comfort. He did yeoman service after 1859 as superintendent of the Concord public schools, and in 1879 presided as the venerable "Dean" of the Concord School of Philosophy.

After the publication of Elizabeth Peabody's *Record*, Alcott began a series of conversations on the Old Testament on Sunday mornings, and in November of 1836 a Friday-evening series on the life of Christ. Dr. Channing grew alarmed, and Alcott murmured, "Whence this pusillanimity of mind in one whom the nations deem the brave and bold defender of sacred truth?"—without, however, bethinking himself for a moment of altering his own course. In the autumn of 1835 he devoted his school to a study of the Gospels, in the method already publicized by the *Record*. Emerson came and approved; Elizabeth Peabody again took notes. Then he determined to publish this account as a logical sequel to the *Record*. Elizabeth took flight and begged him not to include in the work the "questionable parts" on birth and circumcision which she had omitted from the manuscript. Alcott serenely replaced her expurgations in the form of "Notes," and the first volume of *Record of Conversations on the Gospels Held in Mr. Alcott's School, Unfolding the Doctrine and Discipline of Human Culture* was published on December 22, 1836. The second volume was ready early in 1837, and Alcott confidently awaited vindication from liberal and Unitarian Boston.

It seemed to him a natural progression from the elementary level of the *Record* to an application of his method to the Gospels. That he should so reason indicates the religious motive that is the very heart of Transcendentalism. Actually, he aimed not so much at instructing the children about the Bible as using them for an instrument of research. They were to be a litmus paper for testing the true meaning of the New Testament, in order to bring that meaning "within the *apprehension* of *adults.*"

> To *investigate the Consciousness of Childhood,* as to the *Life of Christ,* is to bring as *Evidence of Christianity* all that belongs to the *Young Being.* If these *testimonies* of *children,* confirm the views of adults—that *Christianity is grounded in the essential Nature of Man*—then shall I add . . . to its claims upon our faith . . . No attempt has been made, as yet on truly philosophic principles, to investigate the grounds of our Nature, as developed either in childhood or maturity, for the facts of which Christianity is the Exponent.

Accepting the Transcendental thesis that Christianity is valid, not because it is recorded in history and attested by miracles, but because it coincides with the intuitive religion of nature—and adding to this the Transcendental supposition that the natural intuition is freshest and least unspoiled in children—Alcott employed the children as divining rods for a proper reading of the text. Thus he was laying aside—as utterly useless—the whole apparatus of historical scholarship. As he read his galleys he noted that several works "of this character" were appearing —Emerson's, Brownson's, Furness', Ripley's—and he thoroughly expected that his should be received along with theirs, not merely as the account of an educational experiment, but as a contribution toward constructive theology.]

EDITOR'S PREFACE

The work now presented to the reader, forms the introduction to a course of conversations with children, on the Life of Christ, as recorded in the Gospels. It is the Record of an attempt to unfold the Idea of Spirit from the Consciousness of Childhood; and to trace its Intellectual and Corporeal Relations; its Temptations and Disciplines; its Struggles and Conquests, while in the Flesh. To this end, the character of Jesus has been presented to the consideration of children, as the brightest Symbol of Spirit; and they have been encouraged to express their views regarding it. The Conductor of these conversations has reverently explored their consciousness, for the testimony which it might furnish in favor of the truth of Christianity.

Assuming as a fact the spiritual integrity of the young mind, he was desirous of placing under the inspection of children, a character so much in conformity with their own, as that of Jesus of Nazareth. He believed that children would as readily apprehend the divine beauty of this character, when rightly presented, as adults. He even hoped that, through their simple consciousness, the Divine Idea of a Man, as Imaged in Jesus, yet almost lost to the world, might be revived in the mind of adults, who might thus be recalled into the spiritual kingdom. These views, confirmed by long intimacy with the young, as well as by the tendency of his own mind to regard the bright visions of childhood, as the promise of the soul's future blessedness; as the loadstar to conduct it through this terrestrial Life, led him to undertake this enterprise, and to prosecute it with a deep and kindling interest, which he feels will continue unabated to its close. . . .

CONVERSATION VIII. NATIVITY OF SPIRIT. FAMILY RELATION

Idea of Birthplace and Birth

MR. ALCOTT . . . Now what came into your minds while I was reading?

JOSIAH. The deserts seemed to me a great space covered with sand, like that in the hour-glass. The sun was shining on it, and making it sparkle. There were no trees. John was there alone.

EDWARD J. I thought the deserts meant woods, with paths here and there.

LUCY. I thought of a space covered with grass and some wild flowers, and John walking about.

CHARLES. I thought of a prairie.

ALEXANDER. I thought of a rocky country.

AUGUSTINE. I thought of a few trees scattered over the country, with bees in the trunks.

GEORGE K. I thought of a place without houses, excepting John's; and flowers, trees, and bee-hives.

Birth

MR. ALCOTT. I should like to hear all your pictures, but as I have not time, you may tell me now what interested you most?

CHARLES. The prophecy of Zacharias.

LUCIA. Elisabeth's saying the child's name must be John.

LUCY. Zacharias finding his speech again.

ANDREW. The birth of the child.

MR. ALCOTT. How was it?

ANDREW. I thought, one night, as Elisabeth was sleeping, an angel brought her a child, and made her dream she had one, and she awoke and it was lying at her side.

WILLIAM B. I think he was born like other children except that Elisabeth had visions.

GEORGE K. I thought God sent an angel to give her a child. It cried as soon as it came and waked up its mother to give it something to eat.

LUCIA. When John was first born, his mother did not know it, for he was born in the night; but she found it by her side in the morning.

CHARLES. Elisabeth must have had some vision as well as Zacharias, or how could she know the child was theirs? Zacharias could not speak.

NATHAN. I don't see why John came in the night. All other children come in the day.

Sacredness of Birth

MR. ALCOTT. No; more frequently in the night. God draws a veil over these sacred events, and they ought never to be thought of except with reverence. The coming of a spirit is a great event. It is greater than death. It should free us from all wrong thoughts. (See Note 85.)

NOTE 85

MR. ALCOTT. And now I don't want you to speak; but to hold up your hands, if you have ever heard any disagreeable or vulgar things about birth. (*None raised hands.*)

Men have been brought before Courts of Justice for saying vulgar things about the birth of Christ; and all birth is sacred as Jesus Christ's. And I have heard of children saying very profane things about it; and have heard fathers and mothers do so. I hope that none of us will ever violate the sacredness of this subject.

Travail of Body with Spirit

MR. ALCOTT . . . What is meant by "delivered"?

WILLIAM B. She delivered her child to Zacharias.

OTHERS. No; God delivered the child to Elisabeth.

CHARLES. Elisabeth's thoughts made the child's soul, and when it was fairly born she was delivered from the anxiety of the thought.*

* MR. ALCOTT. Yes, the deliverance of the spirit is the first thing. And I am glad to find, that you have so strong an impression of that. The physiological facts, sometimes referred to, are only a sign of the spiritual birth. You have seen the rose opening from the seed with the assistance of the atmosphere; this is the birth of the rose. It typifies the bringing forth of the spirit, by pain, and labor, and patience. (See Note 86.)

NOTE 86

MR. ALCOTT. Edward B., it seems, had some profane notions of birth, connected with some physiological facts; but they were corrected here. Did you ever hear this line,
"The throe of suffering is the birth of bliss"?

GEORGE K. Yes; it means that Love, and Joy, and Faith, lead you to have suffering, which makes more happiness for you.

MR. ALCOTT. Yes; you have the thought. And a mother suffers when she has a child. When she is going to have a child, she gives up her body to God, and he works upon it, in a mysterious way, and with her aid, brings forth the Child's Spirit in a little Body of its own, and when it has come, she is blissful. But I have known some mothers who are so timid that they are not willing to bear the pain; they fight against God, and suffer much more.

CHARLES. I should think it ought to be the father, he is so much stronger.

MR. ALCOTT. He suffers because it is his part to see the suffering in order to relieve it. But it is thought, and with good reason, that if there were no wrong doing there would be no suffering attending this mysterious act. When Adam and Eve did wrong, it was said that Adam

Emblems of Birth

MR. ALCOTT. You may give me some emblems of birth.

ALEXANDER. Birth is like the rain. It comes from heaven.

LUCIA. I think it is like a small stream coming from a great sea; and it runs back every night, and so becomes larger and larger every day, till at last it is large enough to send out other streams.

LEMUEL. Lives streamed from the ocean first; now smaller streams from the larger ones, and so on.

SAMUEL R. Birth is like the rising light of the sun; the setting is death.

ANDREW. God's wind came upon the ocean of life, and washed up the waters a little into a channel, and that is birth. They run up farther, and that is living.

MR. ALCOTT. I should like to have all your emblems but have not time. There is no adequate sign of birth in the outward world, except the physiological facts that attend it, with which you are not acquainted . . .

Analysis of the Prophecy of Zacharias

MR. ALCOTT . . . How had the Lord "visited his people"?

LEMUEL. He had visited their spirits.

FRANKLIN. By sending John to tell that Jesus was coming.

MR. ALCOTT. What is it to redeem a people?

LUCIA. To make them good.

EDWARD B. To save them from sin.

MR. ALCOTT. A man who loves to eat and drink, an intemperate man, a passionate man, is a slave to the body; and when his spirit is released from his body, by renewing thoughts, that withdraw his attention from his body, he is redeemed, just as a prisoner taken out of a dungeon is said to be redeemed from captivity. What is meant by "horn of salvation"?

CHARLES. A great deal of mercy.

MR. ALCOTT. What is meant by "house of David"?

FRANKLIN. Jesus was a descendant of David.

MR. ALCOTT. What enemies are mentioned here?

CHARLES. Spiritual enemies.

MR. ALCOTT. What fathers are meant here?

CHARLES. All good people who went before.

---

should earn bread by the sweat of his brow, and Eve have pain in bringing her children into the world. We never hear of trees groaning to put forth their leaves.

CHARLES. They have no power to do wrong.

MR. ALCOTT. True; God only gives them power to put forth, and they do it without pain. A rose has no pain in being born.

MR. ALCOTT. What is "holy covenant"? (*No answer*.) It is a promise, on condition of holiness, of giving blessings. And the oath? (*Here it was found necessary to discriminate between profane swearing and judicial oaths, which they had confounded*.) Is there any such promise to us, as was made by that covenant?

CHARLES. It is made to all good people.

MR. ALCOTT. What is meant by "prophet of the highest"?

CHARLES. Announcer of Jesus Christ.

MR. ALCOTT. What is it to "give knowledge of salvation"?

CHARLES. To tell us how to be good, and forgive our sins that are repented of.

MR. ALCOTT. What is "day-spring"?

CHARLES. Righteousness, wisdom.

MR. ALCOTT. What is it to "sit in darkness"?

CHARLES. To be wicked.

Emblems of John and Jesus

MR. ALCOTT. If John was the day-spring, who was the risen sun?

ALL. Jesus.

MR. ALCOTT. What is it to "wax strong in spirit"?

CHARLES. To stand fast by God.

FRANKLIN. To grow better and better.

MR. ALCOTT reads. "And he was in the deserts."

CHARLES. In the country; at his father's house.

Prejudice

MR. ALCOTT. Why are Jews held in such contempt, when Jesus was born a Jew?

FRANKLIN. Because they killed Jesus, and said, "his blood be on us and our children."

EDWARD B. And Jews are mean, avaricious. (*Mr. Alcott explained the last characteristics by the oppressions they had suffered*.)

MR. ALCOTT. Who think it is a wicked prejudice?

WELLES. It is a right prejudice.

ALL. There are no right prejudices.

Subject

MR. ALCOTT. What has been the subject of this conversation?

NATHAN. Putting spirits into bodies.

MR. ALCOTT. And the nativity, or birth of spirit in the flesh.

5

Miracles

I am not aware that Mr. Norton reduced these principles to the form of a connected system, or that he would not have shrunk from the ultimate consequences which they involved. He held them, I think, as incidental to certain theories of dogmatic theology . . . but that their spirit pervaded his writings . . . will not, I believe, be called in question by those who are the most intimately acquainted with the character of his mind and the tendency of his opinions. The influence of Mr. Norton in philosophy, however, was provocative rather than creative; he led to doubt with regard to the ancient foundations rather than to sympathy with his peculiar ideas; he prepared the way for vigorous combat, and not for docile acceptance; and, like the influence of Hume on the virile mind of Kant . . . he inspired not a few of the earnest-minded young men of the day with a passionate zeal for the conquest of the holy Grail,—the discovery of the golden chalice which was brimming with pure wine for the life of the soul.

—GEORGE RIPLEY

1. Andrews Norton (1786–1853)
Ripley's Martineau

[Only a fool or a genius could have so fatally misconceived his surroundings as did Bronson Alcott—and he was both. He should have been thoroughly warned. In the September 1836 number of *The Christian Examiner* —obviously as a counterweight to Brownson's exposition of Cousin—the editors printed the Dudleian lecture given at Harvard the previous May. It was perfectly designed to mark the parting of the ways, and Orville Dewey (1794–1882) was prepared to mark it.

A Williams graduate, class of 1814, Dewey was brought up a Calvinist and had learned his theology at Andover; only thereafter did he become a Unitarian, and he always carried the imprint of his orthodox youth. He served as colleague to Dr. Channing, 1821–1823, and in 1836 had just begun a remarkably successful pastorate at the Second Congregational Church in New York City. He was fully aware, as he delivered this lecture, of the mounting strength of the heresy, and he went to the point more aggressively than his Harvard-trained brethren were yet capable of doing. Christianity, he said, must be vouched for by miracles or else there is no Christianity. The reason is clear: otherwise man is left entirely to himself, and he is too miserable and fallible a creature to attain truth out of his own resources. Edwards himself would hardly have expressed so low an estimate of human powers as did this liberal Unitarian under the stress of the Transcendental challenge:

> Humanity, in fine, especially in its growing cultivation, has too hard a lot, it appears to me, if God has not opened for it the fountains of revelation. Without that great disclosure from above, human nature stands, in my contemplation of it, as an anomaly amidst the whole creation. The noblest existence on earth is not provided with a resource even so poor as instinct. On the heart that is made to bear the weight of infinite interests, sinks the crushing burthen of doubt and despondency, of fear and sorrow, of pain and death, without resource or relief, or comfort, or hope. The cry of the young ravens, the buzzing of insect life in every hedge, is heard; but the call, that comes up from the deep and dark conflict of the over-shadowed soul, dies upon the vacant air; and there is no ear to hear, nor eye to pity. Oh! were it so, what could sustain the human heart sinking under the burthen of its noblest aspirations? "The still, sad music of humanity," sounding on through all time, would lose every soothing tone, and would become a wail, in which the heart of the world would die!

By insinuating a line from Wordsworth, Dewey carried the counterattack into insurgent territory; the frankness with which, in the next number of the *Examiner,* Ripley utilized Martineau was largely provoked by Dewey. The issue was now clear: the division was over the nature of man—of the natural man. Although Unitarianism had been dedicated by Dr. Channing to an assertion of the rational dignity of man as against the debasements of Calvinism, still, when confronted with the Transcendental glorification, they refused to go so far as to permit a man to discover religion for himself without "supernatural" assistance. In Dewey's view, Transcendentalism was simply bringing the defenseless creature face-to-face again with the Calvinist Jehovah, and was renouncing everything that had been won; in Transcendental eyes, Dewey was a renegade to Channing's prophecy. The crucial matter was, therefore, the miracles; hence the war in New England, between 1836 and 1841—although it involved a larger strategy—was fought on this limited front.

The opening gun was fired on the morning of Saturday, November 5, 1836, as *The Boston Daily Advertiser* (XLII, 13933) carried a letter from Andrews Norton, which he submitted to the newspaper because, as he explained, the editors of *The Christian Register* were reluctant, "from personal considerations," to publish it.

Andrews Norton, born in Hingham and graduated from Harvard in 1804, grew up with the cause of liberal Christianity; to him it was the end-all and be-all of the life of the mind. A tutor in 1811, he became Dexter Professor of Sacred Literature in 1819, and thus ruled the Divinity School when Ripley, Emerson, Clarke, Hedge, Furness, and their friends were callow students. He resigned his office in 1830, to devote himself to his forthcoming masterpiece on the "evidence" of Christianity, but he continued to dominate the theological world of Cambridge.

In 1880 George Ripley undertook to reach back into his painful memories and to contribute to *The Memorial History of Boston*, an account of Transcendentalism. He got as far as a sketch of his master and his enemy; the pen literally dropped from his hand as he completed the paragraph used as the motto for this chapter. A few lines before, Ripley paid tribute, out of a magnanimity which was the essence of the man, to the quality that once had been Norton's:

> His thorough scholarship served to give form and substance to the literary enthusiasm which at that time prevailed in Cambridge. His refined and exquisite taste cast an air of purity and elegance around the spirit of the place. His habits were as severe as those of a medieval monk. His love of literature was a passion . . . His hatred of pretension was equalled only by his devotion to truth. He spurned with a beautiful disdain whatever he deemed to be false, or shallow, or insincere.

This was the man who braced himself for the distressing duty of communicating to the vulgar world the tidings that his students were anathema. As a coeditor of the *Examiner*, he served notice that he would no longer be associated with it if it printed such articles—it no longer did!—and he committed the indiscretion of ending with what was to prove the most pathetic of Unitarian defenses, a charge upon the insurgents of professional and academic incompetence.]

To preclude all occasion of mistake I wish distinctly to present to view the sole ground of this communication. It is that, the article in question having appeared in *The Christian Examiner*, others beside the writer seem responsible for the publication of opinions from which they entirely dissent. I have no wish to interfere with the rights of free discussion; but these rights, I may add, are sometimes misunderstood. Without intending any particular or unkind application to the case before us, of which I am not qualified to judge, it may be laid down as a general principle, that he who controverts doctrines, which many, who have thought most concerning them, think of the highest importance to the happiness of man, should thoroughly settle his own belief, that he should satisfy himself that he has ability to discuss the subject and has viewed it, as far as possible, in all its bearings, and that he should further be convinced, after very serious considerations, that the promulgation of his views will serve the interests of truth and goodness. Let him then publish them in such a form, as far as may be, that they will first go into the hands only of those who are capable of judging of their correctness.

2. George Ripley (1802–1880)
To Andrews Norton

[Ripley worked hard and fast that week end, and his reply was in *The Boston Daily Advertiser* on Wednesday, November 9, 1836 (XLII, 13936).

Because the clergy of eastern Massachusetts were almost solidly Harvard alumni, Norton's charge raised an issue which today we would more concisely recognize as that of "academic freedom." The issue quickly was crossed—as it usually is—with the problem of scholarly competence: who is to determine, not only the right to speak, but the reliability of the speaker? Ripley marshaled an array of scholarship, citing theologians from Chrysostom to Coleridge, but the essence of his—and of the Transcendentalists'—position he put succinctly in the following paragraphs.]

DEAR SIR, I was glad to perceive that the views presented by me in the last number of the Christian Examiner were of sufficient importance to attract your attention. I was still more glad to find that you thought them worthy of so much notice, as to require you to disavow in a public print, under your own name, all responsibility for their publication. Nothing seems to me more desirable than a frank expression of opinion on all subjects, which involve important interests, whether of science or of conduct; and I rejoice that you have set the example of an open disclaimer of certain views which I have defended in the article alluded to. It will create a fresh interest in the subject, and lead to a more thorough examination of my opinions, than I could have ventured to hope, from the imperfect manner in which they are set forth.

With regard to the mode, in which you declare your want of agreement with my article, and the step you propose to take in consequence thereof, I have nothing to say; it is a question of individual taste with which no one has a right to interfere. There is, indeed, a tone in your remarks, slightly suppressed, which a stranger to both of us might think betrayed more of the *odium theologicum* than of personal friendship; but presuming that this is not the case, I shall reply to them in the spirit of candor and clarity, by which I will not doubt that they were suggested. I must forget the benefits I have received from the severity of your taste and the minuteness of your learning in a former pupilage, before I can persuade myself to discuss any subject with you in a manner incompatible with your superiority in years and attainments to myself.

I will add, at the same time, that if you find heresies in my Review, I also find them in your comments upon it; but we are both too deeply laden with offences of that kind, to make the spectacle of our flinging stones at each other any thing but ludicrous . . .

Those who are aware of your position in society, your eminence among learned theologians, your freedom of speculation, and the exceeding deference, which for many reasons, we have all been wont to pay to your opinions, will perceive the necessity under which I labor, of doing what I can to turn aside the sharp edge of your denunciation. You have presented me, without the usual formalities of prosecution, before the jury of my fellow citizens, as a dangerous man. You have declared, with singular indefiniteness, that I have uttered views "vitally injurious to the cause of religion," "tending to destroy faith in the only evidence of Christianity—as a revelation;" and you also intimate, that I have done this rashly and unadvisedly, without a wise regard "to the interests of truth and goodness."

A certain sense of decorum, then, towards that portion of the public, whose servant I am, towards my neighbors and friends, with whom I live in relations of mutual trust, forces me to give them a distinct opportunity of judging between you and myself. If you are right, I am unworthy of the confidence, they are pleased to repose in me: if you are wrong, it is due to them that they should be made to know it . . .

The evidence of miracles depends on a previous belief in Christianity, rather than the evidence of Christianity on a previous belief in miracles. In presenting the argument for our faith to an unbeliever, I would begin with establishing its coincidence with the divine testimony of our spiritual nature; and having done that I would proceed to shew the probability of miracles. This, Sir, I suppose is the view for which you are unwilling to be responsible. I am not now required to defend it in its scientific form . . . I am only called upon here to shew that this view is not likely to be so disastrous to our community as you seem to imagine. It will be sufficient for my defence, in this regard, to demonstrate that it is no theological novelty of my own, but one which has had the sanction of devout and thinking minds in every age of the Church. In proof of this, I shall appeal to the Scriptures, to the Fathers, to the Reformers and early Protestants, and to theologians of the present day . . .

As to modern theologians I need not tell you that it is in the country of

Luther, that the science of theology has received its greatest developments, since the time of the Reformation. You are aware that every topic of this science has been discussed there with freedom, learning and strenuous industry. The attacks which were made upon the truth of the miracles, in the early stages of modern German theology, of course gave rise to a profound examination of their character and validity. The result is that they who hold to the reality of the Christian miracles, have been forced to adopt the mode of proof which I have exhibited in the article under consideration. Instead of resting the doctrine on the miracles they rest the miracles on the doctrine . . .

I must own that I am not aware of the reception of these views, to any considerable extent, among English or American theologians. But for many years before I knew any thing of German theology, they seemed so rational, so satisfactory, so entirely in accordance with the present state of science, that I maintained them as I had opportunity; and I cannot conceal my wonder that their expression in the Examiner should have caused you either surprise or regret . . .

I have thus presented some proofs which may shew that I did not utter my opinion without thought or from a vain love of novelty. I am as firmly persuaded of the truth and importance of my views as you are of your own. Perhaps I am not less deeply or practically interested in the progress of religious truth, the cause of human happiness, than yourself. At all events, I would lay no restriction upon the free discussion of the former, or upon any honest efforts for the promotion of the latter. We live in an age of scepticism and vague thought on many of the most important subjects of belief; but for myself I am certain that no cold reserve, no coward fear, no spiritual despotism can remove or mitigate the evil. We want scientific inquiry and discussion, in which the love of truth shall be blended with a heartfelt trust in its power. I see most clearly the work that is to be done for this age, before a return to deep religious conviction is possible. Would that you and others to whom the gift is granted might engage in the work with such wisdom and energy as to prevent so obscure a pen as mine from being called before the public.

There is one thing, Sir, in your article which I confess struck me with much surprise. I allude to the appeals you have made to the fears of the uninstructed. You have not shewn me wherein I have erred. You have made no attempt to set me right. You merely say that my opinions are dangerous, without giving a hint as to the means of their correction. I had thought that we lived at too late a day for this. I had thought that we had breathed the air of freedom too long, to substitute an appeal to popular prejudice in the place of reason and argument. The same course, Sir, that you have taken, has been pursued before against the innovator on traditional ideas. A similar charge was brought against our Saviour by the Pharisees and against the Apostle Paul by the Ephesians. It was uttered by Athanasius against Arius and by Augustine against Pelagius. It has been uttered by monks and inquisitors in all ages, against those who united a free spirit with a frank and fearless zeal. I have found from the whole current of Christian history, that it has seldom been successful to attempt the destruction of an opinion in this mode. The truth has usually survived though the advocate thereof has perished. I would be far, Sir, from impairing your legitimate influence in our theological circles, but when you so far forget the principles of our Protestant fathers, as to wish to place shackles upon the press and to drown the voice of discussion by the cry of alarm, I must take leave to say, that I regret to see you manifesting the spirit of a class of men, who are too well known in the annals of the Church, and with whom I would gladly hope that few among us have any thing in common.

I will add in conclusion, that I have no hope, in these remarks of gaining your assent to the doctrine which I believe. Our differences of opinion arise from a radical difference in our philosophical views. You are a disciple of the school which was founded by Locke—the successor of Hobbes and the precursor of Condillac and Voltaire. For that philosophy I have no respect. I believe it to be superficial, irreligious and false in its primary elements. The evils it has brought upon humanity, by denying to the mind the power of perceiving spiritual truth, are great and lamentable. They have crept over Theology, Literature, Art, and Society. This age has no higher mission than to labor for their cure. I wish to go back to the philosophy of the most enlightened Fathers, to that of the giants of English theology in the days of their unshorn strength, to that lofty spiritual faith which is now held by the most eminent philosophers of the continent of Europe. With the prevalence of this philosophy, a true reform of theology may be predicted; and the living and practical faith of the heart take the place of bondage to a dead letter.

3. Samuel Osgood (1812–1880)

Emerson's Nature

[Graduating from the Harvard Divinity School in 1833, James Freeman Clarke faced the choice of remaining in New England or of going West "to build up a society there." He elected the West, fearing "that if I were settled in an old-fashioned Unitarian society I should gradually subside into routine." The break between the generations was thus, three years before any would openly acknowledge it, an accomplished fact: the most brilliant of the Divinity School's products could see the conventional Harvard man's future only as a gradual subsiding into routine.

Along with Clarke went William G. Eliot and Ephraim Peabody. In 1835 they established in Cincinnati a periodical, advertised as containing "Unitarian views of Christianity," called *The Western Messenger*. The movers, even while responding to their new surroundings, remained Harvard men. Eventually all but one found their way back to New England. (And in Eliot's case, if he himself did not, it remained for his grandson to take the road of the back-trailer.)

Thus, in faraway Cincinnati, the *Messenger* became an organ of insurgent, younger Unitarian opinion, even before insurgency in the homeland had found more of a voice than the Transcendental Club. In the number for December 1836 Clarke praised Furness' *Remarks,* openly declaring that graduates of divinity schools, being taught the conventional doctrine of miracles, emerged with their faith destroyed. If despite their tuition they are saved, he declared—revealing how much he and his generation had imbibed the Germanic terminology—it was "because the heart instructed by God, is wiser than the head taught of men."

So the *Messenger* saluted Furness with greater joy than could *The Christian Examiner,* and also "the author of an article in the last Christian Examiner, upon Martineau's lectures." In a few days Clarke heard of Norton's attack and in his January number deplored the action of Unitarianism's greatest scholar. He insisted that Jesus never worked a miracle until He had first gained faith. Hence the notice of Emerson's *Nature* that he published in the same issue was clearly designed to accentuate the position to which the editors of the *Messenger* had long since come, in opposition to the "old-fashioned Unitarian society" from which they sprang.

Samuel Osgood, born in Charlestown and graduated from Harvard in 1832, was a friend of Clarke. Upon leaving the Divinity School in 1835, he hastened to Cincinnati, and for two years worked with the *Messenger* contingent. In 1837 he returned to New England; after 1849 he was a Unitarian minister in New York, until in 1869 he resigned his pulpit and took orders in the Episcopal Church. Thus he was considered to be one of the many casualties of Transcendentalism.

In *The Western Messenger* for January 1837 (II, 385–393), Osgood was still the vibrant revolutionary. Introducing his review of *Nature* by a quotation from Wordsworth, he served notice upon Norton that Emerson spoke for a world-wide movement, but as a member of the New England cell, he still insisted that Emerson was a Christian because *Nature* is the essence of Christianity. Furthermore— Osgood having encountered the facts of Western civilization—he underscored the positions in Emerson's little book which most challenged the powers of the new society. Thus he first made evident that Transcendentalism was bound, sooner or later, to confront the problem of upon what terms it could live with America.

For Osgood—as for many of Emerson's younger contemporaries—the issue seemed obvious: the new philosophy was unalterably opposed to the "practical" men, to the bankers and the railroad executives who utilized nature without the slightest appreciation of its emblematic character.]

It would be interesting to study the Poetry, Philosophy and Religion of Mankind, in the different stages of its progress, in order to learn the various views and sentiments with which Nature has been regarded. Such a study would lead us to consider all periods of our race:—the infant period when the heart of man had the freshness of childhood, and in childish wonder, he saw Nature clad with the freshness of its new born beauty: the savage period, when man looked upon Nature, only as a means of supplying his physical wants, or drew from it a language for his passions; it would lead us to consider the mystic period in human progress, when as in the central oriental world, Nature was regarded as a dreamy shadow, and the indolent soul, absorbed in its own fond visions, scorned the world of matter as being unreal, or shrunk from it as contaminating: then would come before our view, the period in which the material universe engrossed the mind, and the soul was too intent on the finite to rise to the infinite, and that Grecian taste for beauty prevailed, which admired the beautiful in form, without recognising the spiritual beauty, of which all that is divine in form, is but the faint emblem: then comes the period in which Nature is prized, mainly for her physical uses—the age of natural science and material utility. In this latter period we find our own lot to be cast, and should rejoice to find ourselves emerging from it. We should rejoice at those signs, that are appearing, which promise that Nature shall ere long have her due, and be looked on with the right spirit—that a day is coming, when the world around us shall be regarded, not only for its material uses, but shall be loved as the emblem of the Divine Beauty, and reverenced as being instinct with the Divine Spirit, and an expression of the Divine Wisdom, Love and Power. When this day comes, man will look on Nature with the same eye, as when in the Eden of primitive innocence and joy, and at the same time, with all the lights which science and varied experience afford.

Christianity teaching the immortality of the soul, and revealing to us God in all things, has been the cause of this happy change. It puts a spiritual aspect on all things—on all Providence and all creation. It forbids our being lost in the mazes of the Infinite. It teaches us to ascend to the Infinite from the Finite. It does not take us away from Nature, but in Nature shows to us our God.

Now certainly all those books, which throw a religious light on Nature, should be encouraged by all, who wish to redeem the souls of men from the thraldom of the senses: not only those books which exhibit the argument for religion, drawn from a view of those final causes, which a scientific view of Nature gives, but those which shew the correspondence of the material world, with our own higher nature, and teach us to look on Nature with the spiritual eye—with something of that same spirit in which God made his creation.

The strong hold, which Coleridge and Wordsworth have taken, of so many minds, while it confers a high honor on their sublime genius, also shews, that they have but given expression to thoughts and feelings, which before existed and were growing in the minds of their readers. We rejoice at the influence of such poets. We rejoice that a poetry of Nature, truly Christian, is springing up among us. We rejoice, that those to whom it is given to pass within the veil, and to see in Nature a Beauty, that is hid to common eyes, have so made the Beautiful minister to the Good and True. We hail with joy every inspiration of genius, which connects sentiment with religion. But it is a rightful minister of religion. The Beautiful is the rightful priest of the True—none the less so, because the priest sometimes deserts his proper altar, and beauty of sentiment is made to throw its garlands around the altar of vice and sensuality.

In our own bustling country, where banks, steam boats and rail roads seem to engross the nation's attention, we are happy to find some spirits, who keep aloof from the vulgar melee, and in calm of soul, live for Nature and for God. No greater exception to the common spirit of our nation, could be pointed out, than the author of a little work, recently published at the East . . .

The many will call this book dreamy, and perhaps it is so. It may indeed naturally seem, that the author's mind is somewhat onesided, that he has not mingled enough with common humanity, to avoid running into eccentricity, that he has been so careful to keep his own individuality, that he has confounded his idiosyncrasies, with universal truth. All this may be. But it is not for the vulgar many to call such a man a dreamer. If he does dream, the many are more deluded dreamers. His dreams are visions of the eternal realities of the spiritual world: their's are of the fleeting phantoms of earth. Indeed the real visionary is not to be found, in the mystic's cell, or the philosopher's study, but in the haunts of busy life. The sensualist is a wretched visionary: he sees but a part, and that but a mean part of the reality of things, and sees all in a false light. The man of ambition is a dreamer. Those men, who pride themselves most on their practical turn of mind, are often far more visionary, than their more romantic neighbors, whom they are accustomed to deride. The veriest votary of Mammon, who makes himself an entire drudge to money getting, and boasts, that while other men are chasing shadows, such shadows, as beauty in nature and art, or truth in science or religion, he alone is grasping the substance; this man is constantly pursuing a phantom—he is chasing a joy, that never comes to him: the future, and dreaming of some distant good, as the reward of his labors, and the enjoyment of his wealth. He dreams and toils, and heaps up his treasures, and forms visions of bliss, which are never realized; never finding the time, in which he may enjoy his wealth, he lives in a realm of illusion, until death, the stern teacher of reality, comes and touches him with his cold hand, and heaped treasures and fond visions at once disappear.

Not so with him, who puts his thoughts on things eternal. He sees the world as it really is. He looks on the temporal in the light of the Eternal. "So he comes to look on the world with new eyes." So he learns the high truths which nature teaches.

4. James Freeman Clarke (1810–1888)
Ripley's Discourses

[News from Boston traveled slowly, so that not until March 1837 could Clarke review Brownson's *New Views* in *The Western Messenger* (III, 529–539). He took his stand firmly: there is no middle ground between the optimism of this work and the despair of Calvinism—Andrews Norton having already assumed precisely the middle ground. In the next issue, for April (III, 576–579), Clarke noticed Ripley's *Discourses*, still assuming, in ignorance of what had happened in Boston, that opposition was to be expected only from orthodox Calvinists.]

We like these Discourses, because they show the happy influence of a higher philosophy than generally prevails—a philosophy of Reason and Faith, and not of sensualism and doubt. We thank heaven, that this philosophy is prevailing, and that the young men of all denominations of Christians are rejoicing in it. We are glad that the day of sensual philosophy is past or passing, and men are believing, that the mind has a nature of its own, and is not a mere creature of circumstance, a result of mere sensation, the sport of casual impressions. We are glad that history is so read, the soul so reflected upon, the divine word so studied, as to prove, that the soul of man has divine elements, and that the Divine Spirit has ministered to it, and does minister to it.

People may croak as much as they please about the vanity of philosophising; such croaking is vanity and folly, for every thinking man will and must philosophise, either rightly or wrongly. Look into the writings of those people, who condemn attempts at philosophising on matters of religion, and you will find, that every paragraph they write shows the traces of their own philosophical system. When they condemn, like a Stuart, the philosophy of Coleridge or Marsh, they show that they are followers of a Locke or Edwards, and that their own cherished system is the reason of their condemning the speculations of their opponents. Thinking people must have a philosophy, for they cannot think, without thinking upon the meaning of words and the nature of things; and they cannot arrive at any conclusions upon these subjects without philosophising. Since the world have been philosophised into sensualism, and sensualism has borne such infernal fruits, it is full time that it should be philosophised into something better. The great minds of the day and age are striving to do this, and have wrought a noble revolution.

5. James Freeman Clarke (1810–1888)
Alcott

[In the same issue (March 1837, III, 540–545) in which he discussed Ripley's *Discourses,* Clarke continued *The Western Messenger's* endorsement of the new school by noticing favorably Alcott's *Conversations*—thus indicating how, to the contemporaneous eye, Alcott's educational program was regarded as an integral part of the philosophical and religious movement. Clarke saw Alcott's book as "a running commentary" upon Brownson's *New Views.* "It argues well for Eclecticism that these two works should issue at the same time, from the same press, in the same city. It is Theory and Practice walking hand in hand."

By the time Clarke was going to press with his May number, he realized what had been happening in Boston. There, in February and March, the newspapers bristled with indignation. This man, said "A Parent" in *The Boston Courier,* is motivated only by a lust for novelty, and so pollutes the moral atmosphere. The editor agreed: the *Conversations* is an indecent book, because Alcott questions his pupils "on subjects which are universally excluded from promiscuous companies of men and women." Then came the crushing blow: the *Courier* quoted a clergyman—nobody had the slightest difficulty recognizing Andrews Norton—as saying that of the *Conversations* "one-third was absurd, one-third blasphemous, and one-third obscene."

Alcott was hooted in the streets; frantic parents withdrew their children from the Temple School, and at the end of March—cruelest of all possible results—when Alcott attempted to explain to Dr. Channing the connection of the divine and the human nature, the peerless Unitarian liberal "expressed great dislike, even horror." But Emerson, who had much to lose by the act, wrote a letter to the *Courier* pointing out the unfairness of the methods used against Alcott and attempting to tell the public what Alcott was after: "He aims to make children think, and, in every question of a moral nature, to send them back on themselves for an answer." To Alcott himself he wrote, on March 25, one of the finest letters in the history of authentic American liberalism:

> I hate to have all the little dogs barking at you, for you have something better to do than attend to them; but every beast must do after his kind, and why not these? And you will hold by yourself, and presently forget them.

Clarke, who also wrote to the *Courier* comparing Alcott to Socrates, spoke out in Cincinnati by quoting long sections of the *Conversations,* which, he said, were adequate refutation of the libels, and to his selections prefaced this declaration (*The Western Messenger,* III, 678–681).]

We could easily imagine that the views contained in it would be misunderstood and disliked by many. For these views were *new.* This opposition, too, was likely to come from the wise and good. For feeling a deep interest in the preservation of sound opinions on religious and moral subjects, the good and wise are always ready to begin the attack on any reformer in religion and morals. They mistake him for a rash and foolish innovator, and until they find out their mistake, they are his worst enemies, afterward his staunchest friends. The Conservatives are a good party, but they are always the first to stone the Prophets and hale them into the prison of misrepresentation and abuse.

Now we are very ready to grant that Mr. Alcott's system and Mr. Alcott's book may have many errors in it; but for all that we maintain him to be a prophet. He has made discoveries, so we think, and poured light on the most important subjects of human interest. His *theories* have been of the greatest practical use to us, and we doubt not that he is a lever by which Providence designs to lift to a higher ground the whole business of education. Thinking this, we cannot stop to find fault till we have said it. Thinking this, we feel bound to say a word in reply to some current objections made to the book by those who, we think, do not yet appreciate its high and extraordinary merits . . .

Now these objections are the very ones which are likely to arise in the mind of a person who opens the book without much previous thought on the subject, and without any practical acquaintance with the difficulties of get-

ting at the minds of children, and what success or failure is in this department . . .

The answers of the children are childish, we grant, but far from being
trifling. Is it not evident that they are always *in earnest,* from the connexion
and closeness of application of all which is said. If any thing is clear, this is
so, that these children are exercising the whole force of their attention upon
the subjects before them. Mr. Alcott, it will be seen, does not suffer the conversation to go on when any sign of carelessness appears. The illustrations
are, no doubt, familiar, and drawn from common place objects. We are very
apt to think and call this irreverent . . . The fact is that if religion is to be
any thing more than a form, it must be spoken of familiarly as a household
thing, and when thus spoken of, men will always cry out "How irreverent."
Most people's respect for religion consists in keeping at a respectful distance
from it. They pay it all outward homage and respect, but take care that it
never comes into their homes and hearts. It is the beauty of Mr. Alcott's plan
that religion becomes a familiar, dear and constant inmate in the heart and
thoughts of the child.

This is perhaps the strongest objection brought against Mr. Alcott's plan,
and therefore we have noticed it first. It is an objection to which all reformers are liable—all who wish to change a formal and ceremonious worship into
a living and real one. Another which is dwelt upon a good deal lies against
the method. Mr. Alcott is blamed because he does not teach his own opinions
directly, but rather leads on the mind of the child. This method is unusual
we know, but not unprecedented. The dogmatic style of teaching is the most
common, and on most subjects the right one. But Mr. Alcott has at least one
illustrious precedent to justify him—namely, Socrates. Those who remember
the admirable conversations of that great sage preserved by Xenophon, will
be struck to see how closely and successfully Mr. Alcott has copied his plan
of teaching. The object of Socrates was to lead on and bring out the mind of
his pupil rather than to impress his own opinions, and we certainly think it
the best method of teaching morality. It makes the impression deep, vivid,
and permanent . . .

Another great fear is of errors of opinion, false views, &c. &c. This is the
great bugbear with which we, of this magazine, have to be constantly contending. We have to be always saying what we now say again, that the great
danger is rather that men shall not think at all, than that they should think
erroneously; that the great error is sluggishness of mind and indifference to
the truth; that if the mind is suffered to act freely on great subjects, truth
must be in the end the gainer by it. These are the principles to which all

cheerfully assent in the abstract, but unanimously object to in practice. Few have faith enough in the power of truth and its adaptation to the human mind to allow of free inquiry and examination. The author of this book is one of that few. We also are pledged to these principles in theory, and we shall aim as far as in us lies to uphold and protect their practical application.

6. Martin Luther Hurlbut (1781–1842)

Furness' Remarks

[By the spring of 1837, *The Christian Examiner* was in a difficult position. In its pages the radicals—thanks to James Walker's conciliatory policy— had scored their first successes. And now, was the literary and critical organ of liberalism to call a halt? But if it did not, it stood to lose the support of the Unitarian community.

The editors evaded as long as possible by giving noncommittal notices to Brownson's and Ripley's books, Walker merely admonishing Brownson against a too great "willingness to seem very original and free." But Furness' book, with its explicit attack on miracles, could not be handled so courteously. Martin Luther Hurlbut, a Williams graduate who had lived in Charleston, South Carolina, and was now minister in Southampton, was a bit outside the Boston circle, and so to him the editors entrusted this difficult review. Hurlbut paid tribute to Furness' sincerity and to the esteem in which he was held; still, Hurlbut had no choice but to declare that if the miracles are not historically miraculous, then Unitarianism is lost. The issue now was clear: either Christianity is to be merged in a universal naturalism, or Boston liberalism must decide that there is a definable limit to liberal Christianity. The review was published in March 1837 (XXII, 101–124).]

We have observed, of late, a growing disposition, as we think, on the part of the defenders of Christianity, to get rid of the question of miraculous agency, altogether, as if it were a burden that embarrassed their movement,—something, as it seems to us, like a spirit of compromise,—a disposition to meet the unbeliever half-way . . . There is a class of writers among us, who are, consciously or unconsciously, *philosophizing* away the peculiarities of the Gospel, and reducing it to a level with mere naturalism. Such, we verily believe, to be the *tendency* of Mr. Furness's theory of miracles,—and on this account we are disposed to regret its publication. We are persuaded Mr. Furness would disavow any such purpose . . . Still, it is not in his option to check, limit, or *qualify* the tendency of his book. The arrow has been discharged from the bow; where it may fall, or whom it may wound, is not for him to determine. We say not this from any disposition to discourage

investigation . . . Let the subject of miraculous agency be fearlessly entertained, and examined in all its aspects and bearings . . . But, as we verily
think, that a disbelief of this agency involves the disbelief of Christianity, we
may surely be excused for requiring that it be examined fairly, dispassionately,
and *cautiously,* and with a clear apprehension of the consequences it involves . . .

Mr. Furness's theory represents the miraculous powers of Jesus as native
and inherent, as much a part of his intellectual and moral being as the faculties of his understanding, or conscience; and equally liable, in the nature of
things to misapplication, or perversion . . . But . . . Mr. Furness goes
much further than this. We understand him to maintain, that all men are
endued with miraculous powers; that the human mind, as such, possesses a
"supremacy over" material things. This is to us a very startling proposition;
and we do not wonder that he should have anticipated the very obvious objection, that "if it were true, we should have had more numerous manifestations of the wonder-working power of this spiritual law" . . . To us it seems
quite incredible, that this mighty energy should have lain dormant and un-
discovered, in the human soul from the days of the creation to the times of
the Saviour; and still more so, if more could be, that, having been once revealed, it should again escape from the consciousness of all men, and require
to be discovered anew in the nineteenth century. Here have men been beating
their heads for six thousand years against the adamantine bars, within which
destiny has encaged them, when all the while they carried, each in his own
bosom, a key that might at any moment have set him free. For ourselves, we
could as soon believe that a sixth sense remained to be discovered. No *new*
power of the human mind, we believe, has been developed since the days of
Moses; and if men,—if universal man,—had possessed this power, it must,
for ages, have been as familiar as his power of reasoning and observation.
Mr. Furness intimates, indeed, that glimpses of this consciousness have,
from time to time, shown themselves among men, and instances the exorcists
in the time of Jesus. The mountebanks of the world, then, as it seems, have
been its seers and prophets; and what the profane call quackery is inspiration . . .

To our minds the supposition of miraculous interposition on adequate
occasions involves no difficulty. We deem the supposition of a revelation to be
made by the Father of spirits a *reasonable* one, and we see not how it is
possible there should be a revelation without miracles. Truths, however important, which the human mind should attain to in the ordinary exercise of
its native powers, would not constitute a revelation,—a system of revealed

religion. This must, in its very nature, be miraculous, or it cannot be at all. If the miracles of the Gospel are to be regarded as "natural facts," capable of being reduced to natural laws, and explained by them, it does appear to us, that Christianity, as a system of revealed truth, ceases to be. We are thrown back upon *mere naturalism*. The moral lessons of Jesus must be taken for what they are worth, like those of any other wise and good man; encumbered however with the whole weight of this history of wonderful events, which, on this supposition, *prove* nothing, and *tend* to nothing, but to excite wonder at the outset, and skepticism in the sequel.

7. Francis Bowen (1811–1890)
Emerson's Nature

[At the end of the March issue, the editors of *The Christian Examiner*, F. W. P. Greenwood and James Walker, were obliged to face the fact that their denomination was split. "It remains," they wryly protested, "that we should allow both sides, as Unitarians, to be represented in this work." They hoped that such "a temperate and judicious carrying out of this liberal plan" would give more life to the magazine, and in November, Walker even achieved a temperate notice of Alcott.

But the time for temperateness had run out. Not so much because Ripley, Brownson, and Furness had spoken, or because Alcott had created a scandal, but because Emerson had published. The man to whom the editors assigned *Nature* was, like Norton, neither temperate nor judicious. Born in Charlestown, Francis Bowen had supported himself since boyhood, and his graduation from Harvard with highest honors in 1833 was a hard-won achievement. He taught mathematics at Exeter and in 1836 had become tutor in philosophy at Harvard. A disciple of the Scottish realists, he also knew his Kant. He was an aggressive conservative—in later years a stout defender of protective tariffs—and a serious student. In 1853 he was to become Alford Professor, and his *Modern Philosophy* (1877) is still a rewarding history.

In 1837 he had the wit to pick the real power among the new pamphleteers and the resolution to speak out, despite the Unitarian code of temperateness. The first section of his essay appeared in January (XXI, 371–385). Thereafter, the *Examiner* was effectually closed to the Transcendentalists, and they were forced to seek vehicles of their own. Bowen had the courage to break the surface of good manners and to say what the elders had long been wanting to say: that Transcendentalism was a foreign and un-American fad, and that its adherents were arrogant and dogmatic. The essay tells volumes about the form in which Emerson first appeared in the eyes of many of his contemporaries.]

We find beautiful writing and sound philosophy in this little work; but the effect is injured by occasional vagueness of expression, and by a vein of mysticism, that pervades the writer's whole course of thought. The highest praise that can be accorded to it, is, that it is a *suggestive* book, for no one can read it without tasking his faculties to the utmost, and relapsing into fits of severe meditation. But the effort of perusal is often painful, the thoughts excited are frequently bewildering, and the results to which they lead us, uncertain and obscure. The reader feels as in a disturbed dream, in which shows of surpassing beauty are around him, and he is conversant with disembodied spirits, yet all the time he is harassed by an uneasy sort of consciousness, that the whole combination of phenomena is fantastic and unreal.

In point of taste in composition, some defects proceed from over anxiety to avoid common errors. The writer aims at simplicity and directness, as the ancient philosopher aimed at humility, and showed his pride through the tatters of his cloak. He is in love with the Old Saxon idiom, yet there is a spice of affectation in his mode of using it. He is sometimes coarse and blunt, that he may avoid the imputation of sickly refinement, and writes bathos with malice prepense, because he abhors forced dignity and unnatural elevation . . .

It belongs to a class, and may be considered as the latest representative of that class.

Within a short period, a new school of philosophy has appeared, the adherents of which have dignified it with the title of Transcendentalism. In its essential features, it is a revival of the old Platonic school. It rejects the aid of observation, and will not trust to experiment. The Baconian mode of discovery is regarded as obsolete; induction is a slow and tedious process, and the results are uncertain and imperfect. General truths are to be attained without the previous examination of particulars, and by the aid of a higher power than the understanding. "The hand-lamp of logic" is to be broken, for the truths which are *felt* are more satisfactory and certain than those which are *proved*. The sphere of intuition is enlarged, and made to comprehend not only mathematical axioms, but the most abstruse and elevated propositions respecting the being and destiny of man. Pure intelligence usurps the place of humble research. Hidden meanings, glimpses of spiritual and everlasting truth are found, where former observers sought only for natural facts. The observation of sensible phenomena can lead only to the discovery of insulated, partial, and relative laws; but the consideration of the same phenomena, in a typical point of view, may lead us to infinite and absolute truth,—to a knowledge of the reality of things.

As the object and method of philosophizing are thus altered, it is obvious that language also must be modified, and made to subserve other purposes than those for which it was originally designed. Transcendental philosophy took its rise in Germany, and the language of that country, from the unbounded power which it affords of composition and derivation from native roots, is well adapted to express results that are at once novel and vague. Hence the mysticism and over refinement, which characterize the German school of philosophy, art, and criticism. Our own tongue is more limited and inflexible. It must be enriched by copious importation from the German and Greek, before it can answer the ends of the modern school. And this has been done to such an extent, that could one of the worthies of old English literature rise from his grave, he would hardly be able to recognise his native tongue . . .

The writers of whom we speak, openly avow their preference of such indistinct modes of reflection, and justify loose and rambling speculations, mystical forms of expression, and the utterance of truths that are but half perceived, on the same principle, it would seem, that influences the gambler, who expects by a number of random casts to obtain at last the desired combination . . .

Dogmatism and the spirit of innovation go hand in hand . . . Both the means and the ends, which other philosophers have proposed to themselves, are rejected by the new sect of hierophants. They are among men, but not of men. From the heights of mystical speculation, they look down with a ludicrous self-complacency and pity on the mass of mankind, on the ignorant and the educated, the learners and the teachers, and should any question the grounds on which such feelings rest, they are forthwith branded with the most opprobrious epithets, which the English or the Transcendental language can supply. It is not going too far to say, that to the bitterness and scorn, with which Coleridge and some of his English adherents have replied to modest doubts and fair arguments, no parallel can be found, save in the scholastic controversies of the Middle Ages . . .

Some bounds must be set to the application of views like these. Postulates must not be confounded with axioms . . . The distinction, so much insisted on by the New School, between the Reason and the Understanding, if it mean any thing, must be coincident with that which exists between the mind's active and creating power on the one side, and its passive and recipient faculty on the other. If not so,—if the two faculties agree in being each perceptive of truth,—we ask, what difference in kind can there be between two classes of truths, that separate powers are necessary for their reception? . . . Our assertion is, that the argument for the existence of a God, or the immateriality of the soul, is tested by the same power of mind that discovered and proved any proposition in Euclid . . .

The aim of the Transcendentalists is high. They profess to look not only beyond facts, but without the aid of facts, to principles. What is this but Plato's doctrine of innate, eternal, and immutable ideas, on the consideration of which all science is founded? . . . Again, they are busy in the inquiry (to adopt their own phraseology,) after the Real and the Absolute, as distinguished from the Apparent. Not to repeat the same doubt as to their success, we may at least request them to beware lest they strip Truth of its relation to Humanity, and deprive it of its usefulness. Granted that we are imprisoned in matter, why beat against the bars in a fruitless attempt to escape, when a little labor might convert the prison to a palace, or at least render the confinement more endurable. The frame of mind which longs after the forbidden fruit of knowledge in subjects placed beyond the reach of the human faculties, as it is surely indicative of a noble temperament, may also, under peculiar circumstances, conduce to the happiness of the individual. But if too much indulged, there is danger lest it waste its energies in mystic and unprofitable dreams, and despondency result from frequent failure, till at last, disappointment darkens into despair . . .

Arrogance and self-sufficiency are no less absurd in philosophy, than criminal in morals; and we cannot but think, that these qualities are displayed by men who censure indiscriminately the objects which the wise and good have endeavored to attain, and the means which they have employed in the pursuit. A fair and catholic spirit will ever incline to eclecticism in its inquiries and systems; while it is the mark of a narrow mind to consider novelty as a mark of truth, or to look upon the difficulties of a question as evincing the importance of its solution. To regard Franklin as a greater name than that of Plato, might be unjust, were not the comparison itself fanciful and improper; but we may safely assert, that there are few, very few, who would not do better to look at the American rather than the Grecian sage, as their model of the philosophical character.

8. Francis Bowen (1811–1890)

Locke and Transcendentalists

[The second installment of Bowen's attack was published in *The Christian Examiner* for November 1837 (XXIII, 170–194). There was no longer anything whatsoever to be gained by pretending that the split was not fundamental, and Bowen cast off all restraint.]

If the alteration regard the dress more than the substance, if the transcendental philosophy as yet be a manner rather than a creed, still the departures from the old method are real, and involve important consequences. But we believe, that the change is more sweeping in its nature. It is proposed, not to alter and enlarge, but to construct the fabric anew . . . It is a matter worthy of all inquiry, whether the present revolution be like that effected by Lord Bacon, an evidence of intellectual progress, an epoch in the history of man, or whether it be the mere reaction of mind pushed too far to one extreme, the recoil of systems too much depreciated, and too long forgotten . . .

The arrogant tone has been too quickly assumed, for the new philosophy wants even the first recommendation to notice. There is *prima facie* evidence against it. It is abstruse in its dogmas, fantastic in its dress, and foreign in its origin. It comes from Germany, and is one of the first fruits of a diseased admiration of every thing from that source, which has been rapidly gaining ground of late, till in many individuals it amounts to sheer midsummer madness . . .

We judge the tree by its fruits, when we assert, that the study of such writings tends to heat the imagination, and blind the judgment—that it gives a dictatorial tone to the expression of opinion, and a harsh, imperious, and sometimes flippant manner to argumentative discussion—that it injures the generous and catholic spirit of speculative philosophy by raising up a sect of such a marked and distinctive character that it can hold no fellowship either with former laborers in the cause, or with those, who, at the present time, in a different line of inquiry, are aiming at the same general objects. The difference in the mode of philosophizing between the old and new schools is radical. Either one party or the other is entirely in the wrong. To come over to the new system, we must read our former lessons backwards, give up the old tests of correctness and sincerity, and rely no longer on meek and gentle features without, as indications of truth and goodness dwelling within . . .

Whatever course, therefore, tends to rive the philosophical world into parties, to inflame discussion between them beyond all discreet bounds, to remove the objects of thought still farther from the common pursuits and interests of mankind, is so far positively pernicious and wrong. Let the Transcendentalists look to this point. Their efforts hitherto have tended to undermine the only foundation, on which they could safely rest. They have deepened the gulf between speculative and practical men, and by their innovations in language, they are breaking down the only bridge that spans the chasm. Let them succeed in this end, and they perish by isolation . . .

Originality has become the cant of the day—the magic sign, whose worshippers would fain persuade themselves of the worthlessness of every thing, save that which is too strange, too wild, and fantastical, to have entered human thought before. In such a doctrine as this we have no share. There is that in Truth, which prevents the labors of the humblest of her admirers from becoming degrading or useless to himself or mankind . . . There are mysteries in nature, which human power cannot penetrate; there are problems which the philosopher cannot solve. He may form theories, but his theories will be mere dreams—the futile attempts of human intellect to scan the designs of that Being, "whose judgments are unsearchable, and His way past finding out." Even in that field of discovery, which is open to the philosopher, he must seek to gratify his thirst for further knowledge only by persevering labor and humble trust. That eager self-confidence, which would fain grasp at conclusions, without first examining the premises, which would reach the pinnacle without the previous toil of ascending the steps, must be restrained. Truth would lose its proper estimation, if it were a pearl that could be obtained without price. It can be purchased only by patient observation, by deep and thorough reflection. In the words of Bacon, "*Homo, naturae minister et interpres, tantum facit et intelligit, quantum de naturae ordine re vel mente observaverit; nil amplius scit aut potest.*"

9. Christopher Pearse Cranch (1813–1892)

Emerson's American Scholar

[As unfolded to this point, the narrative may help us to understand against what background Emerson spoke as he delivered *The American Scholar* before the Phi Beta Kappa Society at Harvard on August 31, 1837. The genius of Emerson enabled him, as few of his contemporaries were enabled, to pitch his address upon a level above specific reference to contemporaneous events, and so it survives as a document out of time and out of its context; but Emerson himself, and his contemporaries in either camp, understood the point of many oblique gibes to which the setting gave a delicious—or an acrid—flavor. At this stage of the controversy no one could miss the studied insult in his distinction between "Man Thinking" and the "bookworm," or the defiance thrown down in the sentence: "Not out of those, on whom systems of education have exhausted their culture, comes the helpful giant to destroy the old or to build the new, but out of unhandselled savage nature, out of terrible Druids and Berserkirs, come at last Alfred and Shakespeare."

In Cincinnati the band of exiles rallied at once to the standard, and this time the notice was written by Christopher Pearse Cranch. One of the most delightful of the Transcendental group—if only because he alone had a feeling for frivolity —he ultimately proved one of the most futile and wasted talents. Born in Alexandria, Virginia, of a Massachusetts family—his father was made a judge of the Circuit Court by John Adams—Cranch was graduated from Columbian College in 1831 and then came to the Harvard Divinity School. In 1835 he followed Clarke to the West, preached in St. Louis and Cincinnati, and became an editor of *The Western Messenger*. He endured the West for five full years, then returned to Boston and became a social being; he spent three years in Italy, ten in Paris, and finally settled in Cambridge in 1873. His major work was a translation of the *Æneid,* but he dabbled in painting, music, and poetry. He was charming, witty, sensitive; he gave up the pulpit, not like Emerson and Ripley to take on serious work, but to become, by deliberate intention, a dilettante.

In the *Messenger* for November 1837 (IV, 184–188), upon receiving the printed text of Emerson's speech, Cranch hailed it as "beautiful and masterly," and could not resist giving voice to the homesickness that the Transcendentalists in the Ohio Valley were rapidly succumbing to.

> Would that we had been in the church of old Harvard, when the thinker, the orator, and poet charmed the multitude to silence in such a strain as that we have here so imperfectly reviewed. Let him send abroad more of the productions of his elevated and fervent spirit. The age—the country need them. The stream of human society is stagnant, unspiritual, corrupt. But there are purer elements struggling to the surface. Let all the purifying streams that flow into it be as this little rill, and the needed regeneration must follow.

Shortly thereafter, the *Messenger* received Bowen's second discussion of Emerson, and began to comprehend how old Harvard had in fact reacted to the thinker and the poet. In the number for June 1838 (V, 199), one of the editors— probably Cranch, but possibly Clarke—used the publication of Ripley's *Specimens* as an occasion to express the grief of the Western group over what they had to consider Harvard's abysmal failure.]

We would therefore earnestly recommend these volumes of Mr. Ripley . ... to all teachers of intellectual and moral philosophy in our Colleges, and to all young men whose minds are dissatisfied with the prevailing system of metaphysics. We confess, we shared the grief of many others in finding the occupant of the philosophical chair, in one of our Universities, bent on proving that in John Locke philosophy had its beginning, middle, and end—that the Essay on the Human Understanding was to be the *ne plus ultra* of intellectual inquiry. We were grieved, because during an observation of eight years, since we left the University, and a pretty general acquaintance among the young men in different parts of the country, we felt sure that such views were not adapted to the demands of the times—that they would afford no food to the rising generation, but be rejected by them, as husks and straw. That the article to which we refer should have been inserted in the Christian Examiner was well. We supposed it was the purpose of the Editors, like the well instructed scribe, to bring out of their treasury things new and old. And because they had lately been accused of too great novelty in some speculations, they threw into the other scale the articles on Mr. Emerson and on Locke. But we should be glad if the teachers in the principal colleges of our land, might always sympathise with the views of the present century. And especially should we grieve if an University which demands progress in Theology should be reluctant to allow a like advance in metaphysical and moral science.

10. Orestes A. Brownson (1803–1876)

Introductory Remarks

[Publication by the *Examiner* of Bowen's articles demonstrated the need of a vehicle for the insurgent ideas. Brownson was never the man to hesitate when a job needed doing. In January 1838 he brought out the first number of *The Boston Quarterly Review*, financed and managed by himself, for which he wrote a declaration (I, 1–8).

Several of the Transcendentalists helped out from time to time, but in the main the *Quarterly* was Brownson's own work. In the first issue of *The Dial*, in July 1840, Ripley testified to its importance in the struggle "between the old and the new, between prescription and principle, between the assertions of authority and the suggestions of reason." Only the fact that in 1844 Brownson became a Catholic, and so induced his former friends to erase his name from their memories, explains the otherwise inexplicable negligence with which historians have treated this journal, the most vigorous of its day. Between 1838 and 1842 it was the one effective assailant in America of prescription and authority, and it inflicted upon them an infinitely heavier damage than *The Dial* ever dared attempt.]

No man is able to estimate properly the value of his own individual experience. All are prone to exaggerate, more or less, the importance of what has happened to themselves. This it is altogether likely is the case with me. Yet in my own eyes my experience possesses some value. My life has been one of vicissitude and trial. My mind has passed through more than one scene of doubt and perplexity. I have asked in the breaking up, as it were, of my whole moral and intellectual being, What is the Destiny of Man and of Society? Much of my life has been spent—wasted perhaps—in efforts to decipher the answer to this question. In common with others, I have tried my hand at the riddle of the Sphinx; and in common with others too, I have, it may be, faith in my own explanation. In seeking to solve the problem which has pressed heavily on my heart, as well as on my mind, I have been forced to appeal from tradition and authority to the Universal Reason, a ray of which shines into the heart of every man that cometh into the world; and this, which has been forced upon me, I would force upon others. The answer, which I have obtained and which has restored peace and serenity to my own soul, I would urge others to seek, and aid them to find. For this purpose I undertake this Review.

I ought in justice to the periodical press of the country to say, that it has always been at my service as far as I have sought to use it. With one or two insignificant exceptions, I have never asked the privilege of inserting an article, which has not been granted. The Christian Examiner, a periodical for freedom and freshness unsurpassed in the world, has always been open to me; and, for aught I have reason to think, still would be; but that removes not the difficulty. There is a possibility of refusal. The editor's imprimatur must be obtained. The censorship may be indulgent, liberal, obliging, yet it is censorship, and that is enough. The oracle within will not utter his responses, when it depends on the good will of another whether they shall to the public ear or not. The evil of the thing does not consist in the refusal to publish what is written, but in hindering one from writing what he otherwise might. This is after all a small affair; but who is there that is not disturbed by small affairs more than by great?

I undertake this Review, then, for myself; not because I am certain that the public wants it, but because I want it. I want it for a medium through which I may say to those who may choose to listen to my voice, just what I wish to say, and through which I may say it in my own way and time. This is the specific object for which I undertake it. I cannot say whether what I shall utter will be for the public good or not. What is for the public good? Who knows? I do not. This or that may seem to me to-day for the public good, and to-morrow's eve proves me mistaken; and yet how know I that? That, which I shall to-morrow's eve account a public evil, may turn out to have been a public blessing. Man seeth not the end, and knoweth not the termination of events. He cannot say which is the blessing or which is the curse. All that is for him is, what his hand findeth to do, to do it, and the word which is pressing for utterance, to utter it, and leave results to God, to whom alone they belong. I am not wise enough to say dogmatically what is or what is not for the public good; but I know what I think, what comes to me as truth; and as a watchman I would tell what I see, or seem to see, and let them of the city treat it as they will. Man is a seer and it is each man's duty to declare simply what he sees, without attempting to fix its precise value, and without allowing himself to be disturbed because others may not rate its value precisely as he does . . .

I add the epithet Boston, both to designate the place whence it is published, and to pay a sort of compliment to this goodly city. Boston is, of all the cities in the Union, the one in which thought is freest and boldest, and in which progress finds its warmest and most enlightened friends. I may say this, for I am not a Bostonian. I know Boston is called an aristocratic city, and I know also that democracy is a word for which it has no slight aversion; but in point of fact, it has less aristocracy than any other of our cities, and is more truly democratic in its practice. One may indeed see now and then the representative of a by-gone generation, walking the streets with an antique air and dress, but he is, after all, one who makes us doubt whether we have advanced much on our fathers. True, there is here and there a purse-proud *parvenu,* and a poor worshipper of Fashion, but even these it has been conjectured, and not without reason, have souls, and even hearts which may with proper applications be made to beat with something like sympathy with Humanity, and admiration of a generous sentiment or a heroic deed. Boston is, say what you will of it, the city of "notions," and of new notions too; and in the progress of liberal ideas in this country, it ever has and ever will take the lead. Elsewhere there may be more bustle, more pretence, more profession of liberty, of reform, of progress, of democracy; but when it comes to the reality, Boston need not blush in the presence of any of her sisters. This being the case, it is proper that I should call my Review the *Boston* Review, intimating thereby that it contains in some sort *Boston* notions; and sure am I that in Boston shall I find for it the most sympathy and its best friends.

11. Orestes A. Brownson (1803–1876)

Francis Bowen

[So that there might be no mistake about what he intended *The Boston Quarterly Review* to do, Brownson at once took on Francis Bowen (I, 83–106), and thus stepped into the arena where Emerson would not deign to enter. But Brownson's line of attack was not exactly what Emerson would have taken had he condescended to fight: the difference between Unitarian sensationalism and Transcendental intuitionalism was here presented, not as a contrast between the bookworm and Man Thinking, but as the clash of aristocracy and democracy. The charge was indeed pressed home: it was now the respectable and rational disciples of Locke who found themselves indicted as un-American and their vaunted "common sense" was exposed as a dodge for denying the rights of the masses.]

The article, we are examining, appears to us to assume, that the metaphysician should always restrict himself to what may be called common sense modes of thought and expression, and that the highest philosophy may be so announced as to be comprehended at once, by any one of ordinary capacity, whether accustomed to philosophize or not . . . We trust, therefore, that we shall not be doing a needless work, if we undertake, in what follows, to aid our readers to draw the line between common sense and philosophy, and to determine what is the precise object of philosophy . . .

Philosophy and common sense are not opposed to one another. There is no discrepancy between them. Common sense furnishes the philosopher all his knowledge, all the data from which he reasons. His sole mission is to clear up and legitimate the universal beliefs of mankind, or the facts of common sense. The common sense man is not in the wrong; he does not err; he has the truth, but he does not know that he has it. He believes the truth, but he does not comprehend what he believes, nor wherefore he believes. He cannot tell how he came to believe what he does believe; he knows not what right he has to believe it; and when asked, why he believes it, he can only answer, he believes it because he does believe it. The philosopher believes precisely the same things, as the common sense man, but he knows what he believes, and he can tell wherefore he believes. The common sense man believes, but does not comprehend; the philosopher comprehends, and therefore believes . . .

Nor let it be supposed that we would debar the people at large from the truths the philosopher professes to have demonstrated. These truths are not the peculiar possession of the philosopher. They are the truths of the universal reason, and are the property alike of all men. They are taught to all men by the spontaneous reason, which is the same in kind in every man. These truths are not the philosophy. Philosophy is the explanation and verification of them. The masses, who see nothing mysterious in these truths, and who have never thought of questioning them, do not wish to have them explained or verified. The explanation and verification, which is philosophy, are unintelligible to them. But the truths themselves, are not unintelligible to them. Whoever proclaims to the masses these truths, which the philosopher has demonstrated, cleared up, and legitimated, is sure to be heard and believed and followed.

The fact is, the great mass of mankind are not, as to their beliefs, in so sad a condition, as schoolmen sometimes imagine. The educated, the scientific are prone to look upon the masses as possessing no ideas, as having no knowledge but that which they obtain from human teachers. This is peculiarly the case with Locke and his followers. According to them, the child receives no patrimony from his father; he is born into the world naked and destitute in soul as well as in body, and with no innate power to weave himself a garment. His mind is a *tabula rasa,* on which others indeed may write what they will, but upon which he himself can write nothing, save the summing up of what others have written thereon. Evil as well as good, falsehood as well as truth, may be written thereon. It depends wholly on the external circumstances, the quality of the masters secured, whether the mind's blank sheets shall be written over with truth or falsehood. The masses, after the flesh, it must be admitted, are surrounded with unwholesome influences, and provided with most wretched teachers. They must then be filled with evil thoughts and false notions. Their beliefs, their hopes and fears, likes and dislikes, are deserving no respect. Hence, on the one hand, the contempt of the masses manifested by so large a portion of the educated, even in democratic America, and, on the other hand, the pity and commiseration, the great condescension, and vast amount of baby-talk, which equally characterize another, but more kind-hearted, portion of the more favored classes. Of this last division, we presume, is the writer on whom we are remarking. He is not a man to look with contempt on human beings; he feels that we ought to labor to benefit the masses; but we presume he has no suspicion that the masses have any correct beliefs, but such as they receive from the favored and superior few. Hence his strong desire that all men, who write, should write in a simple style, and so let themselves down, that they will not be above the capacities of the many. He would not, we presume, think of learning from them, or of verifying their beliefs; but merely of teaching them what they ought to believe. We bring not this as a charge against him. It speaks well for his goodness of heart, and proves him to be as good a democrat as a follower of Locke consistently can be.

But in point of fact, the masses are not so poor and destitute as all this supposes. They are not so dependent on *us,* the enlightened few, as we sometimes think them. We need not feel that, if we should die, all wisdom would die with us, and that there would be henceforth no means by which the millions would be able to come at truth and virtue. Reason is the true light, and it enlighteneth every man who cometh into the world. It is, as we have said, the same in all men, and therefore it is that no man is left in darkness. The reason has two modes of activity, one the spontaneous, the other the reflective. In the great majority of men, the reflective reason, which gives philosophy, is never awakened, and consequently but a small minority of mankind ever become philosophers. But the spontaneous reason develops itself in all men, in the highest and the lowest, in the uneducated as well as in the educated. This reason, the spontaneous reason, furnishes the universal beliefs of mankind, which are termed common sense. It furnishes all the ideas we ever have; teaches us all the truths we ever know. As this reason is the same in all men, it gives to all men the same ideas, furnishes them with the same truths, the same beliefs. These masses then, on which we look down with contempt or with pity for their weakness and ignorance, have all the truths we who look down upon them have; they have the same ideas, and the same beliefs. They are not so destitute then as the Lockeites thought them; they are not so erroneous then as the self-complacent aristocrat judged them, nor so dependent on their betters, as *great* men have generally counted them. Their views, beliefs, hopes, fears, likes, dislikes, are worthy to be examined, are to be respected. The masses are not to be pitied then, but respected, and herein is laid the foundation of true philanthropy . . .

Philosophy is not needed by the masses: but they who separate themselves from the masses, and who believe that the masses are entirely dependent on them for truth and virtue, need it, in order to bring them back, and bind them again to universal Humanity. And they need it now, and in this country, perhaps as much as ever. The world is filled with commotions. The masses are heaving and rolling, like a mighty river, swollen with recent rains, and snows dissolving on the mountains, onward to a distant and unknown ocean. There are those among us, who stand awe-struck, who stand amazed. What means this heaving and onward rolling? Whither tend these mighty masses of human beings? Will they sweep away every fixture, every house and barn, every mark of civilization? Where will they end? In what will they end? Shall we rush before them and attempt to stay their progress?

Or shall we fall into their ranks and on with them to their goal? . . . The friends of Humanity need philosophy, as the means of legitimating the cause of the people, of proving that it is the right, and the duty, of every man to bind himself to that cause, and to maintain it in good report and in evil report, in life and in death. They need it, that they may prove to these conservatives, who are frightened almost out of their wits at the movements of the masses, and who are denouncing them in no measured terms, that these movements are from God, and that they, who war against them, are warring against truth, duty, God, and Humanity . . .

It will be seen from this, that our philosophy, notwithstanding certain aristocratic airs, is by no means wanting in its democratic tendencies. Its aim is not utility, but the establishment of truth, and that not for the many, but for the few; nevertheless the truth established, always benefits the world, and the truth established in this case, is the truth which every body is interested in. We by no means reject common sense; we love, we obey it, because we have legitimated its right to be loved and obeyed. All true philosophy accepts, and explains, and legitimates, the instinctive beliefs of mankind. Philosophy therefore, though it is not common sense, is in perfect harmony with it.

Will the respect, the writer in the Examiner has for common sense, carry him as far as this? Does he credit common sense? Does he believe the instinctive beliefs of mankind are true, worthy to be trusted? If so, we pray him to legitimate those beliefs on the ground of Locke's philosophy. If he does not believe them true, if he denies them, we ask him, what right he has to require philosophical writers to respect common sense? Moreover, if common sense, the universal beliefs of mankind, the instinctive beliefs of Humanity, the teachings of the spontaneous reason, be discredited, as they must be by a disciple of Locke, we ask, how it is possible to establish the certainty of any thing whatever? We ask those who rail against Humanity, and look upon the instinctive beliefs of the masses with contempt, how they will save us from universal Skepticism?

12. William Henry Channing (1810–1884)
Emerson's American Scholar

[Brownson adroitly avoided mentioning Emerson in his dissection of Bowen, but followed his article immediately by one on Emerson's Phi Beta Kappa address (I, 106–120).

William Henry Channing, a nephew of Dr. Channing, graduated from Harvard College in 1829 and from the Divinity School in 1833. A mercurial, excitable, generous, and thoroughly likable man, Channing threw himself into every possible reforming movement and from the beginning extracted out of Transcendental metaphysics a program of social regeneration. In 1836 he conducted a church for workers in New York; in 1839 he joined Clarke and Cranch in the West and became an editor of the *Messenger*. He resigned his pulpit in 1841 upon becoming convinced that the Gospels are historically unreliable, organized an independent church in New York, spent some months at Brook Farm, edited short-lived magazines—*The Present* (1844) and *The Spirit of the Age* (1849–50)—and after 1854 spent most of his years in England.

Only Brownson's journal would have blurted out the fact that in drawing rooms, classrooms, and private gatherings, in 1838, the saintly Emerson was being vilified—"gaping wonder, shrewd cavilling, sneering doubt, and even offended dignity." The review is the first to recognize the preëminence that Emerson had achieved on the strength of two short publications; yet it also contains a broad hint that already one segment of the new school found him deficient in one fundamental respect: he is not sufficiently warm toward "the great social idea of our era."

In fact, Channing set Norton and Bowen an example of critical dignity by not praising Emerson too wildly, but at the end, fired by his subject, Channing gave voice to the inspiration that Emerson imparted to his younger contemporaries.]

We look, we say, for an American literature. We feel as if the old strata of thought, in the old world, had been broken up, with the old manners which clothed them and grew out from them; and as if the fused and melted mass had settled here to form a new world of higher beauty. And the rock basis of a new era will be a philosophy, which recognises the divinity of reason in every soul; which sees the identity of reason and faith, and honors common sense as the voice of truth; which feels the mystery of moral freedom in every man of that perfect liberty of the entire obedience to right, and which bows with awe before the conviction that God is in each human soul, that never is the individual so entirely himself as when at one with the indwelling Spirit. And the life, which will pervade this new world of thought, will be a poetry of love and sympathy for the commonest familiar feeling, as well as the higher and holier, and for every human tie and relation. Science is always liberal, for nature is no respecter of persons or of forms. She will speak to the humblest or highest of her children through the light which covers the heavens, as with a canopy for angels, through the swift flashes which rend the mountain, or the unseen influence which follows down the string of the paper kite. And shall not it be, is the world never to see a system of social manners too, growing out from this Christian idea of brotherhood, which shall embody the principles of this philosophy—the spirit of this poetry? Our manners will ever be the leaves to clothe with beauty the trunk and branches of our faith; but through them it must imbibe from the sun of God's love, and the atmosphere of human kindness, a purifying, a vital influence. We shall never have a healthy American Literature, unless we have an American Spirit, an American Manner of Life.

13. Orestes A. Brownson (1803–1876)
Alcott's Conversations

[It took courage, in October of 1838, to say a good word for Alcott, but Brownson had courage in abundance (*Boston Quarterly Review,* I, 417–432). He did not condescend to mere defense; by treating Alcott critically, Brownson demonstrated that his educational ideas deserved sober discussion. Brownson thought that Alcott expected too much from "instinct"—thus indicating the beginnings of his divergence from the more extreme Transcendentalists—but still gallantly insisted that Alcott's system was "neither absurd nor alarming."]

Mr. Alcott has received much reproach, and we fear been made to suffer in the prosperity of his school on account of this book. He has been treated with great illiberality, and made to undergo as severe a persecution as the times allow. As a man he is singularly evangelical, pure minded, in love with all that is beautiful and good, and devoted soul and body to what he deems truth, and the regeneration of mankind. He is conscious of being sent into this world on a high and important mission, and his great study is to discharge that mission to the acceptance of him that sent him. Yet no man among us has been spoken of in severer tones, or been more seriously injured, for the moment, by the misapprehension and ill-nature, the misrepresentation and abuse, he has had to endure from those who affect to lead public opinion. It is painful to record this fact. For there is no man in our country who so well understands the art of education, and who is capable or desirous of doing more for establishing a system of Human Culture, in consonance with our faith as Christians and as republicans. And there is no fault, nor even shadow of a fault to be found with him; save that he will be true to the deepest and holiest convictions of his own mind; and will never sacrifice what he holds as truth, virtue, manhood, independence, to popular opinion, to a sickly taste, or a heartless conventionalism. It is not much to our credit, that we condemn him for this.

Mr. Alcott may not be sound in his philosophy, he may not be correct in all his views, and he may carry, and we believe he does carry, some of his favorite notions to extremes; but he deserves profound reverence for his determination to be a Man; to be true to Human Nature; for his fearless assertion of his own convictions, and for his deep and living faith in God and Humanity. He aims to be himself and not another; to think his own thoughts and not another's; and having done this, he will not lock up his thoughts in his own bosom, and seem to acquiesce in reigning dogmas; but he will utter them, regardless of the reproach or injury he may sustain by so doing. Such a man in these times, when there are so few who feel that they are Men and have a part of their own to act, is not to be cast aside, to be trampled on, without great detriment to our social and moral progress. Did we know what is for our good, we should seek out such men, and honor them as prophets sent from God to foretell and to usher in a more glorious future.

14. Orestes A. Brownson (1803–1876)
Ripley's Specimens

[In 1837 Ripley began to organize the younger scholars of Transcendentalism into an ambitious project—the importance of which has been little appreciated by historians of American culture. For several years they had been writing about the new European literature; was it not, therefore, their responsibility to make some of this literature available to Americans? He assumed the task of editing the translations, and the first two volumes—his own renderings of Cousin, Jouffroy, and Constant—appeared in the fall of 1838. The title for the series was carefully chosen: *Specimens of Foreign Standard Literature.* The word "standard" was a deliberate assertion, as against Norton and Bowen, that what they still regarded as the "new" and suspect literature of Europe had already become, in the capitals of culture, "standard."

Brownson was now a close friend of Ripley, and undoubtedly he led Ripley to open the series with a translation of Cousin. Since Brownson was the pioneer exponent of Cousin in America, reviewing Ripley's volume was a congenial task (*The Boston Quarterly Review,* October 1838, I, 433–444). But even more gratifying was the chance to counter the Unitarian charge that the new movement was un-American because it went whoring after strange Gods from France and Germany. Brownson performed a service for American letters by arguing that American literature is not a department of the English and that a democratic America has more in common with the literature of the Continent than with that of the England to which respectable Bostonians looked for guidance.]

We are now the literary vassals of England, and continue to do homage to the mother country. Our literature is tame and servile, wanting in freshness, freedom, and originality. We write as Englishmen, not as

Americans. We are afraid to think our own thoughts, to speak our own words, or to give utterance to the rich and gushing sentiments of our own hearts. And so must it be so long as we rely on England's literature as exclusively as we have hitherto done. Not indeed so much because that literature is not a good one. English literature, so long as it boasts a Shakspeare and a Milton, cannot suffer in comparison with the literature of any other nation. For ourselves we reverence it, and would on no account speak lightly of it. But it cramps our national genius, and exercises a tyrannical sway over the American mind. We cannot become independent and original, till we have in some degree weakened its empire. This will be best done by the study of the fresher, and in some respects superior literatures of continental Europe. We must bring in France and Germany to combat or neutralize England, so that our national spirit may gain the freedom to manifest itself.

Moreover, excellent as is the English literature, it is not exactly the literature for young republicans. England is the most aristocratic country in the world. Its literature is, with some noble exceptions, aristocratic. It is deficient in true reverence for man as man, wholly unconscious of the fact that man is everywhere equal to man. It is full of reverence for that mass of incongruities, the British Constitution, which contains more of the character of the institutions of the Middle Age, than any other constitution or form of government to be found in Europe. It bristles from beginning to end with Dukes and Duchesses, Lords and Ladies, and overflows with servility to the great, and with contempt, or what is worse, condescension for the little. The constant and exclusive study of a literature like this cannot fail to be deeply prejudicial to republican simplicity of thought and taste, to create a sort of disgust for republican manners and institutions, and to make us sigh to reproduce, on American soil, the aristocratic manners and institutions of England . . .

Now in this situation nothing can be more suitable or more succoring for us, than large importations of French and German literature. France and Germany are monarchical, it is true, but not aristocratic. Monarchy has been, in Europe in general, popular rather than aristocratic in its tendency. The people have in most countries less to dread from the monarch than from the noble. Monarchy raises one man indeed above, far above the people, but in doing this, it lessens or neutralizes to some extent the distinctions which obtain below it. The writings of French or even German scholars breathe altogether more of a democratic spirit than do those of the English. Those of the French are altogether more democratic than the writings of American scholars themselves. Then, again, we have in this country not much to fear from the monarchical tendency. There is nothing monarchical in the genius or temper of the American people. We remember yet the struggles our fathers had with the king, and that we are the descendants of those who dethroned Mary Stuart, and brought Charles Stuart to the scaffold. Then we have no powerful families as yet that could make interest for a throne, no individual influential enough, universally popular enough, or far enough elevated above his brethren, to be thought of in connexion with a crown. We have too long been accustomed to govern ourselves, too large a portion of our citizens have taken a direct share in the affairs of government, and may always hope to take a direct share in them, to think of abandoning them to any one man. We can arrive at monarchy in this country only through aristocracy. We do not apprehend that this will ever be the case. The aristocratic tendency is the only tendency we have to apprehend serious danger from; but even this tendency will, we trust, be arrested before it shall have done any lasting injury to our institutions. The study of French and German literature will arrest this tendency. It will break the dominion of England; and, without excluding English literature, will furnish us new elements, and a broader and more democratic basis for our own . . .

This too is the country in which the noble ideas of man and society, which French and German scholars strike out in their speculations, are to be first applied to practice, realized in institutions. There the scholar may study; there the philosopher may investigate man; there the politician may explore the city, and ascertain how the state should be organized; and there they all may deposit the result of their speculations, their researches, their inspirations in books, but, alas, in books only; for to them is wanting the theatre on which to act them out, the practical world in which to realize them. They have old institutions to combat; old prejudices to overcome; old castles and old churches to clear away; an old people to reyouth, before they can proceed to embody their ideas, or to reduce them to practice. More than all this, they want the freedom to do it. Authority is against them, and armed soldiery are ready to repulse them. But here is a virgin soil, an open field, a new people, full of the future, with unbounded faith in ideas, and the most ample freedom. Here, if any where on earth, may the philosopher experiment on human nature, and demonstrate what man has it in him to be when and where he has the freedom and the means to be himself. Let Germany then explore the mines, and bring out the ore, let France smelt it, extract the pure metal, determine its weight and fineness, and we will work it up into vessels of ornament or utility, apply it to the practical purposes of life.

15. Ralph Waldo Emerson (1803–1882)

An Address Delivered before the Senior Class in Divinity College

[Emerson was invited by a committee of the seniors in the Divinity School to deliver their commencement address; before the faculty could gather their wits or find ways to prevent him, he had accepted. He gave the address on the second floor of Divinity Hall on July 15, 1838.

As with *The American Scholar,* Emerson had larger goals in view than the local situation. But he could not talk to candidates for the Unitarian pulpit—especially with the professors in the room—without at least some glance at the concrete issue upon which all the larger differences depended. Posterity now reads the *Divinity School Address* apart from the time and place, but though it remains thus a classic of the American spirit, much of its point is lost. The issue had focused on the problem of miracles; Emerson would not so have outraged Harvard orthodoxy had he merely preached the Over-Soul. The passages that made him a "martyr" were those that struck the nearest at the foundations of the creed in which he himself had been nurtured.]

Jesus Christ belonged to the true race of prophets. He saw with open eye the mystery of the soul. Drawn by its severe harmony, ravished with its beauty, he lived in it, and had his being there. Alone in all history, he estimated the greatness of man. One man was true to what is in you and me. He saw that God incarnates himself in man, and evermore goes forth anew to take possession of his World. He said, in this jubilee of sublime emotion, "I am divine. Through me, God acts; through me, speaks. Would you see God, see me; or, see thee, when thou also thinkest as I now think." But what a distortion did his doctrine and memory suffer in the same, in the next, and the following ages! There is no doctrine of the Reason which will bear to be taught by the Understanding. The understanding caught this high chant from the poet's lips, and said, in the next age, "This was Jehovah come down out of heaven. I will kill you, if you say he was a man." The idioms of his language and the figures of his rhetoric, have usurped the place of his truth; and churches are not built on his principles, but on his tropes. Christianity became a mythus, as the poetic teaching of Greece and of Egypt, before. He spoke of miracles; for he felt that man's life was a miracle, and all that man doth, and he knew that this his daily miracle shines, as the character ascends. But the word Miracle, as pronounced by Christian churches, gives a false impression; it is Monster. It is not one with the blowing clover and the falling rain.

16. Andrews Norton (1786–1853)
The New School in Literature and Religion

[We must again remind ourselves of the canons of caution and sobriety that Unitarianism inculcated as primary virtues before we can appreciate the violence of Norton's reaction to Emerson's commencement address. He had indeed turned to the public newspaper in 1836, but then he had the excuse that his letter could not properly be printed in the *Examiner*. For him to appeal from a commencement ceremony at the Harvard Divinity School to *The Boston Daily Advertiser* (Monday, August 27, 1838; XLIII, 14475), with the intention of blasting not only the orator but the graduates who chose him, was so unprecedented an act that it could have been inspired by nothing less than pure rage.]

There is a strange state of things existing about us in the literary and religious world, of which none of our larger periodicals has yet taken notice. It is the result of that restless craving for notoriety and excitement, which, in one way or another, is keeping our community in a perpetual stir. It has shown itself, we think, particularly since that foolish woman, Miss Martineau, was among us, and stimulated the vanity of her flatterers by loading them in return with the copper coin of her praise, which they easily believed was as good as gold. She was accustomed to talk about her mission, as if she were a special dispensation of Providence, and they too thought that they must have their missions, and began to "vaticinate," as one of their number has expressed it. But though her genial warmth may have caused the new school to bud and bloom, it was not planted by her.—It owes its origin in part to ill understood notions, obtained by blundering through the crabbed and disgusting obscurity of some of the worst German speculatists, which notions, however, have been received by most of its disciples at second hand, through an interpreter. The atheist Shelley has been quoted and commended in a professedly religious work, called the Western Messenger; but he is not, we conceive, to be reckoned among the patriarchs of the sect. But this honor is due to that hasher up of German metaphysics, the Frenchman, Cousin; and, of late, that hyper-Germanized Englishman, Carlyle, has been the great object of admiration and model of style. Cousin and Carlyle indeed seem to have been transformed into idols to be publicly worshipped, the former for his philosophy, and the latter both for his philosophy and his fine writing; while the veiled image of the German pantheist, Schleiermacher, is kept in the sanctuary.

The characteristics of this school are the most extraordinary assumption, united with great ignorance, and incapacity for reasoning. There is indeed a general tendency among its disciples to disavow learning and reasoning as sources of their higher knowledge.—The mind must be its own unassisted teacher. It discerns transcendental truths by immediate vision, and these truths can no more be communicated to another by addressing his understanding, than the power of clairvoyance can be given to one not magnetized. They announce themselves as the prophets and priests of a new future, in which all is to be changed, all old opinions done away, and all present forms of society abolished. But by what process this joyful revolution is to be effected we are not told; nor how human happiness and virtue is to be saved from the universal wreck, and regenerated in their Medea's caldron. There are great truths with which they are laboring, but they are unutterable in words to be understood by common minds. To such minds they seem nonsense, oracles as obscure as those of Delphi.

The rejection of reasoning is accompanied with an equal contempt for good taste. All modesty is laid aside. The writer of an article for an obscure periodical, or a religious newspaper, assumes a tone as if he were one of the chosen enlighteners of a dark age.—He continually obtrudes himself upon his reader, and announces his own convictions, as if from their having that character, they were necessarily indisputable.—He floats about magnificently on bladders, which he would have it believed are swelling with ideas.— Common thoughts, sometimes true, oftener false, and "Neutral nonsense, neither false nor true," are exaggerated, and twisted out of shape, and forced into strange connexions, to make them look like some grand and new conception. To produce a more striking effect, our common language is abused; antic tricks are played with it; inversions, exclamations, anomalous combinations of words, unmeaning, but coarse and violent, metaphors abound, and withal a strong infusion of German barbarisms. Such is the style of Carlyle, a writer of some talent; for his great deficiency is not in this respect, it is [in] good sense, good taste and soundness of principle; but a writer, who, through his talents, such as they are, through that sort of buffoonery and affectation of manner which throws the reader off his guard, through the indisputable novelty of his way of writing, and through a somewhat too prevalent taste among us for an over-excited and *convulsionary* style, which we mistake for eloquence, has obtained a degree of fame in this country, very disproportioned to what he enjoys at home, out of the Westminster Review. Carlyle, however, as an original, might be tolerated, if one could forget his admirers and imitators.

The state of things described might seem a matter of no great concern, a mere insurrection of folly, a sort of Jack Cade rebellion, which in the nature of things must soon be put down, if those engaged in it were not gathering confidence from neglect, and had not proceeded to attack principles which are the foundation of human society and human happiness. "Silly women," it has been said, and silly young men, it is to be feared, have been drawn away from their Christian faith, if not divorced from all that can properly be called religion. The evil is becoming, for the time, disastrous and alarming; and of this fact there could hardly be a more extraordinary and ill boding evidence, than is afforded by a publication, which has just appeared, entitled, an "Address, delivered before the Senior Class in Divinity College, Cambridge," upon the occasion of that class taking leave of the Institution—"By Ralph Waldo Emerson."

It is not necessary to remark particularly on this composition. It will be sufficient to state generally, that the author professes to reject all belief in Christianity as a revelation, that he makes a general attack upon the Clergy, on the ground that they preach what he calls "Historical Christianity," and that if he believe in God in the proper sense of the term, which one passage might have led his hearers to suppose, his language elsewhere is very ill-judged and indecorous. But what *his* opinions may be is a matter of minor concern; the main question is how it has happened, that religion has been insulted by the delivery of these opinions in the Chapel of the Divinity College of Cambridge, as the last instruction which those were to receive, who were going forth from it, bearing the name of Christian preachers. This is a question in which the community is deeply interested. No one can doubt for a moment of the disgust and strong disapprobation with which it must have been heard by the highly respectable officers of that Institution. They must have felt it not only as an insult to religion, but as personal insult to themselves. But this renders the fact of its having been so delivered only the more remarkable. We can proceed but a step in accounting for it. The preacher was invited to occupy the place he did, not by the officers of the Divinity College, but by the members of the graduating class. These gentlemen, therefore, have become accessories, perhaps innocent accessories, to the commission of a great offence; and the public must be desirous of learning what exculpation or excuse they can offer.

It is difficult to believe that they thought this incoherent rhapsody a specimen of fine writing, that they listened with admiration, for instance, when they were told that the religious sentiment "is myrrh, and storax and chlorine and rosemary;" or that they wondered at the profound views of their present Teacher, when he announced to them that "the new Teacher," for whom he is looking, would "see the identity of the law of gravitation with purity of heart;" or that they had not some suspicion of inconsistency, when a new Teacher was talked of, after it had been declared to them, that religious truth "is an intuition," and "cannot be received at second hand."

But the subject is to be viewed under a far more serious aspect. The words God, Religion, Christianity, have a definite meaning, well understood. They express conceptions and truths of unutterable moment to the present and future happiness of man. We well know how shamefully they have been abused in modern times by infidels and pantheists; but their meaning remains the same; the truths which they express are unchanged and unchangeable. The community know what they require when they ask for a Christian Teacher; and should any one approving the doctrines of this discourse assume that character, he would deceive his hearers; he would be guilty of a practical falsehood for the most paltry of temptations; he would consent to live a lie, for the sake of being maintained by those whom he had cheated. It is not, however, to be supposed that his vanity would suffer him long to keep his philosophy wholly to himself. This would break out in obscure intimations, ambiguous words, and false and mischievous speculations. But should such preachers abound, and grow confident in their folly, we can hardly overestimate the disastrous effect upon the religion and moral state of the community.

17. The Christian Examiner
Emerson's Address

[The now genuinely unhappy editors of *The Christian Examiner* could no longer maintain even a pretense of impartiality; they might continue to say that both parties could be heard as long as both were Unitarians, but Emerson's address relieved them of having to think of him or his friends as any longer so entitled. Henry Ware, Jr., hastened to preach before the Divinity School a sermon on "The Personality of the Deity"; evidently the authorities hoped it would undo Emerson's work. Ware sent it to Emerson for comment, but Emerson replied, "I do not know, I confess, what arguments mean in reference to any expression of a thought." In November (XXV, 266–268), the editors of the *Examiner* paid their last respects to Emerson.]

It is not likely that we should have noticed this Address, had it not received . . . notice already, and caused some stir and speculation. But as we have been asked repeatedly, whether certain strange notions contained in it are regarded as good divinity by the instructors and students of the Divinity School at Cambridge, and whether the gentleman who advanced these notions is to be considered as thereby uttering or representing the opinions of the body of Unitarian ministers, we deem it right to say, and we believe we have the best authority for saying, that those notions, so far as they are intelligible, are utterly distasteful to the instructors of the School, and to Unitarian ministers generally, by whom they are esteemed to be neither good divinity nor good sense. With regard to their reception among the students, we cannot speak so positively; we merely know that the only apparent connexion between the School and these notions is, that a majority of the Senior Class, which consisted altogether of seven students, attracted by Mr. Emerson's reputation as a writer and lecturer, invited him to address them on the occasion of their leaving the School, and perhaps listened to him with pleasure, as to one who seemed to speak a new word. That the notions above referred to will be adopted by their composed thoughts, or the style in which they are expressed be imitated in their own writings, we cannot yet believe. However it may turn out, we are well convinced that the instructors of the School should hereafter guard themselves, by a right of veto on the nomination of the students, against the probability of hearing sentiments, on a public and most interesting occasion, and within their own walls, altogether repugnant to their feelings, and opposed to the whole tenor of their own teachings . . .

[On Ware's sermon:] It will not be necessary for us to point out to persons of the least discernment, that the character of the theology of the Cambridge School is more likely to be learned from the discourses and other publications of its professors, than from the Address which we have just noticed, containing the lucubrations of an individual who has no connexion with the School whatever. We thank the members of the School for having requested the publication of this Sermon, and we thank its author for having published it. It is good; it is seasonable. It is a strong and lucid statement of a doctrine which lies at the very foundation of religion, and will tend to disabuse the minds of many respecting the true character and tendency of a set of newly broached fancies, which, deceived by the high sounding pretensions of their proclaimers, they may have thought were about to quicken and reform the world . . .

There is a personal God, or there is none . . .

This is sense; this is truth; and this is good writing. Here is important doctrine clearly and plainly announced, so that there is no mistaking it, and so that it approves itself equally to the most and the least instructed minds. Here is a style which becomes the subject, simple, manly, straight forward.

Give us such writing and such preaching as this, and defend us from the wordiness and mysticism, which are pretending to be a better literature, a higher theology, and almost a new revelation.

18. Orestes A. Brownson (1803–1876)

Emerson's Address

[John Gorham Palfrey, Dean of the Divinity School, was reputed to have said of Emerson's address that the part of it which was not folly was downright atheism. Parker wrote in August that the general impression seemed to be that chaos had come again; many believed "that Christianity, which has weathered some storms, will not be able to stand this gale."

Brownson had not hesitated to criticize Emerson's two previous publications, and he was not going to be swept off his feet by the furor of the moment into unqualified approval. But, in the face of the situation, Brownson had difficulty maintaining perfect objectivity. Considering that most of the Unitarian opposition took the form of a whispering campaign—few having the bluntness of a Norton—Brownson again showed his contempt for the conventions of Boston society by telling the truth as loudly as possible (*The Boston Quarterly Review*, October 1838, I, 500–514).]

This is in some respects a remarkable address,—remarkable for its own character and for the place where and the occasion on which it was delivered. It is not often, we fancy, that such an address is delivered by a clergyman in a Divinity College to a class of young men just ready to go forth into the churches as preachers of the Gospel of Jesus Christ. Indeed it is not often that a discourse teaching doctrines like the leading doctrines of this, is delivered by a professedly religious man, anywhere or on any occasion.

We are not surprised that this address should have produced some excitement and called forth some severe censures upon its author; for we have long known that there are comparatively few who can hear with calmness the utterance of opinions to which they do not subscribe. Yet we regret to see the abuse which has been heaped upon Mr. Emerson. We ought to learn to tolerate all opinions, to respect every man's right to form and to utter his own opinions whatever they may be. If we regard the opinions as unsound, false, or dangerous, we should meet them calmly, refute them if we can; but be careful to respect, and to treat with all Christian meekness and love, him who entertains them . . .

In dismissing this address, we can only say that we have spoken of it freely, but with no improper feeling to its author. We love bold speculation;

we are pleased to find a man who dares tell us what and precisely what he thinks, however unpopular his views may be. We have no disposition to check his utterance, by giving his views a bad name, although we deem them unsound. We love progress, and progress cannot be effected without freedom. Still we wish to see a certain sobriety, a certain reserve in all speculations, something like timidity about rushing off into an unknown universe, and some little regret in departing from the faith of our fathers.

Nevertheless, let not the tenor of our remarks be mistaken. Mr. Emerson is the last man in the world we should suspect of conscious hostility to religion and morality. No one can know him or read his productions without feeling a profound respect for the singular purity and uprightness of his character and motives. The great object he is laboring to accomplish is one in which he should receive the hearty coöperation of every American scholar, of every friend of truth, freedom, piety, and virtue. Whatever may be the character of his speculations, whatever may be the moral, philosophical, or theological system which forms the basis of his speculations, his real object is not the inculcation of any new theory on man, nature, or God; but to induce men to think for themselves on all subjects, and to speak from their own full hearts and earnest convictions. His object is to make men scorn to be slaves to routine, to custom, to established creeds, to public opinion, to the great names of this age, of this country, or of any other. He cannot bear the idea that a man comes into the world to-day with the field of truth monopolized and foreclosed. To every man lies open the whole field of truth, in morals, in politics, in science, in theology, in philosophy. The labors of past ages, the revelations of prophets and bards, the discoveries of the scientific and the philosophic, are not to be regarded as superseding our own exertions and inquiries, as impediments to the free action of our own minds, but merely as helps, as provocations to the freest and fullest spiritual action of which God has made us capable.

This is the real end he has in view, and it is a good end. To call forth the free spirit, to produce the conviction here implied, to provoke men to be men, self-moving, self-subsisting men, not mere puppets, moving but as moved by the reigning mode, the reigning dogma, the reigning school, is a grand and praiseworthy work, and we should reverence and aid, not abuse and hinder him who gives himself up soul and body to its accomplishment. So far as the author of the address before us is true to this object, earnest in executing this work, he has our hearty sympathy, and all the aid we, in our humble sphere, can give him. In laboring for this object, he proves himself worthy of his age and his country, true to religion and to morals. In calling, as he does, upon the literary men of our community, in the silver tones of his rich and eloquent voice, and above all by the quickening influence of his example, to assert and maintain their independence throughout the whole domain of thought, against every species of tyranny that would encroach upon it, he is doing his duty; he is doing a work the effects of which will be felt for good far and wide, long after men shall have forgotten the puerility of his conceits, the affectations of his style, and the unphilosophical character of his speculations. The doctrines he puts forth, the positive instructions, for which he is now censured, will soon be classed where they belong: but the influence of his free spirit, and free utterance, the literature of this country will long feel and hold in grateful remembrance.

19. James Freeman Clarke (1810–1888), Christopher Pearse Cranch (1813–1892)

R. W. Emerson and the New School

[By November 1838 the text of Emerson's address and the news of the commotion had reached the Ohio Valley. *The Western Messenger* ran two articles, the first probably by Clarke, the second probably by Cranch. From the distance, they attempted to attain a larger perspective and to state in the broadest terms the area of agreement among the radicals. Perhaps they were already aware —Clarke had paid a visit to Boston—that the Brownson–Ripley–Channing group were muttering among themselves that Hedge and Emerson were not as helpful as they might be with the social program. Possibly this explains the rather frantic effort at the end of this article to declare allegiance not to Emerson but to Dr. Channing. Actually, by this time, even Dr. Channing was shaking his head and declaring that the "spiritualists," by asserting the immediate connection of the soul with God, "are in danger of substituting private inspiration for Christianity."]

On the whole, we think that the results of this controversy will be excellent. It will show that our Unitarian plan of church union works better in a case of real or supposed heresy, than any other . . . For ourselves, we are convinced that if Mr. Emerson has taught any thing very wrong, it will be found out, and then he will quietly drop out of the Unitarian church, or the Unitarian church will quietly fall off from him. No *excommunication* is necessary. Where people are held together by no outward bond, if the inward attraction ceases, they will soon drop apart.

The question, however, is, *has* he taught any thing wrong? Is he opposed to historical Christianity? Has he given any ground for supposing that he does not believe in the God of Christianity?

. . . To confess the truth, when we received and read the Address, we did not discover anything in it objectionable at all. We were quite delighted with it . . . Parts seemed somewhat obscure, and for that we were sorry—in places we felt hurt by the phraseology, but we bounded carelessly over these rocks of offence and pit-falls, enjoying the beauty, sincerity and magnanimity of the general current of the Address. As critics, we confess our fault. We should have been more on the watch, more ready to suspect our author when he left the broad road-way of commonplace, and instantly snap him up when he stated any idea new to us, or differing from our pre-conceived opinions.

But we must be serious—we have already, perhaps, treated this subject too ironically. The most serious charges that can be brought against a Christian man, have been laid against our author, founded on the contents of this discourse. He has been accused of Infidelity, disbelief in historical Christianity—and of probable Atheism or Pantheism. That charity which thinketh no evil, rejoiceth not in iniquity and hopeth all things, should induce every man most carefully to pause before he brings such charges against a brother. If Mr. Emerson maintains these sentiments, we can no longer hold any fellowship with him, for a wide chasm yawns between our sympathies. But not for an obscure passage in an address would we believe this of a man whose course of life has been always open—whose opinions never lay hid, and who, being such an one, has preached and still preaches as a Christian Minister . . .

It is too late in the day to put a man down by shouting Atheist, Infidel, Heretic. Formerly you could thus excite a prejudice against him that would prevent men from examining the truth of the charge. Not so now. Men cannot be in this day put down by denunciation. The whole religious pulpit and religious press has united for thirty or forty years in calling Unitarians, Deists. What is the result? That their principles are rapidly spreading. In view of this fact, let us lay aside prejudice and candidly examine every new thing . . .

When in our simplicity, we inserted an article upon Shelley in the Western Messenger, we were not aware that because a man was an Atheist he might not be commended for writing good poetry. We lamented the nature of his opinions, mourned over his want of faith, and expressly stated our aversion to his general views. We did not expect therefore to be accused of commending him, as though we had been praising him for his Atheism—least of all did we expect that we were to become members of a "new school" through the medium of that article . . .

Here then we have some means given us of detecting the members of the New School. If a man praises Shelley, he is to be suspected. If he studies Cousin, the charge is almost brought home against him. But if he admires Carlyle, and occasionally drops dark hints about Schleiermacher, he is a confirmed disciple of this new heresy.

Hic niger est. Hunc tu, Romane, caveto.

But yet, though this seems at first an easy way of detecting these dark disorganizers, some difficulty may arise in its application. Thus, there are some who read and study Cousin, but care nothing for Carlyle, or dislike him. And again, there are admirers of Carlyle, who do not wholly admit the Eclectic philosophy. And as to the admirers of Schleiermacher, veiled or otherwise, it is rather difficult to find them . . .

Now it is very true that there are those who assert that the soul is not like a sheet of white paper—that it does not acquire all knowledge by perception and reasoning, but that it is endowed by the Creator with certain ideas which arise necessarily in the mind of every sane man. The idea of cause and effect, for instance, is one—that of God another—those of time, space, infinity, and our own identity, others. We do not depend upon logic for our conviction of these things. They belong to a common sense which is back of all logic—an impartial God bestows them on all his children, and not merely on those who have been educated at Colleges and Universities . . .

The writer against the New School goes on to speak of them as announcing themselves as prophets and priests of the future—and as about to do away with old things, and abolish all the present forms of society. We do not precisely understand what this charge means. It may answer to terrify with visions of Agrarianism, respectable capitalists, but to what class of person it applies we cannot tell. We have heard indeed of Fanny Wright and Robert Dale Owen preaching against the marriage bond, and other important institutions. The paragraph might apply to them, but then we never heard of their admiring Carlyle or Cousin, or worshipping Schleiermacher even in the most secret and veiled manner. We remain in the dark therefore as to the matter of this sentence.

The writer also says a great deal about the *bad taste* of the new school in their writings. We must remind him that *taste* is, by its nature, a very personal affair, and what to one man may seem bad taste, may appear to another very good. One man may think that good taste requires every one to write like Addison or Hume, another may think it in better taste for every man to write like himself. Bossu and Boileau thought it very bad taste to have less than five acts in a play or to violate the unities or time and space. Modern critics laugh at these rules. Voltaire used to prate about good taste perpetually, and showed his own by calling Shakespeare a barbarian. In fact, he who thinks, by rules of taste, to keep the style of writing always at one point, is as foolish as he who would hold back any other part of the great social movement . . .

From all which we have said, however, we would not have it inferred that we deny the existence of a New School in Religion and Literature; but only that the characteristics as given by the writer before, do not appear to us sufficiently descriptive. They would apply to too many sorts of schools.

The truth is, our friend has failed in his definition of the New School, because he sought it in their opinions and manners, rather than in their principles and spirit. There are many who like Mr. Emerson, but do not like Cousin. Mr. E. himself, in his Dartmouth oration, finds fault with Cousin. There are others who like Cousin, who will have nothing of Emerson or Carlyle . . . We cannot find any certain test in these likes and dislikes.

Yet we agree with our friend that there is a new school. Perhaps we should agree with him as to those who are its chief masters and leaders. But we should describe them quite differently. We should say—there is a large and increasing number of the clergy and laity, of thinking men and educated women, especially of the youth in our different colleges, of all sects and all professions, who are dissatisfied with the present state of religion, philosophy and literature. The common principle which binds them together and makes them if you choose a school, is a desire for more of LIFE, soul, energy, originality in these great departments of thought. If they like Carlyle, it is not that they wholly agree with his opinions, or think his style perfect, but because they find in him a genuine man, full of life and originality. If they listen with delight to Mr. Emerson, and read his works with pleasure, it is not that they agree with all his speculations, but that they sympathize with his independence, manliness, and freedom. They read Mr. Brownson's writings, and perhaps they may not admit his opinions about the subtreasury or acquiesce in all his new views of Christianity, but they honor and esteem the free and ardent energy of thought, which every paragraph displays. In the same way they sympathize with the spirit of Mr. Furness, without accepting all his results. In a word they esteem genuine, earnest, independent thought as the one thing needful in our whole life, and where they find this in a man they are drawn toward him by strong sympathies. Wherever there is reality and not appearance, substance and not form, living energy and not hollow show, sincere conviction and not traditional cast—there they feel their chief wants met and answered. They can sympathize with orthodoxy, though holding liberal opinions, when they find orthodoxy sincere, earnest and true. They can sympathize with the doubts of those who believe less than themselves, if these doubts spring from an earnest pursuit of truth. They can join heart and hand with those who never read a page of Cousin or Carlyle, if they find them earnestly laboring by Sunday schools, city missions, and benevolent associations to put more of moral and spiritual life into society. Their sympathies embrace the secluded scholar, the active preacher, the devoted schoolmaster, the enthusiastic artist, the true poet—every man who feels that life should not be a mechanical routine, but be filled with earnestness, soul and spiritual energy. All who look, and hope, and labor for something better than now is, who believe in progress, who trust in future improvement, and are willing to spend and be spent in bringing forward that better time; all such are members of the New School.

If we are asked who is the leader of this New School, we should not name Mr. Emerson so soon as Dr. Channing. He leads on the new school, because from him has come the strongest impulse to independent thought, to earnest self-supported activity. Dr. Channing is one of those who deeply and mournfully feel the absence of life in our religion, philosophy and literature. We know not whether or not he sympathizes with the speculations of Carlyle, Emerson and Cousin; but we know that he sympathizes with earnest sincere seeking in every shape and form. And when he might condemn the results, he would still tolerate and esteem the honest seeker. He believes in progress, he sympathizes with every effort of struggling humanity to bring on by severe thought or manly action a happier and better day. And this, we take it, is the true definition of a member of the NEW SCHOOL.

20. Sampson Reed (1800–1880)

Preface, Observations, 1838

[At this point a voice from a now distant past tried to speak, but in the preoccupations of the moment he went unheeded. The Transcendentalists had long outgrown their fascination with Sampson Reed, and he, instead of aiding the new movement, seemed to them to have taken refuge in a formal church. In 1838 he brought out a new edition of his *Observations on the Growth of the Mind,* and took the occasion to add a preface in which he disowned whatever these heretics may once have derived from him. The passage is indicative of what a figure the Transcendentalists by now were cutting in the eyes of the religious community.]

The natural mind is ever backward to receive *revealed truth,* both from the character of this truth itself, and from the fact of its being revealed—from the character of the truth, because it is opposed to the affections and principles of the natural mind, and calculated to reform and regenerate them —from the fact of its being revealed, because it leaves no place for the pride of discovery . . .

From these causes it is not to be expected that the truths of the spiritual sense of the Sacred Scripture, which the Lord has now revealed through his servant Emanuel Swedenborg, will find a very ready reception. *Transcendentalism* will rather be caressed. This is the product of man's own brain; and when the human mind has been compelled to relax its grasp on sensualism, and the philosophy based on the senses, it may be expected first to take refuge here. *Transcendentalism,* even now, offers indications of an approaching popularity in this country. It may be something gained, when the idolater no longer literally worships the work of his own hands; even though he be in heart an idolater still, and worships the creations of his own imagination. So it may be a step forwards from *sensualism* to *transcendentalism.* It may be a necessary step in the progress of the human mind. But they still lie near each other—almost in contact. There is among insects a class called parasites. Their instinct leads them to deposit their eggs in the bodies of other insects, where, when the young is hatched, it has only to open its mouth and eat up its brother. It would seem to be in a way analogous to this, that Providence often permits one falsity to be removed by another. *Transcendentalism* is the parasite of *sensualism;* and when it shall have done its work, it will be found to be itself a worm, and the offspring of a worm.

21. Orestes A. Brownson (1803–1876)
Norton's Evidence

[Andrews Norton labored intensely for years upon his masterpiece, published in 1838 as *The Evidence of the Genuineness of the Four Gospels.* It is the perfect summation of Unitarian scholarship, and is everything that Emerson, in the *Divinity School Address,* clearly had in mind when he scorned "historical Christianity." Its appearance at this precise moment gave Brownson a chance upon which he pounced with undisguised glee. What he said amounted in effect to a dismissal of Norton's lifework as irrelevant; however, the peculiar insistence of Brownson begins here to become conspicuous: the real line of the separation between Unitarianism and Transcendentalism is social, and therefore Norton's theology is ultimately reprehensible because he (and Harvard University itself) is at heart antipathetic to the American democracy (*The Boston Quarterly Review*, January 1839, II, 86–113).]

When we heard that this work was announced as actually published, we trusted it would wipe out that suspicion of infidelity, which had long been attached to the author in the minds of some of his religious friends, as well as of his religious enemies; but we are sorry to say, that, to a certain extent at least, we have been disappointed. He bears the reputation of being a first-rate logician, and is said to surpass most men in the acuteness and strength of his reasoning powers; consequently, he must know better than others when he has made out his case, and done all that by the nature of his argument he is required to do. It is, therefore, difficult to believe that he himself can be satisfied with the evidences he has adduced, or that he is not well aware that his argument, taken as a whole and in all its force, falls far short of proving the truth of Christianity.

There are persons who believe that the truths of Christianity bear on their face a certain stamp of divinity, which the soul is capable of recognising . . . To these persons the question of the genuineness of the Four Gospels, is a matter of comparative indifference. They have in themselves a witness for God, and may know the things whereof they affirm. With these Christianity is not a mere matter of opinion, but of experience; and they can speak of it as of something they know, which they have seen, felt, handled. But the author of the work before us, if we rightly apprehend his views, does not arrange himself with these persons; he does not believe that the truths of Christianity bring with them their own vouchers; nor does he believe that the soul possesses any inherent power of perceiving their truth, and of knowing that they are from God. Christianity with him is an historical fact, to be established by historical evidence alone . . . In order to prove Christianity, then, it is necessary to prove that Jesus professed its truth "in the name and upon the authority of God," and that "miraculous displays of God's power" attested the fact that he was sent from God for the express purpose of teaching them. The proof of these positions is necessarily in the main historical. If, therefore, the historical proof of these be insufficient, then the truth of Christianity cannot be established . . .

If we can have no better foundation for our faith in God, Christ, and immortality, than follows from what we have thus far said . . . we confess we see no good reason for believing religion is anything more than a splendid illusion. We trust, therefore, that we shall be believed, when we say that the extraordinary and comparatively novel ground chosen by him and some of his friends, on which to rest the defence of our holy religion, fills us with deep and unaffected concern . . . Religious truth never springs up spontaneously in the human mind; there is no revelation made from God to the human soul; we can know nothing of religion but what is taught us from abroad, by an individual raised up and specially endowed with wisdom from on high to be our instructor. This individual we must hear and obey, because he speaks by divine authority. The fact, that he speaks from divine authority, no man of himself can know. There is no divinity in man to respond to and vouch for the divinity that speaks to him from without. Man has no inward power to recognise the voice of God spoken by the mouth of his inspired messengers. These messengers, when they come to us from God, must bring their credentials, sealed with God's seal; and God's seal is a miracle. Hence the vital importance of miracles. They authenticate the mission of the teacher. Did not the teacher authenticate his mission by working miracles, we, alas for us! could not know whether he came from heaven above or from hell beneath; whether he were a teacher of truth or of falsehood! God has made us all the disclosures of truth, he proposes to make; and has sent us all the messengers he ever intends to send. How much then depends on the records in which are contained those miracles which authenticated the mission of those past messengers! Deprive us of the record of those miracles, or invalidate the testimony by which the genuineness, integrity, and authenticity of those records are established, and we shall be without God or hope in the world, plunged into midnight darkness, with not the glimmering of one feeble star even to direct us . . .

We are not aware that [this doctrine] ever received any very distinct utterance, nor any firm hold upon any portion of the Church, till after the prevalence of Locke's philosophy, of which the author of the work under review is one of the few remaining disciples. Locke was a great and good man, but his philosophy was defective, and altogether unfriendly to religion. It denied the possibility of proving religion by any other arguments than miracles addressed to the outward senses, and in point of fact, it denied even those. Locke reduces man to the capacity of receiving sensations, and the faculty of reflecting on what passes within us. According to him we can have no ideas which do not enter through the senses, or which are not formed by the operations of the mind on ideas received by means of sensation. Consequently, we can have no idea of anything which is not either an object of the senses or an operation of our own minds. Now as the truths of Christianity are confessedly neither objects of the senses nor operations of our own minds, it follows that we can form no idea or conception of what they are, or what is their worth . . .

The system of philosophy, on which we are animadverting, is no less fatal to political liberty than to religion and morality; and the fact, that many generous defenders of freedom in its broadest sense, have sometimes embraced it, makes nothing against this position; for their defence of freedom was a sublime inconsistency, which does them honor. This philosophy necessarily disinherits the mass. It denies to man all inherent power of attaining to truth. In religion, if religion it admits, it refers us not to what we feel and know in ourselves, but to what was said or done in some remote age, by some special messenger from God; it refers us to some authorized teacher, and commands us to receive our faith on his word, and to adhere to it on peril of damnation. It therefore destroys all free action of the mind, all independent thought, all progress, and all living faith. In politics it must do the same. It cannot found the state on the inherent rights of man; the most it can do, is to organize the state for the preservation of such conditions, privileges, and prescriptions, as it can historically verify . . .

The doctrine, that truth comes to us from abroad, cannot coëxist with true liberty . . . The democrat is not he who only believes in the people's capacity of being taught, and therefore graciously condescends to be their instructor; but he who believes that Reason, the light which shines out from God's throne, shines into the heart of every man, and that truth lights her torch in the inner temple of every man's soul, whether patrician or plebian, a shepherd or a philosopher, a Croesus or a beggar. It is only on the reality of this inner light, and on the fact, that it is universal, in all men, and in every man, that you can found a democracy, which shall have a firm basis, and which shall be able to survive the storms of human passions.

But the disciple of Locke denies the reality of this inner light; he denies the teachings and the authority of the universal Reason. Truth may, indeed, by a miracle, kindle her torch in one man's mind, once in a thousand generations; but it is only as they borrow their light from him, that the mass can ever hope to be illuminated. He may be a central sun from which light may emanate, but they must be opaque and shine not save as he shines upon them. It is folly, therefore, to repose confidence in the people, to entertain any respect for popular decisions. The disciple of Locke may compassionate the people, but he cannot trust them; he may patronize the masses, but he must scout universal suffrage, and labor to concentrate all power in the hands of those he looks upon as the enlightened and respectable few. He distrusts the stability and endurance of our institutions. He thinks we have made a hazardous experiment. The ignorance of the people is so great, the influence of the enlightened and respectable is so small, the passions of the multitude are so brutal, blind, and violent, that it is impossible that the experiment should succeed; and our Republic must ere long fall like Athens or Rome, and a despotism be erected on its ruins. His goodness of heart, his love of Humanity may induce him to make no open war upon our institutions, and in some instances, to do what he can to give them a fair trial; but he works against his convictions, and hopes, if he hopes at all, against hope. The history of the University, in which our author is or was a professor, together with that of her favorite sons, may tend to confirm this conclusion, to which invincible logic conducts us. That University, we believe, has not of late years been renowned for her reverence for the people, her faith in democratic institutions, or her efforts to establish universal suffrage and equal rights. We have not heard that she takes any peculiar pains to educate her sons in harmony with those free principles which are the just pride of all true Americans. And we do not expect that she will, so long as Locke is her text-book in philosophy . . .

We war not with the author. He has the same right to adopt his method of proof that we have ours; but then he must expect that it will be commented on, and rejected even by those who think it insufficient, inconclusive, or too bold and hazardous. We can only add, that we have grieved to witness, of late, certain demonstrations of uncharitableness on his part towards some of our friends, and of a determination to check, by the use of hard names, and by severe denunciations, the free action of thought, and the bold utterance of honest opinion. In this he is inexcusable; for it is well known that the brand of heresy is and long has been as deep on him as it can be on any one else; and we presume that were he to recall somewhat of his past history, he would find that he himself has been guilty, if there be guilt in the matter, of the very charges he has recently brought against some of his former pupils, and younger brethren in the ministry. Perhaps he may recollect that he was once severely criticised for praising an infidel. He would do well, then, not to fill the newspapers of this city with too many denunciations of a young man who chances to say a good word for the poet Shelley. The only wise course, the only consistent course, for any man to adopt, who resolves to think for himself, is to respect the right to think for oneself in every other man; and this, too, when that other man comes to conclusions different from his own, as well as when he comes to the same.

22. Andrews Norton (1786–1853)

A Discourse on the Latest Form of Infidelity

["The hard-headed Unitarian Pope" was not the man to let Brownson's attack go unanswered, but he could not compromise his dignity by noticing the name of such a disreputable breed outside the Harvard law as Orestes Brownson. So, at a meeting of the alumni of the Divinity School on July 19, 1839, he delivered himself of the one production by which posterity must remember him. If the old-line Unitarian scholar had any reply to Emerson's address, this was Norton's opportunity. Ostensibly the argument was still over the miracles; actually, as Norton is bound to reveal, the question is the nature of man. Is he a "creature of a day," or is he, as Emerson had cried, "a new-born bard of the Holy Ghost"? Norton's address was published as a pamphlet in Cambridge in 1839.]

The present state of things imposes responsibilities upon all, who know the value of our faith and have ability to maintain it. Let us then employ this occasion in considering some of those opinions now prevalent, which are at war with a belief in Christianity . . .

The latest form of infidelity is distinguished by assuming the Christian name, while it strikes directly at the root of faith in Christianity, and indirectly of all religion, by denying the miracles attesting the divine mission of Christ . . .

If it were not for the abuse of language that has prevailed, it would be idle to say, that, in denying the miracles of Christianity, the truth of Christianity is denied. It has been vaguely alleged, that the internal evidences of our religion are sufficient, and that miraculous proof is not wanted; but this can be said by no one who understands what Christianity is, and what its internal evidences are. On this ground, however, the miracles of Christ were not indeed expressly denied, but were represented by some of the founders of the modern school of German infidelity, as only prodigies, adapted to rouse the attention of a rude people, like the Jews; but not required for the conviction of men of more enlightened minds. By others, the accounts of them in the Gospels have been admitted as in the main true, but explained as only exaggerated and discolored relations of natural events. But now, without taking the trouble to go through this tedious and hopeless process of misinterpretation, there are many who avow their disbelief of all that is miraculous in Christianity, and still affect to call themselves Christians. But Christianity was a revelation from God; and, in being so, it was itself a miracle. No proof of his divine commission could be afforded, but through miraculous displays of God's power. Nothing is left that can be called Christianity, if its miraculous character be denied. Its essence is gone; its evidence is annihilated. Its truths, involving the highest interests of man, the facts which it makes known, and which are implied in its very existence as a divine revelation, rest no longer on the authority of God. All the evidence, if evidence it can be called, which it affords of its doctrines, consists in the real or pretended assertions of an individual, of whom we know very little, except that his history must have been most grossly misrepresented . . .

The rejection of Christianity, in any proper sense of the word, the denial that God revealed himself by Christ, the denial of the truth of the Gospel history, or, as it is called in the language of the sect, the rejection of *historical* Christianity, is, of course, accompanied by the rejection of all that mass of evidence, which, in the view of a Christian, establishes the truth of his religion. This evidence, it is said, consists only of probabilities. We want certainty. The dwellers in the regions of shadows complain, that the solid earth is not stable enough for them to rest on. They have firm footing on the clouds.

To the demand for certainty, let it come from whom it may, I answer, that I know of no absolute certainty, beyond the limit of momentary consciousness, a certainty that vanishes the instant it exists, and is lost in the region of metaphysical doubt. Beyond this limit, absolute certainty, so far as human reason may judge, cannot be the privilege of any finite being. When we talk of certainty, a wise man will remember what he is, and the narrow bounds of his wisdom and of his powers . . . A creature of a day, just endued with the capacity of thought, at first receiving all his opinions from those who have preceded him, entangled among numberless prejudices, confused by his passions, perceiving, if the eyes of his understanding are opened, that the sphere of his knowledge is hemmed in by an infinity of which he is ignorant, from which unknown region, clouds are often passing over, and darkening what seemed clearest to his view,—such a being cannot pretend to attain, by his unassisted powers, any assurance concerning the unseen and the eternal, the great objects of religion. If men had been capable of comprehending their weakness and ignorance, and of reflecting deeply on their condition here, a universal cry would have risen from their hearts, imploring their God, if there were one, to reveal himself, and to make known to them their destiny. Their wants have been answered by God before they were uttered. Such is the belief of a Christian; and there is no question more worthy of consideration than whether this belief be well founded. It can be determined only by the exercise of that reason which God has given us for our guidance in all that concerns us. There can be no intuition, no direct perception, of the truth of

Christianity, no metaphysical certainty. But it would be folly, indeed, to reject the testimony of God concerning all our higher relations and interests, because we can have no assurance, that he has spoken through Christ, except such as the condition of our nature admits of . . .

. . . In one sense, and an obvious sense of the word, religion is a universal want of man. It is required for the development of his moral and spiritual powers. He is suffering, tempted, and imperfect; and he needs it for consolation, for strength to resist, and for encouragement to make progress . . . But religious principle and feeling, however important, are necessarily founded on the belief of certain facts; of the existence and providence of God, and of man's immortality. Now the evidence of these facts is not intuitive; and whatever ground for the belief of them may be afforded by the phenomena of nature, or the ordinary course of events, it is certain, that the generality of men have never been able by their unassisted reason to obtain assurance concerning them. Out of the sphere of those enlightened by divine revelation, neither the belief nor the imagination of them has operated with any considerable effect to produce the religious character . . .

But the rejection of Christianity on the ground just stated, and the pretence that the only true universal source of religion is to be found in the common nature of man, have been connected by many with the rejection of all the reasoning by which those facts that are the basis of religion may be otherwise rendered probable; and often with the rejection of all belief in the facts themselves. The religion of which they speak, therefore, exists merely, if it exists at all, in undefined and unintelligible feelings, having reference perhaps to certain imaginations, the result of impressions communicated in childhood, or produced by the visible signs of religious belief existing around us, or awakened by the beautiful and magnificent spectacles which nature presents. Sometimes, as we have elsewhere seen, they are represented as being excited by a system of pantheism; a doctrine that rejects all proper religious belief, and does not admit of being stated in words expressing a rational meaning. In this case, whatever feelings may exist, they can have no claim to be called religious.

There is, then, no mode of establishing religious belief, but by the exercise of reason, by investigation, by forming a probable judgment upon facts. Christianity, in requiring this process, requires nothing more than any other form of religion must do. He who on this account rejects it, cannot have recourse to Natural Religion. This can offer him no relief from the necessity of reasoning; and still less can it pretend to give him any higher assurance than Christianity affords. If its voice be listened to, it will only direct him back to Christianity. If he will not refrain from using the name of religion, his only resource to escape the difficulty and uncertainty of reasoning, is to take refuge in some cloud of mysticism, that belies the form of religion . . .

But we have not, it may be said, yet removed the difficulty, that the evidence and character of Christianity, in order to be properly understood, require investigations which are beyond the capacity or the opportunities of a great majority of men . . . The reply is, that it is to be received on the same ground as we receive all other truths, of which we have not ourselves mastered the evidences; for the same reason that we do not reject all that vast amount of knowledge which is not the result of our own deductions. Our belief in those truths, the evidence of which we cannot fully examine for ourselves, is founded in a greater or less degree on the testimony of others, who have examined their evidence, and whom we regard as intelligent and trustworthy . . . This reliance on the knowledge of others may be called *belief on trust,* or *belief on authority;* but perhaps a more proper name for it would be *belief on testimony,* the testimony of those who have examined a subject to their conviction of the truth of certain facts . . . The admission of this principle does not weaken the force of its evidences in the mind of any man of correct judgment. In maintaining, therefore, that the thorough investigation of the evidences and character of our religion requires much knowledge and much thought, and the combined and continued labor of different minds, we maintain nothing that gives to Christianity a different character from what belongs to all the higher and more important branches of knowledge, and nothing inconsistent with its being in its nature a universal religion.

23. George Ripley (1802–1880)
The Latest Form of Infidelity Examined

[By publishing his address as an independent pamphlet Norton entered the arena of free debate; he was no longer under the protection of Harvard or of a sympathetic editor. Since 1836 George Ripley was awaiting this opportunity; indeed, once Norton had published, everybody looked to Ripley for the reply. Since Norton made slighting references to Spinoza, Schleiermacher, and De Wette, Ripley—who had his pedantic side—let himself be drawn at length into attempting to prove these men truly religious, with a tedious array of quotations, extended through three *Letters* of 1839 and 1840. But the essence of Ripley at his best was in the first of these pamphlets, *The Latest Form of Infidelity Examined* (Boston, 1839). His major point—not far removed from Brownson's—is that the academic isolation of the Harvard faculty has disqualified them from appreciating the currents of thought and emotion now sweeping through the land and that the Transcendental ideas, which Norton had thought to refute by ridicule, are in fact the expression of this nation. Clinging to the doctrine of miracles is thus an undemocratic, and so a truly un-American, device. If the scholar has a function in America, as Emerson was contending, then perhaps he is called to a greater participation in the life of the society than either Norton or Emerson altogether contemplated.]

In the hope, that the Cambridge Theological School would be true to these momentous obligations, would answer to the piercing cry of our country and age for a free and generous theology, would be a tower of safety and strength against every foe of mental liberty, we have loved it with an exceeding love. Her name has been written on the very palms of our hands; they would sooner forget their cunning, than we could forget her welfare; she had taught us to search boldly, though meekly and reverently, into the mysteries of God and the mind of Christ; we took pleasure in her stones and even honored her dust; we valued her reputation, her influence, her usefulness, as if it had been our own; we looked to her, perhaps with exaggerated, yet with pardonable confidence, as the great hope of a progressive theology in our native land, as the fountain from which a bright and benignant light would radiate beyond the mountains of New England, and shine upon the broad and pleasant meadows of the West. This feeling has been shared in common with almost all our clergymen. We have endeavored to diffuse it in our societies; it has kindled the enthusiasm of our most noble-minded young men; our opulent citizens have not escaped its influence; and nearly the whole of our religious community have regarded the School at Cambridge as their favorite child . . .

In our happy state of society, as there is no very broad line of distinction between the clergy and the rest of the community, they had shared in the influences, which, within the last few years, have acted so strongly on the public mind; with intelligent and reflecting men of every pursuit and persuasion, many of them had been led to feel the necessity of a more thorough reform in theology; they were not satisfied that the denial of the Trinity and its kindred doctrines gave them possession of all spiritual truth; they wished to press forward in the course which they had begun, to ascend to higher views, to gain a deeper insight into Christianity, to imbibe more fully its divine spirit, and to apply the truths of revelation to the wants of society and the progress of man.

Their experience as pastors had brought them into contact with a great variety of minds; some of which were dissatisfied with the traditions they had been taught; the religion of the day seemed too cold, too lifeless, too mechanical for many of their flock; they were called to settle difficulties in theology of which they had not been advised in the school; objections were presented by men of discernment and acuteness, which could not be set aside by the learning of books; it was discovered that many had become unable to rest their religious faith on the foundation of a material philosophy; and that a new direction must be given to their ideas, or they would be lost to Christianity, and possibly to virtue. The wants of such minds could not be concealed; they were known to the ministers, if not to the world; to neglect them would have been a sin; the wandering sheep in the wilderness excited more interest than the ninety and nine which were safe in the fold, and to restore them to the good shepherd was counted a paramount duty.

In the course of the inquiries which they had entered into, for their own satisfaction and the good of their people, they had become convinced of the superiority of the testimony of the soul to the evidence of the external senses; the essential character of Christianity, as a principle of spiritual faith, of reliance on the Universal Father, and of the intrinsic equality and brotherhood of man, was made more prominent than the historical circumstances with which it was surrounded, at its introduction into the world; and the signatures of truth and divinity which it bore on its front were deemed stronger proofs of its origin with God, than even the works of might which were wrought by its Author for the benefit of man. They cherished a firm and sincere conviction of the importance of these views, and their adaptation to the peculiar wants and highest interests of the community. They never disguised the results to which they had come; they gave them a due proportion of attention in their public services; they rejoiced in their discussion, even when it was called forth by rude attacks; though sometimes misunderstood, they were not discouraged; they knew the community they lived in, which will not suffer a good man to be put down; and with a calm confidence in truth, they were content to wait for the prevalence of their views. They regarded them as the natural result of liberal inquiry in theology, chastened and purified by the influence of religious sentiment, and guided by the lights of an elevated spiritual philosophy. In the exercise of their ministry, they had been confirmed in the soundness of their ideas; their benign effects were visible among the people of their charge; and these effects were thought to be in harmony with the spirit of Christ, nay, the necessary product of the religion which he announced. They saw their opinions rapidly spreading among the younger members of the profession, while they were regarded with charity, if not with approbation, by those whom they most honored among their seniors. No difference of speculation had estranged them from the hearts of their brethren; no breach had been made in the sympathy which was the pervading principle of their association; the understanding had been sacredly observed, if not formally expressed, that a profession of faith in Christ, and a sincere and virtuous character were the conditions of fellowship, rather than any agreement in theological opinion . . .

By the exclusive principle, I mean the assumption of the right for an individual, or for any body of individuals, to make their own private opinions the measure of what is fundamental in the Christian faith. As liberal Christians, we have long contended against this principle, as contrary to the very essence of Protestantism; we have claimed the inherent right of private judgment, as essential to Christian freedom; we have resisted, to the uttermost, every attempt to impose controverted points of opinion on the universal belief of the Church. We have welcomed every man as a brother, who acknowledged Christ as his Master; we have not presumed to sit in judgment on any Christian's claim to discipleship; we have refused to entertain the question, whether he were entitled to the Christian name; we have felt that it was not ours to give or to withhold; and that the decision in all cases, must rest with himself. It was not because our exclusive brethren made a belief in the Trinity, a test of allegiance to Christ, that we accused them of inconsistency with the liberty of the Gospel; but because they presumed to erect any standard whatever, according to which the faith of individuals should be made to conform to the judgment of others. It was not any special application of the principle, that we objected to; it was the principle itself; and assuredly, the exercise of this principle does not change its character, by reason of the source from which it proceeds. Nay, is it not aggravated by the fact, that it is sustained, not by those with whom it forms a part of their religion, but by those whose religion is identified with hostility to it?

But the doctrine which lies at the foundation of your whole Discourse is a signal manifestation of the exclusive principle. You propose your own convictions,—and convictions, which it will appear in the sequel of this letter, are directly at war with the prevailing faith of the Church,—as the criterion of genuine Christian belief. You maintain that the truth of Christianity can be supported by no other evidence than that which appears satisfactory to yourself; that unless we are persuaded of the divine origin of our religion by the arguments which you deem valid, we cannot be persuaded at all; and that to speak of faith in the revelations of the Gospel, unless that faith be

built on the only basis which you pronounce to be good, is, in itself, a proof
of delusion or insincerity. You make no allowance for the immeasurable
variety of mind which is found everywhere, for the different direction which
early education, natural temperament, and peculiar associations impart to
men's habits of thinking, for the shifting lights which the same evidence presents, according to the circumstances in which it arrests the attention, or for
the changes acquired by language and the ideas which it conveys, in the
progress of ages; but you advance your principle, with the same want of
reserve or qualification that a teacher of the Infallible Church would have
exhibited before the Reformation; you declare that a certain kind of evidence,
in your view, establishes the truth of Christianity, and that he who rests his
faith on any other is an infidel, notwithstanding his earnest and open professions to the contrary. You thus, in fact, deny the name of Christian to not a
few individuals in your audience, although you avoid discussing the grounds
by which their opinions are supported. For it is perfectly well known that
many of our most eminent clergymen,—I will not refrain from speaking of
them as they deserve, on account of my personal sympathy with their views,
—repose their belief in the divine origin of Christianity on a different foundation from that which you approve as the only tenable one. Men whose names
are almost a passport to the opinions they adopt, whose lives are a guaranty
against all suspicion of guile, whose fervent devotion to every cause that
promises the extension of religion or the good of man has become proverbial,
whose candor and transparency of character is a constant memorial of the
simplicity of Christ, are inclined to rest their convictions of the divinity of
the Gospel on evidence which commends itself to their minds, although you
may pronounce it to be valueless and deceptive. Among those who adopt this
view of Christianity are clergymen who have never enjoyed the benefit of
your instructions, but whose minds have been kept open to every fresh access
of light, as well as their younger brethren who are deeply indebted to your
counsels and example in the pursuit of truth, and who have obtained from
your influence in former years, something of that spirit of freedom, for which
they are now condemned . . .

The doctrine, that miracles are the only evidence of a divine revelation, if
generally admitted, would impair the religious influence of the Christian
ministry. It would separate the pastor of a church from the sympathies of his
people, confine him in a sphere of thought remote from their usual interests,
and give an abstract and scholastic character to his services in the pulpit. The
great object of his endeavors would be to demonstrate the truth of the Christian history; the weapons of his warfare would be carnal, and not spiritual;

drawn from grammars, and lexicons, and mouldy traditions, not from the treasures of the human heart. The miracles being established to the satisfaction of an inquisitive generation, nothing would remain but to announce the truth on their authority; for as all other evidence is without value, and this alone sufficient, it would be a waste of time to direct the attention to the divine glory of Christ and his revelation; this is beyond the reach of human "perception"; none but enthusiasts can make use of it. The minister would rely for success on his skill in argument, rather than on his sympathy with man; on the knowledge he gains within the walls of the University, rather than on the experience which may be learned in the homes of his people. He would trust more to his logical demonstration of the evidences of Christianity, than to the faithful exhibition of Christian truth to the naked human heart. But, I believe, not a wise and experienced pastor can be found, who will not say that, as a general rule, the discussion of the historical evidence is ill adapted to the pulpit, and that the effects of such preaching on society at large, or on the individual conscience, are too minute to be estimated . . .

On the contrary, I have known great and beneficial effects to arise from the simple exhibition of the truth of the Gospel to the heart and conscience, by earnest men, who trusted to the intuitive power of the soul, for the perception of its divinity. The revelation of Christ is addressed to the better nature of man; "my sheep," said he, "hear my voice, and follow me, and I give unto them eternal life"; "the light shines in darkness, and the darkness comprehendeth it not," but the "children of light" look upward and are blest; it meets with a cordial reception from those who are burdened with the consciousness of sin, who are seeking for higher things, who are "feeling after God, if haply they may find him"; and this fact is the foundation of the minister's success. If you confine him to the demonstration of the miracles; if you deny him intimate access to the soul, by the truth which he bears; if you virtually tell him that the internal evidence of Christianity is a delusion, that our personal experience of its power is no proof of its divinity, and that the glorious Gospel of the blessed God is to be believed only because learned men vouchsafe to assure the humble Christian of its truth; you deprive the minister of all inward force; you make him little better than a logical machine; and much as I value a sound logic in its proper place, I am sure it is not the instrument which is mighty through God to the pulling down of the strong holds of sin. It may detect error; but it cannot give so much as a glimpse of the glory of Christ. It may refute fallacies; but it cannot bind the heart to the love of holiness. A higher power is necessary for this purpose; and such a power God has granted to man in the divine gift of Christianity, which corresponds to his inmost wants, and bears the pledge of its truth in its effects on the soul . . .

You maintain that "extensive learning" is usually requisite for those who would influence their fellow-men on religious subjects. But Jesus certainly did not take this into consideration in the selection of the twelve from the mass of the disciples; he committed the promulgation of his religion to "unlearned and ignorant" men; the sublimest truths were entrusted to the most common minds; and, in this way, "God made foolish the wisdom of the world" . . .

Christ honored man. He felt the worth of the soul. He knew its intimate connexion with God. He believed in the omnipresence of the Deity; but taught, that of all temples the "upright heart and pure" was the most acceptable. He saw that the parade of wisdom, which books impart, was as nothing before "the light that enlighteneth every human mind." The whole course of his nation's history was an illustration of the fact, "that poor mechanics are wont to be God's great ambassadors to mankind." Hence, he gave no preference to Nicodemus, that master in Israel, or to the wealthy Joseph of Arimathea, who, we may presume, had devoted his leisure to the cultivation of his mind, over Matthew the publican, or the sons of the fisherman Zebedee; and while the former were hesitating between their convictions and their comforts at home, the latter were going barefoot from city to city to preach the kingdom of God. Christ established no college of Apostles; he did not revive the school of the prophets which had died out; he paid no distinguished respect to the pride of learning; indeed, he sometimes intimates that it is an obstacle to the perception of truth; and thanks God, that while he has hid the mysteries of the kingdom of Heaven from the wise and prudent, he has made them known to men as ignorant as babes of the lore of the schools . . .

Once more, I am obliged to differ from your conclusion with regard to the practical importance of scholars to the interests of religion. Perhaps I may venture to hope, that I am not likely to be accused of indifference to human learning. But I cannot fall in with the extravagant pretensions that you urge in its favor. I deny that it entitles its possessor to the claim of infallibility. True learning, in my opinion, is as modest as it is inquisitive; it searches for truth with a lowly and reverent aspect; it never counts itself to have yet attained; it never presumes to assert that it can gain no further light on any subject; conscious of frailty, it communes with all wise teachers; and in meek self-dependence, compares the lessons they announce with the oracles of God. Such learning blesses both its disciples and those to whom they are sent; the former obtain from the latter no less instruction than they give; their reverence for man is too deep to permit the exercise of scorn; and in free and trusting intercourse with all varieties of their fellow men, they feel that they are living to learn; they are growing old in the pursuit of wisdom, with the freshness of children, γη ράσκουσι διδασκόμενοι; and the thought, that no clearer views of truth were yet to visit their minds, would almost bring them to the grave before their time.

A more sincere veneration for human beings I cannot feel, than for scholars of this character. I honor the learned, when they devote their attainments to the service of society; when they cherish a stronger interest in the welfare of their brethren, than in the luxury of their books; when they bring the researches of science to the illustration of truth, the correction of abuses, and the aid of the sufferer; but if they do not acknowledge a higher light than that which comes from the printed page; if they confound the possession of erudition with the gift of wisdom; and above all, if they presume to interfere in the communion of the soul with God, and limit the universal bounty of Heaven within their "smoky cells," I can only utter my amazement.

24. Richard Hildreth (1807–1865)
A Letter to Andrews Norton

[Richard Hildreth was not a Transcendentalist; in fact, he was the outstanding spokesman in America for Benthamite Utilitarianism. But Norton's defense of miracles on the basis of a sensational psychology was as objectionable from his point of view as from the Transcendental, and so, in *A Letter to Andrews Norton on Miracles as the Foundation of Religious Faith* (Boston, 1840), he offered the Transcendentalists his help. They did not want it and did not welcome it.

Born in Deerfield, Hildreth graduated from Harvard in 1826; he studied law and practiced in Newburyport and Boston. Ultimately he was to devote himself to a monumental *History of the United States,* published between 1849 and 1852. He was appointed consul at Trieste in 1861 and died in Florence.

The Transcendentalists were arguing that the question of miracles versus nature should never arise because all nature is divine; Hildreth agreed that it should never be asked, because all nature is scientific. However, the essence of the Emersonian position was that fact and truth are one because they "correspond"; so the Transcendentalists could not deny, even though they could not wholly welcome, the force of Hildreth's attack on supernaturalism. By either way of reasoning, Norton was demolished.]

REVEREND SIR . . . Summing up your doctrine the best I can, it seems to be this. Religion consists in knowledge, which knowledge leads to certain feelings, called Religious feelings. This Religious knowledge is only to be attained by a critical study of the Greek and Hebrew scriptures; books very difficult to be understood, very liable to be misinterpreted, and which in fact, have been interpreted to your satisfaction by nobody except yourself. As for those of us, who happen not to be skilled in Greek and Hebrew; not to understand the true principles of distinguishing the authentic from the apocryphal portions of Scripture; not to possess the secret of discriminating what in the authentic scriptures, is revealed truth, and what is only a re-statement of Jewish ignorance and prejudices; all of us thus situated, have nothing to do, but to look up for "testimony" to you, "our instructor"; and meekly and faithfully to receive your words, under an awful sense of the "responsibility" we should incur, did we dare, with our small means of knowledge, to suggest a difference or a doubt, or to attempt to exercise any influence upon the opinions of others. Indeed, the rule you lay down as to the propriety of giving publicity to opinions, must condemn all the world to perpetual silence, with the exception of those few privileged individuals, like yourself, who are so lucky as to possess the gift of infallibility . . .

Every thing, you would have us believe, except within the serene precinct of your papal jurisdiction, is instability and uncertainty. Amid the political and moral shocks of the times, amid the fierce collisions of earthly passions and cravings, the human understanding is incapable of distinguishing true from false, or bad from good . . . The human understanding has enabled us to measure the earth, to ascertain the distance of the sun, to trace the planets in their orbits, to decompose the atmosphere we breathe, to resolve material substances into their original elements,—it has enabled us, amid the "blind conflict" of life and death carried on perpetually in the material world, to trace out order, system, the great laws of nature. But to understand our social relations to each other; to discover any new political or moral means of advancing happiness and diminishing sorrow; to be able, by the calm light of an observant philosophy, to find out the springs of human action, and to learn how to control and balance them for the good of man-kind; to carry onward civilization; to advance human happiness a single step;—this, by any study of the actual phenomena of society, you pronounce to be hopeless. Such is your doctrine,—and in the name of all the philosophers of the last three centuries, those men who contributed so much to advance the limits of human knowledge, to root out ridiculous and dangerous errors, and to extend the means of human happiness, I here protest against it, and pronounce it false . . .

I cannot understand you otherwise than as asserting, that the advancement of human happiness, and the improvement of the civilized world, is identified with the spread of Unitarian Christianity of the Cambridge school, and that the only way to attain a true knowledge beneficial to mankind, is, to study the Gospels with your commentary . . .

The doctrine held by your opponents, . . . if not more true, is certainly more modest, and much more coincident with the existing state of opinions. The theologians of the new German Rational school, whom you take it upon yourself so superciliously to excommunicate from the Christian communion, do not place Religion as you do, among the natural sciences, nor yet do they suppose, with the old theologians, that the perception of Religious truth takes place only by a special interposition of the deity, a particular communication to each individual mind. So far from maintaining that Religious knowledge is "the source of all improvements in the civilized world, all advances in human happiness," so far from making the study of the sacred writings the chief occupation of the understanding, they declare and zealously maintain, that the understanding has nothing to do with Religion, or at least that so far as the understanding is at all exercised upon it, the results are nothing more than mere facts of psychology. Religion, in its true and vital sense, is a matter of feeling, which feeling leads to knowledge. This is the reverse of your process, according to which Religious feelings cannot exist, unless preceded by Religious knowledge . . .

The knowledge, however, to which Religious feelings lead, is not according to the new theology, a knowledge in any respect like that which we obtain through the medium of the understanding, by employing the senses, in the observation of outward nature, or the faculty of reflection in observing mental operations. That kind of knowledge, which goes to make up the physical and moral sciences, which together may be called the natural sciences, is confined to our relations to outward material objects, to the operations of the intellect itself, and to our social relations. That is the kind of knowledge which constitutes the exclusive province of the understanding. Religious knowledge, on the other hand, consists in the perception of our relations to infinite nature, and infinite futurity, to that infinite God in whom we, and all things, live, move, and have our being. This is a sort of knowledge which is not the proper province of the understanding. It is above the understanding; it is transcendental. It is perceived by a faculty to which has been given the name of self-consciousness, or the transcendental reason, a sort of intuition, a faculty of which Locke and his followers have denied the existence, and which they have explained away as an operation of memory repeating the lessons of childhood, or as mere play of the imagination.

It is obvious at first sight, that this new view of the nature of religious knowledge presents many advantages. It puts a stop, at once and forever, to that furious war between religion and science, which has been waged for eight centuries at such expense of human suffering, ever since the first dawn of reviving letters, down even to the present hour. It enables the philosophers and the theologians to make a partition of the realms of knowledge, as Abraham and Lot shared the pastures of Palestine, and so to live in peace . . .

Religion is thus withdrawn from those busy scenes of human life in which it has heretofore played so conspicuous, but at the same time, so doubtful, if not so disastrous a part. It sits no longer in the high seats of the synagogue, dictating what men shall believe and how they shall act. It is no longer arrayed in purple robes with a triple crown on its head, treading kings under foot, and contending with carnal weapons for an earthly heritage. Its kingdom is not of this world. It is seen no longer with sleek hair, collarless coat, and a certain hypocritical gravity of demeanor, taking sly advantage of the unwary confidence which its seeming sincerity had inspired. It does not present itself with a harsh and austere aspect, clothed in sackcloth, with a skull and cross bones in one hand, and a scourge of flagellation in the other, frowning upon the sports and vivacity of youth, and accursing all indulgence in the pleasures of sense, as though such indulgence were a defilement and a crime. It does not convert itself into a sour and saturnine spy upon the conduct of others, seeking to palm off the promptings of envy and malice as the fruits of superior enlightenment and love. It does not appear as a fat, sleek clergyman, well fed and well housed, who knows Greek, and who despises mankind. It presents itself in no external shape, neither as a bishop, an inquisitor, a monk, a quaker, a methodist, a jesuit, a church member. It eschews all external forms. It dwells within, and rules and reigns there, and there only . . .

The doctrine, however, that Religious knowledge is not a kind of knowledge perceptible by the understanding, is, and always has been, a doctrine of the Christian church. It has been held, and still is held, by all sects which pretend to call themselves Christians—the Socinians alone excepted,—that the saving and sanctifying faith of the Gospel, is something altogether independent of the understanding, and above it. Most sects have held, and still hold, that this sanctifying faith is something communicated to the soul in a miraculous way, by a special act of divine power, in each individual case. The theologians of the new school, dispense with these particular individual interferences of the deity. They dispense with the special miracle in each particular case, and ascribe the perception of divine truth to a native capacity of the human mind, separate and distinct from the understanding, and as they say above it, a capacity no doubt derived from the deity and immediately dependent upon him, but not in that particular, distinguishable from the other mental capacities . . .

Whether or not their view of the matter does in fact afford a firm foundation for Religious knowledge to rest upon, it is not my present intention to enquire; but since you so freely accuse them of infidelity and atheism, and of sapping all the foundations of Religion, I propose to show, by way of retort, that the foundation upon which you, in your turn, attempt to erect the religious edifice, is wholly incapable of sustaining such a superstructure.

You have drawn down Religion from her ancient and as it were natural fastness of continued revelation, by which she had been sheltered for ages. You refuse to place her behind those new ramparts of self consciousness, and a reason above the understanding, which the metaphysicians and theologians of Germany have of late erected to defend her. You expose her, on the open plain, bare and unsheltered, to the sharp daggers of the understanding. Having enticed her down from her heights, and forth from her strong place, you have stripped her of her heavenly armor, and have betrayed her, naked and helpless, into the hands of scorners and of infidels, even as Judas betrayed his Master into the hands of the Roman soldiers . . .

The only ground then, in your opinion, which we can possibly have for placing any confidence in one who claims to be a messenger from God, is the fact that he works miracles. The fact of his working miracles is the only evidence we can have of his divine mission, and of the truth of what he undertakes to reveal. Such is your statement.

I now proceed to show that this evidence of miracles, upon which you have rested so heavy a burden, does not, and in its nature, cannot, furnish any proof whatever to the mind of any rational man, of the truth of any alleged revelation; in fact, that it is impossible for us to know, except by the mere declarations of the apparent performer, whether an alleged miracle be a miracle or not. Instead of the miracle sustaining the revelation, faith in the revelation can alone sustain the miracle. Hence you and all who take your grounds, ought to conclude, that there is in fact no satisfactory evidence to be had of the truth of the Christian revelation, or of any other revelation, or of the truth of those facts, to wit, the existence and providence of God, and man's immortality, which, according to your account, the Christian revelation undertakes to establish . . .

Till within some three centuries past, it was the custom throughout Christendom, and it still is the custom among the ignorant, to account for whatever is unusual, and which cannot be explained by any known law of nature, by ascribing it to supernatural influence . . . In modern times, and among educated men, science has got the better of this credulity. The regularity of the laws of nature has been tested in so many of the great operations of the universe, that it has come to be received as a general principle, that whatever happens, happens in conformity to some general law.

Should a person now-a-days, present himself, who had the power, or the apparent power, of restoring the dead to life by a word, or of opening the eyes of the blind merely by commanding them to open, howsoever much we might be astonished at these remarkable performances, we should not ascribe them to any supernatural power; we should suppose them to occur in conformity to some law of nature hitherto unknown; and instead of resting in a wondering and superstitious ignorance, the whole science of the age would be turned to discover what that law was . . .

The question then, thus simplified, becomes this. Because a man in my presence, performs a wonderful work, heals the sick, for example, in a sudden and astonishing way, or restores one to life who apparently was dead,—is that a reason itself, why I must implicitly believe everything he chooses to tell me? All that I actually see, is the wonderful work. He who does it, tells me that he does it by the immediate aid of God, and that God enables him to do it, as a testimony that he is a messenger from God, and that all he says ought to be implicitly believed. But how do I know that he tells the truth? What guarantee do I have, that he does not deceive me? None in the world, except his bare word; none in the world, except those general grounds of confidence which may exist in the case of any other witness, and which are just as strong without the wonderful work, as with it . . .

The conclusion then to which we come, is this. The wonderful works recorded in the Gospels, supposing we believe them to have been actually performed, do not afford, and cannot afford, in themselves, any evidence whatever that the Gospel is a revelation from God. This is a conclusion from which no rational man can escape . . . In point of fact, so far from believing the Gospels to contain a revelation because they believe in the performance of the wonderful works therein described, it happens to most rational men, that they believe in the actual performance of the Christian miracles, only

because they believe the Gospels to contain a revelation. It is the revelation
that supports the miracles, not the miracles that support the revelation.

You see then, to what a miserable state of spiritual nakedness and destitu-
tion you have reduced us, through a vain and impotent attempt to place
Christianity at the head of the natural sciences, and to sustain it on the
foundation of the understanding alone.

As a supernatural science it may easily be sustained. The supernaturalists
of the old school, who believe in miraculous changes directly wrought upon
the soul by special acts of the deity, find nothing incredible, or even improb-
able, in the Christian Revelation. The transcendentalists of the new school,
so far at least as doctrine is concerned, find no difficulty with Christianity,
because they find it exactly accordant with the innate teachings of what they
call self-consciousness, or reason. But you, who pretend to rest Religion on
the understanding, rest it, as I have shown, upon a broken reed, a reed not
only unable to sustain it, but which pierces to its very heart. To be true to
your principles, to abide the decision of the test to which you appeal, you
ought to be an infidel, you ought to be an atheist.

25. Theodore Parker (1810–1860)
The Previous Questions between Mr. Andrews Norton and His Alumni

[At this point there entered into the debate the man who next only to
Emerson—and in the world of action even above Emerson—was to give shape and
meaning to the Transcendental movement in America. He entered, appropriately,
disguised as a square-toed, down-to-earth Yankee—which Parker basically was.

Born in Lexington, the youngest of eleven children of a farmer, Parker had
little formal schooling. He earned his living as a farmer and carpenter, and he
read everything. Admitted to Harvard, he was too poor to attend classes but took
and passed all the examinations; he conducted a school in Watertown and managed two years at the Divinity School, 1834–1836, by which time he was master of
twenty languages. He accepted the call from West Roxbury—mainly because it
was near the Boston libraries—and became the close friend of Ripley and Brownson. As his learning was prodigious, the range of his activity was staggering.

Ripley had all but spoiled his argument by wandering from the point in his
zeal for Spinoza and Schleiermacher; Hildreth was an uncomfortable support.
Assuming the rustic garb, Parker undertook to close with Norton on the central
issue, and to put the case for Transcendentalism—which was popularly supposed
to be something esoteric and exotic—in the plain language of common men, so
that the masses could see which side was arguing in their interest. His pamphlet,

*The Previous Question between Mr. Andrews Norton and His Alumni Moved
and Handled in a Letter to all Those Gentlemen,* announced as by "Levi
Blodgett," was published in Boston in 1840.]

Now since all religion in general starts from the germs, and primary
essential truths of religion, which are innate with man; since it is promoted
by religious geniuses who, inspired by God, appeal to these innate germs and
truths, in man; since all religions are fundamentally the same, and only
specific variations of one and the same genus, and since, therefore, Christianity is one religion among many, though it is the highest, and even a perfect
religion—it follows incontestably that Christianity also must start from these
same points. Accordingly we find history verifying philosophy, for Christ
always assumes these great facts, viz. the existence of God, and man's sense
of dependence upon him, as facts given in man's nature. He attempted to
excite in man a more living consciousness of these truths, and to give them
a permanent influence on the whole character and life. His words were attended to, just as the words of Homer or Socrates, and the works of Phidias
or Mozart were attended to. But admiration for his character, and the influence of his doctrines, was immeasurably greater than in their case, because
he stood in the very highest department of human interest, and spoke of
matters more concerning than poetry or philosophy, sculpture or music.
Now, if he assumed as already self-evident and undoubted, these two primary
and essential truths of religion, which had likewise been assumed by all his
predecessors—and if no miracle was needed to attest and give authority to
his doctrines respecting those very foundations and essentials of religion, no
man can consistently demand a miracle as a proof that Christ spoke the truth
when he taught doctrines of infinitely less importance, which were themselves unavoidable conclusions from these two admitted truths. Gentlemen,
I am told by my minister, who is an argumentative man, it is a maxim in
logic, that what is true of the genus, is true also of the species. If, therefore,
the two fundamentals of religion, which in themselves involve all necessary
subordinate truths thereof, be assumed by Christ as self-evident, already acknowledged, and therefore at no time, and least of all at that time, requiring
a miracle to substantiate them, I see not how it can be maintained, that a
miracle was needed to establish inferior truths that necessarily followed from
them. It would be absurd to suppose a miracle needed on the part of Socrates, to convince men that he uttered the truth, since no miracle could be a
direct proof of that fact; and still more absurd would it be, while the most
sublime doctrines, as soon as he affirmed them, were admitted as self-evident,

to demand miraculous proofs for the truth of the legitimate and necessary deductions therefrom.

Still further, Gentlemen, Christianity is either the perfection of a religion whose germs and first truths are innate in the soul, or it is the perfection of a religion whose germs and first truths are not innate in the soul. If we take the latter alternative, I admit, that, following the common opinion, miracles would be necessary to establish the divine authority of the mediator of this religion; for devout men measuring the new doctrines by reason, conscience, and the religious sentiment—the only standard within their reach—and finding this doctrine contrary and repugnant thereto, must, of necessity, repel this religion, because it was unnatural, unsatisfactory, and useless to them. To open my meaning a little more fully by an illustration,—should a man present to my eyes a figure as the Ideal of Beauty, if that figure revolted my taste; were repugnant to my sense of harmony in outline, and symmetry of parts, I should say it could not be so; but if he had satisfactory credentials to convince me that he came direct from God, and to prove that this figure was indeed the Ideal of Beauty to the archangels, who had an aesthetic constitution more perfect than that of men, and therefore understood beauty better than I could do, I should admit the fact; but must, in that case, reject his Ideal Beauty, because it was the Ideal of Deformity, relatively, to my sense, inasmuch as it was repugnant to the first principles of human taste. Now if a religion whose germs and first truths are not innate in man, should be presented by a mediator furnished with credentials of his divine office, that are satisfactory to all men, the religion must yet be rejected. The religion must be made for man's religious nature, as much as the shoe must be made for the foot. God has laid the foundation of religion in man, and the religion built up in man must correspond to that foundation, otherwise it can be of no more use to him than St. Anthony's sermon was to the fishes. There was nothing in the fishes to receive the doctrine. But if we take the other alternative, and admit that Christianity is the perfection of a religion whose germs and first truths are innate in man, and confessed to be so, by him who brings, and those who accept the religion, I see no need, or even any use of miracles, to prove the authority of this mediator. To illustrate as before; if some one brings me an image, as the Ideal of Beauty, and that image correspond to my idea of the Beautiful, though it rise never so much above it, I ask no external fact to convince me of the beauty of the image, or the authority of him who brings it. I have all the evidence of its excellent beauty that I need or wish for; all that is possible. If Raphael had wrought miracles, his works would have had no more value than now, for their value depends on no foreign authority; but on their corresponding to ideal excellence . . .

Gentlemen, I believe that Jesus, like other religious teachers, wrought miracles. I should come to this conclusion, even if the Evangelists did not claim them for him; nay, I should admit that his miracles would be more numerous and extraordinary, more benevolent in character and motive, than the miracles of his predecessors. This would naturally follow, if his power and obedience were more perfect than theirs. But I see not how a miracle proves a doctrine, and I even conjecture we do not value him for the miracles; but the miracles for him. I take it no one would think much of his common miracles, if they were not wrought by the God-man. The divine character of Christ gives value to the miracles, which cannot give divinity to Christ, or even prove it is there, as I take it; for many Christians believed Apollonius of Tyana wrought miracles, but they placed no value on them, because they had little respect for Apollonius of Tyana himself. The miracles of the Greek mythology, seem to have had no influence on the mind of the nation, because no great life lay at the bottom of these miracles. The same may be said of the miracles of the middle ages, and even of more modern times. We say these were not real miracles, and the saying is perhaps true, for the most part, but to such as believed them, they were just as good as true; yet their effect was trifling, because there was no great soul which worked these miracles. It may be said these differ in character from the Christian miracles, and the saying has its side of truth, if only the canonical miracles are included; but it is not true if the other miracles of Christian tradition are taken into account, for here malicious miracles are sometimes ascribed to him. But men found comfort in these stories only because they believed in the divinity of the character which lay at the bottom of the Christian movement . . .

Now, since these things are so, it seems to me much easier, more natural, and above all more true, to ground Christianity on the truth of its doctrines, and its sufficiency to satisfy all the moral and religious wants of man in the highest conceivable state, than to rest it on miracles, which, at best, could only be a sign, and not a proof of its excellence, and which, beside, do themselves require much more evidence to convince man of their truth, than Christianity requires without them. To me, the spiritual elevation of Jesus is a more convincing proof of his divinity, than the story of his miraculous transfiguration; and the words which he uttered, and the life which he lived, are more satisfactory evidence of his divine authority, than all his miracles, from the transformation of water into wine, to the resurrection of Lazarus. I take him to be the most perfect religious incarnation of God, without putting his birth on the same level with that of Hercules. I see the story of his supernatural conception, as a picture of the belief in the early Christian church, and find the divine character in the general instructions and heavenly life of Christ. I need no miracle to convince me that the sun shines, and just as little do I need a miracle to convince me of the divinity of Jesus and his doctrines, to which a miracle, as I look at it, can add just nothing. Even the miracle of the resurrection does not prove the immortality of the soul.

Gentlemen, I would say a word to that portion of your number who rest Christianity solely, or chiefly on the miracles. I would earnestly deprecate your theology. Happily, with the unlearned, like myself, this miracle-question is one of *theology,* and not of *religion,* which latter may, and does exist, under the most imperfect and vicious theology. But do you wish that we should rest our theology and religion—for you make it a religious question—on ground so insecure? on a basis which every scoffer may shake, if he cannot shake down—a basis which you acknowledge to be insecure when other religions claim to rest on it, and one from which your own teachers are continually separating fragments? To the mass of Christians, who are taught to repose their faith on miracles, those of the Old are as good as those of the New Testament, both of which are insecure. One of your number, a man not to be named without respect for his talents, his learning, and, above all, for his conscientious piety, a man whom it delights me to praise, though from afar—at one blow, of his Academic Lectures, fells to the ground all the most stupendous miracles of the Old Testament; and another, a party in this contest, has long ago removed several miracles from the text of the New Testament, and thrown discredit—unconsciously—upon the rest. If the groundwork of Christianity is thus to be left at the mercy of scoffers, or scholars and critics, who decide by principles that are often arbitrary, and must be uncertain, what are we the unlearned, who have little time for investigating such matters—and to whom Latin schools and colleges have not opened their hospitable doors—what are we to do? You tell us that we must not fall back on the germs and first truths of religion in the soul. You tell us that Christ *"established a relation between man and God, that could not otherwise exist,"* and the ONLY proof that this relation is *real,* and that he had authority to establish it, is found in the particular miracles he wrought, which miracles cannot, at this day, be *proved* real. Thus you repel us from the belief that the relation between God and man is founded in the nature of things, and was established at our creation, and that the authority of Christianity is not personal with Jesus, but rests on the eternal nature of Truth. Thus you make us rest our moral and religious faith, for time and

eternity, on evidence too weak to be trusted in a trifling case that comes before a common court of justice. You make our religion depend entirely on
something outside, on strange events which happened, it is said, two thousand years ago, of which we can never be certain, and on which yourselves
often doubt, at least of the more and less. Gentlemen, we cannot be critics,
but we would be Christians. If you strike away a part of the Bible, and deny
—what philosophy must deny—the perfect literal truth of the first chapter
of Genesis, or the book of Jonah, or any part which claims to be literally true,
and is not literally true, for us you have destroyed all value in miracles as
evidence—exclusive and irrefragable—for the truth of Christianity. Gentlemen, with us, Christianity is not a thing of speculation, but a matter of life,
and I beseech you, in behalf of numbers of my fellows, pious and unlearned
as myself, to do one of two things, either to prove that the miraculous stories
in the Bible are perfectly true, that is, that there is nothing fictitious or legend-
ary from Genesis to Revelations, which yet professes to be historical, and that
the authors of the Bible were never mistaken as to facts or judgments thereon;
or leave us to ground our belief in Christianity on its truth,—which is obvious
to every spiritual eye that is open,—on its fitness to satisfy our wants; on its
power to regenerate and restore degraded and fallen man; on our faith in
Christ, which depends not on his birth, or ascension; on his miraculous
powers of healing, creating, or transforming; but on his words of truth and
holiness; on his divine life; on the undisputed fact that he was ONE WITH GOD.
Until you do one of these things, we shall mourn in our hearts, and repeat
the old petition "God save Christianity from its friends, its enemies we care
not for." You may give us your miracles, and tell us they are sufficient witness, but hungering and thirsting, we shall look unto Christ, and say, "Lord,
to whom shall we go, Thou only hast the words of everlasting life," and we
believe on Thee, for thy words and life proclaim themselves divine, and these
no man can take from us.

26. J. W. Alexander, Albert Dod, Charles Hodge

Transcendentalism of the Germans and of Cousin and Its In-
fluence on Opinion in This Country

[It should never be forgotten, if the Transcendental movement is to be
understood, that the struggle in New England was at least a three-cornered one.
Actually it was even more complex, because there were feuds and factions among
the Calvinists, but the Transcendentalists were a great embarrassment to the Uni-

tarians because all varieties of Calvinists saw in them the inevitable fruit of Unitarianism. At the Princeton Theological Seminary a faculty of powerful theologians watched with grim amusement the splintering of New England. They were learned men and read German philosophy with no fear of being seduced— Charles Hodge, who taught until his death in 1878, said with pride that in his fifty years at Princeton there had never been broached a new or original idea. In *The Biblical Repertory and Princeton Review* for January 1839, the three leading professors of the Seminary did two articles analyzing the New England situation; granting that they were solid and militant Calvinists, the articles are masterly studies. It shows to what straights Norton was reduced that he should put aside the old differences between Calvinism and himself and in 1840 publish these two articles in Cambridge under the above title. Whatever his years of contending with orthodoxy may have meant to him, at this point he could join hands with those who, by exhibiting the extravagances imported from Germany, might help "to rouse from their delusion such as have been beguiled by what they do not understand." In other words, despite their verbal disagreements, and despite their century of controversy, when they were confronted with Transcendentalism and with Emerson's *Nature,* old-line Calvinism and old-line Unitarianism turned out to have more in common than they ever held separately.]

In America, the earliest school of metaphysics was founded by the followers of Locke; and, with the clew of this great inquirer in his hand, Jonathan Edwards ventured into a labyrinth from which no English theologian had ever come out safe. By the just influence of his eminently patient and discriminating and conclusive research, this greatest of modern Christian metaphysicians put his contemporaries and their descendants upon a sort of discourse which will perhaps characterize New England Calvinism as long as there is a fibre of it left . . . The theology of this school has always been, in a high degree, metaphysical; but the metaphysics is of a Hyperborean sort, exceedingly cold and fruitless. In the conduct of a feeble or even an ordinary mind, the wire-drawing processes of New England theologizing become jejune and revolting . . . Where this metaphysics was plied by a strong hand, as was that of President Edwards, it was noble indeed; deriving strength and honor from its very independence and self-sufficiency . . .

But, when the same products were sought in a colder climate, and from the hands of common and unrefined men; when every schoolmaster or parish clergyman found himself under a necessity of arguing upon the nature of the soul, the nature of virtue, and the nature of agency; when with some this became the great matter of education, to the neglect of all science and beautiful letters, then the consequences were disastrous; and a winter reigned in the theology of the land, second only to that of the scholastic age, and, like that, dispersed only by the return of the sun of vital religion . . .

Human nature could not be expected to endure such a metaphysics as that of New England. It was not merely that it was false, and that it set itself up against our consciousness and our constitutional principle of self-love; but it was cheerless, it was arctic, it was intolerable; a man might as well carry frozen mercury in his bosom, as this in his soul. In a word, it had nothing cordial in it, and it left the heart in collapse. If it had remained in the cells of speculative adepts, it might have been tolerated; but it was carried to the sacred desk, and doled forth to a hungry people under the species of bread and wine. No wonder nature revolted against such a dynasty. No wonder that, in disgust at such a *pabulum,* men cast about for a substitute, and sought it in tame Arminianism or genteel Deism . . .

In tracing the irresistible progress of thought and opinion, as it regards philosophy, we have seen two sources of that dissatisfaction which for several years has prevailed, with respect to hitherto reigning metaphysics; namely, a disrelish for the coldness, heartlessness, and fruitlessness of the New England methods, and a dread of the doctrine of Utilitarianism. It might have been happy for us, if the proposal for a change had come *ab intra,* if one of our own productive minds had been led to forsake the beaten track, and point out a higher path. But such has not been the case. It has so happened, that no great native philosophical leader has as yet arisen to draw away one scholar from the common routine. This has been very unfortunate. If we are to make experiment of a new system, we would fain have it fully and fairly before our eyes; which can never be the case so long as we receive our *philosophemata* by a double transportation, from Germany *via* France, in parcels to suit the importers; as fast as the French forwarding philosopher gets it from Germany, and as fast as the American consignee can get it from France. There is a great inconvenience in the reception of philosophical theories by instalments; and, if our cisatlantic metaphysicians import the German article, we are sometimes forced to wait until they have learned the language well enough to hold a decent colloquy in it. Such, however, is precisely the disadvantage under which the young philosophers of America now labor. We hear much of German philosophy, and of the revelations which have been made to its adepts; much very adroit use of certain disparaging terms, easily learned by heart, and applied to the old system, as "flat," "unspiritual," "empirical," and "sensuous"; we hear much of the progress made in ontological and psychological discovery in foreign universities. But, if we hear truth, the hierophants of the new system among us are not so much more intimate with the source of this great light than some of their silent readers, as to give them any exclusive right to speak *ex cathedra* about transcendental points. Some of them are busily learning French, in order to read in that language any *rifacimento* of Teutonic metaphysics which may come into their hands. Some are learning German; others have actually learned it. He who cannot do either, strives to gather into one the Sibylline oracles and abortive scraps of the gifted but indolent Coleridge, and his gaping imitators; or, in default of this, sits at the urn of dilute wisdom, and sips the thrice-drawn infusion of English from French and French from German . . .

Every English and American reader must fail to penetrate even the husk of German and mock-German philosophy, unless he has accepted the distinction between the *reason* and the *understanding* . . . "The understanding," says Kant, "is the faculty of judging according to sense." "Reason," says Coleridge, "is the power of universal and necessary convictions, the source and substance of truths above sense, and having their evidence in themselves" . . .

It deserves to be noticed, that Kant, in pursuance of his vocation as a *critical* rather than a constructive philosopher, did not attribute to Reason those divine and active powers which later philosophers have assumed, and which are claimed for her by some of our American imitators, who, we would gladly believe, are ignorant of the apotheosis of reason which they thus subserve. The genuine Kantians have always maintained, that, in what their master delivered concerning the absolute and the infinite, he meant to attribute to pure reason the power of directing the cognitive energy beyond its nearer objects, and to extend its research indefinitely; but by no means to challenge for this power the direct intuition of the absolute, as the veritable object of infallible insight . . .

We can now show the reader the ground which M. Cousin's philosophy affords him for a belief in the objective existence of the world, and God. The system of Kant led to skepticism, inasmuch as it taught, that all the laws of thought are altogether subjective, and the evil consequence was remedied only by assigning an illogical office to the Practical Reason. But M. Cousin has gained the same end, and saved his logic. "All subjectivity expires in the spontaneity of perception. Reason, it is true, becomes subjective by its relation to the free and voluntary *me,* the seat and type of all subjectivity; but in itself it is impersonal; it belongs to no one individual rather than another, within the compass of humanity: it belongs not even to humanity itself" . . . It is to this pure affirmation, sometimes represented as "so pure that it escapes notice," so bright that we cannot see it, that the appeal is made in proof of what is styled the spontaneous reason . . . That is, unless we have strength enough to make the discovery in the recesses of our own minds, a task to which M. Cousin acknowledges that but few men are equal, we must admit, that there exists in our consciousness something of which we nevertheless are not conscious, in order to be satisfied of the objective existence of either the world or God; and we regard this as so uncertain a path for arriving at certainty, that we believe few on this side of the Atlantic will trust their feet in it . . .

We trust that there is, in our country at least, enough of this feebleness of imagination to be affrighted by the bugbear, and to shrink back with horror from such a philosophical aliment as is offered by an infidel philosophy; and the more so when we see, in every new arrival of European journals, that there is scarcely a doctrine of orthodox Christianity, on which these harpies have not descended, claiming it as their own, and so defiling it by impious misuse, as to give us poison under the shape of food . . .

With this for his point of departure, it is not surprising that M. Cousin should be led to reject entirely the God of the Scriptures, and substitute in his stead a shadowy abstraction. In place of the mysterious and incomprehensible Jehovah, whose infinite perfections will be the study and delight of an eternity, we have a God whose nature and essence we can now, while seeing through a glass darkly, thoroughly comprehend, and to whom faith is not permitted to attribute any thing of excellence or glory beyond what the human intellect can clearly discern. In place of the God of Abraham, of Isaac, and of Jacob, the God to whom his people, in all ages, have fled for refuge, crying, Do *Thou* deliver me and save me, we are presented with a vague personification of abstract principles, with a God who is described as the reason; thought, with its fundamental momenta; space, time, and number; the substance of the *me,* or the free personality, and of the fatal *not me,* or nature; who returns to himself in the consciousness of man; of whose divine essence all the momenta pass into the world, and return into the consciousness of man; who is every thing, and, it might with equal significancy be added, nothing . . .

When, in the grave language of philosophy we are told, that the very essence of God is his creative power; that he is a force that was compelled to act and to pass with all his characteristics into the visible world; and that nothing now exists which has not from eternity existed in God; we are concerned, we are alarmed. This necessary transfusion of God into the universe destroys our very idea of God. He is made the substratum, the substance, of all existence; and we are only bubbles thrown up upon the bosom of the mighty ALL, to reflect the rainbow colors, in our brief phenomenal existence, and then be absorbed again into the ocean from which we came . . .

It is an ungracious task to be alarmists, and we should shun the office, if only some specialities of this or that sect were at stake, and not, as we believe, the very basis of all religion and morals. Socinianism is evangelical, when compared with the newest theology of Germany . . .

We need not seek, in the remote deductions and results of M. Cousin's philosophy, for evidence of its irreconcilable hostility to Christianity . . . The spontaneous reason, we are told by M. Cousin, is God, and the truths given by it are "literally a revelation from God" . . . This inspiration is attended always by enthusiasm . . . All men are inspired, and all are inspired in an equal degree. This spontaneity of reason, which is to all men a veritable revelation from God, "does not admit of essential differences" . . . It is too plain for argument, that these principles destroy all that is peculiar and valuable in the Sacred Scriptures. The distinctive claim which they put forth, of containing a revelation from God, is set aside by a similar claim on behalf of every man. Humanity is inspired in all its members, and revelations of truth are made to all men in nearly equal degree. When holy men of God spake of old, as they were moved by the Holy Ghost, they were but giving utterance to the visions of the spontaneous reason, and the truths declared by Christ and his Apostles were from God only in the same sense in which all our own intuitions of truth are from God. The Koran is of equal authority with the Bible; all pretended revelations have one and the same authority, that is, the self-evidence of the truths which they contain. The Gospel of Christ is thus stripped of its high prerogative as a special message from God; and holy prophets and apostles, nay, our Saviour too, were deceived in supposing that they had any other kind of communication with God, than that which every man enjoys . . . Would to God, that our fellow-Christians in America, before abandoning as shallow the philosophy of the great English fathers, would take the trouble to examine the issues of the paths on which they are entering! Let us have any philosophy, however shallow, that leaves us in quiet possession of the Gospel, rather than the dark and hopeless bewilderment into which we are thrown by the deep metaphysics of M. Cousin . . .

As there are certain limits to intellectual powers, which the immortal Locke endeavoured to ascertain, and beyond which we float in the region of midnight, so those who have forgotten these cautions have in their most original speculations only reproduced the delirium of other times, which in the cycle of opinion has come back upon us "like a phantasma or a hideous dream." In the French imitation, no less than the German original, there is a perpetual self-delusion, practised by the philosopher, who plays with words as a child with lettered cards, and combines what ought to be the symbols of thought, into expressions unmeaning and self-contradictory . . .

There is something in this new philosophy which will recommend it to many, and especially to young men. It has the charm of novelty. It affects to be very profound. It puts into the mouths of its disciples a peculiar language, and imparts to them a knowledge which none others can attain. It gives them the privilege of despising all others, and makes them incommensurable with any standard of criticism but their own. If pursued and pressed by argument, they have but to rail, as their master does, at "the paltry measure of Locke's philosophy," and ridicule the bounded, insular character of all science except that in which they are adepts. It flatters the pride of the youthful heart, it takes captive the imagination, and, a still more dangerous recommendation, it tends to lighten and remove the restraints of passion. It recognises no standard of right and wrong but the reason of man, and permits no appeal from the decisions of humanity to the authority of the one living and true God. While it retains the name of God, and does not, therefore, at once startle and shock the feelings like open atheism, it teaches its disciples to deify themselves and nature, and to look upon all phenomena alike, whether of the material universe or of the mind of man, as manifestations of the Deity. Every emotion of the heart is an acting forth of God, and every indulgence of a passion, however depraved, becomes an act of worship. The man who exercises in any way, according to his inspired impulses, his body or his mind, even though God is not in all his thoughts, is really rendering to Him acceptable service, as if his heart were filled with emotions of adoration and reverence. The forge of every smithy, as Thomas Carlyle has taught us, is an altar, and the smith, laboring in his vocation, is a priest offering sacrifice to God.

Such being the recommendations of this philosophy, it cannot be doubted that it will find many willing disciples, some attracted by one set of its charms, and some by another. If any of our most respectable colleges have engaged in teaching it, they will not find refractory pupils. But we warn them, that when this system shall have worked out, as work it must, its pernicious and loathsome results; when our young men shall have been taught to despise the wisdom of their elders, and renounce the reverence and submission which the human intellect owes to God; when, in the pride and vainglory of their hearts, they shall make bold question of the truths which their fathers have held most dear and sacred; when the Holy Bible shall be treated as the mere play-ground of antic and impious fancies, and an undisguised pantheism shall spread its poison through our literature; then shall they who have now stepped forth to introduce this philosophy among us, be held to a heavy responsibility. Are these idle fears? They are at least real. We believe, therefore do we speak. And we point the incredulous to the gradations of folly and wickedness, through which this same philosophy has led the German mind. If neither the internal evidence of the system, nor the lights of ancient and modern experience, are sufficient for conviction, we can only appeal to the verdict that time will give. In the mean while every parent and guardian in the land has an interest in knowing which of our colleges are making experiment of the effects of this philosophy upon the minds of the young men intrusted to their care.

We have another alarming symptom of its progress among us, in the Address delivered in July last, by the Rev. Ralph Waldo Emerson, before the Senior Class in Divinity, at Harvard University. This Address is before us. We have read it, and we want words with which to express our sense of the nonsense and impiety which pervade it. It is a rhapsody, obviously in imitation of Thomas Carlyle, and possessing as much of the vice of his mannerism as the author could borrow, but without his genius. The interest which it possesses for us arises from its containing the application of the Transcendental Philosophy in the form of instruction to young men, about to go forth as preachers of Christianity. The principles upon which Mr. Emerson proceeds, so far as he states them, are the same with those of M. Cousin. We find the same conception of the Deity as the substratum of all things, the same attributes assigned to the reason, and the same claim of inspiration for every man. But here we have a somewhat more distinct avowal of the results to which these principles lead, in their application to Christianity, than M. Cousin has seen fit to give us. What we had charged upon the system, before reading this pamphlet, as being fairly and logically involved in its premises, we have here found avowed by one of its own advocates. Thus we have said, that if the notion which it gives us of God is correct, then he who is concerned in the production of any phenomenon, who employs his agency in any manner, in kindling a fire or uttering a prayer, does thereby manifest the Deity and render to him religious worship. This consequence is frankly avowed and taught by Mr. Emerson. Speaking of the "religious sentiment," he says, "It is mountain air" . . . He even admonishes us, that the time is coming when men shall be taught to believe in "the identity of the law of gravitation with purity of heart" . . . He complains grievously of this want of faith in the infinitude of the soul; he cries out because "man is ashamed of himself, and skulks and sneaks through the world". . . Miracles, in the proper sense of the word, are of course discarded . . . There is not a single truth or sentiment in this whole Address that is borrowed from the Scriptures. And why should there be? Mr. Emerson, and all men, are as truly inspired as the penmen of the sacred volume. Indeed, he expressly warns the candidates for the ministry, whom he was addressing, to look only into their own souls for the truth. He has himself succeeded thus in discovering many truths, that are not to be found in the Bible . . . The present mode of interpreting Christianity, even under the form of Unitarianism, he abhors as utterly repugnant to reason, and insufficient for the wants of our nature; he stigmatizes it as an historical, traditional Christianity, that has its origin in past revelations, instead of placing its faith in new ones . . . He treats Christianity as a Mythos, like the creeds of Pagan Greece and Rome, and does not even pay it sufficient respect, under this aspect, to be at the trouble of interpreting for us more than a few of the hidden meanings, that lie concealed under its allegorical forms. We have at least to thank him, on behalf of those whose eyes might not otherwise have been opened, for giving us so distinct and ample an illustration of the kind of service which M. Cousin professes himself willing to render to Christianity by means of his philosophy. We would call public attention to this Address, as the first fruits of transcendentalism in our country. We hold it up as a warning evidence of the nature of the tree which has produced it . . .

We pretend not, as we have said, to comprehend these dogmas. We know not what they are; but we know what they are *not* . . . No one, who has ever heard such avowals, can forget the touching manner in which pious as well as celebrated German scholars have sometimes lamented their still lingering doubts as to the personality of God. But while these systems rob us of our religious faith, they despoil us of our reason. Let those who will, rehearse to us the empty babble about reason as a faculty of immediate insight of the infinite; we will trust no faculty, which, like Eastern princes, mounts the throne over the corpses of its brethren. We cannot sacrifice our understanding. If we are addressed by appeals to consciousness, to intuition, we will try those appeals. If we are addressed by reasoning, we will endeavour to go along with that reasoning. But in what is thus offered, there is no ratiocination; there is endless assertion, not merely of unproved, but of unreasonable, of contradictory, of absurd propositions. And if any overcome by the *prestige* of the new philosophy, as transatlantic, or as new, are ready to repeat dogmas which neither they, nor the inventors of them, can comprehend, and which approach the dialect of Bedlam, we crave to be exempt from the number, and will contentedly abstain for life from "the high *priori* road." The more we have looked at it, the more we have been convinced of its emptiness and fatuity. It proves nothing; it determines nothing; or, where it seems to have results, they are hideous and godless. Moreover, we think we speak the sentiment of a large body of scholars in our country, when we say, that if we must have a transatlantic philosophy, we desire to have it in its native robustness and freshness. We do not wish to have it through the medium of French declaimers, or of the French language, than which no tongue is less fit to convey the endless distinctions of the German . . . We learn with pain, that, among the Unitarians of Boston and its vicinity, there are those who affect to embrace the pantheistic creed. The time may not be far off, when some new Emerson shall preach pantheism under the banner of a self-styled Calvinism; or when, with formularies as sound as those of Germany, some author among ourselves may, like Dinter, address his reader thus, *O thou Son of God!* For the tendency of German philosophizing is towards impious temerity. We have long deplored the spread of Socinianism, but there is no form of Socinianism, or of rational Deism, which is not immeasurably to be preferred to the German insanity. In fine, we cleave with more tenacity than ever to the mode of philosophizing which has for several generations prevailed among our British ancestors; and especially to that Oracle in which we read, what the investigation of this subject has impressed on us with double force, that God will destroy the wisdom of the wise, and bring to nothing the understanding of the prudent; that the foolishness of God is wiser than men, and that, when men change the truth of God into a lie, he will give them over to a reprobate mind.

27. Orestes A. Brownson (1803–1876)
Two Articles from The Princeton Review

[Parker and Brownson were the only Transcendentalists who commanded the kind of scholarship in systematic theology that could meet the Princeton pundits on their own ground, and Brownson was the only one who so loved a fight for the sake of fighting that he was ready to encounter the Princetonians. In *The Boston Quarterly Review* for July 1840 (III, 265–323), he reviewed Norton's edition of the articles and produced the best of the apologies for Transcendentalism that arose in answer to Norton's accusation of infidelity. By now all the lines of cleavage had been discovered and exposed; it was Brownson's proud contention that the movement in the first place was not an importation but was entirely native, and secondly that it was a profound revolt of the democracy against sacerdotalism. But Brownson's magnificent essay closed on a somewhat disturbing note: he would call himself a Transcendentalist if the term meant an innate capacity for discovering truth, but if it was to mean lawless fancy instead of enlightened understanding, Brownson would reject it. Were the Transcendentalists certain that they would not ever give him reason to suspect that the terms of reproach had some justification?]

No tolerable observer of the signs of the times can have failed to perceive that we are, in this vicinity at least, in the midst of a very important revolution; a revolution, which extends to every department of thought, and threatens to change ultimately the whole moral aspect of our society. Everything is loosened from its old fastenings, and is floating no one can tell exactly whither. The revolution—or movement, if the term be preferred,—has already extended too far to be arrested, and is so radical in its nature, that none who take the least interest in the general condition of their race, can regard it with indifference.

It was not to be expected that all would look upon this movement from the same point of view, or with the same feelings. In reference to this, as to all other important movements, the community is naturally divided into the party of the Hopeful and that of the Fearful. They who have felt the insufficiency of the old systems, creeds, intellectual and social wants, who feel the impulse of this new movement, and labor for its furtherance, must hail it with joy, and contemplate its progress with thanksgiving; but they who are satisfied with the old order of things, who regard all change as necessarily a departure from truth and holiness, must needs behold it with alarm, and unaffected grief . . .

Among those who have taken the most decided stand against this new movement, no man is in this neighborhood more conspicuous than Mr. Andrews Norton . . . It is said he usually sits in a room with the shutters closed, which has the double effect of keeping the light out and the darkness in. This may be slander, but his productions, it must be confessed, afford no satisfactory refutation of it.

But be this as it may, we cannot but respect Mr. Norton for his readiness to oppose publicly what he holds to be mischievous speculation. Many others, who think with him, have in private circles denounced in no measured terms the men and the doctrines of what is termed the new school, but he is almost the only one who has had the manliness to bring his charges before the public, and in a tangible shape. He is almost the only one in this neighborhood, who has been willing to come out publicly in defence of the old school, and to give the advocates of the new an opportunity to speak out in their own behalf . . . Certain it is, that he regards the questions at issue of a momentous character, and their right solution as of immense importance to religion and morals. So far he is right, and should be commended for the stand he has taken.

It is not easy to characterize in a word the new movement, the progress of which Mr. Norton and his friends would arrest. The men who are affected by it are called by their opponents, Transcendentalists, and their doctrines are termed Transcendentalism. The movement is properly threefold; philosophical, theological, and political or social; and they who are affected by it are in pursuit of a sound philosophy of the human mind, a just interpretation of man's relations to his Maker, and with his brother. Their doctrines relate to religion, philosophy, and liberty; and on these three subjects, the new school and the old are at issue.

How the name, Transcendentalist, came to be applied to the members of this movement party, we are not informed. They did not themselves assume it, nor does it with any justice describe them. They differ widely in their opinions, and agree in little except in their common opposition to the old school. They do not swear by Locke, and they recognise no authority in matters of opinion but the human mind, whether termed the reason with some of them, or the soul with others. They have all felt that our old catechisms need revision, and that our old systems of philosophy do not do justice to all the elements of human nature, and that these systems can by no means furnish a solid basis for belief in God, much less in Christianity. Here is the amount of their agreement. Some of them embrace the Transcendental philosophy, some of them reject it, some of them *ignore* all philosophy, plant themselves on their instincts, and wait for the huge world to come round to them. Some of them read Cousin, some Goethe and Carlyle, others none at all. Some of them reason, others merely dream. No single term can describe them. Nothing can be more unjust to them, or more likely to mislead the public than to lump them all together, and predicate the same things of them all.

It is against this movement party that Mr. Norton and his friends direct their efforts . . . Mr. Norton characterizes it as the latest form of infidelity; the Princeton Reviewers labor to fix upon it the charges of impiety, atheism, pantheism, and that of being of a foreign origin.

With regard to the last charge, we would suggest to our patriotic brethren that truth transcends both time and space, and if so be we have it, it matters little whether its first discoverer be a Frenchman, a Dutchman, or a Yankee. But in point of fact the charge is unfounded . . . The movement is really of American origin, and the prominent actors in it were carried away by it before ever they formed any acquaintance with French or German metaphysics; and their attachment to the literatures of France and Germany is the effect of their connexion with the movement, not the cause.

Moreover, there are no members of the movement party, who would adopt entirely the views of any one of the distinguished foreigners named. We are inquiring for ourselves, and following out the direction of our own minds, but willing to receive aid, let it come from what quarter it may. These distinguished foreigners are not our masters, but our fellow disciples, and we feel under no special obligation to defend their opinions. We have nothing to do with Hegel, or Schelling, or Kant, or Cousin, any further than our own inquiries lead us to approve their speculations. We are aiming at truth, and believe that here, where thought is free, and the philosopher may tell his whole thought without any circumlocution or reticence, we may attain to a purer philosophy than can be found in either France or Germany . . .

The real aim of the Transcendentalist is to ascertain a solid ground for faith in the reality of the spiritual world. Their speculations have reference in the main to the grounds of human knowledge. Can we know anything? If so, how and what? Here is the real question with which they are laboring. Some of them ask this question without any ulterior views, merely for the sake of satisfying their own minds; others ask it for the purpose of legitimating their religious beliefs; others still, that they may obtain a firm foundation for political freedom. This question is, as every philosopher knows, fundamental, and must be answered before we can proceed scientifically in the construction of any system of religion, morals, or politics . . .

Mr. Norton seems to us to assume the negative of this question . . . Far be it from us, however, to intimate that Mr. Norton consciously and intentionally adopts the skeptical doctrine . . . all we mean is that his language, if taken in its simple and literal sense, must carry him thus far . . . The philosophical system to which he is attached, affords, it is evident, no solid ground to *religious* faith. This system of philosophy, of which Locke is the greatest modern master, recognises in man no power of knowing anything which transcends the senses, except the operations of our own minds. Adopting this system, Berkeley demonstrated but too easily the non-existence of the external world; and Hume, by showing that we can by no power we possess attain legitimately to the idea of cause, opened the door to universal skepticism. Condillac and the French *philosophes,* by taking it up in relation to its account of the origin of human knowledge, struck out of existence all spiritual beings, and of course all religion, and with it all foundation for morals.

It is this fact which has lead our Transcendentalists to reject it. They felt, if that philosophy was to be adopted as the last word of the reason, that faith and reason must forever be irreconcilable, and that no man could be religious but at the expense of his logic. The senses are merely the medium through which we become acquainted with the facts of the external world. They demand in the soul, distinct from themselves, a power to recognise, to perceive the objects they present. Now, if this power be denied, all knowledge must be denied. This power the old philosophy has denied by representing the mind prior to the affection of the senses as a mere blank sheet.

Furthermore, if all our ideas come through the senses, we can have no idea of anything which transcends them. God, all the objects of the spiritual world, in as much as they confessedly are not objects of the senses, must then be absolutely inconceivable. Add, if you will, to the senses reflection, and you do not help the matter. Reflection can add nothing but itself to the materials furnished by the senses, and reasoning can deduce from those materials only what is contained in them. The spiritual is not contained in them, and therefore cannot be deduced from them.

This the Transcendentalists have seen and felt. They have therefore looked into the consciousness, examined human nature anew, to see if they could not find in man the power of recognising and of knowing objects which transcend the reach of the senses. This power they profess to have discovered. They claim for man the power, not of discovering, but of knowing by intuition the spiritual world. According to them objects of religious faith are not merely objects believed on testimony, but objects of science, of which we may have a true inward experience, of which we may have a direct and immediate knowledge, as much so as of the ideas or sensations of our own minds. We may know that God exists as positively, as certainly, as we may know that we feel hunger or thirst, joy or grief . . .

If Mr. Norton be right in representing the truths of religion as matters transcending human knowledge, it follows that we can assert them and believe in them only on the authority of the miraculous being supposed. This being must be miraculously endowed, or else he himself could know no more of the matter than ordinary mortals, and therefore could speak with no more authority. Hence, we are driven to the necessity of declaring miracles the sole evidence possible of Christianity. . . . The whole definition is therefore based on the hypothesis, that it is not the truths of religion themselves that we believe, but the mere fact that they have been miraculously asserted.

The Transcendentalists would define belief in Christianity somewhat differently. They would say, by a belief in Christianity, we mean a belief in the truths, in the reality of the spiritual objects, which Jesus Christ revealed; and now that these truths are revealed, brought to light, we may have a direct perception of them, may know them, and therefore receive them without reference to the authority or endowments of him who first revealed them. While therefore they would not hesitate to acknowledge Jesus as the one who was divinely commissioned to reveal these truths, they would claim for themselves now, in the actual state of Humanity, the ability to perceive them and to know immediately, by intuition, by a mere looking upon them, that they are truths.

Here is the fundamental difference between Mr. Norton and the Transcendentalists, on this question of the evidences of Christianity . . . Mr. Ripley no more than Mr. Norton denies the supernatural origin of Christianity . . . He also admits that the miracles recorded in the New Testament were actually wrought . . . Mr. Norton asserts that we can at best know only the fact, that the teacher is divinely commissioned, from which it is fair to infer the truth of what he taught; Mr. Ripley maintains that we may know by direct perception, by actual experience, the truths themselves, that what the teacher taught is true, without being under the necessity of inferring it from the fact that the teacher was divinely commissioned.

The difference between the two is very great, and the advantages are altogether on Mr. Ripley's side. On Mr. Norton's ground Christianity can be sustained only by means of those historical proofs, that sustain the miracles by which the authority of the teacher is attested. These historical proofs, Mr. Norton himself admits, do not amount to certainty. But this objection he seeks to obviate by contending that certainty is not for such beings as we are . . . On his own hypothesis, the truth of Christianity is not a certainty but a probability. But it is a probability that rests on historical testimony. It can then be a probability only to those who can avail themselves of that testimony. This everybody knows is but a small portion of mankind. His doctrine, then, not only deprives us of all certain evidence of the certain truth of Christianity, but declares that the great mass of mankind are absolutely disinherited by their Maker, placed out of the condition of ever ascertaining for themselves even the probable truth of that which they must believe, or have no assurance of salvation. They are placed entirely at the mercy of the learned few, and the Gospel which was glad tidings to the poor can be glad tidings only to the erudite.

Mr. Ripley's doctrine, on the contrary, rescues the mass from the power of the learned few, and places the truth of Christianity within the reach of every man. Few only of our race are able to judge of the pretensions of an authorized teacher, to sift the testimony of history, balance probabilities and decide for themselves, whether the miracles recorded in the New Testament were actually wrought or not, or if wrought that they establish the divine authority of the teacher; but all are capable of judging of the doctrine itself, whether it be of God or not. The unlettered ploughman by this is placed, so far as the evidences of his religious faith are concerned, on a level with the most erudite scholar or the profoundest philosopher. Christianity by this is adapted to the masses, and fitted to become an universal religion. Its evidence is simplified, and the necessity of relying on an authorized teacher superseded. It recognises a witness within the soul that testifies for God, and gives us the grounds of a living faith in his being and his providence, in his love and his mercy. It destroys the very foundation of a sacerdotal caste, and saves Humanity from ecclesiastical domination. It paves the way for universal freedom, for every man to become a priest and a king, and gives assurance that the prophets did not merely dream in foretelling the approach of a time, when we shall not "teach every man his neighbor and every man his brother, saying, Know the Lord; for all shall know him from the least to the greatest"...

In conclusion, we should say, that we have thus far accepted the name Transcendentalism, although it is not one of our own choosing, nor the one we approve. So far as Transcendentalism is understood to be the recognition in man of the capacity of knowing truth intuitively, or of attaining to a scientific knowledge of an order of existence transcending the reach of the senses, and of which we can have no sensible experience, we are Transcendentalists. But when it is understood to mean, that feeling is to be placed above reason, dreaming above reflection, and instinctive intimation above scientific exposition; in a word when it means the substitution of a lawless fancy for an enlightened understanding, as we apprehend it is understood in our neighborhood, by the majority of those who use it as a term of reproach, we must disown it, and deny that we are Transcendentalists.

6

Manifestoes

Unitarians having been all along the party whose opinions were new and strange, and opposed to those of the whole Christian community, and being denounced, and misrepresented, and persecuted on this account, have been loudly singing the praises of charity and liberality. They have scarcely ever had an opportunity of trying whether they could be liberal, and tolerant, and charitable themselves . . .

But now here comes Mr. Emerson, and utters some doctrines which sound strange . . . Mr. Emerson they know and acknowledge to be a singularly pure-minded, devout and conscientious person. But what do some of them do? . . . They denounce him, and all who are supposed to think with him; and they get up a popular excitement, and a terror of dreadful heresies, and talk about "the latest form of Infidelity," and ask indignantly or sorrowfully, "what we are coming to?" . . . Are we always to go on in this round? Shall we never learn to tolerate any heresy but our own? In my opinion, if any person ought to be liberal, it is those who have all along been taking, somewhat arrogantly, the name of Liberal Christians.

—JAMES FREEMAN CLARKE

1. Ralph Waldo Emerson (1803–1882)

The Editors to the Reader

[From its first meeting the Transcendental Club talked of founding an "organ of a spiritual philosophy." After *The Christian Examiner* was closed to them, the need became urgent. Brownson offered them his *Quarterly*, but it was becoming evident that he was not in perfect sympathy with the others. At a meeting on September 18, 1839, the decision was taken, and in November, Margaret Fuller agreed to be editor. Alcott suggested the title, *The Dial*, and Ripley promised to undertake "all the business part."

The public in general found *The Dial* laughable, and everybody connected with it professed to find it not what they dreamed of. "I suffer in looking over it now," said Margaret, and Emerson's apologies for it to Carlyle are simply abject. It was to survive only four years, never made any money, and never attained more than three hundred subscribers at the most. In 1842 Emerson became editor and Elizabeth Peabody the publisher. In the perspective of time, the work looms constantly larger in our cultural history—if only as a gallant effort to conduct a free and critical and literate journal.

Margaret Fuller wrote the introductory announcement, but Emerson rewrote it so extensively that he considered it his own. It has not been reprinted in the standard edition of his works, but it is surely one of the finest and most gracious of his utterances. The graciousness was particularly conspicuous against the background of controversy that now was at its most angry pitch. (*The Dial*, July 1840, I, 1–4).]

W E invite the attention of our countrymen to a new design. Probably not quite unexpected or unannounced will our Journal appear, though small pains have been taken to secure its welcome. Those, who have immediately acted in editing the present Number, cannot accuse themselves of any unbecoming forwardness in their undertaking, but rather of a backwardness, when they remember how often in many private circles the work was projected, how eagerly desired, and only postponed because no individual volunteered to combine and concentrate the freewill offerings of many coöperators. With some reluctance the present conductors of this work have yielded themselves to the wishes of their friends, finding something sacred and not to be withstood in the importunity which urged the production of a Journal in a new spirit.

As they have not proposed themselves to the work, neither can they lay any the least claim to an option or determination of the spirit in which it is conceived, or to what is peculiar in the design. In that respect, they have obeyed, though with great joy, the strong current of thought and feeling, which, for a few years past, has led many sincere persons in New England to make new demands on literature, and to reprobate that rigor of our conventions of religion and education which is turning us to stone, which renounces hope, which looks only backward, which asks only such a future as the past, which suspects improvement, and holds nothing so much in horror as new views and the dreams of youth.

With these terrors the conductors of the present Journal have nothing to do,—not even so much as a word of reproach to waste. They know that there is a portion of the youth and of the adult population of this country, who have not shared them; who have in secret or in public paid their vows to truth and freedom; who love reality too well to care for names, and who live by a Faith too earnest and profound to suffer them to doubt the eternity of its object, or to shake themselves free from its authority. Under the fictions and customs which occupied others, these have explored the Necessary, the Plain, the True, the Human,—and so gained a vantage ground, which commands the history of the past and the present.

No one can converse much with different classes of society in New England, without remarking the progress of a revolution. Those who share in it have no external organization, no badge, no creed, no name. They do not vote, or print, or even meet together. They do not know each other's faces or names. They are united only in a common love of truth and love of its work. They are of all conditions and constitutions. Of these acolytes, if some are happily born and well bred, many are no doubt ill dressed, ill placed, ill made—with as many scars of hereditary vice as other men. Without pomp, without trumpet, in lonely and obscure places, in solitude, in servitude, in compunctions and privations, trudging beside the team in the dusty road, or drudging a hireling in other men's cornfields, schoolmasters, who teach a few children rudiments for a pittance, ministers of small parishes of the obscurer sects, lone women in dependent condition, matrons and young maidens, rich and poor, beautiful and hard-favored, without concert or proclamation of any kind, they have silently given in their several adherence to a new hope, and in all companies do signify a greater trust in the nature and resources of man, than the laws or the popular opinions will well allow.

This spirit of the time is felt by every individual with some difference,—to each one casting its light upon the objects nearest to his temper and habits of thought;—to one, coming in the shape of special reforms in the state; to another, in modifications of the various callings of men, and the customs of business; to a third, opening a new scope for literature and art; to a fourth, in philosophical insight; to a fifth, in the vast solitudes of prayer. It is in every form a protest against usage, and a search for principles. In all its movements, it is peaceable, and in the very lowest marked with a triumphant success. Of course, it rouses the opposition of all which it judges and condemns, but it is too confident in its tone to comprehend an objection, and so builds no outworks for possible defence against contingent enemies. It has the step of Fate, and goes on existing like an oak or a river, because it must.

In literature, this influence appears not yet in new books so much as in the higher tone of criticism. The antidote to all narrowness is the comparison of the record with nature, which at once shames the record and stimulates to new attempts. Whilst we look at this, we wonder how any book has been thought worthy to be preserved. There is somewhat in all life untranslatable into language. He who keeps his eye on that will write better than others, and think less of his writing, and of all writing. Every thought has a certain imprisoning as well as uplifting quality, and, in proportion to its energy on the will, refuses to become an object of intellectual contemplation. Thus what is great usually slips through our fingers, and it seems wonderful how a life-like word ever comes to be written. If our Journal share the impulses of the time, it cannot now prescribe its own course. It cannot foretell in orderly propositions what it shall attempt. All criticism should be poetic; unpredictable; superseding, as every new thought does, all foregone thoughts, and making a new light on the whole world. Its brow is not wrinkled with circumspection, but serene, cheerful, adoring. It has all things to say, and no less than all the world for its final audience.

Our plan embraces much more than criticism; were it not so, our criticism would be naught. Everything noble is directed on life, and this is. We do not wish to say pretty or curious things, or to reiterate a few propositions in varied forms, but, if we can, to give expression to that spirit which lifts men to a higher platform, restores to them the religious sentiment, brings them worthy aims and pure pleasures, purges the inward eye, makes life less desultory, and, though raising men to the level of nature, takes away its melancholy from the landscape, and reconciles the practical with the speculative powers.

But perhaps we are telling our little story too gravely. There are always great arguments at hand for a true action, even for the writing of a few pages. There is nothing but seems near it and prompts it,—the sphere in the ecliptic, the sap in the apple tree,—every fact, every appearance seem to persuade to it.

Our means correspond with the ends we have indicated. As we wish not to multiply books, but to report life, our resources are therefore not so much the pens of practised writers, as the discourse of the living, and the portfolios which friendship has opened to us. From the beautiful recesses of private thought; from the experience and hope of spirits which are withdrawing from all old forms, and seeking in all that is new somewhat to meet their inappeasable longings; from the secret confession of genius afraid to trust itself to aught but sympathy; from the conversations of fervid and mystical pietists; from tear-stained diaries of sorrow and passion; from the manuscripts of young poets; and from the records of youthful taste commenting on old works of art; we hope to draw thoughts and feelings, which being alive can impart life.

And so with diligent hands and good intent we set down our Dial on the earth. We wish it may resemble that instrument in its celebrated happiness, that of measuring no hours but those of sunshine. Let it be one cheerful rational voice amidst the din of mourners and polemics. Or to abide by our chosen image, let it be such a Dial, not as the dead face of a clock, hardly even such as the Gnomon in a garden, but rather such a Dial as is the Garden itself, in whose leaves and flowers and fruits the suddenly awakened sleeper is instantly apprised not what part of dead time, but what state of life and growth is now arrived and arriving.

2. George Ripley (1802–1880)

Letter to the Church in Purchase Street

["What a brave thing Mr. Ripley has done," wrote Emerson to Margaret Fuller. "He stands now at the head of the Church militant and his step cannot be without an important sequel." Ripley's resignation from the Purchase Street Church should be remembered as one of the great symbolic gestures of the era, even more than Emerson's departure from the Second Church—if only because Ripley was now a much older man and was making a greater gamble with his own and his wife's future. It has not been widely enough remembered, in part because Ripley managed it with an entire absence of melodrama and in part because Ripley himself has been too much forgotten. But in the circumstances, it was an act of pure heroism, and it merited what Emerson said of it.

There was no real quarrel; Ripley's congregation were devoted to him. But in all honesty, Ripley could no longer serve them under the terms on which he had come to them, and so out of a nice scruple of conscience he felt he must go. He offered to resign on May 21, 1840, and on October 1, after four months of patient discussion, he wrote to the church a letter which is at once a history of the New England mind in the period of his pastorate and an act of secession from the church and fellowship of Bowen and Norton. The text is from O. B. Frothingham, *George Ripley* (Boston, 1888, pp. 63–91).]

I had met you for many years from Sunday to Sunday; the thoughts and feelings, which were perhaps new to many of you when first presented, had lost much of their freshness; my own mind had ceased to take a deep interest in many points which we had fully considered with each other; while at the same time I was aware there were others in which I had a deep concern, which had failed to attract your attention. I was called upon, notwithstanding, to address nearly the same individuals, to pursue the same track on which we had long traveled together, to use great diligence lest I should depart from the usual sphere of the pulpit, and touch on subjects which, by the general consent of our churches, are banished from the ordinary meeting of our public assemblies on the Lord's Day. Such a course must always be productive of depression and embarrassment. Unless a minister is expected to speak out on all subjects which are uppermost in his mind, with no fear of incurring the charge of heresy or compromising the interests of his congregation, he can never do justice to himself, to his people, or the truth which he is bound to declare . . . I was fully sensible that I was suffering from this influence; that I had not strength to resist the formality and coldness which are breathed from the atmosphere of our churches; and that, unless we could all break away from such influences, it was wholly in vain for me to speak any longer in this pulpit. It was my wish, therefore, to leave you perfectly free to make such arrangements as would conduce to your highest welfare . . .

I will confess, also, that I was somewhat influenced in the conclusion at which I had arrived by the present aspect of the times. This is very different from what it was when I became your minister. In 1826 the Unitarian controversy was in the ascendent. It excited general interest; questions of dogmatic theology were in every one's mouth; and a popular exposition of the arguments from reason and Scripture in favor of liberal views always commanded general attention. At the same time, inquiries relating to personal religion were not infrequent; many were aroused from the slumber of worldliness and sin; for the first time, religion became a subject of vast and solemn import to their souls; and the plainest and most elementary instruction on the duties of the Christian life were everywhere welcome. That was a good state of things . . . But this state of things it seems could not last forever. It passed away, and a new order of ideas was brought forward. The essential principles of liberal Christianity, as I had always understood them, made religion to consist, not in any speculative doctrine, but in a divine life. They asserted the unlimited freedom of the human mind, and not only the right, but the duty of private judgment. They established the kingdom of God, not in the dead past, but in the living present; gave the spirit a supremacy over the letter; insisted on the necessity of pointing out the corruptions of the church, of sweeping away the traditions which obscured the simplicity of truth, and urged every soul to press on to the highest attainment; to forget what was behind, and never to be kept back from expressing its convictions by the voice of authority or the fear of man. A portion of the liberal clergy felt it their duty to carry out these views; to be faithful to their principles; not to shrink from their application, but to exercise the freedom which God gave them in the investigation of truth and the enforcement of its practical results. They could not linger around the grave of the past. The experiences of manhood enlarged the conception of their pupilage. They had been taught that no system of divinity monopolized the truth, and they were no more willing to be bound by the prevailing creed of Boston and Cambridge, than their fathers had been by the prescription of Rome or Geneva. But in these conclusions they were divided from some of their brethren. It was thought dangerous to continue the progress which had been commenced. Liberal churches began to fear liberality, and the most heretical sect in Christendom to bring the charge of being so against those who carried out its own principles. They who defended the progress as well as the freedom of thought were openly denounced as infidels; various unintelligible names were applied to them; and, instead of judging the tree by its fruits, and acknowledging the name of Christian to all who possessed Christ's spirit and claimed to have received his revelation, men appealed to the prejudices of the multitude, and sought to destroy the religious influence of their brethren, on account of the speculative opinion which they sincerely believed to be true and Christian. Now it was with this latter class that I always found myself. I had a native aversion to human authority for the soul; truth seemed to me to be supernatural, and our own perception limited. I could not stand still; I had faith in man and in God, and never felt the slightest alarm lest the light from above should lead into paths of danger. But I soon found that this spirit could not pass without rebuke. The plainest expositions of Christian truth, as it seemed to me, were accused of heresy. Every idea which did not coincide with prevailing opinions, and many which had heretofore always been received by liberal churches, were considered hostile to church and state, were spoken of under various appellations which no man understood, and this caused the uninitiated to fear and the good to grieve . . .

If it be an objection that a man speaks in the pulpit, as men speak anywhere else, on subjects that deeply interest them, the true man will soon find that he can speak more to the purpose in some other place. It has moreover always been one of my firmest convictions, that we meet in the church on the broadest ground of a spiritual equality. The true followers of Jesus are a band of brothers; they compose one family; they attach no importance whatever to the petty distinctions of birth, rank, wealth, and station; but feeling that they are one in the pursuit of truth, in the love of holiness, and in the hope of immortal life, they regard the common differences of the world, by which men are separated from each other, as lighter than the dust of the balance . . . These ideas I have perhaps insisted on more strongly than any others, for they have been near my heart; they are a part of my life; they seem to me to be the very essence of the religion which I was taught. The great fact of human equality before God is not one to let the heart remain cold; it is not a mere speculative abstraction; it is something more than a watch-word for a political party to gain power with, and then do nothing to carry it into practical operation; it is a deep, solemn, vital truth, written by the Almighty in the laws of our being, announced with terrible distinctness to the oppressor by his beloved Son, and pleaded for by all that is just and noble in the promptings of our nature. Blame me for it if you will, but I cannot behold the degradation, the ignorance, the poverty, the vice, the ruin of the soul, which is everywhere displayed in the very bosom of Christian society in our own city, while men look idly on, without a shudder. I cannot witness the glaring inequalities of condition, the hollow pretension of pride, the scorn-ful apathy with which many urge the prostration of man, the burning zeal with which they run the race of selfish competition, with no thought for the elevation of their brethren, without the sad conviction that the spirit of Christ has well-nigh disappeared from our churches, and that the fearful doom awaits us, "Inasmuch as ye have not done it unto one of the least of these, ye have not done it unto me" . . .

The idea of social worship can be carried into effect only in a congrega-tion where there is a prevailing harmony of sentiment between the people and the minister; where the questions which most interest his mind are those which they are also most desirous to hear discussed; where the arrangements of the society allow the most perfect freedom of departure to all who have ceased to be interested in the views that are advanced. Whenever the attention of the minister is strongly drawn to subjects which are not regarded as im-portant by the hearer, the free, sympathetic chain which binds heart with heart is disturbed, no electric spark is drawn forth, the speaker loses his power, and the people are not moved.

Now this is precisely the position which one portion of our community holds towards another, and, in many cases, ministers and people share in its embarrassments . . .

The attention of some good men is directed chiefly to individual evils; they wish to improve private character without attacking social principles which obstruct all improvement; while the attention of other good men is directed to the evils of society; they think that private character suffers from public sins, and that, as we are placed in society by Providence, the advance-ment of society is our principal duty. With regard to these questions there is a great difference of opinion. They compose the principal subjects of thought at the present day. They form what is called the exciting questions by which society is now agitated. I should not do justice, my friends, to you or myself, if I were to close this communication without noticing the ground I have occupied in regard to those questions. It has been made, as you are aware, the cause of some reproach. A popular cry has been started by many individuals against the advocates of new views on philosophy and the condition of society, and, in common with many others, you have heard accusations brought against principles by those who have failed even to explain the meaning of the terms by which they were denounced.

There is a class of persons who desire a reform in the prevailing philosophy of the day. These are called Transcendentalists, because they believe in an order of truths which transcends the sphere of the external sense. Their leading idea is the supremacy of mind over matter. Hence they maintain that the truth of religion does not depend on tradition, nor historical facts, but has an unerring witness in the soul. There is a light, they believe, which enlighteneth every man that cometh into the world; there is a faculty in all—the most degraded, the most ignorant, the most obscure—to perceive spiritual truth when distinctly presented; and the ultimate appeal on all moral questions is not to a jury of scholars, a hierarchy of divines, or the prescriptions of a creed, but to the common sense of the human race. These views I have always adopted; they have been at the foundation of my preaching from the first time that I entered the pulpit until now. The experience and reflection of nearly twenty years have done much to confirm, nothing to shake, them; and if my discourses in this house, or my lectures in yonder vestry, have in any instance displayed the vitality of truth, impressed on a single heart a genuine sense of religion, disclosed to you a new prospect of the resources of your own nature, made you feel more deeply your responsibility to God, cheered you in reason of the reality and worth of the Christian revelation, it was because my mind has been trained in the principles of Transcendental Philosophy,—a philosophy which is now taught in every Protestant university on the Continent of Europe, which is the common creed of the most enlightened nations, and the singular misunderstanding of which among ourselves illustrates more forcibly, I am ashamed to say, the heedless enterprise than the literary culture of our countrymen. If you ask, why I have not preached the philosophy in the pulpit, I answer that I could not have preached without it, but my main business as a minister, I conceive, has been, not to preach philosophy or politics or medicine or mathematics, but the Gospel of Christ. If you ask whether I embrace every unintelligible production of the mind that is quoted from mouth to mouth as Transcendentalism, I answer, that if any man writes so as not to be understood, be he Transcendentalist or Materialist, it is his own fault, not another's; for my own part, I agree with Paul, "that I had rather speak five words with my understanding, that by my voice I might teach others also, than ten thousand words in an unknown tongue." There is another class of persons who are devoted to the removal of the abuses that prevail in modern society. They witness the oppressions that are done under the sun, and they cannot keep silence. They have faith that God governs man; they believe in a better future than the past. Their daily prayer is for the coming of the kingdom of righteousness, truth, and love; they look forward to a more pure, more lovely, more divine state of society than was ever realized on earth. With these views, I rejoice to say, I strongly and entirely sympathize. While I do not feel it my duty to unite with any public association for the promotion of these ideas, it is not because I would disavow their principles, but because in many cases the cause of truth is carried forward better by individual testimony than by combined action. I would not be responsible for the measures of a society; I would have no society responsible for me; but in public and private, by word and by deed, by persuasion and example, I would endeavor to help the progress of the great principles which I have at heart. The purpose of Christianity, as I firmly believe, is to redeem society as well as the individual from all sin. As a Christian, then, I feel bound to do what I can for the promotion of universal temperance, to persuade men to abandon every habit which is at war with their physical welfare and their moral improvement, and to produce, by appeals to the reason and conscience, that love of inward order which is beyond the reach of legal authority. As a Christian, I would aid in the overthrow of every form of slavery; I would free the mind from bondage and the body from chains; I could not feel that my duty was accomplished while there was one human being, within the sphere of my influence, held to unrequited labor at the will of another, destitute of the means of education, or doomed to penury, degradation, and vice by the misfortune of his birth. I conceive it to be a large share of the minister's duty to preach the gospel to the poor, to announce glad tidings of deliverance to all that are oppressed. His warmest sympathies should be with those who have none to care for them; he should never be so much in earnest as when pleading the cause of the injured. His most frequent visits will not be to the abodes of fashion and luxury, but to the dwellings where not many of the wise and mighty of this world are apt to enter; and if he can enjoy the poor man's blessing, whom he has treated like an equal and a brother in all the relations of life, whose humble abode he has cheered by the expression of honest sympathy, and whose hard lot draws tears from those unused to sorrow, he will count it a richer reward than the applause of society or the admiration of listening crowds. There is another cause in which I feel the strongest interest, and which I would labor to promote,—that of inward peace between man and man. I have no faith whatever in the efficacy or the lawfulness of public or private wars. If they have ever been necessary in the progress of society, as I know they have been unavoidable, it was owing to the prevalence of the rude, untamed animal passions of man over the higher sentiments of his nature. It should be the effort of every true man to abolish them altogether; to banish the principles from which they proceed; to introduce the empire of justice and love; and to abstain on all occasions from the indulgence of bitterness or wrath in his own conduct, and to offer no needless provocation for its indulgence in others. I believe in the omnipotence of kindness, of moral intrepidity, of divine charity. If society performed its whole duty, the dominion of force would yield to the prevalence of love, our prisons would be converted into moral hospitals, the schoolmaster would supersede the executioner, violence would no more be heard in our land, nor destruction in our borders. Our walls would be salvation, and our gates praise.

I have thus laid before you, my friends, what I proposed to communicate on this occasion. I have used great plainness of speech. I have kept nothing back. I have omitted no topic on which I thought light or explanation was demanded. You will have no further occasion to inquire from others what I believe or think, as you have received as explicit disclosures as I know how to make from my own lips. If, after you have heard the statements now presented, you shall arrive at different conclusions from those contained in the letter of your committee; if you shall think that another's voice can be heard here with greater advantage than my own; if you shrink from one who comes before you laden with so many heresies; I shall claim no privilege in this place. I shall consult your truest interests ever; and I cannot believe that they will be promoted by your being compelled to listen to one with whom you feel a diminished sympathy. If, on the other hand, you do not decline my services, on the conditions which I have stated, it will be my earnest endeavor to build you up in holiness, in freedom, in faith, so long as I stand here. But I can never be a different man from what God has made me. I must always speak with frankness the word that comes into my heart; and my only request is that it may be heard with the same frankness and candor with which it is uttered.

3. George Ripley (1802–1880)
A Farewell Discourse

[The congregation still loved him, but could not accept Ripley's statement of October. On January 1, 1841, he requested permission to resign; the society voted to let him go, and on January 30 the committee wrote him an admiring letter. On March 28 he preached his farewell discourse, which the church proudly printed.

The seventeenth century heretics—Anne Hutchinson, Roger Williams—came to their conclusions reluctantly, and at length were cast out by the authorities for standing firm on what they could not surrender. Ripley eagerly embraced heresy, and then exiled himself. That Transcendentalism produced such "tender" consciences helps to account for several phenomena of the period, for such resignations from the pulpit as Emerson's, Ripley's, W. H. Channing's, as well as for Henry Thoreau's more comprehensive resignation from all institutions he had never joined.]

It might very innocently be supposed that if the pastor were more inclined to conform to ancient usage; if he were more willing to work in the yoke of popular customs, to take his views of truth from his elders, rather than from his own mind; if he would acquiesce more readily in prevalent errors and abuses; if he would take the social standard of Boston at this moment, as the everlasting standard of right; if he would consider all ideas except those of domestic manufacture, as contraband; if he would be content to remain fast anchored to the fixtures of the crudest youth, and preach forever as he preached ten years ago; if he would close his eyes upon the broad light which is now rising upon the nation, and join the popular cry against reform and progress; if he could be induced to humor the prejudices of men, and exert a little more of clerical authority; if his sympathies were more with those who are conspicuous in the rank of wealth and fashion, and he would cease to pour contempt on merely outside distinctions; if his strongest friendships were not with the lowly and wretched, and his most earnest endeavors put forth in their behalf; in short, if it were his aim to be more of a priest and less of a man, it is possible that our affairs might wear a different aspect. It is possible that the church might be completely filled by one who had the burden of no peculiar heresies, and who was more willing to fall in the ways of the world, than to conquer and live above it.

It was natural, I say, that such suggestions should be made even by those of whose friendship and respect, I had no reason to doubt. I honor the frankness, with which at any time, I have been made acquainted with them, but they have never acted strongly on my mind, except in one direction; they have all tended to convince me, that I had too little faith in many popular prevalent ideas, to satisfy a congregation, that was not as far from them as myself. One course only remained for me,—to give a full disclosure of all my heresies; to confess that I was a peace man, a temperance man, an abolitionist, a transcendentalist, a friend of radical reform in our social institutions; and if there be any other name that is contrary to sound doctrine, as now expounded by the masters in our Israel, to consent to bear whatever stigma might be attached to it. I was unwilling to sustain a false position for a moment. As soon as I knew that any suspicion was attached to what forms the very central spring of my life, and which I regard as the essence of reason and of Christianity, I was bound to declare the whole; and if through no fault of mine, I had been misunderstood before, I should be misunderstood no longer.

The only grounds on which I could continue the pastoral care, not being accepted by the congregation, as declared to me by the committee with whom I had an interview for that purpose, I had no alternative but to resign my office. This has been done, and to-day my resignation is carried into effect.

4. Theodore Parker (1810–1860)
A Discourse of the Transient and Permanent in Christianity

[The identity of "Levi Blodgett" was soon known. In January 1840, when it came his turn to deliver a Thursday Lecture, Parker spoke on "Inspiration," and was denounced by one clergyman as "impious." In May 1840 the Unitarian Conference argued the question of whether differences of opinion concerning miracles ought to exclude men from Christian fellowship. "This is the nineteenth century!" Parker wrote in his journal. "This is Boston! This among the Unitarians!"

On May 19, 1841, Charles C. Shackford was to be ordained in the South Boston Church; he invited Parker to give the sermon. Parker delivered the *Transient and Permanent*. The commotion that followed made the furor over Alcott or Emerson seem very pale indeed. A layman, named Bradford, declared in the Boston *Courier* that he would rather have every Unitarian church razed to the ground than to have one man of Parker's sentiments in the pulpit. Some eight or nine ministers supported Parker, or at least refused to condemn him, and his own congregation stood by him, but otherwise he was ostracized from respectable Boston. No other minister would exchange pulpits with him, and what hurt Parker most was the defection of his old friend, Convers Francis, now moving to Harvard: "Francis fell back on acct. of his Professorship at Cambridge!" Parker was a sensitive and affectionate man; he suffered acutely. He acknowledged his utter disillusionment with the Unitarian clergy: "I once thought them noble; that they would be true to an ideal principle of right. I find that no body of men was ever more completely sold to the sense of expediency." As for himself, he resolved that he would not sit down tamely. "I will go eastward and westward, and northward and southward, and make the land *ring*."]

Heaven and earth shall pass away; but my words shall not pass away.
　　　　　　　　　　　　　　　　　　　　　—Luke xxi:33

　　　In this sentence we have a very clear indication that Jesus of Nazareth believed the religion he taught would be eternal, that the substance of it would last forever. Yet there are some who are affrighted by the faintest rustle which a heretic makes among the dry leaves of theology; they tremble lest Christianity itself should perish without hope. Ever and anon the cry is raised, "The Philistines be upon us, and Christianity is in danger." The least doubt respecting the popular theology, or the existing machinery of the church; the least sign of distrust in the religion of the pulpit, or the religion of the street, is by some good men supposed to be at enmity with faith in Christ, and capable of shaking Christianity itself. On the other hand, a few bad men, and a few pious men, it is said, on both sides of the water, tell us the day of Christianity is past. The latter, it is alleged, would persuade us that hereafter piety must take a new form; the teachings of Jesus are to be passed by; that religion is to wing her way sublime, above the flight of Christianity, far away, toward heaven, as the fledged eaglet leaves forever the nest which sheltered his callow youth. Let us therefore devote a few moments to this subject, and consider what is *transient* in Christianity, and what is *permanent* therein. The topic seems not inappropriate to the times in which we live, or the occasion that calls us together.

　　　Christ says his words shall never pass away. Yet, at first sight, nothing seems more fleeting than a word. It is an evanescent impulse of the most fickle element. It leaves no track where it went through the air. Yet to this, and this only, did Jesus intrust the truth wherewith he came laden to the earth,—truth for the salvation of the world. He took no pains to perpetuate his thoughts; they were poured forth where occasion found him an audience,—by the side of the lake, or a well; in a cottage, or the temple; in a fisher's boat, or the synagogue of the Jews. He founds no institution as a monument of his words. He appoints no order of men to preserve his bright and glad relations. He only bids his friends give freely the truth they had

freely received. He did not even write his words in a book. With a noble
confidence, the result of his abiding faith, he scattered them broadcast on
the world, leaving the seed to its own vitality. He knew that what is of God
cannot fail, for God keeps his own. He sowed his seed in the heart, and
left it there, to be watered and warmed by the dew and the sun which
heaven sends. He felt his words were for eternity. So he trusted them to the
uncertain air; and for eighteen hundred years that faithful element has held
them good,—distinct as when first warm from his lips. Now they are translated into every human speech, and murmured in all earth's thousand tongues,
from the pine forests of the North to the palm groves of eastern Ind. They
mingle, as it were, with the roar of a populous city, and join the chime of
the desert sea. Of a Sabbath morn they are repeated from church to church,
from isle to isle, and land to land, till their music goes round the world.
These words have become the breath of the good, the hope of the wise, the
joy of the pious, and that for many millions of hearts. They are the prayers
of our churches; our better devotion by fireside and fieldside; the enchantment of our hearts. It is these words that still work wonders, to which the
first recorded miracles were nothing in grandeur and utility. It is these
which build our temples and beautify our homes. They raise our thoughts
of sublimity; they purify our ideal of purity; they hallow our prayer for
truth and love. They make beauteous and divine the life which plain men
lead. They give wings to our aspirations. What charmers they are! Sorrow
is lulled at their bidding. They take the sting out of disease, and rob adversity of his power to disappoint. They give health and wings to the pious
soul, broken-hearted and shipwrecked in his voyage through life, and encourage him to tempt the perilous way once more. They make all things
ours; Christ our brother; time our servant; death our ally, and the witness
of our triumph. They reveal to us the presence of God, which else we might
not have seen so clearly in the first wind-flower of spring, in the falling of
a sparrow, in the distress of a nation, in the sorrow or the rapture of the
world. Silence the voice of Christianity, and the world is well-nigh dumb;
for gone is that sweet music which kept in awe the rulers and the people,
which cheers the poor widow in her lonely toil, and comes, like light through
the windows of morning, to men who sit stooping and feeble, with failing
eyes and a hungering heart. It is gone—all gone! only the cold, bleak world
left before them.

Such is the life of these words; such the empire they have won for themselves over men's minds since they were spoken first. In the meantime, the
words of great men and mighty, whose name shook whole continents, though

graven in metal and stone, though stamped in institutions, and defended by whole tribes of priests and troops of followers,—their words have gone to the ground, and the world gives back no echo of their voice. Meanwhile the great works, also, of old times, castle and tower, and town, their cities and their empires, have perished, and left scarce a mark on the bosom of the earth to show they once have been. The philosophy of the wise, the art of the accomplished, the song of the poet, the ritual of the priest, though honored as divine in their day, have gone down a prey to oblivion. Silence has closed over them; only their spectres now haunt the earth. A deluge of blood has swept over the nations; a night of darkness, more deep than the fabled darkness of Egypt, has lowered down upon that flood, to destroy or to hide what the deluge had spared. But through all this the words of Christianity have come down to us from the lips of that Hebrew youth, gentle and beautiful as the light of a star, not spent by their journey through time and through space. They have built up a new civilization, which the wisest Gentile never hoped for, which the most pious Hebrew never foretold. Through centuries of wasting these words have flown on, like a dove in the storm, and now wait to descend on hearts pure and earnest, as the Father's spirit, we are told, came down on his lowly Son. The old heavens and the old earth are indeed passed away, but the Word stands. Nothing shows clearer than this how fleeting is what man calls great, how lasting what God pronounces true.

Looking at the word of Jesus, at real Christianity, the pure religion he taught, nothing appears more fixed and certain. Its influence widens as light extends; it deepens as the nations grow more wise. But, looking at the history of what men call Christianity, nothing seems more uncertain and perishable. While true religion is always the same thing, in each century and every land, in each man that feels it, the Christianity of the pulpit, which is the religion taught, the Christianity of the people, which is the religion that is accepted and lived out, has never been the same thing in any two centuries or lands, except only in name. The difference between what is called Christianity by the Unitarians in our times, and that of some ages past, is greater than the difference between Mahomet and the Messiah. The difference at this day between opposing classes of Christians, the difference between the Christianity of some sects and that of Christ himself, is deeper and more vital than that between Jesus and Plato, pagan as we call him. The Christianity of the seventh century has passed away. We recognize only the ghost of superstition in its faded features, as it comes up at our call. It is one of the things which have been, and can be no more; for neither God nor the world goes back. Its terrors do not frighten, nor its hopes allure us. We rejoice that it has gone. But how do we know that our Christianity shall not share the same fate? Is there that difference between the nineteenth century and some seventeen that have gone before it since Jesus, to warrant the belief that our notion of Christianity shall last for ever? The stream of time has already beat down philosophies and theologies, temple and church, though never so old and revered. How do we know there is not a perishing element in what we call Christianity? Jesus tells us *his* word is the word of God, and so shall never pass away. But who tells us that *our* word shall never pass away? that *our notion* of his word shall stand for ever?

Let us look at this matter a little more closely. In actual Christianity,—that is, in that portion of Christianity which is preached and believed, — there seems to have been, ever since the time of its earthly founder, two elements, the one transient, the other permanent. The one is the thought, the folly, the uncertain wisdom, the theological notions, the impiety of man; the other, the eternal truth of God. These two bear, perhaps, the same relation to each other that the phenomena of outward nature, such as sunshine and cloud, growth, decay, and reproduction, bear to the great law of nature, which underlies and supports them all. As in that case more attention is commonly paid to the particular phenomena than to the general law, so in this case more is generally given to the transient in Christianity than to the permanent therein.

It must be confessed, though with sorrow, that transient things form a great part of what is commonly taught as religion. An undue place has often been assigned to forms and doctrines, while too little stress has been laid on the divine life of the soul, love to God, and love to man. Religious forms may be useful and beautiful. They are so, whenever they speak to the soul, and answer a want thereof. In our present state some forms are perhaps necessary. But they are only the accident of Christianity, not its substance. They are the robe, not the angel, who may take another robe quite as becoming and useful. One sect has many forms; another, none. Yet both may be equally Christian, in spite of the redundance or the deficiency. They are a part of the language in which religion speaks, and exist, with few exceptions, wherever man is found. In our calculating nation, in our rationalizing sect, we have retained but two of the rites so numerous in the early Christian Church, and even these we have attenuated to the last degree, leaving them little more than a spectre of the ancient form. Another age may continue or forsake both; may revive old forms, or invent new ones to suit the altered circumstances of the times, and yet be Christians quite as good as we, or our fathers of the dark ages. Whether the apostles designed these rites to be perpetual seems a question which belongs to scholars and antiquarians,—not to us, as Christian men and women. So long as they satisfy or help the pious heart, so long they are good. Looking behind or around us, we see that the forms and rites of the Christians are quite as fluctuating as those of the heathens; from whom some of them have been, not unwisely, adopted by the earlier church.

Again, the doctrines that have been connected with Christianity, and taught in its name, are quite as changeable as the form. This also takes place unavoidably. If observations be made upon nature,—which must take place so long as man has senses and understanding,—there will be a philosophy of nature, and philosophical doctrines. These will differ, as the observations are just or inaccurate, and as the deductions from observed facts are true or false. Hence there will be different schools of natural philosophy, so long as men have eyes and understandings of different clearness and strength. And if men observe and reflect upon religion,—which will be done so long as man is a religious and reflective being,—there must also be a philosophy of religion, a theology, and theological doctrines. These will differ, as men have felt much or little of religion, as they analyze their sentiments correctly or otherwise, and as they have reasoned right or wrong. Now, the true system of nature, which exists in the outward facts, whether discovered or not, is always the same thing, though the philosophy of nature, which men invent, change every month, and be one thing at London and the opposite at Berlin. Thus there is but one system of nature as it exists in fact, though many theories of nature, which exist in our imperfect notions of that system, and by which we may approximate and at length reach it. Now, there can be but one religion which is absolutely true, existing in the facts of human nature and the ideas of infinite God. That, whether acknowledged or not, is always the same thing, and never changes. So far as a man has any real religion,—either the principle or the sentiment thereof,—so far he has that, by whatever name he may call it. For, strictly speaking, there is but one kind of religion, as there is but one kind of love, though the manifestations of this religion, in forms, doctrines, and life, be never so diverse. It is through these, men approximate to the true expression of this religion. Now while this religion is one and always the same thing, there may be numerous systems of theology or philosophies of religion. These, with their creeds, confessions, and collections of doctrines, deduced by reasoning upon the facts observed, may be baseless and false, either because the observation was too narrow in extent, or otherwise defective in point of accuracy, or because the reasoning was illogical, and therefore the deduction spurious. Each of these

three faults is conspicuous in the systems of theology. Now, the solar system
as it exists in fact is permanent, though the notions of Thales and Ptolemy,
of Copernicus and Descartes, about this system, prove transient, imperfect
approximations to the true expression. So the Christianity of Jesus is permanent, though what passes for Christianity with popes and catechisms, with
sects and churches, in the first century or in the nineteenth century prove
transient also. Now, it has sometimes happened that a man took his philosophy of nature at second-hand, and then attempted to make his observations
conform to his theory, and nature ride in his panniers. Thus some philosophers refused to look at the moon through Galileo's telescope; for, according to their theory of vision, such an instrument would not aid the
sight. Thus their preconceived notions stood up between them and nature.
Now, it has often happened that men took their theology thus at second-
hand, and distorted the history of the world and man's nature besides, to
make religion conform to their notions. Their theology stood between them
and God. Those obstinate philosophers have disciples in no small number.

What another has said of false systems of science will apply equally to
the popular theology: "It is barren in effects, fruitful in questions, slow and
languid in its improvement, exhibiting in its generality the counterfeit of
perfection, but ill filled up in its details, popular in its choice, but suspected
by its very promoters, and therefore bolstered up and countenanced with
artifices. Even those who have been determined to try for themselves, to add
their support to learning, and to enlarge its limits, have not dared entirely
to desert received opinions, nor to seek the spring-head of things. But they
think they have done a great thing if they intersperse and contribute something of their own; prudently considering, that by their assent they can save
their modesty, and by their contributions, their liberty. Neither is there, nor
ever will be, an end or limit to these things. One snatches at one thing,
another is pleased with another; there is no dry nor clear sight of anything.
Every one plays the philosopher out of the small treasures of his own fancy;
the more sublime wits more acutely and with better success, the duller with
less success, but equal obstinacy; and, by the discipline of some learned men,
sciences are bounded within the limits of some certain authors which they
have set down, imposing them upon old men and instilling them into young.
So that now (as Tully cavilled upon Caesar's consulship) the star Lyra riseth
by an edict, and authority is taken for truth, and not truth for authority;
which kind of order and discipline is very convenient for our present use, but
banisheth those which are better."

Any one who traces the history of what is called Christianity, will see that nothing changes more from age to age than the doctrines taught as Christian, and insisted on as essential to Christianity and personal salvation. What is falsehood in one province passes for truth in another. The heresy of one age is the orthodox belief and "only infallible rule" of the next. Now Arius, and now Athanasius, is lord of the ascendant. Both were excommunicated in their turn, each for affirming what the other denied. Men are burned for professing what men are burned for denying. For centuries the doctrines of the Christians were no better, to say the least, than those of their contemporary pagans. The theological doctrines derived from our fathers seem to have come from Judaism, Heathenism, and the caprice of philosophers, far more than they have come from the principle and sentiment of Christianity. The doctrine of the Trinity, the very Achilles of theological dogmas, belongs to philosophy and not religion; its subtleties cannot even be expressed in our tongue. As old religions became superannuated, and died out, they left to the rising faith, as to a residuary legatee, their forms and their doctrines; or rather, as the giant in the fable left his poisoned garment to work the overthrow of his conqueror. Many tenets that pass current in our theology seem to be the refuse of idol temples, the off-scourings of Jewish and heathen cities, rather than the sands of virgin gold which the stream of Christianity has worn off from the rock of ages, and brought in its bosom for us. It is wood, hay, and stubble, wherewith men have built on the corner-stone Christ laid. What wonder the fabric is in peril when tried by fire? The stream of Christianity, as men receive it, has caught a stain from every soil it has filtered through, so that now it is not the pure water from the well of life which is offered to our lips, but streams troubled and polluted by man with mire and dirt. If Paul and Jesus could read our books of theological doctrines, would they accept as their teaching what men have vented in their name? Never, till the letters of Paul had faded out of his memory; never, till the words of Jesus had been torn out from the book of life. It is their notions about Christianity men have taught as the only living word of God. They have piled their own rubbish against the temple of Truth where Piety comes up to worship; what wonder the pile seems unshapely and like to fall? But these theological doctrines are fleeting as the leaves on the trees. They—

"Are found
Now green in youth, now withered on the ground:
Another race the following spring supplies;
They fall successive, and successive rise."

Like the clouds of the sky, they are here to-day; tomorrow, all swept off and vanished; while Christianity itself, like the heaven above, with its sun, and moon, and uncounted stars, is always over our head, though the cloud sometimes debars us of the needed light. It must of necessity be the case that our reasonings, and therefore our theological doctrines, are imperfect, and so perishing. It is only gradually that we approach to the true system of nature by observation and reasoning, and work out our philosophy and theology by the toil of the brain. But meantime, if we are faithful, the great truths of morality and religion, the deep sentiment of love to man and love to God, are perceived intuitively, and by instinct, as it were, though our theology be imperfect and miserable. The theological notions of Abraham, to take the story as it stands, were exceedingly gross, yet a greater than Abraham has told us, "Abraham desired to see my day, saw it, and was glad." Since these notions are so fleeting, why need we accept the commandment of men as the doctrine of God?

This transitoriness of doctrines appears in many instances, of which two may be selected for a more attentive consideration. First, the doctrine respecting the origin and authority of the Old and New Testament. There has been a time when men were burned for asserting doctrines of natural philosophy which rested on evidence the most incontestable, because those doctrines conflicted with sentences in the Old Testament. Every word of that Jewish record was regarded as miraculously inspired, and therefore as infallibly true. It was believed that the Christian religion itself rested thereon, and must stand or fall with the immaculate Hebrew text. He was deemed no small sinner who found mistakes in the manuscripts. On the authority of the written word man was taught to believe impossible legends, conflicting assertions; to take fiction for fact, a dream for a miraculous revelation of God, an Oriental poem for a grave history of miraculous events, a collection of amatory idyls for a serious discourse "touching the mutual love of Christ and the Church;" they have been taught to accept a picture sketched by some glowing Eastern imagination, never intended to be taken for a reality, as a proof that the infinite God spoke in human words, appeared in the shape of a cloud, a flaming bush, or a man who ate, and drank, and vanished into smoke; that he gave counsels to-day, and the opposite to-morrow; that he violated his own laws, was angry, and was only dissuaded by a mortal man from destroying at once a whole nation,—millions of men who rebelled against their leader in a moment of anguish. Questions in philosophy, questions in the Christian religion, have been settled by an appeal to that book. The inspiration of its authors has been assumed as infallible. Every fact in the early Jewish history has been taken as a type of some analogous fact in Christian history. The most distant events, even such as are still in the arms of time, were supposed to be clearly foreseen and foretold by pious Hebrews several centuries before Christ. It has been assumed at the outset, with no shadow of evidence, that those writers held a miraculous communication with God, such as he has granted to no other man. What was originally a presumption of bigoted Jews became an article of faith, which Christians were burned for not believing. This has been for centuries the general opinion of the Christian church, both Catholic and Protestant, though the former never accepted the Bible as the *only* source of religious truth. It has been so. Still worse, it is now the general opinion of religious sects at this day. Hence the attempt, which always fails, to reconcile the philosophy of our times with the poems in Genesis writ a thousand years before Christ. Hence the attempt to conceal the contradictions in the record itself. Matters have come to such a pass that even now he is deemed an infidel, if not by implication an atheist, whose reverence for the Most High forbids him to believe that God commanded Abraham to sacrifice his son,—a thought at which the flesh creeps with horror; to believe it solely on the authority of an Oriental story, written down nobody knows when or by whom, or for what purpose; which may be a poem, but cannot be the record of a fact, unless God is the author of confusion and a lie.

Now, this idolatry of the Old Testament has not always existed. Jesus says that none born of a woman is greater than John the Baptist, yet the least in the kingdom of heaven was greater than John. Paul tells us the law—the very crown of the old Hebrew revelation—is a shadow of good things which have now come; only a schoolmaster to bring us to Christ; and when faith has come, that we are no longer under the schoolmaster; that it was a law of sin and death, from which we are made free by the law of the spirit of life. Christian teachers themselves have differed so widely in their notion of the doctrines and meaning of those books that it makes one weep to think of the follies deduced therefrom. But modern criticism is fast breaking to pieces this idol which men have made out of the Scriptures. It has shown that here are the most different works thrown together; that their authors, wise as they sometimes were, pious as we feel often their spirit to have been, had only that inspiration which is common to other men equally pious and wise; that they were by no means infallible, but were mistaken in facts or in reasoning,—uttered predictions which time has not fulfilled; men who in some measure partook of the darkness and limited notions of their age, and were not always above its mistakes or its corruptions.

The history of opinions on the New Testament is quite similar. It has been assumed at the outset, it would seem with no sufficient reason, without the smallest pretence on its writers' part, that all of its authors were infallibly and miraculously inspired, so that they could commit no error of doctrine or fact. Men have been bid to close their eyes at the obvious difference between Luke and John, the serious disagreement between Paul and Peter; to believe, on the smallest evidence, accounts which shock the moral sense and revolt the reason, and tend to place Jesus in the same series with Hercules, and Apollonius of Tyana; accounts which Paul in the Epistles never mentions, though he also had a vein of the miraculous running quite through him. Men have been told that all these things must be taken as part of Christianity, and if they accepted the religion, they must take all these accessories along with it; that the living spirit could not be had without the killing letter. All the books which caprice or accident had brought together between the lids of the Bible were declared to be the infallible word of God, the only certain rule of religious faith and practice. Thus the Bible was made not a single channel, but the *only* certain rule of religious faith and practice. To disbelieve any of its statements, or even the common interpretation put upon those statements by the particular age or church in which the man belonged, was held to be infidelity, if not atheism. In the name of him who forbid us to judge our brother, good men and pious men have applied these terms to others, good and pious as themselves. That state of things has by no means passed away. Men who cry down the absurdities of paganism in the worst spirit of the French "free thinkers," call others infidels and atheist, who point out, though reverently, other absurdities which men have piled upon Christianity. So the world goes. An idolatrous regard for the imperfect scripture of God's word is the apple of Atalanta, which defeats theologians running for the hand of divine truth.

But the current notions respecting the infallible inspiration of the Bible have no foundation in the Bible itself. Which evangelist, which apostle of the New Testament, what prophet or psalmist of the Old Testament, ever claims infallible authority for himself or for others? Which of them does not in his own writings show that he was finite, and, with all his zeal and piety, possessed but a limited inspiration, the bound whereof we can sometimes discover? Did Christ ever demand that men should assent to the doctrines of the Old Testament, credit its stories, and take its poems for histories, and believe equally two accounts that contradict one another? Has he ever told you that all the truths of his religion, all the beauty of a Christian life, should be contained in the writings of those men who, even after his resurrection, expected him to be a Jewish king; of men who were sometimes at variance with one another, and misunderstood his divine teachings? Would not those modest writers themselves be confounded at the idolatry we pay them? Opinions may change on these points, as they have often changed—changed greatly and for the worse since the days of Paul. They are changing now, and we may hope for the better; for God makes man's folly as well as his wrath to praise him, and continually brings good out of evil.

Another instance of the transitoriness of doctrines taught as Christian is found in those which relate to the nature and authority of Christ. One ancient party has told us that he is the infinite God; another, that he is both God and man; a third, that he was a man, the son of Joseph and Mary, born as we are; tempted like ourselves; inspired as we may be if we will pay the price. Each of the former parties believed its doctrine on this head was infallibly true, and formed the very substance of Christianity, and was one of the essential conditions of salvation, though scarce any two distinguished teachers, of ancient or modern times, agree in their expression of this truth.

Almost every sect that has ever been makes Christianity rest on the personal authority of Jesus, and not the immutable truth of the doctrines themselves, or the authority of God, who sent him into the world. Yet it seems difficult to conceive any reason why moral and religious truths should rest for their support on the personal authority of their revealer, any more than the truths of science on that of him who makes them known first or most clearly. It is hard to see why the great truths of Christianity rest on the personal authority of Jesus, more than the axioms of geometry rest on the personal authority of Euclid or Archimedes. The authority of Jesus, as of all teachers, one would naturally think, must rest on the truth of his words, and not their truth on his authority.

Opinions respecting the nature of Christ seem to be constantly changing. In the three first centuries after Christ, it appears, great latitude of speculation prevailed. Some said he was God, with nothing of human nature, his body only an illusion; others, that he was man, with nothing of the divine nature, his miraculous birth having no foundation in fact. In a few centuries it was decreed by councils that he was God, thus honoring the divine element; next, that he was man also, thus admitting the human side. For some ages the Catholic Church seems to have dwelt chiefly on the divine nature that was in him, leaving the human element to mystics and other heretical persons, whose bodies served to flesh the swords of orthodox believers. The stream of Christianity has come to us in two channels,—one within the church, the other without the church,—and it is not hazarding too much to say that since the fourth century the true Christian life has been out of the established church, and not in it, but rather in the ranks of dissenters. From the Reformation till the latter part of the last century, we are told, the Protestant Church dwelt chiefly on the human side of Christ, and since that time many works have been written to show how the two—perfect Deity and perfect manhood—were united in his character. But, all this time, scarce any two eminent teachers agree on these points, however orthodox they may be called. What a difference between the Christ of John Gerson and John Calvin, yet were both accepted teachers and pious men. What a difference between the Christ of the Unitarians and the Methodists, yet may men of both sects be true Christians and acceptable with God. What a difference between the Christ of Matthew and John, yet both were disciples, and their influence is wide as Christendom and deep as the heart of man. But on this there is not time to enlarge.

Now, it seems clear that the notions men form about the origin and nature of the Scriptures, respecting the nature and authority of Christ, have nothing to do with Christianity except as its aids or its adversaries; they are not the foundation of its truths. These are theological questions, not religious questions. Their connection with Christianity appears accidental: for if Jesus had taught at Athens, and not at Jerusalem; if he had wrought no miracle, and none but the human nature had ever been ascribed to him; if the Old Testament had forever perished at his birth,—Christianity would still have been the word of God; it would have lost none of its truths. It would be just as true, just as beautiful, just as lasting, as now it is; though we should have lost so many a blessed word, and the work of Christianity itself would have been, perhaps, a long time retarded.

To judge the future by the past, the former authority of the Old Testament can never return. Its present authority cannot stand. It must be taken for what it is worth. The occasional folly and impiety of its authors must pass for no more than their value; while the religion, the wisdom, the love, which make fragrant its leaves, will still speak to the best hearts as hitherto, and in accents even more divine when reason is allowed her rights. The ancient belief in the infallible inspiration of each sentence of the New Testament is fast changing, very fast. One writer, not a sceptic, but a Christian of unquestioned piety, sweeps off the beginning of Matthew; another, of a different church and equally religious, the end of John. Numerous critics strike off several epistles. The Apocalypse itself is not spared, notwithstanding its concluding curse. Who shall tell us the work of retrenchment is to stop here; that others will not demonstrate, what some pious hearts have long felt, that errors of doctrine and errors of fact may be found in many parts of the record, here and there, from the beginning of Matthew to the end of Acts? We see how opinions have changed ever since the Apostles' time; and who shall assure us that they were not sometimes mistaken in historical, as well as doctrinal matters; did not sometimes confound the actual with the imaginary; and that the fancy of these pious writers never stood in the place of their recollection?

But what if this should take place? Is Christianity then to perish out of the heart of the nations, and vanish from the memory of the world, like the religions that were before Abraham? It must be so, if it rest on a foundation which a scoffer may shake, and a score of pious critics shake down. But this is the foundation of a theology, not of Christianity. That does not rest on the decision of Councils. It is not to stand or fall with the infallible inspiration of a few Jewish fishermen, who have writ their names in characters of light all over the world. It does not continue to stand through the forbearance of some critic, who can cut when he will the thread on which its life depends. Christianity does not rest on the infallible authority of the New Testament. It depends on this collection of books for the historical statement of its facts. In this we do not require infallible inspiration on the part of the writers, more than in the record of other historical facts. To me it seems as presumptuous, on the one hand, for the believer to claim this evidence for the truth of Christianity, as it is absurd, on the other hand, for the sceptic to demand such evidence to support these historical statements. I cannot see that it depends on the personal authority of Jesus. He was the organ through which the Infinite spoke. It is God that was manifested in the flesh by him, on whom rests the truth which Jesus brought to light, and made clear and beautiful in his life; and if Christianity be true, it seems useless to look for any other authority to uphold it, as for some one to support Almighty God. So if it could be proved—as it cannot—in opposition to the greatest amount of historical evidence ever collected on any similar point, that the Gospels were the fabrication of designing and artful men, that Jesus of Nazareth had never lived, still Christianity would stand firm, and fear no evil. None of the doctrines of that religion would fall to the ground; for, if true, they stand by themselves. But we should lose—oh, irreparable loss!—the example of that character, so beautiful, so divine, that no human genius could have conceived it, as none, after all the progress and refinement of eighteen centuries, seems fully to have comprehended its lustrous life. If Christianity were true, we should still think it was so, not because its record was written by infallible pens, nor because it was lived out by an infallible teacher; but that it is true, like the axioms of geometry, because it is true, and is to be tried by the oracle God places in the breast. If it rest on the personal authority of Jesus alone, then there is no certainty of its truth if he were ever mistaken in the smallest matter,—as some Christians have thought he was in predicting his second coming.

These doctrines respecting the Scriptures have often changed, and are but fleeting. Yet men lay much stress on them. Some cling to these notions as if they were Christianity itself. It is about these and similar points that theological battles are fought from age to age. Men sometimes use worst the choicest treasure which God bestows. This is especially true of the use men make of the Bible. Some men have regarded it as the heathen their idol, or the savage his fetich. They have subordinated reason, conscience, and religion to this. Thus have they lost half the treasure it bears in its bosom. No doubt the time will come when its true character shall be felt. Then it will be seen that, amid all the contradictions of the Old Testament,—its legends, so beautiful as fictions, so appalling as facts; amid its predictions that have never been fulfilled; amid the puerile conceptions of God, which sometimes occur, and the cruel denunciations that disfigure both psalm and prophecy,—there is a reverence for man's nature, a sublime trust in God, and a depth of piety, rarely felt in these cold northern hearts of ours. Then the devotion of its authors, the loftiness of their aim, and the majesty of their life, will appear doubly fair, and prophet and psalmist will warm our hearts as never before. Their voice will cheer the young, and sanctify the gray-headed; will charm us in the toil of life, and sweeten the cup death gives us when he comes to shake off this mantle of flesh. Then will it be seen that the words of Jesus are the music of heaven sung in an earthly voice, and that the echo of these words in John and Paul owe their efficacy to their truth and their depth, and to no accidental matter connected therewith. Then can the Word, which was in the beginning and now is, find access to the innermost heart of man, and speak there as now it seldom speaks. Then shall the Bible—which is a whole library of the deepest and most earnest thoughts and feelings, and piety, and love, ever recorded in human speech—be read oftener than ever before,—not with superstition, but with reason, conscience, and faith, fully active. Then shall it sustain men bowed down with many sorrows; rebuke sin, encourage virtue, sow the world broadcast and quick with the seed of love, that man may reap a harvest for life everlasting.

With all the obstacles men have thrown in its path, how much has the Bible done for mankind. No abuse has deprived us of all its blessings. You trace its path across the world from the day of Pentecost to this day. As a river springs up in the heart of a sandy continent, having its father in the skies, and its birth-place in distant unknown mountains; as the stream rolls on, enlarging itself, making in that arid waste a belt of verdure wherever it turns its way; creating palm groves and fertile plains, where the smoke of the cottager curls up at eventide, and marble cities send the gleam of their splendor far into the sky,—such has been the course of the Bible on the earth. Despite of idolaters bowing to the dust before it, it has made a deeper mark on the world than the rich and beautiful literature of all the heathen. The first book of the Old Testament tells man he is made in the image of God; the first of the New Testament gives us the motto, Be perfect as your Father in heaven. Higher words were never spoken. How the truths of the Bible have blessed us! There is not a boy on all the hills of New England; not a girl born in the filthiest cellar which disgraces a capital in Europe, and cries to God against the barbarism of modern civilization; not a boy nor a girl all Christendom through, but their lot is made better by that great book.

Doubtless the time will come when men shall see Christ also as he is. Well might he still say, "Have I been so long with you, and yet hast thou not known me?" No! we have made him an idol, have bowed the knee before him, saying, "Hail, king of the Jews!" called him "Lord, Lord!" but done not the things which he said. The history of the Christian world might well be summed up in one word of the evangelist—"and there they crucified him;" for there has never been an age when men did not crucify the Son of God afresh. But if error prevail for a time and grow old in the world, truth will triumph at the last, and then we shall see the Son of God as he is. Lifted up, he shall draw all nations unto him. Then will men understand the word of Jesus, which shall not pass away. Then shall we see and love the divine life that he lived. How vast has his influence been! How his spirit wrought in the hearts of his disciples, rude, selfish, bigoted, as at first they were! How it has wrought in the world! His words judge the nations. The wisest son of man has not measured their height. They speak to what is deepest in profound men, what is holiest in good men, what is divinest in religious men. They kindle anew the flame of devotion in hearts long cold. They are spirit and life. His truth was not derived from Moses and Solomon; but the light of God shone through him, not colored, not bent aside. His life is the perpetual rebuke of all time since. It condemns ancient civilization; it condemns modern civilization. Wise men we have since had, and good men; but this Galilean youth strode before the world whole thousands of years, so much of divinity was in him. His words solve the questions of this present age. In him the Godlike and the human met and embraced, and a divine life was born. Measure him by the world's greatest sons—how poor they are! Try him by the best of men—how little and low they appear! Exalt him as much as we may, we shall yet perhaps come short of the mark. But still was he not our brother; the son of man, as we are; the son of God, like ourselves? His excellence—was it not human excellence? His wisdom, love, piety,—sweet and celestial as they were, —are they not what we also may attain? In him, as in a mirror, we may see the image of God, and go on from glory to glory, till we are changed into the same image, led by the spirit which enlightens the humble. Viewed in this way, how beautiful is the life of Jesus! Heaven has come down to earth, or, rather, earth has become heaven. The Son of God, come of age, has taken possession of his birthright. The brightest revelation is this of what is possible for all men,—if not now, at least hereafter. How pure is his spirit, and how encouraging its words! "Lowly sufferer," he seems to say, "see how I bore the cross. Patient laborer, be strong; see how I toiled for the unthankful and the merciless. Mistaken sinner, see of what thou art capable. Rise up, and be blessed."

But if, as some early Christians began to do, you take a heathen view, and make him a God, the Son of God in a peculiar and exclusive sense, much of the significance of his character is gone. His virtue has no merit, his love no feeling, his cross no burthen, his agony no pain. His death is an illusion, his resurrection but a show. For if he were not a man, but a god, what are all these things? what his words, his life, his excellence of achievements? It is all nothing, weighed against the illimitable greatness of Him who created the worlds and fills up all time and space! Then his resignation is no lesson, his life no model, his death no triumph to you or me, who are not gods, but mortal men, that know not what a day shall bring forth, and walk by faith "dim sounding on our perilous way." Alas! we have despaired of man, and so cut off his brightest hope.

In respect of doctrines as well as forms, we see all is transitory. "Everywhere is instability and insecurity." Opinions have changed most on points deemed most vital. Could we bring up a Christian teacher of any age, from the sixth to the fourteenth century, for example, though a teacher of undoubted soundness of faith, whose word filled the churches of Christendom, clergymen would scarce allow him to kneel at their altar, or sit down with them at the Lord's table. His notions of Christianity could not be expressed in our forms, nor could our notions be made intelligible to his ears. The questions of his age, those on which Christianity was thought to depend,— questions which perplexed and divided the subtle doctors,—are no questions to us. The quarrels which then drove wise men mad now only excite a smile or a tear, as we are disposed to laugh or weep at the frailty of man. We have other straws of our own to quarrel for. Their ancient books of devotion do not speak to us; their theology is a vain word. To look back but a short period,—the theological speculations of our fathers during the last two centuries, their "practical divinity," even the sermons written by genius and piety, are, with rare exceptions, found unreadable; such a change is there in the doctrines.

Now who shall tell us that the change is to stop here; that this sect or that, or even all sects united, have exhausted the river of life, and received it all in their canonized urns, so that we need draw no more out of the eternal well, but get refreshment nearer at hand? Who shall tell us that another age will not smile at our doctrines, disputes, and unchristian quarrels about Christianity, and make wide the mouth at men who walked brave in orthodox raiment, delighting to blacken the names of heretics, and repeat again the old charge, "He hath blasphemed"? Who shall tell us they will not weep at the folly of all such as fancied truth shone only into the contracted nook of their school, or sect, or coterie? Men of other times may look down equally on the heresy-hunters, and men hunted for heresy, and wonder at both. The men of all ages before us were quite as confident as we, that their opinion was truth, that their notion was Christianity and the whole thereof. The men who lit the fires of persecution, from the first martyr to Christian bigotry down to the last murder of the innocents, had no doubt their opinion was divine. The contest about transubstantiation, and the immaculate purity of the Hebrew and Greek texts of the Scriptures, was waged with a bitterness unequalled in these days. The Protestant smiles at one, the Catholic at the other, and men of sense wonder at both. It might teach us all a lesson, at least of forbearance. No doubt an age will come in which ours shall be reckoned a period of darkness, like the sixth century,—when men groped for the wall, but stumbled and fell, because they trusted a transient notion, not an eternal truth; an age when temples were full of idols, set up by human folly; an age in which Christian light had scarce begun to shine into men's hearts. But while this change goes on, while one generation of opinions passes away, and another rises up, Christianity itself, that pure religion, which exists eternal in the constitution of the soul and the mind of God, is always the same. The Word that was before Abraham, in the very beginning, will not change, for that Word is truth. From this Jesus subtracted nothing; to this he added nothing. But he came to reveal it as the secret of God, that cunning men could not understand, but which filled the souls of men meek and lowly of heart. This truth we owe to God; the revelation thereof to Jesus, our elder brother, God's chosen son.

To turn away from the disputes of the Catholics and the Protestants, of the Unitarian and the Trinitarian, of old school and new school, and come to the plain words of Jesus of Nazareth,—Christianity is a simple thing, very simple. It is absolute, pure morality; absolute, pure religion,—the love of man; the love of God acting without let or hindrance. The only creed it lays down is the great truth which springs up spontaneous in the holy heart,—there is a God. Its watchword is, Be perfect as your Father in heaven. The only form it demands is a divine life,—doing the best thing in the best way, from the highest motives; perfect obedience to the great law of God. Its sanction is the voice of God in your heart; the perpetual presence of him who made us and the stars over our head; Christ and the Father abiding within us. All this is very simple—a little child can understand it; very beautiful—the loftiest mind can find nothing so lovely. Try it by reason, conscience, and faith,—things highest in man's nature,—we see no redundance, we feel no deficiency. Examine the particular duties it enjoins,—humility, reverence, sobriety, gentleness, charity, forgiveness, fortitude, resignation, faith, and active love; try the whole extent of Christianity, so well summed up in the command, "Thou shalt love the Lord thy God with all thy heart, and with all thy soul, and with all thy mind; thou shalt love thy neighbor as thyself;" and is there anything therein that can perish? No, the very opponents of Christianity have rarely found fault with the teachings of Jesus. The end of Christianity seems to be to make all men one with God as Christ was one with him; to bring them to such a state of obedience and goodness that we shall think divine thoughts and feel divine sentiments, and so keep the law of God by living a life of truth and love. Its means are purity and prayer; getting strength from God, and using it for our fellow-men as well as ourselves. It allows perfect freedom. It does not demand all men to *think* alike, but to think uprightly, and get as near as possible at truth; not all men to *live* alike, but to live holy, and get as near as possible to a life perfectly divine. Christ set up no Pillars of Hercules, beyond which men must not sail the sea in quest of truth. He says, "I have many things to say unto you, but ye cannot bear them now. . . . Greater works than these shall ye do." Christianity lays no rude hand on the sacred peculiarity of individual genius and character. But there is no Christian sect which does not fetter a man. It would make all men think alike, or smother their conviction in silence. Were all men Quakers or Catholics, Unitarians or Baptists, there would be much less diversity of thought, character, and life, less of truth active in the world, than now. But Christianity gives us the largest liberty of the sons of God; and were all men Christians after the fashion of Jesus, this variety would be a thousand times greater than now; for Christianity is not a system of doctrines, but rather a method of attaining oneness with God. It demands, therefore, a good life of piety within, of purity without, and gives the promise that whoso does God's will shall know of God's doctrine.

In an age of corruption, as all ages are, Jesus stood and looked up to God. There was nothing between him and the Father of all; no old world, be it of Moses or Esaias, of a living Rabbi or Sanhedrim of Rabbis; no sin or perverseness of the finite will. As the result of this virgin purity of soul and perfect obedience, the light of God shone down into the very deeps of his soul, bringing all of the Godhead which flesh can receive. He would have us do the same; worship with nothing between us and God; act, think, feel, live, in perfect obedience to him: and we never are *Christians* as he was the *Christ,* until we worship, as Jesus did, with no mediator, with nothing between us and the Father of all. He felt that God's word was in him; that he was one with God. He told what he saw,—the truth; he lived what he felt,—a life of love. The truth he brought to light must have been always the same before the eyes of all-seeing God, nineteen centuries before Christ, or nineteen centuries after him. A life supported by the principle and quickened by the sentiment of religion, if true to both, is always the same thing in Nazareth or New England. Now that divine man received these truths from God; was illumined more clearly by "the light that lighteneth every man;" combined or involved all the truths of religion and morality in his doctrine, and made them manifest in his life. Then his words and example passed into the world, and can no more perish than the stars be wiped out of the sky. The truths he taught; his doctrines respecting man and God; the relation between man and man, and man and God, with the duties that grow out of that relation are always the same, and can never change till man ceases to be man, and creation vanishes into nothing. No; forms and opinions change and perish, but the word of God cannot fail. The form religion takes, the doctrines wherewith she is girded, can never be the same in any two centuries or two men; for since the sum of religious doctrines is both the result and the measure of a man's total growth in wisdom, virtue, and piety, and since men will always differ in these respects, so religious *doctrines* and *forms* will always differ, always be transient, as Christianity goes forth and scatters the seed she bears in her hand. But the *Christianity holy men feel in the heart,* the Christ that is born within us, is always the same thing to each soul that feels it. This differs only in degree, and not in kind, from age to age, and man to man. There is something in Christianity which no sect, from the "Ebionites" to the "Latter-Day Saints," ever entirely overlooked. This is that common Christianity which burns in the hearts of pious men.

Real Christianity gives men new life. It is the growth and perfect action of the Holy Spirit God puts into the sons of men. It makes us outgrow any form or any system of doctrines we have devised, and approach still closer to the truth. It would lead us to take what help we can find. It would make the Bible our servant, not our master. It would teach us to profit by the wisdom and piety of David and Solomon, but not to sin their sins, nor bow to their idols. It would make us revere the holy words spoken by "godly men of old," but revere still more the word of God spoken through conscience, reason, and faith, as the holiest of all. It would not make Christ the despot of the soul, but the brother of all men. It would not tell us that even he had exhausted the fulness of God, so that he could create none greater! for with him "all things are possible," and neither Old Testament nor New Testament ever hints that creation exhausts the Creator. Still less would it tell us the wisdom, the piety, the love, the manly excellence of Jesus, was the result of miraculous agency alone, but that it was won, like the excellence of humbler men, by faithful obedience to Him who gave his Son such ample heritage. It would point to him as our brother, who went before, like the good shepherd, to charm us with the music of his words, and with the beauty of his life to tempt us up the steeps of mortal toil, within the gate of heaven. It would have us make the kingdom of God on earth, and enter more fittingly the kingdom on high. It would lead us to form Christ in the heart, on which Paul laid such stress, and work out our salvation by this. For it is not so much by the Christ who lived so blameless and beautiful eighteen centuries ago that we are saved directly, but by the Christ we form in our hearts and live out in our daily life that we save ourselves, God working with us both to will and to do.

Compare the simpleness of Christianity, as Christ sets it forth on the Mount, with what is sometimes taught and accepted in that honored name, and what a difference! One is of God, one is of man. There is something in Christianity which sects have not reached,—something that will not be won, we fear, by theological battles, or the quarrels of pious men; still we may rejoice that Christ is preached in any way. The Christianity of sects, of the pulpit, of society, is ephemeral,—a transitory fly. It will pass off and be forgot. Some new form will take its place, suited to the aspect of the changing times. Each will represent something of truth, but no one the whole. It seems the whole race of man is needed to do justice to the whole of truth, as "the whole church, to preach the whole gospel." Truth is intrusted for the time to a perishable ark of human contrivance. Though often shipwrecked, she always comes safe to land, and is not changed by her mishap. That pure ideal religion which Jesus saw on the mount of his vision, and lived out in the lowly life of a Galilean peasant; which transforms his cross into an emblem of all that is holiest on earth; which makes sacred the ground he trod, and is dearest to the best of men, most true to what is truest in them,—cannot pass away. Let men improve never so far in civilization, or soar never so high on the wings of religion and love, they can never outgo the flight of truth and Christianity. It will always be above them. It is as if we were to fly towards a star, which becomes larger and more bright the nearer we approach, till we enter and are absorbed in its glory.

If we look carelessly on the ages that have gone by, or only on the surfaces of things as they come up before us, there is reason to fear; for we confound the truth of God with the word of man. So at a distance the cloud and the mountain seem the same. When the drift changes with the passing wind, an unpractised eye might fancy the mountain itself was gone. But the mountain stands to catch the clouds, to win the blessing they bear, and send it down to moisten the fainting violet, to form streams which gladden valley and meadow, and sweep on at last to the sea in deep channels, laden with fleets. Thus the forms of the church, the creeds of the sects, the conflicting opinions of teachers, float round the sides of the Christian mount, and swell and toss, and rise and fall, and dart their lightning, and roll their thunder, but they neither make nor mar the mount itself. Its lofty summit far transcends the tumult, knows nothing of the storm which roars below, but burns with rosy light at evening and at morn, gleams in the splendors of the mid-day sun, sees his light when the long shadows creep over plain and moorland, and all night long has its head in the heavens, and is visited by troops of stars which never set, nor veil their face to aught so pure and high.

Let then the transient pass, fleet as it will, and may God send us some new manifestation of the Christian faith, that shall stir men's heart as they were never stirred; some new word, which shall teach us what we are, and renew us all in the image of God; some better life, that shall fulfil the Hebrew prophecy, and pour out the spirit of God on young men and maidens, and old men and children; which shall realize the word of Christ and give us the Comforter, who shall reveal all needed things! There are Simeons enough in the cottages and churches of New England, plain men and pious women, who wait for the consolation, and would die in gladness if their expiring breath could stir quicker the wings that bear him on. There are men enough, sick and "bowed down, in no wise able to lift up themselves," who would be healed could they kiss the hand of their Saviour, or touch but the hem of his garment,—men who look up and are not fed, because they ask bread from heaven and water from the rock, not traditions or fancies, Jewish or heathen, or new or old; men enough who, with throbbing hearts, pray for the spirit of healing to come upon the waters, which other than angels have long kept in trouble; men enough who have lain long time sick of theology, nothing bettered by many physicians, and are now dead, too dead to bury their dead, who would come out of their graves at the glad tidings. God send us a real religious life, which shall pluck blindness out of the heart, and make us better fathers, mothers, and children! a religious life that shall go with us where we go, and make every home the house of God, every act acceptable as a prayer. We would work for this, and pray for it, though we wept tears of blood while we prayed.

Such, then, is the transient, and such the permanent in Christianity. What is of absolute value never changes; we may cling round it and grow to it forever. No one can say his notions shall stand. But we may all say the truth, as it is in Jesus, shall never pass away. Yet there are always some, even religious men, who do not see the permanent element, so they rely on the fleeting, and, what is also an evil, condemn others for not doing the same. They mistake a defence of the truth for an attack upon the holy of holies; the removal of a theological error for the destruction of all religion. Already men of the same sect eye one another with suspicion and lowering brows that indicate a storm, and, like children who have fallen out in their play, call hard names. Now, as always, there is a collision between these two elements. The question puts itself to each man, "Will you cling to what is perishing, or embrace what is eternal?" This question each must answer for himself.

My friends, if you receive the notions about Christianity which chance to be current in your sect or church, solely because they are current, and thus accept the commandment of men instead of God's truth, there will always be enough to commend you for soundness of judgment, prudence, and good sense, enough to call you Christian for that reason. But if this is all you rely upon, alas for you! The ground will shake under your feet if you attempt to walk uprightly and like men. You will be afraid of every new opinion, lest it shake down your church; you will fear "lest if a fox go up, he will break down your stone wall." The smallest contradiction in the New Testament or Old Testament, the least disagreement between the law and the gospel, any mistake of the apostles, will weaken your faith. It shall be with you "as when a hungry man dreameth, and behold, he eateth; but he awaketh, and his soul is empty."

If, on the other hand, you take the true word of God, and live out this, nothing shall harm you. Men may mock, but their mouthfuls of wind shall be blown back upon their own face. If the master of the house were called Beelzebub, it matters little what name is given to the household. The name Christian, given in mockery, will last till the world go down. He that loves God and man, and lives in accordance with that love, needs not fear what man can do to him. His religion comes to him in his hour of sadness, it lays its hand on him when he has fallen among thieves, and raises him up, heals and comforts him. If he is crucified, he shall rise again.

My friends, you this day receive, with the usual formalities, the man you have chosen to speak to you on the highest of all themes,—what concerns your life on earth, your life in heaven. It is a work for which no talents, no prayerful diligence, no piety is too great; an office that would dignify angels, if worthily filled. If the eyes of this man be holden, that he *cannot* discern between the perishing and the true, you will hold him guiltless of all sin in this; but look for light where it can be had, for his office will then be of no use to you. But if he sees the truth, and is scared by worldly motives, and *will* not tell it, alas for him! If the watchman see the foe coming and blow not the trumpet, the blood of the innocent is on him.

Your own conduct and character, the treatment you offer this young man, will in some measure influence him. The hearer affects the speaker. There were some places where even Jesus "did not many mighty works, because of their unbelief." Worldly motives—not seeming such—sometimes deter good men from their duty. Gold and ease have, before now, enervated noble minds. Daily contact with men of low aims takes down the ideal of life, which a bright spirit casts out of itself. Terror has sometimes palsied tongues that, before, were eloquent as the voice of persuasion. But thereby truth is not holden. She speaks in a thousand tongues, and with a pen of iron graves her sentence on the rock forever. You may prevent the freedom of speech in this pulpit if you will. You may hire you servants to preach as you bid; to spare your vices, and flatter your follies, to prophesy smooth things, and say, It is peace, when there is no peace. Yet in so doing you weaken and enthrall yourselves. And alas for that man who consents to think one thing in his closet and preach another in his pulpit! God shall judge him in his mercy, not man in his wrath. But over his study and over his pulpit might be writ, EMPTINESS; on his canonical robes, on his forehead and right hand, DECEIT! DECEIT!

But, on the other hand, you may encourage your brother to tell you the truth. Your affection will then be precious to him, your prayers of great price. Every evidence of your sympathy will go to baptize him anew to holiness and truth. You will then have his best words, his brightest thoughts, and his most hearty prayers. He may grow old in your service, blessing and blest. He will have—

> "The sweetest, best of consolation,
> The thought, that he has given,
> To serve the cause of Heaven,
> The freshness of his early inspiration."

Choose as you will choose; but weal or woe depends upon your choice.

7

The Movement: Philosophical and Religious

Ink and paper can never make us Christians; can never beget a new nature, a living principle in us; can never form Christ, or any true notions of spiritual things, in our hearts. The Gospel, that new law which Christ delivered to the world, is not merely a dead letter without us, but a quickening spirit within us . . . The secret mysteries of a divine life, of a new nature of Christ formed in our hearts, they cannot be written or spoken . . . neither can they be ever truly understood, except the soul itself be kindled from within, and awakened into the life of them.

—RALPH CUDWORTH

1. George Ripley (1802–1880)
Jesus Christ, the Same Yesterday, Today, and Forever

[Ripley first delivered this sermon at the installation of Brownson at Canton on May 14, 1834. From then until his resignation Ripley frequently repeated it; it was regarded as one of the finest expressions of the new doctrine. The sermon was never published, so that this is its first appearance in print. It is reproduced here from the Frothingham Collection in the Massachusetts Historical Society.]

WITH a strong desire for the unchangeable and everlasting the human soul is placed in the midst of perishable and transitory things. Every object with which we are connected, bears the impress of imperfection and change. Nothing appears to rest on such a stable foundation that it may not disappoint our hopes and pass away from our possession. Our lives are subject to the law of universal mutability. The days of which they are composed are themselves made up of moments so fleeting that we take no notice of their passage, and are warned of their existence only by their loss. We are borne onward from change to change by the invisible current of events until the life that now is, is absorbed in that which is to come. While we continue in the present state our experience is diversified by a constant succession of changes. Our feelings vary, our ideas are modified or renounced, our habits of thinking often revised, our souls assume another tone, and even the dust which enters into the composition of our mortal frames receives new shapes, constantly changing and constantly renewed. It is the same with the objects of our sympathy and love. The friends with whom we pursue the journey of life remain with us but a little while and leave us alone. Many who set out with us at the beginning are not with us now; and many who are with us now, must be parted from our company before the journey is finished. Even the material universe is bound by the same law of perpetual change. The planets are speeding their courses, the earth is flying onward in its destined path, the waters are flowing, the tides are heaving, the winds are rushing, not an element of nature is still, not a particle of matter is at rest, not an atom continues long in the same form, but all presents the ever-varying spectacle of changes without number and without end. In the midst of such a transitory world, however, there are certain great principles which are the same now as at the beginning, and which we may believe will endure as long as the human soul exists. It is interesting, amid the changes which are busily going on around us, in the rapid succession of the different generations of men, in the fall of nations and the departure of individuals, to mark those great interests which remain the same, and which appear to be indestructible in the mind of man.

In the words which have been read as the text, Jesus Christ is spoken of as the same, yesterday, today, and forever. It is not meant, by this, that the person of our Saviour is unchangeable, that he is a partaker of the Immutability which belongs to God alone, for we know that he was born of a woman, that he suffered the weaknesses of infancy, that he grew in wisdom and in stature, that he endured pain, privations and distress, and finally ended his earthly career by a bloody death. We know that he was not the same when, a child in the retired dwelling of Joseph and Mary, he wrought at a laborious occupation, that he was, when standing on the banks of Jordan, the spirit of God descended upon him and sent him forth to preach the kingdom of Heaven:— not the same, when despised and rejected of men, he expired on the cross, that he was, when raised by the power of God, he ascended, a conqueror over death.

The Immutability of our Saviour consists in the Immutability of the religious truths which he taught. While everything else with which the human mind is conversant suffers decay and change, the great principles of religion to which Jesus Christ bore Testimony are everlasting realities. Religion has always existed, and in its essential elements is always the same. Its ideas are inseparable from man. They grow out of the unchangeable nature of things. They are contemporaneous with the divine mind. The objects upon which they are founded are eternal and immutable. There never was a time when God did not exist. There never was a time when he did not possess Infinite Perfections, unchangeably Holy and Glorious. There never was a time when all created intelligences did not absolutely depend on him, when they were not sustained by his Spirit and blessed by his Providence, when they were not under an imperative, moral obligation to honor and love him, and destined to find their highest happiness in his service. These truths are in themselves the same, yesterday, today, and forever. They never began, and they can never cease to exist. Man, indeed, has not always had the same views of their nature, the same sense of their importance. At one time, they have been dimly and darkly descried, and then again, have shone into the mind with the full blaze of divine Light. In one age they have been almost enveloped in the cloud of earthly conceptions and erroneous ideas, and again have appeared as radiant and powerful as the noon-day Sun. But, when most obscured from human apprehension, they have been unchangeable themselves, as little altered in their own nature as the starry heavens when concealed from our sight by earthly vapors.

Religious truths, let it be understood are eternal, the same, yesterday, today, and forever. These attributes are applied to our Saviour in the text because his mind was so filled and penetrated with the power of religious Truth, as to be identical with it, as existing in the Divine Mind—as to be himself the Truth, as well as the way and the life. The perpetuity of religious truths is then an appropriate subject for this day, which gives to a Christian Society a Christian Ministry. Let us attend to some proofs and illustrations of this important fact.

I. In the first place, I observe that religious truths always have existed. Can you point to a period, however remote in the depth of ages, in which man was destitute of religion? Can you name the time in which his mind was not haunted with the idea of creating and protecting powers, however crude or, perhaps, grotesque the forms in which it may have been expressed? Can you mark the era when religion began to exist as you can that of the creation of many of the different sciences? Nay, more, is it possible to believe that before the formation of this small planet which we inhabit, before the ancestors of our race were framed from the dust of the Earth, that there were no kinds to behold the glory of God, to be warmed with his love, and elevated with his worship? Was Adam the first of all created intelligences? Were there not Sons of God before him,—the Sons of God who raised their shouts of joy when the stars sung their morning hymn over the new-created World? We cannot doubt that the unfathomable ages of a past Eternity have given birth to bright hosts of intellectual Beings, who were capable of communion with their Maker, and who have found supreme felicity in him. In their minds, did not religion exist—exist essentially the same as it does in ours? For what is religion in its primitive elements, but the intercourse of the creature with the Creator, the uplifting of the Finite to the Infinite? Wherever an intelligent Being, then, has existed, there has been religion, wherever a created mind has sought the presence of the uncreated Spirit, there has been religion; wherever a finite existence has felt the power of the Infinite Existence, there has been religion, and the essential element of religion, the communion of the creature with the Creator, must have been the same in all worlds, in every habitable globe, in every mind made in the Image of God.

But not to insist upon ideas which some may regard merely as matters of doubtful speculations, we know that the religious principle has always existed in this world from earliest ages to the present moment. The history of man is a religious history. The sentiment of religion, often indeed disguised, often perverted, often corrupted, often erroneous, is mingled with all his records; in some form or another, it is never absent from them. It is coeval with his existence. Our earliest memorials of the race are religious memorials. Our earliest documents of history are religious documents. Our oldest book is a religious book. Our first ideas of the parents of the human family, are intimately connected with the dealings of God towards them. The primitive ages were full of Religion. It is inscribed on all the ancestral monuments of our species. Of the elder patriarchs of the human race, we know little but the record of their religious history. We see Adam sinning against his Maker, hiding from his presence, and again communing with him among the trees of the garden. We see Abel and Cain with their respective offerings, in honor of their Creator. We see Enoch walking with God, and taken by him from the earth. All is strongly marked with the impress of religion. It is the one, great, predominant idea, which absorbs all others. The Bible, throughout all its pages, is filled with it. It contains a copious history of the manifestation of those divine truths, which constitute the essence of every religion. And it is this fact which makes the Bible so interesting at the present day. As the depository of the everlasting truths of Religion, those truths which are as natural and necessary to the human mind as the pure air to the body, it is still read with unabated interest in every family of the Christian world . . . In almost every civilised country, it is the first book which is perused by the child, and the last which the aged forsake. It is our guide in the tempting scenes of youth, our light in the inquiries of manhood, our consolation in sorrow, our support in death. Now why is the Bible an object of such general and permanent interest? Why has it not passed away with the nation whose history it relates? What has preserved it from the fate to which every human thing is exposed? Not merely its power to charm the intellect and gratify the taste. Not its strains of sublime poetry, its bursts of lofty eloquence, its inimitable pathos, its felicities of expression and powers of diction; for in that case, it would have been like other remains of ancient learning, accessible only to the studious few. The poems of Homer and the orations of Demosthenes are confined to the hands of the learned. The Bible, on the contrary, is in the hands of all. Its pages are reverently consulted in the retirement of the cloistered student, and in the abodes of laborious poverty. How do you account for it? Not by custom and example; for in that case, it would be known only to those who have been brought up under its influence. Other nations have had their sacred books, but the Koran of Mohamed and the Vedas of the Brahmins have not been diffused beyond the pale of their own followers. But the Bible has taken hold of the human heart in every clime. It has met with a warm and affectionate reception wherever it has been sent. The Greenlander has welcomed it into his frozen cabin, and the swarthy Ethiopian stretched forth his hand to the heavenly gift. It has melted the heart of the wild savage and kindled up his dark forests with the light of civilization and humanity, and it has compelled the tribute of the understanding learning and philosophy in the East. How do you account for it? Because it contains the everlasting Truths of religion. In the midst of other things, among descriptions of bloody wars, and ferocious battles, of the prowess of rude nations, and the slow progress of knowledge, the eternal lights of religion spring up on every page of the Bible like the pillar of fire in the desert, and it is this which has given the Bible its power, its influence, its interest, and its perpetuity. Man's heart is formed for religion, and in the Bible he finds it. Man's soul was formed to drink in religious truth, and in the Bible it gushes up from everlasting fountains. While everything else has changed or passed away, the essential truths of the Bible have remained the same. The permanence of the Bible, then, is a strong proof that religious ideas are congenial with the human mind, and are indestructible and everlasting in their character. And as they have been from the beginning, they continue to be today, and will be forever.

II. The religious ideas which were set forth by Jesus Christ as they had been displayed before in other forms, still exert an efficient influence on the heart of man. From the epoch of our Saviour's appearance to the present moment, there have always been living witnesses of their reality and power. Perhaps there was never a greater number of individuals who cherish a sincere and lively interest in religion than at this time—individuals of every variety of natural endowment, of birth and education, of age, profession, and circumstances in life,—individuals who have been led to religion and closely bound to its interests by different influences which have acted upon their characters, some by the strong convictions of their understandings, and some by the warm emotions of their hearts, some by the power of an early religious education, and some by the free, spontaneous workings of their own minds. It is not now thought necessary that religion should be the monopoly of a few. It is not supposed to belong exclusively to its ministers, or to a small number of professed and assuming friends. Narrow creeds are not, as they once were, universally deemed essential to bind in its expansive spirit—human forms are beginning to drop away, or to stand on their intrinsic utility, and to leave religion more and more to its own motive and independent energies. It is considered more than it ever was before a subject of personal responsibility and of paramount obligation. And it numbers among its earnest votaries not only those with whom the world has gone ill; the aged, who are on the confines of the grave; and the wretched who can find no other resource; but also many to whom the world presents its fairest aspect, whose earthly hopes are of the most promising nature, who are in the prime of youthful energy and happiness, and who cheerfully and gladly, in the fulness of their gratitude, consecrate their hearts to the service of God. Religion has been opposed in its written documents and its external evidences, adversaries of quenchless zeal and untiring perseverence have from time to time been arrayed against it, its authority has been called in question, its promises derided, and its principles submitted to a hostile and unsparing scrutiny. But all this without any material effect. Its hold on the heart of man has not been weakened and fresh illustrations of its power are every day springing up around us. Religion has also been laden with corruptions. Unseemly additions have been often connected with its heavenly spirit. It has been made to assume an ungracious aspect and to utter harsh and ominous tones. Yet it has never been so perverted as to destroy entirely its holy influences. It has never been so overloaded as to conceal the whole of its celestial beauty. No disguise has repelled it altogether from the human heart,—so wedded are we to religion by our nature, that it will be accepted in an uninviting form rather than be rudely and forever repulsed. The present age is not false to this great hope of human nature. Even in nations where the storms of revolution have been succeeded by periods of licentiousness and anarchy, where all prevalent ideas have been vigorously attacked, and those of religion among the number, the reign of unbelief is passing away, and the religious sentiment expanding itself in new forms, with new beauty, and destined we cannot doubt to exert an influence unfelt before. While many principles, once fondly cherished, have been destroyed to revive no more, while errors and prejudices have been pointed out and annihilated, while new truths on all subjects have been elicited in the process of free and sound inquiry, while many religious theories have been examined and rejected, many religious rites exchanged for others more congenial with an improved taste, many religious customs abolished which had no foundation in nation and reason, religion itself—the indestructible religious sentiment in the human heart, the feeling of relationship between man and his Maker—remains unimpaired and untouched. It is the same, today, that it always has been. No power has been found strong enough to pluck it up from the depths of the soul, where it maintains its abiding home.

III. And it may now be asked, if there is any reason to believe that religious truths will continue to exert a powerful influence over the mind? Will the great spiritual principles, announced by Jesus Christ endure unchangeable, yesterday, today, and forever? Or, will the progress of society, as it advances to new degrees of improvement, leave religion in the background, and reject it as an outworn and useless thing? Will the time ever arrive, when the mind shall outgrow its need of religion and the mature reason of the human race demonstrate that it is a delusion? We see great changes taking place on every side; old ideas, old institutions, old habits of thought are giving place to others, supposed to proceed more directly from reason, and the natural wants of man,—will religion share the general fate, or will it survive the besom of destruction which is sweeping over so many human institutions? We can have no doubt that it will always be perpetuated by the same causes which first gave it existence. We regard it as an emanation from the Eternal Mind, a stream from the Everlasting Fountain of Truth and as such we believe it partakes of the immutable duration of its author. But when we say that religion is unchangeable, that no power can push it from the human breast, let us not be misunderstood. Religion is unchangeable in its essential elements, but not in its carnal forms. Everything connected with it is subject to change. Men's conceptions of its nature may undergo indefinite alterations. The means by which they are convinced of its Truth, and receive its sentiments into their hearts, may be as various as their individual dispositions, and their particular opportunities for acquiring instruction. The forms of religion may be varied. They have already changed many times; what shall prevent them from changing as often again? The religious sentiment seeks to express itself in forms, but it is confined to no fixed mode. It is essentially the same whether uttered under the magnificent dome of a cathedral, or on the dreary hill-side with no canopy but the blue vault of Heaven. We assemble in our solemn temples, and worship in the fashion which our fathers have taught us; others may take our place who will deem our rites deficient or superfluous, and adopt more appropriate forms of their own own; but what will be altered? Not the substance, but the shadow; not the reality, but the symbol. Religion will remain the same, though embodied in another shape. If men worship in a way different from our own, it will still be worship. If the sentiment is full which connects the finite creature with the Infinite Creator, there will be religion, and though all its present external accompaniments shall pass away, its eternal realities will never pass away. The speculative doctrines of religion, moreover, may assume new forms and be clothed in new language. We believe that they will. What is called theology has often changed, and may often change again. That depends on the state of men's minds, on their degrees of light, their opportunities for information, their power of seeing clearly and reasoning justly. The doctrines which many of our ancestors clung to with a tenacious grasp, were renounced by their descendants; and who can say that many opinions now held firmly by ourselves will not suffer similar changes hereafter, will not be weighed in the balance by our posterity, and found wanting. But should it be so, religion will lose nothing in itself. That is independent of forms, of modes, of human reasoning, of speculative doctrines, of the systems and refinements of men. Let them be swept away, the vital essence of religion remains. Man would still feel his dependence on his Creator, the Idea of Duty would still spring up within his mind, his connexion with Infinity would still be recognised and felt. When we say, then, that religion is the same yesterday, today, and forever, we mean that the sentiment of religion will never be banished from human nature. We mean that the essential principles of Truth to which Christ bore witness as the Messenger of God, will endure forever. We mean that no change which takes place in the relations of human society, no advance of the mind in sound knowledge and improvement, can permanently injure the power of religion, or for a moment destroy its importance.

We believe that religion will be everlasting according to the explanation which has now been given, from the fact that it is demanded by the universal Reason of Man. Reason seeks to satisfy itself with regard to the mysterious phenomena with which we are surrounded. It thirsts after the primitive, absolute, all pervading Truth. It is not contented with the knowledge of barren, insulated facts, but strives to discover the original principle of those facts. This is the only ground for consistency of opinion, and strength of conviction. Now, there is no principle of reason yet pointed out, which explains the existence of the Universe, the situations of man on earth, and the hopes and fears which agitate his soul, independent of Religion. That admitted, a clear light is shed over the works of creation and the nature and destiny of man; that neglected, everything is an enigma which we cannot solve, and which at once appals and confounds the Reason. Without religion, we are buried in this world as in a living Tomb. Mystery—Darkness—Death—Despair—these are the inscriptions which are borne on the portals of our gloomy prison-house. Doomed and unhappy orphans, we know not whence we came, why we are here, nor whither we go. We look around, and find nothing but the perishing forms of matter; we look within, and nothing there, but a fearful and wonderful nature of which we know not the use, and of which we can give no account. Religion alone explains these mysteries to the satisfaction of the Reason; and while Reason retains its present characteristics, its grasp on Religion will never be renounced.

Again, we believe that Religion will be everlasting from the fact that it is demanded by the Conscience. We are told that man is a Law unto himself, and this Law written upon our hearts informs us of Duties to be done, of hopes to be cherished, of habits to be formed. It points out to us the path of obedience and warns us of the way of transgression. It not only pronounces its sentence of approbation when we do right, and of condemnations when we do wrong, but refers us to the Supreme Law-Giver by whom its decisions will be confirmed. This Law is Universal and Immutable. It is the voice of God in the Soul of Man. Its decrees are always certain, always consistent. They are the same in one age as in another—the same in Rome and in Athens, in Egypt and in Palestine. Take away this attribute of man, you may annihilate Religion. But while Conscience continues, as it now is, an essential part of human nature, the foundation of Religion, in the mind of man, will be indestructible.

Finally, we believe that Religion will be everlasting, from the fact that it is demanded by the Heart. We have capacities for boundless love, which no earthly object can fill. We have a thirst for happiness which no finite sources can satisfy. We are exposed to sorrows which no worldly considerations can console. These deep wants of our nature lead us to God. If we succeed, for a season, in quenching the religious sentiment, it is only to cast a darker gloom over the soul. We are soon taught by the bitterness of experience that when we are false to religion, we are false to ourselves. We look up to Heaven, but no God do we find there. We look within our bosoms but lose sight of our undying souls. We send abroad our thoughts over the wide Universe, but hear no reports of Immortality. The charm of life is then gone; there is no verdure in the summer's field; no brightness in the summer's sky; no beauty on the green earth; no grandeur in the midnight firmament. All is blank, and desolate, and lifeless, for to our darkened eye no God is present there. And God, my friends, is necessary to man. Even in the gloom of doubt and unbelief there are times when the heart is revealed to itself with a clearness that is almost overwhelming, and it perceives, by intuition, its inexpressible need of a Father and a God. There are moments when life seems like a dream, and the shadows which we have pursued are revealed to us in all their emptiness and vanity, and the heart yearns for something purer, holier, and more enduring, upon which it may find repose, and in which it may always trust. There are seasons when the soul is melted in sorrow, and though God has been neglected before, he is thought of then, and our heart and our flesh cry out for the living God. We want a Father to whom we can go—upon whom we can depend—whom we can worship, venerate, and love. We want him when the burdens of life press heavily upon our hearts. We want him when our thoughts, which wander through Eternity, seek to rest upon the Invisible and the Infinite. We want him when we watch over the dying bed of our companions and friends in the pilgrimage of life, when we stand by the open grave to which we commit their mortal remains—when the hour of our own departure is at hand, and our eyes weighed down in that sleep from which we shall not awake save by the voice of the Archangel and the trumpet of God. Then, my friends, we want God. Then we feel that there is none beside him and pray that he may be the strength of our souls and our portion forever. There are the native, spontaneous emotions of the human heart—and until these are eradicated—which all history, all experience, all philosophy demonstrate they never can be—the foundation of religion will remain unshaken. No opposition can weaken, no adversaries destroy it, but it will remain unchanged and unchangeable, yesterday, today, and forever.

2. George Ripley (1802–1880)

Introductory Notice, Specimens of Foreign Standard Literature

[The undertaking by the Transcendental group, under the leadership of Ripley, to produce a respectable series of translations of the new literature of Europe constitutes one of their more heroic enterprises. Ultimately the set included Dwight's translations of Goethe and Schiller, Margaret Fuller's of Eckermann's *Conversations,* Felton's of Menzel, W. H. Channing's of Jouffroy, Clarke's of De Wette, and Brooks's of German lyrics. They did it with no financial backing and in the midst of pressing concerns.

For the first two volumes, *Philosophical Miscellanies from the French of Cousin, Jouffroy, and Benjamin Constant* (which Brownson at once hailed, p. 84), Ripley wrote an introduction which, ostensibly an exposition of Cousin, was a statement of the faith of that segment of the movement which found particular joy in Cousin and which was already moving toward a primary concern with the social problem. The volumes were published in Boston in 1838.]

The aim of his philosophy is to furnish a criterion, taken from the actual observation of human nature, by which to estimate both the phenomena of daily experience, and the speculative systems which have been constructed for their explanation in every age of the world. For these reasons, his followers can never be linked together in the strong bands of an exclusive party. They will possess in common the admirable logical method of their teacher; they will start with him from the rigorous analysis of the facts of consciousness; and they will search like him for the elements of truth in every system, through all ages. But they will not be bound to adopt any of his specific doctrines, except in so far as they can verify them for themselves . . .

This characteristic is adapted to give his philosophy a favorable reception among ourselves. The reign of authoritative, dogmatic systems has never been firmly established over the mind of this nation; every exclusive faith has called forth a host in dissent; and the time appears to have arrived when no opinions can gain a general reception, unless they appeal to the spirit of inquiry, and disdain the aid of prescription or restraint. This tendency of thought will find a congenial object in the philosophy of Cousin . . .

In point of orderly arrangement, of continuous and systematic reasoning, and of admirable taste in the selection of terms, Cousin presents a favorable contrast to the most eminent philosophers of Germany. With the exception of Reinhold and Fries, to whom perhaps Jacobi should be added, I know of no modern German writers on philosophy to whose style we are not obliged to pardon much, through respect for the depth of their thoughts, and the completeness of their investigations. They are compelled to suffer the severe penalty of addressing themselves to scholars and thinkers by profession instead of the great mass of an intelligent population. There is nothing more dangerous to correctness of thought or to clearness of expression, than for the literary men of a nation to withdraw from the sympathies of the common mind, and thus to lose the benefit of comparing the abstractions of speculation with the natural good sense of the body of the people. The most sublime contemplations of the philosopher can be translated into the language of the market; and unless they find a response in the native feelings of humanity, there is probably some error in the doctrine, or some defect in its exposition. This source of difficulty has been avoided by Cousin. Called upon to exhibit the reasonings and conclusions of the German philosophy to a promiscuous audience in the metropolis of France, he has addressed the popular mind with singular success, and solved the cardinal problem of presenting the highest truths of speculation in a form adapted to the average intelligence of enlightened society. He has put the general reader in possession of the most valuable results of a profound philosophy; this is all that can be demanded of a teacher; more than this is beyond the reach of any style, however clear; and in order to comprehend the entire significance and fulness of the truth which is thus obtained, nothing will suffice but the voluntary exertion of our own intellect, the free reproduction in our consciousness of the ideas we have received from the instruction of another.

The characteristic which has now been alluded to, in the writings of Cousin presents an additional claim upon the attention of our countrymen. Our national taste,—as far as it is formed,—may certainly be said to repudiate all mystery and concealment. We have even less patience with obscurity of style than with shallowness of thought. We are often tempted to slight or discard truths of unutterable consequence both to society and to individuals, on account of the unusual, it may be, the repulsive phraseology in which they are conveyed. The first condition of popularity among us is the clear expression of distinct thoughts. We forgive any thing sooner than those entanglements of words which leave us to guess at the meaning of the writer, and at last to remain doubtful whether we have read his riddle aright. For this reason, the German philosophers, in their native costume, will never become extensively popular in this country. The fruits of their inquiries will one day pass into general circulation amongst us; but not till they have been refined and clarified by successive operations in different minds . . .

Intimately connected with its distinctness of expression, is another essential characteristic of the philosophy of Cousin, which will serve to facilitate its advancement among the intelligent thinkers of this nation. I allude to the substantial basis which it gives to the instinctive convictions of the human mind. This is the ultimate aim of all genuine philosophy. No system can be of any permanent utility which does not reproduce and legitimate the indestructible faith, that is cherished by the common sense of the mass of humanity. A philosopher who makes war upon this is guilty of the same absurdity with the artist who should make war on natural beauty. Of this fact, Cousin is not only fully aware himself; but he takes unwearied pains to explain its origin, to justify its importance, and to urge its consequences upon the attention of the reader. Every primitive belief of humanity is invested in his eyes with a character of peculiar, I may say indeed, of awful sanctity. In following the process of his investigations concerning the essential elements of reason, the absolute foundation of faith, the instinctive convictions of our race which are found, to a certain extent, in every mind, and manifested, in a certain form, in every epoch of the world, we are led to forget the impulses of merely intellectual curiosity, and to yield ourselves up,—if I may so express it without temerity,—to a solemn emotion of religious reverence. He gives us the true key to the meaning of those remarkable expressions, which in almost every language, indicate the conviction that the voice of God is uttered in the heart of man, that the light of the soul is a light from Heaven . . .

The respect which is every where testified in the system of Cousin for the spontaneous belief of humanity, presents a bond of sympathy between the highly educated and the masses, which is strikingly adapted to the condition of society among ourselves. The office of the true scholar in our republic is to connect himself in the most intimate and congenial relations with the energetic and busy population of which he is too often merely an insignificant unit. He is never to stand aloof from the concerns of the people; he is never to view them in the pride of superior culture or station as belonging to a distinct order from himself; he is never to set himself above them as their condescending instructor from whom they are to receive wisdom and light, according to his estimate of their capacity; but he is called upon to honor the common mind, to commune with the instinctive expressions of the mighty heart of a free nation, and to bring the aid of learning and philosophy to the endeavor of the people to comprehend their destiny, and to secure its accomplishment. The direct tendency of the system of Cousin is to produce this effect. It abases the proud and exalts the humble. It destroys the arrogance of mere scholarship, and teaches us to listen to the voice of humanity, though uttered from the lowliest shrine. At the same time, it substantiates the principle of social progress, and inspires a serene and patient faith in the promised fortunes of our race . . .

In the opinion of many individuals,—and I own myself to be one of the number,—the prevailing philosophical theories in this country are not completely adequate, to say the least, to the scientific grounding of a spiritual religion. The wedded union of philosophy and religion, so essential to the peace of the meditative mind, has not yet been consummated in the sanctuary of our holiest thoughts. This is the true cause of the ominous fact that an open dread of philosophy and a secret doubt of religion are not unfrequent in the midst of us. This is the most candid, and probably the most just, explanation that can be given of the strange aversion to inquiry, the morbid sensitiveness to new manifestations of truth which is sometimes exhibited by well-meaning and excellent individuals. If we felt the ground firm beneath us, we should not fear the consequences of the most searching scrutiny into the foundation on which we stand . . . But this state of mind can be produced only by establishing an unbroken harmony between feeling and speculation, between the spontaneous impulses of the heart and the profound results of reflection. I should be glad to believe that we have a philosophy among us which is capable of doing this. The experience of several years, with some opportunities for observation, has convinced me however that this is not the case . . . There are few who have not been called to test the validity of their dearest convictions, either by the assaults of skepticism from without, or the course of their own reflections. It must be a mind of extraordinary construction which has not felt the need of comprehending its own instincts more clearly; of looking into the foundation of the primitive truths on which the well-being of man reposes; and of settling the lofty spiritual faith in which it has grown up on the firm ground of a broad and clear philosophy. A sense of this want is widely spread in almost every circle of society, into which we enter. A deep conviction of the reality of spiritual truth, and, at the same time, a strong desire for a philosophical system which shall explain and legitimate it, are every where found among contemplative individuals. Too often, however, the clearness and strength of the former are impaired, by failing to meet with the latter. More than one young man has told me, in sadness of spirit, of the struggle which was going on in the very depths of his being, between reflection and faith, between the convictions to which he clung, and the theories by which they were sustained. The same testimony is given by writers of the most opposite opinions and experience . . .

It is by the prevalence of this feeling that I account for the remarkable popularity of Mr. Coleridge as a philosophical writer, with a great number of individuals who cannot be insensible to his signal defects and imperfections. The works of Mr. Coleridge, in my opinion, are exceedingly valuable to two classes of persons. To those, in the first place, on whom the light of spiritual truth is beginning to dawn; and who are just awakened to the consciousness of the inward powers of their nature, and who need to have the sentiment of religion quickened into more vital activity; and, secondly, to those, who have obtained as the fruit of their own reflections, a living system of spiritual faith. The former will find the elements of congenial truth profusely scattered over his pages; the latter will be able, from their own experience, to construct a systematic whole with the massive fragments which are almost buried beneath the magnificent confusion of his style. But Mr. Coleridge cannot satisfy the mind whose primary want is that of philosophical clearness and precision. He is the inspired poet, the enthusiastic prophet of a spiritual philosophy; but the practical architect, by whose skill the temple of faith is to be restored, cannot be looked for in him.

The objects at which Mr. Coleridge aims, it seems to me, are in a great measure accomplished by the philosophy of Cousin. This philosophy demolishes, by one of the most beautiful specimens of scientific analysis that is any where to be met with, the system of sensation, against which Mr. Coleridge utters such eloquent and pathetic denunciations. It establishes on a rock the truth of the everlasting sentiments of the human heart. It exhibits to the speculative inquirer, in the rigorous forms of science, the reality of our instinctive faith in God, in Virtue, in the Human Soul, in the Beauty of Holiness, and in the Immortality of Man.

Such a philosophy, I cannot but believe, will ultimately find a cherished abode in the youthful affections of this nation, in whose history, from the beginning, the love of freedom, the love of philosophical inquiry, and the love of religion have been combined in a thrice holy bond. We need a philosophy like this to purify and enlighten our politics, to consecrate our industry, to cheer and elevate society. We need it for our own use in the hours of mental misgiving and gloom; when the mystery of the universe presses heavily upon our souls; when the fountains of the great deep are broken up, and the

> Intellectual Power
> Goes sounding on, a dim and perilous way,

over the troubled waters of the stormy sea. We need it for the use of our practical men, who, surrounded on every side with the objects of sense; engrossed with the competitions of business, the rivalries of public life, or the cares of professional duty; and accustomed to look at the immediate and obvious utility of every thing which appeals to their notice, often acquire a distaste for all moral and religious inquiries, and as an almost inevitable consequence, lose their interest, and often their belief, in the moral and religious faculties of their nature. We need it for the use of our young men, who are engaged in the active pursuits of life, or devoted to the cultivation of literature. How many on the very threshold of manly responsibility, by the influence of a few unhappy mistakes, which an acquaintance with their higher nature, as unfolded by a sound religious philosophy would have prevented, have consigned themselves to disgrace, remorse, and all the evils of a violated conscience! How many have become the dupes of the sophists' eloquence, or the victims of the fanatics' terrors, for whom the spirit of a true philosophy—a philosophy "baptized in the pure fountain of eternal love," would have preserved the charm and beauty of life.

3. Christopher Pearse Cranch (1813-1892)

Transcendentalism

[How deeply the rank and file of the Transcendental movement conceived of it as a religious movement—and how they could maintain that despite its borrowings from Europe it was nevertheless a native uprising—is demonstrated by the article which Cranch contributed to *The Western Messenger* in January 1841 (VIII, 405-409).]

Much is said of late by persons not knowing whereof they speak, of what has been termed "Transcendentalism." Now, though not one in a hundred of these talkers can tell what this hard word means, or even explain their own vague idea of its meaning, it is a very convenient word. In the minds of most persons, it signifieth (being interpreted) "new doctrine,"—a modern synonyme for "Heresy." Strangely enough, all the "New Lights" of Philosophy and Theology, in foreign countries as well as in our own, however independent in thought, are, by a singular mode of generalizing, lumped together into a "Sect," honored with the cognomen of "New School" and "Transcendentalists." It might amuse almost, to see how this love of wholesale classification melts down obvious differences—persuading us that this new movement which is commencing on both sides of the Atlantic, for reviving the old well-nigh obscured truths of philosophy and theology, and is going forward in so many ways and by so many minds—is not a many headed monster, a hydra whose heads will grow again, though ever so well lopped off; but is *one*-headed, and may and must die, as only "the latest form of infidelity." It might amuse, to see how Kant, Cousin, Carlyle, Emerson, and about half Germany, are placed side by side, as if reading like schoolboys, out of the same book—stereotyping each other's thoughts—a sort of co-partnership for vending mysticisms, and turning brains. As if the "New School," as it is termed, *could* be a sect, with a fixed creed before it: as if it were not its glory that it is *many*-headed and progressive . . .

But avoiding controversy, and leaving the light tone, let us look upon the new movements of the age, as we would on all great and important movements, with reverence, with faith, with hope. For there are features belonging to such movements, which we are apt to overlook. But we may see something. There is a great lesson taught us by all these periods of time, wherein the same or similar great ideas prevail; and that is that a Divine Providence is here displayed, and displayed more signally than in any other way. Thus it was with the first appearance of Christianity, in a degree never seen before or since. Thus it was with the Reformation—thus it was with the Puritan movement—thus it was with the Unitarian movement. From time to time some grand Truth dawns like light upon nations who sat in darkness. All who are true, who are free, feel its coming, though they only *feel,* in dim vague glimmerings of imagination and hope, but cannot *think* their dreams into shape—much less speak it. They cannot give a *reason,* either to themselves or to others, for the *hope* which is in them. They are like infants who have but a confused inarticulate language of their own, understood by none but one all-loving Parent, who will yet teach them soon an *articulate* tongue, and raise up a philosophy to translate their theology. All hearts are at such times preparing in themselves the way of the Lord: the valleys begin to be exalted, the mountains leveled, the rough places made smooth, and the crooked places straight, and when at length the voice comes crying in the wilderness, the voice which is appointed in God's Providence to be the great interpreter of hidden truths, the "Word made flesh," which in the person or teachings of some great man, comes to speak what all are yearning to hear *plainly* spoken or acted, because all feel in themselves the smouldering heat which those thoughts that breathe and words that burn, are to touch into a blaze—*then* does the light break forth:— from the hills around—from the waste places of society—from across wide seas—from language to language, the echoes of that voice reverbrate. And these echoes are not, most happily, unmeaning, barren responses or repetitions, but are turned into new modulations, into rich variations as of some mountain melody, and constantly growing richer and more varied, as they spread circling round the world.

Hence the charge we so often hear, of Imitation, and of the too enthusiastic reception which young and fresh spirits are apt to give to new views. How superficial this charge of stiff barren conservatives. How scant an insight into the deep places of human character does it betoken. How narrow a view of the forth-goings of God's Mighty Spirit upon the restless deep of human minds! Hence a certain great writer of England is accused of imitating the Germans; and another writer in our country of imitating *him;* and these writers in turn, of being imitated by others. Men cry out that a transcendental epidemic is spreading contagion through our Universities. As if this word *Imitation* settled everything. A convenient word it is, we allow, but what does it prove? Is it anything more than a superficial term for a phenomenon, to the eternal foundations of which, as it looms up from the infinite deep of the Spiritual, those narrow observers will not or cannot look? If this phenomenon—this dawning of truths over the earth, be nothing more than a paroxysm, a temporary enchantment, a spoiled child's cry after whatever is *new*—then why so eagerly received? Why so suggestive to the highest thought? Why so strengthening to the calmest and loftiest faith? I speak not now of any opinions or speculations in particular. There is every variety of such, as there should be. But I speak of that fresh, earnest, truth-loving and truth-seeking SPIRIT, which is abroad;—of that heart's thirst, not of the fever-dream, but of the sober, waking vision of soundest health, after something *always* new and lovely and true,—something always adapted to the soul's deep demands. I allude, I repeat, not to any system, or creed, or philosophy, or party, or sect—to no men or speculations, except so far as such are types of a free, earnest, and humble love of Truth; but rather to a higher and better hope, to fast fulfilling prophecies from the heart of humanity, more wisdom-fraught than ever were the utterances of Sybils and Delphic oracles. The true Transcendentalism is that living and always new *spirit* of truth, which is ever going forth on its conquests into the world, and leading all captivity captive: but which at times arms itself as with new splendors of victory,—which is thus in the only sense *transcendental,* when it labors to *transcend* itself, and soar ever higher and nearer the great source of Truth, Himself. When we see such a spirit abroad, walking the earth in native majesty, yet not in tyranny, but in lowly freedom, like that of the Galilean Prophet, humbling itself to common life, and to fallen man, that it may be only the more exalted in the sight of God—when we see it swaying the universal Heart, as wind sways the forest with all its leaves—when we see mankind lifting up their drooping heads and opening their languid eyes, as the refreshing currents of God's providence circulate and blow around them—their thought quickened, their belief strengthened, their hope brightened, their aspiration enlarged—we cannot say, "This is the work of man— the excitement of a season—the summer-fever of prosperity—the corrupt fruit of unlicensed enquiry." It is God Himself, walking in His garden at the cool of the day. It is the Eternal Spirit breathing down on us the life-giving breeze of Almighty Grace.

It is indeed a remarkable fact, though it seems never to have been sufficiently noticed, that at certain periods, men are penetrated with the same great thoughts, or verge to the same great discoveries; and this without any sufficient cause for such unanimity presenting itself from the circle of known facts which surround us. We cannot find the source of this agreement in the events of past progress or of present excitement. Genius springs across our field of vision, like the rushing of a shooting star from the bosom of the darkness; and we are startled and awed, while we are enchanted by the unaccustomed vision, and strain our eyes in vain to track the beautiful meteor to its place of birth in the empty firmament. It is still a mystery to us.

But the mystery is not confined to solitary genius. As all the mountain tops glow in the coming day, so do all elevated minds feel the coming of a Truth. And without any preconcerted plan—without any inter-communion of minds, the sunlight of Truth seems to flash simultaneously upon lands separated by oceans, by dissimilar languages. On different shores and to insulated minds will the same aspects and applications of truth arise. This holds true in all science, physical or metaphysical, theological or political . . .

Such a spirit, we rejoice to believe, is even now abroad on the earth. Everywhere do we see its evidences. It does not confine itself to opinions; it extends to great and good *acts*. It is seen in the practical developments of our religion. It is not the bare spirit of denial and doubt, but of yearning Faith also. While it empties itself of that which it perceives to be unwholesome or noxious, it also supplies the void by fresh appropriations from the realms of truth which open upon it. So much as it sees to be good in what is old, it retains. So much as it finds good in the new, it adopts. From behind and from before would it gather its treasures. They lie all around it. It has but to seek, as a merchantman seeking goodly pearls.

The friends of truth cannot but rejoice in these signs of progress: to see obstinate prejudices wearing down—old errors falling away by piecemeal— the spirit of bigotry subsiding—and the spirit of liberality extending. Let us trust it may long be so: that God may visit his people. But let it be an *active* trust. Let us prepare in our hearts and lives for the coming of the truth—and the kingdom of God will come.

4. Amos Bronson Alcott (1799–1888)
Orphic Sayings

["Who reads the Dial," asked the orthodoxy of Yale College in 1843, "for any other purpose than to laugh at its baby poetry or at the solemn fooleries of its misty prose." *The Dial* became—and in the popular memory has remained—a butt for ridicule mainly because of Alcott's contribution, the "Orphic Sayings," the first fifty of which appeared in the July 1840 number (I, 85–98). A Boston wit said they were like "a train of fifteen coaches going by, with only one passenger." Even Theodore Parker, who knew what it was to be made fun of, could do little else but snort at them.

At the time Alcott wrote them, he was working in his garden in Concord and occasionally wondering how, if ever, he would pay his debts: he was reading Hesiod, More, Cudworth, Goethe, and Coleridge. The value of the "Orphic Sayings" for the American tradition is probably not anything that they say—assuming that they say something—but that they could be written in America at all. To a generation familiar with Existentialism and with innumerable forms of making statement out of gropings for statement, Alcott's epigrams, even though they may be lacking in pungency, can hardly help suggesting insights which his own generation did not comprehend.]

I

Thou art, my heart, a soul-flower, facing ever and following the motions of thy sun, opening thyself to her vivifying ray, and pleading thy affinity with the celestial orbs. Thou dost

the livelong day
Dial on time thine own eternity.

II. ENTHUSIASM

Believe, youth, that your heart is an oracle; trust her instinctive auguries, obey her divine leadings; nor listen too fondly to the uncertain echoes of your head. The heart is the prophet of your soul, and ever fulfills her prophecies; reason is her historian; but for the prophecy the history would not be. Great is the heart: cherish her; she is big with the future, she forebodes renovations. Let the flame of enthusiasm fire alway your bosom. Enthusiasm is the glory and hope of the world. It is the life of sanctity and genius; it has wrought all miracles since the beginning of time.

III. HOPE

Hope deifies man; it is the apotheosis of the soul; the prophecy and fulfilment of her destinies. The nobler her aspirations, the sublimer her conceptions of the Godhead. As the man, so his God: God is his idea of excellence; the complement of his own being.

IV. IMMORTALITY

The grander my conception of being, the nobler my future. There can be no sublimity of life without faith in the soul's eternity. Let me live superior to sense and custom, vigilant always, and I shall experience my divinity; my hope will be infinite, nor shall the universe contain, or content me. But if I creep daily from the haunts of an ignoble past, like a beast from his burrow, neither earth nor sky, man nor God, shall appear desirable or glorious; my life shall be loathsome to me, my future reflect my fears. He alone, who lives nobly, oversees his own being, believes all things, and partakes of the eternity of God.

V. VOCATION

Engage in nothing that cripples or degrades you. Your first duty is self-culture, self-exaltation: you may not violate this high trust. Your self is sacred, profane it not. Forge no chains wherewith to shackle your own members. Either subordinate your vocation to your life, or quit it forever: it is not for you; it is condemnation of your own soul. Your influence on others is commensurate with the strength that you have found in yourself. First cast the demons from your own bosom, and then shall your word exorcise them from the hearts of others.

VI. SENSUALISM

He who marvels at nothing, who feels nothing to be mysterious, but must needs bare all things to sense, lacks both wisdom and piety. Miracle is the mantle in which these venerable natures wrap themselves, and he, who seeks curiously to rend this asunder, profanes their sacred countenance to enter by stealth into the Divine presence. Sanctity, like God, is ever mysterious, and all devout souls reverence her. A wonderless age is godless: an age of reverence, an age of piety and wisdom.

VII. SPIRITUALISM

Piety is not scientific; yet embosoms the facts that reason develops in scientific order to the understanding. Religion, being a sentiment, is science yet in synthetic relations; truth yet undetached from love; thought not yet severed from action. For every fact that eludes the analysis of reason, conscience affirms its root in the supernatural. Every synthetic fact is supernatural and miraculous. Analysis by detecting its law resolves it into science, and renders it a fact of the understanding. Divinely seen, natural facts are symbols of spiritual laws. Miracles are of the heart; not of the head: indigenous to the soul; not freaks of nature, not growths of history. God, man, nature, are miracles.

VIII. MYSTICISM

Because the soul is herself mysterious, the saint is a mystic to the worldling. He lives to the soul; he partakes of her properties, he dwells in her atmosphere of light and hope. But the worldling, living to sense, is identified with the flesh; he dwells amidst the dust and vapors of his own lusts, which dim his vision, and obscure the heavens wherein the saint beholds the face of God.

IX. ASPIRATION

The insatiableness of her desires is an augury of the soul's eternity. Yearning for satisfaction, yet ever balked of it from temporal things, she still prosecutes her search for it, and her faith remains unshaken amidst constant disappointments. She would breathe life, organize light; her hope is eternal; a never-ending, still beginning quest of the Godhead in her own bosom; a perpetual effort to actualize her divinity in time. Intact, aspirant, she feels the appulses of both spiritual and material things; she would appropriate the realm she inherits by virtue of her incarnation: infinite appetencies direct all her members on finite things; her vague strivings, and Cyclopean motions, confess an aim beyond the confines of transitory natures; she is quivered with heavenly desires: her quarry is above the stars: her arrows are snatched from the armory of heaven.

X. APOTHEOSIS

Every soul feels at times her own possibility of becoming a God; she cannot rest in the human, she aspires after the Godlike. This instinctive tendency is an authentic augury of its own fulfilment. Men shall become Gods.

Every act of admiration, prayer, praise, worship, desire, hope, implies and predicts the future apotheosis of the soul.

XI. DISCONTENT

All life is eternal; there is none other; and all unrest is but the struggle of the soul to reassure herself of her inborn immortality; to recover her lost intuition of the same, by reason of her descent amidst the lusts and worship of the idols of flesh and sense. Her discomfort reveals her lapse from innocence; her loss of the divine presence and favor. Fidelity alone shall instaurate the Godhead in her bosom.

XII. TEMPTATION

Greater is he, who is above temptation, than he, who, being tempted, overcomes. The latter but regains the state from which the former has not fallen. He who is tempted has sinned; temptation is impossible to the holy.

XIII. CHOICE

Choice implies apostacy. The pure, unfallen soul is above choice. Her life is unbroken, synthetic; she is a law to herself, and finds no lusts in her members warring against the instincts of conscience. Sinners choose; saints act from instinct and intuition: there is no parley of alien forces in their being.

XIV. INSTINCT AND REASON

Innocent, the soul is quick with instincts of unerring aim; then she knows by intuition what lapsed reason defines by laborious inference; her appetites and affections are direct and trustworthy. Reason is the left hand of instinct; it is tardy, awkward, but the right is ready and dextrous. By reasoning the soul strives to recover her lost intuitions; groping amidst the obscure darkness of sense, by means of the fingers of logic, for treasures present alway and available to the eye of conscience. Sinners must needs reason; saints behold.

XV. IDENTITY AND DIVERSITY

It is the perpetual effort of conscience to divorce the soul from the dominion of sense; to nullify the dualities of the apparent, and restore the intuition of the real. The soul makes a double statement of all her facts; to conscience and sense; reason mediates between the two. Yet though double to sense, she remains single and one in herself; one in conscience, many in understanding; one in life, diverse in function and number. Sense, in its infirmity, breaks this unity to apprehend in part what it cannot grasp at once.

Understanding notes diversity; conscience alone divines unity, and integrates all experience in identity of spirit. Number is predicable of body alone; not of spirit.

XVI. CONSCIENCE

Ever present, potent, vigilant, in the breast of man, there is that which never became a party in his guilt, never consented to a wrong deed, nor performed one, but holds itself above all sin, impeccable, immaculate, immutable, the deity of the heart, the conscience of the soul, the oracle and interpreter, the judge and executor of the divine law.

XVII. THEOCRACY

In the theocracy of the soul majorities do not rule. God and the saints; against them the rabble of sinners, with clamorous voices and uplifted hand, striving to silence the oracle of the private heart. Beelzebub marshals majorities. Prophets and reformers are alway special enemies of his and his minions. Multitudes ever lie. Every age is a Judas, and betrays its Messiahs into the hands of the multitude. The voice of the private, not popular heart, is alone authentic.

XVIII. SPEECH

There is a magic in free speaking, especially on sacred themes, most potent and resistless. It is refreshing, amidst the inane common-places bandied in pulpits and parlors, to hear a hopeful word from an earnest, upright soul. Men rally around it as to the lattice in summer heats, to inhale the breeze that flows cool and refreshing from the mountains, and invigorates their languid frames. Once heard, they feel a buoyant sense of health and hopefulness, and wonder that they should have lain sick, supine so long, when a word has power to raise them from their couch, and restore them to soundness. And once spoken, it shall never be forgotten; it charms, exalts; it visits them in dreams, and haunts them during all their wakeful hours. Great, indeed, is the delight of speech; sweet the sound of one's bosom thought, as it returns laden with the fragrance of a brother's approval.

XIX. THOUGHT AND ACTION

Great thoughts exalt and deify the thinker; still more ennobling is the effect of great deeds on the actor. The dilation and joy of the soul at these visitations of God is like that of the invalid, again inhaling the mountain breeze after long confinement in chambers: she feels herself a noble bird, whose eyrie is in the empyrean· that she is made to bathe her bosom and plume herself in the ether of thought; to soar and sing amidst the seraphim, beholding the faces of Apollo and Jove.

XX. ACTION

Action translates death into life; fable into verity; speculation into experience; freeing man from the sorceries of tradition and the torpor of habit. The eternal Scripture is thus expurgated of the falsehoods interpolated into it by the supineness of the ages. Action mediates between conscience and sense: it is the gospel of the understanding.

XXI. ORIGINALITY

Most men are on the ebb; but now and then a man comes riding down sublimely in high hope from God on the flood tide of the soul, as she sets into the coasts of time, submerging old landmarks, and laying waste the labors of centuries. A new man wears channels broad and deep into the banks of the ages; he washes away ancient boundaries, and sets afloat institutions, creeds, usages, which clog the ever flowing Present, stranding them on the shores of the Past. Such deluge is the harbinger of a new world, a renovated age. Hope builds an ark; the dove broods over the assuaged waters; the bow of promise gilds the east; the world is again repeopled and replanted. Yet the sons of genius alone venture into the ark: while most pass the rather down the sluggish stream of usage into the turbid pool of oblivion. Thitherward the retreating tide rolls, and wafted by the gales of inglorious ease, or urged by the winds of passion, they glide down the Lethean waters, and are not. Only the noble and heroic outlive in time their exit from it.

XXII. VALOR

The world, the state, the church, stand in awe of a man of probity and valor. He threatens their order and perpetuity: an unknown might slumbers in him; he is an augury of revolutions. Out of the invisible God, he comes to abide awhile amongst men; yet neither men nor time shall remain as at his advent. He is a creative element, and revises men, times, life itself. A new world preëxists in his ideal. He overlives, outlives, eternizes the ages, and reports to all men the will of the divinity whom he serves.

XXIII. CHARACTER

Character is the only legitimate institution; the only regal influence. Its power is infinite. Safe in the citadel of his own integrity, principalities, powers, hierarchies, states, capitulate to the man of character at last. It is the temple which the soul builds to herself, within whose fanes genius and sanctity worship, while the kneeling ages bend around them in admiration and love.

XXIV. BREAD

The hunger of an age is alike a presentiment and pledge of its own supply. Instinct is not only prophetic but provident. When there is a general craving for bread, that shall assuredly be satisfied; bread is even then growing in the fields. Now, men are lean and famishing; but, behold, the divine Husbandman has driven his share through the age, and sown us bread that we may not perish; yea, the reapers even are going forth, a blithe and hopeful company, while yet the fields weep with the dews of the morning, and the harvests wave in yellow ripeness. Soon shall a table be spread, and the age rejoice in the fulness of plenty.

XXV. PROPHET

The prophet, by disciplines of meditation and valor, faithful to the spirit of the heart, his eye purified of the notes of tradition, his life of the vestiges of usage, ascends to the heights of immediate intuition: he rends the veil of sense; he bridges the distance between faith and sight, and beholds spiritual verities without scripture or mediator. In the presence of God, he communes with him face to face.

XXVI. METHOD

To benefit another, either by word or deed, you must have passed from the state in which he is, to a higher. Experience is both law and method of all tuition, all influence. This holds alike of physical as of spiritual truths; the demonstration must be epical; the method living, not empirical.

XXVII. BALANCES

I am not partial to your man who always holds his balance in hand, and must weigh forthwith whatsoever of physical or metaphysical haberdashery chances to be laid on his counter. I have observed that he thinks more of the accuracy and polish of his scales, than of the quality of the wares in which he deals. He never questions his own levity. But yet these balance-men are useful: it is convenient to have standards of market values. These are the public's approved sealers of weights and measures, who determine the worth of popular wares by their favorite weights, lucre and usage. It is well for the ages, that Genius rectifies both scales and men by a truer standard, quite wide of marts or markets.

XXVIII. PRUDENCE

Prudence is the footprint of Wisdom.

XXIX. REVELATION

The standing problem of Genius is to divine the essential verity intimated in the life and literature of the Past, divesting it of historical interpolations; separating the foreign from the indigenous, and translating the letter of the universal scripture into the spirit of contemporaneous life and letters.

XXX. CRITICISM

To just criticism unity of mind is essential. The critic must not esteem difference as real as sameness, and as permanent in the facts of nature. This tendency is fatal to all sound and final thinking: it never penetrates to the roots of things. All creative minds have been inspired and guided by the law of unity: their problem is ever to pierce the coarse and superficial rind of diversity, and discover the unity in whose core is the heart and seed of all things.

XXXI. CALCULUS

We need, what Genius is unconsciously seeking, and, by some daring generalization of the universe, shall assuredly discover, a spiritual calculus, a novum organon, whereby nature shall be divined in the soul, the soul in God, matter in spirit, polarity resolved into unity; and that power which pulsates in all life, animates and builds all organizations, shall manifest itself as one universal deific energy, present alike at the outskirts and centre of the universe, whose centre and circumference are one; omniscient, omnipotent, self-subsisting, uncontained, yet containing all things in the unbroken synthesis of its being.

XXXII. GENERATION AND CORRUPTION

The soul decomposes the substances of nature in the reverse order of their composition: read this backward for the natural history of their genesis and growth. Generation and corruption are polar or adverse facts. The tree first dies at the top: to raze the house we first remove the tiling. The decomposition and analysis are from without, according to the order of sense, not of soul. All investigations of nature must be analytic through the order of decay. Science begins and ends in death; poesy in life; philosophy in organization; art in creation.

XXXIII. EACH AND ALL

Life eludes all scientific analysis. Each organ and function is modified in substance and varied in effect, by the subtile energy which pulsates throughout the whole economy of things, spiritual and corporeal. The each is instinct with the all; the all unfolds and reappears in each. Spirit is all in all. God, man, nature, are a divine synthesis, whose parts it is impiety to sunder. Genius must preside devoutly over all investigations, or analysis, with her murderous knife, will seek impiously to probe the vitals of being.

XXXIV. GOD

God organizes never his attributes fully in single structures. He is instant, but never extant wholly, in his works. Nature does not contain, but is contained in him; she is the memoir of his life; man is a nobler scripture, yet fails to outwrite the godhead. The universe does not reveal, eternities do not publish the mysteries of his being. He subjects his noblest works to minute and constant revision; his idea ever transcends its form; he moulds anew his own idols; both nature and man are ever making, never made.

XXXV. NATURE

Nature seems remote and detached, because the soul surveys her by means of the extremest senses, imposing on herself the notion of difference and remoteness through their predominance, and thereby losing that of her own oneness with it. Yet nature is not separate from me; she is mine alike with my body; and in moments of true life, I feel my identity with her; I breathe, pulsate, feel, think, will, through her members, and know of no duality of being. It is in such moods of soul that prophetic visions are beheld, and evangeles published for the joy and hope of mankind.

XXXVI. FLUX

Solidity is an illusion of the senses. To faith, nothing is solid: the nature of the soul renders such fact impossible. Modern chemistry demonstrates that nine tenths of the human body are fluid, and substances of inferior order in lesser proportion. Matter is ever pervaded and agitated by the omnipresent soul. All things are instinct with spirit.

XXXVII. SEPULTURE AND RESURRECTION

That which is visible is dead: the apparent is the corpse of the real; and undergoes successive sepultures and resurrections. The soul dies out of organs; the tombs cannot confine her; she eludes the grasp of decay; she builds and unseals the sepulchres. Her bodies are fleeting, historical. Whatsoever she sees when awake is death; when asleep dream.

XXXVIII. TIME

Organizations are mortal; the seal of death is fixed on them at birth. The young Future is nurtured by the Past, yet aspires to a nobler life, and revises, in his maturity, the traditions and usages of his day, to be supplanted by the sons and daughters whom he begets and ennobles. Time, like fabled Saturn, now generates, and, ere even their sutures be closed, devours his own offspring. Only the children of the soul are immortal; the births of time are premature and perishable.

XXXIX. EMBRYON

Man is a rudiment and embryon of God: eternity shall develop in him the divine image.

XL. ORGANIZATION

Possibly organization is no necessary function or mode of spiritual being. The time may come, in the endless career of the soul, when the facts of incarnation, birth, death, descent into matter and ascension from it, shall comprise no part of her history; when she herself shall survey this human life with emotions akin to those of the naturalist, on examining the relics of extinct races of beings; when mounds, sepulchres, monuments, epitaphs, shall serve but as memoirs of a past state of existence; a reminiscence of one metempsychosis of her life in time.

XLI. SPIRIT AND MATTER

Divined aright, there is nothing purely organic; all things are vital and inorganic. The microscope is developing this sublime fact. Sense looking at the historic surface beholds what it deems matter, yet is but spirit in fusion, fluent, pervaded by her own immanent vitality and trembling to organize itself. Neither matter nor death are possible: what seem matter and death are sensuous impressions, which, in our sanest moments, the authentic instincts contradict. The sensible world is spirit in magnitude, outspread before the senses for their analysis, but whose synthesis is the soul herself, whose prothesis is God. Matter is but the confine of spirit limning her to sense.

XLII. ORDER

The soul works from centre to periphery, veiling her labors from the ken of the senses. Her works are invisible till she has rounded herself in surface, where she completes her organizations. Appearance, though first to sense, is last in the order of generation: she recoils on herself at the acme of sense, revealing herself in reversed order. Historical is the sequel of genetic life.

XLIII. GENESIS

The popular genesis is historical. It is written to sense not to the soul. Two principles, diverse and alien, interchange the Godhead and sway the world by turns. God is dual. Spirit is derivative. Identity halts in diversity. Unity is actual merely. The poles of things are not integrated: creation globed and orbed. Yet in the true genesis, nature is globed in the material, souls orbed in the spiritual firmament. Love globes, wisdom orbs, all things. As magnet the steel, so spirit attracts matter, which trembles to traverse the poles of diversity, and rest in the bosom of unity. All genesis is of love. Wisdom is her form: beauty her costume.

XLIV. GRAVITATION

Love and gravity are a twofold action of one life, whose conservative instincts in man and nature preserve inviolate the harmony of the immutable and eternal law of spirit. Man and nature alike tend toward the Godhead. All seeming divergence is overruled by this omnipotent force, whose retributions restore universal order.

XLV. LOVE

Love designs, thought sketches, action sculptures the works of spirit. Love is divine, conceiving, creating, completing, all things. Love is the Genius of Spirit.

XLVI. LIFE

Life, in its initial state, is synthetic; then feeling, thought, action are one and indivisible: love is its manifestation. Childhood and woman are samples and instances. But thought disintegrates and breaks this unity of soul: action alone restores it. Action is composition; thought decomposition. Deeds executed in love are graceful, harmonious, entire; enacted from thought merely, they are awkward, dissonant, incomplete: a manufacture, not creations, not works of genius.

XLVII. ACTUAL AND IDEAL

The actual and ideal are twins of one mother, Reality, who failing to incarnate her conceptions in time, meanwhile contents herself with admiring in each the complement of the other, herself integrant of both. Always are the divine Gemini intertwined; Pan and Psyche, man and woman, the soul and nature.

XLVIII. BEAUTY

All departures from perfect beauty are degradations of the divine image. God is the one type, which the soul strives to incarnate in all organizations. Varieties are historical: the one form embosoms all forms; all having a common likeness at the base of difference. Human heads are images, more or less perfect, of the soul's or God's head. But the divine features do not fix in flesh; in the coarse and brittle clay. Beauty is fluent; art of highest order represents her always in flux, giving fluency and motion to bodies solid and immovable to sense. The line of beauty symbolizes motion.

XLIX. TRANSFIGURATION

Never have we beheld a purely human face; as yet, the beast, demon, rather than the man or God, predominate in its expression. The face of the soul is not extant in flesh. Yet she has a face, and virtue and genius shall one day reveal her celestial lineaments: a beauty, a majesty, shall then radiate from her that shall transcend the rapt ideal of love and hope. So have I seen glimpses of this spiritual glory, when, inspired by some thought or sentiment, she was transfigured from the image of the earthly to that of the heavenly, the ignoble melting out of her features, lost in the supersensual life.

L. PROMETHEUS

Know, O man, that your soul is the Prometheus, who, receiving the divine fires, builds up this majestic statue of clay, and moulds it in the deific image, the pride of gods, the model and analogon of all forms. He chiselled that godlike brow, arched those mystic temples from whose fanes she herself looks forth, formed that miraculous globe above, and planted that sylvan grove below; graved those massive blades yoked in armed powers; carved that heaven-containing bosom, wreathed those puissant thighs, and hewed those stable columns, diffusing over all the grandeur, the grace of his own divine lineaments, and delighting in this cunning work of his hand. Mar not its beauty, spoil not its symmetry, by the deforming lines of lust and sin: dethroning the divinity incarnated therein, and transforming yourself into the satyr and the beast.

5. Theodore Parker (1810–1860)

A Discourse of Matters Pertaining to Religion

[Not all the citizens of Boston were as pusillanimous as Convers Francis; in 1842 a group headed by Charles Ellis persuaded Parker to follow the South Boston address with a full exposition of his position. They rented the old Masonic Temple, and he there gave five lectures which he amplified into this most important book, *A Discourse of Matters Pertaining to Religion* (Boston, 1842). He worked intensely upon it; his strategy makes it one of the remarkable achievements of the period.

The essence of his plan—which he carried out in relentless detail—is this segment from Book II (Chapters VI–VII, pp. 197–237). He approached the present through a historical analysis, so that any New Englander could at last comprehend how New England had come to the existing pass. But he did not follow the obvious demarcations of Unitarianism versus Orthodoxy; instead he made new groupings around basic concepts such as Naturalism and Supernaturalism. Thus he could pulverize the current Unitarianism by showing that it was in both camps at once and so was neither one thing nor the other. Philosophically it was naturalistic, but by clinging to miracles it tried to be also supernaturalistic: thus it became "a truncated supernaturalism."

> With a philosophy too rational to go the full length of the supernatural theory; too sensual to embrace the spiritual method, and ask no person to mediate between man and God, it oscillates between the two . . . It censures the traditionary sects, yet sits itself among the tombs, and mourns over things past and gone . . . It blinds men's eyes with the letter, yet bids them look for the spirit; stops their ears with texts of the Old Testament, and then asks them to listen to the voice of God in their heart.

It is hardly surprising that at the next meeting of the Unitarian association, on January 23, 1843, Dr. N. L. Frothingham declared that the difference between Trinitarians and Unitarians was one of Christianity, but "the difference between Mr. Parker and the Association is a difference between no Christianity and Christianity." By 1845 the association excluded him from the Thursday Lecture, and in January a group of gentlemen met and passed a resolution, "That the Rev. Theodore Parker have a chance to be heard in Boston." The result was the organization of the Twenty-eighth Congregational Society, which met for several years in the Melodeon, and became Parker's stronghold.

By organizing theological history around the poles of Naturalism and Supernaturalism, Parker could run the real foe to earth: both schools, although incarnating half-truths, were equally chained to the sensational psychology. Each was therefore out of touch, not only with religious fact, but with natural and scientific.

Parker's book had a historico-logical finality that made it, for thousands to whom Emerson was difficult or obscure, the most powerful statement of the Transcendental argument.]

THE RATIONALISTIC VIEW, OR NATURALISM

This allows that the original powers of Nature, as shown in the inorganic, the vegetable, and the animal world, all came from God at the first; that he is a principle, either material or spiritual, separate from the world, and independent thereof. He made the world, and all things, including man, and stamped on them certain laws which they are to keep. He was but *transiently* present and active in nature at creation; is not *immanently* present and active therein. He has now, nothing to do with the world but—to see it go. Here, then is God on the one side; on the other, Man and Nature. But there is a great gulf fixed between them, over which there passes, neither God nor man.

This theory teaches that man, in addition to his organs of perception, has certain intellectual faculties by which he can reason from effect to cause; can discover truth, which is the statement of a fact; from a number of facts in science can discern a scientific law, the relation of thing to thing; from a number of facts in morals, can learn the relation of man to man; deduce a moral law, which shall teach the most expedient and profitable way of managing affairs. Both its scientific and its moral statement of facts rest solely on experience, and never go beyond their precedents. Still farther, it allows that man can find out there is a God, by reasoning *experimentally* from observations in the material world, and *metaphysically* also, from the connection of notions in the mind. But this conclusion is only to be reached, in either case, by a process that is long, complicated, tortuous, and so difficult that but one man in some thousands has the necessary experimental knowledge, and but one in some millions, the metaphysical subtlety requisite to go through it, and become certain that there is a God. Its notion of God is this, a Being who exists as the Power, Mind and Will that caused the universe.

The metaphysical philosophy of this system may be briefly stated. In man, by nature, there is nothing but man. There is but one channel by which knowledge can come into man, that is *sensation;* perception through the senses. That is an assumption, nobody pretends it is proved. This knowledge is modified by *reflection,* the mind's process of ruminating upon the knowledge which sensation affords. At any given time, therefore, if we examine what is in man, we find nothing which has not first been in the senses. Now the senses converse only with finite phenomena. Reflection—what can it get out of these? The Absolute? The premise does not warrant the conclusion.

Something "as good as Infinite?" Let us see. It makes a *scientific* law a mere generalization from observed facts, which it can never go beyond. Its science, therefore, is in the rear of observation; we do not know whether the next stone shall fall to the ground or from it. All it can say of the universality of any law of science, is this, "So far as we have seen, it is so." It cannot pass from the Particular to the Universal. It makes a *moral* law the result of external experience; merely an induction from moral facts; not the affirmation of man's moral nature declaring the eternal rule of Right. It learns morality by seeing what plan succeeds best in the long run. Its morality, therefore, is Selfishness. A man in a new case, for which he can find no precedents, knows not what to do. He is never certain he is right till he gets the reward. Its moral law at present, like the statute law, is the slowly elaborated product of centuries of experience. It pretends to find out God, as a law in science, solely, by reasoning from effect to cause; from a plan to the designer. Then on what does a man's belief in God depend? On man's nature, acting spontaneously? No; for there is nothing in man, but man, and nothing comes in but sensations, which do not directly give us God. It depends on reflection, argument, that process of reasoning mentioned before. Now admitting that sensation affords sufficient premise for the conclusion, there is a difficulty in the way. The man must either depend on his own reasoning, or that of another. In the one case he may be mistaken, in an argument, so long, crooked, and difficult. 'T is at best an inference. The "Hypothesis of a God," as some impiously call it—may thus rest on no better argument than the hypothesis of Vortices, or Epicycles. In the other case, if we trust another man, he may be mistaken; still worse, may design to deceive the inquirer, as, we are told, the Heathen Sages did. Where, then, is the certain conviction of any God at all? This theory allows none. Its "proof of the existence of God" is a proof of the possibility of a God; perhaps of its probability. Surely no more . . .

It makes no difference between Good and Evil; Expedient and Inexpedient are the better words. These are to be learned only by long study and much cunning. All men have not the requisite skill to find out moral and religious doctrines, and no means of proving either in their own heart; therefore they must take the word of their appointed teachers and philosophers, who "have investigated the matter;" found there is "an expedient way" for men to follow, and a "God" to punish them if they do not follow it. In moral and religious matters the mass of men must rely on the authority of their teachers. Millions of men, who never made an astronomical observation, believe the distance between the Earth and the Sun is what Newton or Laplace declares it to be. Why should not men take moral and religious doctrines on the same evidence? It is true, astronomers have differed a little—some making the Earth the centre, some the Sun—and divines still more. But men must learn the moral law as the statute law. The State is above each man's private notions about good and evil, and controls these, as well as their passions. Man must act always from mean and selfish views, never from Love of the Good, the Beautiful, the True . . .

It is obvious enough that this system of Naturalism is the *philosophy* which lies at the foundation of the popular theology in New England; that is very little understood by the men, out of pulpits and in pulpits, who adhere to it; who, while they hold fast to the theory of the worst of the English Deists—though of only the worst; while they deny the immanence of God in matter and man, and therefore take away the natural possibility of inspiration, and cling to that system which justifies the Doubt of Hume, the Selfishness of Paley, the coarse materialism of Hobbes,—are yet ashamed of their descent, and seek to point out others of a quite different spiritual complexion, as the lineal descendants of that ancient stock . . .

THE ANTI-RATIONALISTIC VIEW, OR SUPERNATURALISM

This system differs in many respects from the other; but its philosophy is at bottom the same. It denies that by natural action there can be any thing in man which was not first in the senses. Whatever transcends the senses can come to man only by a miracle. To develop the natural side of the theory it sets God on the one side and man on the other. However it admits the immanence of God in matter, and talks very little about the laws of matter, which it thinks require revision, amendment, and even repeal, as if the nature of things changed, or God grew wiser by experiment. It does not see that if God is always the same, and immanent in nature, the laws of nature can neither change nor be changed. It limits the power of man still farther than the former theory. It denies that he can, of himself, discover the existence of God; or find out that it is better to love his brother than to hate him, to subject the Passions to Reason, Desire to Duty, rather than to subject Reason to Passion, Duty to Desire. Man can find out all that is needed for his animal and intellectual welfare, with no miracle, but can learn nothing that is needed for his moral and religious welfare. He can invent the steam engine, and calculate the orbit of Halley's comet; but cannot tell Good from Evil, nor determine that there is a God. The Unnecessary is given him; the Indispensable he cannot get by nature. Man, therefore, is the veriest wretch in creation. His mind forces him to inquire on religious matters, but brings him into doubt, and leaves him in the very slough of Despond. He goes up and down sorrowing, seeking rest, but finding none. Nay; it goes farther still, and declares that, by nature, all men's actions are sin, hateful to God.

On the other hand, it teaches that God works a miracle from time to time, and makes to man a positive revelation of moral and religious truth, which man could not otherwise gain. Its history of revelation is this: God revealed his own existence in a visible form to the first man; taught him religious and moral duties by words orally spoken. The first man communicated the knowledge to his descendants, from whom the tradition of the fact has spread over all the world. Men know there is a God, and distinction between right and wrong, only by hearsay, as they know there was a Flood in the time of Noah, or Deucalion. The first man sinned, and fell from the state of frequent communion with God. Revelations have since become rare; exceptions in the history of man. However, as man without a connection with the Infinite must soon perish, God continued to make miraculous revelations to one single people. To them he gave laws, religious and civil; made predictions, and accompanied each revelation by some miraculous sign, for without it none could tell truth from a lie. Other nations received reflections of this light, which was directly imparted to the favored people. At length he made a revelation of all religious and moral truth, by means of his Son, a divine and miraculous being, both God and man, and confirmed the tidings by miracles the most surprising. As this revelation is to last forever, it has been recorded miraculously, and preserved for all coming time. The persons who received direct communication miraculously from God, are of course mediators between Him and the human race . . .

Men ask of this system, How do you know there is in man nothing but the product of sensation, or miraculous tradition; that man cannot approach God except by miracle; that these mediators received truth miraculously; taught all truth; nothing but the truth; that you have their words, pure and unmixed in your scriptures; that God has no farther revelation to make? The answer is—*we find it convenient to assume all this, and accordingly have banished Reason from the premises; she asked troublesome questions. We condescend to no proof of the facts. You must take our word for that.* Thus the main doctrines of the theory rest on assumptions; on no facts.

This system represents the despair of man groping after God. The religious sentiment acts, but is crippled by a philosophy poor and sensual. Is man nothing but a combination of five senses, and a thinking machine, to grind up and bolter sensations, and learn of God only by hearsay? The God of supernaturalism is a God afar off; its Religion worn out and second-handed. We cannot meet God face to face. In one respect it is worse than

Naturalism; that sets great value on the faculties of man, which this depreciates and profanes. But all systems rest on a truth, or they could not be; this on a great truth, or it could not prevail widely. It admits the immanence of God in Nature, and declares, also, that mankind is dependent on Him, for religious and moral truth as for all things else; has a connection with God who really guides, educates and blesses the race, for he is transiently present therein. The doctrine of miraculous events, births, persons, deaths and the like, this is the veil of Poetry drawn over the face of Fact. It has a truth not admitted by Naturalism. Now only a few *"thinking"* men even in fancy can be satisfied without a connection with God, so Naturalism is always confined to a few reflective and cultivated persons; while the mass of men believe in the supernatural theory, at least, in the truth it covers up. Its truth is of great moment. Its vice is to make God transiently active in man, not immanent in him; restrict the divine presence and action to times, places and persons. It overlooks the fact that if religious truth be necessary for all, then it must either have been provided for and put in the reach of all, or else there is a fault in the divine plan. Then again, if God gives a natural supply for the lower wants, it is probable, to say the least, he will not neglect the higher. Now for the religious consciousness of Man, a knowledge of two great truths is indispensable; namely, a knowledge of the existence of the Infinite God, and of the duty we owe to Him, for these two are implied in all religious teaching and life. Now one of two things must be admitted, and a third is not possible; either man *can discover these two truths by the light of nature,* or *he cannot.* If the latter be the case, then is man the most hopeless of all beings. Revelation of these truths is confined to a few; it is indispensably necessary to all. Accordingly the first hypothesis is generally admitted by the supernaturalists, in New England—though in spite of their philosophy— that these two truths *can be discovered by the light of nature.* Then if the two main points, the premises which involve the whole of Morals and Religion, lie within the reach of man's natural powers, how is a miracle, or the tradition of a miracle necessary to reveal the minor doctrines involved in the universal truth? Does not the faculty to discern the greater include the faculty to discern the less? What covers an acre will cover a yard. Where then is the *use of the miraculous interposition?*

Neither Naturalism nor Supernaturalism legitimates the fact of man's religious consciousness. Both fail of satisfying the natural religious wants of the race. Each has merits and vices of its own. Neither gives for the Soul's wants a supply analogous to that so bountifully provided for the wants of the Body, or the Mind.

THE NATURAL-RELIGIOUS VIEW, OR SPIRITUALISM

This theory teaches that there is a natural supply for spiritual as well as for corporeal wants; that there is a connection between God and the soul, as between light and the eye, sound and the ear, food and the palate, truth and the intellect, beauty and the imagination; that as we follow an instinctive tendency, obey the body's law, get a natural supply for its wants, attain health and strength, the body's welfare; as we keep the law of the mind, and get a supply for its wants, attain wisdom and skill, the mind's welfare,— so if, following another instinctive tendency, we keep the law of the moral and religious nature, we get a supply for their wants, moral and religious truth, obtain peace of conscience and rest for the soul, the highest moral and religious welfare. It teaches that the world is not nearer to our bodies than God to the soul; "for in him we live and move, and have our being." As we have bodily senses to lay hold on matter and supply bodily wants, through which we obtain, naturally, all needed material things; so we have spiritual faculties, to lay hold on God, and supply spiritual wants; through them we obtain all needed spiritual things. As we observe the conditions of the body, we have nature on our side; as we observe the Law of the Soul, we have God on our side. He imparts truth to all men who observe these conditions; we have direct access to Him, through Reason, Conscience and the religious Sentiment, just as we have direct access to nature, through the eye, the ear, or the hand. Through these channels, and by means of a law, certain, regular and universal as gravitation, God inspires men, makes revelation of truth, for is not truth as much a phenomenon of God, as motion of matter? Therefore if God be omnipotent and omniactive, this inspiration is no miracle, but a regular mode of God's action on conscious spirit, as gravitation on unconscious matter. It is not a rare condescension of God, but a universal uplifting of man. To obtain a knowledge of duty, man is not sent away, outside of himself to ancient documents, for the only rule of faith and practice; the Word is very nigh him, even in his heart, and by this Word he is to try all documents whatever. Inspiration, like God's omnipresence, is not limited to the few writers claimed by the Jews, Christians, or Mahometans, but is coextensive with the race. As God fills all space, so all spirit; as he influences and constrains unconscious and necessitated matter, so he inspires and helps free and conscious man . . .

This inspiration reveals itself in various forms, modified by the country, character, education, peculiarity of him who receives it, just as water takes the form and the color of the cup into which it flows, and must needs mingle with the impurities it chances to meet. Thus Minos and Moses were inspired to make laws; David to pour out his soul in pious strains, deep and sweet as an angel's psaltery; Pindar to celebrate virtuous deeds in high heroic song; John the Baptist to denounce sin; Gerson, and Luther, and Böhme, and Fenelon, and Fox, to do each his peculiar work, and stir the world's heart, deep, very deep. Plato and Newton, Milton and Isaiah, Leibnitz and Paul, Mozart, Raphael, Phidias, Praxiteles, Orpheus, receive into their various forms the one spirit from God most high. It appears in action not less than speech. The spirit inspires Dorcas to make coats and garments for the poor, no less than Paul to preach the Gospel. As that bold man himself has said, "there are diversities of gifts, but the same spirit; diversities of operations, but the same God who worketh in all." In one man it may appear in the iron hardness of reasoning, which breaks through sophistry, and prejudice, the rubbish and diluvial drift of time. In another it is subdued and softened by the flame of affection; the hard iron of the man is melted and becomes a stream of persuasion, sparkling as it runs . . .

The influence of God in Nature, in its mechanical, vital, or instinctive action, is beautiful. The shapely trees; the leaves that clothe them in loveliness; the corn and the cattle; the dew and the flowers; the bird, the insect, moss and stone, fire and water, and earth and air; the clear blue sky that folds the world in its soft embrace; the light which rides on swift pinions, enchanting all it touches, reposing harmless on an infant's eyelid, after its long passage from the other side of the universe,—all these are noble and beautiful; they admonish while they delight us, these silent counsellors and sovereign aids. But the inspiration of God in man, when faithfully obeyed, is nobler and far more beautiful. It is not the passive elegance of unconscious things which we see resulting from man's voluntary obedience. That might well charm us in nature; in man we look for more. Here the beauty is intellectual, the beauty of Thought which comprehends the world and understands its laws; it is moral, the beauty of Virtue, which overcomes the world and lives by its own laws; it is religious, the beauty of Holiness, which rises above the world and lives by the law of the Spirit of Life. A single good man, at one with God, makes the morning and evening sun seem little and very low. It is a higher mode of the divine Power that appears in him, self-conscious and self-restrained . . .

Now to many men, who have but once felt this; when heaven lay about them, in their infancy, before the world was too much with them, and they laid waste their powers, getting and spending, when they look back upon it, across the dreary gulf, where Honor, Virtue, Religion have made shipwreck and perished with their youth, it seems visionary, a shadow, dream-like, unreal. They count it a phantom of their inexperience; the vision of a child's fancy, raw and unused to the world. Now they are wiser. They cease to believe in inspiration. They can only credit the saying of the priests, that long ago there were inspired men; but none now; that you and I must bow our faces to the dust, groping like the Blind-worm and the Beetle; nor turn our eyes to the broad, free heaven; that we cannot walk by the great central and celestial light that God made to guide all that come into the world, but only by the farthing-candle of tradition, poor and flickering light which we get of the priest, which casts strange and fearful shadows around us as we walk, that "leads to bewilder and dazzles to blind." Alas for us if this be all.

But can it be so? Has Infinity laid aside Its omnipresence, retreating to some little corner of space? No. The grass grows as green; the birds chirp as gaily; the sun shines as warm; the moon and the stars walk in their pure beauty, sublime as before; morning and evening have lost none of their loveliness; not a jewel has fallen from the diadem of night. God is still there; ever present in matter, else it were not; else the serpent of Fate would coil him about the All of things; would crush it in his remorseless grasp, and the hour of ruin, strike creation's knell.

Can it be then, as so many tell us, that God, immanent in matter, has forsaken man; retreated from the shekinah in the holy of holies to the court of the Gentiles; that now he will stretch forth no aid, but leave his tottering child to wander on, amid the palpable obscure, eyeless and fatherless, without a path, with no guide but his feeble brother's words and works; groping after God if haply he may find him; and learning, at last, that he is but a God afar off, to be approached only by mediators and attorneys, not face to face as before? Can it be that Thought shall fly through the Heaven, his wing glittering in the ray of every star, burnished by a million suns, and then come drooping back, with ruffled plume and flagging wing, and eye that once looked undazzled on the sun, now spiritless and cold; come back to tell us God is no Father; that he vails his face and will not look upon his child; his erring child! No more can this be true. Conscience is still God-with-us; a Prayer is deep as ever of old; Reason as true; Religion as blest. Faith still remains the substance of things hoped for, the evidence of things not seen. Love is yet mighty to cast out fear. The soul still searches the deeps of God; the pure in heart see him. The substance of the Infinite is not yet exhausted, nor the well of Life drunk dry. The Father is near us as ever, else Reason were a traitor, Morality a hollow form, Religion a mockery, and Love a hideous lie. Now, as in the days of Adam, Moses, Jesus, he that is faithful to Reason, Conscience, and Religion, will, through them, receive inspiration to guide him through all his pilgrimage.

6. Henry D. Thoreau (1817–1862)
The Natural History of Massachusetts

[The story behind Thoreau's first major article is an illumination of the Transcendental mind. In April 1842 Emerson found himself once more fascinated with geology—discovering a "correspondence" to spiritual law in the preponderance of sandstone over coal, and of coal over the fossil of beast and bird. Thus he chanced to read a series of scientific reports put out by the Commonwealth of Massachusetts on the insects, plants, reptiles and birds, invertebrates and quadrupeds of the state. He went to the State House, begged an issue, and "set Henry Thoreau on the good track of giving an account of them in the Dial, explaining to him the felicity of the subject for him as it admits of the narrative of all his woodcraft boatcraft & fishcraft."

The transaction illustrates, first, the Transcendental attitude toward scientific fact—a self-conscious hospitality as long as something more could be done with it —and secondly, the difficult problem of the relation between Emerson and Thoreau. It exhibits the generous, but still the condescending attitude of the patron to his protégé—and for such munificence neither Thoreau nor posterity quite forgives the well-meaning Emerson. He was to maintain to the end—with only occasional doubts—that Thoreau's thought was his own, only in a more "athletic" dress. He knew that in the presence of the concrete he was often awkward, and so he turned this subject over—in all selflessness—to his disciple. He assured his friends that by such essays, Thoreau's "works & fame may go out into all lands, and, as happens to great Premiers, quite extinguish the titular Master."

Nothing could have been more genuine than Emerson's gesture; nothing could sound more smug. No wonder that in the last years of Thoreau's existence communion between the two became difficult! But in 1842 Thoreau stood to gain everything by the assistance; he dutifully produced his essay according to Emerson's directive (The Dial, July 1842, III, 19–40), and while it is indubitably Thoreau's own, it could stand—even had Thoreau never written more—as an expert demonstration of the Transcendental methodology for coping with the multifarious concreteness of nature. That method is to see the particular as a particular, and yet at the same time so to perceive it as to make it, of itself, yield up the general and the universal. Emerson wanted Thoreau to show the method in operation—and this is exactly what Thoreau did.]

I am singularly refreshed in winter when I hear of service berries, poke-weed, juniper. Is not heaven made up of these cheap summer glories? There is a singular health in those words Labrador and East Main, which no desponding creed recognises. How much more than federal are these states. If there were no other vicissitudes than the seasons, our interest would never tire. Much more is adoing than Congress wots of. What journal do the persimmon and the buckeye keep, and the sharp-shinned hawk? What is transpiring from summer to winter in the Carolinas, and the Great Pine Forest, and the Valley of the Mohawk? The merely political aspect of the land is never very cheering; men are degraded when considered as the members of a political organization. On this side all lands present only the symptoms of decay. I see but Bunker Hill and Sing-Sing, the District of Columbia and Sullivan's Island, with a few avenues connecting them. But paltry are they all beside one blast of the east or the south wind which blows over them.

In society you will not find health, but in nature. Unless our feet at least stood in the midst of nature, all our faces would be pale and livid. Society is always diseased, and the best is the most so. There is no scent in it so wholesome as that of the pines, nor any fragrance so penetrating and restorative as the life-everlasting in high pastures. I would keep some book of natural history always by me as a sort of elixir, the reading of which should restore the tone of the system. To the sick, indeed, nature is sick, but to the well, a fountain of health. To him who contemplates a trait of natural beauty no harm nor disappointment can come. The doctrines of despair, of spiritual or political tyranny or servitude, were never taught by such as shared the serenity of nature. Surely good courage will not flag here on the Atlantic border, as long as we are flanked by the Fur Countries. There is enough in that sound to cheer one under any circumstances. The spruce, the hemlock, and the pine will not countenance despair. Methinks some creeds in vestries and churches do forget the hunter wrapped in furs by the Great Slave Lake, and that the Esquimaux sledges are drawn by dogs, and in the twilight of the northern night, the hunter does not give over to follow the seal and walrus on the ice. They are of sick and diseased imaginations who would toll the world's knell so soon. Cannot these sedentary sects do better than prepare the shrouds and write the epitaphs of those other busy living men? The practical faith of all men belies the preacher's consolation. What is any man's discourse to me, if I am not sensible of something in it as steady and cheery as the creak of crickets? In it the woods must be relieved against the sky. Men tire me when I am not constantly greeted and refreshed as by the flux of sparkling streams. Surely joy is the condition of life. Think of the young fry that leap in ponds, the myriads of insects ushered into being on a summer evening, the incessant note of the hyla with which the woods ring in the spring, the nonchalance of the butterfly carrying accident and change painted in a thousand hues upon its wings, or the brook minnow stoutly stemming the current, the lustre of whose scales worn bright by the attrition is reflected upon the bank.

We fancy that this din of religion, literature, and philosophy, which is heard in pulpits, lyceums, and parlors, vibrates through the universe, and is as catholic a sound as the creaking of the earth's axle; but if a man sleep soundly, he will forget it all between sunset and dawn. It is the three-inch swing of a pendulum in a cupboard, which the great pulse of nature vibrates by and through each instant. When we lift our eyelids and open our ears, it disappears with smoke and rattle like the cars on a railroad. When I detect a beauty in any of the recesses of nature, I am reminded, by the serene and retired spirit in which it requires to be contemplated, of the inexpressible privacy of a life,—how silent and unambitious it is. The beauty there is in mosses must be considered from the holiest, quietest nook. What an admirable training is science for the more active warfare of life. Indeed, the unchallenged bravery, which these studies imply, is far more impressive than the trumpeted valor of the warrior. I am pleased to learn that Thales was up and stirring by night not unfrequently, as his astronomical discoveries prove. Linnaeus, setting out for Lapland, surveys his "comb" and "spare shirt," "leathern breeches" and "gauze cap to keep off gnats," with as much complacency as Bonaparte a park of artillery for the Russian campaign. The quiet bravery of the man is admirable. His eye is to take in fish, flower, and bird, quadruped and biped. Science is always brave, for to know, is to know good; doubt and danger quail before her eye. What the coward overlooks in his hurry, she calmly scrutinizes, breaking ground like a pioneer for the array of arts that follow in her train. But cowardice is unscientific; for there cannot be a science of ignorance. There may be a science of bravery, for that advances; but a retreat is rarely well conducted; if it is, then is it an orderly advance in the face of circumstances.

But to draw a little nearer to our promised topics. Entomology extends the limits of being in a new direction, so that I walk in nature with a sense of greater space and freedom. It suggests besides, that the universe is not rough-hewn, but perfect in its details. Nature will bear the closest inspection; she invites us to lay our eye level with the smallest leaf, and take an insect view of its plain. She has no interstices; every part is full of life. I explore, too, with pleasure, the sources of the myriad sounds which crowd the summer noon, and which seem the very grain and stuff of which eternity is made. Who does not remember the shrill roll-call of the harvest fly? . . .

In the autumn days, the creaking of crickets is heard at noon over all the land, and as in summer they are heard chiefly at nightfall, so then by their incessant chirp they usher in the evening of the year. Nor can all the vanities that vex the world alter one whit the measure that night has chosen. Every pulse-beat is in exact time with the cricket's chant and the tickings of the deathwatch in the wall. Alternate with these if you can . . .

It appears from the Report that there are about forty quadrupeds belonging to the State, and among these one is glad to hear of a few bears, wolves, lynxes, and wildcats . . .

Perhaps of all our untamed quadrupeds, the fox has obtained the widest and most familiar reputation, from the time of Pilpay and Aesop to the present day. His recent tracks still give variety to a winter's walk. I tread in the steps of the fox that has gone before me by some hours, or which perhaps I have started, with such a tiptoe of expectation, as if I were on the trail of the Spirit itself which resides in the wood, and expected soon to catch it in its lair. I am curious to know what has determined its graceful curvatures, and how surely they were coincident with the fluctuations of some mind. I know which way a mind wended, what horizon it faced, by the setting of these tracks, and whether it moved slowly or rapidly, by their greater or less intervals and distinctness; for the swiftest step leaves yet a lasting trace. Sometimes you will see the trails of many together, and where they have gambolled and gone through a hundred evolutions, which testify to a singular listlessness and leisure in nature.

When I see a fox run across the pond on the snow, with the carelessness of freedom, or at intervals trace his course in the sunshine along the ridge of a hill, I give up to him sun and earth as to their true proprietor. He does not go in the sun, but it seems to follow him, and there is a visible sympathy between him and it. Sometimes, when the snow lies light, and but five or six inches deep, you may give chase and come up with one on foot. In such a case he will show a remarkable presence of mind, choosing only the safest direction, though he may lose ground by it. Notwithstanding his fright, he will take no step which is not beautiful. His pace is a sort of leopard canter, as if he were in no wise impeded by the snow, but were husbanding his strength all the while. When the ground is uneven, the course is a series of graceful curves, conforming to the shape of the surface. He runs as though there were not a bone in his back, occasionally dropping his muzzle to the ground for a rod or two, and then tossing his head aloft, when satisfied of his course. When he comes to a declivity, he will put his fore feet together, and slide swiftly down it, shoving the snow before him. He treads so softly that you would hardly hear it from any nearness, and yet with such expression, that it would not be quite inaudible at any distance . . .

It appears that we have eight kinds of tortoises, twelve snakes,—but one of which is venomous,—nine frogs and toads, nine salamanders, and one lizard, for our neighbors.

I am particularly attracted by the motions of the serpent tribe. They make our hands and feet, the wings of the bird, and the fins of the fish seem very superfluous, as if nature had only indulged her fancy in making them. The black snake will dart into a bush when pursued, and circle round and round with an easy and graceful motion, amid the thin and bare twigs, five or six feet from the ground, as a birds flits from bough to bough, or hang in festoons between the forks. Elasticity and flexibleness in the simpler forms of animal life are equivalent to a complex system of limbs in the higher; and we have only to be as wise and wily as the serpent, to perform as difficult feats without the vulgar assistance of hands and feet . . .

Nature has taken more care than the fondest parent for the education and refinement of her children. Consider the silent influence which flowers exert, no less upon the ditcher in the meadow than the lady in the bower. When I walk in the woods, I am reminded that a wise purveyor has been there before me; my most delicate experience is typified there. I am struck with the pleasing friendships and unanimities of nature, as when the moss on the trees takes the form of their leaves. In the most stupendous scenes you will see delicate and fragile features, as slight wreathes of vapor, dewlines, feathery sprays, which suggest a high refinement, a noble blood and breeding, as it were. It is not hard to account for elves and fairies; they represent this light grace, this ethereal gentility. Bring a spray from the wood, or a crystal from the brook, and place it on your mantel, and your household ornaments will seem plebeian beside its nobler fashion and bearing. It will wave superior there, as if used to a more refined and polished circle. It has a salute and a response to all your enthusiasm and heroism.

In the winter, I stop short in the path to admire how the trees grow up without forethought, regardless of the time and circumstances. They do not wait as man does, but now is the golden age of the sapling. Earth, air, sun, and rain, are occasion enough; they were no better in primeval centuries. The "winter of *their* discontent" never comes. Witness the buds of the native poplar standing gaily out to the frost on the sides of its bare switches.

They express a naked confidence. With cheerful heart one could be a sojourner in the wilderness, if he were sure to find there the catkins of the willow or the alder. When I read of them in the accounts of northern adventurers, by Baffin's Bay or Mackenzie's river, I see how even there too I could dwell. They are our little vegetable redeemers. Methinks our virtue will hold out till they come again. They are worthy to have had a greater than Minerva or Ceres for their inventor. Who was the benignant goddess that bestowed them on mankind?

Nature is mythical and mystical always, and works with the license and extravagance of genius. She has her luxurious and florid style as well as art. Having a pilgrim's cup to make, she gives to the whole, stem, bowl, handle, and nose, some fantastic shape, as if it were to be the car of some fabulous marine deity, a Nereus or Triton . . .

The works we have placed at the head of our chapter, with as much license as the preacher selects his text, are such as imply more labor than enthusiasm. The State wanted complete catalogues of its natural riches, with such additional facts merely as would be directly useful.

The Reports on Fishes, Reptiles, Insects, and Invertebrate Animals, however, indicate labor and research, and have a value independent of the object of the legislature.

Those on Herbaceous Plants and Birds cannot be of much value, as long as Bigelow and Nuttall are accessible. They serve but to indicate, with more or less exactness, what species are found in the State. We detect several errors ourselves, and a more practised eye would no doubt expand the list.

The Quadrupeds deserved a more final and instructive report than they have obtained.

These volumes deal much in measurements and minute descriptions, not interesting to the general reader, with only here and there a colored sentence to allure him, like those plants growing in dark forests, which bear only leaves without blossoms. But the ground was comparatively unbroken, and we will not complain of the pioneer, if he raises no flowers with his first crop. Let us not underrate the value of a fact; it will one day flower in a truth. It is astonishing how few facts of importance are added in a century to the natural history of any animal. The natural history of man himself is still being gradually written. Men are knowing enough after their fashion. Every countryman and dairymaid knows that the coats of the fourth stomach of the calf will curdle milk, and what particular mushroom is a safe and nutritious diet. You cannot go into any field or wood, but it will seem as if every stone had been turned, and the bark on every tree ripped up. But after all, it is much easier to discover than to see when the cover is off. It has been well said that "the attitude of inspection is prone." Wisdom does not inspect, but behold. We must look a long time before we can see. Slow are the beginnings of philosophy. He has something demoniacal in him, who can discern a law, or couple two facts. We can imagine a time when,— "Water runs down hill,"—may have been taught in the schools. The true man of science will know nature better by his finer organization; he will smell, taste, see, hear, feel, better than other men. His will be a deeper and finer experience. We do not learn by inference and deduction, and the application of mathematics to philosophy, but by direct intercourse and sympathy. It is with science as with ethics, we cannot know truth by contrivance and method; the Baconian is as false as any other, and with all the helps of machinery and the arts, the most scientific will still be the healthiest and friendliest man, and possess a more perfect Indian wisdom.

8

The Movement: Literary and Critical

W e are sad that we cannot be present at the gathering in of this harvest. And yet we are joyous, too, when we think that though our name may not be writ on the pillar of our country's fame, we can really do far more towards rearing it, than those who come at a later period and to a seemingly fairer task. *Now,* the humblest effort, made in a noble spirit, and with religious hope, cannot fail to be even infinitely useful. Whether we introduce some noble model from another time and clime, to encourage aspiration in our own, or cheer into blossom the simplest wood-flower that ever rose from the earth, moved by the genuine impulse to grow, independent of the lures of money or celebrity; whether we speak boldly when fear or doubt keep others silent, or refuse to swell the popular cry upon an unworthy occasion, the spirit of truth, purely worshipped, shall turn our acts and forebearances alike to profit, informing them with oracles which the latest time shall bless.

—MARGARET FULLER

1. Margaret Fuller (1810–1850)
Memoirs

[The eldest daughter of a stern lawyer and a Congressman of Newburyport, Sarah Margaret Fuller was subjected by him to a strenuous education that shattered her health and made her the most learned woman in America. She once said that she had never met an intellect superior to her own—and the sad fact is that she spoke the truth. As a child she read Ovid, Cervantes, Molière, and Shakespeare. An early friend of Clarke, Hedge, and W. H. Channing, she joined with them in the study of German and made elaborate preparations for writing a life of Goethe. Homely, long-necked, nearsighted, hers was a passionate nature with which the males in the Transcendental group were ill equipped to cope.

Like all Transcendentalists, she kept journals (Transcendentalists signalized the attaining of friendship by exchanging diaries). After conducting her fairly sensational "conversations" in and around Boston, and editing *The Dial* between 1840 and 1842, she went to New York and for two years did brilliant work as a pioneer literary critic on Greeley's *Tribune*. She finally got to Europe in 1846 and in Italy the next year met an Italian marchese, Angelo Ossoli, several years younger than herself and an agreeable, though evidently not an intellectual type. They had a child, born in September 1848. She participated as a nurse in the siege of Rome, performing heroic service. She, Ossoli, and the child were returning to America when they were drowned in a shipwreck off Fire Island, July 19, 1850.

Emerson, Clarke, and W. H. Channing sorted out her papers and in 1852 published two volumes of *Memoirs*. They were self-consciously determined to treat her in the grand manner with which, in Europe, the literary remains of a genius were traditionally handled. Nothing like it had yet been done in America. They did not spare themselves; particularly Emerson did not spare himself, but let it be shown that he had proved emotionally inadequate to Margaret's tempestuous assault upon his friendship. The three may have been too incurably virginal to appreciate all that their selections told of a deeply passionate being, but they too had been immersed in German literature of the *Sturm und Drang,* and they could comprehend that in Margaret they had an authentic American version of a romantic heroine. Certain passages in her journals are such deep revelations of the emotional drive behind the Transcendental movement, such uninhibited and even painful disclosures of the attitudes and terrors of the early nineteenth century, that they are indispensable—quite apart from Margaret's own peculiar personality —to an understanding of the frame of mind and of soul out of which came the Transcendental literature.]

THERE was a vein of haughty caprice in her character, and a love of solitude, which made her at times wish to retire apart, and at these times she would expect to be entirely understood, and let alone, yet to be welcomed back when she returned. She did not thwart others in their humors, but she never doubted of great indulgence from them.

Some singular habits she had, which, when new, charmed, but, after acquaintance, displeased her companions. She had by nature the same habit and power of excitement that is described in the spinning dervishes of the East. Like them she would spin until all around her were giddy, while her own brain, instead of being disturbed, was excited to great action. Pausing, she would declaim verses of others, or her own, or act many parts, with strange catchwords and burdens, that seemed to act with mystical power on her own fancy, sometimes stimulating her to convulse the hearers with laughter, sometimes to melt them to tears. When her power began to languish, she would spin again till fired to re-commence her singular drama, into which she wove figures from the scenes of her earlier childhood, her companions, and the dignitaries she sometimes saw, with fantasies unknown to life, unknown to heaven or earth . . .

May 4th, 1830.—I have greatly wished to see among us such a person of genius as the nineteenth century can afford—*i. e.,* one who has tasted in the morning of existence the extremes of good and ill, both imaginative and real. I had imagined a person endowed by nature with that acute sense of Beauty (*i. e.,* Harmony or Truth) and that vast capacity of desire, which give soul to love and ambition. I had wished this person might grow up to manhood alone (but not alone in crowds); I would have placed him in a situation so retired, so obscure, that he would quietly, but without bitter sense of isolation, stand apart from all surrounding him. I would have had him go on steadily, feeding his mind with congenial love, hopefully confident that if he only nourished his existence into perfect life, Fate would, at fitting season, furnish an atmosphere and orbit meet for his breathing and exercise. I wished he might adore, not fever for, the bright phantoms of his mind's creation, and believe them but the shadows of external things to be met with hereafter. After this steady intellectual growth had brought his powers to manhood, so far as the ideal can do it, I wished this being might be launched into the world of realities, his heart glowing with the ardor of an immortal toward perfection, his eyes searching everywhere to behold it; I wished he might collect into one burning point those withering, palsying convictions, which, in the ordinary routine of things, so gradually pervade the soul, that he might suffer, in brief space, agonies of disappointment commensurate with his unpreparedness and confidence. And I thought, thus thrown back on the representing pictorial resources I supposed him originally to possess, with such material, and the need he must feel of using it, such a man would suddenly dilate into a form of Pride, Power, and Glory,— a centre, round which asking, aimless hearts might rally,—a man fitted to act as interpreter to the one tale of many-languaged eyes!

What words are these! Perhaps you will feel as if I sought but for the longest and strongest. Yet to my ear they do but faintly describe the imagined powers of such a being . . .

From a very early age I have felt that I was not born to the common womanly lot. I knew I should never find a being who could keep the key of my character; that there would be none on whom I could always lean, from whom I could always learn; that I should be a pilgrim and sojourner on earth, and that the birds and foxes would be surer of a place to lay the head than I. You understand me, of course; such beings can only find their homes in hearts. All material luxuries, all the arrangements of society, are mere conveniences to them.

This thought, all whose bearings I did not, indeed, understand, affected me sometimes with sadness, sometimes with pride. I mourned that I never should have a thorough experience of life, never know the full riches of my being; I was proud that I was to test myself in the sternest way, that I was always to return to myself, to be my own priest, pupil, parent, child, husband, and wife. All this I did not understand as I do now; but this destiny of the thinker, and (shall I dare to say it?) of the poetic priestess, sibylline, dwelling in the cave, or amid the Lybian sands, lay yet enfolded in my mind. Accordingly, I did not look on any of the persons, brought into relation with me, with common womanly eyes . . .

[To Clarke, while preparing to write a life of Goethe:]

How am I to get the information I want, unless I go to Europe? To whom shall I write to choose my materials? I have thought of Mr. Carlyle, but still more of Goethe's friend, Von Muller. I dare say he would be pleased at the idea of a life of G. written in this hemisphere, and be very willing to help me. If you have anything to tell me, you will, and not mince matters. Of course, my impressions of Goethe's works cannot be influenced by information I get about his *life;* but, as to this latter, I suspect I must have been hasty in my inferences. I apply to you without scruple. There are subjects on which men and women usually talk a great deal, but apart from one another. You, however, are well aware that I am very destitute of what is commonly *called* modesty. With regard to this, how fine the remark of our present subject: "Courage and modesty are virtues which every sort of society reveres, because they are virtues which cannot be counterfeited; also, they are known by the *same hue.*" When that blush does not come naturally to my face, I do not drop a veil to make people think it is there. All this may be very unlovely, but it is *I* . . .

I was now in the hands of teachers, who had not, since they came on the earth, put to themselves one intelligent question as to their business here. Good dispositions and employment for the heart gave a tone to all they said, which was pleasing, and not perverting. They, no doubt, injured those who accepted the husks they proffered for bread, and believed that exercise of memory was study, and to know what others knew, was the object of study. But to me this was all penetrable. I had known great living minds,—I had seen how they took their food and did their exercise, and what their objects were. *Very early I knew that the only object in life was to grow.* I was often false to this knowledge, in idolatries of particular objects, or impatient longings for happiness, but I have never lost sight of it, have always been controlled by it, and this first gift of thought has never been superseded by a later love . . .

My pride is superior to any feelings I have yet experienced: my affection is strong admiration, not the necessity of giving or receiving assistance or sympathy. When disappointed, I do not ask or wish consolation,—I wish to know and feel my pain, to investigate its nature and its source; I will not have my thoughts diverted, or my feelings soothed; 't is therefore that my young life is so singularly barren of illusions. I know, I feel the time must come when this proud and impatient heart shall be stilled, and turn from the ardors of Search and Action, to lean on something above. But—shall I say it?—the thought of that calmer era is to me a thought of deepest sadness; so remote from my present being is that future existence, which still the mind may conceive. I believe in Eternal Progression. I believe in a God, a Beauty and Perfection to which I am to strive all my life for assimilation. From these two articles of belief, I draw the rules by which I strive to regulate my life. But, though I reverence all religions as necessary to the happiness of man, I am yet ignorant of the religion of Revelation. Tangible promises! well defined hopes! are things of which I do not *now* feel the need. At present, my soul is intent on this life, and I think of religion as its rule; and, in my opinion, this is the natural and proper course from youth to age. What I have written is not hastily concocted, it has a meaning. I have given you, in this little space, the substance of many thoughts, the clues to many cherished opinions. 'T is a subject on which I rarely speak. I never said so much but once before. I have here given you all I know, or think, on the most important of subjects—could you but read understandingly! . . .

TO BEETHOVEN

Saturday Evening, 25th Nov., 1843

MY ONLY FRIEND,

How shall I thank thee for once more breaking the chains of my sorrowful slumber? My heart beats. I live again, for I feel that I am worthy audience for thee, and that my being would be reason enough for thine.

Master, my eyes are always clear. I see that the universe is rich, if I am poor. I see the insignificance of my sorrows. In my will, I am not a captive; in my intellect, not a slave. Is it then my fault that the palsy of my affections benumbs my whole life?

I know that the curse is but for the time. I know what the eternal justice promises. But on this one sphere, it is sad. Thou didst say, thou hadst no friend but thy art. But that one is enough. I have no art, in which to vent the swell of a soul as deep as thine, Beethoven, and of a kindred frame. Thou wilt not think me presumptuous in this saying, as another might. I have always known that thou wouldst welcome and know me, as would no other who ever lived upon the earth since its first creation.

Thou wouldst forgive me, master, that I have not been true to my eventual destiny, and therefore have suffered on every side "the pangs of despised love." Thou didst the same; but thou didst borrow from those errors the inspiration of thy genius. Why is it not thus with me? Is it because, as a woman, I am bound by a physical law, which prevents the soul from manifesting itself? Sometimes the moon seems mockingly to say so,—to say that I, too, shall not shine, unless I can find a sun. O, cold and barren moon, tell a different tale!

But thou, oh blessed master! dost answer all my questions, and make it my privilege to be. Like a humble wife to the sage, or poet, it is my triumph that I can understand and cherish thee: like a mistress, I arm thee for the fight: like a young daughter, I tenderly bind thy wounds. Thou art to me beyond compare, for thou art all I want. No heavenly sweetness of saint or martyr, no many-leaved Raphael, no golden Plato, is anything to me, compared with thee. The infinite Shakespeare, the stern Angelo, Dante,—bittersweet like thee,—are no longer seen in thy presence. And, beside these names, there are none that could vibrate in thy crystal sphere. Thou hast all of them, and that ample surge of life besides, that great winged being which they only dreamed of. There is none greater than Shakspeare; he, too, is a god; but his creations are successive; thy *fiat* comprehends them all.

Last summer, I met thy mood in nature, on those wide impassioned plains flower and crag-bestrown. There, the tide of emotion had rolled over, and left the vision of its smiles and sobs, as I saw to-night from thee.

If thou wouldst take me wholly to thyself——! I am lost in this world, where I sometimes meet angels, but of a different star from mine. Even so does thy spirit plead with all spirits. But thou dost triumph and bring them all in.

Master, I have this summer envied the oriole which had even a swinging nest in the high bough. I have envied the least flower that came to seed, though that seed were strown to the wind. But I envy none when I am with thee.

The heart which hopes and dares is also accessible to terror, and this falls upon it like a thunderbolt. It can never defend itself at the moment, it is so surprised. There is no defence but to strive for an equable temper of courageous submission, of obedient energy, that shall make assault less easy to the foe.

This is the dart within the heart, as well as I can tell it:—At moments, the music of the universe, which daily I am upheld by hearing, seems to stop. I fall like a bird when the sun is eclipsed, not looking for such darkness. The sense of my individual law—that lamp of life—flickers. I am repelled in what is most natural to me. I feel as, when a suffering child, I would go and lie with my face to the ground, to sob away my little life . . .

I went out upon the lonely rock which commands so delicious a panoramic view. A very mild breeze had sprung up after the extreme heat. A sunset of the melting kind was succeeded by a perfectly clear moonrise. Here I sat, and thought of Raphael. I was drawn high up in the heaven of beauty, and the mists were dried from the white plumes of contemplation.

Only by emotion do we know thee, Nature. To lean upon thy heart, and feel its pulses vibrate to our own;—that is knowledge, for that is love, the love of infinite beauty, of infinite love. Thought will never make us be born again . . .

Italy has been glorious to me, and there have been hours in which I received the full benefit of the vision. In Rome, I have known some blessed, quiet days, when I could yield myself to be soothed and instructed by the great thoughts and memories of the place. But those days are swiftly passing. Soon I must begin to exert myself, for there is this incubus of the future, and none to help me, if I am not prudent to face it. So ridiculous, too, this mortal coil,—such small things!

I find how true was the lure that always drew me towards Europe. It was no false instinct that said I might here find an atmosphere to develop me in ways I need. Had I only come ten years earlier! Now my life must be a failure, so much strength has been wasted on abstractions, which only came because I grew not in the right soil. However, it is a less failure than with most others, and not worth thinking twice about. Heaven has room enough, and good chances in store, and I can live a great deal in the years that remain . . .

[After the siege of Rome:]

Oh God! help me, is all my cry. Yet I have little faith in the Paternal love I need, so ruthless or so negligent seems the government of this earth. I feel calm, yet sternly, towards Fate. This last plot against me has been so cruelly, cunningly wrought, that I shall never acquiesce. I submit, because useless resistance is degrading, but I demand an explanation. I see that it is probable I shall never receive one, while I live here, and suppose I can bear the rest of the suspense, since I have comprehended all its difficulties in the first moments. Meanwhile, I live day by day, though not on manna . . . I have been the object of great love from the noble and the humble; I have felt it towards both. Yet I am *tired out,*—tired of thinking and hoping,—tired of seeing men err and bleed. I take interest in some plans,—Socialism for instance,—but the interest is shallow as the plans. These are needed, are even good; but man will still blunder and weep, as he has done for so many thousand years. Coward and footsore, gladly would I creep into some green recess, where I might see a few not unfriendly faces, and where not more wretches should come than I could relieve. Yes! I am weary, and faith soars and sings no more. Nothing good of me is left except at the bottom of the heart, a melting tenderness:—"She loves much" . . .

[Written before embarking for America, the voyage on which she was drowned:]

I am absurdly fearful, and various omens have combined to give me a dark feeling. I am become indeed a miserable coward, for the sake of Angelino. I fear heat and cold, fear the voyage, fear biting poverty. I hope I shall not be forced to be brave for him, as I have been for myself, and that, if I succeed to rear him, he will be neither a weak nor a bad man. But I love him too much! In case of mishap, however, I shall perish with my husband and my child, and we may be transferred to some happier state . . . I feel perfectly willing to stay my threescore years and ten, if it be thought I need so much tuition from this planet; but it seems to me that my future upon earth will soon close. It may be terribly trying, but it will not be so very long, now. God will transplant the root, if he wills to rear it into fruit-bearing . . . I have a vague expectation of some crisis,—I know not what. But it has long seemed, that, in the year 1850, I should stand on a plateau in the ascent of life, where I should be allowed to pause for a while, and take more clear and commanding views than ever before. Yet my life proceeds as regularly as the fates of a Greek tragedy, and I can but accept the pages as they turn . . .

2. D. L.

Shelley

[When Andrews Norton's indignation over Emerson's *Divinity School Address* exploded in *The Boston Daily Advertiser,* it included a sneer at *The Western Messenger*—"a professedly religious work"—for commending "the atheist Shelley" (see p. 193). Actually neither Shelley nor Byron was a favorite among the Transcendentalists. As "D. L." tried to make clear (*The Western Messenger,* March 1837, III, 474–478), the Transcendental aesthetic found the strain in romantic literature which celebrated "common life"—in the spirit of Wordsworth —more attractive than the romantic exploitation of the grand and the fearful. But even so, as Margaret Fuller's *Memoirs* betray, the Transcendentalists were capable of a greater sympathy than were most Americans of their time with young men born with knives in their brain.

Hence the temerity of *The Western Messenger* in publishing even a left-handed defense of Shelley in 1837. D. L. indeed deplored that Shelley was not a Christian, but speaking for the Transcendentalists of the West—who were in daily conflict with the grim Protestantism of the region's dominant Presbyterianism—he spoke for the literary sophistication of the movement by maintaining that even as an atheist, Shelley was more Christian than any Presbyterian.

Clarke and D. L. were undoubtedly prepared to shock the Calvinists of the Ohio Valley, but they themselves were to receive the shock when Andrews Norton blasted their mild apology for a major English poet.]

In power and compass of imagination, Shelley is without a superior, if he have an equal. The elements, sun, moon, stars, storm, lightning, become his willing instruments—the ready alphabet of his thoughts, the symbols of his feelings,—the heralds of his soul. He seems also to have command over the most fearful elements of the moral world. In his Prometheus Unbound, there is a working of mighty passion, a creation of moral sublimity, in comparison with which, thunder and lightning, storm and hail, and the whole force of the elements of earth, sea and air, seem tame and lamb-like. In fact, Shelley is the best representative of the Ideal power, as uncontrolled by the other faculties. Of course we must allow greater merit to those poets, who deal with the more familiar scenes and characters of life, than to those, who deal with the grand and extraordinary. "The grand and fearful," Henry

Heine says truly, "are of much easier representation in Art, than the trifling and the little." Therefore we must rank Shakespeare's and Goethe's creations in the walks of common life, above the grand and fearful creations of Shelley. Still we say, that as representative of the pure unqualified Ideal faculty Shelley is unsurpassed, if he is rivalled.

Among Shelley's moral characteristics, may be numbered an intense sensibility, that seems wonderful, when considered in connection with his great power of intellect. His face, with its singular expression of sensitiveness and thought, shews this characteristic. He could wield the mightiest thought and passion, and yet respond to the gentlest touch of feeling; as the sun, which can raise the tornado, and yet nurture the gentlest flower; as the rushing wind, which can upheave oaks, convulse oceans, and wake the gentle spirit-sounds of the Aeolian.

To this sensitive tenderness, so strangely contrasted with his might, Shelley united a burning love for his race, that sometimes indeed led him into wild schemes of philanthropy: also a faith in man's capacity for progress, and in the goodness of the overruling Deity: a love of freedom, that seemed the great passion of his nature, and which broke forth in condemnation of all the despotism of custom and rulers, and was perverted into a rebel defiance of many of the salutary and proper restraints and institutions of society.

Shelley was an unbeliever. For this, we mourn, and must condemn him for not making better use of his power and intellect, which would have taught him the truth of Christianity, and of his feeling heart, which could have revealed to him the unearthly beauty of the character of Jesus. But we must keep one thing in mind, in passing judgment on Shelley, for his avowed opinions. His opinions in regard to God and Christ, were formed and declared in reference and indignant opposition to the prevalent ideas of bigots on those subjects.—He denies God but it is rather the God, whom bigotry has created, than the God of Nature and Father of Christ. He rejects the doctrine of Christianity, but it is chiefly in view of the dogmas, which human creeds have appended to a Christian Faith—such dogmas for instance, as that God is a God of Love, and yet has predestined, from all eternity, a great part of his creatures to Endless Hell.

But much as we condemn Shelley's extravagancies, and mourn his proud rebellious spirit, we must say, that he often exhibits much more true Christian feeling, and even Christian faith, than many, who scoff at him, as an atheist and outlaw. Where shall we find a purer love of liberty, than in his Revolt of Islam—where a purer friendship, than in Adonais—where a more glowing love for man, than in his Prometheus, and Queen Mab—where a stronger faith in man's capacity for progress and the goodness of the Supreme Power, than in his Hellas? Compare him with many of his revilers, and he takes the palm in point of moral elevation and Christian faith and feeling. Even what is called his atheism is better than the theism of some of his bigoted condemners. His "Spirit of Nature" is more like the God and Father of our Lord Jesus, than is the terrific Jehovah, whom we hear thundered out in such savage terms from some of our Presbyterian pulpits.

3. James Freeman Clarke (1810–1888)

Jones Very

[Jones Very was born in Salem, the son of a sea captain, with whom he made voyages to Russia and New Orleans. Graduated from Harvard in 1836, he was appointed tutor in Greek and at the same time entered the Divinity School. In September 1837 he began to receive pronouncements directly from the Holy Ghost and to behold visions; he wept when Henry Ware doubted them. He composed his essay on epic poetry as an undergraduate; it impressed Elizabeth Peabody, who sent him to Emerson. Thus encouraged, he wrote his essay on Shakespeare in the summer of 1838. In the fall his sanity having been questioned, he was asked to resign from the Harvard faculty, and he spent four weeks in the McLean Aslyum. "Such a mind," Emerson insisted, "cannot be lost."

Very was both a welcome and a trying recruit to Transcendentalism. If, as the world judged, he was crazy, all the more reason that the brotherhood should show their opinion of the world—and their devotion to the conception of poetry as inspiration—by standing with him. Some of them were up to the task, at least for a year or two; Brownson was not. Alcott had Brownson and Very together at dinner in 1839, and even he found the contrast comic: "They tried to speak, but Very was unintelligible to the proud Philistine."

At a meeting in Emerson's house, his host noted that Very passed with the other guests for insane, but that all were struck with his "insight." Emerson engineered the publication of Very's *Essays and Poems* in 1839, and it must be admitted, to Emerson's credit, that he went as far as any could go with Very. Eventually the trial proved almost too much; Very wrote his pieces under divine dictation and so provoked one of Emerson's finest witticisms: "Cannot the spirit parse & spell?"

On a visit to the East, Clarke encountered Very, and not to be outdone by Emerson, he published twenty-seven of Very's poems in *The Western Messenger* of March 1839 (VI, 308–314). By 1839 insanity was a hazard the Transcendentalists were prepared to run; in fact, it was actually gratifying to have at least one poet who vindicated the Reason by serving it exclusively and at the complete

cost of the Understanding. The Transcendental theory of genius practically demanded one or two mad poets; most Transcendentalists were not quite prepared
to sacrifice themselves, and Very vindicated the theory by proving a willing
victim. It was only to be expected that to the non-Transcendental world he would
appear merely a lunatic; one would have had to be initiated into the saturnalia of
faith before he could understand that Very was to be, not pitied, but reverenced.]

We had the pleasure of meeting Mr. Very, a few months since, in
the city of Boston . . . He was said to have adopted some peculiar views on
this important theme, and to consider himself inspired by God to communicate them. Such pretensions had excited the fears of his friends, and by many
he was supposed to be partially deranged. The more intelligent and larger
sort of minds, however, who had conversed with him, dissented from this
view, and although they might admit a partial derangement of the lower
intellectual organs, or perhaps an extravagant pushing of some views to
their last results, were disposed to consider his main thoughts deeply important and vital.

And here we may remark that the charge of Insanity is almost always
brought against any man who endeavours to introduce to the common mind
any very original ideas. And especially is this the case with moral and religious truths. He who insists on taking us out of that sphere of thought which
is habitual to us, into a higher and purer one, is regarded by us with alarm
and dissatisfaction. We must either yield ourselves to him, and suffer our
minds to be taken out of their customary routine, which is always painful—
or we must find some way to set aside his appeals to our reason and conscience and disarm them of their force. The easiest way is to call him insane . . . The moment, therefore, this word is applied to a man, were he
sage, prophet or apostle—were he Socrates or Solon, were he Jesus or Paul—
all men are authorised to look down upon him with pity. And it is so much
more soothing to our vanity to look down than to look up, that it is no
wonder that the worldly-minded, the men of sluggish and shallow intellects,
and those who have arranged and systematised their opinions, are pleased
with this excuse for pitying the man whom they ought to reverence . . .

It is also, however, to be remarked, that the intense contemplation of any
vast theme is apt to disturb the balance of the lower intellectual faculties.
While the Reason, which contemplates absolute truth, is active and strong;
the understanding which arranges and gives coherence to our thoughts, may
be weakened or reduced to a state of torpor. When this reaches an extreme
point, it becomes delirium or mono-mania.

But even in these cases it may be a question which is the *worst* delirium, that by which a man, possessing some great truth, has lost the use of his practical intellect—or that other wide-spread delirium, in which the mind is enslaved to the lowest cares and meanest aims, and all that is loftiest and greatest in the soul is stupefied and deadened in worldliness. When, for instance, we have seen a man in whose intellect all other thoughts have become merged in the great thought of his connexion with God, we have had the feeling very strongly, which we once heard thus expressed, "Is this MONO-MANIA, or is it MONO-SANIA?"

With respect to Mr. Very, we have only to say that the intercourse we have ourselves had with him has given no evidence even of such partial derangement. We have heard him converse about his peculiar views of religious truth, and saw only the workings of a mind absorbed in the loftiest contemplations, and which utterly disregarded all which did not come into that high sphere of thought. We leave it to our readers to decide whether there is any thing of unsoundness in these sonnets. To us, they seem like wells of thought, clear and pellucid, and coming up from profound depths.

4. Jones Very (1813–1880)
Epic Poetry

[If Jones Very was indeed mad, his madness had in it something of the method of the great romanticists. His essay on the epic is practically unique in American criticism because it is an effort to capture the distinction—more carefully investigated in Germany—between the modern and the romantic as being the complex and the dramatic, in contrast to the primitive and the classic, which is characterized by the simple and by the epic. It was an attempt, far from unsuccessful, to domesticate in America the kind of romantic theorizing that flourished in Germany, particularly with the Schlegels; yet, because it also grew out of the peculiar pressures of the New England society, the essay could contend that the root of modern complexity of consciousness is Christianity—though not liberal Unitarianism! It challenged the Protestant culture of America by a startling reading of a classic to which lip-service was still paid; the Byronic Satan was hardly yet recognizable in America of 1838. The essay was first published in *The Christian Examiner* for May 1838 (XXIV, 201–221) and was republished in Emerson's edition of *Essays and Poems* (Boston, 1839).]

All things combined in Homer's age to assist him in giving a perfect outward manifestation of the heroic character of his times. He wrote in that stage of society when man's physical existence assumed an importance in the mind like that of our immortality, and gave to all without a power and dignity not their own. This it was which imparted an heroic greatness to war which cannot be seen in it. That far-reaching idea of time, which seems to expand our thoughts with limitless existence, gives to our mental struggles a greatness they could not have before had. We each of us feel within our own bosoms a great, an immortal foe, which if we have subdued, we may meet with calmness every other, knowing that earth contains no greater; but which if we have not, it will continually appear in those petty contests with others by which we do but show our own cowardice. The Greeks, on the contrary, lived only for their country, and drew everything within the sphere of their national views; their highest exemplification of morality was patriotism. Of Homer's heroes it may with peculiar propriety be said that they were but children of a larger growth, and they could have no conception of power that was not perceived in its visible effects. "The world," as Milton says of our first parents, "was all *before* them," and not *within* them, and their mission was to go forth and make a material impression on the material world. The soul of Homer was the mirror of this outward world, and in his verse we have it shown to us with the distinctness and reality of the painter's page . . .

This state of things gave to the Iliad and Odyssey that intense epic interest which we fail to find in later heroic poems. As the mind advances, a stronger sympathy with the inner man of the heart is more and more felt, and becomes more and more characteristic of literature. In the expanded mind and cultivated affections, a new interest is awakened, *dramatic* poetry succeeds the *epic,* thus satisfying the want produced by the further development of our nature. For the interest of the *epic* consists in that character of greatness that in the infancy of the mind is given to physical action and the objects associated with it; but the interest of the *drama* consists in those mental struggles which precede physical action, and to which in the progress of man the greatness of the other becomes subordinate. For as the mind expands and the moral power is developed, the mightiest conflicts are born within,—outward actions lose their grandeur, except to the eye, for the soul looks upon them but as results of former battles won and lost, upon whose decision, and upon whose alone, its destiny hung . . .

The effect of Christianity was to make the individual mind the great object of regard, the centre of eternal interest, and transferring the scene of action from the outward world to the world within, to give all modern literature the dramatic tendency,—and as the mind of Homer led him to sing of the physical conflicts of his heroes with *visible* gods *without;* so the soul of the modern poet, feeling itself contending with motives of godlike power *within,* must express that conflict in the dramatic form, in the poetry of sentiment . . .

This sense of free agency is what constitutes Adam the hero of "Paradise Lost," and makes him capable of sustaining the immense weight of interest which in this poem is made to rest upon him. But that which renders Adam the hero of the poem makes Satan still more so; for Milton has opened to our gaze, within his breast of flame, passions of almost infinite growth, burning with intensest rage. *There* is seen a conflict of "those thoughts that wander through eternity," at the sight of which we lose all sense of the material terrors of that fiery hell around him, and compared with which the physical conflict of the archangels is a mockery. It is not so much that battles present less a subject for description than they did in the time of Homer, that they fail to awaken those feelings of admiration they then did, but because we have become sensible of a power within which bids the tide of war roll back upon its fountains. For the same reason it is that the *manners* of civilized nations are unsuited for heroic song. They are no longer the representatives of greatness; for the heroism of Christianity is not seen so much in the outward act as in the struggle of the will to control the springs of action. It is this which gives to tragedy its superiority over the epic at the present day; it strikes off the chains of wonder by which man has been so long fettered to the objects of sense, and, instead of calling upon him to admire the torrent-streams of war, it bids the bosom open whence they rushed, and points him downward to their source, the ocean might of the soul,

> Dark—heaving—boundless, endless, and sublime—
> The image of eternity—the throne
> Of the Invisible.

Thus Milton's poem is the most favorable model we can have of a Christian epic. The subject of it afforded him the only field of great epic interest, where the greatest power could be shown engaged in bringing about the greatest results. Adam is not so much the Achilles as the Troy of the poem. And there is no better proof that greatness has left the material throne which she has so long held, for a spiritual one, than that Milton, in putting in motion that vast machinery which he did to effect his purpose, seems as if he made, like Ptolemy, the sun and all the innumerable hosts of heaven again to revolve about this little spot of earth. Though he has not made the Fall of Man a tragedy in *form,* as he first designed, he has yet made it tragic in *spirit;* and the epic form it has taken seems but the drapery of another interest. This proves that, however favored by his subject the epic poet of our day may be, he must by the laws of his own being possess an introspective mind, and give that which Bacon calls an inwardness of meaning to his characters, which, in proportion as the mind advances, must diminish that greatness once shown in visible action.

5. Jones Very (1813–1880)
Shakespeare

["The Essay is a noble production," wrote Emerson upon receiving the manuscript; "not consecutive, filled with one thought; but that so deep & true & illustrated so happily & even grandly, that I account it an addition to our really scanty stock of adequate criticism on Shakespeare."

It can, I believe, be taken as the essence of the romantic conception of Shakespeare and so of the artist, of the great artist capable of the wise passivity that permits "Nature" to speak through him. There was always the danger, of course, that these impulses might come from below rather than from on high, and Emerson had announced that he would live from the Devil if he were the Devil's child. There clearly was much that was Devilish—or at least lewd—in Shakespeare; Very girded the New England conscience for the struggle and proved that Shakespeare's obscenities, because they are as natural as any impulse from the vernal wood, are basically innocent. The essay was published in the *Essays and Poems*.]

With other writers, at our very first acquaintance with their thoughts, we recognize our relationship with the swiftness of intuition; but who of us, however familiar he may have been with his writings, has yet caught a glance of Shakespeare's self, so that he could in any way identify himself with him, and feel himself a sharer in his joys and sorrows, his motives and his life? With views narrowed down to our own peculiar and selfish ends, we cannot well conceive, for we feel little within us that answers to a being like him—whose spirit seemed the antagonist of matter; whose life was as various and all-embracing as nature's; and in whom the individual seemed lost and blended with the universal . . . In speaking of him and what he did as an exception to ordinary rules, we only confess our ignorance of the great law of his existence. If he was natural, and by a common nature kindred with us, as we all confess, that ignorance, which only exists by our own sufferance, will clear up, as we lay aside all that is false and artificial in our characters, and Shakespeare and his creations will stand before us in the clear sunlight of our own consciousness.

My object is to show, by an analysis of the character of Shakespeare, that a desire of action was the ruling impulse of his mind; and consequently a sense of existence its permanent state. That this condition was natural; not the result felt from a submission of the will to it, but bearing the will along with it; presenting the mind as phenomenal and unconscious, and almost as much a passive instrument as the material world.

I shall thus be led to find excuse for much that has seemed impure in his writings, and to change that admiration which has hitherto regarded him as a man, into one which would look upon him and love him as the unconscious work of God.

By doing this I shall show that there is a higher action than that we witness in him; where the will has not been borne down and drawn along by the mind's original impulse, but, though capable of resistance, yields flexibly to all its natural movements, presenting that higher phenomenon which genius and revelation were meant to forward in all men,—conscious nature . . .

As we become more and more conscious of that state of mind which our Saviour calls eternal life, we shall better understand the natural superiority of such a mind as Shakespeare's to the narrowing influences which we have to resist, but which his involuntary activity rendered powerless. That a sense of life would be the accompaniment of this activity would then be apparent; for how could that childlike love of variety and joyous sympathy with all things exist, save from that simple happiness which in him ever flowed from the consciousness of being, but which, alas, by most of us is known but in youth? . . . This life of his in all objects and scenes was the simple result of the movements of a mind which found only in all it saw around it something to correspond with its own condition. Its own activity was its possession; circumstances and things seemed to be, because it was; these were accidents, and not, as with other men, realities. His power, while exerted on every thing, seems independent of its objects . . . Did love succeed necessity, we should need no other explanation of such a mind than our own would give us. We all feel at first that life is more than the meat, but from the corrupt world around us we soon learn to prize the meat more than our spiritual life . . . Instead of this, we should be quickening by our daily life that spiritual consciousness which otherwise, in the hour of death, we shall feel that we have lost; when the eye that saw and ear that heard have done their tasks; when the heavens which that eye has so long gazed upon are rolling together as a scroll, and the thousand tones of music which the ear drank from the earth are hushed, and the affrighted soul turns inward upon itself as the sole remaining monument of all that was once real. Were such a consciousness ours, then indeed might we sympathize with Shakespeare; then might the lofty thought which Milton felt in his kindness and age forever permeate our being, and lift us to that height, from which, like him, we could look down on the world and the objects of sense beneath; and as we gazed with the soul's pure eyes, and a mind irradiated with that celestial light for which he prayed, we too might exclaim,

> For who would lose
> Though full of pain, this intellectual being,
> These thoughts that wander through eternity,
> To perish rather, swallowed up and lost
> In the wide womb of uncreated night,
> Devoid of sense and motion?

From what has been said we may perceive that universality is not a gift of Shakespeare alone, but natural to the mind of man; and that whenever we unburthen ourselves of that load of selfishness under which what is natural in us lies distorted, it will resume as its own estate that diversity of being in which he delighted. That which in the poet, the philosopher, or the warrior, therefore affects us is this higher natural action of the mind, which, though exhibited in one, is felt to be harmonious with all; which imparts to us, as it were, their own universality, and makes us for a while companions of their various life. In the individual act we feel more than that which suffices for this alone; we feel sensible that the blood that is filling one vein, and becoming visible to us in one form, possesses a vitality of which every limb and the whole body are alone the fit expression. This natural action of the mind, in whatever direction applied, is ever revealing to us more than we have before known; for this alone unconsciously moves in its appointed path; the only human actor in the drama of existence, save him who is by duty becoming consciously natural, that can show us any good. In its equable and uninterrupted movements, it harmonizes ever with Nature, giving the spiritual interpretation to her silent and sublime growth. In the movements of Shakespeare's mind, we are permitted to see an explanation of that strange phenomenon in the government of Him who made us, by which that which is most universal appears to be coincident with that which is most particular. In him we see how it is that the mighty laws which bind system upon system should be the same that stoop to order with exactest precision the particles whose minuteness escapes our vision; that could we but feel aright, we should see that the same principle which teaches us to love ourselves could not but lead us to love our neighbors as ourselves; that did we love in ourselves what was truly worthy of our love, there would be no object throughout the wide circle of being whose lot and happiness would not be our own. It is thus by becoming most universal we at the same time become most individual; for they are not opposed to each other, but different faces of the same thing. But selfishness is the farthest removed of all things from the universality of genius or of goodness. For, as the superiority to the objects of sense which the soul naturally has, and which, when lost, love would restore, diminishes, these senseless objects in their turn become masters; we are the servants of sin, bowing to an idol that our own hands have set up, and sweating beneath the burthens of a despot strong in our own transferred power. Like the ancients we too find a deity in each of the objects we pursue;—we follow wealth till we worship Mammon; love, till we see a Venus; are ambitious, till our hands are stained with the bloody rites of Mars. While in the physical world we are waging by our railroads and engines a war of utter extermination against time and space, we forget that it is these very things, as motives, that urge us on. We are exhibiting the folly of kingdoms divided against themselves; for, while in the physical world we are driving to annihilation [of] space and time, it is for the very sake of the things of time and sense that we do it. We are thereby excluding ourselves daily from those *many* mansions which Christ has taught are prepared for us. Our words confess that all things are God's, while our hands are busy in fencing off some corner of the wide universe from which to exclude our brother man . . .

It may seem strange that a mind capable of the conception, as we call it, of a Hamlet or a Lear should yet seem to delight in those apparently so opposite,—in characters of a low or even licentious cast. But this apparent inconsistency admits of an easy explanation from the very nature of that mind's action. To us indeed they seem antipodes; but to him they stood embraced by the same horizon of life and action. If we will but think of his mind as moved by the same desire of action as our own limbs are in childhood, and with as little end in view save that of its own activity; we shall then easily conceive why he should seek to identify himself with every mode of life, and be and act characters of the most apparently opposite nature. That such was the impulse under which they were written, we can only appeal to each one's consciousness in reading for a proof. He delighted in all men of high as well as low estate,—we had almost said, in the licentious as in the virtuous. But how different is that playful and childlike spirit with which he acted a vicious character, from that which seems to have actuated a Byron. The one represents an abandoned man as he actually exists, with the joys of sense and the anguish of the spirit alternately agitating his troubled breast; and the contemplation of such a character, if it does not make us as good as it might have done, had he drawn it with higher motives, will yet make us better, as the sight of it does in actual life. But the latter was not innocent, he imparted something of himself to what he describes; he would not and could not, like Shakespeare, put before us a virtuous man with the same pleasure as he does a vicious one; he has not, like him, held a pure and untarnished mirror up to Nature, but reflected her back upon us from his own discolored and passion-stained bosom . . .

Shakespeare's life . . . was coincident with that of others, from the natural action of his mind; and from its unreserved yielding to events it has exhibited them to us more as they are than any other mind has yet done. But a more perfect coincidence, which shall exhibit more of what man is than he has done can only be brought about by feeling more deeply that all things are ours, and by possessing more of that love which knew what was in man. Had this and a sense of duty been Shakespeare's, they would have rendered more powerful and affecting the influence of his characters without making them in any degree less natural. But, it may be asked, should the poet be more moral than Providence; if he exhibit things as they are, will they not have all the influence that God intended they should have? It is that the poet should represent things as they are, for which we contend. We are not pleading for those sickly beings who, by the handiwork of the mind, are made to fit any prescribed pattern of goodness; but for those who live and move about us; to describe the height and depth of whose thoughts and passions, and interpret their meaning, hidden it may be from themselves, even such a mind as Shakespeare's must have entered into and portrayed characters not only from impulse, but also with a love whose strength was that of duty. Too easily might we else, as he has sometimes done, quicken with our life the dry bones of moral death around us. It is no common lamp that will enable us to thread securely the dark and labyrinthine caverns of sin, to shed that light even amid its damp and fatal vapors that will enable us to draw from their lowest depths the rich treasures of wisdom which they hide. No one can enter more entirely into the lives of others than Shakespeare has done, until he has laid down his own life and gone forth to seek and to save that which is lost. Our more perfect views were not intended to be the substitutes for, but the interpreters of the characters of others. What *ought to be,* if we describe it by itself, becomes but our own teaching; what *is*, if we look upon it with a spirit more nearly allied to His who sees all things as they are, will prove the lessons not of our own insignificance, but of His providence. We need not substitute our ideals of virtue and vice for the living forms around us; we need not brighten the one, nor darken the other; to the spiritual eye, even here, will the just begin to appear as angels of light; and as the sun of Divine Favor sets on the wicked, their lengthening shadows, ever here, are seen to blacken and dilate into more gigantic and awful proportions. Shakespeare's characters are true and natural indeed; but they are not the truest and most natural which the world will yet see. From the states of mind of a Hamlet and Macbeth rise tones of which the words he has made them utter bear but faint intelligence; and which will find a stronger and yet stronger utterance as the will of the poet conforms to that of his Maker. Shakespeare was gifted with the power of the poet; a power which, though he may have employed for the purposes intended, does not seem to have been accompanied by that sense of responsibility which would have lent them their full and perfect effect. His creations are natural, but they are unconsciously so. He could but give to them his own life, which was one of impulse and not of principle. Man's brightest dignity is conscious nature; and virtue when deprived of this is robbed of her nobility; and without it vice is but a pardonable weakness. Shakespeare is not to be esteemed so much a man as a natural phenomenon. We cannot say of him that he conformed to God's will; but that the Divine Will in its ordinary operations moved his mind as it does the material world. *He* was natural from an unconscious obedience to the will of God; *we*, if it acts not so strongly upon us but has left us the greater freedom, must become natural by a conscious obedience to it. He that is least in the kingdom of heaven, is greater than he . . .

In Shakespeare's works, I see but the ordinary power of the Deity acting in mind, as I see it around me moulding to its purpose the forms of matter. But we are too apt to admire as the *man* that which we should only regard as the natural operation of the Divine Power. Struck with wonder by this natural action of the mind, we are too prone to dignify as that image of the Most High in which we were created, something which no more deserves the appellation of man, than the clod on which we tread. To be natural either consciously or unconsciously, is indeed alone to be truly great; for that which is so is God's. The material world, and to a hardly less extent the mental one of those we call great, are passive beneath his influence; they are naturally, but unconsciously so. But man is gifted with a will whose highest exercise, could he but recognize the awfulness of the trust, he would feel to be its perfect accordance with his Maker's. But even from the first moment of his existence, when he dared disobedience to his conscience, he became unnatural; and the fair Eden in which he was placed seemed no longer his home; and he is driven a wanderer through his own Fatherland, and lets himself out as a hired servant to till those very fields which were once his own. To become natural, to find again that Paradise which he has lost, man must be born again; he must learn the true exercise of his own will is only in listening to that voice, which is ever walking in the garden, but of which he is afraid and hides himself. In the words of him who came not to do his own will, as we humble ourselves and become as little children, our minds will not longer be at variance with the world without them, but only a brighter image than nature can be of the creator of both; the true soul will be the conscious expression of nature. Shakespeare was natural; but, if we may judge from his writings and life, he must have been as unconsciously so as a field or a stream. As we have said, he was not moved by common motives; he wished but to live, and he passed without a preference through all the forms of living, and may be said to have been most truly himself in being others. Had he pursued the same course from a sense of duty, there would have been added to his character that strength of will, or remorse at its loss in which we feel them especially wanting. That he acted from impulse and not from principle, this shows us that he is not to be regarded as a man so much as a phenomenon; that the tribute he would ask was admiration rather than praise. The careless manner in which he left his works has been wondered at, and lauded long enough, we hope, for Christian men. When will we learn that the thing we call a man wants that which alone can entitle it to that appellation, when he can think a thought, or do a single act, much less leave the works of a whole life with ostrich-like indifference on the barren sands of a world's neglect, without one look behind at their influence on the eternal happiness or misery of all being? 'T was God's care only that the mind he sent labored not in vain. Action, in which God's will is not the motive, is sending the lightning flashes of heaven to play for men's amusement among the far-off clouds, and not to flash in warning across the dark path of destruction in which they are treading. It is the successive peals of thunder which, instead of purifying the moral atmosphere, are made to roll and burst only to create vainly repeated echoes among the hills. Shakespeare, though at times he may have been possessed of his genius, must, in far the most numerous of his days and years, have been possessed by it. Lost in wonder at the countless beings that thronged uncalled the palace of his soul, and dwelt beneath its "majestical roof fretted with golden fires," he knew not, or if he knew, forgot that even those angel visitants were not sent for him merely to admire and number; but that knowing no will but His who made kings his subjects, he should send them forth on their high mission, and with those high resolves which it was left for him to communicate. Had he done this, we might indeed reverence him as the image of his God; as a sharer in His service, whose service is perfect freedom.

From God's action in the mind of such men, we may learn, though with less clearness, that great lesson of Humility which He has revealed through his word. From genius, as well as revelation, we learn that our actions can alone become harmonious with the universality and naturalness which we see in the outward world, when they are made to accord with the will of our Father. From both we learn, that of ourselves we can do no positive act; but have only the power given us to render of no avail that which is so—that we cannot make one hair white or black; that our seeming strength is weakness, nay, worse than weakness, unless it co-operates with God's. Let us labor then, knowing that the more we can erase from the tablets of our hearts the false fashions and devices which our own perverse wills have written over them, the more will shine forth, with all their original brightness, those ancient primeval characters traced there by the finger of God, until our whole being is full of light.

6. Jones Very (1813–1880)

Hamlet

[The character of Hamlet was as fascinating to American romantics as to the English and German. Jones Very struck the pure romantic note, and although distressed that Hamlet was not a Christian, he still saw in him the perfect symbol of the sensitive poet in conflict with a crass and Philistine world. The essay is from *Essays and Poems*.]

Shakespeare was, as I have said, the childlike embodiment of this sense of existence. It found its *natural* expression in the many forms of his characters; in the circumstances of Hamlet, its *peculiar* one. As has been well observed, the others we love for something that may be called adventitious; but we love him not, we think not of him because he was witty, because he is melancholy, but because he existed and was himself; this is the sum total of the impression. The great foreplane of adversity has been driven over him, and his soul is laid bare to the very foundation. It is here that the poet is enabled to build deep down on the clear groundwork of being. It is because the interest lies here, that Shakespeare's own individuality becomes more than usually prominent. We here get down into his deep mind, and the thoughts that interested him interest us. Here is where our Shakespeare suffered, and, at times, a golden vein of his own fortune penetrates to the surface of Hamlet's character, and enriches with a new value the story of his sorrows.

If Shakespeare's master passion then was, as we have seen it to be, the love of intellectual activity for its own sake, his continual satisfaction with the simple pleasure of existence must have made him more than commonly liable to the fear of death; or, at least, made that change the great point of interest in his hours of reflection. Often and often must he have thought, that to be or not to be forever, was a question which must be settled; as it is the foundation, and the only foundation, upon which we feel that there can rest one thought, one feeling, or one purpose worthy of a human soul. Other motives had no hold upon him; place, riches, favors, the prizes of accident, he could lose and still exclaim, "Fortune and I are friends," but the thought of death touched him in his very centre. However strong the sense of continued life such a mind as his may have had, it could never reach that assurance of eternal existence which Christ alone can give,— which alone robs the grave of victory, and takes from death its sting. Here lie the materials out of which this remarkable tragedy was built up. From the wrestling of his own soul with the great enemy come that depth and mystery which startle us in Hamlet.

It is to this condition that Hamlet has been reduced. This is the low portal of grief to which we must stoop, before we can enter the heaven-pointing pile that the poet has raised to his memory. Stunned by the sudden storm of woes, he doubts, as he looks at the havoc spread around him, whether he himself is left, and fears lest the very ground on which he lies prostrate may not prove treacherous. Stripped of all else, he is sensible on this point alone. Here is the life from which all else grows. Interested in the glare of prosperity around him only because he lives, he is ever turning his eyes from it to the desolation in which he himself stands. His glance ever descends from the lofty pinnacle of pride and false security to the rotten foundation,—and tears follow smiles. He raises his eye to heaven, and "this brave o'erhanging firmament" seems to him but "a pestilential congregation of vapors"; it descends to earth, and "its goodly frame seems a sterile promontory." He fixes it on man, and his noble apostrophe—"What a piece of work is a man! How noble in reason! How infinite in faculties, in form and moving, how express and admirable! in action, how like an angel! in apprehension, how like a god!" is followed fast upon by the sad confession, "Yet man delights me not, nor woman neither." He does not, as we say, "get accustomed to his situation." He holds fast by the wisdom of affliction, and will not let her go. He would keep her, for she is his life. The storm has descended, and all has been swept away but the rock. To this he clings for safety. He will not render unavailing the lessons of Providence by "getting accustomed" to feed on that which is not bread, on which to live is death. He fears nothing save the loss of existence. But this thought thunders at the very base of the cliff on which, shipwrecked of every other hope, he had been thrown. That which to everybody else seems common presses upon him with an all-absorbing interest; he struggles with the mystery of his own being, the root of all other mysteries, until it has become an overmastering element in his own mind, before which all others yield and seem as nothing.

This is the hinge on which his every endeavor turns. Such a thought as this might well prove more than an equal counterpoise to any incentive to what we call action. The obscurity that lies over these depths of Hamlet's character arises from this unique position in which the poet exhibits him; a position which opens to us the basis of Shakespeare's own being, and which, though dimly visible to all, is yet familiar to but few. There is action indeed, but projected on so gigantic a scale, that, like the motion of some of the heavenly bodies, from which we are inconceivably removed, it seems a perpetual rest. With Dr. Johnson, and other commentators, we are at first inclined to blame Hamlet's inactivity and call him weak and cowardly; but as we proceed, and his character and situation open upon us, such epithets seem least of all applicable to him. So far is he from being a coward, in the common meaning of that term, that he does not set this life at a pin's fee. He is contending in thought with the great realities beyond it; the dark clouds that hang over the valley of the shadow of death, and float but dimly and indistinct before *our* vision, have, like his father's ghost, become fixed and definite "in *his* mind's eye"; he has looked them into shape, and they stand before him wherever he turns, with a presence that will not be put by. Thus it is, that to most he seems a coward, and that enterprises which to others appear of great pith and moment,

> With this regard, their currents turn awry
> And lose the name of action.

Macbeth is contending with the realities of this world, Hamlet with those of the next. The struggle which is going on in the far-seeing mind of Hamlet never arrives at its consummation; Macbeth, on the contrary, is short-sighted enough to contend with the whips and scorns of time, and with him, therefore, the mental conflict is soon over.

7. Jones Very (1813–1880)
Poems

[After 1840 Very's religious ecstasy began to wane and with its subsiding his poetry became more and more mechanical. He was licensed to preach in 1843, held temporary pastorates, but finally retired to live for forty years in utter seclusion in Salem. When the news of his death reached Concord, Alcott remembered how shadowy his aspect had been. "While walking by his side, I remember, he seemed spectral,—and somehow using my feet instead of his own, keeping as near me as he could, and jostling me frequently." But, said Alcott with that accuracy of judgment which is one of his more astonishing traits, Very's sonnets and essays "surpass any that have since appeared in subtlety and simplicity of execution."

In 1886 Clarke brought out what was supposed to be a complete edition of Very's works, now entitled *Poems and Essays;* for some unaccountable reason Clarke left out several lyrics which he himself had originally printed in the *Messenger,* such as "The Fox and the Bird."]

THE WIND-FLOWER

Thou lookest up with meek confiding eye
Upon the clouded smile of April's face,
Unharmed though Winter stands uncertain by
Eyeing with jealous glance each opening grace.
Thou trustest wisely! In thy faith arrayed
More glorious thou than Israel's wisest king;
Such faith was his whom men to death betrayed
As thine who hear'st the timid voice of Spring,
While other flowers still hide them from her call
Along the river's brink and meadow bare.
Thee will I seek beside the stony wall
And in thy trust with childlike heart would share,
O'erjoyed that in thy early leaves I find
A lesson taught by him who loved all human kind.

THE COLUMBINE

Still, still my eye will gaze long fixed on thee,
Till I forget that I am called a man,
And at thy side fast-rooted seem to be,
And the breeze comes my cheek with thine to fan.
Upon this craggy hill our life shall pass,
A life of summer days and summer joys,
Nodding our honey-bells mid pliant grass
In which the bee half hid his time employs;
And here we'll drink with thirsty pores the rain,
And turn dew-sprinkled to the rising sun,
And look when in the flaming west again
His orb across the heaven its path has run;
Here left in darkness on the rocky steep,
My weary eyes shall close like folding flowers in sleep.

THE NEW BIRTH

'Tis a new life; thoughts move not as they did
With slow uncertain steps across my mind;
In thronging haste fast pressing on they bid
The portals open to the viewless wind
That comes not save when in the dust is laid
The crown of pride that gilds each mortal brow,
And from before man's vision melting fade
The heavens and earth; their walls are falling now.
Fast crowding on, each thought asks utterance strong;
Storm-lifted waves swift rushing to the shore,
On from the sea they send their shouts along,
Back through the cave-worn rocks their thunders roar;
And I a child of God by Christ made free
Start from death's slumbers to Eternity.

THE SON

Father, I wait thy word. The sun doth stand
Beneath the mingling line of night and day,
A listening servant, waiting thy command
To roll rejoicing on its silent way;

The tongue of time abides the appointed hour,
Till on our ear its solemn warnings fall;
The heavy cloud withholds the pelting shower,
Then every drop speeds onward at thy call;
The bird reposes on the yielding bough,
With breast unswollen by the tide of song;
So does my spirit wait thy presence now
To pour thy praise in quickening life along,
Chiding with voice divine man's lengthened sleep,
While round the Unuttered Word and Love their vigils keep.

THE MORNING WATCH

'Tis near the morning watch; the dim lamp burns,
But scarcely shows how dark the slumbering street;
No sound of life the silent mart returns;
No friends from house to house their neighbors greet;
It is the sleep of death; a deeper sleep
Than e'er before on mortal eyelids fell;
No stars above the gloom their places keep;
No faithful watchmen of the morning tell;
Yet still they slumber on, though rising day
Hath through their windows poured the awakening light;
Or, turning in their sluggard trances, say—
"There yet are many hours to fill the night";
They rise not yet; while on the bridegroom goes
Till he the day's bright gates forever on them close!

THE GARDEN

I saw the spot where our first parents dwelt;
And yet it wore to me no face of change,
For while amid its fields and groves I felt
As if I had not sinned, nor thought it strange;
My eye seemed but a part of every sight,
My ear heard music in each sound that rose,
Each sense forever found a new delight,
Such as the spirit's vision only knows;
Each act some new and ever-varying joy

Did by my Father's love for me prepare;
To dress the spot my ever fresh employ,
And in the glorious whole with Him to share;
No more without the flaming gate to stray,
No more for sin's dark stain the debt of death to pay.

THE PRESENCE

I sit within my room, and joy to find
That Thou who always lov'st art with me here,
That I am never left by Thee behind,
But by thyself Thou keep'st me ever near;
The fire burns brighter when with Thee I look,
And seems a kinder servant sent to me;
With gladder heart I read Thy holy book,
Because Thou art the eyes by which I see;
This aged chair, that table, watch and door
Around in ready service ever wait;
Nor can I ask of Thee a menial more
To fill the measure of my large estate,
For Thou thyself, with all a father's care,
Where'er I turn, art ever with me there.

THY BROTHER'S BLOOD

I have no Brother,—they who meet me now
Offer a hand with their own wills defiled,
And, while they wear a smooth unwrinkled brow,
Know not that Truth can never be beguiled;
Go wash the hand that still betrays thy guilt;
Before the spirit's gaze what stain can hide?
Abel's red blood upon the earth is spilt,
And by thy tongue it cannot be denied;
I hear not with the ear,—the heart doth tell
Its secret deeds to me untold before;
Go, all its hidden plunder quickly sell,
Then shalt thou cleanse thee from thy brother's gore,
Then will I take thy gift; that bloody stain
Shall not be seen upon thy hand again.

NATURE

The bubbling brook doth leap when I come by,
Because my feet find measure with its call,
The birds know when the friend they love is nigh,
For I am known to them both great and small;
The flowers that on the lovely hill-side grow
Expect me there when Spring their bloom has given;
And many a tree and bush my wanderings know,
And e'en the clouds and silent stars of heaven;
For he who with his Maker walks aright,
Shall be their lord, as Adam was before;
His ear shall catch each sound with new delight,
Each object wear the dress which then it wore;
And he, as when erect in soul he stood,
Hear from his Father's lips that all is good.

THE MEEK

I would be meek as He who bore His cross,
And died on earth that I in Him might live,
And, while in sin I knew not of my loss,
Suffered with gentle love His hope to give;
May I within the manger too be laid,
And mid the thieves His childlike meekness show;
And though by him who kisses me betrayed,
May I no will but His, my Master's know;
Thus sheltered by the lonely vale of tears,
My feet shall tread secure the path He trod;
Mid lying tongues that pierce my side like spears,
I too shall find within the peace of God;
And though rejected shall possess the earth,
And dead in Christ be witness of His birth.

THE BARBERRY-BUSH

The bush that has most briers and bitter fruit
Waits till the frost has turned its green leaves red,
Its sweetened berries will thy palate suit,
And thou mayst find e'en there a homely bread;

Upon the hills of Salem scattered wide,
Their yellow blossoms gain the eye in Spring;
And straggling e'en upon the turnpike's side,
Their ripened branches to your hand they bring;
I've plucked them oft in boyhood's early hour,
That then I gave such name, and thought it true;
But now I know that other fruit as sour,
Grows on what now thou callest *Me* and *You;*
Yet wilt thou wait the autumn that I see,
Will sweeter taste than these red berries be.

THE CHILDREN

I saw, strange sight! the children sat at meat,
When they their Parent's face had never known;
Nor rose they, when they heard His step, to greet,
But feasted there upon His gifts alone;
'Twas morn, and noon, and evening hour the same;
They heeded not 'twas He who gave them bread,
For they had not yet learned to call His name;
They had been children, but they now were dead;
Yet still their Father, with a father's care,
Early and late stood waiting by their board,
Hoping each hour that they his love could share,
And at his table sit to life restored;
Alas! for many a day and year I stood
And saw them feasting thus, yet knew not Him how good.

THE HAND AND FOOT

The hand and foot that stir not, they shall find
Sooner than all the rightful place to go:
Now in their motion free as roving wind,
Though first no snail more limited and slow;
I mark them full of labor all the day,
Each active motion made in perfect rest;
They cannot from their path mistaken stray,
Though 'tis not theirs, yet in it they are blest;
The bird has not their hidden track found out,
Nor cunning fox, though full of art he be;

It is the way unseen, the certain route,
Where ever bound, yet thou art ever free;
The path of Him, whose perfect law of love
Bids spheres and atoms in just order move.

THE NEW WORLD

The night that has no star lit up by God,
The day that round men shines who still are blind,
The earth their grave-turned feet for ages trod,
And sea swept over by His mighty wind,—
All these have passed away; the melting dream
That flitted o'er the sleepers' half-shut eye,
When touched by morning's golden-darting beam;
And he beholds around the earth and sky
What ever real stands; the rolling spheres,
And heaving billows of the boundless main,
That show, though time is past, no trace of years,
And earth restored he sees as his again,
The earth that fades not, and the heavens that stand,
Their strong foundations laid by God's right hand!

TO THE FOSSIL FLOWER

Dark fossil flower! I see thy leaves unrolled,
With all thy lines of beauty freshly marked,
As when the eye of Morn beamed on thee first,
And thou first turned'st to meet its welcome smile.
And sometimes in the coal's bright rainbow hues
I dream I see the colors of thy prime,
And for a moment robe thy form again
In splendor not its own. Flower of the past!
Now, as I look on thee, life's echoing tread
Falls noiseless on my ear; the present dies;
And o'er my soul the thoughts of distant time,
In silent waves, like billows from the sea,
Come rolling on and on, with ceaseless flow,
Innumerable. Thou mayst have sprung unsown
Into thy noon of life, when first earth heard
Its Maker's sovereign voice; and laughing flowers

Waved o'er the meadows, hung on mountain crags,
And nodded in the breeze on every hill.
Thou mayst have bloomed unseen, save by the stars
That sang together o'er thy rosy birth,
And came at eve to watch thy folded rest.
None may have sought thee on thy fragrant home,
Save light-voiced winds that round thy dwelling played,
Or seemed to sigh, as oft their wingèd haste
Compelled their feet to roam. Thou mayst have lived
Beneath the light of later days, when man
With feet free-roving as the homeless wind
Scaled the thick-mantled height, coursed plains unshorn,
Breaking the solitude of nature's haunt
With voice that seemed to blend in one sweet strain
The mingled music of the elements.
And when against his infant frame they rose,
Uncurbed, unawed by his yet feeble hand,
And when the muttering storm and shouting wave
And rattling thunder, mated, round him raged
And seemed at times like daemon foes to gird,
Thou mayst have won with gentle look his heart,
And stirred the first warm prayer of gratitude,
And been his first, his simplest altar-gift.
For thee, dark flower! the kindling sun can bring
No more the colors that it gave, nor morn,
With kindly kiss, restore thy breathing sweets:
Yet may the mind's mysterious touch recall
The bloom and fragrance of thy early prime:
For He who to the lowly lily gave
A glory richer than to proudest king,
He painted not those darkly-shining leaves,
With blushes like the dawn, in vain; nor gave
To thee its sweetly-scented breath, to waste
Upon the barren air. E'en though thou stood'st
Alone in Nature's forest-home untrod,
The first-love of the stars and sighing winds,
The mineral hold with faithful trust thy form,
To wake in human hearts sweet thoughts of love,
Now the dark past hangs round thy memory.

THE PRAYER

Wilt Thou not visit me?
The plant beside me feels Thy gentle dew;
  And every blade of grass I see,
From Thy deep earth its quickening moisture drew.

Wilt Thou not visit me?
Thy morning calls on me with cheering tone;
  And every hill and tree
Lends but one voice, the voice of Thee alone.

Come, for I need Thy love,
More than the flower the dew, or grass the rain;
  Come, gently as Thy holy dove;
And let me in thy sight rejoice to live again.

I will not hide from them,
When Thy storms come, though fierce may be their wrath;
  But bow with leafy stem,
And strengthened follow on Thy chosen path.

Yes, Thou wilt visit me,
Nor plant nor tree Thine eye delights so well,
  As when from sin set free
My spirit loves with Thine in peace to dwell.

THE SILENT

There is a sighing in the wood,
  A murmur in the beating wave;
The heart has never understood
  To tell in words the thoughts they gave.

Yet oft it feels an answering tone,
  When wandering on the lonely shore;
And could the lips its voice make known,
  'Twould sound as does the ocean's roar.

And oft beneath the wind-swept pine,
 Some chord is struck the strain to swell;
Nor sounds nor language can define,
 'Tis not for words or sounds to tell.

'Tis all unheard; that Silent Voice,
 Whose goings forth unknown to all,
Bids bending reed and bird rejoice,
 And fills with music Nature's hall.

And in the speechless human heart
 It speaks, where'er man's feet have trod;
Beyond the lips' deceitful art,
 To tell of Him, the Unseen God.

THE FOX AND THE BIRD

The bird that has no nest,
 The Fox that has no hole;
He's wiser than the rest,
 Her eggs are never stole.

She builds where none can see,
 He hides where none can find;
The bird can rest where'er she be,
 He freely moves as wind.

Thou hast not found her little young,
 E'en though thou'st sought them long;
Though from thine earliest day they've sung,
 Thou hast not heard their song.

Thou hast not found that Fox's brood,
 That nestle under ground;
Though through all time his burrow's stood,
 His whelps thou'st never found.

8. Margaret Fuller (1810–1850)

A Short Essay on Critics

[One respect in which the Transcendental movement seems most admirable to our view (although also most poignant) was the way in which, even while being torn apart by new and hitherto unknown emotions (unknown in New England, that is)—by such emotions of literary and artistic discovery as Margaret Fuller recorded in her *Memoirs*—even in the throes of this excitement the group strove mightily for standards. Furthermore, most of them knew that they were not themselves creative artists, even though they all exerted themselves to the utmost; hence they were perforce thrown back on criticism as their principal literary endeavor. But also, they understood, and tried to make their fellow countrymen understand, that in America, where literature had to be created *de novo*, criticism had a vital function to perform.

The second article in the first issue of *The Dial* (July 1840, I, 5–11) was Margaret Fuller's attempt to expound this critical mission.]

An essay on Criticism were a serious matter; for, though this age be emphatically critical, the writer would still find it necessary to investigate the laws of criticism as a science, to settle its conditions as an art. Essays entitled critical are epistles addressed to the public through which the mind of the recluse relieves itself of its impressions. Of these the only law is, "Speak the best word that is in thee." Or they are regular articles, got up to order by the literary hack writer, for the literary mart, and the only law is to make them plausible. There is not yet deliberate recognition of a standard of criticism, though we hope the always strengthening league of the republic of letters must ere long settle laws on which its Amphictyonic council may act. Meanwhile let us not venture to write on criticism, but by classifying the critics imply our hopes, and thereby our thoughts.

First, there are the subjective class, (to make use of a convenient term, introduced by our German benefactors.) These are persons to whom writing is no sacred, no reverend employment. They are not driven to consider, not forced upon investigation by the fact, that they are deliberately giving their thoughts an independent existence, and that it may live to others when dead to them. They know no agonies of conscientious research, no timidities of self-respect. They see no Ideal beyond the present hour, which makes its mood an uncertain tenure. How things affect them now they know; let the future, let the whole take care of itself. They state their impressions as they rise, of other men's spoken, written, or acted thoughts. They never dream of going out of themselves to seek the motive, to trace the law of another nature. They never dream that there are statures which cannot be measured from their point of view. They love, they like, or they hate; the book is detestable, immoral, absurd, or admirable, noble, of a most approved scope;—these statements they make with authority, as those who bear the evangel of pure taste and accurate judgment, and need be tried before no human synod. To them it seems that their present position commands the universe . . .

The value of such comments is merely reflex. They characterize the critic. They give an idea of certain influences on a certain act of men in a certain time or place. Their absolute, essential value is nothing. The long review, the eloquent article by the man of the nineteenth century are of no value by themselves considered, but only as samples of their kind. The writers were content to tell what they felt, to praise or to denounce without needing to convince us or themselves. They sought not the divine truths of philosophy, and she proffers them not, if unsought.

Then there are the apprehensive. These can go out of themselves and enter fully into a foreign existence. They breathe its life; they live in its law; they tell what it meant, and why it so expressed its meaning. They reproduce the work of which they speak, and make it better known to us in so far as two statements are better than one. There are beautiful specimens in this kind. They are pleasing to us as bearing witness of the genial sympathies of nature. They have the ready grace of love with somewhat of the dignity of disinterested friendship. They sometimes give more pleasure than the original production of which they treat, as melodies will sometimes ring sweetlier in echo. Besides there is a peculiar pleasure in a true response; it is the assurance of equipoise in the universe. These, if not true critics, come nearer the standard than the subjective class, and the value of their work is ideal as well as historical.

Then there are the comprehensive, who must also be apprehensive. They enter into the nature of another being and judge his work by its own law. But having done so, having ascertained his design and the degree of his success in fulfilling it, thus measuring his judgment, his energy, and skill, they do also know how to put that aim in its place, and how to estimate its relations. And this the critic can only do who perceives the analogies of the universe, and how they are regulated by an absolute, invariable principle. He can see how far that work expresses this principle as well as how far it is excellent in its details. Sustained by a principle, such as can be girt with no rule, no formula, he can walk around the work, he can stand above it, he can uplift it, and try its weight. Finally he is worthy to judge it . . .

The critic, then, should be not merely a poet, not merely a philosopher, not merely an observer, but tempered of all three. If he criticize the poem, he must want nothing of what constitutes the poet, except the power of creating forms and speaking in music. He must have as good an eye and as fine a sense; but if he had as fine an organ for expression also, he would make the poem instead of judging it. He must be inspired by the philosopher's spirit of inquiry and need of generalization, but he must not be constrained by the hard cemented masonry of method to which philosophers are prone. And he must have the organic acuteness of the observer, with a love of ideal perfection, which forbids him to be content with mere beauty of details in the work or the comment upon the work.

There are persons who maintain, that there is no legitimate criticism, except the reproductive; that we have only to say what the work is or is to us, never what it is not. But the moment we look for a principle, we feel the need of a criterion, of a standard; and then we say what the work is *not,* as well as what it *is;* and this is as healthy though not as grateful and gracious an operation of the mind as the other. We do not seek to degrade but to classify an object by stating what it is not. We detach the part from the whole, lest it stand between us and the whole. When we have ascertained in what degree it manifests the whole, we may safely restore it to its place, and love or admire it there ever after . . .

Nature is ever various, ever new, and so should be her daughters, art and literature. We do not want merely a polite response to what we thought before, but by the freshness of thought in other minds we have new thought awakened in our own. We do not want stores of information only, but to be roused to digest these into knowledge. Able and experienced men write for us, and we would know what they think, as they think not for us but for themselves. We would live with them, rather than be taught by them how to live; we would catch the contagion of their mental activity, rather than have them direct us how to regulate our own. In books, in reviews, in the senate, in the pulpit, we wish to meet thinking men, not schoolmasters or pleaders. We wish that they should do full justice to their own view, but also that they should be frank with us, and, if now our superiors, treat us as if we might some time rise to be their equals. It is this true manliness, this firmness in his own position, and this power of appreciating the position of others, that alone can make the critic our companion and friend. We would converse with him, secure that he will tell us all his thought, and speak as man to man. But if he adapts his work to us, if he stifles what is distinctively his, if he shows himself either arrogant or mean, or, above all. if he wants faith in the healthy action of free thought, and the safety of pure motive, we will not talk with him, for we cannot confide in him. We will go to the critic who trusts Genius and trusts us, who knows that all good writing must be spontaneous, and who will write out the bill of fare for the public as he reads it for himself,—

> "Forgetting vulgar rules, with spirit free
> To judge each author by his own intent,
> Nor think one standard for all minds is meant."

Such an one will not disturb us with personalities, with sectarian prejudices, or an undue vehemence in favor of petty plans or temporary objects. Neither will he disgust us by smooth obsequious flatteries and an inexpressive, life-less gentleness. He will be free and make free from the mechanical and dis-torting influences we hear complained of on every side. He will teach us to love wisely what we before loved well, for he knows the difference between censoriousness and discernment, infatuation and reverence; and, while de-lighting in the genial melodies of Pan, can perceive, should Apollo bring his lyre into audience, that there may be strains more divine than those of his native groves.

9. Margaret Fuller (1810–1850)

Menzel's View of Goethe

[Although Shakespeare, by speaking so often as the Devil's child, threat-ened to confront Transcendental doctrine with a conflict between art and morality, he could somehow be dealt with and, as in Very's essay, be enrolled on the side of natural morality. But Goethe was the real problem. On the one hand he was clearly the greatest poet of modern times; on the other, he was quite as clearly an im-moral man. Transcendentalist criticism struggled endlessly with this conundrum, and while the Transcendentalists could not give up their adoration of Goethe, neither could they ever condone his behavior.

Ripley induced Cornelius C. Felton to translate Menzel's history of German literature for the *Specimens*. It was a good survey for the instruction of Americans, but Menzel was a stern Prussian nationalist who condemned Goethe—both for immorality and for lack of patriotism—as severely as would a New England Cal-vinist. Because the attack came from Germany itself, it caused much uneasiness among the faithful, which Margaret Fuller attempted to assuage by a frank dis-cussion of the issue in *The Dial* for January 1841 (I, 340–347). That a woman should dare to talk of such matters in public seemed to many of her contemporaries proof that she was already as abandoned as her subject. The article exhibits an unresolved struggle that is everywhere present in the Transcendental literature: these new writers wanted to be free and at their ease in the literature of the world, but at the same time did not want to let go the simple moral virtues of New England. The question that was haunting all Margaret's friends as she started on the voyage home with Ossoli and a child was what sort of balance she had finally struck; her sudden death left the question as unanswered as she had left it in this discussion in *The Dial*.]

Historically considered, Goethe needs no apology. His so called faults fitted him all the better for the part he had to play. In cool possession of his wide-ranging genius, he taught the imagination of Germany, that the highest flight should be associated with the steady sweep and undazzled eye of the eagle. Was he too much the conoisseur, did he attach too great an importance to the cultivation of taste, where just then German literature so much needed to be refined, polished, and harmonized? Was he too skeptical, too much an experimentalist; how else could he have formed himself to be the keenest, and, at the same time, most nearly universal of observers, teaching theologians, philosophers, and patriots that nature comprehends them all, commands them all, and that no one development of life must exclude the rest. Do you talk (in the easy cant of the day) of German obscurity, extravagance, pedantry, and bad taste,—and will you blame this man, whose Greek–English–Italian–German mind steered so clear of these rocks and shoals, clearing, adjusting, and calming on each side, wherever he turned his prow? Was he not just enough of an idealist, just enough of a realist, for his peculiar task? If you want a moral enthusiast, is not there Schiller? If piety, of purest mystic sweetness, who but Novalis? Exuberant sentiment, that treasures each withered leaf in a tender breast, look to your Richter. Would you have men to find plausible meaning for the deepest enigma, or to hang up each map of literature, well painted and dotted on its proper roller, there are the Schlegels. Men of ideas were numerous as migratory crows in autumn, and Jacobi wrote the heart into philosophy (as well as he could). Who could fill Goethe's place to Germany, and to the world, of which she is now the teacher? His much-reviled, aristocratic turn was at that time a reconciling element. It is plain why he was what he was, for his country and for his age . . .

Most men, in judging another man, ask, Did he live up to our standard?

But to me, it seems desirable to ask rather, Did he live up to his own?

So possible is it that our consciences may be more enlightened than that of the Gentile under consideration. And if we can find out how much was given him, we are told, in a pure evangelium, to judge thereby how much shall be required.

Now Goethe has given us both his own standard, and the way to apply it. "To appreciate any man, learn first what object he proposed to himself; next, what degree of earnestness he showed with regard to attaining that object . . ."

This office of a judge, who is of purer eyes than to behold iniquity, and of a sacred oracle, to whom other men may go to ask when they should choose a friend, when face a foe, this great genius does not adequately fulfil. Too often has the priest left the shrine, to go and gather simples by the aid of spells whose might no pure power needs. Glimpses are found in his works of the highest spirituality, but it is blue sky through chinks, in a roof which should never have been built. He has used life to excess. He is too rich for his nobleness, too judicious for his inspiration, too humanly wise for his divine mission. He might have been a priest; he is only a sage.

An Epicurean sage, says the foregoing article. This seems to me unjust. He is also called a debauchee. There may be reason for such terms, but it is partial, and received, as they will be by the unthinking, they are as false as Menzel's abuse, in the impression they convey. Did Goethe value the present too much? It was not for the Epicurean aim of pleasure, but for use. He, in this, was but an instance of reaction, in an age of painful doubt and restless striving as to the future. Was his private life stained by profligacy? That far largest portion of his life, which is ours, and which is expressed in his works, is an unbroken series of efforts to develop the higher elements of our being. I cannot speak to private gossip on this subject, nor even to well-authenticated versions of his private life. Here are sixty volumes, by himself and others, which contain sufficient evidence of a life of severe labor, steadfast forbearance, and an intellectual growth almost unparalleled. That he failed of the highest fulfilment of his high vocation is certain, but he was neither epicurean nor sensualist, if we consider his life as a whole.

Yet he had failed to reach his highest development, and how was it that he was so content with this incompleteness, nay, the serenest of men? His serenity alone, in such a time of skepticism and sorrowful seeking, gives him a claim to all our study. See how he rides at anchor, lordly, rich in freight, every white sail ready to be unfurled at a moment's warning. And it must be a very slight survey, which can confound this calm self-trust with selfish indifference of temperament. Indeed, he in various ways . . . lets us see how little he was helped in this respect by temperament. But we need not his declaration; the case speaks for itself. Of all that perpetual accomplishment, that unwearied constructiveness, the basis must be sunk deeper than in temperament. He never halts, never repines, never is puzzled, like other men; that tranquillity, full of life, that ceaseless but graceful motion, "without haste, without rest," for which we all are striving, he has attained. And is not his lore of the noblest kind,—Reverence the highest, have patience with the lowest. Let this day's performance of the meanest duty be thy religion. Are the stars too distant, pick up that pebble that lies at thy foot, and from it learn the All. Go out, like Saul, the son of Kish, look earnestly after the meanest of thy father's goods, and a kingdom shall be brought thee. The least act of pure self-renunciation hallows, for the moment, all within its sphere. The philosopher may mislead, the devil tempt, yet innocence, though wounded and bleeding as it goes, must reach at last the holy city. The power of sustaining himself, and guiding others, rewards man sufficiently for the longest apprenticeship. Is not this lore the noblest?

10. Elizabeth Palmer Peabody (1804–1894)
The Word Aesthetic

[Despite the collapse of *The Dial* in 1844, the dream of a Transcendental magazine died hard. In 1849 Elizabeth Peabody attempted to start one in her bookshop; under the title *Aesthetic Papers* it achieved a single issue. (Disregarded at the time, it is now a collector's item because it contains Thoreau's *Civil Disobedience*.) Elizabeth chose the title deliberately, intending to underline what she considered the primary concern, and to expound it she wrote a prefatory essay on the meaning of "aesthetic."

No two Transcendentalists could wholly agree upon any theoretical statement, particularly upon any theory of literature; Emerson, who shied away from such abstractions, was unimpressed by Elizabeth's effort. Still, what she here formulated is an element, in varying degrees, in all the literature of the movement. The dialectical progress which she outlined as a philosophy of literary history—from primitive unconsciousness to civilized self-consciousness, to the ultimate, the modern and the Transcendental, self-conscious achievement of the primitive—constitutes a scale of values that is always in the background of the writings. Parker's dialectic of the process in theology, in the *Discourse,* is analogous. In every case the ultimate goal is "Nature"—hence the prophetic insight of Emerson's *Nature* in 1836.]

The "aesthetic element," then, is in our view neither a theory of the beautiful, nor a philosophy of art, but a component and indivisible part in all human creations which are not mere works of necessity; in other words, which are based on idea, as distinguished from appetite.

Sundry pairs of words, dualistic philosophical terms, have been long growing into use, and exercising, by the ideas they represent, an influence on the world of thought; such as subjective and objective, personal and impersonal, the Me and the Not-me; all having a reference to the central fact of the constant relation of the individual to the universal, and of their equally constant separation. The one always "works and lives in the other"; and, according to the preponderance of the one or the other element, the most various results appear in individuals and in nations . . .

Into the world of art also, as into that of politics and life, these self-opposing and neutralizing elements enter. Each man, according to his personal and unpersonal mode of being, according to the predominance of the subjective or the objective in his nature, takes the one or the other position. The French school of criticism, the personal, is based upon *taste*. It inquires, Does this work satisfy and please my taste, that is the taste of cultivated persons; the taste of the best judges or authorities? A shifting standard, offering no absolute criterion; which places the highest aim of art in pleasing; asking triumphantly, What, then, becomes of art, if its object be not to please? According to the German formula, this is to subordinate the object to the observer. The contrary position, the unpersonal, which sinks and subordinates the observer to the object,—which, by putting my personality aside, enables me to see the object in a pure uncolored light,—is the aesthetic.

Germany is the discoverer of the aesthetic, because the German mind, more than any other, embodies the unpersonal principle that underlies the aesthetic view. It became conscious of its own possession, as soon as its criticism began to apply itself to the region of literature and the arts. But it is singular, that, armed with this talisman to explore and expound the mysteries of art, there is a peculiar deficiency in the modern German attempts in the arts that address themselves to the eye. It reminds us of a man, trying, in a painstaking manner, to imitate the sports and feats that he failed to learn in his youth; so that the untaught, unscientific skill of a vigorous child shoots at a bound far beyond him.

How, then, do we account for the wonders that German art achieved in architecture in old time, and lately in music? Simply by the recollection, that these arts were German growths, antecedent to any conscious aesthetic criticism. Moreover, the arts may be classified, as partaking, in a greater or less degree, of the individual or the universal. Music and architecture, by their nature, are of a more universal expression than painting and sculpture, and belong more naturally to the German.

The progress of art, considered with relation to these two principles, is as follows:—All art, in its origin, is national and religious. The feeling expressed is of far greater importance than the vehicle in which it is conveyed. The practical portion of early art is conventional: the spiritual is profoundly significant, confined in its range, narrow but exalted. An expression of the infinite by means of the beautiful, inadequate indeed as expression, but deeply interesting, as is all inadequate expression, to those who can read the intention through the uncertain and vague embodiment.

The second step in art is when the practical, resting on this deep spiritual basis, advances by means of individual powers, by the personal skill, set free from the national conventionality, yet still confined within certain bounds, the limit and frame, as it were, of true art;—a second expression of the infinite by the beautiful, in which the beauty and satisfactoriness of the expression balances the less deep significance of the idea.

In the first stage, the aesthetic element prevailed unconsciously; for neither taste nor the aesthetic principle has any conscious place in creative, but only in critical ages. The progress of criticism is the reverse of that of art. In the creative age, appreciation is simple, intuitive, passionate, of which the delight of the people in national songs, the passionate enthusiasm with which the Florentines welcomed Cimabue's Madonna, are examples. When criticism springs up, it is first in the form of *taste*. The individual subjects the productions of art to his own personality. He says, "This is good, for it pleases me." Of course, however perfect this taste may be, it is still limited by the individuality: it is based on the degree of pleasure and satisfaction conveyed by a work to a cultivated person. It comes to be really believed, that the end and object of art is to please. Art becomes a luxury; its pleasures can be bought and sold; its appreciation becomes more and more external.

Such was the condition of criticism, when the profound self-subordinating genius of Germany perceived, in the deep significance of ancient works, the presence of an element which the individual mind, with its standard of beauty, and its idea of gratification to the senses, was utterly unable to account for. The Germans went to school to their own ancient paintings, those singularly national works in which a childlike, simple, often unartistic exterior is made to convey the consciousness of the highest spiritual ideal.

The word *aesthetic* is difficult of definition, because it is the watchword of a whole revolution in criticism. Like Whig and Tory, it is the standard of a party; it marks the progress of an idea. It is as a watchword we use it, to designate, in our department, that phase in human progress which subordinates the individual to the general, that he may re-appear on a higher plane of individuality.

11. Ralph Waldo Emerson (1803–1882)
The New Poetry

[In 1871, after even Alcott's patience had been tried by many altercations with the younger William Ellery Channing, he exclaimed, "Whim, thy name is Channing." Born in Boston and named for his illustrious uncle, Channing entered Harvard in 1834, but finding chapel services a bore, he walked out, and hid himself in the country to write poetry. He spent a year in Illinois and Cincinnati and in 1842 married Ellen Fuller, a demure sister of Margaret. They settled in Concord, in order to be near Emerson; Channing became the friend and walking-companion of Thoreau. His literary style, said Thoreau, is "sublimo-slipshod."

Once committed, Emerson was always the loyal champion. Some of Channing's poems were sent to him in 1839, and though he noticed that the poet "defies a little too disdainfully his dictionary & logic," still he proposed to make himself useful to the author. He persisted in being useful, in the conviction that Channing's works were "more new & more charactered than anything we are likely to have." Hence he nominated himself to present to the public—or such of the public as read *The Dial*—a sheaf of Channing's poems in October 1840 (I, 222–232). Critical opinion has generally agreed that Emerson said more that is pertinent to modern poetry than the poems themselves quite justify.]

The tendencies of the times are so democratical, that we shall soon have not so much as a pulpit or raised platform in any church or town-house, but each person, who is moved to address any public assembly, will speak from the floor. The like revolution in literature is now giving importance to the portfolio over the book. Only one man in the thousand may print a book, but one in ten or one in five may inscribe his thoughts, or at least with short commentary his favorite readings in a private journal. The philosophy of the day has long since broached a more liberal doctrine of the poetic faculty than our fathers held, and reckons poetry the right and power of every man to whose culture justice is done. We own that, though we were trained in a stricter school of literary faith, and were in all our youth inclined to the enforcement of the straitest restrictions on the admission of candidates to the Parnassian fraternity, and denied the name of poetry to every composition in which the workmanship and the material were not equally excellent, in our middle age we have grown lax, and have learned to find pleasure in verses of a ruder strain,—to enjoy *verses of society,* or those effusions which in persons of a happy nature are the easy and un-premeditated translation of their thoughts and feelings into rhyme. This new taste for a certain private and household poetry, for somewhat less pretending than the festal and solemn verses which are written for the nations, really indicates, we suppose, that a new style of poetry exists. The number of writers has increased. Every child has been taught the tongues. The universal communication of the arts of reading and writing has brought the works of the great poets into every house, and made all ears familiar with the poetic forms. The progress of popular institutions has favored self-respect, and broken down that terror of the great, which once imposed awe and hesitation on the talent of the masses society. A wider epistolary intercourse ministers to the ends of sentiment and reflection than ever existed before; the practice of writing diaries is becoming almost general; and every day witnesses new attempts to throw into verse the experiences of private life.

What better omen of true progress can we ask than an increasing intellectual and moral interest of men in each other? What can be better for the republic than that the Capitol, the White House, and the Court House are becoming of less importance than the farm-house and the book-closet? If we are losing our interest in public men, and finding that their spell lay in number and size only, and acquiring instead a taste for the depths of thought and emotion, as they may be sounded in the soul of the citizen or the countryman, does it not replace man for the state, and character for official power? Men should be treated with solemnity; and when they come to chant their private griefs and doubts and joys, they have a new scale by which to compute magnitude and relation. Art is the noblest consolation of calamity. The poet is compensated for his defects in the street and in society, if in his chamber he has turned his mischance into noble numbers.

Is there not room then for a new department in poetry, namely, *Verses of the Portfolio?* We have fancied that we drew greater pleasure from some manuscript verses than from printed ones of equal talent. For there was herein the charm of character; they were confessions; and the faults, the imperfect parts, the fragmentary verses, the halting rhymes, had a worth beyond that of a high finish; for they testified that the writer was more man than artist, more earnest than vain; that the thought was too sweet and sacred to him, than that he should suffer his ears to hear or his eyes to see a superficial defect in the expression.

The characteristic of such verses is, that being not written for publication, they lack that finish which the conventions of literature require of authors. But if poetry of this kind has merit, we conceive that the prescription which demands a rhythmical polish may be easily set aside; and when a writer has outgrown the state of thought which produced the poem, the interest of letters is served by publishing it imperfect, as we preserve studies, torsos, and blocked statues of the great masters. For though we should be loath to see the wholesome conventions, to which we have alluded, broken down by a general incontinence of publication, and every man's and woman's diary flying into the bookstores, yet it is to be considered, on the other hand, that men of genius are often more incapable than others of that elaborate execution which criticism exacts. Men of genius in general are, more than others, incapable of any perfect exhibition, because, however agreeable it may be to them to act on the public, it is always a secondary aim. They are humble, self-accusing, moody men, whose worship is toward the Ideal Beauty, which chooses to be courted not so often in perfect hymns, as in wild ear-piercing ejaculations, or in silent musings. Their face is forward, and their heart is in this heaven. By so much are they disqualified for a perfect success in any particular performance to which they can give only a divided affection. But the man of talents has every advantage in the competition. He can give that cool and commanding attention to the thing to be done, that shall secure its just performance. Yet are the failures of genius better than the victories of talent; and we are sure that some crude manuscript poems have yielded us a more sustaining and a more stimulating diet, than many elaborated and classic productions.

We have been led to these thoughts by reading some verses, which were lately put into our hands by a friend with the remark, that they were the production of a youth, who had long passed out of the mood in which he wrote them, so that they had become quite dead to him. Our first feeling on reading them was a lively joy. So then the Muse is neither dead nor dumb, but has found a voice in these cold Cisatlantic States. Here is poetry which asks no aid of magnitude or number, of blood or crime, but finds theatre enough in the first field or brookside, breadth and depth enough in the flow of its own thought. Here is self-repose, which to our mind is stabler than the Pyramids; here is self-respect which leads a man to date from his heart more proudly than from Rome. Here is love which sees through surface, and adores the gentle nature and not the costume. Here is religion, which is not of the Church of England, nor of the Church of Boston. Here is the good wise heart, which sees that the end of culture is strength and cheerfulness. In an age too which tends with so strong an inclination to the philosophical muse, here is poetry more purely intellectual than any American verses we have yet seen, distinguished from all competition by two merits; the fineness of perception; and the poet's trust in his own genius to that degree, that there is an absence of all conventional imagery, and a bold use of that which the moment's mood had made sacred to him, quite careless that it might be sacred to no other, and might even be slightly ludicrous to the first reader.

We proceed to give our readers some selections, taken without much order from this rich pile of manuscript. We first find the poet in his boat.

BOAT-SONG

The river calmly flows,
Through shining banks, through lonely glen,
Where the owl shrieks, though ne'er the cheer of men
Has stirred its mute repose,
Still if you should walk there, you would go there again.

The stream is well alive.
Another passive world you see,
Where downward grows the form of every tree;
Like soft light clouds they thrive:
Like them let us in our pure loves reflected be.

A yellow gleam is thrown
Into the secrets of that maze
Of tangled trees, which late shut out our gaze,
Refusing to be known;
It must its privacy unclose,—its glories blaze.

Sweet falls the summer air
Over her frame who sails with me:
Her way like that is beautifully free,
Her nature far more rare,
And is her constant heart of virgin purity.

A quivering star is seen
Keeping his watch above the hill,
Though from the sun's retreat small light is still
Poured on earth's saddening mien:—
We all are tranquilly obeying Evening's will.

Thus ever love the POWER;
To simplest thoughts dispose the mind;
In each obscure event a worship find
Like that of this dim hour,—
In lights, and airs, and trees, and in all human kind.

We smoothly glide below
The faintly glimmering worlds of light:
Day has a charm, and this deceptive night
Brings a mysterious show;—
He shadows our dear earth,—but his cool stars are white.

Is there any boat-song like this? any in which the harmony proceeds so
manifestly from the poet's mind, giving to nature more than it receives? In
the following stanzas the writer betrays a certain habitual worship of genius,
which characterizes many pieces in the collection, breaking out sometimes
into very abrupt expression.

OCTOBER

Dry leaves with yellow ferns,—they are
Fit wreath of Autumn, while a star
Still, bright, and pure, our frosty air
    Shivers in twinkling points
    Of thin celestial hair,
And thus one side of heaven anoints.

I am beneath the moon's calm look
Most quiet in this sheltered nook
From trouble of the frosty wind
    Which curls the yellow blade;
    Though in my covered mind
A grateful sense of change is made.

To wandering men how dear this sight
Of a cold tranquil autumn night,
In its majestic deep repose;
    Thus will their genius be
    Not buried in high snows,
Though of as mute tranquillity.

An anxious life they will not pass,
Nor, as the shadow on the grass,
Leave no impression there to stay;
    To them all things are thought;
    The blushing morn's decay,—
Our death, our life, by this is taught.

O find in every haze that shines,
A brief appearance without lines,

A single word,—no finite joy;
   For present is a Power
   Which we may not annoy,
Yet love him stronger every hour.

I would not put this sense from me,
If I could some great sovereign be;
Yet will not task a fellow man
   To feel the same glad sense,
   For no one living can
Feel—save his given influence . . .

We will close our extracts from this rare file of blotted paper with a lighter strain, which, whilst it shows how gaily a poet can chide, gives us a new insight into his character and habits.

TORMENTS

Yes! they torment me
Most exceedingly:—
I would I could flee.
A breeze on a river—
I listen forever;
The yellowish heather
Under cool weather,—
These are pleasures to me.

What do torment me?
Those living vacantly,
Who live but to see;
Indefinite action,
Nothing but motion,
Round stones a rolling,
No inward controlling;—
Yes! they torment me.

Some cry all the time,
Even in their prime
Of youth's flushing clime.
O! out on this sorrow!
Fear'st thou to-morrow?
Set thy legs going,
Be stamping be rowing,—
This of life is the lime.

Hail, thou mother Earth!
Who gave me thy worth
For my portion at birth:
I walk in thy azure,
Unfond of erasure,
But they who torment me
So most exceedingly
Sit with feet on the hearth.

We have more pages from the same hand lying before us, marked by the same purity and tenderness and early wisdom as these we have quoted, but we shall close our extracts here. May the right hand that has so written never lose its cunning! May this voice of love and harmony teach its songs to the too long silent echoes of the Western Forest.

12. William Ellery Channing (1818–1901)

Poems

[With Emerson's patronage, Channing continued to write poems for *The Dial*, although most of the world agreed with Poe's strictures upon them. He lived the rest of his life in Concord, becoming separated from his family, eking out his last years in the house of F. B. Sanborn.

These two poems (*The Dial*, IV, 64, 103), if not demonstrably his best, are fair samples of what the Transcendental organ offered to the world as Transcendental poetry.]

THE EARTH

My highway is unfeatured air,
My consorts are the sleepless stars,
And men, my giant arms upbear,
My arms unstained and free from scars.

I rest forever on my way,
Rolling around the happy sun,
My children love the sunny day,
But noon and night to me are one.

My heart hath pulses like their own,
I am their mother, and my veins,
Though built of the enduring stone,
Thrill as do theirs with godlike pains.

The forests and the mountains high,
The foaming ocean and its springs,
The plains,—O pleasant company,
My voice through all your anthems rings.

Ye are so cheerful in your minds,
Content to smile, content to share,
My being in your silence finds
The echo of my spheral air.

No leaf may fall, no pebble roll,
No drop of water lose the road,
The issues of the general soul,
Are mirrored in their round abode.

AN OLD MAN

Heavy and drooping,
By himself stooping,
Half of his body left,
Of all his mind bereft,
Antiquate positive,
Forgotten causative,—
Yet he still picks the ground,
Though his spade makes no sound,
Thin fingers are weak,
And elbows a-peak.

He talks to himself,
Of what he remembers,
Rakes over spent embers,
Recoineth past pelf,
Dreams backwards alone,
Of time gnawing the bone.
Too simple for folly,
Too wise for content,
Not brave melancholy,
Or knave eminent,
Slouched hat, and loose breeches,
And gaping with twitches,—

Old coin found a-ploughing,
Curious but cloying,
How he gropes in the sun,
And spoils what he's done.

13. Frederic Henry Hedge (1805–1890)
Questionings

[Hedge was not by temperament or profession a poet, but on one sleepless night, riding in the mail coach to Bangor, he watched the stars and upon reaching home wrote down these lines. They were published in *The Dial* for January 1841 (I, 290–291); the poem was later widely reprinted under the title "The Idealist," which possibly gives more of a clue to the theme. It is not surprising that even the most scholarly of the Transcendentalists—even one who barely approved of *The Dial*—should break into verse; Transcendental doctrine maintained that every man is at least potentially a poet. Since Hedge was deeply read in German idealism, he inevitably put into his one poetic utterance the basic epistemological problem with which Transcendental philosophy commenced.]

QUESTIONINGS

Hath this world, without me wrought,
Other substance than my thought?
Lives it by my sense alone,
Or by essence of its own?
Will its life, with mine begun,
Cease to be when that is done,
Or another consciousness
With the self-same forms impress?

Doth yon fireball, poised in air,
Hang by my permission there?
Are the clouds that wander by,
But the offspring of mine eye,
Born with every glance I cast,
Perishing when that is past?
And those thousand, thousand eyes,
Scattered through the twinkling skies,
Do they draw their life from mine,
Or, of their own beauty shine?

Now I close my eyes, my ears,
And creation disappears;
Yet if I but speak the word,
All creation is restored.
Or—more wonderful—within,
New creations do begin;
Hues more bright and forms more rare,
Than reality doth wear,
Flash across my inward sense,
Born of the mind's omnipotence.

Soul! that all informest, say!
Shall these glories pass away?
Will those planets cease to blaze,
When these eyes no longer gaze?
And the life of things be o'er,
When these pulses beat no more?

Thought! that in me works and lives,—
Life to all things living gives,—
Art thou not thyself, perchance,
But the universe in trance?
A reflection inly flung
By that world thou fanciedst sprung
From thyself;—thyself a dream;—
Of the world's thinking thou the theme.

Be it thus, or be thy birth
From a source above the earth—
Be thou matter, be thou mind,
In thee alone myself I find,
And through thee alone, for me,
Hath this world reality.
Therefore, in thee will I live,
To thee all myself will give,
Losing still, that I may find,
This bounded self in boundless Mind.

14. Christopher Pearse Cranch (1813–1892)
Poems

[To *The Western Messenger* Cranch contributed some of the most banal, not to say maudlin, verses of the period, but the existence of *The Dial* aroused a deeper strain within him. The five poems he contributed in 1840–41 were resolute attempts to turn Transcendental metaphysics into poetry. "Correspondences" is probably the best statement, outside of Emerson, of a doctrine which the Transcendentalists derived from Swedenborg by way of Sampson Reed, and which for them was the final confirmation of the link between mind and nature.

In 1875, after Cranch had ceased to pretend that he was a militant Transcendentalist, after he had amused himself with travel and with sketching, he published a volume, *The Bird and the Bell with Other Poems* (Boston, 1875). Although these productions fall outside the period of this volume, "The Spirit of the Age" deserves reprinting as a belated statement of a conception that had been exceedingly strong among the radicals of 1840. Also, running through the literature of that strenuous period had been a tendency toward defying a busy and practical America by flaunting an unabashed aestheticism; this was the turning that Cranch finally took, and in the light of his career, "The Garden" may be taken as a resolution, by one who had commenced as an eager Transcendentalist, of the conflicting claims of religion and literature, of action and leisure.]

STANZAS

Thought is deeper than all speech,
Feeling deeper than all thought:
Souls to souls can never teach
What unto themselves was taught.

We are spirits clad in veils:
Man by man was never seen:
All our deep communing fails
To remove the shadowy screen.

Heart to heart was never known:
Mind with mind did never meet:
We are columns left alone
Of a temple once complete.

Like the stars that gem the sky,
Far apart though seeming near,

In our light we scattered lie;
All is thus but starlight here.

What is social company
But a babbling summer stream?
What our wise philosophy
But the glancing of a dream?

Only when the Sun of Love
Melts the scattered stars of thought,
Only when we live above
What the dim-eyed world hath taught,

Only when our souls are fed
By the Fount which gave them birth,
And by inspiration led
Which they never drew from earth,

We, like parted drops of rain,
Swelling till they meet and run,
Shall be all absorbed again,
Melting, flowing into one.

THE OCEAN

—— "In a season of calm weather
Though inland far we be,
Our souls have sight of that immortal sea
That brought us hither,
Can in a moment travel thither,
And see the children sport upon the shore,
And hear the mighty waters rolling evermore."—

Wordsworth

Tell me, brother, what are we?
Spirits bathing in the sea
    Of Deity!
Half afloat, and half on land,
Wishing much to leave the strand,
Standing, gazing with devotion,

Yet afraid to trust the ocean,—
Such are we.

Wanting love and holiness,
To enjoy the wave's caress;
Wanting faith and heavenly hope,
Buoyantly to bear us up;
Yet impatient in our dwelling,
When we hear the ocean swelling,
And in every wave that rolls
We behold the happy souls
Peacefully, triumphantly
Swimming on the smiling sea,
Then we linger round the shore,
Lovers of the earth no more.

Once,—'t was in our infancy,
We were drifted by this sea
To the coast of human birth,
To this body and this earth:
Gentle were the hands that bore
Our young spirits to the shore;
Gentle lips that bade us look
Outward from our cradle-nook
To the spirit-bearing ocean
With such wonder and devotion,
As, each stilly sabbath day,
We were led a little way,
Where we saw the waters swell
Far away from inland dell,
And received with grave delight
Symbols of the Infinite:—
Then our home was near the sea;
"Heaven was round our infancy";—
Night and day we heard the waves
Murmuring by us to their caves;—
Floated in unconscious life
With no later doubts at strife,
Trustful of the Upholding Power,
Who sustained us hour by hour.

Now we've wandered from the shore,
Dwellers by the sea no more;
Yet at times there comes a tone
Telling of the visions flown,
Sounding from the distant sea
Where we left our purity:
Distant glimpses of the surge
Lure us down to ocean's verge;
There we stand with vague distress,
Yearning for the measureless,
By half-wakened instincts driven,
Half loving earth, half loving heaven,
Fearing to put off and swim,
Yet impelled to turn to Him,
In whose life we live and move,
And whose very name is Love.

Grant me, courage, Holy One,
To become indeed thy son,
And in thee, thou Parent-Sea,
Live and love eternally.

CORRESPONDENCES

All things in Nature are beautiful types to the soul that will read them;
   Nothing exists upon earth, but for unspeakable ends.
Every object that speaks to the senses was meant for the spirit:
   Nature is but a scroll,—God's hand-writing thereon.
Ages ago, when man was pure, ere the flood overwhelmed him,
   While in the image of God every soul yet lived,
Everything stood as a letter or word of a language familiar,
   Telling of truths which *now* only the angels can read.
Lost to man was the key of those sacred hieroglyphics,—
   Stolen away by sin,—till with Jesus restored.
Now with infinite pains we here and there spell out a letter;
   Now and then will the sense feebly shine through the dark.
When we perceive the light which breaks through the visible symbol,
   What exultation is ours! *we* the discovery have made!
Yet is the meaning the same as when Adam lived sinless in Eden,
   Only long-hidden it slept and now again is restored.

Man unconsciously uses figures of speech every moment,
　Little dreaming the cause why to such terms he is prone,—
Little dreaming that everything has its own correspondence
　Folded within it of old, as in the body the soul.
Gleams of the mystery fall on us still, though much is forgotten,
　And through our commonest speech illumines the path of our thoughts.
Thus does the lordly sun shine out a type of the Godhead;
　Wisdom and Love the beams that stream on a darkened world.
Thus do the sparkling waters flow, giving joy to the desert,
　And the great Fountain of Life opens itself to the thirst.
Thus does the word of God distil like the rain and the dew-drops,
　Thus does the warm wind breathe like to the Spirit of God,
And the green grass and the flowers are signs of the regeneration.

　O thou Spirit of Truth; visit our minds once more!
Give us to read, in letters of light, the language celestial,
　Written all over the earth,—written all over the sky:
Thus may we bring our hearts at length to know our Creator,
　Seeing in all things around types of the Infinite Mind.

INWORLD

　　Amid the watches of the windy night
　　A poet sat and listened to the flow
　　Of his own changeful thoughts, until there passed
　　A vision by him, murmuring, as it moved,
　　A wild and mystic lay—to which his thoughts
　　And pen kept time, and thus the measure ran:—

　　　All is but as it seems.
　　　The round green earth,
　　　With river and glen;
　　　The din and the mirth
　　　Of the busy, busy men;
　　　The world's great fever
　　　Throbbing forever;
　　　The creed of the sage,
　　　The hope of the age,
　　　All things we cherish,
　　　All that live and all that perish,
　　　These are but inner dreams.

The great world goeth on
To thy dreaming;
To thee alone
Hearts are making their moan,
Eyes are streaming.
Thine is the white moon turning night to day,
Thine is the dark wood sleeping in her ray;
Thee the winter chills;
Thee the spring-time thrills;
All things nod to thee—
All things come to see
If thou art dreaming on.
If thy dream should break,
And thou shouldst awake,
All things would be gone.

Nothing is, if thou art not.
From thee as from a root
The blossoming stars upshoot,
The flower cups drink the rain.
Joy and grief and weary pain
Spring aloft from thee,
And toss their branches free.
Thou art under, over all;
Thou dost hold and cover all;
Thou art Atlas—thou art Jove;—
The mightiest truth
Hath all its youth
From thy enveloping thought—
Thy thought itself lay in thy earliest love.

Nature keeps time to thee
With voice unbroken;
Still doth she rhyme to thee,
When thou hast spoken.
When the sun shines to thee,
'Tis thy own joy
Opening mines to thee
Nought can destroy.

When the blast moans to thee,
Still doth the wind
Echo the tones to thee
Of thy own mind.
Laughter but saddens thee
When thou art glad,
Life is not life to thee
But as thou livest,
Labor is strife to thee,
When thou least strivest:—

More did the spirit sing, and made the night
Most musical with inward melodies,
But vanished soon and left the listening Bard
Wrapt in unearthly silence—till the morn
Reared up the screen that shuts the spirit-world
From loftiest poet and from wisest sage.

OUTWORLD

The sun was shining on the busy earth,
All men and things were moving on their way—
The old, old way which we call life. The soul
Shrank from the giant grasp of Space and Time.
Yet—for it was her dreamy hour, half yielded
To the omnipotent delusion—and looked out
On the broad glare of things, and felt itself
Dwindling before the Universe. Then came unto the Bard
Another spirit with another voice,
And sang:—

Said he that all but seems?
  Said he, the world is void and lonely,
A strange vast crowd of dreams
  Coming to thee only?
And that thy feeble soul
Hath such a strong control
O'er sovereign Space and sovereign Time
  And all their train sublime?
Said he, thou art the Eye
  Reflecting all that is—

The Ear that hears while it creates
  All sounds and harmonies—
The central sense that bides amid
All shows, and turns them to realities?
Listen, mortal, while the sound
  Of this life intense is flowing!
Dost thou find all things around
  Go as thou art going?
Dost thou dream that thou art free,
Making, destroying all that thou dost see,
In the unfettered might of thy soul's liberty?
  Lo, an atom troubles thee,
  One bodily fibre crushes thee,
    One nerve tortures and maddens thee,
    One drop of blood is death to thee.
Art thou but a withering leaf,
For a summer season brief
  Clinging to the tree,
Till the winds of circumstance,
Whirling in their hourly dance,
  Prove too much for thee?
Art thou but a speck, a mote
  In the system universal?
Art thou but a passing note
  Woven in the great Rehearsal?
Canst thou roll back the tide of Thought
  And unmake the creed of the age,
And unteach the wisdom taught
  By the prophet and the sage?
Art thou but a shadow
Chasing o'er a meadow?
The great world goes on
  Spite of thy dreaming.
Not to thee alone
Hearts are making their moan,
  And tear drops streaming,
And the mighty voice of Nature
Is thy parent, not thy creature,
Is no pupil, but thy teacher;

And the world would still move on,
Were thy soul forever flown.
For while thou dreamest on, enfolded
   In Nature's wide embrace,
All thy life is daily moulded
   By her informing grace.
And time and space must reign
   And rule o'er thee forever,
And the Outworld lift its chain
   From off thy spirit never;
But in the dream of thy half-waking fever,
   Thou shalt be mocked with gleam and show
Of truths thou pinest for and yet canst never know.

And then the Spirit fled and left the Bard
Still wondering—for he felt that voices twain
Had come from different spheres with different truths,
That seemed at war and yet agreed in one.

THE SPIRIT OF THE AGE

A wondrous light is filling the air,
And rimming the clouds of the old despair;
And hopeful eyes look up to see
Truth's mighty electricity,—
Auroral shimmerings swift and bright,
That wave and flash in the silent night,—
Magnetic billows travelling fast,
And flooding all the spaces vast
From dim horizon to farthest cope
Of heaven, in streams of gathering hope.
Silent they mount and spread apace,
And the watchers see old Europe's face
Lit with expression new and strange,—
The prophecy of coming change.

Meantime, while thousands, wrapt in dreams,
Sleep heedless of the electric gleams,
Or ply their wonted work and strife,
Or plot their pitiful games of life;

While the emperor bows in his formal halls,
And the clerk whirls on at the masking balls;
While the lawyer sits at his dreary files,
And the banker fingers his glittering piles,
And the priest kneels down at his lighted shrine,
And the fop flits by with his mistress fine,—
The diplomat works at his telegraph wires:
His back is turned to the heavenly fires.
Over him flows the magnetic tide,
And the candles are dimmed by the glow outside.
Mysterious forces overawe,
Absorb, suspend the usual law.
The needle stood northward an hour ago;
Now it veers like a weathercock to and fro.
The message he sends flies not as once;
The unwilling wires yield no response.
Those iron veins that pulsed but late
From a tyrant's will to a people's fate,
Flowing and ebbing with feverish strength,
Are seized by a Power whose breadth and length,
Whose height and depth, defy all gauge
Save the great spirit of the age.
The mute machine is moved by a law
That knows no accident or flaw,
And the iron thrills to a different chime
Than that which rang in the dead old time.
For Heaven is taking the matter in hand,
And baffling the tricks of the tyrant band.
The sky above and the earth beneath
Heave with a supermundane breath.
Half-truths, for centuries kept and prized,
By higher truths are polarized.
Like gamesters on a railroad train,
Careless of stoppage, sun or rain,
We juggle, plot, combine, arrange,
And are swept along by the rapid change.
And some who from their windows mark
The unwonted lights that flood the dark,
Little by little, in slow surprise

Lift into space their sleepy eyes;
Little by little are made aware
That a spirit of power is passing there,—
That a spirit is passing, strong and free,—
The soul of the nineteenth century.

THE GARDEN

Naught know we but the heart of summer here.
On the tree-shadowed velvet lawn I lie,
And dream up through the close leaves to the sky,
And weave Arcadian visions in a sphere
Of peace. The steaming heat broods all around,
But only lends a quiet to the hours.
The aromatic life of countless flowers,
The singing of a hundred birds, the sound
Of rustling leaves, go pulsing through the green
Of opening vistas in the garden walks.
Dear Summer, on thy balmly breast I lean,
And care not how the moralist toils or talks;
Repose and Beauty preach a gospel too,
Deep as that sterner creed the Apostles knew.

Is there no praise of God amid the bowers
Of summer idleness? Still must we toil
And think, and tease the conscience, and so soil
With over-careful fingering the flowers
That blow within the garden of the heart?
Still must we be machines for grinding out
Thin prayers and moralisms? Much I doubt,
Pale priest of a thorn-girded church, thy part
Is small in this wide breathing universe.
Least can I find thy title and thy worth
Here, where with myriad chords the musical earth
Is rhyming to the enraptured poet's verse.
Better thy cowl befits thy cloister's gloom;
It's shadow blots the garden and its bloom.

15. Henry D. Thoreau (1817–1862)

Poems

[Thoreau began writing verse after leaving Harvard in 1837; all those published in *The Dial* were written between 1837 and 1841. "Sic Vita" he tied to a bunch of violets and tossed into a window for Mrs. Lucy Brown, who showed it to Emerson. This was probably the beginning of Emerson's interest in Thoreau as a writer; for three years before Thoreau published anything, Emerson stoutly insisted that Thoreau was a real poet—"who writes genuine poetry that rarest product of New England wit." One of his reasons for starting *The Dial* was that Thoreau could be heard: "My Henry Thoreau will be a great poet for such a company, and one of these days for all companies."

Margaret Fuller did not estimate Thoreau so highly and rejected his manuscripts; those published under her editorship were generally at Emerson's urging. "Sympathy," in the first number (I, 71–72), was written in June 1839 when Thoreau met the eleven-year-old Edmund Sewall, brother of the Ellen Sewall with whom Thoreau was in love. "Stanzas" was published in January 1841 and "Sic Vita" in July (I, 314; II, 81). "The Inward Morning" and "Free Love"— which are Thoreau's best verse—appeared under Emerson's editorship, in October 1842 (III, 198–199). They are efforts to turn the Transcendental epistemology into poetry, as were the poems of Cranch and Hedge.]

SYMPATHY

Lately alas I knew a gentle boy,
Whose features all were cast in Virtue's mould,
As one she had designed for Beauty's toy,
But after manned him for her own stronghold.

On every side he open was as day,
That you might see no lack of strength within,
For walls and ports do only serve alway
For a pretence to feebleness and sin.

Say not that Caesar was victorious,
With toil and strife who stormed the House of Fame;
In other sense this youth was glorious,
Himself a kingdom wheresoe'er he came.

No strength went out to get him victory,
When all was income of its own accord;

For where he went none other was to see,
But all were parcel of their noble lord.

He forayed like the subtle breeze of summer,
That stilly shows fresh landscapes to the eyes,
And revolutions worked without a murmur,
Or rustling of a leaf beneath the skies.

So was I taken unawares by this,
I quite forgot my homage to confess;
Yet now am forced to know, though hard it is,
I might have loved him, had I loved him less.

Each moment, as we nearer drew to each,
A stern respect withheld us farther yet,
So that we seemed beyond each other's reach,
And less acquainted than when first we met.

We two were one while we did sympathize,
So could we not the simplest bargain drive;
And what avails it now that we are wise,
If absence doth this doubleness contrive?

Eternity may not the chance repeat,
But I must tread my single way alone,
In sad remembrance that we once did meet,
And know that bliss irrevocably gone.

The spheres henceforth my elegy shall sing,
For elegy has other subject none;
Each strain of music in my ears shall ring
Knell of departure from that other one.

Make haste and celebrate my tragedy;
With fitting strain resound ye woods and fields;
Sorrow is dearer in such case to me
Than all the joys other occasion yields.

Is 't then too late the damage to repair?
Distance, forsooth, from my weak grasp hath reft

The empty husk, and clutched the useless tare,
But in my hands the wheat and kernel left.

If I but love that virtue which he is,
Though it be scented in the morning air,
Still shall we be dearest acquaintances,
Nor mortals know a sympathy more rare.

STANZAS

Nature doth have her dawn each day,
  But mine are far between;
Content, I cry, for sooth to say,
  Mine brightest are, I ween.

For when my sun doth deign to rise,
  Though it be her noontide,
Her fairest field in shadow lies,
  Nor can my light abide.

Sometimes I bask me in her day,
  Conversing with my mate;
But if we interchange one ray,
  Forthwith her heats abate.

Through his discourse I climb and see,
  As from some eastern hill,
A brighter morrow rise to me
  Than lieth in her skill.

As 't were two summer days in one,
  Two Sundays come together,
Our rays united make one Sun,
  With fairest summer weather.

SIC VITA

I am a parcel of vain strivings tied
  By a chance bond together,
Dangling this way and that, their links

Were made so loose and wide,
                    Methinks,
    For milder weather.

A bunch of violets without their roots,
    And sorrel intermixed,
  Encircled by a wisp of straw
    Once coiled about their shoots,
                    The law
    By which I'm fixed.

A nosegay which Time clutched from out
    Those fair Elysian fields,
  With weeds and broken stems, in haste,
    Doth make the rabble rout
                    That waste
    The day he yields.

And here I bloom for a short hour unseen,
    Drinking my juices up,
  With no root in the land
    To keep my branches green,
                    But stand
    In a bare cup.

Some tender buds were left upon my stem
    In mimicry of life,
  But ah! the children will not know
    Till time has withered them,
                    The wo
    With which they're rife.

But now I see I was not plucked for nought,
    And after in life's vase
  Of glass set while I might survive,
    But by a kind hand brought
                    Alive
    To a strange place.

That stock thus thinned will soon redeem its hours,
    And by another year

Such as God knows, with freer air,
  More fruits and fairer flowers
        Will bear,
  While I droop here.

THE INWARD MORNING

Packed in my mind lie all the clothes
  Which outward nature wears,
And in its fashion's hourly change
  It all things else repairs.

In vain I look for change abroad,
  And can no difference find,
Till some new ray of peace uncalled
  Illumes my inmost mind.

What is it gilds the trees and clouds,
  And paints the heavens so gay,
But yonder fast abiding light
  With its unchanging ray?

Lo, when the sun streams through the wood
  Upon a winter's morn,
Where'er his silent beams intrude
  The murky night is gone.

How could the patient pine have known
  The morning breeze would come,
Or humble flowers anticipate
  The insect's noonday hum?

Till the new light with morning cheer
  From far streamed through the aisles,
And nimbly told the forest trees
  For many stretching miles.

I've heard within my inmost soul
  Such cheerful morning news,
In the horizon of my mind
  Have seen such orient hues,

As in the twilight of the dawn,
  When the first birds awake,
Are heard within some silent wood,
  Where they the small twigs break,

Or in the eastern skies are seen,
  Before the sun appears,
The harbingers of summer heats
  Which from afar he bears.

FREE LOVE

My love must be as free
  As is the eagle's wing,
Hovering o'er land and sea
  And every thing.

I must not dim my eye
  In thy saloon,
I must not leave my sky
  And nightly moon.

Be not the fowler's net
  Which stays my flight,
And craftily is set
  T' allure the sight,

But be the favoring gale
  That bears me on,
And still doth fill my sail
  When thou art gone.

I cannot leave my sky
  For thy caprice,
True love would soar as high
  As heaven is.

The eagle would not brook
  Her mate thus won,
Who trained his eye to look
  Beneath the sun.

16. Margaret Fuller (1810–1850)

A Dialogue

[Margaret Fuller responded to the Transcendental excitement by attempting, as did the others, to write poetry. Her effusions are not memorable. This lyric, from the first issue of *The Dial* (I, 134), is worth preserving, not only as a fair sample of the average level of Transcendental verse, but also for its startling use of a highly charged sexual imagery, a manner often employed by poets in the group. Whether they did this in innocence, or as part of their effort to extend the boundaries of American literature, is a question which students will have to resolve for themselves.]

DAHLIA

My cup already doth with light o'errun.
    Descend, fair sun;
I am all crimsoned for the bridal hour,
    Come to thy flower.

THE SUN

Ah, if I pause, my work will not be done,
    On I must run,
The mountains wait.—I love thee, lustrous flower,
    But give to love no hour.

17. Ellen Sturgis Hooper (1815–1841)

I Slept, and Dreamed That Life Was Beauty

[Ellen Sturgis was born in Boston and married a physician, Robert Hooper. Margaret Fuller wrote from Rome in 1849, "I have seen in Europe no woman more gifted by nature than she." The lyric appeared in the first number of *The Dial* (I, 123); it was universally admired among the Transcendental fraternity. Considering the temper of America at the time and the scorn which solid businessmen and industrialists would feel for verse of this character, the publication, and the admiration, of it can be viewed as one of the ways in which *The Dial* endeavored to go against the materialistic current of American life.]

I slept, and dreamed that life was Beauty;
I woke, and found that life was Duty.
Was thy dream then a shadowy lie?

Toil on, sad heart, courageously,
And thou shalt find thy dream to be
A noonday light and truth to thee.

18. Caroline Sturgis Tappan (1818–1888)
Poems

[Born in Boston, a sister of Ellen Sturgis Hooper, Caroline was an intimate friend of Margaret Fuller and a confidante of Emerson. She was a woman of
great charm. Her poetry joined the protest of Transcendentalism against an America where things were in the saddle. The best two of her poems were published in
The Dial for October 1840 (I, 195, 217–218).]

LIFE

Greatly to Be
Is enough for me,
Is enough for thee.

Why for work art thou striving,
Why seek'st thou for aught?
To the soul that is living
All things shall be brought.

What thou art thou wilt do,
And thy work will be true.

But how can I Be
Without labor or love?
Life comes not to me
As to calm gods above.

Not only above
May spirit be found,
The sunshine of love
Streams all around.

The sun does not say,
"I will not shine
Unless every ray
Falls on planets divine."

He shines upon dust,
Upon things mean and low,
His own inward thought
Maketh him glow.

LYRIC

The stars coldly glimmer—
    And I am alone.
The pale moon grows dimmer,
    And now it has gone.
Loud shrieks the owl, night presses round,
The little flowers lie low on the ground
    And sadly moan.

Why is the earth so sad?
    Why doth she weep?
Methinks she would be glad
    Calmly to sleep.
But the dews are falling, heavy and fast,
Sadly sighs the cold night-blast,
    Loud roars the deep.

I press my hands upon my heart,—
    'Tis very cold!
And swiftly through the forest dart
    With footsteps bold.
What shall I seek? Where shall I go?
Earth and ocean shudder with woe!
    Their tale is untold!

19. Margaret Fuller (1810–1850)
A Record of Impressions

[One of the really gallant—but at the same time pathetic—endeavors of
the Transcendental fellowship was to act as if society in America had already
achieved among the arts the maturity of a London and Paris. They strove by might
and main to talk not only of literature—which they could read extensively—but of
painting, architecture, sculpture, and music as though they were perfectly at home
with them. Actually, unless they could go to Europe, they knew of sculpture only

the plaster casts in the Athenaeum, of architecture only what they could read, of painting little or nothing, and of music only what a few amateur orchestras could manage to perform. Yet the heroism of *The Dial* is in no way more evident than in the aplomb with which it treated these subjects or reviewed such exhibitions and concerts as Boston could then afford, for all the world as though these cultural events were established features of Boston life.

Washington Allston, having returned from years abroad in the great world, gave an exhibition of his paintings in the summer of 1839. Margaret Fuller went and adored. In the first issue of *The Dial* (I, 73–84) she took upon herself to be an art critic—although what she was bound to reveal was her confusion and ignorance before an art form with which her experience had been pitifully limited. What does come through is the charming intoxication of these children of the Puritans at being at last permitted even to discuss painting, and at trying to play the critic.]

This is a record of impressions. It does not aspire to the dignity of criticism. The writer is conscious of an eye and taste, not sufficiently exercised by study of the best works of art, to take the measure of one who has a claim to be surveyed from the same platform. But, surprised at finding that an exhibition, intended to promote thought and form the tastes of our public, has called forth no expression of what it was to so many, who almost daily visited it; and believing that comparison and discussion of the impressions of individuals is the best means to ascertain the sum of the whole, and raise the standard of taste, I venture to offer what, if not true in itself, is at least true to the mind of one observer, and may lead others to reveal more valuable experiences.

Whether the arts can ever be at home among us; whether the desire now manifested to cultivate them be not merely one of our modes of imitating older nations; or whether it springs from a need of balancing the bustle and care of daily life by the unfolding of our calmer and higher nature, it is at present difficult to decide. If the latter, it is not by unthinking repetition of the technics of foreign connoisseurs, or by a servile reliance on the judgment of those, who assume to have been formed by a few hasty visits to the galleries of Europe, that we shall effect an object so desirable, but by a faithful recognition of the feelings naturally excited by works of art, not indeed flippant, as if our raw, uncultivated nature was at once competent to appreciate those finer manifestations of nature, which slow growths of ages and peculiar aspects of society have occasionally brought out, to testify to us what we may and should be. We know it is not so; we know that if such works are to be assimilated at all by those who are not under the influences that produced them, it must be by gradually educating us to their own level. But it is not blind faith that will educate us, that will open the depths and clear the eye of the mind, but an examination which cannot be too close, if made in the spirit of reverence and love . . .

The calm and meditative cast of these pictures, the beauty that shone *through* rather than *in* them, and the harmony of coloring were as unlike anything else I saw, as the Vicar of Wakefield to Cooper's novels. I seemed to recognise in painting that self-possessed elegance, that transparent depth, which I most admired in literature; I thought with delight that such a man as this had been able to grow up in our bustling, reasonable community, that he had kept his foot upon the ground, yet never lost sight of the rose-clouds of beauty floating above him. I saw, too, that he had not been troubled, but possessed his own soul with the blandest patience; and I hoped, I scarce know what, probably the *mot d'enigme* for which we are all looking. How the poetical mind can live and work in peace and good faith! how it may unfold to its due perfection in an unpoetical society! . . .

Yet, probably, I am too little aware of the difficulties the artist encounters, before he can produce anything excellent, fully to appreciate the greatness he has shown. Here, as elsewhere, I suppose the first question should be, What ought we to expect under the circumstances?

There is no poetical ground-work ready for the artist in our country and time. Good deeds appeal to the understanding. Our religion is that of the understanding. We have no old established faith, no hereditary romance, no such stuff as Catholicism, Chivalry afforded. What is most dignified in the Puritanic modes of thought is not favorable to beauty. The habits of an industrial community are not propitious to delicacy of sentiment.

He, who would paint human nature, must content himself with selecting fine situations here and there; and he must address himself, not to a public which is not educated to prize him, but to the small circle within the circle of men of taste.

If, like Wilkie or Newton, he paints direct from nature, only selecting and condensing, or choosing light and draperies, I suppose he is as well situated now as he could ever have been; but if, like Mr. Allston, he aims at the Ideal it is by no means the same. He is in danger of being sentimental and picturesque, rather than spiritual and noble. Mr. Allston has not fallen into these faults; and if we can complain, it is never of blemish or falsity, but of inadequacy. Always he has a high purpose in what he does, never swerves from his aim, but sometimes fails to reach it . . .

The Italian shepherd boy is seated in a wood. The form is almost nude, and the green glimmer of the wood gives the flesh the polished whiteness of marble. He is very beautiful, this boy; and the beauty, as Mr. Allston loves it best, has not yet unfolded all its leaves. The heart of the flower is still a perfumed secret. He sits as if he could sit there forever, gracefully lost in reverie, steeped, if we may judge from his mellow brown eye, in the present loveliness of nature, in the dimly anticipated ecstacies of love.

Every part of nature has its peculiar influences. On the hill top one is roused, in the valley soothed, beside the waterfall absorbed. And in the wood, who has not, like this boy, walked as far as the excitement of exercise would carry him, and then, with "blood listening in his frame," and heart brightly awake, seated himself on such a bank. At first he notices everything, the clouds doubly soft, the sky deeper blue, as seen shimmering through the leaves, the fyttes of golden light seen through the long glades, the skimming of a butterfly ready to light on some starry wood-flower, the nimble squirrel peeping archly at him, the flutter and wild notes of the birds, the whispers and sighs of the trees,—gradually he ceases to mark any of these things, and becomes lapt in the Elysian harmony they combine to form. Who has ever felt this mood understands why the observant Greek placed his departed great ones in groves. While during this trance he hears the harmonies of Nature, he seems to become her and she him; it is truly the mother in the child, and the Hamadryads look out with eyes of tender twilight approbation from their beloved and loving trees. Such an hour lives for us again in this picture.

20. Sophia Dana Ripley (died 1861)
Painting and Sculpture

[Philosophizing about the nature of art was one of the more enthralling liberties to which Transcendentalism and *The Dial* invited their adherents. If it had to be done in ignorance of European galleries and museums, at least there was the compensation that for the first time in America it could even be undertaken, and that there was at least one journal which would print it. But of course much of the effort would need to be expended in demonstrating to the satisfaction of the New England conscience that these arts—upon which the Puritans had long looked with open distrust—were basically moral and noble. In the sensational aesthetic this might be difficult to prove, but by the Transcendental doctrine, Sophia Ripley, the wife of George Ripley, could find a high dedication for painting and sculpture. She published this paper in *The Dial* for July 1841 (II, 78–81).]

Such are the limitations of humanity that inequality is a proof of the inspiration of our work, perhaps also of our life. We are vessels too frail to receive the divine influx, except in small measure, at wide intervals; hence the patched up nature, the flagging and halting of an epic, often of a drama of high merit.

Goethe has said that "art has its origin in the effort of the individual to preserve himself from the destroying power of the whole." This for the origin of the useful arts seems an adequate explanation, but not for the fine arts; for if any one thing constitutes the difference between the two, is it not that the useful resist nature, and the others work with it and idealize it? Architecture, as it arises protectingly against the unfriendly external powers, takes a lower place than the other fine arts, and at its commencement can hardly be considered as one of them. It is hardly a satisfactory definition of art, though nearly allied to Goethe's, that it perpetuates what is fleeting in nature; not even of statuary, which snatches the attitude and expression of the moment, and fixes it forever.

I have been watching the flight of birds over a meadow near me, not as an augur, but as a lover of nature. A certain decorousness, and precision, about their delicate course has, for the first time, struck my eye. They are free and bold—but not alone free and bold. Perhaps perfect freedom for man would have the same result, if he grew up in it, and did not ruffle his plumage by contending for it. If it were his unalienable birthright, and not his hard-earned acquisition, would he not wear it gracefully, gently, reservedly? Poor human being, all education is adjusting fetters to thy delicate limbs, and all true manhood is the strife to burst them; happy art thou, if aught remains to thee but strength!

In the days of Michel Angelo, perhaps even in the earlier time of Grecian Art, certainly often since, the question has been discussed of the comparative dignity of Painting and Sculpture. The generous critic shrinks from the use of the words higher and lower, when applied to art, and yet I sometimes feel that these terms of comparison are among the limitations to which we must submit, while we continue human, as we accept our bodies and language itself, availing ourselves of them as best we may, until we gain that mount of vision, from which nothing is high nor low nor great nor small. Doubtless for everything that is gained something is lost, and yet if the thing gained is more than the lost, then comes in legitimately the idea of superiority. In my lonely hours of thought, I love to substitute, for these objectionable terms of comparison, those of means and ends, results, causes and effects, and so forth, and though deeply conscious of my ignorance on the subject of Art, I have often thought of the relation of its different departments to each other, and always end with the conclusion that Sculpture is the result of all the other arts, the lofty interpreter of them all; not in the order of time, but in the truer one of affinities. Phidias sits by the side of Plato uttering in marble, as his brother philosopher in words, his profound interpretation of all that had gone before, the result of his deep penetration into what Greece had acted, Homer sung, and Aeschylus and Sophocles elevated into the region of sculpture and philosophy. The Homeric poem, the Orphic hymn, the Delphic temple, the Persian war, each was entire of itself, and contained within itself the hint, the germ of all that after time might ever be, but it waited the sculptor's touch, the sage's insight, to tell its history, to detect its immortality, to transmute it from an historical fact to a prophecy. The preparatory art of painting probably existed too in Greece, as certainly as the epic and the drama, though the traces of this art are faint in her history, for painting is the epic poem, the drama, uttering itself in another form, and the soil that produces one will produce the other. My theory is confirmed to me by the experience of life. With every individual, after the feeling that prompts to action has died away, and the action is achieved, the mind pauses, and without any conscious reviewing of the details of experience, looks with quiet eye into its present state, which is the result of all before. This state of lofty contemplation, of deepening knowledge of oneself and the universe, is the end for which feeling warms and action strengthens the intellect. He that doeth shall know. Love prompted the divine essence to pass into the varied existence of this fair outward creation. Then followed the pause, and the sentence passed in the three words, "it is good," contains all that the highest thought has since discovered of the universe in which we dwell. Sculpture is the pause of art in the swift current of the life of nations, which is depicted glowing in the drama and on canvas; poetry and color idealizing it somewhat for its master's hand. The drama and painting are transfigured by philosophy and sculpture, as the human countenance by death. The departing soul, in the pause between its two lives, impresses itself as it never did before on the form of our friend. We read in this last impress the interpretation of its past history, the clear prophecy of its high possibilities, always deciphered confusedly before amid the changing hues, the varying lights and shadows of its distracted earthly life.

It seems to me that sculpture has not completed its circle. It is finished for Grecian life, and so is philosophy; but the modern world, modern life, is yet to be stamped with the seal of both. The materials for a future philosophy will be less pure and simple, but richer and more varied than those of the elder world. There can be no pure epic, no single motive for a nation's action, no severely chaste drama (almost approaching sculpture in its simplicity), no bursting forth of burning lyric, one gush from the soul in its primal freshness. Modern life is too complicated for this, but a nobler and sterner sculpture in words or marble, than our race has yet known, may be in reserve for it,—gifted with a restoring power that may bring it back to unity. Jesus loved and lived, then came the pause—It is finished. This little sentence summed up all the agitated moments of his yet unrecorded individual earthly history. The Plato of *Christianity* is yet waited for. "The hands of color and design" have reproduced to Christendom every event of Jesus's sacred history, working in the church and for the church. Will the gazing world wait in vain for the Christian Phidias, who shall lift this history out of the dim twilight of experience, and plant it in marble for eternity?

The old fable of the stones arising and forming themselves into noble structures at the sound of the lyre, has been used to prove that Music and Architecture are sister arts. Does it not prove quite the reverse, that Architecture arose at the bidding of Music, is kindred, but inferior, not a vassal or equal, but an humble friend, unless the Scripture announcement holds good in arts as in the moral world—let him that is greatest among you be as a servant?

21. John Sullivan Dwight (1813–1893)
Music

[Born in Boston and graduated from Harvard in 1832, Dwight had a natural, untrained, and profound love of music; as an undergraduate he was active in the Pierian Sodality, but in New England of that time there was no place for a mere musician to go and no living to be made from music. Dwight went to the Divinity School, where he became a close friend of Parker and Cranch. He read German fluently and for Ripley's *Specimens* translated lyrics of Goethe and Schiller. He was ordained at Northampton, but could stand the ministry for only a year; he occupied temporary pulpits, then dropped out of a profession which he could not find congenial.

Becoming an ardent associationist, he went to Brook Farm, where he organized the musical activities that were part of the charm of the idyllic years. Finally he became the pioneer musical journalist of America, editing from 1852 to 1881

Dwight's Journal of Music, the importance of which in forming American musical taste can hardly be exaggerated.

To *The Dial* Dwight contributed reviews of musical events, similar to Margaret Fuller's comments on painting, which treated the fragmentary seasons as though they constituted a full fare. For Elizabeth Peabody's *Aesthetic Papers* (pp. 25–36) he wrote in 1849 a theoretical explanation of music which perfectly expresses the Transcendental method of dealing with art in general.]

Music is both body and soul, like the man who delights in it. Its body is beauty in the sphere of sound,—*audible beauty.* But in this very word *beauty* is implied a soul, a moral end, a meaning of some sort, a something which makes it of interest to the inner life of man, which relates it to our invisible and real self. This beauty, like all other, results from the marriage of a spiritual fact with a material form, from the rendering external, and an object of sense, what lives in essence only in the soul. Here the material part, which is measured sound, is the embodiment and sensible representative, as well as the re-acting cause, of that which we call impulse, sentiment, feeling, the spring of all our action and expression. In a word, it is the language of the heart;—not an arbitrary and conventional representative, as a spoken or written word is; but a natural, invariable, pure type and correspondence. Speech, so far as it is distinct from music, sustains the same relation to the head. Speech is the language of ideas, the communicator of thought, the Mercury of the intellectual Olympus enthroned in each of us. But behind all thought, there is something deeper, and much nearer life. Thought is passive, involuntary, cold, varying with what it falls upon like light, a more or less clear-sighted guide to us, but not a prompting energy, and surely not our very essence; not the source either of any single act, or that whole complex course and habit of action which we call our character. Thought has no impulse in itself, any more than the lungs have. "Out of the *heart* are the issues of life." Its loves, its sentiments, its passions, its prompting impulses, its irresistible attractions, its warm desires and aspirations,—these are the masters of the intellect, if not its law; these people the blank consciousness with thoughts innumerable; these, though involuntary in one sense, are yet the principle of will in us, and are the spring of all activity, and of all thought too, since they, in fact, strike out the light they see to act by. The special moments and phases of this active principle we call emotions; and music, which I hold to be its natural language, has for its very root and first principle, and is actually born from, motion.

Sound is generated by motion; rhythm is measured motion; and this is what distinguishes music from every other art of expression. Painting, sculpture, architecture, are all quiescent: they address us in still contemplation. But music is all motion, and it is nothing else.

And so in its effects. It does not rest, that we may contemplate it; but it hurries us away with it. Our very first intimation of its presence is, that we are moved by it. Its thrilling finger presses down some secret spring within us, and instantly the soul is on its feet with an emotion. Painting and sculpture rather give the idea of an emotion, than directly move us; and, if speech can raise or quell a passion, it is because there is kneaded into all speech a certain leaven of the divine fire called music. The same words and sentences convey new impressions with every honest change of tone and modulation in the speaker's voice; and, when he rises to any thing like eloquence, there is a certain buoyant rhythmical substratum of pure tone on which his words ride, as the ship rides on the ocean, borrowing its chief eloquence from that. Take out the consonants which break up his speech, and the vowels flow on musically. How often will the murmur of a devout prayer overcome a remote hearer with more of a religious feeling, than any apprehension of the distinct words could, if he stood nearer!

Music is a universal language, subtly penetrating all the walls of time and space. It is no more local than the mathematics, which are its impersonal reason, just as sound is its body, and feeling or passion is its soul. The passions of the human heart are radically alike, and answer to the same tones everywhere and always, except as they may be undeveloped; and music has a power to develope them, like an experience of life. It can convey a foretaste of moods and states of feeling yet in reserve for the soul, of loves which yet have never met an object that could call them out. A musical composition is the best expression of its author's inmost life. No persons in all history are so intimately known to those that live away from them or after them, as are Handel, Mozart, Beethoven, Weber, Schubert, Bellini, and others, to those who enter into the spirit of their musical works. For they have each bequeathed the very wine of his peculiar life in this form, that it sparkles still the same as often as it is opened to the air. The sounds may effervesce in each performance; but they may be woke to life again at any time. So it is with the passions and emotions which first dictated melodious creations . . .

Music is religious and prophetic. She is the real Sibyl, chanting evermore of unity. Over wild, waste oceans of discord floats her silvery voice, the harbinger of love and hope. Every genuine strain of music is a serene prayer, or bold, inspired demand, to be united with all, at the Heart of things. Her appeal to the world is more loving than the world can yet appreciate. Kings and statesmen, and men of affairs, and men of theories, would stand aside from their own over-rated occupations to listen to her voice, if they knew how nearly it concerned them, how much more it goes to the bottom of the matter, and how clearly she forefeels humanity's great destiny. The soul that is truly receptive of music learns angelic wisdom, and grows more child-like with experience. The sort of experience which music gives does not plough cunning furrows in the brow of the fresh soul, nor darken its expressive face by knitting there the tangled lines of Satan. Here, the most deeply initiated are in spirit the most youthful; and Hope delights to wait on them.

The native impulses of the soul, or what are variously called the passions, affections, propensities, desires, are, all of them, when considered in their essence and original unwarped tendency, so many divinely implanted loves. Union, harmony of some sort, is their very life. To meet, to unite, to blend, by methods intricate as swift, is their whole business and effort through eternity. As is their attraction, such must be their destiny; not to collision, not to excess followed by exhaustion; not to discord, chaos, and confusion; but to binding ties of fitness and conjunction through all spheres, from the simplest to the most universal accords. Through these (how else?) are the hearts of the human race to be knit into one mutually conscious, undivided whole, one living temple not too narrow, nor too fragmentary for the reception of the Spirit of God. Is not this foretold in music, the natural language of these passions, which cannot express corruption nor any evil feeling, without ceasing to be music; which has no tone for any bad passion, and translates into harmony and beauty whatever it expresses? The blending of all these passions harmoniously into one becomes the central love, the deepest and most undivided life of man. This is the love of God, as it also, from the first, is the inbreathing of God, who is love; to whom the soul seeks its way, by however blind an instinct, through all these partial harmonies, learning by degrees to understand the universal nature of its desire and aim. The sentiment of unity, the strongest and deepest sentiment of which man is capable, the great affection into which all his affections flow—to find, not lose themselves; which looks to the source when little wants conflict, and straightway they are reconciled in emulous ardor for the glory of the whole; which lifts a man above the thought of self, by making him in every sense fully himself, by reuniting his prismatic, party-colored passions into one which is as clear and universal as the light; the sentiment which seeks only universal harmony and order, so that all things, whether of the inner or of the outer world, may be perfectly transparent to the love in which they have their being, and that the sole condition of all peace and happiness, the consciousness of one in all and all in one, may never more be wanting;—that is what the common sense of mankind means by the *religious* sentiment,—that is the pure essence of religion. Music is its natural language, the chief rite of its worship, the rite which cannot lose its sacredness; for music cannot cease to be harmony, cannot cease to symbolize the sacred relationship of each to all, cannot contract a taint, any more than the sunbeam which shines into all corners. Music cannot narrow or cloak the message which it bears; it cannot lie; it cannot raise questions in the mind, or excite any other than a pure enthusiasm. It is God's alphabet, and not man's; unalterable and unpervertible; suited for the harmony of the human passions and affections; and sent us, in this their long winter of disharmony and strife, to be a perpetual type and monitor, rather say an actual foretaste, of that harmony which must yet come. How could there be religion without music? That sentiment would create it again, would evoke its elements out of the completest jargon of discords, if the scale and the accords, and all the use of instruments, were forgotten. Let that feeling deepen in our nation, and absorb its individual ambitions, and we shall have our music greater than the world has known . . .

It is not alone in the music of the church of any form, whether mass or plainer choral, that this sentiment is strongest. Perhaps no music ever stirred profounder depths in the hearer's religious consciousness, than some great orchestral symphonies, say those of Beethoven. Even a waltz of his, it has been said, is more religious than a prayer of Rossini's. His symphonies are like great conflagrations of some grand piles of architecture, in which the material substance seems consumed, while the spirit soars in the graceful but impatient crackling shapes of the devouring element, and is swiftly lost in upper air.

23. Theodore Parker (1810–1860)
The Writings of Ralph Waldo Emerson

[In 1847 Parker organized a group of contributors, some of whom were not particularly Transcendentalists, to conduct a new magazine, *The Massachusetts Quarterly Review,* which lasted three years. Parker always held *The Dial* in considerable scorn, and announced that his *Quarterly* was to be "*The Dial* with a beard." Devoted mainly to reform and scholarship, the *Quarterly* does not figure greatly in the history of American literature, but some of its reviews are the most distinguished of the time. For the March 1850 issue (III, 200–255), Parker wrote the best of contemporaneous estimates of Emerson, which is not only a critique of the writer but a resumé of the literary creed of the movement as a whole.]

It is now almost fourteen years since Mr. Emerson published his first book: Nature. A beautiful work it was and will be deemed for many a year to come. In this old world of literature, with more memory than wit, with much tradition and little invention, with more fear than love, and a great deal of criticism upon very little poetry, there came forward this young David, a shepherd, but to be a king, "with his garlands and singing robes about him"; one note upon his new and fresh-strung lyre was "worth a thousand men." Men were looking for something original, they always are; when it came, some said it thundered, others that an angel had spoke. How men wondered at the little book! It took nearly twelve years to sell the five hundred copies of Nature. Since that time Mr. Emerson has said much, and if he has not printed many books, at least has printed much; some things far surpassing the first essay, in richness of material, in perfection of form, in continuity of thought; but nothing which has the same youthful freshness, and the same tender beauty as this early violet, blooming out of Unitarian and Calvinistic sand or snow. Poems and essays of a later date, are there, which show that he has had more time and woven it into life; works which present us with thought deeper, wider, richer, and more complete, but not surpassing the simplicity and loveliness of that maiden flower of his poetic spring . . .

All of Mr. Emerson's literary works, with the exception of the Poems, were published before they were printed; delivered by word of mouth to various audiences. In frequently reading his pieces, he had an opportunity to see any defect of form and amend it. Mr. Emerson has won by his writings a more desirable reputation, than any other man of letters in America has yet attained. It is not the reputation which brings him money or academic honors, or membership of learned societies; nor does it appear conspicuously in the literary Journals as yet. But he has a high place among thinking men, on both sides of the water; we think no man who writes the English tongue has now so much influence in forming the opinions and character of young men and women. His audience steadily increases, at home and abroad, more rapidly in England than America. It is now with him as it was, at first, with Dr. Channing; the fairest criticism has come from the other side of the water; the reason is that he, like his predecessor, offended the sectarian and party spirit, the personal prejudices of the men about him; his life was a reproach to them, his words an offence, or his doctrines alarmed their sectarian, their party, or their personal pride, and they accordingly condemned the man. A writer who should bear the same relation to the English mind as Emerson to ours, for the same reason would be more acceptable here than at home. Emerson is neither a sectarian nor a partisan, no man less so; yet few men in America have been visited with more hatred,—private personal hatred, which the authors poorly endeavored to conceal, and perhaps did hide from themselves. The spite we have heard expressed against him, by men of the common morality, would strike a stranger with amazement, especially when it is remembered that his personal character and daily life are of such extraordinary loveliness. This hatred has not proceeded merely from ignorant men, in whom it could easily be excused; but more often from men who have had opportunities of obtaining as good a culture as men commonly get in this country. Yet while he has been the theme of vulgar abuse, of sneers and ridicule in public, and in private; while critics, more remarkable for the venom of their poison than the strength of their bow, have shot at him their little shafts, barbed more than pointed, he has also drawn about him some of what old Drayton called "the idle smoke of praise." Let us see what he has thrown into the public fire to cause this incense; what he has done to provoke the immedicable rage of certain other men; let us see what there is in his works, of old or new, true or false, what American and what cosmopolitan; let us weigh his works with such imperfect scales as we have, weigh them by the universal standard of Beauty, Truth and Love, and make an attempt to see what he is worth . . .

Mr. Emerson is the most American of our writers. The Idea of America, which lies at the bottom of our original institutions, appears in him with great prominence. We mean the idea of personal freedom, of the dignity and value of human nature, the superiority of a man to the accidents of a man. Emerson is the most republican of republicans, the most protestant of the dissenters. Serene as a July sun, he is equally fearless. He looks every thing in the face modestly, but with earnest scrutiny, and passes judgment upon its merits. Nothing is too high for his examination; nothing too sacred. On earth only one thing he finds which is thoroughly venerable, and that is the nature of man; not the accidents, which make a man rich or famous, but the substance, which makes him a man. The man is before the institutions of man; his nature superior to his history. All finite things are only appendages of man, useful, convenient, or beautiful. Man is master, and nature his slave, serving for many a varied use. The results of human experience—the state, the church, society, the family, business, literature, science, art—all of these are subordinate to man: if they serve the individual, he is to foster them, if not, to abandon them and seek better things. He looks at all things, the past and the present, the state and the church, Christianity and the market-house, in the daylight of the intellect. Nothing is allowed to stand between him and his manhood. Hence, there is an apparent irreverence; he does not bow to any hat which Gessler has set up for public adoration, but to every man, canonical or profane, who bears the mark of native manliness. He eats show-bread, if he is hungry. While he is the most American, he is almost the most cosmopolitan of our writers, the least restrained and belittled by the popular follies of the nation or the age.

In America, writers are commonly kept in awe and subdued by fear of the richer class, or that of the mass of men. Mr. Emerson has small respect for either; would bow as low to a lackey as a lord, to a clown as a scholar, to one man as a million. He spurns all constitutions but the law of his own nature, rejecting them with manly scorn. The traditions of the churches are no hindrances to his thought; Jesus or Judas were the same to him, if either stood in his way and hindered the proportionate develop- ment of his individual life. The forms of society and the ritual of scholar- ship are no more effectual restraints. His thought of today is no barrier to freedom of thought tomorrow, for his own nature is not to be sub- ordinated, either to the history of man, or his own history. "Tomorrow to fresh fields and pastures new," is his motto.

Yet, with all this freedom, there is no wilful display of it. He is so con- fident of his freedom, so perfectly possessed of his rights, that he does not talk of them. They appear, but are not spoken of. With the hopefulness and buoyant liberty of America, he has none of our ill-mannered boasting. He criticizes America often; he always appreciates it; he seldom praises, and never brags of our country. The most democratic of democrats, no disciple of the old régime is better mannered, for it is only the vulgar democrat or aristocrat who flings his follies in your face. While it would be difficult to find a writer so uncompromising in his adhesion to just principles, there is not in all his works a single jeer or ill-natured sarcasm. None is less ad- dicted to the common forms of reverence, but who is more truly reveren- tial?

While his Idea is American, the form of his literature is not less so. It is a form which suits the substance, and is modified by the institutions and natural objects about him. You see that the author lives in a land with free institutions, with town-meetings and ballot-boxes; in the vicinity of a decaying church; amongst men whose terrible devils are Poverty and Social Neglect, the only devils whose damnation is much cared for. His geography is American. Catskill and the Alleghenies, Monadnock, Wachusett, and the uplands of New Hampshire, appear in poetry or prose; Contocook and Agiochook are better than the Ilyssus, or Pactolus, or "smooth-sliding Mincius, crowned with vocal reeds." New York, Fall River, and Lowell have a place in his writings, where a vulgar Yankee would put Thebes or Paestum. His men and women are American—John and Jane, not Coriolanus and Persephone. He tells of the rhodora, the club-moss, the blooming clover, not of the hibiscus and the asphodel. He knows the humblebee, the blackbird, the bat, and the wren, and is not ashamed to say or sing of the things under his own eyes. He illustrates his high thought by common things out of our plain New England life—the meeting in the church, the Sunday school, the dancing-school, a huckleberry party, the boys and girls hastening home from school, the youth in the shop, beginning an unconscious courtship with his unheeding customer, the farmers about their work in the fields, the bustling trader in the city, the cattle, the new hay, the voters at a town meeting, the village brawler in a tavern full of tipsy riot, the conservative who thinks the nation is lost if his ticket chance to miscarry, the bigot worshipping the knot hole through which a dusty beam of light has looked in upon his darkness, the radical who declares that nothing is good if established, and the patent reformer who screams in your ears that he can finish the world with a single touch,—and out of all these he makes his poetry, or illustrates his philosophy. Now and then he wanders off to other lands, reports what he has seen, but it is always an American report of what an American eye saw. Even Mr. Emerson's recent exaggerated praise of England is such a panegyric as none but an American could bestow . . .

From what has been said, notwithstanding the faults we have found in Emerson, it is plain that we assign him a very high rank in the literature of mankind. He is a very extraordinary man. To no English writer since Milton can we assign so high a place; even Milton himself, great genius though he was, and great architect of beauty, has not added so many thoughts to the treasury of the race; no, nor been the author of so much loveliness. Emerson is a man of genius such as does not often appear, such as has never appeared before in America, and but seldom in the world. He learns from all sorts of men, but no English writer, we think, is so original. We sincerely lament the want of logic in his method, and his exaggeration of the intuitive powers, the unhappy consequences of which we see in some of his followers and admirers. They will be more faithful than he to the false principle which he lays down, and will think themselves wise because they do not study, learned because they are ignorant of books, and inspired because they say what outrages common sense. In Emerson's poetry there is often a ruggedness and want of finish which seems wilful in a man like him. This fault is very obvious in those pieces he has put before his several essays. Sometimes there is a seed-corn of thought in the piece, but the piece itself seems like a pile of rubbish shot out of a cart which hinders the seed from germinating. His admirers and imitators not unfrequently give us only the rubbish and probably justify themselves by the example of their master. Spite of these defects, Mr. Emerson, on the whole, speaks with a holy power which no other man possesses who now writes the English tongue. Others have more readers, are never sneered at by respectable men, are oftener praised in the Journals, have greater weight in the pulpits, the cabinets and the councils of the nation; but there is none whose words so sink into the mind and heart of young men and maids; none who work so powerfully to fashion the character of the coming age. Seeing the power which he exercises, and the influence he is likely to have on generations to come, we are jealous of any fault in his matter, or its form, and have allowed no private and foolish friendship to hinder us from speaking of his faults.

This is his source of strength: his intellectual and moral sincerity. He looks after Truth, Justice, and Beauty. He has not uttered a word that is false to his own mind or conscience; has not suppressed a word because he thought it too high for men's comprehension, and therefore dangerous to the repose of men. He never compromises. He sees the chasm between the ideas which come of man's nature and the institutions which represent only his history; he does not seek to cover up the chasm, which daily grows wider between Truth and Public Opinion, between Justice and the State, between Christianity and the Church; he does not seek to fill it up, but he asks men to step over and build institutions commensurate with their ideas. He trusts himself, trusts man, and trusts God. He has confidence in all the attributes of infinity. Hence he is serene; nothing disturbs the even poise of his character, and he walks erect. Nothing impedes him in his search for the true, the lovely and the good; no private hope, no private fear, no love of wife or child, of gold, or ease, or fame. He never seeks his own reputation; he takes care of his Being, and leaves his seeming to take care of itself. Fame may seek him; he never goes out of his way a single inch for her.

He has not written a line which is not conceived in the interest of mankind. He never writes in the interest of a section, of a party, of a church, of a man, always in the interest of mankind. Hence comes the ennobling influence of his works. Most of the literary men of America, most of the men of superior education, represent the ideas and interests of some party; in all that concerns the welfare of the Human Race, they are proportionably behind the mass who have only the common cultures; so while the thought of the people is democratic, putting man before the accidents of a man, the literature of the nation is aristocratic, and opposed to the welfare of mankind. Emerson belongs to the exceptional literature of the times—and while his culture joins him to the history of man, his ideas and his whole life enable him to represent also the nature of man, and so to write for the future. He is one of the rare exceptions amongst our educated men, and helps redeem American literature from the reproach of imitation, conformity, meanness of aim, and hostility to the progress of mankind. No faithful man is too low for his approval and encouragement; no faithless man too high and popular for his rebuke.

A good test of the comparative value of books, is the state they leave you in. Emerson leaves you tranquil, resolved on noble manhood, fearless of the consequences; he gives men to mankind, and mankind to the laws of God. His position is a striking one. Eminently a child of Christianity and of the American idea, he is out of the Church and out of the State. In the midst of Calvinistic and Unitarian superstition, he does not fear God, but loves and trusts Him. He does not worship the idols of our time—Wealth and Respectability, the two calves set up by our modern Jeroboam. He fears not the damnation these idols have the power to inflict—neither poverty nor social disgrace. In busy and bustling New England comes out this man serene and beautiful as a star, and shining like "a good deed in a naughty world." Reproached as an idler, he is active as the sun, and pours out his radiant truth on Lyceums at Chelmsford, at Waltham, at Lowell, and all over the land. Out of a cold Unitarian Church rose this most lovely light. Here is Boston, perhaps the most humane city in America, with its few noble men and women, its beautiful charities, its material vigor, and its hardy enterprise; commercial Boston, where honor is weighed in the public scales, and justice reckoned by the dollars it brings; conservative Boston, the grave of the Revolution, wallowing in its wealth, yet grovelling for more, seeking only money, careless of justice, stuffed with cotton yet hungry for tariffs, sick with the greedy worm of avarice, loving money as the end of life, and bigots as the means of preserving it; Boston, with toryism in its parlors, toryism in its pulpits, toryism in its press, itself a tory town, preferring the accidents of man to man himself—and amidst it all there comes Emerson, graceful as Phoebus-Apollo, fearless and tranquil as the sun he was supposed to guide, and pours down the enchantment of his light, which falls where'er it may, on dust, on diamonds, on decaying heaps to hasten their rapid rot, on seeds new sown to quicken their ambitious germ, on virgin minds of youth and maids to waken the natural seed of nobleness therein, and make it grow to beauty and to manliness. Such is the beauty of his speech, such the majesty of his ideas, such the power of the moral sentiment in men, and such the impression which his whole character makes on them, that they lend him, everywhere, their ears, and thousands bless his manly thoughts.

9

The Movement: Political and Social

It is not to be denied that the principles of this system, are those of reform in church, state and society, and for this cause they are unpopular . . . We find it working its way everywhere; in governments we find nations in their intercourse adopt rules less exclusive and more Christian. Individual rights are more respected and protected. Education is provided, the comforts of life secured with less partiality. Cruel and sanguinary punishments are dying out. Society shows its influence. Instead of one man born to wealth and education, and ten thousand, his serfs, to ignorance and beggary, the distinctions of rank are fading away, and each is educated, and has a chance in the scramble of life. The work must go on till there shall be no more scrambling or snatching, but a fair and equal chance for each.

—CHARLES MAYO ELLIS

1. George Bancroft (1800–1891)
On the Progress of Civilization

[Born in Worcester, graduated from Harvard in 1817, Bancroft spent the next four years in Europe, where he knew Schleiermacher. He drew his inspiration from the same books and ideas as did the Transcendentalists; in fact, he was a thorough German scholar and a master of German philosophy. Yet he was never one of the Transcendental group, although his relations with Emerson were cordial. Upon his return to America he conducted an experimental school for boys at Round Hill, Northampton (1823–1831); as much as Alcott's schools, it illustrates the potentialities for educational theory implicit in the Transcendental premises. Thereafter Bancroft became a politician, the only one among the Transcendentalists who was prepared to sully his hands by actual party politics; he soon became a power in the Democratic party and so fell out of sympathy with those apostles of the movement who disdained political action.

He published the first volume of his *History of the United States* in 1834, the second in 1837—a book, said Emerson, "whereon all good givers of opinions must purse their lips." Actually, it was as much a declaration of Transcendentalism as any of the proclamations of 1836. When Bancroft came to Fox and the Quaker inner light, he linked them with Kant and the Transcendental literature:

> The professor of Konigsberg, like Fox and Barclay and Penn, derived philosophy from the voice in the soul; like them, he made the oracle within the categorical rule of practical morality, the motive to disinterested virtue; like them, he esteemed the Inner Light, which discerns universal and necessary truths, an element of humanity; and therefore his philosophy claims for humanity the right of ever renewed progress and reform. If the Quakers disguised their doctrine under the form of theology, Kant concealed it for a season under the jargon of a nervous but unusual diction. But Schiller has reproduced the great idea in beautiful verse; Chateaubriand avowed himself its advocate; Coleridge has repeated the doctrine in misty language; it beams through the poetry of Lamartine and Wordsworth; while in the country of beautiful prose, the eloquent Cousin, listening to the same eternal voice which connects humanity with universal reason, has gained wide fame for "the divine principle," and in explaining the harmony between that light and the light of Christianity, has often unconsciously borrowed the language, and employed the arguments of Barclay and Penn.

Bancroft's celebration of the divine principle even included the now regulation attack on Locke, who "derives the idea of infinity from the senses."

But Bancroft was one to whom the great idea did mean, inescapably, progress and reform—not merely self-culture. Hence his associates in the movement were those who likewise found the logic of the position leading to active participation in politics. By 1836 he was a friend of Brownson, who like himself and Ripley had "philosophized himself into democracy." Bancroft was coaching Brownson to the conclusion: "The merchants and the lawyers, that is, the monied interest, broke up feudalism. The day for the multitude has now dawned."

To *The Boston Quarterly Review* for October 1838 (I, 389–407), Bancroft contributed an analysis of the universe as seen by Transcendental theory, uncovering the issue upon which the movement—in so far as it had any coherent form—was to fall asunder. The title was prophetic: "On the Progress of Civilization, or Reasons Why the Natural Association of Men of Letters Is with the Democracy." If Bancroft was correct, the Transcendental metaphysic made reform and democracy the goals of cosmic history.]

THE material world does not change in its masses or in its powers. The stars shine with no more lustre, than when they first sang together in the glory of their birth. The flowers that gemmed the fields and the forests, before America was discovered, now bloom around us in their season. The sun that shone on Homer still shines on us in unchanging lustre. The bow that beamed on the patriarch still glitters in the clouds. Nature is the same. For her no new powers are generated; no new capacities are discovered. The earth turns on its axis, and perfects its revolutions, and renews its seasons, without increase or advancement.

Does the same passive destiny attach to the inhabitants of the earth? Is there for us no increase of capacity; no gathering of intellectual riches? Are the expectations of social improvement a delusion; and the hopes of philanthropy but a dream? Or is there an advancement of the human condition? Can there be progress in the human race? . . .

I. Matter is passive. If at rest it would remain so forever; if set in motion, it continues its unmeaning course, without reason, purpose, or result. The capacity of the human race for improvement is connected with the universal diffusion of the gifts of mind.

The five senses do not constitute the whole inventory of our sources of knowledge. They are the organs by which thought connects itself with the external universe; but the power of thought is not merged in the exercise of its instruments. We have functions which connect us with heaven, as well as organs which set us in relation with earth. We have not merely the senses opening to us the external world, but an internal moral sense, which places us in connexion with the world of intelligence and the decrees of God.

It is the possession of this higher faculty which renders advancement possible. There is *a spirit in man:* not in the privileged few; not in those of us only who by the favor of Providence have been nursed in public schools: IT IS IN MAN: it is the attribute of the race. The spirit, which is the guide to truth, is the gracious gift to each member of the human family; not one is disfranchised; not one is cut off from the heavenly inheritance.

Reason exists within every breast. I mean not that faculty which deduces inferences from the experience of the senses, but that higher faculty, which from the infinite treasures of its own consciousness, originates truth, and assents to it by the force of intuitive evidence; that faculty which raises us beyond the control of time and space, and gives us faith in things eternal and invisible. There is not the difference between one mind and another, which the pride of philosophy might conceive. To Plato or Aristotle, to Leibnitz and Locke, there was no faculty given, no intellectual function conceded, which did not belong to the meanest of their countrymen. In them there could not spring up a truth, which did not equally have its source in the mind of every one. They had not the power of creation: they could but reveal what God has implanted in the breast of every one. On their minds not a truth could dawn, of which the seed did not equally live in every heart . . .

Our age has seen a revolution in works of imagination. The poet has sought his theme in common life. Never is the genius of Scott more pathetic, than when, as in the Antiquary, he delineates the sorrows of a poor fisherman, or as in the Heart of Midlothian, takes his heroine from a cottage. And even Wordsworth, the purest and most original poet of the day, in spite of the inveterate character of his political predilections, has done homage to the spirit of the age. With magic power he has thrown the divine light of genius on the walks of commonest life; he finds a moral in every grave of the village churchyard; he discloses the immense wealth of affection in the humblest minds, the peasant and shepherd, the laborer and artisan; the strolling pedlar is, under the powerful action of his genius, a teacher of the sublimest morality; and the solitary wagoner, the lonely shepherd, and even the feeblest mother of an idiot boy, furnishes the highest lessons in the reverence for Humanity . . .

Here I am met by an interrogation. What! Do you despise learning? Shall one who has spent nearly all his life in schools and universities plead the equality of uneducated nature? Is there no difference between the man of refinement and the savage?

I am a man, said Black Hawk nobly to the chief of the first republic in the world, *I am a man,* said the barbarous chieftain, *and you are another* . . .

If it be true, that the gifts of mind and heart are universally diffused, if the sentiment of truth, justice, love, and beauty exists in every one, then it follows, as a necessary consequence, that the common judgment in politics, morals, character, and taste is the highest authority on earth, and the nearest possible approach to an infallible decision. This inference I dare not avoid; and if from the consideration of individual powers we turn to the action of the human mind in masses, we shall still retain our good hopes for the race.

If reason is a universal faculty, the decision of the common mind is the nearest criterion of truth. The public mind winnows opinions; it is the sieve which separates error from certainty . . .

Time would fail me, were I to pursue this subject in all its bearings. I pass therefore to a point, which has been less considered. The sentiment of beauty, as it exists in the human mind, is the criterion in works of art, inspires the conceptions of genius, and exercises a final judgment on its productions.

For who are the best judges in matters of taste? Do you think the cultivated individual? Undoubtedly not; but the collective mind. The public is wiser than the wisest critic. In Athens, where the arts were carried to perfection, it was done when "the fierce democracie" was in the ascendant; the temple of Minerva and the works of Phidias were invented and perfected to please the common people. When Greece yielded to tyrants, her genius for excellence in arts expired; or rather purity of taste disappeared, because the artist then endeavored to please the individual, and therefore humored his caprice; while before he had endeavored to please the race . . .

If with us the arts are destined to be awakened into a brilliant career, the inspiration must spring from the triumphs of democracy. Genius will not create, to flatter individuals or decorate saloons. It yearns for larger influences; it feeds on wider sympathies; and its perfect display can never exist, except in an appeal to the general sentiment for the beautiful . . .

Who are by way of eminence the poets of all mankind? Surely Homer and Shakspeare. Now Homer formed his taste, as he wandered from door to door, a vagrant minstrel, paying for hospitality by a song; and Shakspeare wrote for an audience, wholly composed of the common people . . .

But it is unnecessary to seek examples in detail. At the revival of letters a distinguishing feature of the rising literature was the employment of the vulgar tongue. Dante used the language of the populace and won immortality; Wickliffe, Luther, and at a later day Descartes, each employed his native language, and carried truth directly to all, who were familiar with its accents. Every beneficent revolution in letters has the character of popularity; every great reform among authors has sprung from the power of the people in its influence on the development and activity of mind.

The same influence continues unimpaired. Scott spurned a drawing-room reputation; the secret of Byron's power lay in part in the harmony which existed between his muse and the democratic tendency of the age; Wordsworth, even in the midst of his passion for a hierarchy, pleads earnestly for the rights of labor. German literature is almost entirely a popular creation. It was fostered by no monarch; it was dandled by no aristocracy. It was plebeian in its origin and manly in its results. "The public," says Schiller, "is my study and my sovereign. Of this and of no other tribunal do I acknowledge the jurisdiction. Its decrees I fear and reverence. My mind is exalted by the intention to submit to no restraints but the invisible decisions of the unbiased world; to know no court of appeals but the soul of Humanity."

The same confidence may exist in the capacity of the human race for political advancement. The absence of the prejudices of the old world leaves us here the opportunity of consulting independent truth; and man is left to apply the instinct of freedom to every social relation and public interest. We have approached so near to nature, that we can hear her gentlest whispers; we have made Humanity our lawgiver and our oracle; and, therefore, principles, which in Europe the wisest receive with distrust, are here the common property of the public mind. The spirit of the nation receives and vivifies every great doctrine, of which the application is required; no matter how abstract it may be in theory, or how remote in its influence, the intelligence of the multitude embraces, comprehends, and enforces it. Freedom of mind, freedom of the seas, freedom of industry, each great truth is firmly grasped; and whenever a great purpose has been held up, or a useful reform proposed, the national mind has calmly, steadily, and irresistibly pursued its aim.

II. A devotion to the cause of mind is therefore a devotion to the cause of Humanity, and assures its progress.

Every great object, connected with the benevolent exertions of the day, has reference to the culture of mind. The moral and intellectual powers are alone become the common inheritance; and every victory in the cause of Humanity is due to the progress of moral and intellectual culture. For this the envoys of religion cross seas, and visit remotest isles; for this the press in its freedom teems with the productions of maturest thought; for this the philanthropist plans new schemes of education; for this halls in every city and village are open to the public instructor. Not that we view with indifference the glorious efforts of material industry; the vast means of internal intercourse; the accumulations of thrifty labor; the varied results of concentrated action. But even here it is mind that achieves the triumph, and that exults in expectation. It is the genius of the architect, that gives beauty to the work of human hands, and makes the temple, the dwelling, or the public edifice an outward representation of the spirit of propriety and order. It is science, that guides the blind zeal of cupidity to the construction of the vast channels of intercourse, which are fast binding the world into one family. And it is as a method of moral improvement, that these increased means of intercourse derive their greatest value. Mind becomes universal property; the poem, that is invented on the soil of England, finds its response on the shores of lake Erie and the banks of the Missouri, and is admired near the sources of the Ganges. The defence of public liberty in our own halls of legislation penetrates the plains of Poland, is echoed along the mountains of Greece, and pierces the darkest night of eastern despotism . . .

It is alone by infusing great principles into the common mind, that revolutions in human society are effected. They never have been, they never can be, effected by superior *individual* excellence. Time will allow but a single illustration. The age of the Antonines is the age of the greatest glory of the Roman empire. Men distinguished by every accomplishment of prowess and science, for a century in succession, possessed undisputed sway over more than a hundred millions of men; till at last, in the person of Mark Aurelian, philosophy herself seemed to mount the throne. And did she stay the downward tendencies of the Roman empire? Did she infuse new elements of life into the decaying constitution? Did she commence one great, beneficent reform? Not one permanent amelioration was effected; philosophy was clothed with absolute power; and yet absolute power accomplished nothing for Humanity. It could accomplish nothing. Had it been possible, Aurelian would have done it. Society can be changed, the human race can be advanced, only by moral principles diffused through the multitude . . .

Paul, who was a Roman citizen, was beheaded, just outside the walls of the eternal city; and Peter, who was a plebeian, and could not claim the distinction of the axe and the block, was executed on the cross, with his head downwards to increase the pain and the indignity. Do you think the Roman emperor took notice of the names of these men, when he signed their death warrant? And yet, as they poured truth into the common mind, what series of kings, what lines of emperors can compare with them, in their influence on the destinies of mankind, in their powerful aid in promoting the progress of the human race?

Yes, reforms in society are only effected through the masses of the people.

III. And such action does take place. Human life has gone forward; the mind of the race has been quickened and edified. New truths have been constantly developed, and, becoming the common property of the human family, they have improved its condition and ensured its progress.

This progress is advanced by every sect, precisely because each sect, to obtain vitality, does of necessity embody a truth. The irresistible tendency of the human race is to advancement. Absolute power has never succeeded in suppressing a single truth. An idea once generated may find its admission into every living breast and live there. Like God it becomes immortal and omnipresent. The tendency of the species is upward, irresistibly upward. The individual is often lost; Providence never disowns the race. The individual is often corrupt; Humanity is redeemed. No principle, once promulgated, has ever been forgotten. No "timely tramp" of a despot's foot ever trod out one idea. The world cannot retrograde; the dark ages cannot return. Dynasties perish; cities are buried; nations have been victims to error, or martyrs for right; Humanity has always been on the advance; its soul has always been gaining maturity and power.

Yes, truth is immortal; it cannot be destroyed; it is invincible, it cannot long be resisted. Not every great principle has yet been generated; but when once developed, it lives without end, in the safe custody of the race. States may pass away; every just principle of legislation which has been once established will endure without end. The ark has mouldered; the tabernacle disappeared; the Urim and the Thummim lost their lustre; but God, who revealed himself on Sinai, is still the God of the living. Jerusalem has fallen, and the very foundations of the temple have been subverted; but Christian truth still lives in the hearts of millions. Do you think that infidelity is spreading? And are you terrified by a handful of skeptics? When did the Gospel of all truth, that redeems, and blesses, and sanctifies the world, live in the hearts of so many millions, as at this moment? The forms under which it is produced may decay; for they, like all that is the work of man's hands, are subject to the changes and chances of mortal being; but the spirit of truth is incorruptible; it may be developed, illustrated, and applied; it never can die; it never can decline.

No truth can perish; no truth can pass away. Succeeding generations transmit to each other the undying flame. Thus the progress of the race is firm and sure. Wherever moral truth has started into being, Humanity claims and guards the bequest. Each generation gathers together the imperishable children of the past, and increases them by new sons of light, alike radiant with immortality.

2. William Henry Channing (1810–1884)

An Ideal of Humanity

[William Henry Channing needed no instruction from Bancroft to interpret Transcendentalism into a reforming faith. He went West already persuaded of that logic. In October 1839 The Western Messenger ceased publication; in May of 1840 Channing reorganized it and, as sole editor, maintained it for another year. Under his conduct, it concentrated not upon the literary but the social teachings of the new creed. His manifesto (VIII, 1–8), although clouded in Transcendental rhetoric, underscores the basic difference between him and the previous editors, like Clarke and Cranch, who had been generally reformers and anti-slavery men, but who had thought of their mission primarily in religious and literary terms. Channing spoke for that wing of the Transcendental community which now looked to Brownson rather than to Emerson for leadership, that segment through whom the millennial hope of Jonathan Edwards and revivalistic Protestantism once more became articulate, even though no longer in a strictly theological dress.]

The leading aim of the Western Messenger we think then should be the inculcation of a spirit of Life—individual and social Life. We would seek to conceive and realise an Ideal of Humanity. The temple in which the Holy Spirit loves to dwell is a true man; the acceptable worship is a pure character, manifested in acts of dignity and love. The end of existence is growth; progress is the vital law of the soul; hope will admit no limit but perfection. Man's restlessness is a sign of his grand destiny. Even misdirected energies reveal his greatness. The whole discipline of providence is a proof of God's interest and regard. In Jesus we see our perfected nature. In this view the whole of being, all powers, all circumstances, the grand relations, the minute details of earthly existence become sublime. As the Master teaches his pupils to draw straight marks and outlines; so by the ever returning perplexities of this work-day world, God is training man to the art of virtue. We would strive in every way, by essays, tales, biographies, poems, translations, extracts, maxims, to show the worth of true Manhood. Again; we see a progress in the past history of our race; we feel that a mighty power of good is stirring now in society; we believe in the coming of the kingdom of God. We have full faith that the time is approaching, though it may yet be distant, when national greatness will be tested by virtue and wisdom, and not by numbers, wealth, or extent of possession; when the only policy tolerated will be rectitude; when the object of legislation will be not only the common weal, but the highest good of individuals; when those men will be raised to power, who in their characters embody true greatness, and thus prove their right to rule; when measures will be the result, not of artful manoeuvring or party sway, but of the consenting judgments of an intelligent and upright people; when castes will be broken down, and reverence and courtesy act freely; when servitude, military glory, the sway of fashion and the tyranny of public opinion will be banished; when all will seek to give the most favourable opportunities to each, and each will find his highest joy in blending his energies with the best designs of all; when among men, as "with God there will be no respect of persons." We would lend what aid we can to bring on this glorious consummation, by the statement of great principles, by the exhibition of social needs, by encouraging all enterprises of true charity, of moral or intellectual improvement, by descriptions of scenes now occurring, by illustrating in every way the idea of Brotherhood.

3. Orestes A. Brownson (1803–1876)

Emerson

[Once comprehended in the manner of a Bancroft or of a W. H. Channing, Transcendental philosophy would inevitably result in totally different emphases in the realms of art and literature from those propounded in *The Dial*. To the task of expounding these differences, from the point of view of an orientation primarily social in character, Brownson frequently addressed himself in his *Review*, through a series of articles that were forgotten in the latter half of the nineteenth century, but which to the America of the mid-twentieth century may speak with the strongest voice of them all.

In the *Review* Brownson was always, as we have seen, the valiant champion for Emerson when it came to fending off a Norton, a Bowen, or the Princeton theologues. However, when he addressed himself to Emerson directly, from the beginning he recognized an incipient disagreement. Even in 1841 and 1842, when the divergence reached the point that Brownson was compelled to accuse Emerson of the "fatal error" of "Ideal Pantheism," he never doubted that the *Essays* "must take rank with the best in the language." But the real ground upon which Brownson was forced to part with Emerson was not metaphysics; it was a radically different conception of the relation of art to society, of the artist to the democracy. He first brought the issue into the open by reviewing Emerson's Dartmouth Address for *The Boston Quarterly Review* in January 1839 (II, 1–27); here he began to work out practically alone in so thinking—his doctrine of literature as an organic expression of the whole community.]

Few things are less dependent on mere will or arbitrariness than literature. It is the expression and embodiment of the national life. Its character is not determined by this man or that, but by the national spirit. The time and manner of its creation are determined by as necessary and invariable laws, as the motions of the sun, the revolutions of the earth, the growth of a tree, or the blowing of a flower . . . It depended not on Homer alone to sing. He sang because his song was in him and would be uttered. The God moved, and he must needs give forth his oracle. The choice of his subject, and the manner of treating it, depended not alone on his individual will.

It was given him by the belief in which he had been brought up, the education which he had received, the spirit, habits, beliefs, prejudices, tastes, cravings of the age and country in which he lived, or for which he sang . . .

The notion, which some entertain, that a national literature is the creation of a few great men, is altogether fallacious. Chaucer, Shakespeare, and Milton, Spenser, Pope, and Johnson are not the creators of English literature; but they are themselves the creatures of the spirit of the English nation, and of their times. Bacon, Hobbes, and Locke are not the authors of English philosophy, they are but its interpreters. Great men do not make their age; they are its effect . . . A great man is merely the glass which concentrates the rays of greatness scattered through the minds and hearts of the people; not the central sun from which they radiate. To obtain an elevated national literature, it is not necessary then to look to great men, or to call for distinguished scholars; but to appeal to the mass, wake up just sentiments, quicken elevated thoughts in them, and direct their attention to great and noble deeds; the literature will follow as a necessary consequence. When a national literature has been quickened in the national mind and heart, the great man is sure to appear as its organ, to give it utterance, form, embodiment. Before then his appearance is impossible.

We find also some difficulty in admitting the notion that the scholar must be a solitary soul, living apart and in himself alone; that he must shun the multitude and mingle never in the crowd, or if he mingle, never as one of the crowd; that to him the thronged mart and the peopled city must be a solitude; that he must commune only with his own thoughts, and study only the mysteries of his own being. We have no faith in this ascetic discipline. Its tendency is to concentrate the scholar entirely within himself, to make him a mere individual, without connexions or sympathies with his race; and to make him utter his own individual life, not the life of the nation, much less the universal life of Humanity . . . We can make the people listen to us only so far as we are one of them. When God sent us a Redeemer, he did not make him of the seed of angels, but of the seed of Abraham. He gave him a human nature, made him a partaker of flesh and blood, in like manner as those he was to redeem were partakers of flesh and blood, so that he might be touched with a sense of human infirmities, sympathize with our weakness, and through sympathy redeem us. So he who would move the people, influence them for good or for evil, must have like passions with them; feel as they feel; crave what they crave; and resolve what they resolve. He must be their representative, their impersonation . . .

The scholar must have an end to which his scholarship serves as a means.

Mr. Emerson and his friends seem to us to forget this. Forgetfulness of this is the reigning vice of Goethe and Carlyle. They bid the scholar make all things subsidiary to himself. He must be an artist, his sole end is to produce a work of art. He must scorn to create for a purpose, to compel his genius to serve, to work for an end beyond the work itself. All this which is designed to dignify art is false, and tends to render art impossible. Did Phidias create but for the purpose of creating a statue? Was he not haunted by a vision of beauty which his soul burned to realize? . . . Never yet has there appeared a noble work of art which came not from the artist's attempt to gain an end separate from that of producing a work of art. Always does the artist seek to affect the minds or the hearts of his like, to move, persuade, convince, please, instruct, or ennoble. To this end he chants a poem, composes a melody, laughs in a comedy, weeps in a tragedy, gives us an oration, a treatise, a picture, a statue, a temple. In all the masterpieces of ancient and modern literature, we see the artist has been in earnest, a real man, filled with an idea, wedded to some great cause, ambitious to gain some end. Always has he found his inspiration in his cause, and his success may always be measured by the magnitude of that cause, and the ardor of his attachment to it.

American scholars we shall have; but only in proportion as the scholar weds himself to American principles, and becomes the interpreter of American life . . . The idea of this nation is that of democratic freedom, the equal rights of all men. No man, however learned he may be, however great in all the senses of greatness, viewed simply as an individual, who does not entertain this great idea, who does not love it, and struggle to realize it in all our social institutions, in our whole practical life, can be a contributor to American literature . . .

In order to rear up American scholars and produce a truly American literature, we would not do as the author of the oration before us, declaim against American literature as it is, against the servility, and want of originality and independence of the American mind; nor would we impose a specific discipline on the aspirants to scholarship. We would talk little about the want of freedom; we would not trouble ourselves at all about literature, as such. We would engage the heart and soul in the great American work. We would make all the young men around us see and feel that there is here a great work, a glorious work, to be done. We would show them a work *they* can do, and fire them with the zeal and energy to do it . . . When our educated men acquire faith in democratic institutions, and a love for the Christian doctrine of the brotherhood of the human race, we shall have scholars enough, and a literature which will disclose to the whole world the superiority of freedom over slavery.

Let Mr. Emerson, let all who have the honor of their country or of their race at heart, turn their whole attention to the work of convincing the educated and the fashionable, that democracy is worthy of their sincerest homage, and of making them feel the longing to labor in its ennobling cause; and then he and they may cease to be anxious as to the literary results. It will be because a man has felt with the American people, espoused their cause, bound himself to it for life or for death, time or eternity, that he becomes able to adorn American literature; not because he has lived apart, refused "to serve society," held lone reveries, and looked on sunsets, and sunrise. If he speak a word, "posterity shall not willingly let die," it will not be because he has prepared himself to speak, by a scholastic asceticism, but by loving his countrymen and sympathizing with them.

4. Orestes A. Brownson (1803–1876)
Wordsworth

[By 1839 the new school, which could actually agree on very little, did agree on the proposition that Wordsworth was the greatest poet of the age. The Transcendentalists went to him for ideas and phrases, philosophy and technique; they used him, as Cranch did publicly (see p. 386), for the inspiration of their own poetry. It is symptomatic of their political naïveté that seldom in their adulation is there the slightest hint of an awareness that Wordsworth was concerned with politics. The Americans appeared incapable of recognizing a Tory when they saw one. It took Brownson to break the spell; while in the ordinary respects he appreciated Wordsworth, he would not let aesthetic prejudice blind him to that fact that Wordsworth was a black reactionary. He denounced him in *The Boston Quarterly Review* of April 1839 (II, 137–168).]

Wordsworth's great defect is not his want of intellect, nor his want of poetic sensibility, for he possesses both in a high degree; but the fact that he frames all his poems in accordance with a theory. We say not that his theory is false, for in the main it may be true; but no man can write poetry according to a theory. Genius spurns all fetters, all systems of philosophy, and makes and follows his own rules. From the practice of Genius, we are to learn the laws of Genius. We, critics and system-makers, have no right to attempt to frame a code of laws for his observance. Our glory is to take our law from him, and interpret it faithfully. But Wordsworth, as the theorizer, has attempted to legislate for Wordsworth, as the poet, and hence his failure. Whenever he loses sight of his theory, and abandons himself to the workings of spontaneity, he sings a true song. Would that this were not so seldom! . . .

We are inclined to believe that those, who admire Wordsworth, admire him more for his supposed philosophy than for his poetry. They, who have outgrown the material, soulless philosophy of the last century, and turned their minds inward to seek a more spiritual and living philosophy, seem to themselves to find in Wordsworth a congenial soul. They find after the great events and intense activity which closed the last century, and the echo of which hath not yet died away, something attractive in his gentle spirit, in his quiet smile, and kindly feeling for all animate and inanimate nature . . .

But the passive virtues, after all, are not the highest, nor those best fitted for song. Man was made for action, and the universal sentiment of the race awards the highest rank to the active virtues. He who chants the quiet scenes of nature, the gentle affections of the heart, may have listeners, but only at a certain age and in a certain mood of mind; but he who chants the active virtues, though displayed in war, in acts from which the soul shrinks with horror, is sure of the race for his audience and his chorus . . .

We have little faith in Wordsworth's democracy. He is a kind-hearted man, that would hurt no living thing, and who shudders to see a single human being suffer. So far, so good. But he has no faith in anything like social equality. He compassionates the poor, and would give the beggar an "awmous"; but measures which would prevent begging, which would place the means of a comfortable subsistence in hands of all men, so that there should be no poor, he apparently contemplates not without horror. A man is not necessarily inclined to democracy because he sings wagoners, pedlers, and beggars, any more than he is necessarily inclined to aristocracy because he brushes his coat, and maintains his personal dignity and independence . . . Wordsworth sings beggars, we admit, and shows very clearly that a man who begs is not to be despised; but does he ever fire our souls with a desire so to perfect our social system, that beggary shall not be one of its fruits? A Wordsworthian society without beggars, or such feeble old paupers as Simon Lee, would be shorn of all its poetic beauty. Herein lies the defect we discover in his democracy . . .

The tendency of a man's soul is usually to be ascertained by the party with which he arranges himself. Wordsworth goes with the high Tory party of his country, and opposes, as much as a man of his inertness can, the efforts of the friends of freedom . . . We are aware that the French Revolution is a bugbear to many; but we dare be known among those who see in it a great, though terrible effort of Humanity to gain possession of those rights which Christianity had taught her to regard as her inalienable patrimony, and to cherish as the apple of her eye, and we can own no man as a friend to his God, to his race, or to his country, who sided with those who took up arms against it, and sought to perpetuate old wrongs, time-hallowed oppressions. He must repent of his doings in sackcloth and ashes, with deep humility, with all the marks of sincere contrition, acknowledge his error, before we can believe the love of liberty lives in his heart. That Revolution had doubtless its excesses, but it needs no apology. Its apology stands in the fact that it has been. Its excesses will be forgotten much sooner than the excesses, the proscriptions, the murders, the soul-destroying tyrannies, of kings and aristocracies. The day will come when Humanity shall regard the chapter which records that Revolution as the brightest in her history. We should be the most shameless of all the world, citizens as we are of a country which owes its national existence to a Revolution, whose institutions are based on the very principles of Liberty and Equality, which France sought, but sought in vain, yet not wholly in vain, to make the basis of her own, did we not sympathize with the French Revolution, and pity the blindness of a Wordsworth, who could not see that the cause of Humanity was in it.

5. Orestes A. Brownson (1803–1876)
The Laboring Classes

[Brownson's voracious readings in the literature of Europe took him not only through its poetry and philosophy, but into territory that most of his colleagues did not penetrate, into social speculation. He read not only Fourier, as did Ripley and W. H. Channing, but the early socialists, and particularly Saint-Simon, from whom he learned to analyze history as a struggle between successive social classes. This at a time when in America the very concept of a "class" was hardly comprehensible! Up to the depression of 1837 Brownson saw no inconsistency between the Simonian view and the Transcendental version of history as spiritual progress; the two are mingled in his New Views of 1836.

The economic crisis jolted him severely, because it gave the lie direct to the spiritualist's optimism. He applied himself, with all his tremendous passion, to extending his analysis, and to applying Saint-Simon's pattern to America. He discovered, as a wholly novel insight, that this country had never had a feudal class. Therefore it was clear that the struggle in America—which accounted for the horrors of the panic—was not, as in Europe, between nobles and merchants, but between merchants and workers. The spiritual hope could be realized only through the resolution of this conflict, only through the victory of the mass of the laborers.

Meanwhile, through his friendship with Bancroft, Brownson had become an avowed member of the Democratic party; he was convinced that through it the victory of the masses was to be won. By the same token the Whig party, the party of property (Unitarians of the Bowen-Norton variety were Whigs to a man) was the enemy of freedom just as Norton was the enemy of the spirit. When the Whig convention nominated Harrison and commenced the shameless "log cabin and hard cider" campaign, Brownson felt it was time that a good man should come to the aid of his party. In the July issue, 1840, of *The Boston Quarterly Review* (III, 358–395) he published "The Laboring Classes." Commencing as a review of Carlyle's *Chartism,* he corrected Carlyle's interpretation of the plight of British workmen, by arguing that they were exploited not by the aristocracy but by the "middle class." Actually, the Duke of Wellington was more likely to be a friend of labor than "an Abbot Lawrence." Then, leaving Carlyle behind, Brownson launched his revolutionary thesis.]

No one can observe the signs of the times with much care, without perceiving that a crisis as to the relation of wealth and labor is approaching. It is useless to shut our eyes to the fact, and like the ostrich fancy ourselves secure because we have so concealed our heads that we see not the danger. We or our children will have to meet this crisis. The old war between the King and the Barons is well nigh ended, and so is that between the Barons and the Merchants and Manufacturers,—landed capital and commercial capital. The business man has become the peer of my Lord. And now commences the new struggle between the operative and his employer, between wealth and labor. Every day does this struggle extend further and wax stronger and fiercer; what or when the end will be God only knows . . .

What we would ask is, throughout the Christian world, the actual condition of the laboring classes, viewed simply and exclusively in their capacity of laborers? They constitute at least a moiety of the human race . . . In any contest they will be as two to one, because the large class of proprietors who are not employers, but laborers on their own lands or in their own shops will make common cause with them.

Now we will not so belie our acquaintance with political economy, as to allege that these alone perform all that is necessary to the production of wealth. We are not ignorant of the fact, that the merchant, who is literally the common carrier and exchange dealer, performs a useful service, and is therefore entitled to a portion of the proceeds of labor. But make all necessary deductions on his account, and then ask what portion of the remainder is retained, either in kind or in its equivalent, in the hands of the original producer, the workingman? All over the world this fact stares us in the face, the workingman is poor and depressed, while a large portion of the non-workingmen, in the sense we now use the term, are wealthy. It may be laid down as a general rule, with but few exceptions, that men are rewarded in an inverse ratio to the amount of actual service they perform. Under every government on earth the largest salaries are annexed to those offices, which demand of their incumbents the least amount of actual labor either mental or manual. And this is in perfect harmony with the whole system of re-partition of the fruits of industry, which obtain in every department of society. Now here is the system which prevails, and here is its result. The whole class of simple laborers are poor, and in general unable to procure anything beyond the bare necessaries of life . . .

Now, what is the prospect of those who fall under the operations of this system? We ask, is there a reasonable chance that any considerable portion of the present generation of laborers, shall ever become owners of a suffi-cient portion of the funds of production, to be able to sustain themselves by laboring on their own capital, that is, as independent laborers? We need not ask this question, for everybody knows there is not. Well, is the condition of a laborer at wages the best that the great mass of the working people ought to be able to aspire to? Is it a condition,—nay can it be made a con-dition,—with which a man should be satisfied; in which he should be con-tented to live and die?

In our own country this condition has existed under its most favorable aspects, and has been made as good as it can be. It has reached all the excel-lence of which it is susceptible. It is now not improving but growing worse. The actual condition of the workingman today, viewed in all its bearings, is not so good as it was fifty years ago. If we have not been altogether mis-informed, fifty years ago, health and industrious habits, constituted no mean stock in trade, and with them almost any man might aspire to competence and independence. But it is so no longer. The wilderness has receded, and already the new lands are beyond the reach of the mere laborer, and the employer has him at his mercy. If the present relation subsist, we see noth-ing better for him in reserve than what he now possesses, but something altogether worse . . .

Now the great work for this age and the coming, is to raise up the laborer, and to realize in our own social arrangements and in the actual condition of all men, that equality between man and man, which God has established between the rights of one and those of another. In other words, our business is to emancipate the proletaries, as the past has emancipated the slaves. This is our work. There must be no class of our fellow men doomed to toil through life as mere workmen at wages. If wages are tolerated it must be, in the case of the individual operative, only under such conditions that by the time he is of a proper age to settle in life, he shall have accumulated enough to be an independent laborer on his own capital,—on his own farm or in his own shop. Here is our work. How is it to be done? . . .

For our part, we yield to none in our reverence for science and religion; but we confess that we look not for the regeneration of the race from priests and pedagogues. They have had a fair trial. They cannot construct the temple of God. They cannot conceive its plan, and they know not how to build. They daub with untempered mortar, and the walls they erect tumble down if so much as a fox attempt to go up thereon. In a word they always league with the people's masters, and seek to reform without disturbing the social arrangements which render reform necessary. They would change the consequents without changing the antecedents, secure to men the rewards of holiness, while they continue their allegiance to the devil. We have no faith in priests and pedagogues. They merely cry peace, peace, and that too when there is no peace, and can be none . . .

The truth is, the evil we have pointed out is not merely individual in its character. It is not, in the case of any single individual, of any one man's procuring, nor can the efforts of any one man, directed solely to his own moral and religious perfection, do aught to remove it. What is purely individual in its nature, efforts of individuals to perfect themselves, may remove. But the evil we speak of is inherent in all our social arrangements, and cannot be cured without a radical change of those arrangements. Could we convert all men to Christianity in both theory and practice, as held by the most enlightened sect of Christians among us, the evils of the social state would remain untouched. Continue our present system of trade, and all its present evil consequences will follow, whether it be carried on by your best men or your worst. Put your best men, your wisest, most moral, and most religious men, at the head of your paper money banks, and the evils of the present banking system will remain scarcely diminished. The only way to get rid of its evils is to change the system, not its managers. The evils of slavery do not result from the personal characters of slave masters. They are inseparable from the system, let who will be masters. Make all your rich men good Christians, and you have lessened not the evils of existing inequality in wealth. The mischievous effects of this inequality do not result from the personal character of either rich or poor, but from itself, and they will continue, just so long as there are rich men and poor men in the same community. You must abolish the system or accept its consequences. No man can serve both God and Mammon. If you will serve the devil, you must look to the devil for your wages; we know no other way . . .

For our part we are disposed to seek the cause of the inequality of conditions of which we speak, in religion, and to charge it to the priesthood . . . Through awe of the gods, through fear of divine displeasure, and dread of the unforeseen chastisements that displeasure may inflict, and by pretending, honestly or not, to possess the secret of averting it, and of rendering the gods propitious, the priests are able to reduce the people to the most wretched subjection, and to keep them there; at least for a time . . .

In every age the priests, the authorized teachers of religion, are the first to oppose the true prophet of God, and to condemn his prophecies as blasphemies. They are always a let and a hindrance to the spread of truth. Why then retain them? Why not abolish the priestly office? Why continue to sustain what the whole history of man condemns as the greatest of all obstacles to intellectual and social progress?

The next step in this work of elevating the working classes will be to resuscitate the Christianity of Christ . . . According to the Christianity of Christ no man can enter the kingdom of God, who does not labor with all zeal and diligence to establish the kingdom of God on the earth . . . No man can be a Christian who does not labor to reform society, to mould it according to the will of God and the nature of man; so that free scope shall be given to every man to unfold himself in all beauty and power, and to grow up into the stature of a perfect man in Jesus Christ . . . It is the Gospel of Jesus you must preach, and not the gospel of the priests . . . We must preach no Gospel that permits men to feel that they are honorable men and good Christians, although rich and with eyes standing out with fatness, while the great mass of their brethren are suffering from iniquitous laws, from mischievous social arrangements, and pining away for the want of the refinements and even necessaries of life . . .

Having, by breaking down the power of the priesthood and the Christianity of the priests, obtained an open field and freedom for our operations, and by preaching the true Gospel of Jesus, directed all minds to the great social reform needed, and quickened in all souls the moral power to live for it or to die for it; our next resort must be to government, to legislative enactments. Government is instituted to be the agent of society, or more properly the organ through which society may perform its legitimate functions. It is not the master of society; its business is not to control society, but to be the organ through which society effects its will. Society has never to petition government; government is its servant, and subject to its commands . . .

But what shall government do? Its first doing must be an *un*doing. There has been thus far quite too much government, as well as government of the wrong kind. The first act of government we want, is a still further limitation of itself. It must begin by circumscribing within narrower limits its powers. And then it must proceed to repeal all laws which bear against the laboring classes, and then to enact such laws as are necessary to enable them to maintain their equality. We have no faith in those systems of elevating the working classes, which propose to elevate them without calling in the aid of the government. We must have government, and legislation expressly directed to this end.

But again what legislation do we want so far as this country is concerned? We want first the legislation which shall free government, whether State or Federal, from the control of the Banks. The Banks represent the interest of the employer, and therefore of necessity interests adverse to those of the employed; that is, they represent the interests of the business community in opposition to the laboring community. So long as the government remains under the control of the Banks, so long it must be in the hands of the natural enemies of the laboring classes, and may be made, nay, will be made, an instrument of depressing them yet lower . . . Uncompromising hostility to the whole banking system should therefore be the motto of every working man, and of every friend of Humanity. The system must be destroyed. On this point there must be no misgiving, no subterfuge, no palliation. The system is at war with the rights and interest of labor, and it must go. Every friend of the system must be marked as an enemy to his race, to his country, and especially to the laborer. No matter who he is, in what party he is found, or what name he bears, he is, in our judgment, no true democrat, as he can be no true Christian.

Following the destruction of the Banks, must come that of all monopolies, of all PRIVILEGE. There are many of these. We cannot specify them all; we therefore select only one, the greatest of them all, the privilege which some have of being born rich while others are born poor. It will be seen at once that we allude to the hereditary descent of property, an anomaly in our American system, which must be removed, or the system itself will be destroyed . . . We only say now, that as we have abolished hereditary monarchy and hereditary nobility, we must complete the work by abolishing hereditary property. A man shall have all he honestly acquires, so long as he himself belongs to the world in which he acquires it. But his power over his property must cease with his life, and his property must then become the property of the state, to be disposed of by some equitable law for the use of the generation which takes his place. Here is the principle without any of its details, and this is the grand legislative measure to which we look forward. We see no means of elevating the laboring classes which can be effectual without this. And is this a measure to be easily carried? Not at all. It will cost infinitely more than it cost to abolish either hereditary monarchy or hereditary nobility. It is a great measure, and a startling. The rich, the business community, will never voluntarily consent to it, and we think we know too much of human nature to believe that it will ever be effected peaceably. It will be effected only by the strong arm of physical force. It will come, if it ever come at all, only at the conclusion of war, the like of which the world as yet has never witnessed, and from which, however inevitable it may seem to the eye of philosophy, the heart of Humanity recoils with horror.

We are not ready for this measure yet. There is much previous work to be done, and we should be the last to bring it before the legislature. The time, however, has come for its free and full discussion. It must be canvassed in the public mind, and society prepared for acting on it. No doubt they who broach it, and especially they who support it, will experience a due share of contumely and abuse. They will be regarded by the part of the community they oppose, or may be thought to oppose, as "graceless varlets," against whom every man of substance should set his face. But this is not, after all, a thing to disturb a wise man, nor to deter a true man from telling his whole thought. He who is worthy of the name of man, speaks what he honestly believes the interests of his race demand, and seldom disquiets himself about what may be the consequences to himself. Men have, for what they believed the cause of God or man, endured the dungeon, the scaffold, the stake, the cross, and they can do it again, if need be. This subject must be freely, boldly, and fully discussed, whatever may be the fate of those who discuss it.

[Brownson's article was ferociously attacked, but he—who, as Parker said, looked battles—continued the attack with a further installment of "The Laboring Classes" in his October issue (III, 420–512). The two parts make a single essay, which is, with the possible exception of Calhoun's "Disquisition," the most remarkable study of society written by an American before the Civil War; long forgotten, it has only lately begun to receive the appreciation that is its due.]

Our account of the condition of the laboring classes, we have been told, is exaggerated and false. This objection would have some weight with us, were it not urged exclusively by those who live by availing themselves of the labors of the workingmen, and who, therefore, have a direct interest in keeping them as they are . . .

For ourselves, we were born and reared in the class of proletaries; and we have merely given utterance to their views and feelings. We have said little concerning their condition not warranted by what we have ourselves either seen or felt. We have made no random statement, and drawn no hasty inference. We know whereof we affirm; and shall abide by what we have already affirmed; at least, until the laboring classes themselves rise up and accuse us of misrepresenting them . . .

The class of persons, who have been loudest in their condemnation of us, are the *Nouveaux riches, parvenus,* upstarts, men who have themselves come up from the class of proletaries, and who have made it a virtue to forget "the rock whence they were hewn." Standing now on the shoulders of their brethren, they are too elevated to see what is going on at the base of the social organization. Would you know what is going on down there, you must interrogate those who dwell there, and feel the pressure that is on them. One would not interrogate the rider in order to ascertain the sensations the horse has in being ridden . . .

"But *we* have risen and so may others." Yes, doubtless; *some* others; but *all* others? How have you risen? By the productive industry of our own hands? By hard work. Aye, but by what kind of hard work? Has it not been by hard work in studying how you could turn the labors of others to your own profit; that is, transfer the proceeds of labor from the pockets of the laborer to your own? If you had had no laboring class, dependent entirely on its labor for the means of living, whose industry you could lay under contribution, would you ever have risen to your present wealth? Of course not. Of course, then, only a certain number of individuals of the laboring classes could, even with your talents, skill, and matchless virtues, rise as you have done. One rises from the class of proletaries only by making those, he leaves behind, the lever of his elevation. This, therefore, necessarily implies that there must always be a laboring class, and of course that the means, which this or that laborer uses for his individual elevation, cannot in the nature of things be used by all of his class . . .

"But what would you that we should do? Do we not pay the market price for labor?" Ay, the market price; but who fixes the market price; you, or the laborer? Why do you employ him? Is it not that you may grow rich? Why does he seek employment? Is it not that he may not die of hunger, he, his wife, and little ones? Which is the more urgent necessity, that of growing rich, or that of guarding against hunger? You can live, though you do not employ the laborer; but, if he find not employment, he must die. He is then at your mercy. You have over him the power of life and death. It is then of his necessity that you avail yourselves, and by taking advantage of that you reduce the price of labor to the minimum of human subsistence, and then grow rich by purchasing it. Would you be willing to labor through life as he does, and live on the income he receives? Not at all. You would regard, as the greatest of calamities which could befall you, that of losing your property, and being reduced to the necessity of supporting yourselves and families on the wages you could receive as common laborers. Do you not then see that you condemn in the most positive terms the condition of the proletary, that you declare plainer than any words we can use, that you look upon that condition as a serious calamity? What right have you then to maintain that a condition, which you regard with horror so far as concerns yourselves, is good enough for your brethren? And why complain of us for calling upon you to do all in your power, so to arrange matters, that no one shall be doomed to that condition? Why do you not, as the Christian law, of doing unto others as you would be done by, commands you, set yourselves at work in earnest to remodel the institution of property, so that all shall be proprietors, and you be relieved from paying wages, and the proletary from the necessity of receiving them? This is what we would have you do; what we hold you bound to do, and which you must do, or the wrongs and sufferings of the laborer will lie at your door, and his cries will ascend to the ears of an avenging God against you,— a God who espouses the cause of the poor and needy, and has sworn to avenge them on their oppressors. This you know, if you believe at all in that Gospel, which you so wrongfully accuse us of denying . . .

We have been accused of proposing to rob the rich of their estates, and of proposing to do it by physical force. We think we have shown, in the foregoing, that ours is no scheme of robbery and plunder. We have planted ourselves on the Christian idea of man's equality to man, and on the innate sense of justice, which belongs to all men. What we have demanded, we have demanded in the name of Justice. Show us, that what we demand is unjust, or that it is not in accordance with natural right, and we have nothing more to say. Perhaps, however, that to some, who accuse us, the justice of our propositions is their greatest condemnation. There are people in the world, at least it is so said, whose chief apprehensions are, that justice may be done. We will hope, however, that these are but few, and that their number is daily diminishing.

With regard to physical force, we have not much to say. We see an immense system of wrong everywhere established, and everywhere upheld. This system is the growth of a hundred ages, and is venerable in the eyes of many; but it must be overthrown. Man must be free, and SHALL be free, —free to develop his lofty and deathless nature, and prove himself a child of God. This is in his destiny. But how can he become thus free? How can the huge system of accumulated wrongs, under which he now groans, be overthrown, and a new and better system introduced and established? Peaceably? We would fain hope so; but we fear not. We are well assured of one thing; that the reform party will not be the first to take up arms. It will proceed calmly and peaceably, but energetically to its work. It will use no arms but those of the intellect and the heart. It fixes its eye on Justice, and marches steadily towards its realization. Will the conservatives yield up peaceably their exclusive privileges? Will they consent that justice shall be realized? If so, there will be no war. But we think we know the conservatives too well to believe this. A party that could collect together in this city, by hundreds, to mob a poor itinerant lecturer, and by thousands to consult on demolishing the post-office, because the postmaster insisted on obeying the laws, we do not believe will suffer the reform party to proceed quietly to the realization of its hopes. The proletaries will never resort to physical forces; but that the masters may, for the purpose of keeping the proletaries in their present condition, we must believe, till we have some evidence to the contrary. They have already threatened it here. Distinguished members of Congress have said publicly, that they would resort to force, if necessary, to effect a change in the policy of the Federal Administration, in case they should fail in their efforts to elect General Harrison to the Presidency. And what in England, in France, throughout all Europe, but armed soldiery, sustains the existing order of things? We know the conservative spirit. It fights against all reforms; it would hold the human race back to the past, and never suffer it to take a single step forward. Hitherto, it has been only on the battlefield; a Marathon, a Plataea, a Marston Moor, a Naseby, a Bunker's Hill, a Saratoga, or a Yorktown, that Humanity has conquered her power to advance. The Past has always stood in the gate, and forbid the Future to enter; and it has been only in mortal encounter, that the Future has as yet ever been able to force its entrance. It may be different in the future; we hope it will be. We would rather be found, on this subject, a false prophet than a true one. But we fear the age of peace has not yet dawned. Commerce has indeed spread her meshes all over the world, but she cannot hold it quiet. We need but glance at Europe, Asia, Africa, and even our own country, at the present moment, to see that no permanent peace has as yet been established. Everywhere are warlike preparations going on, and our speculators are already beginning to count on their means of turning the coming contest to their own profit. If a general war should now break out, it will involve all quarters of the globe, and it will be in the end more than a war between nations. It will resolve itself into a social war, a war between two social elements; between the aristocracy and the democracy, between the people and their masters. It will be a terrible war! Already does it lower on the horizon, and, though the storm may be long in gathering, it will roll in massy folds over the whole heavens, and break in fury upon the earth. Stay it, ye who can. For ourselves, we merely stand on the watch-towers, and report what we see. Would that we had a different report. But the war, if it comes, will not be brought about by reformers, but by conservatives, in order to keep the people out of their rights; and on the heads of conservatives, then, must fall the blame.

6. William Henry Channing (1810–1884)
Brownson's Laboring Classes

[The reaction of American society to *The Laboring Classes* was for Brownson a more harrowing ordeal than the attack on the *Conversations* had been for Alcott. The Whigs pounced upon it, gleefully reprinted it as an unmasking of the true design of the Democrats, and made of it powerful propaganda against Brownson's own cause. Democratic politicians tried to call him off, and when he would not stop, they disowned him. Bancroft explained that the Democrats of Massachusetts were no more responsible for Brownson than the Whigs were for Mormonism. *The Methodist Quarterly Review* accused him of everything subversive, including free love. The few friends who had helped him with his magazine deserted, and he had to fill up pages with his old sermons. His humiliation was completed in November when Harrison was overwhelmingly elected. Thereupon Brownson was rapidly propelled along the highway of disillusion that led, in four years, to a renunciation of Transcendentalism, of Cousin and of the *New Views*, and of democracy. In 1844 he became a Catholic, and for political doctrine turned to John C. Calhoun.

In Boston of 1840 all Brownson's old Unitarian foes were, of course, aghast over *The Laboring Classes*. Dr. Channing sounded more like Andrews Norton than his earlier self, and John Quincy Adams sneered at "Brownson and the Marat-Democrats." Emerson kept his head, and wrote gaily to Margaret Fuller that Brownson was "a Cobbett of a scribe": "Let him wash himself & he shall write for the immortal Dial." *The Dial* for July had already set in type Ripley's fine tribute to Brownson, so the magazine had the appearance of coming out in Brownson's favor in the very month of the first *Laboring Classes.* But it was in Cincinnati that Brownson found his one real defender, and Channing's action, though it ruined *The Western Messenger,* is an unsung deed of courage in the annals of American journalism.

In October 1840 (VIII, 288), Channing wrote a brief editorial explaining that the furor over Brownson's article had led him to a rereading of *New Views.*]

Mr. B. is held in such horror just now, because of some late heterodox political views, that it is as much as one's life is worth to mention him without execration. The Dial, of Boston, is pronounced "libertine" and "licentious" for no greater crime than praising Mr. B.'s "philosophical analysis," and "fearless energy." However, though we believe our Whig friends have deceived themselves into thinking Mr. B. an enemy of all goodness, because he looks upon Priests and Ordinances as William Penn and his band of Friends did and do; and though we fear their eyes are blind to his true power and worth, because they differ from him on some points, yet we feel obliged to say that we think few writers of equal clearness, vigor and boldness have appeared in these United States.

Right or wrong, he has a mind of his own, and does not follow any leader, as most of us do, like blind mice holding by the tails of a few open-eyed ones. We do not believe there is as much thought, well expressed, and deserving careful consideration, in any equal number of periodical pages, as there is in the pages of Brownson's Review, beginning with its establishment, and coming down to this time. The very article on the Laboring Classes, which has shaken our nerves so, we think worthy of careful study. We believe with Mr. B., that the cause of Property against Birth being decided, that of Man against Property must come on and be tried; and all this howling and shrieking of Conservative men and women seems to us like the uproar by which the Peruvians tried to stop the moon's eclipse. As respects the spirit of Mr. B.'s article, and the mode of action he proposes, we are in the strongest opposition to him: we think his spirit unchristian, and his plan of action unwise; but we believe him as honest as Luther, as fearless as Knox, and as capable, either for good or evil, as any writer of our day.

[In November, Channing ran an article criticizing *The Laboring Classes,* to which he appended an editorial note saying he did not agree with his criticism, but as a true liberal he wanted all sides to be heard.

By Transcendental doctrine it ought logically to have followed that, if Nature is in truth the present expositor of the divine mind, citizens of the new West, who lived more directly in relation with nature than the citizens of Boston, should have spectacularly vindicated the freedom and liberality of man in the open air. Emerson himself could fall into this logic and write in *The Dial* for April 1843 (III, 511–512) a passage that has been discreetly omitted from the reprinting of the article in the standard edition of his works; discussing "Europe and European Books" (one of the central critical documents of the movement), Emerson rebelled against the domination of the American mind by European importations:

> Our eyes will be turned westward, and a new and stronger tone in literature will be the result. The Kentucky stump-oratory, the exploits of Boone and David Crockett, the journals of western pioneers, agriculturalists, and socialists, and the letters of Jack Downing, are genuine growths, which are sought with avidity in Europe, where our European-like books are of no value. It is easy to see that soon the centre of population and property of the English race, which long ago began its travels, and which is still on the eastern shore, will shortly hover midway over the Atlantic main, and then as certainly fall within the American coast, so that the writers of the English tongue shall write to the American and not to the island public, and then will the great Yankee be born.

Brownson also had looked for great things to the West; he wrote to Clarke in January of 1837 commending *The Western Messenger,* and Clarke published the letter (III, 602):

> The real American character is to be formed and developed in the great and noble valley of the Mississippi . . . There the mission of the American people, which is to prove what man may be when and where he has free scope for the full and harmonious development of all his faculties, is to receive its first fulfilment . . . In the old world he is down-trodden by kings, priests and nobility; and even here a heartless conventionalism, a timid and sickly public restrains him, and checks the utterance of great thoughts and noble sentiments. But with you he is free, fresh, and unaffected by time-consecrated but barbarous customs. All the elements of humanity exist with you on a scale as gigantic as that of your physical nature; and when they shall have been moulded into an harmonious and perfect whole, they will form the true MAN of which there has been on earth but one prototype.

By December of 1840 Channing was overwhelmed by an avalanche of protest from the free, fresh, and unaffected humanity of the noble valley. He lost subscribers by the score. In December (VIII, 384) he reviewed the story, and announced that he had been informed "the whole of the *respectable* world" considered Brownson an outlaw. Channing thereupon declared himself. The *Messenger* lasted only four more issues and expired in April 1841.]

Oh respectable friends! Pity our misfortune, that, having entered the cave of this Cyclops, we did not find him so hideous as represented, and saw no human bones. In a word, to speak seriously, we think a most uncalled for hue-and-cry has been got up against one, whom we believe to be quite as pure in purpose and sound in judgment, as most of his opponents; and we have no idea of standing quietly by without a word of protest. More than that, we think that Mr. Brownson has discussed with uncommon ability questions which ought to be calmly, fully, and on all sides considered. For ourselves, though we by no means agree with him in all his opinions, we thank him, that he has led us to some views of truth, which we have not seen stated so forcibly elsewhere. We wish our friends, who disapprove of our course, would read him for themselves. They ought in justice to hear before they condemn. They would then, we doubt not, confess that this man whom they have been taught thus to dread, is nowise a fool or a villain, but really a person possessed of quite an average share of philanthropy, information and shrewdness. But Mr. Brownson can defend himself. One thing, friends, we would have you fully understand: We became editors of this periodical, supposing ourselves to be freemen, and the Western Messenger an organ of Freedom; and, so long as we continue editors, we shall assuredly act on this supposition.

7. Theodore Parker (1810–1860)

A Sermon of Merchants

[Upon moving to Boston and mounting the pulpit—in the Melodeon!—of the Twenty-eighth Congregational Society, Parker threw himself into every possible reforming movement: the Sabbath, capital punishment, crime, prostitution, temperance, jails, women's rights, marriage. Eventually his crusading energies were to be absorbed entirely in the slavery controversy. But in 1840 he had been one of the few to read Brownson's *The Laboring Classes* with comprehension. He did not agree with Brownson's notions of property, but he could perceive that the present system entails evils upon society: "This question first, of inherited property, and, next, of all private property, is to be handled in the nineteenth century."

He too began to read Saint-Simon and Fourier. In *The Dial* for October 1840 (I, 196–216), he published "A Lesson for the Day, or the Christianity of Christ, of the Church and of Society," and for April 1841 (I, 497–519), "Thoughts on Labor." These articles should be reprinted in this volume were there space enough, or were they not mainly diluted versions of Brownson (so much so that Brownson accused Parker of plagiarizing). Once installed in the Melodeon, and before he had entirely concentrated on slavery, Parker, on August 30, 1846, delivered his sensational sermon, "Of the Perishing Classes in Boston," and followed it on November 30 with his still more sensational "A Sermon of Merchants" (published in *Speeches, Addresses, and Occasional Sermons,* Boston, 1852).

It has been the fashion in some quarters to hold against Parker the fact that he could propose no more realistic remedy for social evils than moral regeneration. Considering the ethos of the time, this charge need not be weighed too heavily; the great fact is that he did address himself to a critique of American society, and he addressed himself specifically to the businessmen. While so doing, he gave them a definition of government in a democracy, a passage that W. H. Herndon read in Springfield, Illinois—in the great and noble valley of the Mississippi—and called to the attention of his law partner.]

Here in America the position of this class is the most powerful and commanding in society. They own most of the property of the nation. The wealthy men are of this class; in practical skill, administrative talent, in power to make use of the labor of other men, they surpass all others. Now, wealth is power, and skill is power—both to a degree unknown before. This skill and wealth are more powerful with us than any other people, for there is no privileged caste, priest, king, or noble, to balance against them. The strong hand has given way to the able and accomplished head. Once head armor was worn on the outside, and of brass, now it is internal and of brain . . .

Now the merchants in America occupy the place which was once held by the fighters and next by the nobles. In our country we have balanced into harmony the centripetal power of the government, and the centrifugal power of the people: so have national unity of action, and individual variety of action—personal freedom. Therefore a vast amount of talent is active here which lies latent in other countries, because that harmony is not established there. Here the army and navy offer a few inducements to able and aspiring young men. They are fled to as the last resort of the desperate, or else sought for their traditional glory, not their present value. In Europe, the army, the navy, the parliament or the court, the church and the learned professions offer brilliant prizes to ambitious men. Thither flock the able and the daring. Here such men go into trade.

It is better for a man to have set up a mill than to have won a battle. I deny not the exceptions. I speak only of the general rule. Commerce and manufactures offer the most brilliant rewards—wealth, and all it brings. Accordingly the ablest men go into the class of merchants. The strongest men in Boston, taken as a body, are not lawyers, doctors, clergymen, bookwrights, but merchants . . .

In virtue of its strength and position, this class is the controlling one in politics. It mainly enacts the laws of this State and the nation; makes them serve its turn. Acting consciously or without consciousness, it buys up legislators when they are in the market; breeds them when the market is bare. It can manufacture governors, senators, judges, to suit its purposes, as easily as it can make cotton cloth. It pays them money and honors; pays them for doing its work, not another's. It is fairly and faithfully represented by them. Our popular legislators are made in its image; represent its wisdom, foresight, patriotism and conscience. Your Congress is its mirror.

This class is the controlling one in the churches, none the less, for with us fortunately the churches have no existence independent of the wealth and knowledge of the people. In the same way it buys up the clergymen, hunting them out all over the land; the clergymen who will do its work, putting them in comfortable places. It drives off such as interfere with its work, saying, "Go starve, you and your children!" It raises or manufactures others to suit its taste.

The merchants build mainly the churches, endow theological schools; they furnish the material sinews of the church. Hence metropolitan churches are in general as much commercial as the shops . . .

This class owns the machinery of society, in great measure,—the ships, factories, shops, water privileges, houses and the like. This brings into their employment large masses of working men, with no capital but muscles or skill. The law leaves the employed at the employer's mercy. Perhaps this is unavoidable. One wishes to sell his work dear, the other to get it cheap as he can. It seems to me no law can regulate this matter, only conscience, reason, the Christianity of the two parties. One class is strong, the other weak. In all encounters of these two, on the field of battle, or in the marketplace, we know the results: the weaker is driven to the wall. When the earthen and iron vessel strike together, we know beforehand which will go to pieces. The weaker class can seldom tell their tale, so their story gets often suppressed in the world's literature, and told only in outbreaks and revolutions. Still the bold men who wrote the Bible, Old Testament and

New, have told truths on this theme which others dared not tell—terrible words which it will take ages of Christianity to expunge from the world's memory.

There is a strong temptation to use one's power of nature or position to the disadvantage of the weak. This may be done consciously or unconsciously. There are examples enough of both. Here the merchant deals in the labor of men. This is a legitimate article of traffic, and dealing in it is quite indispensable in the present condition of affairs. In the Southern States, the merchant, whether producer, manufacturer or trader, owns men and deals in their labor, or their bodies . . . That is slavery. He steals the man and his labor. Here it is possible to do a similar thing: I mean it is possible to employ men and give them just enough of the result of their labor to keep up a miserable life, and yourself take all the rest of the results of that labor. This may be done consciously or otherwise, but legally, without direct violence, and without owning the person. This is not slavery, though only one remove from it. This is the tyranny of the strong over the weak; the feudalism of money; stealing a man's work, and not his person. The merchants as a class are exposed to this very temptation. Sometimes it is yielded to. Some large fortunes have been made in this way. Let me mention some extreme cases; one from abroad, one near at home. In Belgium the average wages of men in manufactories is less than twenty-seven cents a day . . . How much better off are many women in Boston who gain their bread by the needle? yes, a large class of women in all our great cities? The ministers of the poor can answer that; your police can tell of the direful crime to which necessity sometimes drives women whom honest labor cannot feed! . . .

Then, too, there is the temptation to abuse their political power to the injury of the nation, to make laws which seem good for themselves, but are baneful to the people; to control the churches, so that they shall not dare rebuke the actual sins of the nation, or the sins of trade, and so the churches may be made apologizers for lowness, practising infidelity as their sacrament, but in the name of Christ and God. The ruling power in England once published a volume of sermons, as well as a book of prayers, which the clergy were commanded to preach. What sort of a gospel got recommended therein, you may easily guess; and what is recommended by the class of merchants in New England, you may as easily hear . . .

There is always a conservative element in society; yes, an element which resists the further application of Christianity to public affairs. Once the fighters and their children were uppermost, and represented that element.

Then the merchants were reformatory, radical, in collision with the nobles. They were "Whigs"—the nobles were "Tories." The merchants formed themselves into companies, and got power from the crown to protect themselves against the nobles, whom the crown also feared. It is so in England now. The great revolution in the laws of trade lately effected there, was brought about by the merchants, though opposed by the lords. The anti-corn law league was a trades-union of merchants contending against the owners of the soil. There the lord of land, and by birth, is slowly giving way to the lord of money, who is powerful by his knowledge or his wealth. There will always be such an element in society. Here I think it is represented by the merchants. They are backward in all reforms, excepting such as their own interest demands. Thus they are blind to the evils of slavery, at least silent about them . . . Yes, it is through their influence that the chivalry, the wisdom, patriotism, eloquence, yea, religion of the free States, are all silent when the word slavery is pronounced . . .

The merchant-manufacturers want a protective tariff; the merchant-importers, free trade; and so the national politics hinge upon that question. When Massachusetts was a carrying State, she wanted free trade; now a manufacturing State, she desires protection. That is all natural enough; men wish to protect their interests, whatsoever they may be. But no talk is made about protecting the labor of the rude man, who has no capital, nor skill, nothing but his natural force of muscles. The foreigner underbids him, monopolizing most of the brute labor of our large towns and internal improvements. There is no protection, no talk of protection for the carpenter, or the bricklayer. I do not complain of that. I rejoice to see the poor wretches of the old world finding a home where our fathers found one before. Yet if we cared for men more than for money, and were consistent with our principles of protection, why we should exclude all foreign workmen, as well as their work, and so raise the wages of the native hands. That would doubtless be very foolish legislation—but perhaps not, on that account, very strange . . .

This same preference of money over men appears in many special statutes. In most of our manufacturing companies the capital is divided into shares so large that a poor man cannot invest therein! This could easily be avoided. A man steals a candlestick out of a church, and goes to the State Prison for a year and a day. Another quarrels with a man, maims him for life, and is sent to the common jail for six months. A bounty is paid, or was until lately, on every gallon of intoxicating drink manufactured here and sent out of the country. If we begin with taking care of the rights of man, it seems easy to take care of the rights of labor and of capital. To begin the other way is quite another thing. A nation making laws for the nation is a noble sight. The Government of all, by all and for all, is a democracy. When that Government follows the eternal laws of God, it is founding what Christ called the kingdom of heaven. But the predominating class making laws not for the nation's good but only for its own, is a sad spectacle; no reasoning can make it other than a sorry sight. To see able men prostituting their talents to such a work, that is one of the saddest sights! I know all other nations have set us the example, yet it is painful to see it followed, and here . . .

Here trade takes the place of the army, navy, and court in other lands. That is well, but it takes also the place in great measure of science, art and literature. So we become vulgar and have little but trade to show. The rich man's son seldom devotes himself to literature, science, or art; only to getting more money, or to living in idleness on what he has inherited. When money is the end, what need to look for any thing more? He degenerates into the class of consumers, and thinks it an honor. He is ashamed of his father's blood, proud of his gold. A good deal of scientific labor meets with no reward, but itself. In our country this falls almost wholly upon poor men. Literature, science and art are mainly in their hands, yet are controlled by the prevalent spirit of the nation. Here and there an exceptional man differs from that, but the mass of writers conform. In England, the national literature favors the church, the crown, the nobility, the prevailing class. Another literature is rising, but is not yet national, still less canonized. We have no American literature which is permanent. Our scholarly books are only an imitation of a foreign type; they do not reflect our morals, manners, politics, or religion, not even our rivers, mountains, sky. They have not the smell of our ground in their breath. The real American literature is found only in newspapers, and speeches, perhaps in some novel, hot, passionate, but poor, and extemporaneous. That is our national literature. Does that favor man—represent man? Certainly not. All is the reflection of this most powerful class. The truths that are told are for them, and the lies. Therein the prevailing sentiment is getting into the form of thought. Politics represent the morals of the controlling class, the morals and manners of rich Peter and David on a large scale. Look at that index, you would sometimes think you were not in the Senate of a great nation, but in a board of brokers, angry and higgling about stocks. Once in the nation's loftiest hour, she rose inspired and said: "All men are born equal, each with unalienable rights; that is self-evident." Now she repents her of the vision and the saying. It does not appear in her literature, nor church, nor state. Instead of that, through this controlling class, the nation says: "All dollars are equal, however got; each has unalienable rights. Let no man question that!" This appears in literature and legislation, church and state. The morals of a nation, of its controlling class, always get summed up in its political action. That is the barometer of the moral weather. The voters are always fairly represented . . .

Would that my words could reach all of this class. Think not I love to speak hard words, and so often; say not that I am setting the poor against the rich. It is no such thing. I am trying to set the strong in favor of the weak. I speak for man. Are you not all brothers, rich or poor? I am here to gratify no vulgar ambition, but in Religion's name to tell their duty to the most powerful class in all this land. I must speak the truth I know, though I may recoil with trembling at the words I speak; yes, though their flame should scorch my own lips. . . . Trade is silently making a wonderful revolution. We live in the midst of it, and therefore see it not. All property has become movable, and therefore power departs from the family of the first-born, and comes to the family of mankind. God only controls this revolution, but you can help it forward, or retard it. The freedom of labor, and the freedom of trade, will work wonders little dreamed of yet; one is now uniting all men of the same nation; the other, some day, will weave all tribes together into one mighty family. Then who shall dare break its peace? I cannot now stop to tell half the proud achievements I foresee resulting from the fierce energy that animates your yet unconscious hearts. Men live faster than ever before. Life, like money, like mechanical power, is getting intensified and condensed. The application of science to the arts, the use of wind, water, steam, electricity, for human works, is a wonderful fact, far greater than the fables of old times. . . . Even now these new achievements have greatly multiplied the powers of men. They belong to no class; like air and water they are the property of mankind. It is for you, who own the machinery of society, to see that no class appropriates to itself what God meant for all. Remember it is as easy to tyrannize by machinery as by armies, and as wicked; that it is greater now to bless mankind thereby, than it was of old to conquer new realms. Let men not curse you, as the old nobility, and shake you off, smeared with blood and dust. Turn your power to goodness, its natural transfiguration, and men shall bless your name, and God bless your soul. If you control the nation's politics, then it is your duty to legislate for the nation,—for man. You may develop the great national idea, the equality of all men; may frame a government which shall secure man's unalienable rights. It is for you to organize the rights of man, thus balancing into harmony the man and the many, to organize the rights of the hand, the head, and the heart. If this be not done, the fault is yours. If the nation play the tyrant over her weakest child, if she plunder and rob the feeble Indian, the feebler Mexican, the Negro, feebler yet, why the blame is yours. Remember there is a God who deals justly with strong and weak. The poor and the weak have loitered behind in the march of man; our cities yet swarm with men half-savage. It is for you, ye elder brothers, to lead forth the weak and poor! If you do the national duty that devolves on you, then are you the saviours of your country, and shall bless not that alone, but all the thousand million sons of men. Toil then for that. If the church is in your hands, then make it preach the Christian truth. Let it help the free development of religion in the self-consciousness of man, with Jesus for its pattern. It is for you to watch over this work, promote it, not retard. Help build the American church. The Roman church has been, we know what it was, and what men it bore; the English church yet stands, we know what it is. But the church of America—which shall represent American vigor aspiring to realize the ideas of Christianity, of absolute religion,—that is not yet. No man has come with pious genius fit to conceive its litany, to chant its mighty creed, and sing its beauteous psalm. The church of America, the church of freedom, of absolute religion, the church of mankind, where Truth, Goodness, Piety, form one trinity of beauty, strength, and grace—when shall it come? Soon as we will. It is yours to help it come . . .

To this class let me say: Remember your Position at the head of the nation; use it not as pirates, but Americans, Christians, men. Remember your Temptations, and be warned in time. Remember your opportunities —such as no men ever had before. God and man alike call on you to do your duty. Elevate your calling still more; let its nobleness appear in you. Scorn a mean thing. Give the world more than you take. You are to serve the nation, not it you; to build the church, not make it a den of thieves, nor allow it to apologize for your crime, or sloth. Try this experiment and see what comes of it. In all things govern yourselves by the eternal law of right. You shall build up not a military despotism, nor a mercantile oligarchy, but a State, where the government is of all, by all, and for all; you shall found not a feudal theocracy, nor a beggarly sect, but the church of mankind, and that Christ which is the same yesterday, to-day, and for ever, will dwell in it, to guide, to warn, to inspire, and to bless all men. And you, my brothers, what shall you become? Not knaves, higgling rather than earn; not tyrants, to be feared whilst living, and buried at last amid popular hate, but men, who thrive best by justice, conscience, and have now the blessedness of just men making themselves perfect.

8. Margaret Fuller (1810–1850)
The Great Lawsuit

[Margaret Fuller made the greatest impression on her times with a booklet, *Woman in the Nineteenth Century,* published in New York in 1845. It is a pioneer work for the "feminist" movement in America and influenced the calling of the Seneca Falls Conference in 1848. When Margaret reached London in 1846, she found herself already famous because of it.

Just as the Transcendental metaphysic inevitably supplied bases for a new critique of the social structure, so it could not avoid posing the problem of the relation between the sexes in new terms, arguing for sexual equality. Not only could man become Man Thinking by walking in the open air, but so also, at least theoretically, could woman. Margaret Fuller could actually think better than a great many men. Men who had other ideals of womanhood disliked her intensely —Dr. Oliver Wendell Holmes, for example—and Edgar Poe took delight in classifying the race into three categories: men, women, and Margaret Fuller. Emerson looked with benignity upon the agitation for women's rights, but shrank from the prospect of their actually going to the polls; Parker, Ripley, Sophia Ripley, and W. H. Channing had no such scruples. The debate kept getting sidetracked onto the superficial issue of the vote. Margaret was the woman to go to fundamentals.

The book was a reworking of an article that she first dashed off, at white heat, for *The Dial* of July 1843 (IV, 1–48). Emerson characteristically reported to her that "The Great Lawsuit" was felt by all the circle "to be a piece of life, so much better than a piece of grammar" (it certainly was not the latter!), but he did add Thoreau's opinion: "rich extempore writing, talking with pen in hand." This from Henry, who Emerson explained, "will never like anything." The book turned out to be a fairly scholarly and reasoned presentation, but the *Dial* article has all the headlong impetuosity which is to me, as it was to some of her contemporaries— but by no means to all—the peculiar delight of Margaret Fuller's writings.]

THE GREAT LAWSUIT

MAN *versus* MEN. WOMAN *versus* WOMEN

Could we . . . say what we want, could we give a description of the child that is lost, he would be found. As soon as the soul can say clearly, that a certain demonstration is wanted, it is at hand . . .

No doubt, a new manifestation is at hand, a new hour in the day of man. We cannot expect to see him a completed being, when the mass of men lie so entangled in the sod, or use the freedom of their limbs only with wolfish energy. The tree cannot come to flower till its root be freed from the cankering worm, and its whole growth open to air and light. Yet something new shall presently be shown of the life of man, for hearts crave it now, if minds do not know how to ask it . . .

Here, as elsewhere, the gain of creation consists always in the growth of individual minds, which live and aspire, as flowers bloom and birds sing, in the midst of morasses; and in the continual development of that thought, the thought of human destiny, which is given to eternity to fulfil, and which ages of failure only seemingly impede. Only seemingly, and whatever seems to the contrary, this country is as surely destined to elucidate a great moral law, as Europe was to promote the mental culture of man . . .

Of all its banners, none has been more steadily upheld, and under none has more valor and willingness for real sacrifices been shown, than that of the champions of the enslaved African. And this band it is, which, partly in consequence of a natural following out of principles, partly because many women have been prominent in that cause, makes, just now, the warmest appeal in behalf of woman . . .

Thus vaguely are these questions proposed and discussed at present. But their being proposed at all implies much thought, and suggests more. Many women are considering within themselves what they need that they have not, and what they can have, if they find they need it. Many men are considering whether women are capable of being and having more than they are and have, and whether, if they are, it will be best to consent to improvement in their condition.

The numerous party, whose opinions are already labelled and adjusted too much to their mind to admit of any new light, strive, by lectures on some model-woman of bridal-like beauty and gentleness, by writing or lending little treatises, to mark out with due precision the limits of woman's sphere, and woman's mission, and to prevent other than the rightful shepherd from climbing the wall, or the flock from using any chance gap to run astray . . .

Under these circumstances, without attaching importance in themselves to the changes demanded by the champions of woman, we hail them as signs of the times. We would have every arbitrary barrier thrown down. We would have every path laid open to woman as freely as to man. Were this done, and a slight temporary fermentation allowed to subside, we believe that the Divine would ascend into nature to a height unknown in the history of past ages, and nature, thus instructed, would regulate the spheres not only so as to avoid collision, but to bring forth ravishing harmony.

Yet then, and only then, will human beings be ripe for this, when inward and outward freedom for woman, as much as for man, shall be acknowledged as a right, not yielded as a concession. As the friend of the negro assumes that one man cannot, by right, hold another in bondage, so should the friend of woman assume that man cannot, by right, lay even well-meant restrictions on woman. If the negro be a soul, if the woman be a soul, apparelled in flesh, to one master only are they accountable. There is but one law for all souls, and, if there is to be an interpreter of it, he comes not as man, or son of man, but as Son of God.

Were thought and feeling once so far elevated that man should esteem himself the brother and friend, but nowise the lord and tutor of woman, were he really bound with her in equal worship, arrangements as to function and employment would be of no consequence. What woman needs is not as a woman to act or rule, but as a nature to grow, as an intellect to discern, as a soul to live freely, and unimpeded to unfold such powers as were given her when we left our common home. If fewer talents were given her, yet, if allowed the free and full employment of these, so that she may render back to the giver his own with usury, she will not complain, nay, I dare to say she will bless and rejoice in her earthly birth-place, her earthly lot . . .

It is not the transient breath of poetic incense, that women want; each can receive that from a lover. It is not life-long sway; it needs but to become a coquette, a shrew, or a good cook, to be sure of that. It is not money, nor notoriety, nor the badges of authority, that men have appropriated to themselves. If demands made in their behalf lay stress on any of these particulars, those who make them have not searched deeply into the need. It is for that which at once includes all these and precludes them; which would not be forbidden power, lest there be temptation to steal and misuse it; which would not have the mind perverted by flattery from a worthiness of esteem. It is for that which is the birthright of every being capable to receive it,—the freedom, the religious, the intelligent freedom of the universe, to use its means, to learn its secret as far as nature has enabled them, with God alone for their guide and their judge.

Ye cannot believe it, men; but the only reason why women ever assume what is more appropriate to you, is because you prevent them from finding out what is fit for themselves. Were they free, were they wise fully to develop the strength and beauty of woman, they would never wish to be men, or manlike. The well-instructed moon flies not from her orbit to seize on the glories of her partner. No; for she knows that one law rules, one heaven contains, one universe replies to them alike . . .

The especial genius of woman I believe to be electrical in movement, intuitive in function, spiritual in tendency. She is great not so easily in classification, or re-creation, as in an instinctive seizure of causes, and a simple breathing out of what she receives that has the singleness of life, rather than the selecting or energizing of art.

More native to her is it to be the living model of the artist, than to set apart from herself any one form in objective reality; more native to inspire and receive the poem than to create it. In so far as soul is in her completely developed, all soul is the same; but as far as it is modified in her as woman, it flows, it breathes, it sings, rather than deposits soil, or finishes work, and that which is especially feminine flushes in blossom the face of earth, and pervades like air and water all this seeming solid globe, daily renewing and purifying its life. Such may be the especially feminine element, spoken of as Femality. But it is no more the order of nature that it should be incarnated pure in any form, than that the masculine energy should exist unmingled with it in any form.

Male and female represent the two sides of the great radical dualism. But, in fact, they are perpetually passing into one another. Fluid hardens to solid, solid rushes to fluid. There is no wholly masculine man, no purely feminine woman.

History jeers at the attempts of physiologists to bind great original laws by the forms which flow from them. They make a rule; they say from observation, what can and cannot be. In vain! Nature provides exceptions to every rule. She sends women to battle, and sets Hercules spinning; she enables women to bear immense burdens, cold, and frost; she enables the man, who feels material love, to nourish his infant like a mother. Of late she plays still gayer pranks. Not only she deprives organizations, but organs, of a necessary end. She enables people to read with the top of the head, and see with the pit of the stomach. Presently she will make a female Newton, and a male Syren.

Man partakes of the feminine in the Apollo, woman of the masculine as Minerva.

Let us be wise and not impede the soul. Let her work as she will. Let us have one creative energy, one incessant revelation. Let it take what form it will, and let us not bind it by the past to man or woman, black or white. Jove sprang from Rhea, Pallas from Jove. So let it be.

If it has been the tendency of the past remarks to call woman rather to the Minerva side,—if I, unlike the more generous writer, have spoken from society no less than the soul,—let it be pardoned. It is love that has caused this, love for many incarcerated souls, that might be freed could the idea of religious self-dependence be established in them, could the weakening habit of dependence on others be broken up.

Every relation, every gradation of nature, is incalculably precious, but only to the soul which is poised upon itself, and to whom no loss, no change, can bring dull discord, for it is in harmony with the central soul.

If any individual live too much in relations, so that he becomes a stranger to the resources of his own nature, he falls after a while into a distraction, or imbecility, from which he can only be cured by a time of isolation, which gives the renovating fountains time to rise up. With a society it is the same. Many minds, deprived of the traditionary or instinctive means of passing a cheerful existence, must find help in self-impulse or perish. It is therefore that while any elevation, in the view of union, is to be hailed with joy, we shall not decline celibacy as the great fact of the time. It is one from which no vow, no arrangement, can at present save a thinking mind. For now the rowers are pausing on their oars, they wait a change before they can pull together. All tends to illustrate the thought of a wise contemporary. Union is only possible to those who are units. To be fit for relations in time, souls, whether of man or woman, must be able to do without them in the spirit.

It is therefore that I would have woman lay aside all thought, such as she habitually cherishes, of being taught and led by men. I would have her, like the Indian girl, dedicate herself to the Sun, the Sun of Truth, and go no where if his beams did not make clear the path. I would have her free from compromise, from complaisance, from helplessness, because I would have her good enough and strong enough to love one and all beings, from the fulness, not the poverty of being.

Men, as at present instructed, will not help this work, because they also are under the slavery of habit. I have seen with delight their poetic impulses. A sister is the fairest ideal, and how nobly Wordsworth, and even Byron, have written of a sister.

There is no sweeter sight than to see a father with his little daughter. Very vulgar men become refined to the eye when leading a little girl by the hand. At that moment the right relation between the sexes seems established, and you feel as if the man would aid in the noblest purpose, if you ask him in behalf of his little daughter. Once two fine figures stood before me, thus. The father of very intellectual aspect, his falcon eye softened by affection as he looked down on his fair child, she the image of himself, only more graceful and brilliant in expression. I was reminded of Southey's Kehama, when lo, the dream was rudely broken. They were talking of education, and he said,

"I shall not have Maria brought too forward. If she knows too much, she will never find a husband; superior women hardly ever can."

"Surely," said his wife, with a blush, "you wish Maria to be as good and wise as she can, whether it will help her to marriage or not."

"No," he persisted, "I want her to have a sphere and a home, and some one to protect her when I am gone."

It was a trifling incident, but made a deep impression. I felt that the holiest relations fail to instruct the unprepared and perverted mind. If this man, indeed, would have looked at it on the other side, he was the last that would have been willing to have been taken himself for the home and protection he could give, but would have been much more likely to repeat the tale of Alcibiades with his phials.

But men do *not* look at both sides, and women must leave off asking them and being influenced by them, but retire within themselves, and explore the groundwork of being till they find their peculiar secret. Then when they come forth again, renovated and baptized, they will know how to turn all dross to gold, and will be rich and free though they live in a hut, tranquil, if in a crowd. Then their sweet singing shall not be from passionate impulse, but the lyrical overflow of a divine rapture, and a new music shall be elucidated from this many-chorded world.

Grant her then for a while the armor and the javelin. Let her put from her the press of other minds and meditate in virgin loneliness. The same idea shall reappear in due time as Muse, or Ceres, the all-kindly, patient Earth-Spirit.

I tire every one with my Goethean illustrations. But it cannot be helped.

Goethe, the great mind which gave itself absolutely to the leadings of truth, and let rise through him the waves which are still advancing through the century, was its intellectual prophet. Those who know him, see, daily, his thought fulfilled more and more, and they must speak of it, till his name weary and even nauseate, as all great names have in their time. And I cannot spare the reader, if such there be, his wonderful sight as to the prospects and wants of women.

As his Wilhelm grows in life and advances in wisdom, he becomes acquainted with women of more and more character, rising from Mariana to Macaria.

Macaria, bound with the heavenly bodies in fixed revolutions, the centre of all relations, herself unrelated, expresses the Minerva side.

Mignon, the electrical, inspired lyrical nature.

All these women, though we see them in relations, we can think of as unrelated. They all are very individual, yet seem nowhere restrained. They satisfy for the present, yet arouse an infinite expectation.

The economist Theresa, the benevolent Natalia, the fair Saint, have chosen a path, but their thoughts are not narrowed to it. The functions of life to them are not ends, but suggestions.

Thus to them all things are important, because none is necessary. Their different characters have fair play, and each is beautiful in its minute indications, for nothing is enforced or conventional, but everything, however slight, grows from the essential life of the being.

Mignon and Theresa wear male attire when they like, and it is graceful for them to do so, while Macaria is confined to her arm chair behind the green curtain, and the Fair Saint could not bear a speck of dust on her robe.

All things are in their places in this little world because all is natural and free, just as "there is room for everything out of doors." Yet all is rounded in by natural harmony which will always arise where Truth and Love are sought in the light of freedom.

Goethe's book bodes an era of freedom like its own, of "extraordinary generous seeking," and new revelations. New individualities shall be developed in the actual world, which shall advance upon it as gently as the figures come out upon his canvas.

A profound thinker has said "no married woman can represent the female world, for she belongs to her husband. The idea of woman must be represented by a virgin."

But that is the very fault of marriage, and of the present relation between the sexes, that the woman does belong to the man, instead of forming a whole with him. Were it otherwise there would be no such limitation to the thought.

Woman, self-centred, would never be absorbed by any relation; it would be only an experience to her as to man. It is a vulgar error that love, *a* love to woman is her whole existence; she also is born for Truth and Love in their universal energy. Would she but assume her inheritance, Mary would not be the only Virgin Mother. Not Manzoni alone would celebrate in his wife the virgin mind with the maternal wisdom and conjugal affections. The soul is ever young, ever virgin.

And will not she soon appear? The woman who shall vindicate their birthright for all women; who shall teach them what to claim, and how to use what they obtain? Shall not her name be for her era Victoria, for her country and her life Virginia? Yet predictions are rash; she herself must teach us to give her the fitting name.

9. Elizabeth Palmer Peabody (1804–1894)
Plan of the West Roxbury Community

[Whether Brook Farm is properly to be considered a manifestation of Transcendentalism is a question that became to the actors themselves as clouded as it remains for the historian. Assuredly, when in 1844 the enterprise transformed itself from a happy-go-lucky Institute of Agriculture and Education into an articulated Phalanx, after the blue-print of the French socialist, Charles Fourier, it became something foreign and forlorn in West Roxbury. But in the original intention of the band that gathered about George Ripley in the autumn of 1840 there was no such elaborate system in view. They were merely attempting, in all simplicity, to realize in a community of the chosen the aims of Transcendental philosophy. In this spirit, on November 9, Ripley invited Emerson to join:

> Our objects, as you know, are to insure a more natural union between intellectual and manual labor than now exists; to combine the thinker and the worker, as far as possible, in the same individual; to guarantee the highest mental freedom, by providing all with labor, adapted to their tastes and talents, and securing to them the fruits of their industry; to do away [with] the necessity of menial services, by opening the benefits of education and the profits of labor to all; and thus to prepare a society of liberal, intelligent, and cultivated persons, whose relations with each other would permit a more simple and wholesome life, than can be led amidst the pressure of our competitive institutions.

In April 1841 the first of the combined thinkers and workers—including a highly sceptical one, Nathaniel Hawthorne—took over Brook Farm, and Utopia was begun.

Brownson's excursion into political action was so much on his own, and its consequences were worked out on such a national scale, that his debacle did not effect alignments within the group itself. But when Ripley undertook Brook Farm, he had to ask Emerson to come along, and Emerson had to refuse. Henceforth there were two opposing poles in Transcendentalism—the associationists and the Emersonian individualists. Communication across the gulf was still kept up, but to the enthusiasts of Brook Farm, Emerson was as much a lost leader as Dr. Channing or Norton. His philosophy and his works were now found to be marked by "a profound indifference to the great humanitarian movements of the age." The fellowship of 1836 had been bound together by nothing more than gossamer threads, but with the creation of Brook Farm they all had to face the issue of society versus solitude—and thereafter could never meet, all of them, as compatriots.

In replying to Ripley's invitation, Emerson drew the sword of cleavage and sharpened the blade: "It seems to me a circuitous & operose way of relieving myself of any irksome circumstances, to put on your community the task of my emancipation which I ought to take on myself." In the privacy of his journal he phrased it even more trenchantly, telling himself that this scheme—like all schemes —amounts to no more than arithmetic and comfort—"a room in the Astor House hired for the Transcendentalists." He asked himself the now famous question, whether he should raise the siege of his hencoop, "and march baffled away to a pretended siege of Babylon?" The Ripleys, as it turned out, did not find the Farm a matter of mere arithmetic, and still less of comfort; in their heart of hearts, they could never forgive Waldo Emerson.

None the less, neither Emerson nor Margaret Fuller, however stubbornly they insisted that the self could be emancipated only by the self's private culture, could let *The Dial* do otherwise than give Brook Farm and the associationist point of view all the publicity at its command. Elizabeth Peabody was interested in everything new—she was, according to Clarke, "always engaged in supplying some want that had first to be created"—and she visited the Farm in all reverence. For *The Dial* of January 1842 (II, 361–372), she wrote without partisanship this description of the Brook Farm that lasted for only the first two careless years, when it was the creation of sheer Transcendental exuberance, before it chained itself to the rigidity of a socialistic dogma. In the last issue of *The Dial,* for March 1844 (IV, 473–478), after the Fouricrists had captured the Farm, she was to put with rare felicity the really divisive question: "The question is whether the Phalanx acknowledges its own limitations of nature in being an organization, or opens up any avenue into the source of life that shall keep it sweet, enabling it to assimilate to itself contrary elements and consume its own waste; so that, phoenix-like, it may renew itself forever in greater and finer forms."]

A few individuals, who, unknown to each other, under different disciplines of life, reacting from different social evils, but aiming at the same object,—of being wholly true to their natures as men and women; have been made acquainted with one another, and have determined to become the Faculty of the Embryo University.

In order to live a religious and moral life worthy the name, they feel it is necessary to come out in some degree from the world, and to form them-

selves into a community of property, so far as to exclude competition and the
ordinary rules of trade;—while they reserve sufficient private property, or
the means of obtaining it, for all purposes of independence, and isolation at
will. They have bought a farm, in order to make agriculture the basis of their
life, it being the most direct and simple in relation to nature.

A true life, although it aims beyond the highest star, is redolent of the
healthy earth. The perfume of clover lingers about it. The lowing of cattle
is the natural bass to the melody of human voices.

On the other hand, what absurdity can be imagined greater than the institution of cities? They originated not in love, but in war. It was war that
drove men together in multitudes, and compelled them to stand so close, and
build walls around them. This crowded condition produces wants of an unnatural character, which resulted in occupations that regenerated the evil, by
creating artificial wants. Even when that thought of grief,

> "I know, where'er I go
> That there hath passed away a glory from the Earth,"

came to our first parents, as they saw the angel, with the flaming sword of
self-consciousness, standing between them and the recovery of spontaneous
Life and Joy, we cannot believe they could have anticipated a time would
come, when the sensuous apprehension of Creation—the great symbol of God
—would be taken away from their unfortunate children,—crowded together
in such a manner as to shut out the free breath and the Universal Dome of
Heaven, some opening their eyes in the dark cellars of the narrow, crowded
streets of walled cities. How could they have believed in such a conspiracy
against the soul, as to deprive it of the sun and sky, and glorious apparelled
Earth! . . .

The plan of the Community, as an Economy, is in brief this; for all who
have property to take stock, and receive a fixed interest thereon; then to keep
house or board in commons, as they shall severally desire, at the cost of pro-
visions purchased at wholesale, or raised on the farm; and for all to labor in
community, and be paid at a certain rate an hour, choosing their own number of hours, and their own kind of work. With the results of this labor, and
their interest, they are to pay their board, and also purchase whatever else they
require at cost, at the warehouses of the Community, which are to be filled by
the Community as such. To perfect this economy, in the course of time they
must have all trades, and all modes of business carried on among themselves,
from the lowest mechanical trade, which contributes to the health and comfort of life, to the finest art which adorns it with food or drapery for the mind.

All labor, whether bodily or intellectual, is to be paid at the same rate of wages; on the principle, that as the labor becomes merely bodily, it is a greater sacrifice to the individual laborer, to give his time to it; because time is desirable for the cultivation of the intellect, in exact proportion to ignorance. Besides, intellectual labor involves in itself higher pleasures, and is more its own reward, than bodily labor . . .

Besides, after becoming members of this community, none will be engaged merely in bodily labor. The hours of labor for the Association will be limited by a general law, and can be curtailed at the will of the individual still more; and means will be given to all for intellectual improvement and for social intercourse, calculated to refine and expand. The hours redeemed from labor by community, will not be reapplied to the acquisition of wealth, but to the production of intellectual goods. This community aims to be rich, not in the metallic representative of wealth, but in the wealth itself, which money should represent; namely, LEISURE TO LIVE IN ALL THE FACULTIES OF THE SOUL. As a community, it will traffic with the world at large, in the products of Agricultural labor; and it will sell education to as many young persons as can be domesticated in the families, and enter into the common life with their own children. In the end, it hopes to be enabled to provide—not only all the necessaries, but all the elegances desirable for bodily and for spiritual health; books, apparatus, collections for science, works of art, means of beautiful amusement. These things are to be common to all; and thus that object, which alone gilds and refines the passion for individual accumulation, will no longer exist for desire, and whenever the Sordid passion appears, it will be seen in its naked selfishness. In its ultimate success, the community will realize all the ends which selfishness seeks, but involved in spiritual blessings, which only greatness of soul can aspire after.

And the requisitions on the individuals, it is believed, will make this the order forever. The spiritual good will always be the condition of the temporal. Every one must labor for the community in a reasonable degree, or not taste its benefits. The principles of the organization, therefore, and not its probable results in future time, will determine its members. These principles are coöperation in social matters, instead of competition or balance of interests; and individual self-unfolding, in the faith that the whole soul of humanity is in each man and woman. The former is the application of the love of man; the latter of the love of God, to life. Whoever is satisfied with society, as it is; whose sense of justice is not wounded by its common action, institutions, spirit of commerce, has no business with this community; neither has any one who is willing to have other men (needing more time for intellectual cultivation than himself) give their best hours and strength to bodily labor, to secure himself immunity therefrom. And whoever does not measure what society owes to its members of cherishing and instruction, by the needs of the individuals that compose it, has no lot in this new society. Whoever is willing to receive from his fellow men that, for which he gives no equivalent, will stay away from its precincts forever.

But whoever shall surrender himself to its principles, shall find that its yoke is easy and its burden light. Everything can be said of it, in a degree, which Christ said of his kingdom, and therefore it is believed that in some measure it does embody his Idea. For its Gate of entrance is straight and narrow. It is literally a pearl *hidden in a field*. Those only who are willing to lose their life for its sake shall find it. Its voice is that which sent the young man sorrowing away. "Go sell all thy goods and give to the poor, and then come and follow me." "Seek first the kingdom of Heaven, and its righteousness, and all other things shall be added to you."

This principle, with regard to labor, lies at the root of moral and religious life; for it is not more true that "money is the root of all evil," than that *labor is the germ of all good* . . .

It seems impossible that the little organization can be looked on with any unkindness by the world without it. Those, who have not the faith that the principles of Christ's kingdom are applicable to real life in the world, will smile at it, as a visionary attempt. But even they must acknowledge it can do no harm, in any event. If it realizes the hopes of its founders, it will immediately become a manifold blessing. Its moral *aura* must be salutary. As long as it lasts, it will be an example of the beauty of brotherly love. If it succeeds in uniting successful labor with improvement in mind and manners, it will teach a noble lesson to the agricultural population, and do something to check that rush from the country to the city, which is now stimulated by ambition, and by something better, even a desire for learning. Many a young man leaves the farmer's life, because only by so doing can he have intellectual companionship and opportunity; and yet, did he but know it, professional life is ordinarily more unfavorable to the perfection of the mind, than the farmer's life; if the latter is lived with wisdom and moderation, and the labor mingled as it might be with study. This community will be a school for young agriculturalists, who may learn within its precincts, not only the skilful practice, but the scientific reasons of their work, and be enabled afterwards to improve their art continuously. It will also prove the best of normal schools, and as such, may claim the interest of those, who mourn over the inefficiency of our common school system, with its present ill-instructed teachers . . .

There may be some persons, at a distance, who will ask, to what degree has this community gone into operation? We cannot answer this with precision, for we do not write as organs of this association, and have reason to feel, that if we applied to them for information, they would refuse it, out of their dislike to appear in public. We desire this to be distinctly understood. But we can see, and think we have a right to say, that it has purchased the Farm, which some of its members cultivated for a year with success, by way of trying their love and skill for agricultural labor;—that in the only house they are as yet rich enough to own, is collected a large family, including several boarding scholars, and that all work and study together. They seem to be glad to know of all, who desire to join them in the spirit, that at any moment, when they are able to enlarge their habitations, they may call together those that belong to them.

10. George Ripley (1802–1880)
The Harbinger

[Nobody knows what went on in Ripley's mind as he consented, by January 18, 1844, to change Brook Farm from a Transcendental picnic into a regimented Phalanx. "It must have been," as Lindsay Swift said, "that he came to lay more stress on the method by which individual freedom was to become assured, than on the fact of personal liberty in itself." The burning of the expensively constructed "Phalanstery" on March 3, 1846, ruined both Ripley and the method. He sold his library and is said to have declared that he understood how a man would feel at his own funeral.

In 1844 *The Dial* gave up. On June 14, 1845, appeared the magazine published at Brook Farm, *The Harbinger*. (Emerson evaded a request for support by assuring Dwight that he would "heartily rejoice to aid an uncommitted journal.") Inspired by the loftiest devotion to the cause, Ripley conducted it not as an organ of the Farm—although the Farm needed help—but of Fourierism in general and of international socialism. In 1847 it had to be transferred to New York, where it died in 1849. For the first issue (I, 9) he wrote a declaration of policy which may well be taken for the culmination of that line of Transcendental thinking which led, through an increasing absorption in method, to a socialistic and totalitarian conclusion.]

The interests of Social Reform, will be considered as paramount to all others, in whatever is admitted into the pages of the Harbinger. We shall suffer no attachment to literature, no taste for abstract discussion, no love of purely intellectual theories, to seduce us from our devotion to the cause of the oppressed, the down trodden, the insulted and injured masses of our fellow men. Every pulsation of our being vibrates in sympathy with the wrongs of the toiling millions, and every wise effort for their speedy enfranchisement will find in us resolute and indomitable advocates. If any imagine from the literary tone of the preceding remarks, that we are indifferent to the radical movement for the benefit of the masses, which is the crowning glory of the nineteenth century, they will soon discover their mistake. To that movement, consecrated by religious principle, sustained by an awful sense of justice, and cheered by the brightest hopes of future good, all our powers, talents, and attainments are devoted. We look for an audience among the refined and educated circles, to which the character of our paper will win its way; but we shall also be read by the swart and sweaty artizan; the laborer will find in us another champion; and many hearts, struggling with the secret hope which no weight of care and toil can entirely suppress, will pour on us their benedictions as we labor for the equal rights of All.

The Harbinger will be devoted to the cause of a radical, organic social reform as essential to the highest development of man's nature, to the production of those elevated and beautiful forms of character of which he is capable, and to the diffusion of happiness, excellence, and universal harmony upon earth. The principles of universal unity as taught by Charles Fourier, in their application to society, we believe, are at the foundation of all genuine social progress; and it will ever be our aim, to discuss and defend these principles, without any sectarian bigotry, and in the catholic and comprehensive spirit of their great discoverer. While we bow to no man as an authoritative, infallible master, we revere the genius of Fourier too highly, not to accept, with joyful welcome, the light which he has shed on the most intricate problems of human destiny. The social reform, of whose advent the signs are every where visible, comprehends all others; and in laboring for its speedy accomplishment, we are conscious that we are devoting our best ability to the removal of oppression and injustice among men, to the complete emancipation of the enslaved, to the promotion of genuine temperance, and to the elevation of the toiling and down-trodden masses to the inborn rights of humanity.

In literature, the Harbinger will exercise a firm and impartial criticism, without respect of persons or parties. It will be made a vehicle for the freest thought, though not of random speculations; and with a generous appreciation of the various forms of truth and beauty, it will not fail to expose such instances of false sentiment, perverted taste, and erroneous opinion, as may tend to vitiate the public mind, or degrade the individual character. Nor will the literary department of the Harbinger be limited to criticism alone. It will receive contributions from various pens, in different spheres of thought; and free from dogmatic exclusiveness, will accept all that in any way indicates the unity of Man with Man, with Nature, and with God. Consequently, all true science, all poetry and arts, all sincere literature, all religion that is from the soul, all wise analyses of mind and character will come within its province.

We appeal for aid in our enterprise to the earnest and hopeful spirits in all classes of society. We appeal to all who, suffering from a resistless discontent in the present order of things, with faith in man and trust in God, are striving for the establishment of universal justice, harmony, and love. We appeal to the thoughtful, the aspiring, the generous everywhere, who wish to see the reign of heavenly truth triumphantly supplanting the infernal discords and falsehoods, on which modern society is built, for their sympathy, friendship, and practical co-operation, in the undertaking which we announce to day.

11. Frederic Henry Hedge (1805–1890)
The Art of Life

[In December 1841 and January 1842 Emerson delivered at the Masonic Temple three lectures on the age; this was the first winter of Brook Farm, and of his consciousness that in Ripley's judgment the existence of the Farm was a standing rebuke to him. He worked out a subtle dialectic by opposing "the Times" of the first lecture to "the Conservative" of the second, and then finding a kind of synthesis of the two—or more accurately an escape from them both—in "The Transcendentalist." (Were there space enough, that lecture should be reprinted at this point.) It was a plea for those who "withdraw" from society—from any form of society. "They are lonely; the spirit of their writing and conversation is lonely; they repel influences; they shun general society; they incline to shut themselves in their chamber in the house, to live in the country rather than in the town, and to find their tasks and amusements in solitude." It was an almost angry justification of those who retire into uninhabitable deserts of thought, on the argument that only the solitary heroes find the highway of health and benefit to mankind. "Will you not tolerate"—he raised his voice to a, for him, shrill and defiant tone—"one or two solitary voices in the land, speaking for thoughts and principles not marketable or perishable?" Emerson thus assumed the offensive not merely because he was striking at social Boston but because he was haunted by the socialism of Ripley and his followers.

The supreme expression of this Transcendental individualism is, of course, Thoreau's "Civil Disobedience," published in *Aesthetic Papers* in 1849. Out of the imperative to withdrawal Thoreau constructed an aggressive social philosophy, an absolute anarchism. A free and enlightened state must recognize the individual as a higher and independent power, and must not think it inconsistent with its security if "a few" live aloof from it. "A State which bore this kind of fruit, and suffered it to drop off as fast as it ripened, would prepare the way for a still more perfect and glorious State, which also I have imagined, but not yet anywhere seen."

In the second number of *The Dial*, for October 1840 (I, 175–182), Frederic Hedge took the lead in indicating the road that Emerson and Thoreau must travel. He invoked the word "scholar," which Emerson in 1837 had made the word to conjure with. The unity of sentiment within the group, which a few short years before had seemed sufficient guarantee of their unanimity, was lost in the abyss between society and solitude. The great utterances of Emerson and Thoreau, which survive as classics of a kind of political wisdom, must be interpreted against the contemporaneous setting of the debate. Of course, it should be noted that this separation into factions was not, at the time, an earth-shaking event; the Transcendentalists were not numerous, and they exerted no influence on practical politics. But even so, it is in the perspective of American intellectual history, in terms of the ultimate significance of the division, that the sundering of Transcendental optimism becomes a portent for the American spirit and for the twentieth century. "These two states of thought," said Emerson, "diverge every moment, and stand in wild contrast."]

The work of life, so far as the individual is concerned, and that to which the scholar is particularly called, is *self-culture,*—the perfect unfolding of our individual nature. To this end above all others the art, of which I speak, directs our attention and points our endeavor. There is no man, it is presumed, to whom this object is wholly indifferent,—who would not willingly possess this too, along with other prizes, provided the attainment of it were compatible with personal ease and worldly good. But the business of self-culture admits of no compromise. Either it must be made a distinct aim, or wholly abandoned . . .

Of self-culture, as of all other things worth seeking, the price is a single devotion to that object,—a devotion which shall exclude all aims and ends, that do not directly or indirectly tend to promote it. In this service let no man flatter himself with the hope of light work and ready wages. The work is hard and the wages are slow. Better pay in money or in fame may be found in any other path than in this. The only motive to engage in this work is its own inherent worth, and the sure satisfaction which accompanies the consciousness of progress, in the true direction towards the stature of a perfect man. Let him who would build this tower consider well the cost, whether in energy and endurance he have sufficient to finish it. Much, that he has been accustomed to consider as most desirable, he will have to renounce. Much, that other men esteem as highest and follow after as the grand reality, he will have to forgo. No emoluments must seduce him from the rigor of his devotion. No engagements beyond the merest necessities of life must interfere with his pursuit. A meagre economy must be his income. "Spare fast that oft with gods doth diet" must be his fare. The rusty coat must be his badge. Obscurity must be his distinction. He must consent to see younger and smaller men take their places above him in Church and State. He must become a living sacrifice, and dare to lose his life in order that he may find it . . .

On all hands man's existence is converted into a preparation for existence. We do not properly live in these days, but, everywhere, with patent inventions and complex arrangements, are getting ready to live; like that King of Epirus, who was all his lifetime preparing to take his ease, but must first conquer the world. The end is lost in the means. Life is smothered in appliances. We cannot get to ourselves, there are so many external comforts to wade through. Consciousness stops half way. Reflection is dissipated in the circumstances of our environment. Goodness is exhausted in aids to goodness, and all the vigor and health of the soul is expended in quack contrivances to build it up. O! for some moral Alaric, one is tempted to exclaim, who should sweep away, with one fell swoop, all that has been in this kind, —all the manuals and false pretensions of modern culture, and place man once more on the eternal basis of original Nature. We are paying dearer than we imagine for our boasted improvements. The highest life,—the highest enjoyment, the point at which, after all our wanderings, we mean to land, is the life of the mind—the enjoyment of thought. Between this life and any point of outward existence, there is never but one step, and that step is an act of the will, which no aids from without can supersede or even facilitate. We travel round and round in a circle of facilities, and come at last to the point from which we set out. The mortal leap remains still to be made.

With these objects and tendencies the business of self-culture has nothing to do. Its objects are immediate and ultimate. Its aim is to live now, to live in the present, to live in the highest. The process here is one with the end. With such opposite views the scholar must expect nothing from Society, but may deem himself happy, if for the day-labor, which necessity imposes, Society will give him his hire, and beyond that leave him free to follow his proper calling, which he must either pursue with exclusive devotion, or wholly abandon. The more needful is it that he bring to the conflict the Prometheus spirit of endurance, which belongs of old to his work and line . . .

Whatever selfishness there may seem to be in such a discipline as this, exists only in appearance. The influence it would have upon Society would, in fact, be hardly less beneficial than its influence on the individual himself. In self-culture lies the ground and condition of all culture. Not those, who seem most earnest in promoting the culture of Society, do most effectually promote it. We have reformers in abundance, but few who, in the end, will be found to have aided essentially the cause of human improvement; either because they have failed to illustrate in themselves the benefits they wished to confer, and the lesson they wished to inculcate, or because there is a tendency in mankind to resist overt efforts to guide and control them. The silent influence of example, where no influence is intended, is the true reformer. The only efficient power, in the moral world, is attraction. Society are more benefited by one sincere life, by seeing how one man has helped himself, than by all the projects that human policy has devised for their salvation. The Christian church—the mightiest influence the world has known—was the product of a great example . . .

On this ground I am disposed to rejoice in those radical movements, which are everywhere springing up in the discontented spirits and misguided efforts of modern reform. Perfectionism, Grahamism, Nonresistance, and all the forms of ultraism, blind and headlong as they seem, have yet a meaning which, if it cannot command assent, must at least preclude contempt. They are the gropings of men who have waked too soon, while the rest of mankind are yet wrapt in sleep, and the new day still tarries in the East. The philosopher sees through these efforts, and knows that they are not the light that is to come; but he feels that they are sent to bear witness of the light, and hails them as the welcome tokens of approaching day. However our reason may disallow, however our taste may reject them, the thoughtful mind will perceive there the symptoms of a vitality which appears nowhere else. They are the life, however spasmodic, of this generation. There, or nowhere, beats the heart of the century. Thus the new in Church and State is always preceded by a cynical, radical spirit, which wages war with the old. Every genuine reform has its preacher in the wilderness. First the Cynic John with hair cloth and fasts, then the God-man Jesus with the bread of life.

Meanwhile the scholar has his function, too, in this baptism of repentance. For him, too, the age has its problem and its task. What other reformers are to the moral culture, he must be to the mind of his age. By taste averse, by calling exempt, from the practical movements around him, to him is committed the movement of thought. He must be a radical in speculation, an ascetic in devotion, a Cynic in independence, an anchorite in his habits, a perfectionist in discipline. Secluded from without, and nourished from within, self-sustained and self-sufficing, careless of praise or blame, intent always on the highest, he must rebuke the superficial attainments, the hollow pretensions, the feeble efforts, and trivial productions, of his contemporaries, with the thoroughness of his acquisitions, the reach of his views, the grandeur of his aims, the earnestness of his endeavor.

It is to such efforts and to such men that we must look for the long expected literature of this nation. Hitherto our literature has been but an echo of other voices and climes. Generally, in the history of nations, song has preceded science, and the feeling of a people has been sooner developed than its understanding. With us this order has been reversed. The national understanding is fully ripe, but the feeling, the imagination of the people, has found as yet no adequate expression. We have our men of science, our Franklins, our Bowditches, our Clevelands; we have our orators, our statesmen; but the American poet, the American thinker is yet to come. A deeper culture must lay the foundation for him, who shall worthily represent the genius and utter the life of this continent. A severer discipline must prepare the way for our Dantes, our Shakespeares, our Miltons. "He who would write an epic," said one of these, "must have his life an epic." This touches our infirmity. We have no practical poets,—no epic lives. Let us but have sincere livers, earnest, whole-hearted, heroic men, and we shall not want for writers and for literary fame. Then shall we see springing up, in every part of these Republics, a literature, such as the ages have not known, a literature, commensurate with our idea, vast as our destiny and varied as our clime.

12. George B. Loring (1817–1891)
Hawthorne's Scarlet Letter

[The importance with which the dissension inside Transcendentalism over the social question may legitimately be invested by the historian can further be emphasized by noting that around the middle of the century certain large Transcendental ideas were becoming commonplace. As these attitudes became more widely diffused, they also became less precise, until at last they entered the general American tradition as perhaps no more than sentimental assumptions.

Dr. George Bailey Loring is a case in point. He was not a Transcendentalist; indeed, he was a man of no great originality or profundity of thought. But he had just graduated from Harvard College in 1838 when Emerson delivered the *Divinity School Address,* and being this much younger than men like Clarke or Cranch or Hedge, he matured in an atmosphere where the Transcendental notions could be taken for granted. He received his M.D. from the Harvard Medical School in 1842 and served until 1851 as surgeon at the Marine Hospital in Chelsea. Later he moved to Salem, became a gentleman farmer, a popular orator, and a politician. He served with distinction as Commissioner of Agriculture and from 1888 to 1890 was Minister to Portugal.

When Ripley invited Emerson to Brook Farm and Emerson declined, both agreed that their goal was "emancipation." In 1850, when Parker asked Dr. Loring to review *The Scarlet Letter* for *The Massachusetts Quarterly Review* (III, 484–500), the young surgeon was already so imbued with the no longer new notions that he naturally read the novel as an attack upon society and upon convention, under the banner of self-reliance.

That Hawthorne intended *The Scarlet Letter* to preach the Transcendental revolt against Unitarian rationalism and Bostonian proprieties may well be doubted; nevertheless Hawthorne was—despite his often satirical criticism of the movement—not entirely untouched by it. In his own curious way, he too was infected. From the beginning there was always present a latent possibility that the Transcendental doctrine of trusting the promptings of one's own genius might mean trusting the promptings of sexual passion. But Margaret Fuller's relation with Ossoli was the only "affair"—if it was that—which came out of the Transcendental emancipation. Still, Loring had no difficulty in making out of Hester Prynne a Transcendental heroine. Because his interpretation approached the one really dangerous theme, he demanded that Parker keep his authorship a profound secret. The review illustrates how handily the Transcendental attitude toward society could now be utilized for literary criticism, and how, by 1850, it had indeed become a part of the thinking—or at any rate the feeling—of many Americans who, like Hawthorne himself, did not consider themselves specifically Transcendentalists.]

It would be hard to conceive of a greater outrage upon the freezing and self-denying doctrines of that day, than the sin for which Hester Prynne was damned by society, and for which Arthur Dimmesdale damned himself. For centuries, the devoted and superstitious Catholic had made it a part of his creed to cast disgrace upon the passions; and the cold and rigid Puritan, with less fervor, and consequently with less beauty, had driven them out of his paradise, as the parents of all sin. There was no recognition of the intention or meaning of that sensuous element of human nature which, gilding life like a burnishing sunset, lays the foundation of all that beauty which seeks its expression in poetry, and music, and art, and gives the highest apprehension of religious fervor. Zest of life was no part of the Puritan's belief. He scorned his own flesh and blood. His appetites were crimes. His cool head was always ready to temper the hot blood in its first tendency to come bounding from his heart. He had no sympathy, no tenderness, for any sinner, more especially for that hardened criminal who had failed to trample all his senses beneath his feet. Love, legalized, was a weakness in the mind of that mighty dogmatist, who, girt with the "sword of the Lord and of Gideon," subdued his enemies, and, with folios of texts and homilies, sustained and cheered his friends; and love, illegalized, was that burning, scarlet sin which had no forgiveness in these disciples of Him who said to the woman, "neither do I condemn thee." The state of society which this grizzly form of humanity created, probably served as little to purify men as any court of voluptuousness; and, while we recognize with compressed lip that heroism which braved seas and unknown shores, for opinion's sake, we remember, with a warm glow, the elegances and intrepid courage and tropical luxuriance of the cavaliers whom they left behind them. Asceticism and voluptuarism on either hand, neither fruitful of the finer and truer virtues, were all that men had arrived at in the great work of sensuous life . . .

It was as heir of these virtues, and impressed with this education, that Arthur Dimmesdale, a clergyman, believing in and applying all the moral remedies of the times, found himself a criminal. We learn nothing of his experience during the seven long years in which his guilt was secretly gnawing at his breast, unless it be the experience of pain and remorse. He speaks no word of wisdom. He lurks and skulks behind the protection of his profession and his social position, neither growing wiser nor stronger, but, day after day, paler and paler, more and more abject. We do not find that, out of his sin, came any revelation of virtue. No doubt exists of his repentance, —of that repentance which is made up of sorrow for sin, and which grows out of fear of consequences; but we learn nowhere that his enlightened conscience, rising above the dogmas and catechistic creeds of the day, by dint of his own deep and solemn spiritual experiences, taught him what obligations had gathered around him, children of his crime, which he was bound to acknowledge before men, as they stood revealed to God. Why had his religious wisdom brought him no more heroism? He loved Hester Prynne— he had bound himself to her by an indissoluble bond, and yet he had neither moral courage nor moral honesty, with all his impressive piety, to come forth and assert their sins and their mutual obligations. He was, evidently, a man of powerful nature. His delicate sensibility, his fervor, his influence upon those about him, and, above all, his sin, committed when the tides of his heart rushed in and swept away all the bulrush barriers he had heaped up against them, through years of studious self-discipline, —show what a spirit, what forces, he had. Against none of these forces had he sinned. And yet he was halting, and wavering, and becoming more and more perplexed and worn down with woe, because he had violated the dignity of his position, and had broken a law which his education had made more prominent than any law in his own soul. In this way, he presented the twofold nature which belongs to us as members of society; —a nature born from ourselves and our associations, and comprehending all the diversity and all the harmony of our individual and social duties. Violation of either destroys our fitness for both. And when we remember that, in this development, no truth comes except from harmony, no beauty except from a fit conjunction of the individual with society, and of society with the individual, can we wonder that the great elements of Arthur Dimmesdale's character should have been overbalanced by a detestable crowd of mean and grovelling qualities, warmed into life by the hot antagonism he felt radiating upon himself and all his fellow-men—from the society in which he moved, and from which he received his engrafted moral nature? He sinned in the arms of society, and fell almost beyond redemption; his companion in guilt became an outcast, and a flood of heroic qualities gathered around her. Was this the work of social influences? . . .

In this matter of crime, as soon as he became involved, he appeared before himself no longer a clergyman, but a man—a human being. He answered society in the cowardly way we have seen. He answered himself in that way which every soul adopts, where crime does not penetrate. The physical facts of crime alone, with which society has to do, in reality constitute sin. Crimes are committed under protest of the soul, more or less decided, as the weary soul itself has been more or less besieged and broken. The war in the individual begins, and the result of the fierce struggle is the victory of the sensual over the spiritual, when the criminal act is committed. If there is no such war, there is no crime; let the deed be what it may, and be denominated what it may, by society. The soul never assents to sin, and weeps with the angels when the form in which it dwells violates the sacred obligations it imposes upon it. When this human form, with its passions and tendencies, commits the violation, and, at the same time, abuses society, it is answerable to this latter tribunal, where it receives its judgment; while the soul flees to her God, dismayed and crushed by the conflict, but not deprived of her divine inheritance. Between the individual and his God, there remains a spot, larger or smaller, as the soul has been kept unclouded, where no sin can enter, where no mediation can come, where all the discords of his life are resolved into the most delicious harmonies, and his whole existence becomes illuminated by a divine intelligence. Sorrow and sin reveal this spot to all men—as, through death, we are born to an immortal life. They reveal what beliefs and dogmas becloud and darken. They produce that intense consciousness, without which virtue can not rise above innocency. They are the toil and trial which give strength and wisdom, and which, like all other toil, produce weariness and fainting and death, if pursued beyond the limit where reaction and the invigorating process begin. We can not think with too much awe upon the temptations and trials which beset the powerful. The solemn gloom which shuts down over a mighty nature, during the struggle, which it recognizes with vivid sense, between its demon and its divinity, is like that fearful night in which no star appears to relieve the murky darkness. And yet, from such a night as this, and from no other, the grandeur of virtue has risen to beautify and warm and bless the broad universe of human hearts, and to make the whole spiritual creation blossom like the rose. The Temptation and Gethsemane,—these are the miracles which have redeemed mankind.

Thus it stands with the individual and his soul. With himself and society come up other obligations, other influences, other laws. The tribunal before which he stands as a social being can not be disregarded with impunity. The effects of education and of inheritance cling around us with the tenacity of living fibres of our own bodies, and they govern, with closest intimacy, the estimate of deeds which constitute the catalogue of vice and virtue, and which in their commission elevate or depress our spiritual condition.

We doubt if there is a stronger element in our natures than that which forbids our resisting with impunity surrounding social institutions. However much we may gain in the attempt, it is always attended with some loss. The reverence which enhanced so beautifully the purity and innocence of childhood, often receives its death-blow from that very wisdom out of which comes our mature virtue. Those abstractions whose foundation is the universe, and without an apprehension of which we may go handcuffed and fettered through life, may draw us away from the devotion which deepened and gilded the narrow world in which we were strong by belief alone.

The institutions in which we were born controlled in a great degree the mental condition of our parents, as surrounding nature did their physical, and we owe to these two classes of internal and external operations the characters we inherit. An attack, therefore, upon these institutions, affects us to a certain degree as if we were warring against ourselves. Reason and conscience, and our sublimest sense of duty, may call us to the work of reform,—instinct resists. And the nervous energy called for in the struggle is felt through our whole frames with a convulsive influence, while our children seem to have been born with the spirit of unrest. That harmonious calm, out of which alone healthy creations can arise, appeals to all man's interests, even when the quiet sky he is admiring overhangs an ill-cultivated and sterile field. As he puts in his ploughshare for the upturning of the first furrow, he looks over the expanse which the rest of ages has sanctified, and sighs a farewell to the failure of the past, and a sad and sorrowful welcome to the toil and doubt and undeveloped promise of the future.

This law of our nature, which applies to the well-directed and honest efforts of good progressive intentions, applies also to misguided and sinful actions. The stormy life of the erring mother affords no rest for the healthy development of her embryonic child. It amounts to but little for her to say, with Hester Prynne, "what we did had a consecration of its own," unless that consecration produces a heavenly calm, as if all nature joined in harmony. Pearl, that wild and fiery little elf, born of love, was also born of conflict; and had the accountability of its parents extended no farther than the confines of this world, the prospective debt due this offspring involved fearful responsibilities. How vividly this little child typified all their startled instincts, their convulsive efforts in life and thought, their isolation, and their self-inflicted contest with and distrust of all mankind. Arthur Dimmesdale, shrinking from intimate contact and intercourse with his child, shrunk from a visible and tangible representation of the actual life which his guilty love had created for himself and Hester Prynne;—love, guilty, because, secured as it may have been to them, it drove them violently from the moral centre around which they revolved . . .

It is no pleasant matter to contemplate what is called the guilt of this woman; but it may be instructive, nevertheless. We naturally shrink from any apparent violation of virtue and chastity, and are very ready to forget, in our eager condemnation, how much that is beautiful and holy may be involved in it. We forget that what society calls chastity is often far the reverse, and that a violation of this perverted virtue may be a sad, sorrowful, and tearful beauty, which we would silently and reverently contemplate,—

silently, lest a harsh word of the law wound our hearts,—reverently, as we would listen to the fervent prayer. While we dread that moral hardness which would allow a human being to be wrecked in a storm of passion, let us not be unmindful of the holy love which may *long and pray for its development.* Man's heart recognizes this, whether society will or not. The struggle and the sacrifice which the latter calls a crime, the former receives as an exhilarating air of virtue . . . It is this recognition which brought forth the words, "Neither do I condemn thee." And it is only when we harden our hearts to a capacity for receiving the utmost rigor of the law, and render them cold, keen, and glittering, by the formularies of social virtue, that we are ready to cast out the sinner. Properly attuned, we look earnestly into his life, in search of that *hidden virtue, which his crime may stand pointing at.*

We would not condemn the vigilance and sensitiveness of society, were it really a tribute paid to the true sanctity of virtue. But is there no deeper sense, which wears out a life of martyrdom in obedience to the demands of the world? Is there no suffering which goes unrecognized, because it interferes with no avowed rights? Is there no violation of social law more radical and threatening than any wayward act of passion can be? It may be necessary, perhaps, that the safety of associated man demands all the compromises which the superficiality of social law creates, but the sorrow may be none the less acute because the evil is necessary. We see in the lives of Arthur Dimmesdale and Hester Prynne, that the severity of puritanic law and morals could not keep them from violation; and we see, too, that this very severity drove them both into a state of moral insanity. And does any benefit arise from such a sacrifice? Not a gentle word, or look, or thought, met those two erring mortals. Revenge embittered the heart of the old outraged usurper. Severity—blasting, and unforgiving, and sanctimonious— was the social atmosphere which surrounded them. We doubt not that, to many minds, this severity constitutes the saving virtue of the book. But it is always with a fearful sacrifice of all the gentler feelings of the breast, of all the most comprehensive humanity, of all the most delicate affections and appreciations, that we thus rudely shut out the wanderer from us; especially when the path of error leads through the land whence come our warmest and tenderest influences. We gain nothing by this hardness, except a capability to sin without remorse. The elements of character upon which vice and virtue hang are so nearly allied, that the rude attempts to destroy the one may result in a fatal wounding of the other; the harvest separates the tares from the wheat with the only safety. Who has not felt the forbidding aspect of that obtrusive and complacent virtue which never cherishes the thought of forgiveness? And who, that has recognized the deep and holy meaning of the human affections, has not been frozen into demanding a warm-hearted crime as a relief for the cold, false, vulgar, and cowardly asperity which is sometimes called chastity?

10

Recollections

Last night I dreamed of walking with Dr. Channing, and as we descended the hill, I asked him what interested him now; to which he replied that the signs of the times seemed auspicious for furthering spiritual illumination and culture, and he had been wishing a school of Divinity were established, especially for bright young men and women, remarking that New England thought had led now for a quarter of a century, and it was time to begin to organize and cherish itself in this its highest form for the enlightenment and discipline of its preachers and teachers . . .

I said, perceiving the Doctor still clung to his city and denomination, at least practically and socially: "The young students look elsewhere for what they seek. They, indeed, have quoted us in their graduating essays, read our books in preference to most others, and the late graduating class propose to visit Emerson and myself tomorrow for the very conversation about which I was speaking. They say there is something in the atmosphere of Cambridge, classic as are its shades, that paralyses and obscures, and that Concord somehow seems delightfully classical, as if the Academy, the Lyceum, were transplanted from Athens, and the Orchard overshadowed the new School of Divinity."

Here the colloquy came suddenly to a close, by my wife appearing bearing a pail of water in each hand, tugging them up the lane, leaving me to wonder where I was and why I was permitting her to do what belonged to me.—And on this hint, I awoke to find my Academium was all a dream and that the Orchard well was dry, the water having failed during these days of drought, and my Castalia was elsewhere.

—AMOS BRONSON ALCOTT (1871)

1. Theodore Parker (1810–1860)

Theodore Parker's Experience as a Minister

[I have not attempted to furnish this collection with a "historical introduction" as is the fashion in anthologies. Not only can the selections themselves
tell the history, but there exist two summations of the movement which no modern
scholar can expect, within a similar space, to equal.

In January 1859 Parker suffered a hemorrhage of the lungs, and wrote in his
journal, "When I see the inevitable, I fall in love with her." His doctors sent him
to the West Indies, where on April 19 he finished his farewell letter to the Twenty-
eighth, which the Church published as a pamphlet under the title, *Theodore
Parker's Experience as a Minister*. Too long to quote in full, much of it is devoted
to his multifarious activities; I have extracted those portions that constitute one
of the two best narratives of that episode in the life of the American spirit which
we call the Transcendental movement.]

In due time I entered the Theological School at Cambridge, then
under the charge of the Unitarians, or "Liberal Christians." I found excellent
opportunities for study: there were able and earnest professors, who laid no
yoke on any neck, but left each man free to think for himself, and come to
such conclusions as he must. Telling what they thought they knew, they
never pretended they had learned all that may be known, or winnowed out
all error from their creed. They were honest guides, with no more sophistry
than is perhaps almost universal in that calling, and did not pretend to be
masters. There, too, was a large library, containing much valuable ancient
lore, though, alas! almost none of the new theologic thought of the German
masters. Besides, there was leisure, and unbounded freedom of research; and
I could work as many hours in the study as a mechanic in his shop, or a
farmer in his field. The pulpits of Boston were within an easy walk, and
Dr. Channing drew near the zenith of his power . . .

Connected with this Biblical study, came the question of inspiration and
of miracles. I still inconsistently believed, or half believed, in the direct miraculous interposition of God, from time to time, to set things right which else
went wrong, though I found no historic or philosophic reason for limiting it
to the affairs of Jews and Christians, or the early ages of the Church. The
whole matter of miracles was still a puzzle to me, and for a long time a
source of anxiety; for I had not studied the principles of historic evidence,
nor learned to identify and scrutinize the witnesses. But the problem of in-

spiration got sooner solved. I believed in the immanence of God in man, as well as matter, His activity in both; hence, that all men are inspired in proportion to their actual powers, and their normal use thereof; that truth is the test of intellectual inspiration, justice of moral, and so on. I did not find the Bible inspired, except in this general way, and in proportion to the truth and justice therein. It seemed to me that no part of the Old Testament or New could be called the "Word of God," save in the sense that all truth is God's word . . .

I studied assiduously the metaphysics and psychology of religion. Religious consciousness was universal in human history. Was it then natural to man, inseparable from his essence, and so from his development? In my own consciousness I found it automatic and indispensable; was it really so likewise in the human race? The authority of Bibles and Churches was no answer to that question. I tried to make an analysis of humanity, and see if by psychologic science I could detect the special element which produced religious consciousness in me, and religious phenomena in mankind—seeking a cause adequate to the facts of experience and observation. The common books of philosophy seemed quite insufficient; the sensational system, so ably presented by Locke in his masterly Essay, developed into various forms by Hobbes, Berkeley, Hume, Paley, and the French Materialists, and modified, but not much amended, by Reid and Stewart, gave little help; it could not legitimate my own religious instincts, nor explain the religious history of mankind, or even of the British people, to whom that philosophy is still so manifold a hindrance. Ecclesiastical writers, though able as Clarke and Butler, and learned also as Cudworth and Barrow, could not solve the difficulty; for the principle of authority, though more or less concealed, yet lay there, and, like buried iron, disturbed the free action of their magnetic genius, affecting its dip and inclination. The brilliant mosaic, which Cousin set before the world, was of great service, but not satisfactory. I found most help in the works of Immanuel Kant, one of the profoundest thinkers in the world, though one of the worst writers, even of Germany; if he did not always furnish conclusions I could rest in, he yet gave me the true method, and put me on the right road.

I found certain great primal intuitions of human nature, which depend on no logical process of demonstration, but are rather facts of consciousness given by the instinctive action of human nature itself. I will mention only the three most important which pertain to religion.

1. The instinctive intuition of the divine, the consciousness that there is a God.

2. The instinctive intuition of the just and right, a consciousness that there is a moral law, independent of our will, which we ought to keep.

3. The instinctive intuition of the immortal, a consciousness that the essential element of man, the principle of individuality, never dies.

Here, then, was the foundation of religion, laid in human nature itself, which neither the atheist nor the more pernicious bigot, with their sophisms of denial or affirmation, could move, or even shake. I had gone through the great spiritual trial of my life, telling no one of its hopes or fears; and I thought it a triumph that I had psychologically established these three things to my own satisfaction, and devised a scheme which to the scholar's mind, I thought, could legitimate what was spontaneously given to all, by the great primal instincts of mankind . . .

The years of my preliminary theological study, and of my early ministry, fell in the most interesting period of New England's spiritual history, when a great revolution went on—so silent that few men knew it was taking place, and none then understood its whither or its whence.

The Unitarians, after a long and bitter controversy, in which they were often shamelessly ill-treated by the "orthodox," had conquered, and secured their ecclesiastical right to deny the Trinity, "the Achilles of dogmas"; they had won the respect of the New England public; had absorbed most of the religious talent of Massachusetts, founded many churches, and possessed and liberally administered the oldest and richest college in America. Not yet petrified into a sect, they rejoiced in the large liberty of "the children of God," and owning neither racks nor dungeons, did not covet any of those things that were their neighbor's. With less education and literary skill, the Universalists had fought manfully against Eternal Damnation—the foulest doctrine which defiles the pages of man's theologic history—secured their ecclesiastical position, wiping malignant statutes from the law books, and, though in a poor and vulgar way, were popularising the great truth that God's chief attribute is LOVE, which is extended to all men. Alone of all Christian sects, they professedly taught the immortality of man in such a form that it is no curse to the race to find it true! But, though departing from those doctrines which are essential to the Christian ecclesiastic scheme, neither Universalist nor Unitarian had broken with the authority of Revelation, the word of the Bible, but still professed a willingness to believe both Trinity and Damnation, could they be found in the miraculous and infallible Scripture.

Mr. Garrison, with his friends, inheriting what was best in the Puritan founders of New England, fired with the zeal of the Hebrew prophets and Christian martyrs, while they were animated with a spirit of humanity rarely found in any of the three, was beginning his noble work, but in a style so humble that, after much search, the police of Boston discovered there was nothing dangerous in it, for "his only visible auxiliary was a negro boy." Dr. Channing was in the full maturity of his powers, and after long preaching the dignity of man as an abstraction, and piety as a purely inward life, with rare and winsome eloquence, and ever progressive humanity, began to apply his sublime doctrines to actual life in the individual, the state, and the church. In the name of Christianity, the great American Unitarian called for the reform of the drunkard, the elevation of the poor, the instruction of the ignorant, and, above all, for the liberation of the American slave. A remarkable man, his instinct of progress grew stronger the more he travelled, and the further he went, for he surrounded himself with young life. Horace Mann, with his coadjutors, began a great movement, to improve the public education of the people. Pierpont, single-handed, was fighting a grand and two-fold battle—against drunkenness in the street, and for righteousness in the pulpit—against fearful ecclesiastic odds maintaining a minister's right and duty to oppose actual wickedness, however popular and destructive. The brilliant genius of Emerson rose in the winter nights, and hung over Boston, drawing the eyes of ingenuous young people to look up to that great, new star, a beauty and a mystery, which charmed for the moment, while it gave also perennial inspiration, as it led them forward along new paths, and towards new hopes. America has seen no such sight before; it is not less a blessed wonder now.

Besides, the Phrenologists, so ably represented by Spurzheim and Combe, were weakening the power of the old supernaturalism, leading men to study the constitution of man more wisely than before, and laying the foundation on which many a beneficent structure was soon to rise. The writings of Wordsworth were becoming familiar to the thoughtful lovers of nature and of man, and drawing men to natural piety. Carlyle's works got reprinted at Boston, diffusing a strong, and then also, a healthy influence on old and young. The writings of Coleridge were reprinted in America, all of them "aids to reflection," and brilliant with the scattered sparks of genius; they incited many to think, more especially young Trinitarian ministers; and, spite of the lack of both historic and philosophic accuracy, and the utter absence of all proportion in his writings; spite of his haste, his vanity, prejudice, sophistry, confusion, and opium—he yet did great service in New England, helping to emancipate enthralled minds. The works of Cousin, more systematic, and more profound as a whole, and far more catholic and comprehensive, continental, not insular, in his range, also became familiar to the Americans—reviews and translations going where the eloquent original was not heard—and helped to free the young mind from the gross sensationalism of the academic philosophy on one side, and the grosser supernaturalism of the ecclesiastic theology on the other.

The German language, hitherto the priceless treasure of a few, was becoming well known, and many were thereby made acquainted with the most original, deep, bold, comprehensive, and wealthy literature in the world, full of theologic and philosophic thought. Thus, a great storehouse was opened to such as were earnestly in quest of truth. Young Mr. Strauss, in whom genius for criticism was united with extraordinary learning and rare facility of philosophic speech, wrote his "Life of Jesus," where he rigidly scrutinised the genuineness of the Gospels and the authenticity of their contents, and with scientific calmness, brought every statement to his steady scales, weighing it, not always, justly, as I think, but impartially always, with philosophic coolness and deliberation. The most formidable assailant of the ecclesiastical theology of Christendom, he roused a host of foes, whose writings—mainly illtempered, insolent, and sophistical—it was yet profitable for a young man to read.

The value of Christian miracles, not the question of fact, was discussed at Boston, as never before in America. Prophecy had been thought the Jachin, and miracles the Boaz, whereon alone Christianity could rest; but, said some, if both be shaken down, the Lord's house will not fall. The claims of ecclesiastical tradition came up to be settled anew; and young men, walking solitary through the moonlight, asked, "Which is to be permanent master—a single accident in human history, nay, perchance only the whim of some anonymous dreamer, or the substance of human nature, greatening with continual development, and

'Not without access of unexpected strength!' "

The question was also its answer . . .

Of course a strong reaction followed. At the Cambridge Divinity School, Professor Henry Ware, Jun., told the young men, if there appeared to them any contradiction between the reason of man and the letter of the Bible, they "must follow the written Word," "for you can never be so certain of the correctness of what takes place in your own mind, as of what is written in the Bible." In an ordination sermon, he told the young minister not to preach himself, but Christ; and not to appeal to human nature for a proof of doctrines, but to the authority of revelation. Other Unitarian ministers declared, "There are limits to free inquiry"; and preached, "Reason must be put down, or she will soon ask terrible questions"; protested against the union of philosophy and religion, and assumed to "prohibit the banns" of marriage between the two. Mr. Norton—then a great name at Cambridge, a scholar of rare but contracted merit, a careful and exact writer, born for controversy, really learned and able in his special department, the interpretations of the New Testament—opened his mouth and spoke: the mass of men must accept the doctrines of religion solely on the authority of the learned, as they do the doctrines of mathematical astronomy; the miracles of Jesus—he made merry at those of the Old Testament—are the only evidence of the truth of Christianity; in the popular religion of the Greeks and Romans, there was no conception of God; the new philosophic attempts to explain the fact of religious consciousness were "the latest form of infidelity"; the great philosophical and theological thinkers of Germany were "all atheists"; "Schleiermacher was an atheist," as was also Spinoza, his master, before him; and Cousin, who was only "that Frenchman," was no better; the study of philosophy, and the neglect of "Biblical criticism," were leading mankind to ruin—everywhere was instability and insecurity! . . .

The movement party established a new quarterly, the *Dial*, wherein their wisdom and their folly rode together on the same saddle, to the amazement of lookers-on. The short-lived journal had a narrow circulation, but its most significant papers were scattered wide by newspapers which copied them. A *Quarterly Review* was also established by Mr. Brownson, then a Unitarian minister and "sceptical democrat" of the most extravagant class, but now a Catholic, a powerful advocate of material and spiritual despotism, and perhaps the ablest writer in America against the rights of man and the welfare of his race. In this he diffused important philosophic ideals, displayed and disciplined his own extraordinary talents for philosophic thought and popular writing, and directed them towards Democracy, Transcendentalism, "New Views," and the "Progress of the Species."

I count it a piece of good fortune that I was a young man when these things were taking place, when great questions were discussed, and the public had not yet taken sides . . .

The critical study of the Bible only enhanced my reverence for the great and good things I found in the Old Testament and New. They were not the less valuable because they were not the work of "miraculous and infallible inspiration," and because I found them mixed with some of the worst doctrines ever taught by men; it was no strange thing to find pearls surrounded by sand, and roses beset with thorns. I liked the Bible better when I could consciously take its contradictory books each for what it is, and felt nothing commanding me to accept it for what it is not; and could freely use it as a help, not slavishly serve it as a master, or worship it as an idol. I took no doctrine for true, simply because it was in the Bible; what therein seemed false or wrong, I rejected as freely as if I had found it in the sacred books of the Buddhists or Mormons.

I had not preached long before I found, as never before, that practically, the ecclesiastical worship of the Bible hindered the religious welfare and progress of the Christians more than any other cause . . .

I continued my humble studies, philosophical and theological; and as fast as I found a new truth, I preached it to gladden other hearts in my own parish, and elsewhere, when I spoke in the pulpits of my friends. The neighbouring ministers became familiar with my opinions and my practice, but seldom uttered a reproach. At length, on the 19th of May, 1841, at the ordination of Mr. Shackford, a thoughtful and promising young man, at South Boston, I preached a "Discourse of the Transient and Permanent in Christianity." The Trinitarian ministers who were present joined in a public protest; a great outcry was raised against the sermon and its author. Theological and commercial newspapers rang with animadversions against its wickedness. "Unbeliever," "Infidel," "Atheist," were the titles bestowed on me by my brothers in the Christian ministry; a venerable minister, who heard the report in an adjoining county, printed his letter in one of the most widely circulated journals of New England, calling on the Attorney-General to prosecute, the grand jury to indict, and the judge to sentence me to three years' confinement in the State Prison for blasphemy!

I printed the sermon, but no bookseller in Boston would put his name to the title-page—Unitarian ministers had been busy with their advice. The Swedenborgian printers volunteered the protection of their name; the little pamphlet was thus published, sold, and vehemently denounced. Most of my clerical friends fell off; some would not speak to me in the street, and refused to take me by the hand; in their public meetings they left the sofas or benches when I sat down, and withdrew from me as Jews from contact with a leper. In a few months most of my former ministerial coadjutors forsook me, and there were only six who would allow me to enter their pulpits. But yet one Unitarian minister, Rev. John L. Russell, though a stranger till then, presently after came and offered me his help in my time of need! The controlling men of the denomination determined, "This young man must be silenced!" The Unitarian periodicals were shut against me and my friends—the public must not read what I wrote. Attempts were secretly made to alienate my little congregation, and expel me from my obscure station at West

Roxbury. But I had not gone to war without counting the cost. I well knew beforehand what awaited me, and had determined to fight the battle through, and never thought of yielding or being silenced. I told my opponents the only man who could "put me down" was myself, and I trusted I should do nothing to bring about that result. If thrust out of my own pulpit, I made up my mind to lecture from city to city, from town to town, from village to village, nay, if need were from house to house, well assured that I should not thus go over the hamlets of New England till something was come. But the little society came generously to my support and defence, giving me the heartiest sympathy, and offered me all the indulgence in their power. Some ministers and generous-minded laymen stood up on my side, and preached or wrote in defence of free thought and free speech, even in the pulpit. Friendly persons, both men and women, wrote me letters to cheer and encourage, also to warn —this against fear, that against excess and violence; some of them never gave me their names, and I only have this late opportunity to thank them for their anonymous kindness. Of course scurrilous and abusive letters did not fail to appear . . .

Under these circumstances you formed your society. A few earnest men thought the great principle of religious freedom was in danger; for, indeed, it was ecclesiastically repudiated, and that, too, with scorn and hissing, by the Unitarians—the "liberal Christians!" the "party of progress"—not less than by the orthodox. Some of you came together, privately first, and then in public, to look matters in the face, and consider what ought to be done. A young man proposed this resolution: *"Resolved,* That the Rev. Theodore Parker shall have a chance to be heard in Boston." That motion prevailed, and measures were soon taken to make the resolution an event . . . So, one rainy Sunday, the streets full of snow, on the 16th of February, 1845, for the first time I stood before you to preach and pray: we were strangers then! . . . I was then in my thirty-fifth year, and had some knowledge of the historical development of religion in the Christian world. I knew that I came to a "thirty years' war," and I had enlisted for the whole, should life hold out so long. I knew well what we had to expect at first; for we were committing the sin which all the great world-sects have held unpardonable—attempting to correct the errors of theory and the vices of practice in the Church . . . But I knew that I had thoroughly broken with the ecclesiastical authority of Christendom; its God was not my God, nor its Scriptures my Word of God, nor its Christ my Saviour; for I preferred the Jesus of historic fact to the Christ of theologic fancy. Its narrow, partial, and unnatural heaven I did not wish to enter on the terms proposed, nor did I fear, since earliest youth, its mythic, roomy hell, wherein the triune God, with his pack of devils to aid, tore the human race in pieces for ever and ever. I came to preach "another Gospel," sentiments, ideas, actions, quite unlike what belonged to the theology of the Christian Church. Though severely in earnest, I came to educate men into true religion as well as I could, I knew I should be accounted the worst of men, ranked among triflers, mockers, infidels, and atheists. But I did not know all the public had to offer me of good or ill; nay, I did not know what was latent in myself, nor foresee all the doctrines which then were hid in my own first principles, what embryo fruit and flowers lay sheathed in the obvious bud. But at the beginning I warned you that if you came, Sunday after Sunday, you would soon think very much as I did on the great matters you asked me to teach—because I had drawn my doctrine from the same human nature which was in you, and that would recognise and own its child . . .

To me, human life in all its forms, individual and aggregate, is a perpetual wonder; the flora of the earth and sea is full of beauty and of mystery which science seeks to understand; the fauna of land and oceans is not less wonderful; the world which holds them both, and the great universe that folds it on every side, are still more wonderful, complex, and attractive, to the contemplating mind. But the universe of human life, with its peculiar worlds of outer sense and inner soul, the particular faunas and floras which therein find a home, are still more complex, wonderful, and attractive; and the laws which control it seem to me more amazing than the mathematic principles that explain the celestial mechanics of the outward world. The Kosmos of matter seems little compared to this Kosmos of immortal and progressive man; it is my continual study, discipline, and delight. Oh, that some young genius would devise the "novum organum" of humanity, determine the "principia" thereof, and with deeper than mathematic science, write out the formulas of the human universe, the celestial mechanics of mankind!

In your busy, bustling town, with its queerly-mingled, heterogeneous population, and its great diversity of work, I soon learned to see the unity of human life under all this variety of circumstances and outward condition. It is easy for a simple-hearted man, standing on a central truth, to reduce them all to one common denomination of humanity, and ascertain the relative value of individuals in this comparative morality. The huckster, with a basket, where apples, pea-nuts, candy, and other miscellaneous small stores, are huddled together, is a small merchant; the merchant, with his warehouse, his factory, or bank, his ships on many a sea, is a great huckster; both buy to sell, and sell to gain; the odds is quantitative, not in kind, but in bulk. The cunning lawyer, selling his legal knowledge and forensic skill to promote a client's gainful wickedness; the tricksy harlot, letting out her person to a stranger's unholy lust; the deceitful minister, prostituting his voice and ecclesiastical position to make some popular sin appear decent and Christian, "accordant with the revealed word of God"—all stand in the same column of my religious notation. In the street I see them all pass by, each walking in a vain show, in different directions, but all consilient to the same end! . . .

When a young man, it was part of my original plan to leave the practical work of continual preaching, a little before I should be fifty years old, and devote the residue of my life to publishing works which I hoped might be of permanent value . . . But, when I found the scholarly class more unfriendly than the multitude, I began to think I had chosen the wrong audience to address; that it was the people, not the scholars, who were to lead in philosophic thought; and when you gave me a chance to be heard in Boston, and I preached on from year to year, great crowds of men, who were not readers but workers in the week, coming and continuing to listen to the longest of sermons, wherein great subjects were treated without respect to popular prejudice, ecclesiastical, political, or social, and that, too, without sparing the severest attention of the hearers; when I found these multitudes seemed to comprehend the abstractest reasoning, and truths most universal, and appeared to be instructed, set free, and even elevated to higher hopes both here and hereafter, and to noble character; when, with all my directness of homely speech, I found myself welcome in most of the lecture halls between the Mississippi and the Penobscot, and even beyond them, having thence two or three hundred invitations a-year; when the national crisis became nearer and more threatening, and I saw my sentiments and ideas visibly passing into the opinion and the literature of the people, and thence coming out in the legislation of New England and the other Northern states—I thought it not quite time to withdraw, and my early purposes were a little shaken. I intended to continue some ten years more in severe practical work, till about sixty, then retire, not to lie down in the grave like a camel under his load at night, but hoping to enjoy a long, quiet autumn of twenty years or so, when I might accomplish my philosophic and literary works, and mow up as provender for future time what I had first raised as green grass, and then mowed down to make into sound hay, but have now left, alas! either strewn where it grew or but loosely raked together, not yet carted into safe barns for the long winter, or even stacked up and sheltered against immediate spoiling by a sudden rain in harvest.

2. Ralph Waldo Emerson (1803–1882)
Historic Notes of Life and Letters in New England

[The other of the two accounts was given by Emerson, then aging rapidly, as his hundredth lecture before the Concord Lyceum in 1880. The second half of it wanders off into a story of Brook Farm, which he treats with tender humor, a sign, perhaps, that he was still uneasy in his conscience—assuming, what the elder Henry James denied, that he had one—over his rejection of Ripley's proposal forty years before. In 1880 Emerson was hardly in a condition to compose a formal history or an analysis; with the help of his secretary and his daughter this address was pieced together out of older jottings; the result, at least in flashes, is a deft and comprehensive recapturing of the mood that generated the "movement."]

The ancient manners were giving way. There grew a certain tenderness on the people, not before remarked. Children had been repressed and kept in the background; now they were considered, cosseted and pampered. I recall the remark of a witty physician who remembered the hardships of his own youth; he said, "It was a misfortune to have been born when children were nothing, and to live till men were nothing."

There are always two parties, the party of the Past and the party of the Future; the Establishment and the Movement. At times the resistance is reanimated, the schism runs under the world and appears in Literature, Philosophy, Church, State and social customs. It is not easy to date these eras of activity with any precision, but in this region one made itself remarked, say in 1820 and the twenty years following.

It seemed a war between intellect and affection; a crack in Nature, which split every church in Christendom into Papal and Protestant; Calvinism into Old and New schools; Quakerism into Old and New; brought new divisions in politics; as the new conscience touching temperance and slavery. The key to the period appeared to be that the mind had become aware of itself. Men grew reflective and intellectual. There was a new consciousness. The former generations acted under the belief that a shining social prosperity was the beatitude of man, and sacrificed uniformly the citizen to the State. The modern mind believed that the nation existed for the individual, for the guardianship and education of every man. This idea, roughly written in revolutions and national movements, in the mind of the philosopher had far more precision; the individual is the world.

This perception is a sword such as was never drawn before. It divides and detaches bone and marrow, soul and body, yea, almost the man from himself. It is the age of severance, of dissociation, of freedom, of analysis, of detachment. Every man for himself. The public speaker disclaims speaking for any other; he answers only for himself. The social sentiments are weak; the sentiment of patriotism is weak; veneration is low; the natural affections feebler than they were. People grow philosophical about native land and parents and relations. There is an universal resistance to ties and ligaments once supposed essential to civil society. The new race is stiff, heady and rebellious; they are fanatics in freedom; they hate tolls, taxes, turnpikes, banks, hierarchies, governors, yea, almost laws. They have a neck of unspeakable tenderness; it winces at a hair. They rebel against theological as against political dogmas; against mediation, or saints, or any nobility in the unseen.

The age tends to solitude. The association of the time is accidental and momentary and hypocritical, the detachment intrinsic and progressive. The association is for power, merely,—for means; the end being the enlargement and independency of the individual. Anciently, society was in the course of things. There was a Sacred Band, a Theban Phalanx. There can be none now. College classes, military corps, or trades-unions may fancy themselves indissoluble for a moment, over their wine; but it is a painted hoop, and has no girth. The age of arithmetic and of criticism has set in. The structures of old faith in every department of society a few centuries have sufficed to destroy. Astrology, magic, palmistry, are long gone. The very last ghost is laid. Demonology is on its last legs. Prerogative, government, goes to pieces day by day. Europe is strewn with wrecks; a constitution once a week. In social manners and morals the revolution is just as evident. In the law courts, crimes of fraud have taken the place of crimes of force. The stockholder has stepped into the place of the warlike baron. The nobles shall not any longer, as feudal lords, have power of life and death over the churls, but now, in another shape, as capitalists, shall in all love and peace eat them up as before. Nay, government itself becomes the resort of those whom government was invented to restrain. "Are there any brigands on the road?" inquired the traveler in France. "Oh, no, set your heart at rest on that point," said the landlord; "what should these fellows keep the highway for, when they can rob just as effectually, and much more at their ease, in the bureaus of office?"

In literature the effect appeared in the decided tendency of criticism. The most remarkable literary work of the age has for its hero and subject precisely this introversion: I mean the poem of Faust. In philosophy, Immanuel Kant has made the best catalogue of the human faculties and the best analysis of the mind. Hegel also, especially. In science the French *savant,* exact, pitiless, with barometer, crucible, chemic test and calculus in hand, travels into all nooks and islands, to weigh, to analyze and report. And chemistry, which is the analysis of matter, has taught us that we eat gas, drink gas, tread on gas, and are gas. The same decomposition has changed the whole face of physics; the like in all arts, modes. Authority falls, in Church, College, Courts of Law, Faculties, Medicine. Experiment is credible; antiquity is grown ridiculous.

It marked itself by a certain predominance of the intellect in the balance of powers. The warm swart Earth-spirit which made the strength of past ages, mightier than it knew, with instincts instead of science, like a mother yielding food from her own breast instead of preparing it through chemic and culinary skill,—warm negro ages of sentiment and vegetation,—all gone; another hour had struck and other forms arose. Instead of the social existence which all shared, was now separation. Every one for himself; driven to find all his resources, hopes, rewards, society and deity within himself.

The young men were born with knives in their brain, a tendency to introversion, self-dissection, anatomizing of motives. The popular religion of our fathers had received many severe shocks from the new times; from the Arminians, which was the current name of the backsliders from Calvinism, sixty years ago; then from the English philosophic theologians, Hartley and Priestley and Belsham, the followers of Locke; and then I should say much later from the slow but extraordinary influence of Swedenborg; a man of prodigious mind, though as I think tainted with a certain suspicion of insanity, and therefore generally disowned, but exerting a singular power over an important intellectual class; then the powerful influence of the genius and character of Dr. Channing.

Germany had created criticism in vain for us until 1820, when Edward Everett returned from his five years in Europe, and brought to Cambridge his rich results, which no one was so fitted by natural grace and the splendor of his rhetoric to introduce and recommend. He made us for the first time acquainted with Wolff's theory of the Homeric writings, with the criticism of Heyne. The novelty of the learning lost nothing in the skill and genius of his relation, and the rudest undergraduate found a new morning opened to him in the lecture-room of Harvard Hall.

There was an influence on the young people from the genius of Everett which was almost comparable to that of Pericles in Athens. He had an inspiration which did not go beyond his head, but which made him the master of elegance. If any of my readers were at that period in Boston or Cambridge, they will easily remember his radiant beauty of person, of a classic style, his heavy large eye, marble lids, which gave the impression of mass which the slightness of his form needed; sculptured lips; a voice of such rich tones, such precise and perfect utterance, that, although slightly nasal, it was the most mellow and beautiful and correct of all the instruments of the time. The word that he spoke, in the manner in which he spoke it, became current and classical in New England. He had a great talent for collecting facts, and for bringing those he had to bear with ingenious felicity on the topic of the moment. Let him rise to speak on what occasion soever, a fact had always just transpired which composed, with some other fact well known to the audience, the most pregnant and happy coincidence. It was remarked that for a man who threw out so many facts he was seldom convicted of a blunder. He had a good deal of special learning, and all his learning was available for purposes of the hour. It was all new learning, that wonderfully took and stimulated the young men. It was so-coldly and weightily communicated from so commanding a platform, as if in the consciousness and consideration of all history and all learning,—adorned with so many simple and austere beauties of expression, and enriched with so many excellent digressions and significant quotations that, though nothing could be conceived beforehand less attractive or indeed less fit for green boys from Connecticut, New Hampshire and Massachusetts, with their unripe Latin and Greek reading, than exegetical discourses in the style of Voss and Wolff and Ruhnken, on the Orphic and Ante-Homeric remains,—yet this learning instantly took the highest place to our imagination in our unoccupied American Parnassus. All his auditors felt the extreme beauty and dignity of the manner, and even the coarsest were contented to go punctually to listen, for the manner, when they had found out that the subject-matter was not for them. In the lecture-room, he abstained from all ornament, and pleased himself with the play of detailing erudition in a style of perfect simplicity. In the pulpit (for he was then a clergyman) he made amends to himself and his auditor for the self-denial of the professor's chair, and, with an infantine simplicity still, of manner, he gave the reins to his florid, quaint and affluent fancy.

Then was exhibited all the richness of a rhetoric which we have never seen rivalled in this country. Wonderful how memorable were words made which were only pleasing pictures, and covered no new or valid thoughts. He abounded in sentences, in wit, in satire, in splendid allusion, in quotation impossible to forget, in daring imagery, in parable and even in a sort of defying experiment of his own wit and skill in giving an oracular weight to Hebrew or Rabbinical words;—feats which no man could better accomplish, such was his self-command and the security of his manner. All his speech was music, and with such variety and invention that the ear was never tired. Especially beautiful were his poetic quotations. He delighted in quoting Milton, and with such sweet modulation that he seemed to give as much beauty as he borrowed; and whatever he quoted will be remembered by any who heard him, with inseparable association with his voice and genius. He had nothing in common with vulgarity and infirmity, but, speaking, walking, sitting, was as much aloof and uncommon as a star. The smallest anecdote of his behavior or conversation was eagerly caught and repeated, and every young scholar could recite brilliant sentences from his sermons, with mimicry, good or bad, of his voice. This influence went much farther, for he who was heard with such throbbing hearts and sparkling eyes in the lighted and crowded churches, did not let go his hearers when the church was dismissed, but the bright image of that eloquent form followed the boy home to his bed-chamber; and not a sentence was written in academic exercises, not a declamation attempted in the college chapel, but showed the omnipresence of his genius to youthful heads. This made every youth his defender, and boys filled their mouths with arguments to prove that the orator had a heart. This was a triumph of Rhetoric. It was not the intellectual or the moral principles which he had to teach. It was not thoughts. When Massachusetts was full of his fame it was not contended that he had thrown any truths into circulation. But his power lay in the magic of form; it was in the graces of manner; in a new perception of Grecian beauty, to which he opened our eyes. There was that finish about this person which is about women, and which distinguishes every piece of genius from the works of talent,—that these last are more or less matured in every degree of completeness according to the time bestowed on them, but works of genius in their first and slightest form are still wholes. In every public discourse there was nothing left for the indulgence of his hearer, no marks of late hours and anxious, unfinished study, but the goddess of grace had breathed on the work a last fragrancy and glitter.

By a series of lectures largely and fashionably attended for two winters in Boston he made a beginning of popular literary and miscellaneous lecturing, which in that region at least had important results. It is acquiring greater importance every day, and becoming a national institution. I am quite certain that this purely literary influence was of the first importance to the American mind.

In the pulpit Dr. Frothingham, an excellent classical and German scholar, had already made us acquainted, if prudently, with the genius of Eichhorn's theologic criticism. And Professor Norton a little later gave form and method to the like studies in the then infant Divinity School. But I think the paramount source of the religious revolution was Modern Science; beginning with Copernicus, who destroyed the pagan fictions of the Church, by showing mankind that the earth on which we live was not the centre of the Universe, around which the sun and stars revolved every day, and thus fitted to be the platform on which the Drama of the Divine Judgment was played before the assembled Angels of Heaven,—"the scaffold of the divine vengeance" Saurin called it,—but a little scrap of a planet, rushing round the sun in our system, which in turn was too minute to be seen at the distance of many stars which we behold. Astronomy taught us our insignificance in Nature; showed that our sacred as our profane history had been written in gross ignorance of the laws, which were far grander than we knew; and compelled a certain extension and uplifting of our views of the Deity and his Providence. This correction of our superstitions was confirmed by the new science of Geology, and the whole train of discoveries in every department. But we presently saw also that the religious nature in man was not affected by these errors in his understanding. The religious sentiment made nothing of bulk or size, or far or near; triumphed over time as well as space; and every lesson of humility, or justice, or charity, which the old ignorant saints had taught him, was still forever true.

Whether from these influences, or whether by a reaction of the general mind against the too formal science, religion and social life of the earlier period,—there was, in the first quarter of our nineteenth century, a certain sharpness of criticism, an eagerness for reform, which showed itself in every quarter. It appeared in the popularity of Lavater's Physiognomy, now almost forgotten. Gall and Spurzheim's Phrenology laid a rough hand on the mysteries of animal and spiritual nature, dragging down every sacred secret to a street show. The attempt was coarse and odious to scientific men, but had a certain truth in it; it felt connection where the professors denied it, and was a leading to a truth which had not yet been announced. On the heels of this intruder came Mesmerism, which broke into the inmost shrines, attempted the explanation of miracle and prophecy, as well as of creation. What could be more revolting to the contemplative philosopher! But a certain success attended it, against all expectation. It was human, it was genial, it affirmed unity and connection between remote points, and as such was excellent criticism on the narrow and dead classification of what passed for science; and the joy with which it was greeted was an instinct of the people which no true philosopher would fail to profit by. But while society remained in doubt between the indignation of the old school and the audacity of the new, a higher note sounded. Unexpected aid from high quarters came to iconoclasts. The German poet Goethe revolted against the science of the day, against French and English science, declared war against the great name of Newton, proposed his own new and simple optics; in Botany, his simple theory of metamorphosis;—the eye of a leaf is all; every part of the plant from root to fruit is only a modified leaf, the branch of a tree is nothing but a leaf whose serratures have become twigs. He extended this into anatomy and animal life, and his views were accepted. The revolt became a revolution. Schelling and Oken introduced their ideal natural philosophy, Hegel his metaphysics, and extended it to Civil History.

The result in literature and the general mind was a return to law; in science, in politics, in social life; as distinguished from the profligate manners and politics of earlier times. The age was moral. Every immorality is a departure from nature, and is punished by natural loss and deformity. The popularity of Combe's Constitution of Man; the humanity which was the aim of all the multitudinous works of Dickens; the tendency even of Punch's caricature, was all on the side of the people. There was a breath of new air, much vague expectation, a consciousness of power not yet finding its determinate aim.

I attribute much importance to two papers of Dr. Channing, one on Milton and one on Napoleon, which were the first specimens in this country of that large criticism which in England had given power and fame to the Edinburgh Review. They were widely read, and of course immediately fruitful in provoking emulation which lifted the style of Journalism. Dr. Channing, whilst he lived, was the star of the American Church, and we then thought, if we do not still think, that he left no successor in the pulpit. He could never be reported, for his eye and voice could not be printed, and his discourses lose their best in losing them. He was made for the public; his cold temperament made him the most unprofitable private companion; but all America would have been impoverished in wanting him. We could not then spare a single word he uttered in public, not so much as the reading a lesson in Scripture, or a hymn, and it is curious that his printed writings are almost a history of the times; as there was no great public interest, political, literary or even economical (for he wrote on the Tariff), on which he did not leave some printed record of his brave and thoughtful opinion. A poor little invalid all his life, he is yet one of those men who vindicate the power of the American race to produce greatness.

Dr. Channing took counsel in 18[34] with George Ripley, to the point whether it were possible to bring cultivated, thoughtful people together, and make society that deserved the name. He had earlier talked with Dr. John Collins Warren on the like purpose, who admitted the wisdom of the design and undertook to aid him in making the experiment. Dr. Channing repaired to Dr. Warren's house on the appointed evening, with large thoughts which he wished to open. He found a well-chosen assembly of gentlemen variously distinguished; there was mutual greeting and introduction, and they were chatting agreeably on indifferent matters and drawing gently towards their great expectation, when a side-door opened, the whole company streamed in to an oyster supper, crowned by excellent wines; and so ended the first attempt to establish aesthetic society in Boston.

Some time afterwards Dr. Channing opened his mind to Mr. and Mrs. Ripley, and with some care they invited a limited party of ladies and gentlemen. I had the honor to be present. Though I recall the fact, I do not retain any instant consequence of this attempt, or any connection between it and the new zeal of the friends who at that time began to be drawn together by sympathy of studies and of aspiration. Margaret Fuller, George Ripley, Dr. Convers Francis, Theodore Parker, Dr. Hedge, Mr. Brownson, James Freeman Clarke, William H. Channing and many others, gradually drew together and from time to time spent an afternoon at each other's houses in a serious conversation. With them was always one well-known form, a pure idealist, not at all a man of letters, nor of any practical talent, nor a writer of books; a man quite too cold and contemplative for the alliances of friendship, with rare simplicity and grandeur of perception, who read Plato as an equal, and inspired his companions only in proportion as they were intellectual,—whilst the men of talent complained of the want of point and precision in this abstract and religious thinker.

These fine conversations, of course, were incomprehensible to some in the company, and they had their revenge in their little joke. One declared that "It seemed to him like going to heaven in a swing"; another reported that, at a knotty point in the discourse, a sympathizing Englishman with a squeaking voice interrupted with the question, "Mr. Alcott, a lady near me desires to inquire whether omnipotence abnegates attribute?"

I think there prevailed at that time a general belief in Boston that there was some concert of *doctrinaires* to establish certain opinions and inaugurate some movement in literature, philosophy and religion, of which design the supposed conspirators were quite innocent; for there was no concert, and only here and there two or three men or women who read and wrote, each alone, with unusual vivacity. Perhaps they only agreed in having fallen upon

Coleridge and Wordsworth and Goethe, then on Carlyle, with pleasure and sympathy. Otherwise, their education and reading were not marked, but had the American superficialness, and their studies were solitary. I suppose all of them were surprised at this rumor of a school or sect, and certainly at the name of Transcendentalism, given nobody knows by whom, or when it was first applied. As these persons became in the common chances of society acquainted with each other, there resulted certainly strong friendships, which of course were exclusive in proportion to their heat: and perhaps those persons who were mutually the best friends were the most private and had no ambition of publishing their letters, diaries or conversation.

From that time meetings were held for conversation, with very little form, from house to house, of people engaged in studies, fond of books, and watchful of all the intellectual light from whatever quarter it flowed. Nothing could be less formal, yet the intelligence and character and varied ability of the company gave it some notoriety and perhaps waked curiosity as to its aims and results.

Nothing more serious came of it than the modest quarterly journal called The Dial, which, under the editorship of Margaret Fuller, and later of some other, enjoyed its obscurity for four years. All its papers were unpaid contributions, and it was rather a work of friendship among the narrow circle of students than the organ of any party. Perhaps its writers were its chief readers: yet it contained some noble papers by Margaret Fuller, and some numbers had an instant exhausting sale, because of papers by Theodore Parker.

Theodore Parker was our Savonarola, an excellent scholar, in frank and affectionate communication with the best minds of his day, yet the tribune of the people, and the stout Reformer to urge and defend every cause of humanity with and for the humblest of mankind. He was no artist. Highly refined persons might easily miss in him the element of beauty. What he said was mere fact, almost offended you, so bald and detached; little cared he. He stood altogether for practical truth; and so to the last. He used every day and hour of his short life, and his character appeared in the last moments with the same firm control as in the midday of strength. I habitually apply to him the words of a French philosopher who speaks of "the man of Nature who abominates the steam-engine and the factory. His vast lungs breathe independence with the air of the mountains and the woods."

Bibliography

BIBLIOGRAPHY

Although in recent years scholars have produced a flood of articles and monographs on aspects of the Transcendental movement, or upon the minor figures involved, most of these are too restricted in scope to be of interest to the general reader. Since the complete array of titles has been listed in the relevant sections of *Literary History of the United States,* Volume III (New York, 1948), it need not be duplicated here. The following bibliography contains only the major studies and writings upon central figures or themes.

GENERAL

George Boas, editor. *Romanticism in America.* Baltimore, 1940.

E. D. Branch. *The Sentimental Years, 1836–1860.* New York, 1934.

Van Wyck Brooks. *The Flowering of New England, 1815–1865.* Revised edition, New York, 1941.

Katherine Burton. *Paradise Planters: The Story of Brook Farm.* New York, 1939.

Arthur E. Christy. *The Orient in American Transcendentalism.* New York, 1932.

John T. Codman. *Brook Farm: Historic and Personal Memoirs.* Boston, 1894.

Moncure Conway. *Autobiography, Memoirs, and Experiences.* 2 vols., London, 1904.

George W. Cooke. *Early Life at Brook Farm and Concord.* New York, 1894.

—— *The Poets of Transcendentalism: An Anthology.* Boston, 1903.

—— *Unitarianism in America.* Boston, 1902.

Merle Curti. "The Great Mr. Locke: America's Philosopher, 1783–1861," *Huntington Library Bulletin,* XI (1937), 107–155.

—— *The Growth of American Thought.* New York, 1943.

Marianne Dwight. *Letters from Brook Farm,* edited by Amy L. Reed. Poughkeepsie, 1928.

Arthur A. Ekirch, Jr. *The Idea of Progress in America, 1815–1860.* New York, 1944.

Samuel A. Eliot, editor. *Heralds of a Liberal Faith.* 3 vols., Boston, 1910.

Edward W. Emerson. *The Early Years of the Saturday Club.* Boston, 1918.

Clarence H. Faust. "The Background of the Unitarian Opposition to Transcendentalism," *Modern Philology,* XXXV (1938), 297–324.

Mary E. Sargent Fiske. *Sketches and Reminiscences of the Radical Club.* Boston, 1880.

Octavius B. Frothingham. *Boston Unitarianism, 1820–1850.* New York, 1890.

—— *Recollections and Impressions, 1822–1890.* New York, 1891.

Octavius B. Frothingham. *Transcendentalism in New England: A History.* New York, 1876.

Ralph H. Gabriel. *The Course of American Democratic Thought.* New York, 1940.

William Girard. "De l'influence exercée par Coleridge et Carlyle sur la formation du transcendentalisme," *University of California Publications in Modern Philology,* IV (1916), 404–411.

Harold C. Goddard. *Studies in New England Transcendentalism.* New York, 1908.

Clarence F. Gohdes. *The Periodicals of American Transcendentalism.* Durham, North Carolina, 1931.

M. A. DeWolfe Howe. *Later Years of the Saturday Club.* Boston, 1927.

Howard M. Jones. "The Influence of European Ideas in Nineteenth-Century America," *American Literature,* VII (1935), 241–273.

Walter L. Leighton. *French Philosophers and New-England Transcendentalism.* Charlottesville, Virginia, 1908.

F. O. Matthiessen. *American Renaissance.* New York, 1941.

Lewis Mumford. *The Golden Day.* New York, 1926.

Vernon L. Parrington. *Main Currents in American Thought.* 3 vols., New York, 1927–1930 (Volume II: *The Romantic Revolution in America*).

Andrew P. Peabody. *Harvard Reminiscences.* Boston, 1880.

Stow Persons. *Free Religion, An American Faith.* New Haven, 1947.

Henry A. Pochmann. *New England Transcendentalism and St. Louis Hegelianism.* Philadelphia, 1948.

I. Woodbridge Riley. *American Thought from Puritanism to Pragmatism.* New York, 1923.

Frank B. Sanborn. *Recollections of Seventy Years.* 2 vols., Boston, 1909.

Arthur M. Schlesinger, Jr. *The Age of Jackson.* New York, 1945.

Herbert W. Schneider. *A History of American Philosophy.* New York, 1946.

Lindsay Swift. *Brook Farm.* New York, 1900.

Edgerly W. Todd. "Philosophical Ideas at Harvard College, 1817–1837," *New England Quarterly,* XVI (1943), 63–90.

H. G. Townsend. *Philosophical Ideas in the United States.* New York, 1934.

David A. Wasson. *Essays Religious, Social, Political.* Boston, 1889.

René Wellek. "The Minor Transcendentalists and German Philosophy," *New England Quarterly,* XV (1942), 652–680.

AMOS BRONSON ALCOTT

The Journals of Bronson Alcott, edited by Odell Shepard. Boston, 1938.

George E. Haefner. *A Critical Estimate of the Educational Theories and Practices of A. Bronson Alcott.* New York, 1937.

Dorothy McCuskey. *Bronson Alcott, Teacher.* New York, 1940.

Elizabeth P. Peabody. *Record of a School, Exemplifying the General Principles of Spiritual Character.* Boston, 1835.

Frank B. Sanborn and William T. Harris. *A. Bronson Alcott: His Life and Philosophy.* 2 vols., Boston, 1893.

Clara E. Sears. *Bronson Alcott's Fruitlands.* Boston, 1915.

Odell Shepard. *Pedlar's Progress: The Life of Bronson Alcott.* Boston, 1937.

ORESTES A. BROWNSON

The Works of Orestes A. Brownson, edited by Henry F. Brownson, 20 vols., Detroit, 1882–1902.

Henry F. Brownson. *Orestes A. Brownson's Early Life, Middle Life, Latter Life.* 3 vols., Detroit, 1898–1900.

A. Robert Caponigri. "Brownson and Emerson: Nature and History," *New England Quarterly,* XVIII (1945), 368–390.

Theodore Maynard. *Orestes Brownson: Yankee, Radical, Catholic.* New York, 1943.

Helen S. Mims. "Early American Democratic Theory and Orestes Brownson," *Science and Society,* III (1939), 1–35.

Arthur M. Schlesinger, Jr. *Orestes A. Brownson.* Boston, 1939.

WILLIAM ELLERY CHANNING

The Works of William E. Channing. 6 vols., Boston, 1841–1843.

John W. Chadwick. *William Ellery Channing.* Boston, 1903.

William Henry Channing. *The Life of William Ellery Channing.* Boston, 1880.

——— *Memoir of William Ellery Channing.* 3 vols., Boston, 1848.

Arthur I. Ladu. "Channing and Transcendentalism," *American Literature,* XI (1939), 129–137.

Elizabeth P. Peabody. *Reminiscences of Rev. William Ellery Channing.* Boston, 1880.

Herbert W. Schneider. "The Intellectual Background of William Ellery Channing," *Church History,* VII (1938), 3–23.

WILLIAM HENRY CHANNING

Octavius B. Frothingham. *Memoir of William H. Channing.* Boston, 1886.

CHRISTOPHER PEARSE CRANCH

Leonora Cranch Scott. *The Life and Letters of Christopher Pearse Cranch.* Boston, 1917.

JAMES FREEMAN CLARKE

Autobiography, Diary and Correspondence, edited by E. E. Hale. Boston, 1891.

JOHN SULLIVAN DWIGHT

George W. Cooke, editor. *Early Letters of George W. Curtis to John S. Dwight.* New York, 1898.

—— *John Sullivan Dwight.* Boston, 1898.

RALPH WALDO EMERSON

The Complete Works of Ralph Waldo Emerson, edited by Edward Waldo Emerson. 12 vols., Boston, 1903–1904.

The Correspondence of Thomas Carlyle and Ralph Waldo Emerson, edited by C. E. Norton. 2 vols., Boston, 1883.

Journals, edited by Edward Waldo Emerson and Waldo Emerson Forbes. 10 vols., Boston, 1909–1914.

Letters from Ralph Waldo Emerson to a Friend, edited by C. E. Norton. Boston, 1899.

The Letters of Ralph Waldo Emerson, edited by Ralph L. Rusk. 6 vols., New York, 1939.

Uncollected Lectures by Ralph Waldo Emerson, edited by Clarence F. Gohdes. New York, 1933.

The Uncollected Writings, edited by Charles C. Bigelow. New York, 1912.

Young Emerson Speaks, edited by Arthur C. McGiffert. Boston, 1938.

Stewart G. Brown. "Emerson's Platonism," *New England Quarterly,* XVIII (1945), 325–45.

Kenneth W. Cameron. *Emerson the Essayist.* 2 vols., Raleigh, North Carolina, 1945.

Frederic I. Carpenter. *Emerson and Asia.* Cambridge, 1930.

Merrell R. Davis. "Emerson's 'Reason' and the Scottish Philosophers," *New England Quarterly,* XVII (1944), 209–228.

Horace Howard Furness. *Records of a Lifelong Friendship, 1807–1882.* Boston, 1910.

Henry D. Gray. *Emerson: A Statement of New England Transcendentalism as Expressed in the Philosophy of Its Chief Exponent.* Stanford, California, 1917.

Vivian C. Hopkins. "The Influence of Goethe on Emerson's Aesthetic Theory," *Philological Quarterly,* XXVII (1948), 325–344.

Perry Miller. "From Edwards to Emerson," *New England Quarterly,* XIII (1940), 587–617.

Bliss Perry. *Emerson Today.* Princeton, 1931.

Ralph L. Rusk. *The Life of Ralph Waldo Emerson.* New York, 1949.

Frank B. Sanborn, editor. *The Genius and Character of Emerson.* Boston, 1885.

Frank T. Thompson. "Emerson's Indebtedness to Coleridge," *Studies in Philology,* XXIII (1926), 55–76.

—— "Emerson and Carlyle," *Studies in Philology,* XXIV (1927), 438–453.

———— "Emerson's Theory and Practice of Poetry," *Publications of the Modern Language Association*, XLIII (1928), 1170–84.

Fred B. Wahr. *Emerson and Goethe*. Ann Arbor, Michigan, 1915.

René Wellek. "Emerson and German Philosophy," *New England Quarterly*, XVI (1943), 41–62.

Charles L. Young. *Emerson's Montaigne*. New York, 1941.

CONVERS FRANCIS

William Newall. *Memoir of Rev. Convers Francis, D.D.* Cambridge, Massachusetts, 1866.

Mosetta Vaughan. *Sketch of the Life and Work of Convers Francis, D.D.* Watertown, Massachusetts, 1944.

MARGARET FULLER

The Writings of Margaret Fuller, edited by Mason Wade. New York, 1941.

R. W. Emerson, W. H. Channing, J. F. Clarke. *Memoirs of Margaret Fuller.* 2 vols., Boston, 1852.

Katherine Anthony. *Margaret Fuller: A Psychological Biography*. New York, 1920.

Frederick Augustus Braun. *Margaret Fuller and Goethe*. New York, 1910.

Thomas W. Higginson. *Margaret Fuller Ossoli*. Boston, 1884.

Madeline B. Stern. *The Life of Margaret Fuller*. New York, 1942.

Mason Wade. *Margaret Fuller: Whetstone of Genius*. New York, 1940.

FREDERIC HENRY HEDGE

Orie W. Long. *Frederic Henry Hedge: A Cosmopolitan Scholar*. Portland, Maine, 1940.

Ronald V. Wells. *Three Christian Transcendentalists: James Marsh, Caleb Sprague Henry, Frederic Henry Hedge*. New York, 1943.

SYLVESTER JUDD

Margaret, A Tale of the Real and Ideal. Boston, 1845 (revised edition, 2 vols., 1851).

Arethusa Hall. *Life and Character of the Rev. Sylvester Judd.* Boston, 1854.

CHARLES KING NEWCOMB

The Journals of Charles King Newcomb, edited by Judith K. Johnson. Providence, 1946.

JAMES MARSH

The Remains of the Rev. James Marsh, edited by Joseph Torrey. Boston, 1843.

John Dewey. "James Marsh and American Philosophy," *Journal of the History of Ideas*, II (1941), 131–150.

Marjorie H. Nicolson. "James Marsh and the Vermont Transcendentalists," *Philosophical Review*, XXXIV (1925), 28–50.

THEODORE PARKER

The Works of Theodore Parker. 15 vols., Boston, 1907–1913.
John W. Chadwick. *Theodore Parker, Preacher and Reformer*. Boston, 1900.
Henry Steele Commager. *Theodore Parker*. Boston, 1936.
Octavius B. Frothingham. *Theodore Parker*. Boston, 1874.
John Weiss. *Life and Correspondence of Theodore Parker*. 2 vols., New York, 1864.

GEORGE RIPLEY

Octavius B. Frothingham. *George Ripley*. Boston, 1882.

SOPHIA DANA RIPLEY

Katherine Burton. "Sophia Dana Ripley," *Missionary*, LXIII (1939), 40.

HENRY DAVID THOREAU

Collected Poems of Henry Thoreau, edited by Carl Bode. Chicago, 1943.
The Writings of Henry David Thoreau. 20 vols., Boston, 1906.
Henry Seidel Canby. *Thoreau*. Boston, 1939.
William Ellery Channing. *Thoreau, the Poet-Naturalist*. Boston, 1873.
Joseph Wood Krutch. *Henry David Thoreau*. New York, 1948.
Sherman Paul. "The Wise Silence: Sound as the Agency of Correspondence in Thoreau," *New England Quarterly*, XXII (1949), 511–527.
Frank B. Sanborn. *Henry D. Thoreau*. Boston, 1886.

JONES VERY

Poems and Essays, edited by J. F. Clarke. Boston, 1883.
Carlos Baker. "Emerson and Jones Very," *New England Quarterly*, VII (1934), 90–99.
William Irving Bartlett. *Jones Very, Emerson's "Brave Saint."* Durham, North Carolina, 1942.
Yvor Winters. *Maule's Curse*. Norfolk, Connecticut, 1938.

Index

INDEX